Financial Crises, Contagion, and the Lender of Last Resort

A Reader

Edited by
CHARLES GOODHART
GERHARD ILLING

OXFORD
UNIVERSITY PRESS

OXFORD
UNIVERSITY PRESS

Great Clarendon Street, Oxford OX2 6DP

Oxford University Press is a department of the University of Oxford.
It furthers the University's objective of excellence in research, scholarship,
and education by publishing worldwide in

Oxford New York

Auckland Bangkok Buenos Aires Cape Town Chennai
Dar es Salaam Delhi Hong Kong Istanbul Karachi Kolkata
Kuala Lumpur Madrid Melbourne Mexico City Mumbai Nairobi
São Paulo Shanghai Singapore Taipei Tokyo Toronto

with an associated company in Berlin

Published in the United States
by Oxford University Press Inc., New York

First published 2002

British Library Cataloguing in Publication Data
Data available

Library of Congress Cataloging in Publication Data

Financial crises, contagion, and the lender of last resort: a reader / edited
by Charles Goodhart, Gerhard Illing.
p. cm.
Includes bibliographical references.
1. Loans, Foreign. 2. Lenders of last resort. 3. Financial crises.
4. International Monetary Fund. I. Goodhart, C. A. E. (Charles Albert Eric) II. Illing, Gerhard.
HG3891.5 .F555 2002 332.1′5—dc21 2001046492

ISBN 0-19-924720-X
ISBN 0-19-924721-8 (pbk.)

1 3 5 7 9 10 8 6 4 2

Typeset by Newgen Imaging Systems (P) Ltd., Chennai, India
Printed in Great Britain
on acid-free paper by
T.J. International Ltd., Padstow, Cornwall

Contents

1

Introduction

CHARLES GOODHART AND GERHARD ILLING

During the nineteenth and at the beginning of the twentieth century, financial crises were a common phenomenon in many countries. Frequently, bank runs and currency crises occurred at the same time, forming twin crises. Under the gold standard, bank runs caused a drain on the gold reserves of central banks. What at first sight might have seemed to be a natural response, the contraction of credit, would just make the crisis worse. Only since central banks learnt that they should do exactly the opposite—to be ready to supply credit to stop a panic—did banking panics become a rare event. By acting as a lender of last resort (LOLR), central banks provided a stabilizing insurance mechanism against liquidity shocks. This practice, first suggested by Henry Thornton in 1802, was refined by Walter Bagehot in 1873 with his famous advice, the now so-called *Bagehot principle*: '*lend freely at a high rate against good collateral*.'

The Bank of England was, perhaps, the first to adopt this principle, having been chastened by the panic that followed the failure of the Overend Gurney Company in 1866. Since then, LOLR became standard practice among central banks. For a long time, however, there was little theoretical analysis of LOLR, nor formal models of financial crises. Crises were not a fashionable subject; among theorists, the topic was mainly left to economic historians. That is not surprising, since the period in the middle third of the twentieth century, from about the mid-1930s until 1973, was one of unusual financial stability.

Things changed dramatically from the early 1970s onwards. Successive waves of crises occurred around the world. Immediately after the turmoil of 1972–73, with widespread inflationary pressures, the oil shock, and the breakdown of the Bretton Woods pegged exchange rate system, there were occasions of financial instability, for example, the Herstatt bank failure in Germany in 1974 and the fringe bank crisis in the UK in 1974–75. Probably, the most dangerous crisis of the whole period, the LDC crisis, which threatened the stability of financial systems both in developing and developed countries, broke in 1982. Thereafter, during the 1990s, emerging countries faced financial problems with increasing intensity: the Mexican peso crisis in 1994 was followed by the Asian crisis in 1997 with dramatic effects on the economies in the East Asian region. The default on Russian GKO

We wish to thank Curzio Giannini for helpful comments on an earlier draft.

bonds in August 1998 caused contagion effects around the world; amongst them the near bankruptcy of the LTCM hedge fund a month later.

This increased frequency of financial crises and the perceived danger of systemic risk caused a dramatic revival of interest in the subject within the economic profession. Financial crises became a hot research topic. In particular, these recent events renewed interest in the analysis of LOLR. On the one hand, such LOLR support actions have been accused of contributing to the increased frequency of (systemic) crises experienced during recent decades: By providing a safety net for banking activities, they are said to encourage excessive risk-taking (moral hazard), thus provoking the very crises they are supposed to prevent. On the other hand, the (surprisingly) fast recovery experienced after (most of) these crises may, perhaps, be attributed to the safety net provided by LOLR facilities, which may have dampened real effects by containing contagion.

Currently, the need for, and the appropriate design of, a LOLR both at the national and international level is hotly debated. There are fierce controversies about how to handle crisis management. How should a LOLR operate in a modern economy? What, if anything, can be learned from studying the history of LOLR? Are the Bagehot principles still relevant? How should they be adapted, if at all, to changes in the structure of financial markets? Modern controversies focus on the following central questions:

1. Is there a need for any public sector provision of liquidity at all? Why should private arrangements not work? Proponents of the free banking school argue that liquidity management should best be left to private markets. The banking community has a self-interest to maintain financial stability, for example, by issuing emergency circulation during a potential crisis. On this view, private institutions could, and would, allocate liquidity efficiently. Examples of such private sector mechanisms are the clearinghouses in the US before the creation of the Fed. Timberlake gives a detailed description of the experience of clearinghouses during financial crises in the US until the beginning of the twentieth century. Historical evidence suggests, however, that private arrangements had to cope with severe coordination problems, often preventing an efficient management of panics. Consequently, there is widespread agreement that there is a need for a LOLR to avert crises at the national level.

2. According to the Bagehot principles, liquidity support should be given to illiquid, but solvent individual banks. Is this principle still relevant for modern financial markets? Most liquidity provision by central banks, nowadays, is usually not directed to specific banks; rather it is done via open market operations (OMO). One view, generally adopted by monetarists, the 'money view', argues that LOLR activities should be confined to the aggregate provision of liquidity via pure OMO; individual banks should not be rescued. Efficient interbank markets will smoothly distribute liquidity to those banks who need it most urgently. So solvent banks should never become illiquid. If a bank gets into trouble, being denied access to funds on the interbank market, it should be seen as a clear indication of insolvency.

3. The 'banking view' takes the opposite position. It sees a need for assistance to individual banks, based on their inherent fragility. Via relationship lending, banks build up specific informational capital whose destruction would be socially wasteful: the break-up value of a bank is less than its value as an ongoing concern. That, and the inherent difficulty of valuing the present value of a bank's loan book, makes it difficult for outsiders, even when they may be the bank's own supervisor, to distinguish between a solvency and a liquidity crisis. Similar informational asymmetries may prevent interbank markets from operating smoothly. This problem is aggravated by spillover effects across banks via contagion. In the presence of informational externalities, the notion of liquidity allocation via efficient markets is rather dubious, so public support of individual banks may be justified. On the other hand, support and bail-outs for insolvent banks may encourage excessive risk-taking and limit private incentives to reduce contagion effects. Neither individual nor systemic risk-taking is exogenous.

Obviously, there are complex trade offs between different types of externalities. The design of efficient mechanisms requires a detailed understanding of the nature of these externalities. What are the costs and benefits of LOLR? What is the nature of financial contagion; how can it be contained? How should incentives be structured to limit moral hazard? Are there other, superior or complementary, mechanisms for managing crises? Such mechanisms include regulation, supervision, deposit insurance and contingency financing arrangements. Is there room for constructive ambiguity?

4. The same issues as considered on a national level are also relevant for the international financial system. Whereas there is widespread agreement on the need for a LOLR at the national level, there are hot debates whether the same holds at the international level. What are the crucial differences between national and international levels? Since currencies are mostly created nationally by national central banks (with the ESCB in the Euro-zone being the main counter-example), can there be an international LOLR? Per contra, can a LOLR be confined to national boundaries given the increasing globalization of modern financial markets? Is the IMF an international LOLR? Whether, or not, it is, how should it be designed? Should it focus primarily on crisis management, or, given its limited resources and concerns about moral hazard, on crisis prevention? But how could an international body without sovereign powers go about preventing crises?

All such questions have been the focus of two conferences in 1999 at the Center for Financial Studies in Frankfurt and at the Financial Markets Group at the London School of Economics and Politics in London, independently organized by the editors of this volume. A number of theoretical and policy oriented papers were presented at these conferences. Since then, many of these papers have been published in various professional journals. Given the importance of the topic, we, the conference organizers, thought it useful to collect the papers also in a Reader. In order to provide a more comprehensive understanding of the subject, we have supplemented these contributions with previous classic papers on the subject, starting with excerpts from the works of Thornton and Bagehot. While we ourselves have our own personal views about the more controversial aspects of this subject (see e.g. Goodhart in Part II) we have tried to select a balanced presentation of the range of views among economists.

In this introduction, we do not need to go at great length through all the issues involved, since, fortunately, we were able to find a comprehensive review of the literature by Freixas, Giannini, Hoggarth and Soussa. It is reprinted as the first paper of our book of Readings. The remainder of the introduction describes the content of the book, and is organized in the same way as the following parts. Part I gives an account of the historical evolution of the notion of LOLR, followed by Part II on contemporary analysis. Since a thorough analysis of the nature of financial contagion is essential for the debate on LOLR, Part III on bank runs and contagion documents recent advances on this issue. Part IV is concerned with the question whether there is a need for, and the design of, an international LOLR in the context of reforming the IMF. These questions will remain controversial in the foreseeable future. Given limitations of space, we decided not to cover the debate to what extent the European Central Bank should act as LOLR within the European Union. This heated debate may soon be only of historical interest with the evolution of the European Monetary Union. The academic contributions are anyhow documented extensively in Goodhart (2000).

PART I: HISTORICAL ANALYSIS

Financial crises are dramatic events. They evoke radical thinking, strong reactions and regime changes. Not only are most changes to financial regulation, and to the financial 'architecture', made in response to such crises, but also many of the most seminal studies and papers are similarly stimulated by such events.[1] Bagehot's great work, *Lombard Street* (1873) was largely written as a tract about the actual failings, and the theoretically better policy response, of the Bank of England in the Overend Gurney crisis of 1866 (see chapter 7 in particular).

Many, though not all, of Bagehot's proposals had been anticipated seventy years earlier by Henry Thornton in an even greater work, *An Enquiry into the Nature and Effects of the Paper Credit of Great Britain* (1802). This book was also prompted by a crisis, that is, the suspension of the Bank of England's commitment to redeem its notes in gold (1797). Thus, Thornton starts his introduction with the following words:

> The first intention of the Writer of the following pages was merely to expose some popular errors which related chiefly to the suspension of the cash payments of the Bank of England,

[1] Although we focus in this study of LOLR on the works of Thornton and Bagehot, mention should also be made of G. Rae, whose book *The Country Banker*, written in 1890 largely in response to the prior failure of the City of Glasgow Bank in 1878, was an early seminal work on risk control in banking and of the importance of transparency and good accounting as a protection against misdeeds and an incentive to maintain high standards in banking.

and to the influence of our paper currency on the price of provisions. But in pursuing this purpose, many questions occurred which it seemed important to discuss, partly on account of their having some bearing on the topics under consideration, and partly because they appeared to be of general importance, and had either been left unexplained, or had been inaccurately stated by those English writers who have treated of paper credit. This work has, therefore, assumed, in some degree, the character of a general treatise.

These two writers, but especially perhaps Bagehot, laid down the principles which central banks should follow in response to crises. These Bagehot principles appear to have been now generally accepted, though the exact interpretation of what they may mean remains subject to some continuing discussion; compare Goodhart with Humphrey and Keleher. In one respect this is ironic because Bagehot's main opponent in the discussion of the Bank's behaviour was a Mr Hankey (an experienced Bank director), who based his argument—against supporting the banking system in a crisis—squarely on the moral hazard argument.[2]

Bagehot himself, as is well known, was highly sympathetic to arguments for 'free banking', that is, a system with no central bank or any public sector involvement in the banking system at all. Under such circumstances he believed that market incentives would lead individuals to behave sufficiently prudently, for example, with respect to liquidity and capital, so that crises would be averted. But he recognized that the Bank of England was a fixed part of the financial system. Given the Bank's central role in the market place, there would be an inevitable tendency for the commercial banks to look to the Bank for support in a crisis, and the Bank had to provide it.

Thus, Bagehot's first response to Hankey was as follows (p. 171):

First. He should have observed that the question is not as to what 'ought to be', but as to what is. The 'Economist' did not say that the system of a single bank reserve was a good system, but that it was the system which existed, and which must be worked, as you could not change it.

[2] Bagehot reprints Hankey's arguments (*Lombard St*, 1999 edition, John Wiley & Sons, pp. 169–71), as follows:

Mr. Hankey, one of the most experienced bank directors, not long after, took occasion to observe:

'The "Economist" newspaper has put forth what in my opinion is the most mischievous doctrine ever broached in the monetary or banking world in this country; viz. that it is the proper function of the Bank of England to keep money available at all times to supply the demands of bankers who have rendered their own assets unavailable. Until such a doctrine is repudiated by the banking interest, the difficulty of pursuing any sound principle of banking in London will be always very great. But I do not believe that such a doctrine as that bankers are justified in relying on the Bank of England to assist them in time of need is generally held by the bankers in London. . . . If it were practicable for the Bank to retain money unemployed to meet such an emergency, it would be a very unwise thing to do so. But I contend that it is quite impractical, and if it were possible, it would be most inexpedient; and I can only express my regret that the Bank, from a desire to do everything in its power to afford general assistance in times of banking or commercial distress, should ever have acted in a way to encourage such an opinion. The more the conduct of the affairs of the Bank is made to assimilate to the conduct of every other well-managed bank in the United Kingdom, the better for the Bank, and the better for the community at large.'

There are delicious overtones connecting this to the modern debate. Many, especially those of the 'money view', continue to argue that the optimal system would be one with minimum public sector involvement, for example, in the guise of regulation and supervision. Absent the public sector, market incentives will bring about a good equilibrium. But at the national level not only do central banks continue to exist, but the (foolish?) government insists on providing (explicit or implicit) deposit insurance, and effectively guarantees the continuing operation of the main financial institutions (Too Big to Fail). So private sector incentives are thereby distorted towards excessive risk-taking, and regulation, supervision and LOLR become (regrettably) necessary.

Whether there ever really could be a Garden of Eden, a golden age, in which pure private sector market forces could work, untrammelled by public sector interference, to achieve good equilibria is contentious and largely counterfactual. At the national level we have surely been thrown out of that Garden of Eden. One reason why the debate about the questions of an International LOLR, and the role of the International Monetary Fund (IMF), is so intense is that the international system does not share the same structure as national systems (see Part IV). There is no exact equivalent international central bank, and no one to guarantee deposits or financial stability on a world-wide scale. Within this context the arguments about moral hazard on the one hand versus contagion on the other can proceed in a system where the financial architecture has not already predisposed the answers in one direction. Indeed, one of the main questions is exactly what form the financial architecture should adopt.

Thornton

Given the early date of this book, it is a wonderfully clear exposition of monetary and banking issues, and can still be read, with profit, today. Thornton came from a family which mixed financial business with evangelical Christianity. He was a philanthropist as well as an economist; besides his monetary writing, he composed books of prayers and lectures on the Ten Commandments (edited later by Sir R. Inglis).

He wrote from personal experience. He worked in the family bank of Downe, Free, and Thornton from 1778 till his death in 1815. His elder brother, Samuel Thornton, was a Director of the Bank of England, and Henry will have followed the Bank's actions with close interest. Besides his financial business, and evangelical activities, he became an MP for Southwark in 1782 as an independent, but leaning strongly towards the Whigs. His entry in the Dictionary of National Biography states that he 'was not an effective speaker, but became well known in Parliament as a high authority upon all matters of finance'. In this capacity he was also made a member of the famous Bullion Committee, in which he was prominent.

But his reputation as a monetary economist and financial expert rests on his 1802 book. The excerpts published here indicate his thoughts on how the Bank of England, or any other central bank, should respond to a crisis. He argues, as later did Bagehot, that in a system with a central bank, the commercial banks will turn to it for assistance in any such crisis, and that the central bank must stand ready to supply that, despite the likely concurrent drain on its gold reserves. While Thornton advocates a policy of liberal lending in crises, he would have the Bank protect its own position by taking good collateral. He is fully aware of the moral hazard argument, but suggests that good judgment and discretion will find the happy medium between moral hazard on the one hand and contagion on the other, as set out in the following extract.

It is by no means intended to imply, that it would become the Bank of England to relieve every distress which the rashness of country banks may bring upon them: the bank, by doing this, might encourage their improvidence. There seems to be a medium at which a public bank should aim in granting aid to inferior establishments, and which it must often find very difficult to be observed. The relief should neither be so prompt and liberal as to exempt those who misconduct their business from all the natural consequences of their fault, nor so scanty and slow as deeply to involve the general interests. These interests, nevertheless, are sure to be pleaded by every distressed person whose affairs are large, however indifferent or even ruinous may be their state.

One distinction between Thornton and Bagehot is that the former does not emphasize any particular need to lend at high interest rates during crises. This may have been because the usury laws then in force prevented any increase beyond 5 per cent.

Bagehot

Bagehot's book, *Lombard Street*, is the best known text on how to cope with financial crises, and includes the Bagehot Principles. We present these again here in the key excerpts from his chapters II and VII.

His background was succinctly described by Peter Bernstein, in his foreword to the 1999 re-issue, as follows:

Bagehot was born in 1826 and lived for only 51 years. He came from a banking family, but writing was his passion. He was recognized as one of England's greatest essayists as well as one of her most distinguished economists, and his collected works fill five fat volumes. After succeeding his father as head of the family banking business, he subsequently succeeded his father-in-law as editor of *The Economist* magazine. His importance was so great in understanding and articulating developments in the world of finance that Gladstone referred to him as 'Permanent Chancellor of the Exchequer.'

Lombard Street is a compilation of articles that Bagehot wrote for *The Economist* during the 1850s and that subsequently appeared in book form in 1873. Although the stated purpose of the book was to describe the money market, Bagehot's mind was much too fertile and his range of interests much too wide for his writings to comprise a dull textbook in monetary theory. Indeed, he declares straight off, in his very first sentence, that he chose this particular title rather than 'The Money Market' because he plans to deal 'with concrete realities.' Personalities, sociology, political considerations, and anecdotes appear all through the analysis, and especially personalities. Bagehot felt strongly that individuals shape history. He also enjoyed their idiosyncrasies—why else would he have reproduced those entertaining full texts in the appendixes to *Lombard Street*?

> . . . Bagehot invented crisis management; after nearly 150 years, his wise words are still the prescription of choice for containing financial crises, as well as a handbook for avoiding them . . . Bagehot deals explicitly with panic and with the administration of the reserve under crisis conditions. It is here that he establishes the guidelines for the function of lender-of-last-resort.

These guidelines are set out in full in the excerpts reprinted in Part I.

Humphrey and Keleher

Financial crises re-emerged in the 1970s and 1980s, having been largely dormant for the previous forty years. With interest in the question of how to deal with such crises revived, it was natural for there to be a re-examination and re-assessment of the historical work on LOLR. The classic article in this genre is by Humphrey and Keleher (Cato Journal, 1984).

They begin with a general description of how both the short and long run LOLR provision of liquidity should be undertaken, strongly leaning to the view that it should be done primarily, or entirely, by general OMO operations, rather than by lending to individual banks. They continue with an assessment of Thornton's analysis, which takes them into the debates between the Currency and Banking Schools and the background to the Bank Charter Act of 1844, and the crises that followed. This then leads onto their assessment of Walter Bagehot's contribution, the centrepiece of their paper.

They reach six main conclusions in the domestic case, that is,

1. The LOLR's emergence depends critically on fractional reserve banking and central bank monopoly over legal tender issuance.
2. The LOLR is essentially a monetary, rather than a banking or credit function.
3. The LOLR function applies to all monetary regimes.
4. The LOLR function in no way conflicts with the monetary control function of the central bank.
5. The LOLR has a macroeconomic rather than a microeconomic responsibility.
6. The LOLR function can be accomplished either through open market operations or loans made at the penalty rate.[3]

They conclude with a discussion whether, or not, the case for a domestic LOLR also carries over to the international context. This section of their paper should be read in conjunction with the studies specifically concentrating on this topic, here grouped in Part IV.

[3] The question of whether Bagehot ever proposed a 'penalty' rate, and, whether or not he did, if such a penalty rate should be applied on LOLR lending remains a contentious issue between those supporting the 'money' and the 'banking' views.

Bordo

Bordo begins by examining a variety of arguments about the appropriate role of an LOLR, beginning once again with Thornton and Bagehot, and then continuing with viewpoints that are mostly to be found in the papers contained in Part II. The main reason for including this paper is that it provides evidence on the historical record of banking panics and their resolution over the last two centuries, and, of course, of the use of central bank LOLR functions as a means of mitigating such crises.

He draws the following conclusions from this historical survey:

1. Banking panics are rare events.
2. Successful LOLR actions prevented panics on numerous occasions.
3. Some public authority must provide the LOLR function.
4. Such an authority does not have to be a central bank.
5. The advent of federal deposit insurance in 1934 solved the problem of banking panics in the US.
6. Assistance to insolvent banks was the exception rather than the rule until the 1970s.

Timberlake

The belief of advocates of 'free banking', that is, a system without a central bank, is that market pressures would induce more prudence among commercial banks, so that banking panics would be less frequent, at best non-existent. In practice, however, banking crises have occurred in most countries, with or without Central Banks; though some would point to Scotland before 1844 or Canada before 1935, as examples of crisis-free decades in a free banking system (see Dowd 1992).

The question then arises whether, if such a banking crisis should occur, the private sector might be able to develop an alternative to the public sector provision of LOLR. Timberlake shows how such an alternative developed in the USA, during the period of the national banking system, 1857–1907, in the guise of 'an extension of the functions of the clearing-house association'. The novelty of their practice was that they could, after a fashion (and somewhat illegally!), provide 'for the creation of new reserves as they were needed'.

Timberlake's paper briefly records the history of such clearinghouses in the USA, and then describes in detail how they operated during crises, for example, in issuing loan certificates to members losing reserves. He concludes that,

> The issue of clearing-house currency put the brakes on the development of an unstable bank credit contraction. It fulfilled the increased demand for money and allowed the banks to extend credit in their customary manner. It did not prevent the demise of inefficient banks; it only stopped the fractional reserve collapse that might otherwise have occurred . . .
>
> The Federal Reserve alternative, however, was critically different from the clearing-house system. It introduced a discretionary political element into monetary decision-making and thereby divorced the authority for determining the system's behavior from those who had a

self-interest in maintaining its integrity. Of such stuff are disasters built. The clearing-house system, while it was not formalized and did not operate under the guidance of 'human wisdom', was constrained effectively by the undesigned order of the marketplace.

PART II: CONTEMPORARY ANALYSIS

The Bagehot principle states that the LOLR should lend to illiquid, yet solvent banks. Is this principle still relevant for modern financial markets, when liquidity is provided via open market operations? According to the 'money view', central banks should restrict their activities to the provision of sufficient aggregate liquidity via OMO; they should abstain from supporting individual banks. Milton Friedman (1959) recommended such a policy; among others, it has been advocated by Anna Schwartz, Allan Meltzer, and Chari and Kehoe (1999).

The 'money view' is based on two pillars: First, it emphasizes the potential costs involved in supporting individual banks—the negative externalities arising from moral hazard. Second, it claims that overall financial stability can be obtained without incurring such costs: aggregate liquidity provision to the general market would, (so it is argued), deliver the benefits at no cost. A crucial requirement is that financial markets have to operate smoothly even in times of a crisis. If that is correct, the Bagehot principles, based on the distinction between illiquidity and insolvency, would be irrelevant: As long as interbank markets work as an efficient screening mechanism even in a crisis, solvent banks would never be illiquid. Excess liquidity would be redirected to those banks needing it most. Obviously, there is no reason why banks should then seek to borrow against good collateral at a high rate from a lender of last resort, when the market would be cheaper and easier.

In contrast, according to the 'banking view', market failures preventing the smooth provision of liquidity are the very characteristic of financial crises. Informational externalities may cause disruptions on the interbank market so that illiquid, yet solvent, banks may be denied assistance. Since the cost of disruption is likely to increase with the size of the failed banks, an implicit or explicit guarantee for large financial institutions may be an adequate response to this market failure.[4] To understand this debate, a careful analysis of the notion of liquidity risk and the nature of the externalities involved is required. How might informational imperfections cause liquidity problems? What is special about banks?

Part II collects leading contributions to this debate. The first two papers describe the arguments behind the 'money view'. Goodfriend and King present a detailed and comprehensive outline of it. Traditionally, the main concern of the LOLR has been with a collapse in the money stock. George Kaufman extends the notion to the prevention of fire sales on asset markets in general. The remaining papers in Part II deal with reasons for possible failures of the interbank market. Hirsch and Solow characterize the nature of the externalities which may lead to market failure,

[4] Goodhart and Huang (1999) provide a rationale for the 'too big to fail' doctrine.

supporting the intuition outlined by earlier writers. They argue that the costs of those failures have to be weighed against the cost of moral hazard. The model presented by Flannery illustrates how the interbank market may break down in times of crises due to adverse selection. Goodhart gives a (provocative) presentation of the arguments in favour of the banking view.

Goodfriend and King

The authors argue that a central bank can protect the banking system against crises via open market operations. LOLR policy is seen as equivalent to the routine provision of an elastic currency. By interest rate smoothing via OMO, monetary policy works as an endogenous stabilizer responding automatically to aggregate liquidity shocks. Excess demand for aggregate liquidity is met via an endogenous increase in money supply.

Given that today's financial markets provide highly efficient means of allocating credit privately, solvent institutions will never be prevented from getting access to liquid funds. The interbank market takes care of an efficient allocation of liquidity within the banking sector. Consequently, specific intervention for individual banks (Goodfriend and King call it banking policy) is not needed. They concede that financial markets may not be able to determine readily the status of a particular institution. They argue, however, that central banks have no relative advantage in screening strong from weak banks. If an individual bank is unable to get funds on the interbank market, that should be seen as a sign of insolvency and the need of recapitalization. Any support for insolvent banks, however, is an implicit subsidy for excessive risk-taking. So any attempts to support individual banks, by encouraging moral hazard, will lead to an inefficient outcome.

Kaufman

In the same vein, Kaufman states that no assistance to specific institutions should be given unless the central bank has superior information about the solvency of the participants. He again stresses negative externalities arising from individual support: in addition to the moral hazard problem, regulators face political pressure and regulatory capture.

According to the 'money view', rather than helping individual banks, a LOLR should aim at preventing a financial panic. A general flight out of bank deposits (into currency or foreign exchange) must not be allowed to contract the money stock. Kaufman, however, notices that there has been a substantial change in the concept of LOLR intervention towards protection of equilibrium asset prices from (temporary) liquidity problems, with the aim of preventing fire-sale losses and the destruction of real wealth. As financial markets have become more efficient, on the one hand mechanisms for providing liquidity have improved, but at the same time the increased speed of transactions may have increased the potential for abrupt price changes (liquidations) and fire sales. As an example of a successful policy,

Kaufman cites the Fed's easing of monetary conditions after the October 1987 stock market crash.[5]

Hirsch

Fred Hirsch's contribution is the first paper rationalizing the existence of central banks (not only in their LOLR capacity, but also as supervisor and regulator) as a way to cope with market frictions arising from imperfect information. He draws an analogy between LOLR and the provision of insurance. Problems of imperfect information and enforceability of contracts impede smooth insurance against illiquidity risk, motivating a role for the public provision of financial stability. Just like health insurance, support of banking stability comes at a cost: By reducing the private cost of risk taking, it encourages moral hazard among banks. So there is a need for control and regulation. Hirsch points out that such arrangements are bound to have some costs: informal discretionary controls by regulatory authorities lead to cartelization. On the other hand, a policy of denying official public support encourages banking concentration, since depositors do not consider a commitment to let big banks fail to be credible. Neither strategy, therefore, is dominant as a means of promoting efficiency. Hirsch emphasizes that the 'optimal' way to discharge central banking functions depends on the features of the overall institutional context–which is also a key point in understanding why replicating the LOLR function at the international level is so difficult.

Solow

Robert Solow extends the analogy to insurance theory. He stresses the externalities arising from the fact that any fractional-reserve banking system is vulnerable to runs. The network of interrelated debtor–creditor relations may cause cumulative chain reactions, undermining confidence in the banking system. In his view, confidence inspiring stabilization of the monetary-financial system is a public good. Solow suggests partial insurance as a way to cope with moral hazard.

Flannery

Flannery presents a model indicating how the interbank market may break down in a crisis. The underlying reason is the familiar 'lemons' problem. For lenders with surplus liquidity, it is difficult to distinguish between those banks that are in trouble because of poor loan performance and those having simply high liquidity needs. Since banks with low asset values will also apply for loans, for example, as those with 'inside' information withdraw their deposits from such banks, the

[5] Remarkably, others blame this same policy for causing moral hazard effects: trusting that the Fed is ready to prevent a stock market crash, investors are tempted to ignore downside risk. This, in turn, may generate a bubble on the stock market.

adverse selection problem makes banks reluctant to give credit, interrupting the interbank market. In Flannery's model, banks differ in their efficiency for screening applicants. Less efficient banks suffer from a 'winner's curse' problem: since those bad risks rejected by more efficient banks will apply again for credit, the average quality of the applicant pool is lower. In normal times, the screening mechanism of financial markets functions rather well—banks have a fairly good judgement of their relative screening abilities. But during crises, established information channels may break down and uncertainty about one's own screening abilities rises dramatically. Thus, the non diversifiable risk of the winner's curse (bad quality of the applicants' pool) increases. This may reduce risk-taking capacity in times of crisis. Banks become more cautious and are less willing to give interbank credit. As a result, the interbank loan market may break down. So liquid funds would not be allocated efficiently.

In principle, the problem might be solved via a pooling of private sector liquidity—a loan consortium of all banks with surplus liquidity might provide it to those banks in need. But, as Flannery argues, high coordination costs and pressure for quick action make such an outcome unlikely. In contrast, the central bank as LOLR is in a position to lend in a non-discriminatory fashion. If all private lenders withdrew completely from the market, the LOLR would not even be affected by the 'winner's curse' problem, and so could break even. Otherwise, social costs from tax finance to cover potential losses have to be weighed against the benefits from preventing financial distress.

Goodhart

Charles Goodhart criticizes the 'money view' interpretation of the Bagehot principles as non-operational and suggests that the term LOLR should be used only for central bank liquidity support to individual banks. He argues that—within the relevant time scale—it is very often difficult, or impossible for a central bank to distinguish between insolvency and illiquidity. Whenever a commercial bank asks for central bank assistance, there must always be the suspicion of insolvency—otherwise the market would be willing to provide liquidity. The Bagehot rules do not depend on the solvency of the individual borrower but on the security; according to Goodhart, they were intended to prevent significant losses on central bank's LOLR loans and to prevent an excessive expansion of the money stock.

As a key issue—both at the national and international level—he singles out the question how potential losses are to be shared. National LOLR capacities are restricted by the central bank's ability to absorb losses, and so are ultimately limited by the taxing power of the government. Unless potentiality for losses is small, systemic problems nowadays require joint management and resolution by the supervisory body, the central bank and the government. The fundamental difference on the international level is that the decision process about burden sharing involves much more intricate coordination problems in the absence of a single authority with international taxing powers.

In Goodhart's view, it will not be possible to dispense with LOLR altogether. So when the central bank (or, internationally, the IMF) would not act as LOLR, alternative, possibly inferior *ad hoc* systems would be established. The real challenge is how best to organize the LOLR function rather than to abolish it.

PART III: BANK RUNS AND CONTAGION

Contemporary analysis suggests that the key debate is about how two types of externalities should be weighed. On the one hand, there are inefficiencies resulting from moral hazard as a consequence of the safety net. On the other hand, inefficiencies arising from contagion could bring a danger of systemic risk. A detailed analysis of the nature of these externalities is needed. During recent decades, economic modelling has made substantial progress in understanding these issues. The contributions in Part III on bank runs and contagion provide a comprehensive microeconomic foundation.

What is special about the banking system? What are the reasons for its vulnerability? Why are banks susceptible to runs? What externalities may cause spillovers (contagion) across banks? For a long time, these questions have been answered mainly historically; there have been only very few theoretical models. Recently, however, a number of innovative papers collected in this part give deeper insights into the nature of the problem, offering a better understanding of the externalities involved both in liquidity and systemic risk.

All these models build on the seminal contribution of Diamond and Dybvig. This classic paper provides a fundamental insight into the nature of the financial fragility of the banking system: Deposit contracts with a sequential service constraint introduce a payoff externality. If I expect that others will run, it is rational to run myself. Therefore, bank runs may be the result of self-fulfilling expectations even when fundamentals are sound. Insolvency may be the endogenous result of a sudden change in expectations.

Diamond and Dybvig are concerned with a run on a single bank; they abstract from spillover effects across banks. Their model, however, provides a robust framework, flexible enough to incorporate transmission channels of contagion. A variety of channels have been analysed in detail. Due to the interconnectedness of the financial sector, the failure of one bank may lead to contagion effects involving other financial institutions, creating distress among market participants.

1. Panics induced by purely random events (e.g. sunspots). The failure of one bank may trigger a run on others simply because it triggers a change in expectations about the probability of a bank run equilibrium. Such a mechanism (as suggested in Freixas, Parigi and Rochet), however, is not entirely convincing; unless a reason for the original run is found, how can depositors elsewhere assess which other banks, if any, have now become more fragile?

2. Information based panics. When depositors receive 'noisy' signals, they may misinterpret liquidity shocks as negative signals about the bank's asset returns.

This effect, first analysed in Chari and Jaghannathan (1988), has been adapted to a multi-bank context by Chen. The paper shows how a combination of pay-off externalities and information externalities (generating herding behaviour) may induce 'inefficient' panics.

3. Cumulative chain reactions via links, for example, in the payments system, the interbank markets, or in other 'nodes' in the financial system. As pointed out by Solow, the interconnectedness of banks creates a fragile network of interrelated debtor–creditor relations. Such exposures, for example, on the interbank market, may amplify small negative shocks. Allen and Gale, and Freixas, Parigi, and Rochet model this cascade effect and compare the fragility of different market structures. These papers provide a better understanding of the contagion mechanism, and highlight the importance of market structure. They can be seen as a first step towards a deeper understanding of the risk of breakdowns in different kinds of financial market mechanisms.

De Bandt and Hartmann

De Bandt and Hartmann give a broad survey of both theoretical models and empirical analysis of systemic risk. First, they provide a conceptual framework for the analysis of systemic risk, stressing that contagion effects are at the heart of systemic risk. Then, they consider different channels through which contagion can work, distinguishing between risks in banking markets and risks in the interbank payment infrastructure. The diversity of contagion channels illustrates the need for careful empirical research about such transmission mechanisms. De Bandt and Hartmann survey a large number of econometric tests and some other quantitative assessments of the various facets of systemic risk. Their results, however, point to a general difficulty of developing empirical tests that can make a clear distinction between the various different types of contagion.

Diamond and Dybvig

Diamond and Dybvig (1983) is the classic paper demonstrating the inherent fragility of banks. Banks provide maturity transformation. They accept deposits payable on demand, and invest the proceeds in longer term, often illiquid projects, funding complex, informationally intense positions. The maturity mismatch between deposits and assets makes them susceptible to runs. Banks may be forced into costly liquidation of illiquid assets (leading to the destruction of informational capital). Moreover, the attempt to liquidate (complex) positions can result in large changes of asset prices. A flight out of its deposits—triggered by aggregate shocks in the economy, bad news about the bank, unforeseen liquidity needs, or simply a change in mood among depositors causing fire sales in a panic—can make a bank insolvent. Attempts by any bank facing liquidity problems to realize assets or to borrow may then pass on, and possibly even intensify, liquidity pressures elsewhere (though Diamond and Dybvig do not themselves model this latter generalization).

Diamond and Dybvig show that a bank run may be a self-fulfilling equilibrium. If depositors expect that other depositors will withdraw their money and force the bank to liquidate its long term assets, it is optimal to do the same. So runs can be triggered by a change of expectations even with no change in fundamentals. The nature of deposits with sequential service constraint creates a pay-off externality, leading to runs as a consequence of a coordination failure among depositors. The distinction between insolvency and illiquidity becomes blurred; insolvency may be the endogenous result of a sudden change in expectations. In the Diamond and Dybvig model, a LOLR may prevent a 'sunspot' panic without costs. It can eliminate the inferior Nash equilibrium simply by announcing that it will lend freely to banks in trouble. In this context, a LOLR works as a mechanism to coordinate expectations and direct them towards the good equilibrium.

The classic model by Diamond and Dybvig provides the starting point for a formal analysis of LOLR issues, allowing for extensions in many directions.[6] The following papers use it as the basis for analysing various contagion channels.

Allen and Gale, Optimal Currency Crises

The Diamond and Dybvig model does not yield any insight into the nature of economic events which might trigger a crisis. In reality, crises do not happen out of the blue. Empirical evidence suggests that crises have been related to weak fundamentals—banking panics occur mainly during recessions (see Gorton (1988) and Kaminsky and Reinhart (1999). Allen and Gale modify the set-up so as to generate this feature. First, they analyse financial crises in a closed economy and then extend the model to include an international bond market. Allen and Gale dispense with the sequential service constraint and concentrate on the impact of aggregate shocks in an economy with fixed nominal deposits. In their model, banking crises are a response to falling asset returns during the course of the business cycle. In this context, runs can even have a positive effect, since they introduce contingent outcomes via bankruptcy, into deposit contracts that might allow early and late consumers to share the risks associated with stochastic asset returns.

Banks offer deposit contracts to consumers facing liquidity preference shocks. They can invest in a safe and in an illiquid, risky asset. In period 1, consumers get informed about the return of the risky asset. When it turns out to be lower than the safe asset, there will be a run on the banks, forcing liquidation of all assets. Bank runs allow for some risk sharing among early and late consumers. When early

[6] Due to the multiplicity of equilibria, there is an indeterminacy in the Diamond and Dybvig model, calling for additional selection criteria to specify under what conditions a specific equilibrium will prevail. Morris and Shin (1998) have shown that there is a unique equilibrium when depositors get only imperfect information (noisy signals) about fundamentals. Goldstein and Pauzner (2000) adopt these methods to demonstrate that panic-based withdrawals will trigger bank runs when fundamentals get sufficiently bad: with deteriorating fundamentals, more depositors receive bad signals and demand early withdrawals, driven by the fear that others withdraw as well. Using the same method, Rochet and Vives (2000) provide a theoretical foundation for the notion of 'solvent but illiquid' banks.

liquidation is costless such runs can achieve the first best outcome. In general, however, it is costly and inefficient to liquidate all long term real assets. The central bank, as lender of last resort, can prevent costly liquidation: providing fiat money when economy-wide asset returns are low raises the price level and so lowers the real value of depositors' nominal claims. Effectively, the central bank's policy introduces state contingent deposit contracts: The deposits of the early consumers can be paid out, leaving the banks enough assets to make it worthwhile for (most of the) late consumers not to withdraw.

Many of the recent currency and banking crises after the deregulation of financial markets in the 1980s have been 'twin crises'. So the relationship between banking and currency crises needs to be analysed in an international context. Chang and Velasco (2000) model currency crises as sunspot events in a straightforward extension of Diamond and Dybvig. In contrast, the approach of Allen and Gale relates crises to weak fundamentals. They consider the case of a small country, so risk is diversifiable for international investors. In principle, when domestic debt is denominated in domestic currency, the bond market could provide perfect insurance in a flexible exchange rate regime. The central bank adjusts the price level (the exchange rate) to local shocks such that returns will be positively correlated with the strength of their own currency. Banks could perfectly hedge the risk of their assets by issuing domestic currency bonds to foreigners and investing the proceeds in foreign currency assets. Low local returns are compensated by capital gains on foreign assets, and the other way round with high returns. Optimal risk sharing, however, would require large (unbounded) international financial positions.

But most countries are constrained in the amount of domestic currency debt they can issue on international markets. Severe incentive problems prevent well functioning international insurance markets: When foreign debt is denominated in terms of domestic currency, there is a strong temptation for a surprise inflation to expropriate foreign lenders even in the absence of negative shocks. So, as an incentive constraint, most international debt has to be denominated in foreign currency, drastically reducing the scope for risk shifting via international bond market. When returns are so low that commitments to depositors and foreign lenders cannot be met, bankruptcy and inefficient liquidation cannot be avoided by the local central bank.

Allen and Gale's model also provides an interesting perspective on the role of the IMF as an international LOLR. In the absence of frictionless markets for risk, it can be welfare improving in several ways. First, the conditionality of IMF support could work as a commitment device, providing appropriate incentives not to misuse the possibility of inflating (or more generally, defaulting on) foreign debt. Second, an international LOLR could prevent banking and currency crises, avoiding inefficient liquidation and the risk of contagion.

Chen

Chen considers externalities arising from the transmission of information. He shows that banking panics can be the outcome of individually rational, but socially wasteful, information-based herding. The combination of two different externalities drives this result: (1) the pay-off externality imposed by the sequential service constraint. (2) An information externality creating herding behaviour: it may be rational to ignore one's own information and instead follow the crowd.

Chen extends the Diamond and Dybvig model to a setting with many banks. All banks invest in risky projects. The probability of failure is correlated across banks: the failure of other banks gives some (noisy) information about one's own bank. For each bank, some fraction of depositors (the insiders) are assumed to get precise information about their bank's returns at some stage. For some banks, this information comes sooner than for other banks. The informed depositors can condition their withdrawal on exact information, whereas uninformed depositors have to rely on aggregate information.

Since it is efficient to close banks with failing projects (in order to prevent moral hazard–gambling for resurrection) a bank run by informed depositors has a welcome disciplinary effect. But due to the correlation of returns across banks, observing a high bank failure rate is also a signal of overall low average returns. Thus, uninformed depositors will be induced to run on all remaining banks. Anticipating this, even those depositors in other banks that might have received good information about the state of their own bank would ignore that information and instead run themselves as well. Thus, after observing a high failure rate, a run could set in even on fundamentally sound banks, imposing high social costs.

Chen suggests a simple solution to the herding problem: deposit insurance of uninformed depositors eliminates their incentive to run. Consequently, informed depositors will only run on banks with failing projects, providing an efficient disciplinary mechanism. If informed depositors can be given an incentive to invest in (uninsured) subordinated debt, while uninformed depositors are (fully) insured, then such a separating equilibrium would be desirable.

Allen and Gale, Financial Contagion

The paper by Chen illustrates how the transmission of information about real shocks (the observation of a high failure rate) may trigger banking panics. In that set up, contagion occurs without direct real links among the banks. It is caused by correlation of returns. Financial interdependence of banks due to their interconnected exposure, for example, on the interbank market, provides another important transmission mechanism. Mutual credit lines create a dense, interrelated network among banks. These links allow diversification of local risks, but they increase the system's fragility against aggregate shocks. A real shock depressing the asset value of one bank may trigger a chain reaction via such financial links.

Allen and Gale present a simple model demonstrating this effect. They expand the Diamond and Dybvig model to consider regional liquidity shocks. Without credit relations between different regions, local liquidity shocks may force costly liquidation of illiquid investments resulting in bankruptcy. When liquidity shocks are imperfectly correlated across regions, interbank deposits held by banks at other regions can provide insurance against local liquidity preference shocks. In the absence of (economy wide) aggregate shocks, a variety of market structures can implement the first-best outcome.

The paper shows, however, that market structures can be financially fragile: when bankruptcy has occurred in one region (banks having exhausted their liquidity buffer), the crisis may spread to all other regions if there is an aggregate liquidity shortage. So interbank links can create contagion effects. When there is an excess aggregate demand for liquidity, banks simultaneously try to liquidate their claims on each other, until banks in one region go bankrupt. This bankruptcy imposes losses on the creditor banks in the next, connected region. If losses of creditor banks are so large that their buffer is exhausted too, bankruptcy will spill over to that region. The more regions go bankrupt, the more severe the problem, so a cascade effect will set in.

The paper points to a trade-off between the individual benefits of access to liquidity and the social costs of contagion. It illustrates that contagion depends on the endogenous pattern of financial claims. It occurs most likely when interbank deposits are connected by a chain of overlapping bank liabilities. In contrast, a complete and more complex market structure (with interbank links across all regions) would be more robust to liquidity shocks. The paper demonstrates that the nature of interbank interconnectedness is crucial for understanding financial fragility.

Freixas, Parigi and Rochet

A similar route is taken by Freixas, Parigi and Rochet. In their model, inter-regional financial connections arise because depositors face uncertainty about where, that is, in which locality, they need to consume. Interbank credit lines minimize the need for liquid reserves and allows banks to invest more in illiquid high-return technologies. On the other hand, these credit lines introduce fragility.

Freixas, Parigi and Rochet first analyse contagion via sunspot effects—a coordination failure due to the multiplicity of equilibria (as in Diamond and Dybvig). Insolvency of one bank may cause depositors of solvent banks to withdraw as well (contagion triggered by sunspot information?). Liquidity may dry up in the interbank market simply because each bank refuses to lend if it cannot be confident that it will itself be able to borrow in the interbank market—a self-fulfilling run. In that case, the central bank can act simply as a coordinating device and guide expectations towards the no-run equilibrium.

Contagion effects may also arise when one bank becomes insolvent for fundamental reasons (a low return). As in Allen and Gale, the authors compare different payment structures, for example, interbank funding via a credit chain (overlapping liabilities) versus diversified uniform lending across all banks (analogous to the complete market case). They show that contagion is more likely in the credit chain case. They also analyse asymmetric structures with a large money centre bank and small banks at the periphery. Not surprisingly, contagion is more likely when the centre bank fails.

PART IV: AN INTERNATIONAL LENDER OF LAST RESORT?

The main features of a national central bank's LOLR role receive widespread, if not unanimous, support. It should act, via OMO, to maintain such steady growth in the monetary aggregates as will maintain medium-term price stability, and at the same time stability in the financial system. These two objectives are complementary, not conflicting. As the contributions in Parts I to III show, there do, however, remain strong differences of view about the precise form of the LOLR function at the national level. But such differences of view become magnified when we move from the domestic to the international level. The domestic LOLR function is closely linked to a central bank's ability to create (high-powered) currency. There is no international currency. Does it then follow (as a matter of logic) that there cannot be an international lender of last resort (ILOLR)? Or, if there is such an ILOLR, will it be the central bank with the most widely internationally accepted, leading currency, that is, the Fed?

Of course, banks and banking systems have been bailed out, supported and recapitalized by Ministries of Finance (Treasuries), and through them by the taxpayer. This has happened in recent decades time and time again, for example, in Scandinavia, Japan, Chile, S & Ls in USA, Crédit Lyonnais in France, to name but a few. A banking panic is likely to entail considerable financial loss. When it is decided, by the responsible authorities, that the financial institution(s) should be kept in business, (but the loss is too big for its owners to bear, or for its other creditors, e.g. debt and deposit holders, to be prepared to absorb and to recapitalize), then someone else has to bear the burden.

Often, in such circumstances, the potential capital loss is too great for the central bank to sustain by itself. In earlier pre-1970 decades when the banking systems in most countries were cartelized and protected from competition, the central bank could call on financial support from the other commercial banks in order to share out the burden of potential loss more widely amongst the associates of a financial institution facing difficulties. The pressures of deregulation and global competition have largely blocked that route, though there were overtones of such a mechanism in the handling of the Long Term Capital Management (LTCM) crisis in 1998.

So, when a national central bank does not have the capital resources to handle a domestic crisis, it turns to its Finance Ministry and to the taxpayer. When the Ministry takes over, does that still count as LOLR? Similarly, neither the central bank, nor the Ministry, will have, or will be able to create, unlimited reserves of foreign currency, when the (liquidity) shortage takes the form of a shortage of foreign currency. In such a case they have to appeal for assistance to other bodies with access to foreign currency funds, either to national bodies, for example, to the US Treasury and the Fed, or to international bodies. The international institution established in order to deal with, and—one would hope—to prevent the need for such applications is, of course, the IMF.

This leads, first of all, to a semantic problem. Is such lending *ever* to be counted as ILOLR; or just when it is done by a (foreign) central bank, for example, the Fed;

or when the IMF does it; or is *any* lending to a country, irrespective of its source, subject to a critical shortage of foreign exchange to be counted as ILOLR?

The vastly more important question, however, rather than what do you call it, is whether such lending is desirable and effective, or not? Few doubt that national authorities can effectively recapitalize a loss-making financial institution(s), but many more doubt whether the IMF's procedures, for example, conditionality, do provide much benefit to the country applying for crisis funding. If so, why then do they apply? On the other hand, conditionality may be so severe, that they apply much later than would be desirable, or most efficacious.

The whole process is far more complex than in the national case, with a multiplicity of participants, (governments, central banks, creditors and debtors), of legal systems and infrastructures. So besides the standard concerns about contagion on one side, and moral hazard on the other, (which remain just as strong in the international as in the national contexts), questions about the design and conduct of any exercise of an *international* LOLR are complicated by externalities due to coordination problems among many agents and the lack of enforcement mechanisms among sovereign states. Furthermore, it may be the case that certain arrangements, while containing moral hazard to the greatest possible extent, are collectively inefficient because they place the burden on actors that have only limited capacity to take preventive measures—so social efficiency may be a crucial issue for an adequate design. Any institutional arrangement has to tackle these issues. In such circumstances it is not surprising that the discussion of this issue has been, and remains, highly charged. As all the contributors to this chapter bear witness, there is uncertainty and disquiet about how the IMF should be reformed, (or in the view of some disbanded); and whether, and what, is the role of an ILOLR. It is, indeed, an on-going policy issue.

Again, the authors put different relative weights on the three types of externalities. Capie and Schwartz stress the moral hazard issue and argue that it can be avoided by leaving liquidity provision to private markets. For emerging market economies, the Meltzer report sees a role for the public provision of LOLR, but within a strictly quasi market framework: Analogous to credit lines by private banks, the IMF should lend, but only to those countries which qualified in advance by meeting specified standards. Ideally, the qualification criteria are meant to prevent crises. If the commitment to prequalification were credible, coordination problems ex post would not arise.

But whenever contagion is at stake, serious doubts arise about the credibility (not to mention desirability) of any commitment not to lend to those countries which did not prequalify (or, even more seriously, to those which should be dequalified). Whenever contagion is at issue, arrangements have to be found for coping with the coordination problem. A main challenge is to design efficient, incentive compatible mechanisms for international burden sharing of potential losses. Concluding Part IV, Fischer and Giannini discuss various mechanisms to accomplish that goal. Giannini emphasizes the role of international adaptations, including changes in international contract practices and possibly an amendment of the IMF Articles of Agreement, to facilitate participation of the private sector and standstills.

Capie

Forrest Capie argues that a LOLR is defined by virtue of the fact that it alone provides the ultimate means of payment. According to Capie, 'there is no international money and so there can be no international lender of last resort.'

Moreover the function of such a lender is to provide liquidity to the system as a whole, not to individual applicants. By construction, applications for assistance are made to the IMF (or to the US authorities) by individual countries. 'Such rescues involve too much moral hazard.'[7]

Schwartz

Anna Schwartz argues, like Forrest Capie, that the IMF cannot be an ILOLR by definition, because 'It cannot create high-powered money in any national currency, so it cannot create international reserves.' Besides this (semantic?) point, she argues that the IMF suffers from some practical drawbacks as an ILOLR. Unlike national LOLRs, it has not proven possible for it to act quickly, or without lengthy consultations with its (prominent) members. She argues that worries about contagion, in the international arena, have been greatly overstated, whereas moral hazard is a serious problem. The wrong group of people have been supported in practice by the IMF's ILOLR actions, wealthy investors in developed countries, not the poorer people in the applicant countries or the taxpayers in countries funding the IMF.

In any case the resolution of financial crises is better done through private sector market mechanisms.

> The IMF was established in 1944 to serve as a lender to countries when private international capital markets were limited and repressed IMF lending had a proper role in that regime but it no longer exists. In the 1990s, private international capital markets are deregulated and flush with funds. IMF lending in the regime that now exists is a carryover for which there is no proper role.

Brealey

Brealey is more concerned with examining whether the IMF's LOLR operations work effectively than with (more ideological) questions whether the IMF should, or should not, act as a LOLR in principle. Indeed, he is sceptical about the validity of claims of the extent of either contagion or of moral hazard. On contagion, Brealey states that

> Underlying public policy towards international crises is the view that markets are subject to a succession of contagious bubbles and panics, which the authorities can, and should,

[7] Chari and Kehoe (1999) argue in a similar vein.

2

Lender of Last Resort: A Review of the Literature

XAVIER FREIXAS, CURZIO GIANNINI, GLENN HOGGARTH, AND FAROUK SOUSSA

The concept of lender of last resort (LOLR) originated at the beginning of the nineteenth century when Henry Thornton (1802) spelt out the basic elements of sound central bank practice with respect to distress lending. Walter Bagehot (1873), who is most often credited with establishing modern LOLR theory, expanded on Thornton's work (although without referring to him by name). Both authors justified the need for a LOLR whose role, they argued, was:

> . . . (1) to protect the money stock, (2) to support the whole financial system rather than individual financial institutions, (3) to behave consistently with the longer-run objective of stable money growth, and (4) to preannounce its policy in advance of crises so as to remove uncertainty. (Humphrey, 1989).

Bagehot suggested that, in a liquidity crisis, a central bank should lend freely, at a high rate of interest relative to the pre-crisis period, to any borrower with good collateral, where good collateral was any paper normally accepted by the central bank, valued at between panic and pre-panic prices. He also recommended that the quality standards on collateral taken by the Bank of England during a crisis should be relaxed. Institutions without good collateral were assumed to be insolvent and should, Bagehot argued, be allowed to fail.

Although this description of the LOLR function continues to influence central bank policy makers today, current LOLR practices have also been shaped by changes in the financial and regulatory system over the past century.

This paper addresses the issues set out in the recent literature on LOLR support. It starts with the fundamental question of whether an LOLR is necessary and then reviews the modern debate on LOLR. This is followed by a discussion of when and why capital injections to insolvent banks might be necessary and, finally, the costs of LOLR and capital injections.

We would like to thank Alastair Clark, Paul Tucker and Geoffrey Wood for helpful comments.

This article first appeared in the Bank of England's *Financial Stability Review*, November 1999 (www.bankofengland.co.uk/fsr/).

THE NEED FOR A LENDER OF LAST RESORT

The term 'LOLR' is used in different ways in the literature. In this paper, LOLR is taken to mean the *discretionary* provision of liquidity to a financial institution (or the market as a whole) by the central bank in reaction to an adverse shock which causes an abnormal increase in demand for liquidity which cannot be met from an alternative source.

The central bank provides liquidity (reserve money) in exchange for, or against the security of, financial assets. Although this increases the liquidity of a bank's balance sheet it does not change the overall value of its assets.

Asymmetric Information

This section addresses cases of emergency lending to illiquid but *solvent* institutions. The distinction between solvent and insolvent banks is a feature of the academic literature. In practice, however, a central bank may not always be able to make this distinction, particularly in the short time-scale in which a lending decision may have to be made.[1]

Bank Runs

A distinguishing feature of banks is that their assets are largely illiquid term loans while their liabilities comprise predominantly unsecured short term deposits. Moreover, deposits are paid out in full on a first-come-first-served basis. Most economists agree that these features of banks' balance sheets make them susceptible to depositor runs. Since, in general, banks' assets are not readily marketable, such runs can result in the forced disposal of these assets at depressed 'fire sale' prices and thence to the insolvency of an otherwise fundamentally sound bank. This potentially involves a welfare loss to the public as a whole which would justify public sector intervention, assuming that the benefit of such intervention outweighs the costs involved.

In the literature on bank runs, it is usually assumed that depositors are individuals or firms who have placed funds in a bank for an indefinite period but with the understanding that these funds may be redeemed at face value on demand or at short notice. This literature does not cover other types of bank liability such as interbank borrowing, CDs, bonds and commercial paper, all of which typically have a pre-specified maturity. Although in practice some of these may be the source of liquidity problems for banks—for example, short-term interbank lending may not be rolled over—the literature reviewed here focuses on deposits as defined above.

The first paper formally to model the possibility of bank runs was that of Diamond and Dybvig (1983), where it was demonstrated that despite certainty

[1] Hawtrey (1932) argues that the central bank can avoid having to make a decision as to the solvency of a bank if it lends only on collateral. If the bank fails, however, the central bank will avoid losses only if sufficient margin had been taken to cover any fall in the value of the collateral.

of financial instability. These costs of financial instability are normally proportionately higher for large banks, notwithstanding higher support costs, although not necessarily so (Freixas, 1999).

Interbank Credit Risk Exposures

Because of the extensive network of interbank exposures of various kinds, the failure of one bank to fulfil its obligations may have an immediate and direct knock-on effect on other banks.

One mechanism through which this may occur is interbank lending, which is usually unsecured. Although intuitively this is clearly a possible source of systemic risk, careful modelling of interbank market exposures has not been widely developed. Rochet and Tirole (1996) present a general model, the purpose of which is to '. . . provide a framework in which some of the issues surrounding systemic risk can start being analysed.' Their contribution to this discussion is that they provide a model of the inter-linkages that exist between banks, grouped under the generic heading 'interbank lending'. In their model, peer monitoring is presented as a potential source of systemic risk via interbank lending. This is because, if peer monitoring is to be encouraged, the authorities must commit to closing all banks who suffer losses from interbank loan exposures: if the failure of one bank causes the failure of another which had lent to it, both banks must be allowed to fail. If this is not the case, there would be no incentive for peer monitoring. Because it is difficult for the central bank to commit to a closure policy that would allow knock-on effects to occur, Rochet and Tirole conclude that the practical relevance of peer monitoring is seriously reduced.

Empirical analysis of the magnitude of interbank market exposures, and thus their likely systemic consequences, is constrained by a lack of available data. However, in one study of interbank exposures, Michael (1998) concludes that such exposures in the United Kingdom interbank market are significant, particularly amongst the large settlement banks which provide payment services to other banks.

Another source of systemic risk lies in the operation of settlement and payment arrangements.[5] Humphrey (1986), McAndrews and Wasilyew (1995) and Angelini, Maresca and Russo (1996) all examine the risks posed by payment system exposures and conclude that they are significant, although to varying degrees, depending on system characteristics. The most fundamental difference is that between payment systems with deferred (uncollateralised) net settlement and those with real-time gross settlement.[6] Systems with deferred uncollateralised net settlement generate substantial interbank exposures. From the time payment instructions are exchanged until the settlement is completed, the receiving bank is exposed to the

[5] See Bank of England (1989) and Hills and Rule (1999) in this issue for a discussion of the potential risks inherent in payments and settlement systems.

[6] A deferred net settlement system is one in which a bank's net position—the difference between the sum of the value of transfers it is owed and owes—is calculated at a point in time, such as the end of day, and at the same time a corresponding payment/receipt is made (see BIS, 1997a).

sending bank. Kobayakawa (1997) and Schoenmaker (1995) discuss the possibility of systemic disturbances in a deferred net settlements system.

A real-time gross settlement system (RTGS) eliminates these exposures between members. However, if the central bank provides uncollateralised intra-day liquidity (as is the case with Fedwire in the United States) to facilitate the process of real-time settlement, the central bank takes on the credit risk. In the European Union, central banks have addressed this risk by themselves taking collateral from members of the systems in overdraft.

Freixas and Parigi (1997) compare the benefits and costs of a real time gross settlement system and a deferred net settlement system. They conclude that a gross payment system is preferable when the probability of bank failures is high (for a given cost of bank failures), the cost of holding reserves is low and the volume of payments is low.[7]

Empirical evidence on interbank exposures arising from payment and settlement systems is limited. Using data from the Federal Reserve's large value transfer system, Fedwire, Furfine (1999) concludes that the threat to systemic risk posed by bilateral payment system exposures relative to capital is exaggerated. However, as Furfine's data represent just twenty per cent of the interbank exposures in the US system, he concedes that his results may represent a conservative estimate of the importance of system risk via interbank exposures as a whole.

Contagion

The possibility of runs on individual banks as a result of the combination of the deposit contract and asymmetric information was considered in the section on bank runs. Widespread runs which affect several banks in a domino fashion (contagion) are considered in this section.

The failure of one bank may lead to runs on another bank if depositors perceive similarities between the two (Docking, Hirschey, and Jones, 1997). Although bank portfolios may vary, certain banks may specialise in similar types of business (e.g. commercial real estate, automobile loans etc.) or geographic areas (e.g. regional banks) and may therefore hold similar assets. If the failure of a bank leads depositors in similar banks to withdraw their deposits, while depositors in dissimilar banks do not, the contagion is said to be information-based (Chari and Jagannathan, 1988). That is, depositors take the decision to withdraw their funds based on information about the similarity of the two banks. If, however, the failure of a bank results in widespread runs regardless of any assessment of similarities or differences between banks, such a situation is referred to as 'pure panic' contagion.

The idea that the failure of a bank may change depositors' confidence in the solvency of other banks, independently of the correlation in asset quality, has been expressed often but seldom modelled. This view assumes that depositors' irrational

[7] In practice, RTGS may not require higher reserves but would operate on the basis of intra-day credit by the central bank. The cost would therefore be the conditions imposed by the central bank in providing such credit (e.g. collateral, interest etc.).

behaviour may lead to a run on a sound bank in reaction to another bank's failure. Such an occurrence is implied, for example, by the Diamond and Dybvig (1983) model, described earlier.[8]

Kaufman (1994) presents evidence addressing the question of whether past episodes of widespread bank runs were motivated by pure panic, or were information-based. He reviews empirical studies that assess the reaction of uninsured depositors (for which equity-holders are used as a proxy) to the failure, or announcement of significant losses, of another bank.[9] These studies examine whether, following a bank failure, share prices fall more for banks with similar characteristics than those with dissimilar ones (e.g. size, geographical location) to the failed bank. Similar studies published since Kaufman's review include Liu and Ryan (1995), Aharony and Swary (1996), and Docking, Hirschey, and Jones (1997). They all support the view that contagion very rarely takes place due to pure panic. Rather, information-based contagion through perceived similarities between banks is found to be far more significant, although these studies are not directly based on deposit contracts.

CENTRAL BANKS' RESPONSE TO ILLIQUIDITY PROBLEMS

If LOLR implies the exchange of illiquid assets (whether for a bank or for a market) for reserve money, in order to be fully credible the provider of LOLR facilities needs to have unlimited capacity to supply reserve money. The issues are somewhat different however depending on whether the shortage is at the level of a firm or the market generally.[10]

Lending to the Market

Since Bagehot's day, there has been a substantial widening and deepening of interbank markets. One view in the academic literature is that in the light of these

[8] Krugman (1999) argues that the recent east Asian crisis appears to have had some characteristics of a panic. In particular, the pattern of capital outflows from Asian countries in 1997–98 only partly reflected the pre-crisis fundamentals in the affected economies (see Haldane, 1999 in this issue).

[9] These include studies by Wicker (1980), Aharony and Swary (1983), Swary (1986), Lamy and Thompson (1986), Cornell and Shapiro (1986), Federal Reserve Bank of Cleveland (1986), Smirlock and Kaufold (1987), Peavy and Hempel (1988), Madura and McDaniel (1989), Wall and Peterson (1990), Smith and White (1990), Musumeci and Sinkey (1990), Dickinson, Peterson, and Christiansen (1991), Gay, Timme, and Yung (1991), Karafiath, Mynatt, and Smith (1991), Kane (1992), and Aharony and Swary (1992). These are all event-studies (i.e. measure share-price reaction to particular events). Other studies (not reviewed by Kaufman) include Saunders and Wilson (1996), Gorton (1988), Schoenmaker (1996), and Calomiris and Mason (1997).

[10] Since usually one important source of information in assessing solvency is from supervisory returns and there is risk involved in using public funds, the provision of LOLR will usually require close co-operation and exchange of information amongst the central bank, the supervisor (in countries where this is located outside the central bank) and the government. In the United Kingdom this has been formalised in the Memorandum of Understanding (MoU) between the Bank of England, the Financial Services Authority and HM Treasury. The MoU is set out as an annex in the Bank of England Quarterly Bulletin, May 1998.

developments, emergency liquidity provision need only ever be made to the market as a whole through open market operations (OMOs) (see, e.g. Goodfriend and King (1988), Bordo (1990), Schwartz (1992, 1995)).[11] This is because, as discussed earlier, the interbank market would ensure the allocation of liquidity from banks with surpluses to those with deficits, provided that the latter are considered creditworthy.[12]

Open market operations are also the principal mechanism through which monetary policy is implemented by the central bank on a day-to-day basis in normal circumstances. The question of whether or not a distinction can be made between monetary policy and LOLR support to the market as a whole therefore arises. Goodfriend and King (1988) draw no distinction between the two, arguing that LOLR to the market as a whole is monetary policy aimed at smoothing interest rates (the supply of reserve money is increased to match an increase in reserve money demand, thus stemming upward pressure on interest rates). There is little other modern literature on the matter, but Thornton (1802) suggested LOLR support is to satisfy extraordinary *short-term* increases in the demand for reserve money whereas monetary policy is aimed at targeting medium-long run growth in monetary aggregates (and thus inflation).[13] However, regardless of the motive, LOLR support to the money market as a whole will involve an increase in the supply of reserve money in order to satisfy the increase in reserve money demand. Since there is no distinction between the operations used for LOLR to the market and for monetary purposes, Goodhart (1999) argues that the term LOLR should be used only for central bank liquidity support to individual banks.[14]

Liquidity Support to Individual Institutions

The main reason put forward in the literature for central bank lending to individual banks is that the inefficiencies in the interbank market described earlier could result in some solvent banks becoming illiquid because they cannot borrow from other banks. While LOLR support to the market as a whole increases the supply of reserve money, lending to specific banks need not. Any bilateral lending may be offset through reduced provision of liquidity to the market as a whole via OMOs,

[11] It should be noted that in practice most central banks have a limited number of counterparties in OMOs who are expected to on-lend to the market more generally. These counterparties are selected on the basis of strict criteria. The Bank of England, for example, requires that counterparties (i) have the technical capability to respond to OMOs, (ii) maintain an active presence in gilt repo/bill markets, (iii) participate regularly in OMOs, and (iv) provide useful information on market conditions and developments.

[12] As discussed in the section on the failure of the interbank market, this view implies that the central bank has no informational advantage over the interbank market.

[13] In practice, faced with a sudden increase in financial instability, for example, the 1987 stock market crash, central banks have sometimes loosened monetary policy in order to maintain monetary stability.

[14] It is possible, however, as with the arrangements for Y2K, for central banks to satisfy temporary increases in the financial system's demand for liquidity through either discretionary increases in the supply of reserves, or passive increases where standing facilities are provided, without changing their monetary policy interest rate.

implying that although the composition of the central bank's assets change, the supply of total reserve money does not.

It is important to note too that the distinction between illiquidity and insolvency discussed in the analysis above is seldom clear-cut in practice. Goodhart (1995), Lastra (1997) and Goodhart and Huang (1999) all argue that the time-scale required for making a decision as to whether or not to lend to a bank is often too short to be able to arrive at firm conclusions over its solvency. Even where the potential sources of pressure were observable far in advance, for example, Y2K, or build-up slowly, such as the small bank crisis in the UK in the early 1990s, and the authorities can thus plan somewhat, the need for action at short notice is still possible. Moreover, a bank which is solvent *ex ante* may not be so *ex post*; for example, a future deterioration in the general economic situation may mean that a bank which was solvent at the time of the liquidity injection becomes insolvent later. Central banks which lend in such circumstances should have a clear exit strategy.

RISK-CAPITAL SUPPORT

Justification

So far this article has described LOLR as being largely motivated by the negative consequences bank failures originating in liquidity problems have on the stability of the financial system. The stability of the financial system can of course also be threatened by the failure of an obviously *insolvent* bank. Moreover, it is possible that the failure of an insolvent non-bank financial institution could also pose a systemic threat. In such circumstances the *ex ante* provision of risk capital rather than liquidity support may need to be considered by the authorities.

Systemic risk aside, it is possible that it may be less costly to restructure an insolvent bank than allow it to fail.[15] James (1991), among others, has obtained results showing that the liquidation value of a bank is lower than its market value as a going concern. Guttentag and Herring (1983) also make this point, stating that 'banks usually are worth more alive than dead even when their worth alive is negative.' This is primarily a justification for the take-over of bad banks by good banks. However, some argue that, failing this, capital injection by the public sector accompanied by restructuring of a bad bank may be justified where the benefits outweight the costs of doing so.

Goodhart and Huang (1999) argue that financial instability resulting from the failure of a bank is characterised by panic in which the behaviour of depositors becomes unpredictable. Mistakes in the conduct of monetary policy are thus more likely to occur. They argue that when the central bank is approached by a bank for

[15] Note that this also provides further justification for extending liquidity support to illiquid, solvent but non-systemic banks.

liquidity support, it does not have time to verify whether or not the bank is solvent. If the central bank provides support to a bank that is revealed later to be insolvent, it will incur a direct financial loss as well as suffering a reputational cost. The central bank will therefore in practice need to weigh the probable cost of providing capital to a possibly insolvent bank against the cost of the instability that its failure could generate.

The Provision of Risk Capital in Practice

Empirical analyses of the resolution of cases of bank default indicate that failing banks are more often dealt with through the injection of capital rather than being liquidated. Goodhart and Schoenmaker (1995), for example, gather evidence on the effective resolution policies in 24 countries. Out of a sample of 104 failing banks, they find that 73 resulted in rescue and 31 in liquidation. Santomero and Hoffman's (1998) review of bank default resolution similarly establishes that access to the discount window in the US between 1985 and 1991 was often granted to banks with poor CAMEL ratings that later failed.[16] (Access was granted, they argue, in order to keep institutions afloat—even those which were known to be insolvent—so as not to impose further costs on the deposit insurance fund which had suffered large losses.)

Who Should Provide Capital to Banks?

There are a number of reasons why the provision of LOLR support and the provision of risk capital for insolvent banks may or should fall to different institutions.

In theory, emergency support in its strictest sense to solvent but illiquid banks implies no risk to the central bank. In practice, as discussed in the section on liquidity support to individual institutions, the value of the collateral may fall below the value of the loan thus creating a risk to the central bank. Therefore, lending to a bank—particularly a large one—that is not clearly solvent, could expose the central bank to potential loss. Many central banks would not be in a position to take on such risk independently and therefore it would require a government guarantee to cover the central bank exposure (Goodhart and Schoenmaker, 1993; Goodhart, 1999).

Stella (1997) argues that a central bank may not need capital in the same way as commercial banks. Capital is necessary for commercial banks in order to provide a buffer against losses, to provide start-up funds, and to overcome moral hazard problems with creditors. He argues that none of these factors applies in the same way to central banks. Stella calculates a central bank's net worth taking into account the net present value of future income (including seignorage revenue), so that the importance of subscribed capital for central banks is reduced. However, he

[16] CAMEL ratings are scores assigned by US supervisors that reflect their judgement of a bank's Capital, Asset quality, Management, Earnings and Liquidity.

argues that a weak balance sheet (resulting perhaps partly from exposures to troubled banks) may compromise its independence and ability to retain flexibility in its conduct of monetary (and foreign exchange) policy.

In practice, if an institution were *clearly* insolvent the government would need to make a decision on whether or not to provide risk capital to prevent its failure. Although the central bank would probably advise on the systemic consequences of the failure of the institution, the government's decision for support might also be made on other criteria (e.g. for social reasons).

THE COSTS OF LOLR/CAPITAL INJECTIONS–MORAL HAZARD

Any form of insurance, and liquidity and capital support are no exception in this respect, creates moral hazard. Moral hazard arises when the provision of insurance, by modifying the incentives for the insured party to take preventive actions, increases the probability of occurrence of the event being insured against. Moral hazard is inherently forward-looking: a particular episode 'creates' moral hazard only to the extent that it influences expectations of how a similar situation will be dealt with in the future. In principle, where liquidity support can be clearly separated from provision of risk capital, the moral hazard created will be limited to possible mismanagement of liquidity risk. Capital support, however, may raise expectations that the financial institution is insured against mismanagement of virtually all types of risk, including credit and market risk (from which particular benefits may accrue).

Moral Hazard in Emergency Assistance and Bailouts of Individual Institutions

If exercised too leniently, LOLR may lead to banks expecting liquidity support from the central bank '. . .as a matter of course' (Bagehot, 1873). Indeed, if liquidity support is extended on terms more favourable than are available in the market, it ceases to be lending of *last resort* altogether. It is for this reason that Bagehot's 'rules' proposed, among other things, that lending be made at a rate high relative to the pre-crisis rate. This, he believed, would ration access to liquidity and decrease the moral hazard problem. Also, a penalty rate was thought to be a fair price to pay for the protection offered to the failing bank through the provision of liquidity or to cover the central bank's risk exposure (Humphrey, 1989).

An injection of capital, on the other hand, may have two effects on bank behaviour (Freixas and Rochet, 1997). First, it gives the bank managers and shareholders incentives to take additional risks so as to maximise the subsidy implicit in such a rescue. Second, the possibility that the official sector will provide risk-capital to a failed financial institution may reduce the incentives for uninsured creditors to monitor the behaviour and performance of the institutions to which they have lent (Kaufman, 1991; Rochet and Tirole, 1996). Whereas deposit insurance is explicit and typically covers only retail depositors, and then usually only up to a certain amount, capital injections *implicitly* insure all investors.[17] They will thus further reduce the incentives of partially insured depositors to monitor *and* also weaken the incentives of uninsured investors and peer banks as well.

Both Thornton (1802) and Bagehot (1873) were well aware of this risk of moral hazard. As Bagehot put it, 'any aid to a present bad bank is the surest mode of preventing the establishment of a future good bank'. Bagehot's proposal to lend only on security reflects the attempt to eliminate the moral hazard capital provision entails.

Under modern financial conditions, however, the applicability of Bagehot's rules is questionable. To begin with, the idea of lending at a penalty rate is often challenged and in practice emergency lending to individual solvent institutions has sometimes been made without applying a premium over the current national market rate (Goodhart and Schoenmaker, 1995; Prati and Schinasi, 1999). This occurred, for example, during the Savings and Loans crisis in the United States. This divergence from Bagehot's rules has several justifications: lending at a high rate may (i) aggravate the bank's crisis (Crockett, 1996; Garcia and Plautz, 1988); (ii) send a signal to the market that precipitates an untimely run, unless it is provided covertly; and (iii) give the managers incentives to pursue a higher risk/reward strategy to get themselves out of trouble ('gamble for resurrection'). These risks may be more likely in modern financial systems where clearly solvent financial institutions should normally be able to obtain liquidity from the interbank market.

However, as we have seen, it may be socially desirable for the public sector to intervene even when faced with a clearly insolvent institution. Prati and Schinasi (1999) and Giannini (1999) point out that in many industrial countries, authorities have often felt the need to advance support even when confronted with a genuine insolvency problem.

One means of limiting the moral hazard leads to the notion of 'constructive ambiguity'. As Corrigan (1990) has argued, by introducing an element of uncertainty into the provision of support, pressure can, in principle, be maintained on banks to act prudently, since the latter will not know individually whether they will be rescued or not. Constructive ambiguity is, by definition, difficult to pin down and formalise. An informal definition of the notion can be found in a recent G10 Report which states that:

> . . . any pre-commitment to a particular course of action in support of a financial institution should be avoided by the authorities, who should retain discretion as to whether, when and under what conditions support would be provided. In addition, when making such a decision, it is important to analyse rigorously whether there is a systemic threat and, if so, what options there may be for dealing with systemic contagion effects in ways that limit the adverse impact on market discipline. (BIS, 1997b)

[17] One exception is the current deposit insurance scheme in Japan which covers all depositors and creditors. However, mainly in recognition of moral hazard concerns, this scheme is planned to end in March 2001 (see Nakaso, 1999).

As this passage makes clear, *ex ante* constructive ambiguity is a complex notion, encompassing, besides uncertainty as to whether intervention will take place at all, also uncertainty regarding both the *exact timing* of the intervention and the *terms* and *penalties* attached to any particular intervention.

Ambiguity regarding whether intervention is actually taking place, which implies that liquidity assistance may be provided covertly, might be desirable either to avoid 'imitation effects' within the banking system or where, due to the bank's size and operational ramifications, the handling of an individual bank's problem risks itself triggering systemic repercussions (Enoch, Stella, and Khamis, 1997). The rationale for this type of secrecy, in circumstances where widespread panic has not yet occurred, was, for example, set out in a speech by Eddie George, Governor of the Bank of England, where he stated that:

> . . .we usually try to keep the fact that we are providing systemic support secret at the time. . . . If people know that we are so concerned about systemic fragility that we have judged it necessary to provide support, that could lead to a wider loss of confidence. They would wonder how far that support would be extended, and we could rapidly find ourselves in the position where we were in practice underwriting all the liabilities of the banking system. (George, 1994)

When a panic has already set in, however, it is sometimes recognised that management of the crisis, including support operations, may usefully be made public. This is because transparency during a crisis may reduce uncertainty and thereby have a calming effect on financial markets (Bagehot, 1873).

Ambiguity regarding the conditions attached to liquidity support, in turn, may be needed to keep managers and shareholders uncertain as to the cost they will have to bear should a firm's illiquidity result from imprudent behaviour (Crockett, 1996).

The downside of constructive ambiguity is that it places a large degree of discretion in the hands of the agency responsible for crisis management. As in other fields of economic policy-making, discretion raises a time-consistency problem: while it is in the interest of the authorities to deny their willingness to provide a safety-net, *ex post* they may later find it optimal to intervene. Lack of transparency enables them to avoid having to justify treating differently what the general public may perceive as identical situations. Enoch, Stella and Khamis (1997) argue that central bank discretion in handling individual cases could be balanced against firm rules for disclosure after the event.[18] Indeed, as the IMF's Code of Good Practices on Transparency in Monetary and Financial Policies itself testifies, an effort is currently being made in this direction (IMF, 1999).[19]

[18] This is exemplified by the Bank of England's handling of the small banks crisis in the early 1990s where, at the time, it was not made public that the Bank was providing assistance to a small number of small banks. After the direct systemic threats were averted, however, the Bank then disclosed its operations to the public and accounted for its actions (see, e.g. *Bank of England Annual Report*, various issues).

[19] '. . . aggregate information on emergency financial support by financial institutions should be publicly disclosed through an appropriate statement when such disclosure will not be disruptive to financial stability' (IMF, 1999 para 7.3.1).

In practice, the effectiveness of constructive ambiguity as a check on moral hazard can be expected to be greater to the extent that there exist procedures for 'punishing' the managers and shareholders of imprudently managed intermediaries. Furthermore, the effects of moral hazard have often been contained by rules directly constraining or indirectly encouraging banks and other financial intermediaries to act prudently, including in managing their capital and liquidity.

'Punishing' the managers and shareholders of imprudently managed intermediaries is widely regarded as crucial in the context of official capital injection. As Andrew Crockett has recently put it:

> . . . if it is clear that management will always lose their jobs, and shareholders their capital, in the event of a failure, moral hazard should be alleviated. (Crockett, 1996)

The extent to which moral hazard and time consistency problems have been limited in practice in individual countries is, of course, debatable. Unsurprisingly, countries that experienced serious banking problems have also felt it necessary to modify their institutional set-up. In the United States, for example, the S&L crisis stirred a heated debate on whether limits should be placed on the degree of forbearance authorities may show in deciding when to trigger 'punishment strategies'. The debate led to the revision of the overall safety net through the FDIC Improvement Act (1991), which aimed at making it 'more incentive-compatible by providing for a graduated series of regulatory sanctions to mimic market discipline' (Benston and Kaufman, 1998). The notion of Prompt Corrective Action—according to which sanctions become mandatory after a certain threshold has been reached—is an important component of the reform.

Concerted Private Sector Lending—a Possible Solution to the Moral Hazard Problem

As discussed earlier, disruptions in the interbank market may justify a role for the central bank as LOLR if such problems cannot be overcome in some other way. However, the central bank may be able to overcome the market's co-ordination and information problem through organising private sector liquidity support rather than lending itself.

The central bank may have a role of bringing potential lenders together where individual banks, even when known to be solvent, are unable to obtain funds due to co-ordination problems among creditors. This is the basis of the interbank market failure in Freixas, Parigi, and Rochet (1998) (which builds on the co-ordination failure literature of Diamond and Dybvig, 1983), described in the section on failure of the interbank market. Such co-ordination problems could be resolved by the central bank bringing all banks together and encouraging dialogue: if banks are able to reassure one another that liquidity will be forthcoming, interbank lending will resume.

The other failures of the interbank market described earlier are related to uncertainty about the solvency of the bank in question. In such cases, some pressure by the central bank on surplus banks to lend may be warranted if the former has superior information to markets participants (via the supervisor, involvement in the payment system or as part of an application for emergency liquidity assistance).

Giannini (1999) points out that often in the past central banks have acted as an agent organising the channelling of other banks' private funds—concerted lending—to the bank in difficulty. In principle, organising such private sector support could be either the responsibility of the central bank or another official agency (Fischer, 1999). The central bank, however, as the bankers' bank and at the heart of the monetary and payments system, has an advantage in organising private sector liquidity support because it can provide agency (e.g. escrow) facilities or act as a principal intermediary.

Central bank involvement in organising private liquidity support is targeted at overcoming co-ordination problems.[20] The central bank should not need to 'coerce' other banks to lend as all parties should be better off doing so. If the central bank does pressure banks to lend, or to lend on terms that would improve the failing bank's position relative to what it would otherwise have been, then this would indicate that the problem is not purely one of co-ordination. In such a case, private sector support is still, in effect, subsidising the failing bank (Goodfriend and Lacker, 1999).

More generally, co-ordination problems may be difficult to overcome because of the short-term competitive advantage surplus banks experience during a crisis. In these circumstances, 'moral suasion' and regulatory powers may be required to instil a co-operative attitude into what are otherwise keen competitors. This seems to underlie Kindleberger's view that:

> . . . the optimum may be a small number of actors, closely attuned to one another in an oligarchic relation, like-minded, applying strong pressure to keep down the chiselers and free-riders, prepared ultimately to accept responsibility. (Kindleberger, 1989)

Historical evidence seems to confirm the existence of a tension between the effectiveness of concerted support and the degree of competition in the financial system. Orchestrated liquidity support operations occurred often in the past. The Bank of England's co-ordination of the rescue of Baring Bros. in 1890 and its organisation of a 'life-boat' during the secondary banking crisis in the early 1970s (see Reid, 1982) are prominent examples, as is the Clearinghouse System—a private institutional framework in place for dealing with liquidity problems—operating in the United States from the 1860s up to the 1910s. Such private sector solutions, however, became less feasible as the degree of competition in the market increased. The Clearinghouse System was brought down, at the beginning of the century, by the marked increase in competition in the key US financial centre, New York. Likewise, orchestrated operations became more difficult to organise in the United

[20] An analogy can be drawn with the Bank of England's 'London Approach', which is aimed at overcoming co-ordination problems amongst creditors of non-financial institutions (see Kent, 1997; Brierley and Vlieghe, 1999).

Kingdom during the 1980s, when the difficulties encountered in the rescue of Johnson Matthey Bankers Ltd., a London bank which had been an active market-maker in the gold bullion sector, in an environment of heightened competition led the authorities to rethink their approach to LOLR support (Capie *et al.* 1994).[21]

The notion that liquidity support should be seen primarily as the responsibility of the institutions operating in the market has, however, remained in countries where competition in the financial system has until recently been somewhat limited, e.g. France, Italy, and Germany: in the last of these it was formalised with the creation, in the 1970s, of the so-called LikoBank to deal with liquidity problems at smaller banks. The US authorities at the beginning of the 1990s were concerned that the climate of competition characteristic of their financial markets prevented this feature of continental European banking practices from being reproduced on the other side of the Atlantic. As Corrigan put it:

> Private institutions either are more willing, or feel more compelled, to participate in stabilisation or rescue efforts in foreign countries than they are in the United States. (. . .) Where a handful of banks dominate national banking systems, that handful of banks feels more directly threatened by potential dangers of a systemic nature than do banks here in the United States. (Corrigan, 1990)

However, the handling of the crisis of Long Term Capital Management (LTCM), in 1998, may reflect a change in view of the importance of systemic risk to counterparties of financial institutions. As William McDonough (1998) recently stated, the failure of LTCM would have had substantial repercussions on financial markets, on which LTCM's counterparties 'voiced their own concerns' so that, in the end, 'a private sector solution . . . involving an investment of new equity by Long-Term Capital's creditors and counterparties' was reached.[22] This may suggest that in some circumstances a financial institution can be 'too big to fail' even from the perspective of the rest of the private sector.

SUMMARY

This paper has identified, from the literature, two main reasons for the existence of the central bank's role as LOLR:

- informational asymmetry which makes otherwise solvent banks vulnerable to deposit withdrawals and/or the drying up of interbank lending in times of crisis; this can result in insolvency for otherwise sound banks, and thus a welfare loss to the bank's stakeholders.

[21] It should be noted, however, that the more recent failure of Barings in 1995 was because the magnitude of Barings' losses were uncertain since open positions in derivatives markets made the risk to potential creditors unquantifiable (see the evidence given before the Treasury Select Committee by Eddie George, Governor of the Bank of England (Treasury and Civil Service Committee, 1995)).

[22] Statement before the Committee on Banking and Financial Services in the United States Congress, October 1998.

- the potential risk to the stability of the financial system as a whole following the failure of a solvent bank. Widespread financial instability may prevent the financial system from performing its primary functions including the smooth operation of the payments system, and intermediating between savers and borrowers with an efficient pricing of risk. Such problems may be induced by the failure of a large financial institution, or a group of smaller ones, which have ripple effects on other financial institutions through direct credit or payments exposures or via contagion.

Risks to the stability of the financial system as a whole also arise with the failure of a large insolvent bank (and possibly non-bank financial institutions). In such cases, the government would make a decision on whether or not to provide risk capital to prevent its failure. The central bank would likely play a role in providing objective expert advice on the systemic consequences of the failure of the institution concerned.

LOLR and/or capital support should be considered only when the benefits from intervention outweigh the costs, particularly of moral hazard and also potential losses to the tax-payer.

Two channels of possible LOLR support are identified in the literature—(i) lending to the market as a whole and (ii) lending to individual institutions. LOLR support to the market as a whole is used to deal with generalised liquidity shortages. Such operations (which are made against high quality collateral) reduce the general level of short-term interest rates or prevent them from rising further. Put another way, such support increases the supply of reserve money. The distinction between LOLR support to the market and a loosening in monetary policy is not easily made leading some academics to suggest that they are one and the same thing.

Central bank emergency liquidity support to individual illiquid but solvent institutions occurs when such institutions cannot borrow from other banks or from the central bank through normal facilities. Unlike lending to the market as a whole, lending to individual institutions need not increase the size of the central bank's balance sheet, but will change its composition. This implies that there need be no conflict with monetary policy. It is likely that such lending is made against collateral not acceptable in normal monetary operations or on the interbank market. Therefore, emergency assistance may expose the central bank to risk should the bank which receives it become insolvent and the value of the collateral taken subsequently fall below the value of the loan. In practice, when an institution faces a sudden liquidity crisis, it is sometimes difficult for the central bank to obtain timely and detailed information to assess whether the institution is fundamentally solvent or not. A central bank may therefore mistakenly lend to an insolvent bank. Moreover, what may start as an illiquidity problem may evolve into an insolvency one. In such circumstances it is important that the central bank has a clear exit strategy.

The literature identifies a number of costs from providing liquidity and especially solvency support. There is a direct financial cost involved in the explicit provision of risk-capital to insolvent institutions and in losses incurred through providing liquidity to banks which turn out subsequently to be insolvent. Moreover, by insuring banks against the costs of liquidity or solvency problems, the provision of support may result in banks being less concerned than would be the case otherwise to avoid such problems (i.e. it promotes moral hazard). In particular, if LOLR is given to individual firms on too favourable terms, it may cease to be last resort lending altogether and banks may come to rely on it as a matter of course. More importantly, the expectation of bail out in an insolvency situation may result in bank managers and shareholders taking excessive risks and creditors and uninsured depositors not properly monitoring their banks.

A potential method to reduce, although not eliminate, the moral hazard problem is, as suggested by Bagehot more than a century ago, through imposing a high rate (relative to the pre-crisis period) but this may: (i) aggravate the bank's crisis; (ii) send a signal to the market that precipitates an untimely run; and (iii) give the managers incentives to pursue a higher risk-reward strategy in order to repay the higher rate ('gamble for resurrection'). In practice, moral hazard has often been reduced through maintaining a degree of uncertainty about which financial institutions receive support and which will be allowed to fail ('constructive ambiguity') coupled with procedures for 'punishing' the managers and shareholders of imprudently managed intermediaries. In addition, safeguards have been used to limit the impact of moral hazard and the amount of discretion allowed in liquidity support. The cost to the public sector has also been minimised through the central bank/supervisor encouraging liquidity support from the private sector.

REFERENCES

Aharony, J and Swary, I (1983) 'Contagion Effects of Bank Failures: Evidence from Capital Markets', *Journal of Business* (July), Vol 56(3), pp. 305–22.

Aharony, J and Swary, I (1992) 'Local Versus Nation-wide Contagion Effects of Bank Failures: The Case of the South West', Working Paper, Israel Institute of Business Research.

Aharony, J and Swary, I (1996) 'Additional Evidence on the Information-based Contagion Effects of Bank Failures', *Journal of Banking and Finance*, Vol. 20, pp. 57–69.

Allen, F and Gale, D (1997) 'Innovation in Financial Services, Relationships and Risk Sharing', University of Pennsylvania Working Paper, pp. 97–126.

Angelini, P and Giannini, C (1994) 'On the Economics of Interbank Payment Systems', *Economic Notes*, Vol 23, No 2, pp. 191–215.

Angelini, P, Maresca, G and Russo, D (1996) 'Systemic Risk in the Netting System', *Journal of Banking and Finance*, Vol. 20, pp. 853–68.

Avery, R B, Belton, T M and Goldberg, M A (1988) 'Market Discipline in Regulating Bank Risk: New Evidence from the Capital Markets', *Journal of Money, Credit, and Banking*, Vol. 20, pp 597–610.

Bagehot, W (1873) 'Lombard Street: A Description of the Money Market', London, H S King.

Bank for International Settlements (1994) 'Public Disclosure of Market and Credit Risks by Financial Intermediaries', Basel, September.

Bank for International Settlements (1997a) 'G10 Report on Financial Stability in Emerging Market Economies', Basel.

Bank for International Settlements (1997b) 'Real-time Gross Settlement Systems: A Report Prepared by the Committee on Payment and Settlement Systems of the Central Banks of the G10 Countries', Basel.

Bank for International Settlements (1998) 'Report of the Working Group on Strengthening Financial Systems', Basel.

Bank of England (1998) 'The Bank of England Act 1998', *Quarterly Bulletin*, May, pp. 93–99.

Bank of England (1989) 'Payment and Settlement Systems Risk and Efficiency: A Discussion Paper', mimeo.

Begg, D, De Grauwe, P, Giavazzi, F, Uhlig, H and Wyplosz, C (1998) 'The ECB: Safe at Any Speed?', *Monitoring the Central Bank 1*, CEPR, London.

Benston, G J and Kaufman, G (1998) 'Deposit Insurance Reform in the FDIC Improvement Act: The Experience to Date', *Federal Reserve Bank of Chicago*, second quarter, vol 22(2) pp. 2–20.

Berger, A, Davies, S and Flannery, M (1998) 'Comparing Market and Regulatory Assessments of Bank Performance: Who Knows What When?', Federal Reserve Board Working Paper, March.

Berger, A and Davies, S (1994) 'The Information Content of Bank Examinations', Proceedings, Conference on Bank Structure and Competition, Federal Reserve Bank of Chicago.

Bernanke, B and Gertler, M (1995) 'Inside the Black Box: The Credit Channel of Monetary Policy Transmission', *Journal of Economic Perspectives*, Vol. 9, Autumn, pp. 27–48.

Bhattacharya, S and Gale, D (1987) 'Preference Shocks, Liquidity, and Central Bank Policy' in Barnett, W and Singleton, K (eds.) 'New Approaches to Monetary Economics', Cambridge University Press, Cambridge pp. 69–88.

Bhattacharya, S and Fulghieri, P (1994) 'Uncertain Liquidity and Interbank Contracting', *Economics Letters*, Vol. 44, pp. 287–94.

Bordo, M D (1986) 'Financial Crises, Banking Crises, Stock Market Crashes and the Money Supply: Some International Evidence, 1870–1933', in Capie, F and Wood, G E (eds.) 'Financial Crises and the World Banking System', MacMillan, London pp. 190–248.

Bordo, M D (1990) 'The Lender of Last Resort: Alternative Views and Historical Experience', *Federal Reserve Bank of Richmond Economic Review*, Jan/Feb, pp. 18–29.

Briault, C (1999) 'The Rationale for a Single National Financial Services Regulator', Financial Services Authority, Occasional Paper, No. 2, May.

Brierley, P G and Vlieghe, G W (1999) 'Corporate Workouts, the London Approach and Financial Stability', *Financial Stability Review*, Bank of England, issue 7, November.

Brimmer, A F (1989) 'Distinguished Lecture on Economics in Government: Central Banking and Systemic Risks in Capital Markets', *Journal of Economic Perspectives*, Vol. 3, pp. 3–16.

Bryant, J (1980) 'A Model of Bank Reserves, Bank Runs and Deposit Insurance', *Journal of Banking and Finance*, Vol. 4, pp. 335–44.

Calomiris, C and Gorton, G (1991) 'The Origins of Banking Panics: Models, Facts and Bank Regulation', in Hubbard, G R (ed.), 'Financial Markets and Financial Crises', University of Chicago Press, Chicago pp. 107–73.

Calomiris, C and Khan, C (1991) 'The Role of Demandable Debt in Restructuring Optimal Banking Arrangements', *American Economic Review*, June, Vol 81(3) pp. 497–513.

Calomiris, C and Khan, C (1996) 'The Efficiency of Self-Regulated Payment Systems: Learning from the Suffolk System', *Journal of Money Credit and Banking*, Vol 28(4) Part 2 pp. 767–96.

Calomiris, C and Mason, J R (1997) 'Contagion and Bank Failures During the Great Depression: The June 1932 Chicago Banking Panic', *American Economic Review*, Vol. 87, pp. 863–83.

Capie, F, Goodhart, C A E, Fischer, S and Schnadt, N (1994) 'The Future of Central Banking: The Tercentenary Symposium of the Bank of England', Cambridge University Press, Cambridge.

Chari, V and Jagannathan, R (1988) 'Banking Panics, Information and Rational Expectations Equilibrium', *Journal of Finance*, Vol. 43, pp. 749–61.

Clark, J and Perfect, S (1996) 'The Economic Effects of Client Losses on OTC Bank Derivative Dealers: Evidence from the Capital Markets', *Journal of Money Credit and Banking*, vol 28(3) Part 2 pp. 527–45.

Cornell, B and Shapiro, A (1986) 'The Reaction of Bank Stock Prices to the International Debt Crisis', *Journal of Banking and Finance*, March, vol (10) 1 pp. 55–73.

Corrigan, E G (1990) 'Statement Before US Senate Committee on Banking, Housing and Urban Affairs', Washington D.C.

Crockett, A (1996) 'The Theory and Practice of Financial Stability', *De Economist*, vol. 144(4) pp. 531–68.

Davies, H (1997) 'Financial Regulation: Why, How and by Whom?' *Bank of England Quarterly Bulletin*, February pp. 107–12.

Davies, S (1993) 'The Importance of Market Behaviour in Predicting Bank Performance', Board of Governors of The Federal Reserve System Working Paper, March.

Davis, K (1991) 'Assessing Financial Institution Risk', in Johnson M R, Kriesler P and Owen, A D (eds.) 'Contemporary Issues in Australian Economics', MacMillan, Melbourne.

Davis, K (1995) 'Bank Deregulation, Supervision and Agency Problems', *Australian Economic Review*, 3rd Quarter, pp. 43–54.

De Bandt, O and Hartmann, P (1998) 'What is Systemic Risk Today?', Risk Measurement and Systemic Risk: Proceedings of the Second Joint Central Bank Research Conference', Bank of Japan, November pp. 37–84.

De Bonis, R, Giustiniani, A and Gomel, G (1999) 'Crises and Bail-Outs of Banks and Countries: Linkages, Analogies and Differences', *The World Economy*, Vol. 22(1).

Demirgüçç-Kunt, A and Detragiache, E (1999) 'Does Deposit Insurance Increase Banking System Stability? An Empirical Investigation', World Bank, unpublished.

Diamond, D (1984) 'Financial Intermediation and Delegated Monitoring', *Review of Economics Studies*, July, pp. 393–414.

Diamond, D (1989) 'Reputation Acquisition in Debt Markets', *Review of Economic Studies*, Vol. 99, pp. 689–721.

Diamond, D (1991a) 'Monitoring and Reputation: The Choice Between Bank Loans and Directly Placed Debt', *Journal of Political Economy*, Vol. 99, pp. 689–721.

Diamond, D (1991b) 'Debt Maturity Structure and Liquidity Risk', *Quarterly Journal of Economics*, Vol. 106, pp. 709–37.

Diamond, D and Dybvig, P (1983) 'Bank Runs, Deposit Insurance and Liquidity', *Journal of Political Economy*, Vol. 91, pp. 401–19.

Dickinson, A, Peterson, D and Christiansen, W (1991) 'An Empirical Investigation into the Failure of the First Republic Bank: Is There a Contagion Effect?', *Financial Review*, Summer, pp. 303–18.

Docking, D, Hirschey, M and Jones, E (1997) 'Information and Contagion Effects of Bank Loan-Loss Reserve Announcements', *Journal of Financial Economics*, pp. 219–39.

Dowd, K (1992) 'Models of Banking Instability: A Partial Review of the Literature', *Journal of Economic Surveys*, Vol. 6, pp. 107–32.

Enoch, C, Stella, P and Khamis, M (1997) 'Transparency and Ambiguity in Central Bank Safety Net Operations', IMF Working Paper, WP/97/138.

Euro-Currency Standing Committee (1997) 'Report of a Task Force on The Implications of Structural Change for the Nature of Systemic Risk', paper discussed at ECSC meeting, December.

Federal Reserve Bank of Cleveland (1986) 'An Analysis of the Timing of Deposit Reductions Prior to Suspension in a Selected Group of Banks', *Annual Report 1985*, pp. 468–76.

Fischer, S (1999) 'On the Need for an International Lender of Last Resort', Paper prepared for the American Economic Association and the American Finance Association Meetings, IMF, mimeo.

Flannery, M (1996) 'Financial Crises, Payment System Problems and Discount Window Lending', *Journal of Money, Credit and Banking*, Vol. 28, pp. 804–24.

Freixas, X (1999) 'Optimal Bail Out Policy, Conditionality and Creative Ambiguity', mimeo, Bank of England.

Freixas, X and Parigi, B (1997) 'Contagion and Efficiency in Gross and Net Payment Systems', *Journal of Financial Intermediation*.

Freixas, X, Parigi, B and Rochet, J C (1998a) 'Systemic Risk, Interbank Relations and Liquidity Provision by the Central Bank', mimeo, IDEI.

Freixas, X, Parigi, B and Rochet, J C (1998b) 'The Lender of Last Resort: A Theoretical Foundation', mimeo, IDEI.

Freixas, X and Rochet, J C (1997) 'Microeconomics of Banking', MIT Press, Cambridge, MA.

Friedman, M (1959) 'A Program for Monetary Stability', Number Three, Fordham University Press, New York.

Furfine, C (1999) 'Interbank Exposures: Quantifying the Risk of Contagion', Bank for International Settlements Working Paper, no. 70.

Garcia, G and Plautz, E (1988) 'The Federal Reserve: Lender of Last Resort'. Ballinger, Cambridge, MA.

Gay, G, Timme, S and Yung, K (1991) 'Bank Failure and Contagion Effects: Evidence from Hong Kong', *Journal of Financial Research*, Summer, pp. 153–65.

George, E A J (1994) 'The Pursuit of Financial Stability', *Bank of England Quarterly Bulletin*, February pp. 60–66.

George, E A J (1997) 'Are Banks Still Special?', *Bank of England Quarterly Bulletin*, February pp. 113–118.

Giannini, C (1999) 'Enemy of None but a Common Friend of All? An International Perspective on the Lender of Last Resort Function', Princeton *Essays in International Finance*, No. 214.

Goodfriend, M and King, R G (1988) 'Financial Deregulation, Monetary Policy and Central Banking', *Federal Reserve Bank of Richmond Economic Review*, Vol. 74, No. 3.

Goodfriend, M and Lacker, J M (1999): 'Limited Commitment and Central Bank Lending', *Federal Reserve Bank of Richmond Working Paper, 99–2*.

Goodhart, C A E (1988) 'The Evolution of Central Banks', MIT Press, Cambridge, MA.

Goodhart, C A E (1995) 'The Central Bank and the Financial System', MIT Press, Cambridge, MA.

Goodhart, C A E (1999) 'Myths About the Lender of Last Resort', International Finance 2:3.

Goodhart, C A E and Huang, H (1999) 'A Model of the Lender of Last Resort', LSE Financial Markets Group Discussion Paper, dpo 131.

Goodhart, C A E and Schoenmaker, D (1993) 'Institutional Separation between Supervisory and Monetary Agencies', LSE Financial Markets Group Special Paper, No. 52.

Goodhart, C A E and Schoenmaker, D (1995) 'Should the Functions of Monetary Policy and Bank Supervision be Separated?', *Oxford Economic Papers*, Vol. 39, pp. 75–89.

Gorton, G (1988) 'Banking Panics and Business Cycles', *Oxford Economic Papers*, Vol. 40, pp. 751–81.

Greenbaum, S I, Kanatas, G and Venezia, I (1989) 'Equilibrium Loan Pricing Under the Bank-Client Relationship', *Journal of Banking and Finance*, Vol. 13, pp. 221–35.

Greenbaum, S I and Thakor, A (1995) 'Contemporary Financial Intermediation', The Dryden Press, Orlando, FI.

Greenbaum, S I and Venezia, I (1985) 'Partial Exercise of Loan Commitments Under Adaptive Pricing', *Journal of Financial Research*, Vol. 8, pp. 251–63.

Greenspan, A (1996) 'Remarks on Evolving Payment System Issues', *Journal of Money Credit and Banking*, Vol. 28, pp. 689–95.

Guttentag, J and Herring, R (1983) 'The Lender of Last Resort Function in an International Context', *Princeton Essays in International Finance*, Number 151, May.

Haldane, A G (1999) 'Private Sector Involvement in Financial Crisis: Analytics and Public Policy Approaches', *Financial Stability Review*, Bank of England, Issue 7, November.

Hawtrey, R (1932) 'The Art of Central Banking', London.

Heeler, H R (1991) 'Prudential Supervision and Monetary Policy', in Downs, P and Vaez-Zadeh, R (eds.), 'The Evolving Role of Central Banks', IMF, Washington.

Hills, B and Rule, D S (1999) 'Counterparty Credit Risk in Wholesale Payment and Settlement Systems' *Financial Stability Review*, Bank of England, Issue 7, November.

Hirsch, F (1977) 'The Bagehot Problem', The Manchester School of Economic and Social Studies, March.

Hölmstrom, B and Tirole, J (1993) 'Financial Intermediation, Loanable Funds and the Real Sector', *Quarterly Journal of Economics*, Vol. 112, pp. 663–91.

Humphrey, D B (1986) 'Payments Finality and Risk of Settlement Failure', in Saunders, A S and White, L J (eds.), 'Technology and Regulation of Financial Markets: Securities, Futures and Banking', Lexington Books, Lexington, MA pp. 97–120.

Humphrey, T (1989) 'The Lender of Last Resort: The Concept in History', *Federal Reserve Bank of Richmond Economic Review*, March/April, pp. 8–16.

International Monetary Fund (1999) 'Code of Good Practices on Transparency in Monetary and Financial Policies: Declaration of Principles', IMF, Washington.

Jacklin, C (1987) 'Demand Deposits, Trading Restrictions and Risk Sharing', in 'Contractual Arrangements for Intertemporal Trade', Prescott, E and Wallace, N (eds.), University of Minnesota Press, Minneapolis.

Jacklin, C and Bhattacharya, S (1988) 'Distinguishing Panics and Information-based Bank Runs: Welfare and Policy Implications', *Journal of Political Economy*, Vol. 96, pp. 568–92.

James, C (1991) 'The Losses Realised in Bank Failures', *Journal of Finance*, September, pp. 1223–42.

Kahn, C and Roberds, W (1996a) 'On The Role of Bank Coalitions in the Provisions of Liquidity', Federal Reserve Bank of Atlanta Working Paper, June.

Kahn, C and Roberds, W (1996b) 'Payment System Settlement and Bank Incentives', Federal Reserve Bank of Atlanta Working Paper, September.

Kane, E J (1992) 'How Incentive-Incompatible Deposit Insurance Plans Fail', in Kaufman, G (ed.), *Research in Financial Services, Vol. 4*, JAI Press, Greenwich, Conn.

Karafiath, I, Mynatt, R and Smith, K L (1991) 'The Brazillian Default Announcement and the Contagion Effect Hypothesis', *Journal of Banking and Finance*, June, pp. 699–716.

Kaufman, G (1991) 'Lender of Last Resort: A Contemporary Perspective', *Journal of Financial Services Research*, Vol. 5, pp. 95–110.

Kaufman, G (1994) 'Bank Contagion: A Review of the Theory and Evidence', *Journal of Financial Services Research*, pp. 123–150.

Kent, P (1997) 'Corporate Workouts: A UK Perspective', *International Insolvency Review*, Vol. 6 pp. 165–82.

King, M A and Goodhart, C A E (1987) 'Financial Stability and the Lender of Last Resort: A Note', LSE Financial Markets Group Special Paper Series, Special Paper No. 2.

Kindleberger, C (1989) 'Manias, Panics and Crashes: A History of Financial Crises', Basic Books, New York.

Kobayakawa, S (1997) 'The Comparative Analysis of Settlement Systems', CEPR Discussion Paper No. 1667.

Krugman, P (1999) 'Balance Sheets, the Transfer Problem and Financial Crises', *Journal of Money, Credit, and Banking*, Vol. 11, pp. 311–25.

Lamy, R E and Thompson, G R (1986) 'Penn Square, Problem Loans and Insolvency Risk', *Journal of Financial Research*, Summer, pp. 103–12.

Lastra, R M (1997) 'Lender of Last Resort', paper presented at EBRD seminar; unpublished.

Liu, C and Ryan, S G (1995) 'The Effect of Bank Loan Portfolio Composition on the Market Reaction to an Anticipation of Loan Loss Reserves', *Journal of Accounting Research*, Vol. 33, pp. 77–94.

Madura, J and McDaniel, W (1989) 'Market Reaction to Increased Loan-Loss Reserves at Money-Center Banks', *Journal of Financial Services Research*, December, pp. 359–69.

McAndrews, J and Roberds, W (1995) 'Banks, Payments and Co-ordination', *Journal of Financial Intermediation*, Vol. 4, pp. 305–27.

McAndrews, J and Wasilyew, G (1995) 'Simulations of Failure in a Payments System', Federal Reserve Bank of Philadelphia Working Paper 95–119.

McDonough, W J (1998) 'Statement Before the Committee on Banking and Financial Services, U.S. House of Representatives', Washington D.C.

Michael, I (1998) 'Financial Interlinkages and Systemic Risk', *Financial Stability Review*, Bank of England, Issue 4, Spring pp. 26–33.

Miron, J (1986) 'Financial panics, the seasonality of the nominal interest rate, and the founding of the Fed', *American Economic Review*, Vol. 76, pp. 125–40.

Mishkin, F (1995) 'Symposium on the Monetary Transmission Mechanism', *Journal of Economic Perspectives*, Vol. 9, Autumn.

Mishkin, F (1995) 'Comments on Systemic Risk' in Kaufman, G (ed.) *Banking Financial Markets and Systemic Risk: Research in Financial Services, Private and Public Policy*, Vol. 7, JAI Press Inc., Hampton pp. 31–45.

Mishkin, F (1999) 'Moral Hazard and Reform of the Government Safety Net', paper prepared for FRB Chicago conference 'Lessons from Recent Global Financial Crises', Chicago, September 30 – October 2.

Morris, S and Shin, H (1999) 'Co-ordination Risk and the Price of Debt', mimeo.

Musemeci, J and Sinkey, J Jr (1990) 'The International Debt Crisis, Investor Contagion and Bank Security Returns in 1987: The Brazilian Experience', *Journal of Money Credit and Banking*, May, pp. 209–30.

Nakaso H (1999) 'Recent Banking Sector Reforms in Japan', *Economic Policy Review*, Federal Reserve Bank of New York, July pp. 1–7.

Park, S (1995) 'Market Discipline by Depositors: Evidence from Reduced-Form Equations', *The Quarterly Review of Economics and Finance*, Vol. 35, pp. 497–514.

Peavey III, J W and Hempel, G H (1998) 'The Penn Square Bank Failure', *Journal of Banking and Finance*, pp. 141–50.

Prati, A and Schinasi, G (1999): 'Financial Stability in European Economic and Monetary Union', mimeo.

Rajan, G (1992) 'Insiders and Outsiders: The Choice Between Informed and Arm's-length Debt', *Journal of Finance*, Vol. 47, pp. 1367–1400.

Reid, M (1982) 'The Secondary Banking Crisis, 1973–75: Its Causes and Course', Macmillan, London.

Rochet, J C and Tirole, J (1996) 'Interbank Lending and Systemic Risk', *Journal of Money Credit and Banking*, Vol. 28, pp. 733–62.

Santomero, A and Hoffman, P (1998) 'Problem Bank Resolution: Evaluating the Options', The Wharton School Financial Institutions Center Discussion Paper 98-05.

Saunders, A (1987) 'The Interbank Market, Contagion Effects and International Financial Crises', in Portes and Swoboda (eds.) 'Threats to International Financial Stability', CEPR pp. 196–232.

Saunders, A and Wilson, B (1996) 'Contagious Bank Runs: Evidence from the 1929–1933 Period', *Journal of Financial Intermediation*, Vol. 5, pp. 409–23.

Schoenmaker, D (1995) 'A Comparison of Alternative Interbank Settlement Systems', LSE Financial Markets Group Discussion Paper No. 204.

Schoenmaker, D (1996) 'Contagion Risk in Banking', LSE Financial Markets Group Discussion Paper No. 239.

Schwartz, A (1986) 'Real and Pseudo-Financial Crises', in Capie, F and Woods, G (eds.), 'Financial Crises and the World Banking System', Macmillan, London pp. 11–40.

Schwartz, A (1992) 'The Misuse of the Fed's Discount Window', *Federal Reserve Banks of St. Louis Review*, September/October, pp. 58–69.

Schwartz, A (1995) 'Systemic Risk and the Macroeconomy' in Kaufman, G (ed.), *Banking Financial Markets and Systemic Risk: Research in Financial Services, Private and Public Policy*, Vol. 7, JAI Press Inc., Hampton pp. 19–30.

Selgin, G (1993) 'In Defence of Bank Suspension', *Journal of Financial Services Research*, Vol. 7, pp. 347–64.

Sharpe, A (1990) 'Asymmetric Information, Bank Lending and Implicit Contracts - A Stylised Model of Customer Relationships', *Journal of Finance*, Vol. 45, pp. 1069–87.

Smirlock, M and Kaufold, H (1987) 'Bank Foreign Lending, Mandatory Disclosure Rules and the Reaction of Bank Stock Prices to the Mexican Debt Crisis', *Journal of Business*, July, pp. 347–64.

Smith, B F and White, R W (1990) 'The Capital Market Impact of Recent Bank Failures', *Canadian Journal of Administrative Sciences*, June, pp. 41–47.

Stella, P (1997) 'Do Central Banks Need Capital?' IMF working paper, WP/97/83.

Summers, B J (ed.) (1994) 'The Payment System, Design, Management and Supervision', International Monetary Fund, Washington, D.C.

Swary, I (1986) 'Stock Market Reaction to Regulatory Action in the Continental Illinois Crisis', *Journal of Business*, July, pp. 451–73.

Thornton, H (1802) 'An Enquiry into the Nature and Effects of the Paper Credit of Great Britain'.

Treasury and Civil Service Committee (1995) 'Sixth Report: The Regulation of Financial Services in the U.K., Volume II', HC1994–95 332 II.

Wall, L and Peterson, D R (1990) 'The Effect of Continental Illinois' Failure on the performance of Other Banks', *Journal of Monetary Economics*, August, pp. 77–99.

Wicker, E (1980) 'A Reconsideration of the Causes of the Banking Panic of 1930', *Journal of Economic History*, September, pp. 571–83.

PART I

HISTORICAL ANALYSIS

3

An Enquiry into the Nature and Effects of the Paper Credit of Great Britain (*excerpts*)

HENRY THORNTON

Now a high state of confidence contributes to make men provide less amply against contingencies. At such a time, they trust, that if the demand upon them for a payment, which is now doubtful and contingent, should actually be made, they shall be able to provide for it at the moment; and they are loth to be at the expence of selling an article, or of getting a bill discounted, in order to make the provision much before the period at which it shall be wanted. When, on the contrary, a season of distrust arises, prudence suggests, that the loss of interest arising from a detention of notes for a few additional days should not be regarded.

It is well known that guineas are hoarded, in times of alarm, on this principle. Notes, it is true, are not hoarded to the same extent; partly because notes are not supposed equally likely, in the event of any general confusion, to find their value, and partly because the class of persons who are the holders of notes is less subject to weak and extravagant alarms. In difficult times, however, the disposition to hoard, or rather to be largely provided with Bank of England notes, will, perhaps, prevail in no inconsiderable degree.

This remark has been applied to Bank of England notes, because these are always in high credit; and it ought, perhaps, to be chiefly confined to these. They constitute the coin in which the great mercantile payments in London, which are payments on account of the whole country, are effected. If, therefore, a difficulty in converting bills of exchange into notes is apprehended, the effect both on bankers, merchants, and tradesmen, is somewhat the same as the effect of an apprehension entertained by the lower class of a difficulty in converting Bank of England notes or bankers' notes into guineas. The apprehension of the approaching difficulty makes men eager to do that to-day, which otherwise they would do to-morrow.

The truth of this observation, as applied to Bank of England notes, as well as the importance of attending to it, may be made manifest by adverting to the events of the year 1793, when, through the failure of many country banks, much general distrust took place. The alarm, the first material one of the kind which had for a long time happened, was extremely great. It does not appear that the Bank of England notes, at that time in circulation, were fewer than usual. It is certain, however, that the existing number became, at the period of apprehension, insufficient for giving punctuality to the payments of the metropolis; and it is not to be doubted, that the insufficiency must have arisen, in some measure, from that slowness in the circulation of notes, naturally attending an alarm, which has been just described. Every one fearing lest he should not have his notes ready when the day of payment should come, would endeavour to provide himself with them somewhat beforehand. A few merchants, from a natural though hurtful timidity, would keep in their own hands some of those notes, which, in other times, they would have lodged with their bankers; and the effect would be, to cause the same quantity of bank paper to transact fewer payments, or, in other words, to lessen the rapidity of the circulation of notes on the whole, and thus to encrease the number of notes wanted. Probably, also, some Bank of England paper would be used as a substitute for country bank notes suppressed.

The success of the remedy which the parliament administered, denotes what was the nature of the evil. A loan of exchequer bills was directed to be made to as many mercantile persons, giving proper security, as should apply. It is a fact, worthy of serious attention, that the failures abated greatly, and mercantile credit began to be restored, not at the period when the exchequer bills were actually delivered, but at a time antecedent to that aera. It also deserves notice, that though the failures had originated in an extraordinary demand for guineas, it was not any supply of gold which effected the cure. That fear of not being able to obtain guineas, which arose in the country, led, in its consequences, to an extraordinary demand for bank notes in London; and the want of bank notes in London became, after a time, the chief evil. The very expectation of a supply of exchequer bills, that is, of a supply of an article which almost any trader might obtain, and which it was known that he might then sell, and thus turn into bank notes, and after turning into bank notes might also convert into guineas, created an idea of general solvency. This expectation cured, in the first instance, the distress of London, and it then lessened the demand for guineas in the country, through that punctuality in effecting the London payments which it produced, and the universal confidence which it thus inspired. The sum permitted by parliament to be advanced in exchequer bills was five millions, of which not one half was taken. Of the sum taken, no part was lost. On the contrary, the small compensation, or extra interest, which was paid to government for lending its credit (for it was mere credit, and not either money or bank notes that the government advanced), amounted to something more than was necessary to defray the charges, and a small balance of profit accrued to the public. For this seasonable interference, a measure at first not well understood and opposed at the time, chiefly on the ground of constitutional jealousy, the mercantile as well as the manufacturing interests of the country were certainly much indebted to the parliament, and to the government.

Some very solid objections, however, may be urged against the system of banking in the country.

The first which I shall mention, is, the tendency of country banks to produce, occasionally, that general failure of paper credit, and with it that derangement and suspension of commerce, as well as intermission of manufacturing labour, which have been already spoken of.

Country bank notes, and especially the smaller ones, circulate, in a great measure, among people out of trade, and pass occasionally into the hands of persons of the lower class; a great proportion, therefore, of the holders of them, have few means of judging of the comparative credit of the several issuers, and are commonly almost as ready to take the paper of any one house calling itself a bank, as that of another. A certain degree of currency being thus given to inferior paper, even the man who doubts the ultimate solvency of the issuer is disposed to take it; for the time during which he intends to detain it is very short, and his responsibility will cease almost as soon as he shall have parted with it.[1] Moreover, the amount of each note is so small, that the risk seems, also, on that account, insignificant. The notes of the greater and of the smaller country banks, thus obtaining, in ordinary times, a nearly similar currency, they naturally fall at a season of alarm into almost equal discredit. If any one bank fails, a general run upon the neighbouring ones is apt to take place, which, if not checked in the beginning by pouring into the circulation a large quantity of gold, leads to very extensive mischief. Many country bankers, during a period of danger, prescribe to themselves a principle of more than ordinary reserve in the issue of their notes, because they consider these as the more vulnerable part of their credit. They know, that if the character of their house should be brought into question, through the fear or even the caprice of any of those strangers into whose hands their circulating paper passes, some distrust may be excited among their customers, the effect of which may be a sudden demand for the payment of large deposits. The amount, therefore, of the country bank notes circulating in the kingdom is liable to great fluctuation. The country banker, in case of an alarm, turns a part of the government securities, bills of exchange, or other property which he has in London, into Bank of England notes, and those notes into money; and thus discharges many of his own circulating notes, as well as enlarges the fund of gold in his coffers. The Bank of England has, therefore, to supply these occasional wants of the country banker; and, in order to be fully prepared to do this, it has, ordinarily, to keep a quantity of gold equal to that of the notes liable to be extinguished, as well as a quantity which shall satisfy the other extraordinary demands which may be made at the same season of consternation either by banking houses, or by individuals. Thus the country banker by no means bears his own burthen, while the Bank of England sustains a burthen which is not

[1] I apprehend that, supposing a country bank to fail, the holder of one of its notes, who should have parted with it in sufficient time to afford to the next holder an opportunity of applying for the discharge of it before the day of failure, could not be called upon for the payment of the value of it. The responsibility, therefore, of him who has been the holder of a country bank note commonly ceases in about one or two days after it has been parted with. That of the holder of a bill continues till after the bill is due, namely, for a period, perhaps, of one or two months.

its own, and which we may naturally suppose that it does not very cheerfully endure.[2]

The national bank, indeed, may fairly be called upon, in consideration of the benefits enjoyed through its monopoly, to submit to a considerable expence in supplying gold for the country; but there must be some bounds to the claims which can equitably be made upon it: and, in estimating the benefit arising to the kingdom from the use of country bank notes, we have either to deduct the loss which the Bank of England incurs by maintaining an additional supply of gold sufficient to answer the demands which they occasion, or else we have to take into consideration the risk which the bank incurs by only keeping a fund of gold which is somewhat inadequate. The country banks may, perhaps, cause the bank in some measure to encrease its general fund of gold, though not to hold so much of this unproductive article as to afford a security equal to that which the bank would enjoy if no country bank notes existed.

It is obvious, that the additional capital given to the kingdom through the use of country bank notes must not be measured by the amount of those notes, but that a deduction must be made of the sum kept in gold in the coffers of the issuers, as their provision for the occasional payments to which their bank paper subjects them. The other deduction, which has been spoken of, is of the same nature. It is a second deduction, which must be made on account of a similar, and, perhaps, no less considerable provision for the payment of country bank notes, which is rendered necessary to be kept in the coffers of the Bank of England. In other words, the capital given to the country, through the use of country bank notes, is only equal (and it was so stated in speaking of that subject) to the amount of the gold which they cause to be exported.

I shall endeavour here to explain more particularly than has yet been done, some of those circumstances which cause a great diminution of country bank notes to bring distress on London, and to end in a general failure of commercial credit.

In a former chapter it was observed, that when that alarm among the common people, which produces an unwillingness to take country bank paper, and an eagerness for gold has risen to a considerable height, some distrust is apt to be excited among the higher class of traders; and that any great want of confidence in this quarter produces an encreased demand for that article, which is, among London bankers and merchants, in much the same credit as gold; I mean Bank of England notes, and which forms, at all times, the only circulating medium of the metropolis in all the larger transactions of its commerce. This more than usual

[2] At the time of the distress of 1793, some great and opulent country banks applied to the Bank of England for aid, in the shape of discount, which was refused on account of their not offering approved London securities: some immediate and important failures were the consequence. The Bank of England was indisposed to extend its aid to houses in the country. The event, however, shewed that the relief of the country was necessary to the solvency of the metropolis. A sense of the unfairness of the burthen cast on the bank by the large and sudden demands of the banking establishments in the country, probably contributed to produce an unwillingness to grant them relief.

demand for Bank of England notes the bank is at such a time particularly unwilling to satisfy, for reasons which I shall endeavour fully to detail. The reader will have been prepared to enter into them by the observations on the subject of the bank, introduced towards the close of the chapter which treated of that institution.

First, the bank may be supposed to be unwilling to satisfy that somewhat *encreased* demand for its notes which a season of consternation is apt to produce, because it is not unlikely to partake, in some degree, in the general alarm, especially since it must necessarily be supposed to have already suffered, and to be still experiencing a formidable reduction of the quantity of its gold. The natural operation of even this general sort of fear must be to incline it to contract its affairs, and to diminish rather than enlarge its notes.

But it must also be recollected, that the bank has necessarily been led already to encrease its loans in the same degree in which its gold has been reduced, provided it has maintained in circulation the accustomed quantity of notes. This point was explained in the chapter on the subject of the bank. The directors, therefore, must seem to themselves to act with extraordinary liberality towards those who apply to them for discounts, if they only go so far as to maintain the usual, or nearly the usual, quantity of notes. The liberality in lending which they must exercise, if, when the gold is low, they even augment their paper, must be very extended indeed.

In order to render this subject more clear, let us suppose that an extra demand on the Bank of England for three millions of gold has been made through the extinction of the paper of country banks, and through the slower circulation and hoarding of gold which have attended the general alarm. Let us assume, also, that the bank, during the time of its supplying this gold, has thought proper to reduce its notes one million. It will, in that case, have necessarily increased its loans two millions. Let us further assume, as we not very unreasonably may, that the two millions of additional loans have been afforded, not to the government, who owe a large and standing sum to the bank (suppose eight or ten millions besides the bank capital), but exclusively to the merchants; and let the total amount of loans antecedently afforded to the merchants be reckoned at four millions. The bank, in this case, will have raised its discounts to the merchants from four millions to six; that is, it will have encreased them one half, even though it has diminished its notes one million. This extension of the accustomed accommodation to the mercantile world must appear to call for the thanks of that body, rather than to leave any room for complaint; and yet it is plain from reasoning, and, I believe, it might be also proved from experience, that it will not ease the pressure. The difficulties in London, notwithstanding the additional loan of *two* millions to the merchants, will be somewhat encreased; for a sum in gold, amounting to *three* millions, has been drawn from the bank by the London agents of the country bankers and traders, and has been sent by those agents into the country. London, therefore, has furnished for the country circulation three millions of gold; and it has done this by getting discounted at the bank two additional millions of bills, for which it has received two of the millions of gold, and by sparing one million of its circulating notes as a means of obtaining the other million. This reduction of the usual quantity of notes is borne by the metropolis with peculiar difficulty at a time of general alarm. However liberally, therefore, the bankers and merchants may acknowledge themselves to have been already relieved by the bank, they will repeat, and will even urge more than ever, their application for discounts.

It may be observed, with a view to the further elucidation of this part of our subject, that both the bank, and they who borrow of it, are naturally led to fix their attention rather on the amount of the loans furnished than on that of the notes in circulation. The bank is used to allow to each borrower a sum bearing some proportion to his supposed credit; but seldom or never exceeding a certain amount. It is true, the various borrowers do not always in an equal degree avail themselves of their power of raising money at the bank; and, therefore, a material enlargement of the sum total of the bank loans may take place at a moment of difficulty, through the encreased use which some of the richer merchants then make of their credit, as well as through the creation of a few new borrowers at the bank. The directors also, in particular cases, may suffer their rule to be relaxed. The circumstance, however, of the general principle on which the bank ordinarily, and, indeed, naturally proceeds, being that of a limitation of the amount of each of its loans to individuals, must tend, as I conceive, to place something like a general limit to the total sum lent. It must conduce to prevent the fluctuation in the bank loans from keeping pace with the variation in the necessities of the public, and must contribute to produce a reduction of notes at that season of extraordinary distrust, when the state of the metropolis, as was more fully remarked in a former part of this Work, calls rather for their encrease.

That the borrowers at the bank are likely to pay no attention to the subject of the total quantity of notes in circulation is easily shewn. They have, indeed, no means of knowing their amount. They can only judge of the liberality of the bank by the extent of its loans; and of this they form an imperfect estimate by the sum which they or their connexions have been able to obtain. Scarcely any one reflects, that there may be a large encrease of the general loans of the bank, as well as possibly an extension of each loan to individuals, while there is a diminution of the number of bank notes; and that the amount of the notes, not that of the loans, is the object on which the eye should be fixed, in order to judge of the facility of effecting the payments of the metropolis.

It was remarked, in a former chapter, that the bank, at the time antecedent to the suspension of its cash payments, having diminished the sum lent by it to government, and enlarged, though not in an equal degree, that furnished to the merchants, the pressure on the merchants was not relieved, as was expected, by the encreased loan afforded them, but even grew more severe. It was also shewn, that this could not fail to be the case, since the bank notes necessary for effecting the current payments of the metropolis were then diminished, and since the additional loans afforded to the merchants only in part compensated for the new pressure which was created in the general money market of the kingdom, by the circumstance of the government being obliged to become a great borrower in that market. Whenever the bank materially lessens its paper, a similar pressure is likely to be felt. Neither the transfer of the bank loans from the government to the merchants, nor even a large encrease of its loans, when that encrease is not carried so far as is necessary to the maintenance of the accustomed, or nearly the accustomed, quantity of bank paper, can prevent, as I apprehend, distress in the metropolis; and this distress soon communicates itself to all parts of the kingdom. The short explanation of the subject is this. Many country bank notes having disappeared, a quantity of gold is called for, which is so much new capital suddenly needed in the country. The only place in which any supply of gold exists is the Bank of England. Moreover, the only quarter from whence the loan of the new capital, under all the circumstances of the case, can come, is also the Bank of England: for the gold in the bank is the only dead or sleeping stock in the kingdom which is convertible into the new active capital which is wanted. The bank, therefore, must *lend*, the gold which it furnishes; it must lend, that is to say, to some individuals a sum equal to the gold which other individuals have taken from it: otherwise it does not relieve the country.

If it should be asked, Why does not the bank in such case demand something intrinsically valuable, instead of contenting itself with mere paper in return?–the answer is, first, that if the bank were to receive goods in exchange for its gold, or, in other words, were to purchase goods, it would have afterwards to sell them; and it would then become a trading company, which it is forbid to be by its charter; it is allowed to traffic only in bullion. The answer is, secondly, that if it were to take goods as a mere security, and to detain them as such, it would then prevent their passing into consumption with the desirable expedition. By proceeding on either of these plans, it would also involve itself in a degree of trouble which would not be very consistent with the management of the business of a banking Company.[3] It may be answered, thirdly, that the bills which the bank discounts, are, generally speaking, so safe, that the security either of goods, or stocks, or land, none of which are received in pledge by the directors, may be considered as nearly superfluous. A very small proportion of the five per cent discount, gained upon the bills turned into ready money at the bank, has compensated, as I believe, for the whole of the loss upon them, even in the years of the greatest commercial failures which have yet been known.

The observations which have now been made sufficiently shew what is the nature of that evil of which we are speaking. It is an evil which ought to be charged not to any fault in the mercantile body, but to the defects of the banking system. It is a privation which the merchants occasionally experience of a considerable part of that circulating medium which custom has rendered essential to the punctual fulfilment of their engagements. In good times, the country banks furnish this necessary article, which they are enabled to do through the confidence of the people in general; but when an alarm arises, the country banks cease to give it out, the

[3] Of the parliamentary loan of exchequer bills in 1793, which was directed to be granted on the security either of sufficient bondsmen, or of a deposit of goods, only a small proportion was taken on the latter principle, on account of the great obstruction to the sale of goods, which was thought to arise from warehousing them on the account of the commissioners appointed by parliament. It has been already remarked, that no part of the sum lent was lost.

people refusing what they had before received; and the Bank of England, the only body by whose interposition the distress can be relieved, is somewhat unwilling to exercise all the necessary liberality, for the reasons which have been so fully mentioned. The merchants are some of the chief sufferers, and they are generally, also, loaded with no inconsiderable share of censure; but the public, the country banks, and the Bank of England, may properly divide the blame.

The mischief produced by a general failure of paper credit is very considerable. How much such a failure interrupts trade and manufacturing industry, and, therefore, ultimately also tends to carry gold out of the country, has been already stated at large. It also causes a great, though merely temporary, fall in the market price of many sorts of property; and thus inflicts a partial and very heavy loss on some traders, and throws extraordinary gain into the hands of others; into the hands, I mean, of those who happen to have superior powers of purchasing at the moment of difficulty. By giving to all banking, as well as mercantile, transactions the appearance of perilous undertakings, it deters men of large property, and of a cautious temper, from following the profession of bankers and merchants. It creates no small uneasiness of mind, even among traders who surmount the difficulties of the moment. Above all, it reduces many respectable, prudent, and, ultimately, very solvent persons to the mortifying necessity of stopping payment; thus obliging them to share in that discredit, in which, it is much to be desired, that traders of an opposite character only should be involved. If, indeed, we suppose, as we necessarily must, that, on account of the multitude of failures which happen at the same time, the discredit of them is much diminished, then another evil is produced, which, in a commercial country, is very great. Acts of insolvency, leaving less stigma on the character, become not so much dreaded as might be wished. The case of some, who bring difficulties on themselves, being almost unavoidably confounded with that of persons whose affairs have been involved through the entanglement of paper credit, to stop payment is considered too much as a misfortune or accident, and too little as a fault; and thus a principal incentive to punctuality in mercantile payments is weakened, and an important check to adventurous speculation is in some measure lost.

The observations which have been made, will, however, shew that the tendency of country bank paper to produce a general failure of paper credit, is an evil which may be expected to diminish; for, first, if the Bank of England, in future seasons of alarm, should be disposed to extend its discounts in a greater degree than heretofore, then the threatened calamity may be averted through the generosity of that institution.[4] If, secondly, the country bankers should be taught (as, in some degree,

[4] It is by no means intended to imply, that it would become the Bank of England to relieve every distress which the rashness of country banks may bring upon them: the bank, by doing this, might encourage their improvidence. There seems to be a medium at which a public bank should aim in granting aid to inferior establishments, and which it must often find very difficult to be observed. The relief should neither be so prompt and liberal as to exempt those who misconduct their business from all the natural consequences of their fault, nor so scanty and slow as deeply to involve the general interests. These interests, nevertheless, are sure to be pleaded by every distressed person whose affairs are large, however indifferent or even ruinous may be their state.

unquestionably they must), by the difficulties which they have experienced, to provide themselves with a larger quantity of that sort of property which is quickly convertible into Bank of England notes, and, therefore, also, into gold, then the country bankers will have in their own hands a greater power of checking the progress of an alarm. Still, indeed, their resource will be the gold which is in the bank. The encreased promptitude, however, with which the greater convertibility of their funds will enable them to possess themselves of a part of the bank treasure, will render a smaller supply of it sufficient; and this smaller supply may be expected to be furnished, without difficulty, either by means of such a trifling addition to the bank loans as the bank will not refuse, or by sparing the necessary sum from the paper circulation of the metropolis, which, if commercial confidence is not impaired, will always admit of some slight and temporary reduction. The Bank of England will itself profit by the circumstance of its gold becoming more accessible to the country banks; for the untoward event of a general failure of paper credit will thus be rendered less probable, and, therefore, a smaller stock of gold will be an equally sufficient provision for the extraordinary demands at home to which the bank will be subject. Or if, thirdly, those among whom country bank notes circulate should learn to be less variable as to the confidence placed by them in country paper, or even to appreciate more justly the several degrees of credit due to the notes of different houses, then the evil which was before supposed to be obviated by the liberality of the Bank of England, or by the prudence of the country banker, will abate through the growth of confidence and the diffusion of commercial knowledge among the public. It seems likely that by each of these means, though especially in the second mode which was mentioned, the tendency of country bank notes to produce an occasional failure of commercial credit will be diminished. In time past, the mischief has been suffered to grow till it appeared too formidable to be encountered; and this has happened partly in consequence of our wanting that knowledge and experience which we now possess.

4

A General View of Lombard Street (*excerpts*)

WALTER BAGEHOT

Such a reserve as we have seen is kept to meet sudden and unexpected demands. If the bankers of a country are asked for much more than is commonly wanted, then this reserve must be resorted to. What then are these extra demands? and how is this extra reserve to be used? Speaking broadly, these extra demands are of two kinds—one from abroad to meet foreign payments requisite to pay large and unusual foreign debts, and the other from at home to meet sudden apprehension or panic arising in any manner, rational or irrational.

A domestic drain is very different. Such a drain arises from a disturbance of credit within the country, and the difficulty of dealing with it is the greater, because it is often caused, or at least often enhanced, by a foreign drain. Times without number the public have been alarmed mainly because they saw that the Banking reserve was already low, and that it was daily getting lower. The two maladies—an external drain and an internal—often attack the money market at once. What then ought to be done?

In opposition to what might be at first sight supposed, the best way for the bank or banks who have the custody of the bank reserve to deal with a drain arising from internal discredit, is to lend freely. The first instinct of everyone is the contrary. There being a large demand on a fund which you want to preserve, the most obvious way to preserve it is to hoard it—to get in as much as you can, and to let nothing go out which you can help. But every banker knows that this is not the way to diminish discredit. This discredit means, 'an opinion that you have not got any money,' and to dissipate that opinion, you must, if possible, show that you have money: you must employ it for the public benefit in order that the public may know that you have it. The time for economy and for accumulation is before. A good banker will have accumulated in ordinary times the reserve he is to make use of in extraordinary times.

Ordinarily discredit does not at first settle on any particular bank, still less does it at first concentrate itself on the bank or banks holding the principal cash reserve. These banks are almost sure to be those in best credit, or they would not be in that position, and, having the reserve, they are likely to look stronger and seem stronger than any others. At first, incipient panic amounts to a kind of vague conversation: Is A. B. as good as he used to be? Has not C. D. lost money? and a thousand such questions. A hundred people are talked about, and a thousand think,—'Am I talked about, or am I not?' 'Is my credit as good as it used to be, or is it less?' And every day, as a panic grows, this floating suspicion becomes both more intense and more diffused; it attacks more persons, and attacks them all more virulently than at first. All men of experience, therefore, try to 'strengthen themselves,' as it is called, in the early stage of a panic; they borrow money while they can; they come to their banker and offer bills for discount, which commonly they would not have offered for days or weeks to come. And if the merchant be a regular customer, a banker does not like to refuse, because if he does he will be said, or may be said, to be in want of money, and so may attract the panic to himself. Not only merchants but all persons under pecuniary liabilities—present or imminent—feel this wish to 'strengthen themselves,' and in proportion to those liabilities. Especially is this the case with what may be called the auxiliary dealers in credit. Under any system of banking there will always group themselves about the main bank or banks (in which is kept the reserve) a crowd of smaller money dealers, who watch the minutiæ of bills, look into special securities which busy bankers have not time for, and so gain a livelihood. As business grows, the number of such subsidiary persons augments. The various modes in which money may be lent have each their peculiarities, and persons who devote themselves to one only lend in that way more safely, and therefore more cheaply. In time of panic, these subordinate dealers in money will always come to the principal dealers. In ordinary times, the intercourse between the two is probably close enough. The little dealer is probably in the habit of pledging his 'securities' to the larger dealer at a rate less than he has himself charged, and of running into the market to lend again. His time and brains are his principal capital, and he wants to be always using them. But in times of incipient panic, the minor money dealer always becomes alarmed. His credit is never very established or very wide; he always fears that he may be the person on whom current suspicion will fasten, and often he is so. Accordingly he asks the larger dealer for advances. A number of such persons ask all the large dealers—those who have the money—the holders of the reserve. And then the plain problem before the great dealers comes to be—'How shall we best protect ourselves? No doubt the immediate advance to these second-class dealers is annoying, but may not the refusal of it even be dangerous? A panic grows by what it feeds on; if it devours these second-class men, shall we, the first-class, be safe?'

A panic, in a word, is a species of neuralgia, and according to the rules of science you must not starve it. The holders of the cash reserve must be ready not only to keep it for their own liabilities, but to advance it most freely for the liabilities of others. They must lend to merchants, to minor bankers, to 'this man and that man,' whenever the security is good. In wild periods of alarm, one failure makes many, and the best way to prevent the derivative failures is to arrest the primary failure which causes them. The way in which the panic of 1825 was stopped by advancing money has been described in so broad and graphic a way that the passage has become classical. 'We lent it,' said Mr. Harman, on behalf of the Bank of England, 'by every

5

The Lender of Last Resort: A Historical Perspective

THOMAS M. HUMPHREY AND ROBERT E. KELEHER

INTRODUCTION

The current international debt situation has led some analysts to suggest the possibility of a scenario whereby international debt defaults quickly lead to severe strains on domestic commercial banks. In this context, monetary and central bank policy become especially important, and references are often made to the central bank's function as lender of last resort (LLR). In considering stopgap versus permanent solutions to financial crises, the role of the lender of last resort assumes special pertinence.

Although often mentioned, few thorough assessments of the domestic LLR function exist. Moreover, the analytical foundations or theoretical framework underlying the LLR function are rarely if ever spelled out. Discussions of this central bank role are often premised on differing definitions or understandings of the function. As a result, semantic problems often cloud such discussions. Then too, clarifications of the LLR function under alternative monetary and exchange rate regimes have never been made. Consequently, analyses of the concept are frequently ambiguous. Because of this lack of clarity, analyses of this role often leave important issues unresolved. For example, is the LLR essentially a banking or a monetary function? Is the function microeconomic or macroeconomic in nature; that is, does LLR responsibility pertain to individual banks or to the market as a whole? Are the monetary control and LLR functions of a central bank irreconcilable? Does the LLR function differ under alternative monetary regimes? Is current Federal Reserve policy in accord with the original conceptions of this function? Can the role be carried out via open market operations or must the discount window always be used? This lack of clarity of the LLR function is evident in discussions of the domestic LLR. But the confusion becomes especially apparent in analyses of international financial crises and particularly when a role for an international LLR is proposed.

In an effort to dispel this confusion, it is useful to reassess this important central bank function. The purpose of this paper is to examine both the domestic and possible international roles of an LLR. We begin with a discussion of the function of

This article first appeared in the *Cato Journal* 4(1) (Spring/Summer 1984).

an LLR. Next, a brief outline of the role of an LLR under various monetary regimes is presented. We then consider the historical development of the concept of a domestic LLR. Special attention is given to the work of Henry Thornton, the Banking School, and Walter Bagehot. A discussion of the possible role for an international LLR and some conclusions complete the paper.

THE FUNCTION OF THE LENDER OF LAST RESORT

The call for an LLR arises because of two important institutional characteristics of contemporary monetary systems, fractional reserve banking and governmental monopoly of legal tender issuance.[1] The monopoly of legal tender issuance ensures that the central bank is the ultimate provider of currency and thereby the guarantor of deposit-to-currency convertibility. Once banks believed they could always obtain currency in a crisis from such a monopoly issuer, they reduced their holdings of reserves and began to hold assets they believed could be easily transformed into reserves (or legal tender). This contributed to a centralization of reserves under the custody of the monopoly issuer, the 'central' reserve bank. The discussion of the LLR in this paper is premised on these given institutional arrangements. Thus, while we believe strongly in free competitive markets for all goods (perhaps including money) and are sympathetic in principle to the arguments of free-money advocates and their case against the LLR, we nevertheless intend to examine the function of existing LLRs under existing institutional arrangements.[2] We hope that such an examination will provide a better understanding of the role existing LLRs may play in banking crises and help us evaluate various proposals for an international LLR.

Given existing institutional arrangements, monetary systems are vulnerable to sharp increases in the demand for the safest and most readily acceptable form of money, namely currency (or, under a metallic standard, gold). Such sharp increases in demand for currency or gold can bring about a widespread call-in of loans and a dramatic fall (or collapse) of asset prices. Historically, such increases in demand

[1] With 100 percent reserve requirements, an LLR would not be necessary. Moreover, monetary systems characterized by multiple issuers of transactions media could be proposed and indeed have existed without any apparent need for an LLR. The monopoly of legal tender issuance applied to the Bank of England by 1833. Even for several decades before that date, the Bank of England's notes were de facto legal tender (White, 1981a, b; Smith, 1936). In addition, it should be noted that FDIC insurance does not nullify the need for an LLR. First, current FDIC pricing schemes are likely to be changed in the near future. Second, an LLR is essential (ultimately) to back up FDIC insurance. Third, the United States has one of the very few government-supported deposit insurance schemes.

[2] For an excellent discussion of the arguments relating to the existence of LLRs, see White (1981a, b) and Smith (1936). While sympathetic to these arguments, we follow arguments of the Public Choice School and thereby remain skeptical that the objectives of free-money advocates can be realized in the political world in which we live. That is, we doubt that many governments and bureaucracies will be willing to relinquish the power inherent in governmental central banking. See Mundell (1983a, pp. 30–32).

were often associated with runs on banks and a collapse of loans and deposits. Consequently, a role of the LLR is as a backstop or guarantor to prevent a panic-induced collapse of a fractional-reserve banking system. Since such banking systems connect movements in credit (chiefly bank loans and investments) to movements in money, the primary function of the LLR is to prevent *credit* crises from becoming *monetary* crises; that is, to prevent credit/debt contraction from producing monetary contraction.

Thus, while the LLR should prevent systemwide runs on banks, large-scale loan call-ins, and collapses of asset prices, loans, and credit, its ultimate purpose is to prevent collapses of money—to promote monetary stability. The LLR has both the power and the duty to achieve this goal. For, whereas government has little or no reason to intervene in the lending decisions of financial intermediaries, the granting of monopoly powers to a single note issuer carries certain governmental responsibilities with it. Specifically, since certain negative externalities (such as disruptions to real activity, to the payments system, and to financial intermediation) are commonly associated with monetary instability, a governmental role for preventing such negative externalities and consequently providing for monetary stability is implied by the creation of monopoly note issuance.

The monetary stabilization responsibility of the LLR relates to marketwide (macroeconomic) effects and not to individual bank (microeconomic) effects. The LLR function, then, pertains to the responsibility of guaranteeing the liquidity of the entire economy but not necessarily of particular institutions. Moreover, the LLR role is not to prevent all shocks to the financial system, but rather to minimize the secondary repercussions of those shocks. Accordingly, the LLR is charged with averting contagion, spillover, or domino effects which may adversely affect the stability of the entire monetary system. In essence, the purpose of the LLR is to maintain sufficient confidence in the financial system so that there will be no need to provide last-resort liquidity.

One indirect implication of this liquidity-provision responsibility is worth mentioning. The effective exercise of this liquidity responsibility will prevent a drastic and widespread call-in of loans as well as a dramatic fall (or collapse) of asset prices. Thus, in providing this function, the LLR indirectly ensures that banks needing to sell liquid assets will not have to do so at large losses that might otherwise bring about insolvency and its adverse effects.

These objectives should be fully acknowledged and widely announced to the public before any crisis occurs. Credible assurance of this kind is necessary to reduce the uncertainty about the central bank's willingness to act. This, in turn, promotes confidence and generates stabilizing expectations that help to avert future panics. To minimize so-called 'moral-hazard' problems, such an advance announcement should indicate that assistance will not be available to unsound banks but only 'to the market.'

The LLR function, therefore, is a short-run stabilization function which need not necessarily conflict with longer-run central bank objectives. Such longer-run objectives may differ somewhat under alternative monetary regimes. Accordingly, the precise operational mechanism or tools needed to provide LLR services may differ under alternative regimes.[3]

LENDER-OF-LAST-RESORT SERVICES UNDER ALTERNATIVE MONETARY REGIMES

Historically, explanations of the LLR function have developed out of the peculiarities of time and place. Many authors who initially explained the LLR function did so from the perspective of a small open economy often operating under fixed exchange rates; that is, under an international commodity (or gold) standard. These economists had a tendency to generalize from their own knowledge or experience of a particular time and place to situations under which the experience may not be relevant (Mundell, 1983b, p. 286). Accordingly, the influence of fixed exchange rates in an open economy clearly dominated many of the early explanations of the LLR.

In the case of a small open economy under fixed exchange rates (or a gold standard), for example, the longer-run objective of a domestic central bank is not to directly control the total money supply but rather to maintain (fixed-rate) convertibility of currency into international reserves (or gold). If this convertibility is maintained, the growth of the money supply is tied to the (presumably stable) growth of world international reserves (or gold stock). To maintain the stock of international reserves, the central bank has to ensure that the domestic paper note component of the money supply does not grow so fast as to force an efflux of international reserves through the balance of payments, thereby endangering convertibility. Thus, control over the domestic note component of the money stock is a necessary condition for the long-run maintenance of convertibility. In short, central bank responsibility under this regime involves keeping the domestic credit component of the money stock on a target path consistent with protection of the specie reserve and hence with long-run maintenance of convertibility. Also, under this regime, widespread bank runs and a collapse of the fractional reserve banking system could trigger large internal drains of specie that would threaten to exhaust the gold reserve and endanger convertibility. The function of the LLR under these circumstances, therefore, is to prevent such a collapse and thereby to complement and promote the goal of maintaining convertibility. Thus, the role of the LLR is to prevent credit crises and the associated runs on specie reserves from adversely affecting the longer-run monetary objectives of the central bank.

Crisis situations involving the LLR frequently followed excessive credit expansions. Such credit expansions often were large and prolonged enough to produce outflows of specie and to foster doubts about the ability of commercial banks to redeem their paper in gold. More precisely, when an overexpansion of loans and thereby of bank-created money occurred in a small open economy, an

[3] For a brief summary of alternative monetary regimes and their implications, see Humphrey and Keleher (1982).

external drain of international reserves (or gold) normally followed as a necessary element of the balance-of-payments adjustment mechanism. Under such circumstances, restrictive monetary policy was deemed appropriate to stem the reserve (or gold) outflow and thereby maintain convertibility. However, because some banks typically had been overzealous or imprudent in their lending, the quality of their loan portfolios sharply deteriorated in the adjustment phase of the credit cycle. Depositors and note holders, fearing for the safety of their deposits and notes, withdrew deposits (or requested conversion of deposits and notes into currency or gold) and thereby created an *internal* drain. Appropriate policy action under an internal drain was expansionary in order to accommodate demands for currency, to promote confidence, and thereby to stem the possibility of widespread bank runs, the collapse of the fractional reserve banking system, sharp contractions of the money supply, and the suspension of convertibility.

The policy prescription for simultaneously meeting external and internal drains was to 'lend freely at a high (penalty) rate.' A high bank rate attracted foreign capital and hence stemmed the external drain. At the same time, a high bank rate rationed the scarce reserves among eager borrowers and ensured that central bank lending was indeed last-resort lending by providing an incentive for banks to exhaust market sources of liquidity before coming to the central bank.[4] Yet, lending freely ensured that credit remained available, so that a sharp fall in bank asset prices would not have to occur (since a market for these assets was provided). This helped to promote confidence in the banking system and thereby prevented secondary runs or contagion. Since the discount rate was the principal and convenient policy tool under a regime of fixed exchange rates, last-resort liquidity was normally provided via the discount window. The provision of such liquidity, therefore, became synonymous with discount-window lending by the 'lender' of last resort. In short, the LLR function complemented, rather than conflicted with, the central bank's monetary objectives of maintaining a convertible currency and stable growth of the domestic note issue.

In the cases of a small open economy under flexible exchange rates and a closed economy, direct monetary control becomes a viable target of monetary policy. That is, when the convertibility requirement no longer exists to influence policy, monetary and price-level stability may become a direct objective of central bank policy. Given fractional-reserve banking and governmental monopoly of legal tender issuance, however, economies under both of these regimes still remain vulnerable to bank runs and the collapse of fractional-reserve banking, and thereby to sharp contractions of the money supply. Again, the function of the LLR under these regimes is to prevent credit crises and instability from creating monetary crises and contraction; that is, to prevent banking collapses from affecting the money supply.

[4] There was an additional rationale for the high bank rate. Specifically, it ensured that the domestic-credit component of the money stock would be kept on a noninflationary path. For when bankers are forced to borrow money from the LLR at a penalty rate, they will be eager to pay off those loans when the panic expires. The resulting loan repayment will extinguish the emergency increase in the money stock, bringing that stock back on path.

Under both the closed-economy and flexible-exchange-rate regimes, the pursuit of monetary stability automatically results in the provision of last-resort liquidity. Achieving monetary stability necessarily means that sharp increases in the demand for coin and currency be accommodated in order to prevent sharp contractions in the money stock. Stability in monetary growth will also tend to minimize the volatility of credit and therefore lessen the likelihood both of sharp collapses in the prices of bank assets and of widespread bank runs. Such policy objectives typically are most conveniently provided through open market operations. Although many economists still do not associate open market purchases with the LLR function, such purchases are a particularly efficient way of providing liquidity to the market. They have the advantage of speed as well as that of regulating the total amount of reserves, but *not* their allocation among particular users.

LLR provision of liquidity during a crisis via open market operations does not conflict with longer-run monetary control. Specifically, prompt and vigorous LLR action will stop any panic within a very short time, long before the supply of high-powered money strays very far off its stable long-run path. Also, to the extent that the emergency expansion of high-powered money merely offsets panic-induced rises in currency and reserve ratios, the money stock will remain largely unchanged. As a result, any deviation of the money supply from its long-run target path will be small both in magnitude and duration. Thus, the LLR function is essentially a very short-run function of a central bank which is only activated during temporary periods of emergency. The stabilization of money and prices is a continuous and longer-run function. Consequently, the functions are not in conflict. Indeed, since the LLR function works to prevent sudden decreases (shocks) of the money stock, it is fully consistent with a 'gradualist' approach to monetary control. The monetary control and LLR functions, therefore, are complementary rather than conflicting functions.

In sum, the lender of last resort has the same objective under different regimes: to prevent short-run credit instabilities from affecting longer-run monetary objectives. The short-run LLR function does not conflict with, but rather complements, the longer-run monetary objectives.

Lucid explanations of the above-described central bank LLR function were presented by several early monetary theorists. The concept of the LLR was developed and refined during the course of important monetary debates of the 19th century and often after a monetary crisis. Indeed, as Charles Rist (1966, p. 380) emphasized: 'Central banks of issue, and consequently their functions and operations, really developed in the course of the nineteenth century.' These earlier monetary writers spelled out the LLR function both more clearly and more consistently than many modern authors. For this reason, a thorough and clear understanding of this function and its important implications can best be obtained by reviewing its historical development, and by recognizing the different monetary regimes under which these important authors developed their interpretations.

HENRY THORNTON'S EARLY PRESENTATION OF THE THEORY OF A LENDER OF LAST RESORT

The term 'lender of last resort' owes its origin to Sir Francis Baring, who in his *Observations on the Establishment of the Bank of England* (1797) referred to the Bank as 'the dernier resort' from which all banks could obtain liquidity in times of crisis. But the concept itself received its first—and in many respects still its most rigorous, complete, and systematic—treatment in the hands of Henry Thornton. It was Thornton who, in his testimony before Parliament, in his speeches on the Bullion Report, and in his classic *An Enquiry Into the Nature and Effects of the Paper Credit of Great Britain* (1802), identified the Bank of England's distinguishing characteristics as an LLR. It was he who also specified the LLR's primary function, who distinguished between the microeconomic versus macroeconomic and shock-preventing versus shock-absorbing aspects of this function, and who analyzed its relationship with the monetary control function of the central bank. Finally, it was he who first enunciated the so-called 'moral hazard' problem confronting the LLR.

Thornton identified three distinguishing characteristics of the LLR. First was its unique position as the ultimate source of liquidity for the financial system. The LLR, he pointed out, maintained and created a strategic stock of high-powered money that could be used to satisfy demands for liquidity at critical times. More precisely, it held the central gold reserve from which all banks could draw. Equally important, it supplied the other (non-gold) component of the monetary base in the form of its own notes—notes which, by virtue of their unquestioned soundness and universal acceptability, were considered the equivalent of gold and therefore constituted de facto legal tender. The Bank's effective monopolistic power to issue these notes gave it sole control over an inexhaustible source of domestic legal tender—the first requisite of an LLR.

The second distinguishing characteristic of the LLR identified by Thornton was its special responsibilities as custodian of the central gold reserve. Not only must it hold sufficient reserves to inspire full confidence in their ready availability in times of stress, but it must also rely on its own resources (since as the last resort, it can turn to no other source) to protect the reserve from gold-depleting specie drains. Specifically, it must stand ready to freely issue its own paper to stem the panics that bring about internal specie drains. And, while relying on its control over the issue of monetary notes to prevent external drains caused by persistent inflationary over-issue of paper, it must hold so large a reserve as to be able to withstand those temporary and self-reversing external drains originating in real shocks to the balance of payments. Should the Bank nevertheless find its reserve exhausted and the gold in circulation depleted by an extraordinary succession of such shocks (Thornton mentions three successive crop failures), it must take steps to ensure that the eventual return flow of gold is not delayed by domestic monetary contractions that depress aggregate production and thus reduce output available for export.

For, according to Thornton (1939, p. 118), given downward inflexibility of wages and prices in the face of money-induced declines in aggregate demand,

> the manufacturer, on account of the unusual scarcity of money, may even . . . be absolutely compelled by necessity to slacken, if not suspend, his operations. To inflict such a pressure on the mercantile world as necessarily causes an intermission of manufacturing labour, is obviously not the way to increase that exportable produce, by the excess of which, above the imported articles, gold is to be brought into the country.

In short, the central bank must ensure that temporary external drains originating in a succession of transitory real disturbances are not prolonged by secondary monetary shocks. To do this, it must sterilize or neutralize those gold drains with temporary increases in its own note issue. In so doing, it maintains the base of high-powered money and prevents sharp contractions in the money stock, contractions which, by depressing manufacturing activity and thus reducing output available for export, would prolong the deficit in the balance of trade and hinder the return flow of gold. By judicious expansion of its own paper, the Bank of England arrests and reverses these specie drains that imperil its gold reserve.

The third characteristic of the LLR, according to Thornton, was that it was not just like any other bank; it had public responsibilities. Unlike an ordinary commercial banker, whose responsibilities extend only to his stockholders, an LLR's responsibility, Thornton asserted, extends to the entire economy. Specifically, the LLR's duties include preserving the aggregate quantity and hence purchasing power of the circulating medium during bank runs and panics, and assisting the entire financial system in times of crisis. This responsibility, he argued, dictates that the LLR behave in a way precisely the opposite of that of a commercial banker in times of distress, expanding its note issue and loans at the very time the banker is contracting his. For whereas the individual banker can justify his loan and note contraction on the grounds that it will enhance his own liquidity and safety while not materially worsening that of the whole economy, the LLR can make no such assumption. On the contrary, the LLR must assume that, because of its influence over the total money supply, any contractionary policy on its part would adversely affect the economy. Consequently, the LLR must expand its note issue and loans at a time when the prudent commercial banker is contracting his. To be in a position to do this, the LLR, Thornton noted, must hold much larger cash reserves than the ordinary bank.

Having outlined the distinctive features of the LLR, Thornton next expounded on many issues relating to central banking, but four in particular are especially relevant to the LLR. The first concerns a possible conflict between the central bank's responsibility as controller of that part of the monetary stock which consists of domestic notes and its function as lender of last resort. To the extent that the central bank bears the responsibility for providing a stable framework of the domestic note component of monetary growth, it must exercise a moderate and continued restraint on the rate of expansion of its own note issue. It must exercise such restraint either to protect its international reserves from displacement by excess paper so that it can maintain the convertibility of its currency under fixed exchange rates or to prevent domestic inflation under floating exchange rates. But coping with unusual liquidity strains or panics through exercise of the LLR function calls for abandonment of this restraint and relinquishing control over the rate of expansion of the note component of the monetary base. Hence, some banking specialists have noted an apparent conflict between these two central banking objectives.

Thornton, however, saw no inconsistency between a policy of stable monetary growth and the actions required to deal with liquidity crises. In the following passage, which Joseph Schumpeter has called the 'Magna Carta of central banking,' Thornton distinguishes between the long-run target growth path of the note component of the monetary base and temporary emergency deviations from the path. The proper policy of the Bank of England, Thornton (1939, p. 259) said, is

> [T]o limit the total amount of paper issued, and to resort for this purpose, whenever the temptation to borrow is strong, to some effectual principle of restriction; in no case, however, materially to diminish the sum in circulation, but to let it vibrate only within certain limits; to afford a slow and cautious extension of it, as the general trade of the kingdom enlarges itself; to allow of some special, though temporary, increase in the event of any extraordinary alarm or difficulty, as the best means of preventing a great demand at home for guineas;[5] and to lean to the side of diminution, in the case of gold going abroad, and of the general exchanges continuing long unfavourable; this seems to be the true policy of the directors of an institution circumstanced like that of the Bank of England. To suffer either the solicitations of merchants, or the wishes of government, to determine the measure of the bank issues, is unquestionably to adopt a very false principle of conduct.

Thus, to Thornton, the main responsibility of the central bank was to regulate the domestic paper component of the money stock so that it expands at a steady noninflationary pace roughly comparable to the long-term growth rate of output. The bank must also counter those specie drains that periodically threatened to deplete its gold reserve and force suspension of convertibility. As previously mentioned, these drains were of two types: external (or foreign), composed of exports of gold to cover an adverse balance of payments in the country's international accounts and, internal, consisting of panic-induced increases in the quantity of gold held by domestic residents. Temporary (self-reversing) external drains arising from transitory real shocks to the balance of payments can normally be met from the large buffer stock of gold reserves held precisely for that purpose, the temporary runoff of gold being offset by a reverse flow later on. But an extraordinary succession of such drains, if sufficient to exhaust the metallic reserve and deplete the gold in circulation, may require expansionary policy. Such policy, Thornton argued, would neutralize (sterilize) the gold outflow, prevent needless monetary contraction and the resulting disruption of the export industries ('those sources of our returning wealth'), and thereby contribute to the prompt correction of the trade

[5] Thornton is here referring to the public's demond for gold coin, the guinea being the name of a standard gold coin in use in England at the time.

deficit and the speedy return of gold. By contrast, persistent external drains arising from inflationary over-issue of paper call for restrictive policy. Either by reducing inflated British prices relative to foreign prices or by creating an excess demand for money which domestic residents attempt to satisfy by selling more goods and buying less, such restrictive policy spurs exports, checks imports, eliminates the trade-balance deficit, and halts the outflow of gold. Clearly monetary contraction, he thought, is the correct remedy for persistent external drains.

In the case of a panic and internal drain, however, the Bank should be prepared temporarily to expand sharply both its note issue and its loans to satisfy the public's demand for high-powered money. This means that the Bank must step off its path of stable note growth to prevent the money stock from shrinking. Indeed, Thornton argued that emergency expansions of Bank of England notes were required to keep the stock of paper money (Bank notes plus notes issued by commercial banks) on path in the face of panic-induced rises in currency and reserve ratios. There need be no conflict between the functions of monetary control and lender of last resort, however, since the first refers to the long run and the second to temporary periods of emergency that may last for only a few days. Although he had no penalty rate mechanism to extinguish the emergency increase of base money and return it to path once the panic was over, he did argue that if the central bank, in its role as an LLR, responds promptly and vigorously to the threat of a liquidity crisis, the panic will be averted quickly. Indeed, Thornton held that the mere expectation of such a response may be sufficient to stop the panic before additional notes are issued. Thus, the deviation of the money stock from its long-run target path will be small, both in magnitude and duration.

The second issue considered by Thornton concerns the extent of the lender of last resort's responsibility to individual banks as opposed to the banking system as a whole. Suppose these individual banks are unsound. Must the LLR act to prevent their failure; that is, are bailout operations necessary to preserve the stability of the payments mechanism? According to Thornton (1939, p. 188):

> It is by no means intended to imply, that it would become the Bank of England to relieve every distress which the rashness of country banks may bring upon them: the bank, by doing this, might encourage their improvidence. There seems to be a medium at which a public bank should aim in granting aid to inferior establishments, and which it must often find very difficult to be observed. The relief should neither be so prompt and liberal as to exempt those who misconduct their business from all the natural consequences of their fault, nor so scanty and slow as deeply to involve the general interests. These interests, nevertheless, are sure to be pleaded by every distressed person whose affairs are large, however indifferent or even ruinous may be their state.

Thorton made four key points in this passage. First, the lender of last resort's primary responsibility is to the market ('the general interests') and not to the individual bank. The central bank has no duty to sustain particular institutions. Second, the LLR must take account of the moral hazard problem. That is, it must recognize that when it makes liberal accommodation available, it may create incentives that encourage laxity and recklessness in the lending practice of individual banks. Thornton's solution to this problem was to advise against bail-out operations for banks whose distress arises from 'rashness,' 'improvidence,' or 'misconduct.' By subsidizing the risk-bearing function of poorly managed banks, such rescue operations, he asserts, would encourage other banks to take excessive speculative risks without fear of the consequences. In short, individual imprudence should be punished by losses. Only if the financial repercussions of such punishment threaten to become widespread should the lender of last resort intervene. His third point, however, was that even in this latter case, aid should be extended sparingly and on relatively unfavorable terms. Finally, he was skeptical of the claim that economic welfare is inevitably harmed when a bank fails. This argument, he noted, would provide every large bank, no matter how poorly run, with an automatic justification for aid. He was aware that occasionally the public interest may be better served by the demise of inefficient banks, because the resulting improvements in resource allocation may outweigh any adverse spillover side effects of the failure.

The third issue addressed by Thornton was whether the lender of last resort should try to prevent shocks to the financial system. Here Thornton answered in the negative. The lender of last resort exists, he said, not to prevent shocks but to minimize their secondary repercussions. He argued that a panic could be triggered by any kind of 'alarm'; for example, rumors of a foreign invasion, an initial bank failure, and so on. The central bank has no responsibility for stopping these triggering events, but it does have a responsibility for arresting the panic, stopping it from spreading throughout the system. 'If any one bank fails,' said Thornton (1939, p. 180), 'a general run on the neighboring ones is apt to take place, which if not checked at the beginning by a pouring into the circulation a large quantity of gold, leads to very extensive mischief.'

The proper response, according to Thornton, is not to stop the initial failure, but to pump liquidity into the market. In Thornton's view, the actual occurrence of a widespread panic would be properly attributable not to the initial bank failure, but to the central bank's failure to insulate the economy from the impact of that event. He distinguished between the effect of closing an individual bank and the policy errors of the lender of last resort. Closing an individual bank, he said, contributes very little to 'general distress' or 'general commercial difficulty.' By contrast, policy errors of the lender of last resort create a 'general shock to credit' that 'produces Distress through the whole Kingdom' (Thornton, pp. 287–8, 304–5).

Finally, Thornton identified the paramount objective or primary purpose of the lender of last resort. Today, opinion varies as to the lender's ultimate objective, with all of the following being mentioned: preventing widespread bank failures; preserving confidence in the banking system; preventing a massive dumping of assets and the consequent collapse of asset values; guarding against the danger of massive currency withdrawals; and ensuring that banks and other lending institutions will be able to meet their loan commitments. Thornton, however, saw the lender of last resort's overriding objective as the prevention of panic-induced declines in the money stock, declines that could produce depressions in the level of economic activity. That is, he viewed the LLR as essentially a monetary rather than a banking function. While recognizing that the LLR also functions to forestall bank runs and avert credit crises, he insisted that these functions, although undeniably important, were nevertheless ancillary and incidental to the LLR's main task of protecting the money supply. In other words, the LLR's crisis-averting and run-arresting duties were simply the means (albeit the most efficient and expeditious ones) through which it pursued its ultimate objective of preserving the quantity, and hence the purchasing power, of the money stock. The important point was to prevent sharp short-run shrinkages in the quantity of money, since hardship ensued from these rather than from bank runs or credit crises per se.

In this connection, he drew a sharp distinction between bank *credit* (loans and discounts) on the one hand and the stock of *money* on the other. He then argued that, while the two aggregates tend to rise and fall together, it is the fall of the money stock that does the damage to the real economy. More precisely, he asserted that, while credit indeed finances and supports business activity, such credit arises from money rather than vice versa. Since credit springs from money and not money from credit, it follows that monetary contractions rather than credit collapses per se are the root cause of lapses in economic activity. Regarding this point, Thornton (1939, p. 307) asserted that a run-induced contraction in bank credit is not as harmful as the corresponding decline in the money stock: 'It is not the limitation of Discounts or Loans, but . . . the limitation of Bank Notes or of the Means of Circulation that produces the Mischiefs [of unemployment and lost output].'

To show how such monetary contractions and the resulting fall in output and employment would occur in the absence of an LLR, Thornton traced a chain of causation running from an alarm or rumor to financial panic to the demand for high-powered money to the money stock itself and thence to aggregate spending and the level of real economic activity. Panics, he noted, trigger doubts about the solvency of country banks and the safety of their note and deposit liabilities. As a result, moneyholders seek to convert these assets into money of unquestioned soundness, namely gold or Bank of England notes. These two items, he noted, comprise the base of high-powered money, an unaccommodated increase in the demand for which in a fractional reserve banking system is capable of causing a multiple contraction of the money stock. The demand for base money, he said, is doubly augmented during panics; for at the same time that moneyholders are attempting to convert suspect country bank notes and deposits into gold or its equivalent, country banks are also seeking to augment their reserve holdings of these high-powered monetary assets, not only to meet anticipated cash withdrawals but also to allay public suspicion of financial weakness. The result is a massive rise in the demand for base money—a rise that, if not satisfied by increased issues, produces sharp contractions in the money stock and equally sharp contractions in spending. Since Thornton contended that wages and prices were downwardly sticky and therefore responded sluggishly to declines in spending, it follows, he said, that output and employment will bear most of the burden of adjustment; that is, the monetary contraction will fall most heavily on real activity.

the Act were put to severe tests by three turbulent financial crises in 1847, 1857, and 1866. All of these financial crises were characterized by sharp internal drains or panics. As indicated above, however, the Bank Act prevented the Bank from acting as an LLR. In all of these crises, the government found it necessary to temporarily suspend the Bank Act. Thus, these crises showed the government always ready, on the only occasions when it was necessary, to exempt the Bank from the provisions of the Bank Act (Smith 1936, p. 18), allowing it to issue notes uncovered by gold in excess of the statutory limits imposed in the Bank Charter Act.[13] Such note expansion was considered necessary to stem the internal drain or panic. In short, the government rescinded the restriction and thereby enabled the Bank to serve as an LLR. In all three cases, either the mere suspension of the Act (as in 1847) or the expanded note issue was sufficient to stop the internal drain; that is, the provision of LLR services halted the panics.

These crises and the need for special government action to deal with them forced a reconsideration of certain provisions of the Bank Act. In particular, a deficiency of the Act appeared to be its prohibition of last-resort lending. Several Parliamentary committees recommended the incorporation of a 'relaxing clause' (or an 'elastic clause') into the Act. Such a clause would enable the Bank to temporarily provide LLR services in the special case of an internal drain or panic.

A 'relaxation clause' had been opposed by Currency School writers on the grounds that it would lead the public to believe that an increase in note issues would easily and promptly occur should any perceived problems arise. They also thought there was a danger that the clause would be used too soon and too often, thereby becoming the rule rather than the exception. Consequently, incentives would be created for banks to forego adopting necessary correctives and instead take more risks; that is, a moral hazard problem would arise. Banks, for example, would have an incentive to hold smaller reserves and liquid assets, thereby increasing the likelihood of financial crises (Mints, 1945, p. 119). Currency School writers also believed that if the public anticipated relaxation, foreign drains would not be stopped. Finally, such a clause would allow discretion and, in addition, introduce a departure from the principles of metallic currency (Daugherty, 1943, p. 243).

The Banking School

Banking School writers (such as Tooke, Fullarton, Wilson, and Gilbart) disagreed with Currency School writers on many of these issues and, indeed, opposed the Bank Act of 1844. The principal writers of the Banking School did not begin to attack Currency School theories until shortly before the Bank Charter Act was passed (Daugherty, 1943, p. 148). Events after 1844, however, provided support for their views of the LLR function.

In opposing the views of the Currency School, Banking School writers insisted that the Bank of England should not behave 'just like any other bank.'[14] They

[13] In 1847 there was no actual infringement of these limits. See Daugherty (1943, p. 242).

[14] See, for example, Thomas Tooke, who stated: 'A great mistake was committed by the framers of the Act of 1844, in the assumption that the Banking Department of the Bank of England admits of being

believed that a special role existed for the Bank of England and that in the case of an internal drain, any individual commercial bank's attempt to expand would result in an immediate loss of reserves without significantly changing the overall situation. An individual bank, therefore, would be induced to contract rather than expand its operation (Smith, 1936, p. 66). In the case of an internal drain, Banking School writers argued, it was essential for some nonprofit-seeking holder (or creator) of the ultimate reserve of the system to pursue an expansionary policy (Mints, 1945, p. 248). No other institution would be able to inspire the same degree of confidence or have its notes accepted as readily. The bank which holds (or creates) the ultimate reserve has the ability to lend in a crisis and thereby has the great advantage over other institutions, which run the risk of stopping payment if their reserves are exhausted (Hawtrey, 1962, p. 131). In short, Banking School writers contended that, unlike other banks, a loss of reserves should not normally result in a restriction of the issue of Bank of England notes. In their view, the Bank of England should expand its note issuance during an internal drain or panic and be a lender of last resort. By providing these services, the bank would stem the panic and might prevent the suspension of convertibility as well.

In carrying out such LLR responsibilities, there were other ways in which the Bank of England should not behave 'just like any other bank.' Banking School writers insisted that the Bank of England should hold larger reserves than other banks (Fetter, 1965, p. 261), which would promote confidence in the Bank's ability to manage various types of drains. Larger reserves would also permit the Bank to easily manage temporary external drains without disrupting domestic circulation by serving as an 'exchange defense fund' (Wood, 1939, p. 155). Since Banking School writers (such as Tooke and Fullarton) believed that most foreign gold flows were caused by temporary factors, a large reserve would enable the Bank to deal with frequent temporary external drains and not affect the domestic economy (Daugherty, 1943, p. 154; Mints, 1945, p. 120). Finally, larger reserves would also give the Bank more ability to use discretion in its treatment of various gold drains.

Banking School writers opposed the Bank Act of 1844 for several reasons. In their view, one of its defects was that it failed to allow for different policy prescriptions in the case of alternative types of drains; the Act obliged the Bank to deal with all drains in the same way—with restrictive policies.[15] Banking School writers endorsed a definite LLR role for the Bank of England, maintaining that three distinct types of drains existed and discretion was necessary so that the Bank of England could distinguish among them before applying a proper policy remedy for each. A mechanistic rule was inappropriate because of the different causes and

conducted in the same way, and with the same effects on the interest and convenience of the Public, as any other non-issuing Joint Stock Bank,' *On the Bank Charter Act of 1844* (London, 1856), p. 142, reprinted in Fetter (1965, p. 261).

[15] Indeed, John Stuart Mill supported the Banking School writers on this issue. He indicated that 'the [Bank] Act hindered the Bank from taking the steps which would give relief when a crisis had occurred.' See Viner (1965, p. 234).

types of these drains. Instead, proper policy prescriptions included expansion for an internal drain, contraction for a permanent external drain, and the use of its large reserve stock to manage a temporary (self-correcting) external drain. In short, according to Banking School writers (and contrary to Currency School writers), contractionary policy was inappropriate in both the cases of an internal drain and a temporary external drain.[16] The view that the various types of drains should not be dealt with in the same manner, of course, was not new. Henry Thornton had stated that the Bank should deal differently with the alternative types of drains (Wood, 1939, p.154).

As mentioned above, the Currency School's support of the Bank Act was based on the view that convertibility was not, in and of itself, sufficient to prevent financial crises. Some additional mechanism was necessary to control the note component of the domestic monetary base, and the Bank Act's nondiscretionary rule was supposed to provide that control. Banking School writers believed that in the case of the small open economy, convertibility, together with bank lending against real bills, would suffice to provide control of the domestic note component of the monetary base and thereby prevent financial crises. Modern scholars have recently demonstrated that under a convertible currency, the real bills criterion would indeed function to control the paper component of the money stock.[17]

The events after 1844 tended to support Banking School views on the role of the Bank of England as an LLR during an internal drain. Financial crises had encouraged various monetary writers to delineate their views on the proper role of the Bank of England, and the crisis of 1866 stimulated one particularly well known monetary writer. He subsequently put the capstone on the 19th-century debate concerning the domestic LLR. His name was Walter Bagehot.

THE CONTRIBUTION OF WALTER BAGEHOT

The post-1844 case for the lender of last resort received its strongest and most influential exposition in the writings of Walter Bagehot. In his seminal 1873 volume, *Lombard Street*, Bagehot at once clarified, refined, and advanced many of the pro-LLR propositions underlying the position of the Banking School. In so

[16] As Viner has indicated, J. S. Mill also made 'distinctions between internal drains, external drains which were self-corrective in character, and external drains which could be checked only by a change in relative price levels, and criticized the Act of 1844 on the grounds that it forced the Bank to apply identical treatment to all three types of drains. [Mill] claimed that a mechanical rule for the regulation of note issue was objectionable because it would prevent different treatment of the different types of drains.' See Viner (1965, p. 262).

[17] See, for example, Thomas M. Humphrey (1982) and David Laidler (1983). These authors, for example, point out that the Banking School relied on convertibility to fix the price level of the small open economy and on the real bills criterion to tie the growth rate of the paper component of the money stock to the growth rate of real output. They also argue that when convertibility is absent (so that nothing exists to anchor the price level), the real bills criterion by itself offers no constraint or limitation to the price level or the quantity of money in existence. Hence the traditional Mints/monetarist criticism is correct in an *inconvertible* paper currency regime but is not valid if convertibility reigns.

doing, he revived and restated many of the points made earlier by Thornton. Following Thornton, he emphasized the Bank of England's special position as the holder of the ultimate reserve. This position, he noted, not only rendered the central bank different from ordinary commercial banks, but also gave it the power as well as the duty to lend freely in a crisis, the very time when other bankers would be contracting their loans. He also followed Thornton in advocating that the Bank of England hold large buffer stocks of gold reserves, from which periodic drains could be met without adversely affecting the quantity of money in circulation. Finally, like Thornton, he distinguished between the appropriate response to internal versus external cash drains. An internal drain, he said, should be countered by a policy of lending freely and vigorously to erase all doubt about the availability of bank accommodation. An external drain, however, should be met by a sharp rise in the central bank's lending rate, the high interest rate serving to attract foreign gold and encouraging the retention of domestic gold. This latter action, Bagehot thought, was necessary to protect the nation's gold reserve, the gold component of the monetary base. According to Bagehot (1962, p. 155), 'the first duty of the Bank of England was to protect the ultimate cash of the country, and to raise the rate of interest so as to protect it.'

A sufficient gold reserve, of course, was necessary both for the preservation of the gold standard and for the maintenance of public confidence in the convertibility of paper currency into gold. Regarding public confidence, Bagehot (1962, pp. 156–7) argued that 'a panic is sure to be caused' if the gold reserve falls below 'a certain minimum which I will call the "apprehension minimum." ' It follows that the lender of last resort should strive to keep its gold reserves above this critical threshold.

Bagehot (1962, pp. 27–8) thought that a persistent external drain would trigger an internal drain as the public, observing the diminution of the gold stock and fearing a prospective suspension of cash payments, would seek to convert deposits and country bank notes into gold. 'Unless you can stop the foreign export,' he said, 'you cannot allay the domestic alarm.' In this case, in which 'periods of internal panic and external demand for bullion commonly occur together,' the lender of the last resort must 'treat two opposite maladies at once—one requiring stringent remedies, and especially a rapid rise in the rate of interest; and the other, an alleviative treatment with large and ready loans.' Therefore, 'the best remedy . . . when a foreign drain is added to a domestic drain' is the provision of 'very large loans at very high rates.' Here is the origin of the famous Bagehot Rule: 'lend freely at a high rate.'

Like Thornton, Bagehot stressed that last-resort lending should not be a continuous practice but rather a temporary emergency measure applicable only in times of banking panics. And, in perfect accord with his predecessor, Bagehot argued that if the central bank responded promptly and vigorously, the panic would be ended in a few days, by implication an interval not long enough for the domestic note component of the money stock to depart significantly from its appropriate long-run growth track.

Bagehot also viewed the role of the leader of last resort as primarily macroeconomic. The central bank, he said, bears the responsibility of guaranteeing the liquidity of the whole economy but not that of particular institutions. Thus, he prescribed last-resort lending as a remedy solely for emergencies affecting the entire banking system, not for isolated emergency situations affecting an individual bank or a few specific banks. Nor did he intend it to be used to prevent very large or key banks from failing as a consequence of poor management and inefficiency. As shown below, he did not think that support of such distressed key banks was necessary to forestall panics. Like Thornton, he emphasized that the task of the central bank was not to prevent initial failures but rather to prevent a subsequent wave of failures spreading through the system.

Bagehot also followed Thornton in arguing that the lender of last resort exists not to prevent shocks but to minimize the secondary repercussions following them. His views on this point are contained in his analysis of panics, which, said Bagehot (1962, p. 61), can be triggered by a variety of exogenous events—'a bad harvest, an apprehension of foreign invasions, a sudden failure of a great firm which everybody trusted.' But 'no cause is more capable of producing a panic, perhaps none is so capable, as the failure of a first-rate joint stock bank in London' (Bagehot, 1962, p. 29). The shock of this initial failure must be contained before it gets out of hand, for 'in wild periods of alarm, one failure makes many.' The problem is how to 'arrest the primary failure' that causes 'the derivative failures.' Bagehot's solution, quoted below (1962, p. 25), stresses the liberal provisions of liquidity to the whole system rather than loans to the distressed bank:

> A panic, in a word, is a species of neuralgia, and according to the rules of science you must not starve it. The holders of the cash reserve must be ready not only to keep it for their own liabilities, but to advance it most freely for the liabilities of others. They must lend to merchants, to minor bankers, to 'this man and that man,' whenever the security is good. . . . The way in which the panic of 1825 was stopped by advancing money has been described in so broad and graphic a way that the passage has become classical. 'We lent it,' said Mr. Harmon, on behalf of the Bank of England, 'by every possible means and in modes we had never adopted before; we took in stock on security, we purchased Exchequer bills, we made advances on Exchequer bills, we not only discounted outright but we made advances on the deposit of bills of exchange to an immense amount, in short, by every possible means consistent with the safety of the bank, and we were not on some occasions overnice. Seeing the dreadful state in which the public were, we rendered every assistance in our power.' After a day or two of this treatment, the entire panic subsided, and the 'City' was quite calm.

Conspicuously absent is any mention of the need to channel aid to specific institutions, as would be implied by bail-out operations. Bagehot's emphasis is clearly on aid to the market rather than to the initially distressed bank. He obviously did not think it necessary to prevent the initial failure at all costs.

Up to this point, Bagehot has been depicted largely as a follower or disciple of Thornton. But Bagehot did more than just elaborate, refine, and coordinate Thornton's analysis. He also contributed several original points that added substance to the lender-of-last-resort doctrine and advanced it beyond Thornton's formulation. At least five of these points deserve mention.

First, Bagehot distinguished between the central bank's extending support to the market after a crisis began, and its giving assurance of support in advance of an impending crisis. He argued that the lender of last resort's duty did not stop with the actual provision of liquidity in times of crisis, but also involved making it clear in advance that it would lend freely in all future crises. As Bagehot (1962, p. 85) put it, 'the public have a right to know whether [the central bank]—the holders of our ultimate bank reserve—acknowledge this duty, and are ready to perform it.' This assurance alone, he thought, would dispel uncertainty about and promote confidence in the central bank's willingness to act; thus generating a pattern of stabilizing expectations that would help avert future panics.

Second, he advocated that last-resort accommodation be made at a penalty rate. Borrowers should have relief in times of crises, but they should be prepared to pay a price that implied a stiff penalty. The central bank has a duty to lend, but it should extract a high price for its loans, a price that would ration scarce liquidity to its highest-valued uses just as a high price rations any scarce commodity in a free market. Moreover, a penalty rate also had the appeal of distributional equity, it being only fair that borrowers should pay handsomely for the protection and security afforded by the lender of last resort. Allocative efficiency and distributive justice aside, the penalty rate, Bagehot claimed, would produce at least four additional beneficial results. First, it would encourage the importation and prevent the exportation of specie, thus protecting the nation's gold reserve. It would achieve this result by attracting short-term capital from abroad and by exerting a deflationary influence on the level of economic activity and domestic prices, thereby improving the external balance of trade by spurring exports and reducing imports. Second, consistent with the objective of maintaining stable growth of the note component of the money stock, a penalty rate would ensure the quick retirement of emergency expansions of the note issue once the emergency ends. The very unprofitability of borrowing at the above-market rate would encourage the prompt repayment of loans when the panic subsides, and the resulting loan repayment would extinguish the emergency issue so that the money stock would return to its noninflationary path. Third, the high rate of interest would reduce the quantity of precautionary cash balances that overcautious wealth-holders would want to hold. Without the high rate to deter them, these cashholders might deplete the central gold reserve. As Bagehot put it, the penalty rate would serve as 'a heavy fine on unreasonable timidity,' prompting potential cashholders to economize on the nation's scarce gold reserve. In this connection, he advocated that the penalty rate be established 'early in the panic, so that the fine may be paid early; that no one may borrow out of idle precaution without paying well for it; that the Banking reserve may be protected as far as possible' (Bagehot, 1962, p. 97).

Last and most important, the penalty rate would, in addition to rationing the scarce gold reserve, provide an incentive for banks to exhaust all market sources of liquidity and even develop new sources before coming to the central bank. By encouraging individual banks to develop better techniques of money management and the capital market to develop new channels to mobilize existing liquidity, the penalty rate would promote allocative efficiency in the financial system. In short, the penalty rate would protect the gold reserve, minimize deviations of the growth of the domestic note component from its stable path, allocate resources by market price, discourage reliance on the central bank, and ensure that recourse to the latter's lending facilities was truly a last resort.

Bagehot's analysis, it should be noted, implies still another use for the penalty rate: providing a test of the soundness of distressed borrowers. A penalty rate set a couple of percentage points above the market rate on alternative sources of funds would encourage illiquid banks to turn to the market first. Success in obtaining accommodation at the market rate would indicate that lenders judge these borrowers to be sound risks, for the borrowers and their assets would pass the market test. On the other hand, resort to the central bank would tend to indicate weaknesses in the borrowing institutions, suggesting that the banks may be unable to borrow in the market at the lower rate. Fearing default, lenders may demand a risk premium in excess of the difference between the market rate and the penalty rate, forcing the banks to close, to arrange a merger with other banks, or to resort to the central bank's lending facility. Thus, the penalty rate will have provided a test of the banks' soundness.

Bagehot's third contribution was his specification of the types of borrowers the lender of last resort should accommodate, the kinds of assets it should lend on, and the criteria it should use to determine the acceptability of those assets. Regarding the types of borrowers, he stated that the Bank of England should be willing to accommodate anyone with good security. Last-resort loans, said Bagehot (1962, p. 25), should be available 'to merchants, to minor bankers, to this man and that man.' The objective of the central bank in time of panic is to satisfy the market's demand for liquidity. It makes little difference, he said, whether this objective is accomplished via loans to merchants, to bankers, or to whomever.

Concerning the type of collateral on which the central bank should lend, Bagehot's answer was clear. The bank should stand ready to lend on any and all sound assets, or, as he put it, 'on every kind of current security, or every sort on which money is ordinarily and usually lent' (Bagehot, 1962, p. 97). Besides the conventionally eligible bills and government securities, acceptable collateral should include 'all good banking securities,' and perhaps even 'railway debenture stock' (pp. 97, 101). In another passage he makes the point that the '*amount* of the advance is the main consideration . . . not the nature of the security on which the advance is made, always assuming the security to be good' (p. 101). The basic criterion was that the paper be indisputably good in *ordinary or normal times*. The latter qualification is important. It implies that the lender of last resort should not be afraid to extend loans on normally sound assets whose current market value is temporarily below book value owing to depression in the securities market.

To summarize, Bagehot felt that few restrictions should be placed on the types of assets on which the central bank might lend, or the kinds of borrowers it might accommodate. This position was consistent with his advocacy of price as opposed to non-price rationing mechanisms. He recommended that the central bank eschew qualitative restraints—eligibility rules, moral suasion, administrative discretion and the like—and instead rely on the penalty rate to ration borrowing.

Fourth, Bagehot provided a precise delineation of the extent of the lender of last resort's responsibility to individual banks as distinguished from the banking system as a whole. Concerning the question of whether this responsibility included assistance to insolvent banks, Bagehot's answer was an unequivocal no. The central bank's duty, he said, is not to rescue 'the "unsound" people' who constitute 'a feeble minority.' Such businesses, he said, 'are afraid even to look frightened for fear their unsoundness may be detected' (Bagehot, 1962, p. 97). In short, the job of the central bank is not to prevent failure at all costs but rather to confine the impact of such failure to the unsound institutions alone.

Bagehot meant for his strictures to apply even to those key banks whose failure, in the absence of central bank action, could shatter public confidence and start a falling-dominoes sequence of financial collapse. Thus, Bagehot (1962, p. 129) acknowledged that if

> owing to the defects in its government, one even of the greater London joint stock banks failed, there would be an instant suspicion of the whole system. One *terra incognita* being seen to be faulty, every other *terra incognita* would be suspected. If the real government of these banks had for years been known, and if the subsisting banks had been known not to be ruled by the bad mode of government which had ruined the bank that had fallen, then the ruin of that bank would not be hurtful. The other banks would be seen to be exempt from the cause which had destroyed it. But at present the ruin of one of these great banks would greatly impair the credit of all. Scarcely any one knows the precise government of any one; in no case has that government been described on authority; and the fall of one by grave misgovernment would be taken to show that the others might easily be misgoverned also. And a tardy disclosure even of an admirable constitution would not much help the surviving banks: as it was extracted by necessity, it would be received with suspicion. A skeptical world would say 'of course they say they are all perfect now; it would not do for them to say anything else.'

Even in this case, however, Bagehot did not think it appropriate for the central bank to extend aid to poorly managed key banks. It is, instead, 'the "sound" people, the people who have good security to offer' who constitute 'the majority to be protected.' The lender-of-last-resort function should not be interpreted to mean that unsound banks should not be permitted to fail, but it implies that failure should not be allowed to spread to sound institutions. To Bagehot, the distinction is crucial. In his words, 'no advances indeed need be made' on assets on 'which the [central] Bank will ultimately lose.' Again, in another passage, he offers assurance that if the lender of last resort 'should refuse bad bills or bad securities' it 'will not make the panic really worse.' To arrest a panic, he says, it is sufficient that the bank guarantee to provide liquidity to the 'solvent merchants and bankers' who comprise the 'great majority' of the market. This policy ensures that 'the alarm of the solvent merchants and bankers will be stayed' (Bagehot, 1962, p. 97).

Finally, Bagehot warned against undue reliance on the lender of last resort and stressed the need to strengthen individual banks. The lender of last resort, he pointed out, was not meant to be a substitute for prudent bank practices.

money) which can supply such an international medium of exchange. Under these particular circumstances, an international LLR may be needed.[20]

In the domestic case, when domestic bank notes are not convertible into a common legal tender (as in the case of a free banking system), there is no necessary role for an LLR since there would be no increase in the demand for any type of bank note. Indeed, before the existence of a domestic LLR, suspensions of cash payments (or suspensions of the convertibility of deposits and bank notes into currency or gold), as well as bank holidays, sometimes therapeutically served to limit runs and, hence, to prevent sharp decreases in the domestic money stocks.[21] An analogy holds in the international case. If in the international case described above, central banks face a run on their international reserves and cannot attain (or borrow) the international medium of exchange, they may suspend convertibility and allow their currencies to depreciate and thereafter fluctuate freely against other currencies and the international medium of exchange. Just as in the domestic case (without a monopoly of legal tender issuance), an LLR may not be necessary in this instance. Under flexible exchange rates, an international LLR may not be as essential as a domestic LLR with monopolized legal tender issuance (Smith, 1936, p. 164, n. 1; Moggridge, 1981, p. 50; Aliber, 1984, p. 27).

An International LLR: Historical Precedents?

Although exact parallels cannot easily be drawn, the purpose of any international LLR would be to provide a backstop or a mechanism to prevent sharp contractions of the world money supply, preventing world shocks (such as credit crises) from developing into world monetary crises. Several economists have asserted that at certain times, international LLRs have (in effect) already existed, and others maintain that the lack of an international LLR has caused some major world financial crises.

Under the pre-1914 gold standard, for example, it is sometimes asserted that the Bank of England took responsibility for stabilizing the international monetary system (Withers, 1909, pp. 212, 221, 236). The Bank of England at this time was the world's premier central bank and well understood the role of an LLR. According to Withers (1909, p. 210):

> The fact that London has remained the only market in which every draft and every credit are immediately convertible into gold as a matter of course, has greatly intensified the responsibility of the Bank of England as custodian of a gold reserve, which is liable to be drawn on at any time from all quarters of the habitable globe from which a draft on London may be presented.

[20] See Hawtrey (1962, pp. 228, 278) and Smith (1936, p. 169). See also Robert Aliber (1984, p. 26), where he suggests the following instances of the need for an international lender of last resort: a shift in investor (or central bank) demand from assets with high credit multipliers to those with lower credit multipliers—from dollar assets to gold or to SDR; and a shift from commercial bank liabilities in one country to central bank liabilities in another.

[21] See, for example, Smith (1936, pp. 38, 40, 45, 134, and 136); and Friedman and Schwartz (1963, pp. 8, 109–10, 124, 157, 160, 163–4, 167, 328).

Such an assertion led to the belief that the Bank of England served as an international LLR. Fetter (1965, p. 255), for instance, stated in his text:

> [A] widely held belief of economists—expressed more in oral tradition than in formal presentation—[was] that the successful operation of the international economy before 1914 was due to the Bank of England's action as managing director, or as executive secretary, of the international gold standard, and to the City of London's role as an international lender of last resort.

Although the Bank of England may have provided critical central bank services, it did not meet the requirements for an international LLR—the Bank was not the ultimate creator of international reserves.

The lack of an international LLR has been singled out by some economists, notably Charles Kindleberger (1973; 1978), as the primary reason for the worldwide financial and monetary collapse of the 1930s. Certainly, no mechanism was available at that time to prevent the contraction of the world money stock that occurred (Mundell, 1983, p. 289; Humphrey and Keleher, 1982, pp. 95–100). In fact, the experience of this period led to proposals to create such an institution.[22]

Although established in 1944, the IMF was created, in part, as a response to the events of the 1930s. Some analysts contend that the IMF already acts as an international LLR since it possesses substantial unused financial resources, the power to raise additional funds, a large unpledged gold stock, and the power to issue SDRs (Dean and Giddy, 1981, p. 33; Weintraub, 1983, pp. 43–4). The IMF, however, was not created to be an international LLR. Indeed, various proposals for an international bank that could create international reserves were explicitly rejected by the United States and other countries at the time because of a fear that excessive international money might be created. The signers of the Bretton Woods agreements definitely wanted to 'guard against the possibility of its becoming a factory of international money' (Machlup, 1969, p. 340). They therefore did not give the IMF reserve-creating powers. Instead, the IMF was designed to promote world trade and assist member countries with short-term balance of payments deficits through extensions of short-term loans. But the IMF could not then, and cannot today, serve as an international LLR since it cannot create money or international reserves. The only funds it can make available are those resulting from limited contributions made and agreed upon by the member countries. Once the IMF reaches this quota, its funds are exhausted; it cannot simply create money.[23] Since the ability to create money is the critical distinguishing feature of a LLR, the IMF, lacking that feature, falls well short of being a genuine, full-fledged LLR.

[22] In 1932, for example, a report was issued by a cabinet committee in Britain recommending the development of an international institution that would be allowed to issue paper gold, to be called international certificates. (Kindleberger, 1978, p. 196).

[23] Actually, the IMF may borrow from any source and in the currency of any member country. However, it must first obtain the consent of the government of the member country in whose currency it proposes to borrow. Thus far it has borrowed limited funds from member countries but never from the markets. Furthermore, in January 1982, the IMF's Executive Board confirmed that quotas should continue to be the main source of funds. See Group of Thirty (1983, p. 2).

The Bretton Woods system was handicapped at its outset by an inadequate supply of liquidity in the form of gold. Because of this shortage, the fact that the United States emerged from the war as the world's largest economy, and the fact that a large portion of world trade was denominated in dollars, the dollar became an international reserve and medium of exchange. During Bretton Woods, then, the world functioned on a dollar standard. Since the Federal Reserve could create such reserves and had an important impact on world monetary growth, the Federal Reserve may have met the criteria for a full-fledged international LLR. The dollar still serves as an international reserve currency, so some economists (see below) believe that the Federal Reserve still meets these criteria.

Do We Need an International LLR?

In assessing whether we need an international LLR, most economists would agree that some reliable mechanism for preventing sharp decreases in world reserves (or world money) should be established.[24] The question is: What should this mechanism be?

In general, there are two principal positions on this issue, each supported by various groups of economists from various schools of thought. One is that no international LLR is necessary. Some monetarist-oriented economists, for example, assert that under purely flexible exchange rates with reliable (decentralized) domestic LLRs, no international LLR is necessary. In this view, each domestic LLR has the power and ability to maintain and preserve the stability of its domestic money stock. If all domestic LLRs reliably pursue their LLR responsibilities, then sharp contractions of any aggregation of domestic monies will be prevented.[25] These arrangements will be sufficient to prevent monetary contractions, so the creation of an additional international agency is unnecessary.

Ironically, advocates of free money presumably join with most monetarists on this issue. The former contend that an international LLR is not necessary for many of the same reasons that they believe domestic LLRs are not necessary.[26] They endorse a decentralized multi-currency system with competition between monies—a system which was explicitly endorsed by Bagehot[27]—and they oppose the monopolization of the creation of world reserves. Free-money proponents also argue that although individual domestic LLRs have the monopoly of legal tender issuance within their own countries, they are forced to compete with one another

[24] We are not directly addressing the closely related and important issue of alternative monetary arrangements to provide for price stability, but are focusing only on the case for an international LLR.

[25] In the case of the current international debt situation, domestic LLRs can prevent any serious impacts of such debt disturbances on the domestic money stock.

[26] See, for example, White (1981a, b); Smith (1936); and the references cited therein.

[27] Specifically, Bagehot indicated that if he were starting *de novo*, he would have preferred decentralized multiple reserve, competitive note issue arrangements rather than the 'unnatural' system that existed when he wrote. But he believed attempting to create such arrangements was not politically feasible.

in the international realm (as suggested by the literature on currency substitution). All other things equal, such competition (albeit among government-created banks) is beneficial since it compels central banks to impose discipline upon their monetary policies. If their monies are to be acceptable, the central banks must be expected to maintain a stable value, so the dangers of excessive monetary instability are reduced. These economists, therefore, oppose the creation of an international LLR.

Another group of economists who join with monetarists and free-money advocates on this issue are proponents of the Public Choice School. These economists oppose the creation of an international LLR because of the dangers of further centralizing the power to make decisions. They contend that the bureaucrats who would manage such an institution would (like anyone else) pursue their own interests and service the needs of their constituents rather than the public interest. Such international agencies, once created, seem never to 'die or fade away,' but to continue to grow regardless of whether they serve a useful purpose. If an international LLR were allowed to create international reserves, for example, what mechanism would reliably control this institution and shape the incentives of those managing it? A super-governmental agency unconstrained in its power over creation of international reserves can be expected systematically to abuse that power. Public choice economists contend that an international LLR would likely lead to more world inflation and monetary instability, so they oppose its creation.

The case against an international LLR is supported by monetarists, who believe the set of existing decentralized domestic LLRs is sufficient to prevent sharp contraction of aggregations of the world's monies and reserves; free-money advocates, who support competition among multiple monies and who oppose the monopolization of world reserve creation; and public choice economists, who emphasize the dangers of creating centralized decision-making powers in a super-governmental bureaucracy.

Other economists, however, support the creation of an international LLR. Some of these economists, for example, contend that *under existing institutional arrangements*, the most reliable mechanism for preventing sharp contractions in world reserves and world monies entails the creation of an international LLR.[28] In supporting this position, these economists (unlike many monetarists) have recognized that during the 1970s the magnitude of international reserve flows actually increased, rather than decreased, under existing floating exchange rate arrangements.[29] Robert Mundell (1983b, p. 290), for example, contends:

> From 1952 to 1969 foreign exchange reserves, mainly dollars and sterling, rose from $16 billion to $33 billion, a little more than doubling over seventeen years. Then from 1969 to 1981 they rose by $272 billion, to $305 billion, almost a *tenfold* increase in only twelve years. . . .

[28] Historically, many proposals have been made for the creation of a world LLR or world central bank. See, for example, Machlup (1964) and references therein.

[29] Monetarists implicitly contend that under a purely flexible exchange rate regime, no international component of the monetary base need exist.

Thus, Mundell recognizes that under current institutional arrangements, the U.S. dollar has served and is serving as an international reserve currency. Indeed, it is possible that this role has actually increased in recent years. Whether we like it or not, we have no choice but to recognize that even under current floating rates the Federal Reserve can create world reserves and that its policy importantly affects world reserves. Consequently, the responsibilities of an international LLR currently fall on the Federal Reserve. Mundell contends that under such circumstances, it would be far better to have a formal international LLR with well-specified objectives than to have the Federal Reserve performing this role. For the other 'four-fifths of the world economy does not want a world monetary system based solely on the U.S. dollar, subject to the vicissitudes of U.S. politics and arbitrary management' (Mundell, 1983b, p. 287). Moreover, in this view, a system of decentralized domestic LLRs is *not* sufficient to reliably prevent contraction of world reserves and money. Specifically, under current arrangements, there are components of the world money stock which are outside the control of domestic LLRs.[30] And the system of floating exchange rates and currency substitution leads not only to destabilizing movements in world reserves and world money, but to volatile fluctuations in exchange rates and increasing pressures for trade restrictions. Thus, given the world as it exists, it would be preferable to construct alternative institutional arrangements which would more reliably prevent sharp decreases in world money.

Accordingly, Mundell (1983b, p. 292) proposes an international LLR that would have powers to create world reserves. He contends that the issues of this international institution 'should be acceptable everywhere and accorded the status of legal tender in every . . . country,' and should be constrained by a combination of commodity (gold) convertibility and constitutional rules.[31] By advocating a package of commodity convertibility plus a global LLR, Mundell extends the Thornton–Banking School–Bagehot LLR prescription to the international sphere.

SOME CONCLUDING THOUGHTS

The purpose of this paper was to trace the development of the LLR concept in the literature and to dispel some of the confusion surrounding it. The LLR concept has long been shrouded in controversy, originally pertaining to the need for and functions of a domestic LLR. Indeed, these issues were central to some key policy disputes in the 19th century and served to polarize important groups of monetary writers into competing schools. These disputes, far from being sterile, served to

[30] Such components, for example, consist of Eurodollars as well as changes in the value of gold reserves due to changes in the price of gold. See Mundell (1983b, pp. 287–8).

[31] A third alternative also exists in the literature. Specifically, several proposals have been made whereby key countries (such as the United States, Japan, and Germany) closely coordinate their monetary policies with the objective of stabilizing the growth of an aggregate of the dollar, yen, and mark. Ronald McKinnon (1982) has made proposals along these lines. Such proposals are a sort of middle ground between a single international LLR and the decentralized domestic LLRs supported by most monetarists.

refine and sharpen the LLR concept, identifying it as a monetary rather than a credit or a banking function and as a protector of the money supply in times of panic.

For the most part, these classical controversies referred to *national* money stocks and *domestic* LLRs. Recently, however, many of the disagreements have been elevated to the level of the international domain, where the key question refers to the necessity for a global LLR.[32] Assuming that this necessity depends on the demand for international reserves (that is, *world* money), and that such demand ceases to exist only in the ideal textbook case of perfectly floating exchange rates, then nations have at least three possible choices with regard to a global LLR. First, they can move to a regime of more perfectly floating exchange rates, in which the need for a world LLR vanishes. Second, they can maintain the existing system of managed floating, in which the U.S. dollar (provided its value remains relatively stable) continues to serve as the key reserve currency and the international LLR responsibility (if indeed it exists) rests essentially with the Federal Reserve. Third, and perhaps most radically, they can create a new supranational institution with reserve-creating powers along the lines suggested by Mundell. Whichever alternative is chosen, the important point is that there must be some mechanism for preventing sharp contractions in world and national money supplies. This is the central message of the LLR literature surveyed in this article. If this message is correct, then stabilizing national and world money stocks, rather than increasing IMF quotas and/or creating new credit facilities, is the appropriate policy prescription for international debt problems.

REFERENCES

Aliber, Robert Z. 'Bagehot, the Lender of Last Resort, and the International Financial System.' Working paper, University of Chicago Graduate School of Business, 1984.

Bagehot, Walter. *Lombard Street*. 1873. Reprint. Homewood, Ill.: Richard D. Irwin, 1962.

Barth, James R., and Keleher, Robert E. ' "Financial Crises" and the Role of the Lender of Last Resort.' Federal Reserve Bank of Atlanta *Economic Review* 69 (January 1984): 58–67.

Daugherty, Marion R. 'The Currency-Banking Controversy,' Pt. 1. *Southern Economic Journal* 9 (October 1942): 140–55.

—. 'The Currency-Banking Controversy,' Pt. 2. *Southern Economic Journal* 9 (January 1943): 241–51.

Dean, James W., and Giddy, Ian H. *Averting International Banking Crises*. The Monograph Series in Finance and Economics. New York: New York University, 1981.

Edwards, Franklin. 'Financial Institutions and Regulations in the 21st Century: After the Crash.' New York: Columbia University, 1980. Mimeographed.

Fetter, Frank W. *Development of British Monetary Orthodoxy 1797–1875*. Cambridge, Mass.: Harvard University Press, 1965.

[32] Free-money advocates, of course, continue to insist on the abolishment of domestic LLRs.

failures. Sound banks are rendered insolvent by the fall in the value of their assets resulting from a scramble for liquidity. By intervening at the point when the liquidity of solvent banks is threatened—that is, by supplying whatever funds are needed to meet the demand for cash—the monetary authority can allay the panic.

Private arrangements can also reduce the likelihood of panics. Branch banking allows funds to be transferred from branches with surplus funds to those in need of cash (e.g. from branches in a prosperous region to those in a depressed region). By pooling the resources of its members, commercial bank clearing houses, in the past, provided emergency reserves to meet the heightened liquidity demand. A clearing house also represented a signal to the public that help would be available to member banks in time of panic. Neither branch banking nor clearing houses, however, can stem a nationwide demand for currency occasioned by a major aggregate shock, like a world war. Only the monetary authority—the ultimate supplies of high-powered money—could succeed. Of course, government deposit insurance can prevent panics by removing the reason for the public to run to currency.[1] Ultimately, however, a LLR is required to back up any deposit scheme.

III. ALTERNATIVE VIEWS ON THE LLR FUNCTION

Four alternative views on the lender of last resort function are outlined below, including:

- The Classical View: the LLR should provide whatever funds are needed to allay a panic;
- Goodfriend and King: an open market operation is the only policy required to stem a liquidity crisis;
- Goodhart (and others): the LLR should assist illiquid and insolvent banks;
- Free Banking: no government authority is needed to serve as LLR.

The Classical Position

Both Henry Thornton's *An Enquiry into the Effects of the Paper Credit of Great Britain* (1802) and Walter Bagehot's *Lombard Street* (1873) were concerned with the role of the Bank of England in stemming periodic banking panics. In Thornton's time, the Bank of England—a private institution which served as the government's bank—had a monopoly of the note issue within a 26-mile radius of London, and Bank of England notes served as high-powered money for the English

[1] In theory private deposit insurance could also be used. In practice, to succeed in the U.S., such arrangements would require the private authority to have the power, currently possessed by the FDIC, to monitor, supervise, and declare insolvent its members. Also the capacity of the private insurance industry is too limited to underwrite the stock of government-insured deposits. (Benston *et al.* 1986, ch. 3). Alternatives to deposit insurance include requiring banks to hold safe assets (treasury bills), charging fees for service, and one hundred percent reserves.

banking system.[2] For Thornton, the Bank's responsibility in time of panic was to serve as LLR, providing liquidity to the market and discounting freely the paper of all solvent banks, but denying aid to insolvent banks no matter how large or important (Humphrey, 1975, 1989).

Bagehot accepted and broadened Thornton's view. Writing at a time when the Bank had considerably enhanced its power in the British financial system, he stated four principles for the Bank to observe as lender of last resort to the monetary system:

- Lend, but at a penalty rate[3]: 'Very large loans at very high rates are the best remedy for the worst malady of the money market when a foreign drain is added to a domestic drain.' (Bagehot, 1873, p. 56);
- Make clear in advance the Bank's readiness to lend freely;
- Accommodate anyone with good collateral (valued at pre-panic prices);
- Prevent illiquid but solvent banks from failing.[4,5]

Recent monetarist economists have restated the classical position. Friedman and Schwartz (1963), in *A Monetary History*, devote considerable attention to the role of banking panics in producing monetary stability in the United States (also see Cagan, 1965). According to them, the peculiarities of the nineteenth century U.S. banking system (unit banks, fractional reserves, and pyramiding of reserves in New York) made it highly susceptible to banking panics. Federal deposit insurance in 1934 provided a remedy to this vulnerability. It served to assure the public that their insured deposits would not be lost, but would remain readily available.

[2] Bank of England notes served as currency and reserves for the London banks. Country banks issued bank notes but kept correspondent balances in the London banks. From 1797 to 1821, Bank of England notes were inconvertible into gold.

[3] Bagehot distinguished between the response to an external gold drain induced by a balance of payment deficit (raising the Bank rate) and the response to an internal drain (lending freely).

[4] Bagehot has been criticized for not stating clearly when the central bank should intervene (Rockoff, 1986), for not giving specific guidelines to distinguish between sound and unsound banks (Humphrey, 1975). and for not realizing that provision of the LLR facility to individual banks would encourage them to take greater risks than otherwise (Hirsch, 1977).

[5] In part, Humphrey's summary of the Classical position is:

'. . . The lender of last resort's responsibility is to the entire financial system and not to specific institutions.'
'The lender of last resort exists not to prevent the occurrence but rather to neutralize the impact of financial shocks.'
'The lender's duty is a twofold one consisting first, of lending without stint during actual panics and second, of acknowledging beforehand its duty to lend freely in all future panics.'
'The lender should be willing to advance indiscriminately to any and all sound borrowing on all sound assets no matter what the type.'
'In no case should the central bank accommodate unsound borrowers. The lender's duty lay in preventing panics from spreading to the sound institutions, and not in rescuing unsound ones.'
'All accommodations would occur at a penalty rate, i.e., the central bank should rely on price rather than non-price mechanisms to ration use of its last resort lending facility.'
'The overriding objective of the lender of last resort was to prevent panic-induced declines in the money stock, . . .' (Humphrey, 1975 p. 9)

Friedman and Schwartz highlight the importance in the pre-FDIC system of timely judgment by strong and responsible leadership in intervening to allay the public's fear. Before the advent of the Fed, the New York Clearing House issued clearing house certificates and suspended convertibility, and, on occasion, the Treasury conducted open market operations. In two episodes, these interventions were successful; in three others, they were not effective in preventing severe monetary contraction. The Federal Reserve System, established in part to provide such leadership, failed dismally in the 1929–33 contraction. According to Friedman and Schwartz, had the Fed conducted open market operations in 1930 and 1931 to provide the reserves needed by the banking system, the series of bank failures that produced the unprecedented decline in the money stock could have been prevented.

Schwartz (1986) argues that all the important financial crises in the United Kingdom and the United States occurred when the monetary authorities failed to demonstrate at the beginning of a disturbance their readiness to meet all demands of sound debtors for loans and of depositors for cash. Finally, she views deposit insurance as not necessary to prevent banking panics. It was successful after 1934 in the U.S. because the lender of last resort was undependable. Had the Fed acted on Bagehot's principles, federal deposit insurance would not have been necessary, as the record of other countries with stable banking systems but no federal deposit insurance attests.

Meltzer (1986) argues that a central bank should allow insolvent banks to fail, for not to do so would encourage financial institutions to take greater risks. Following such an approach would 'separate the risk of individual financial failures from aggregate risk by establishing principles that prevent banks' liquidity problems from generating an epidemic of insolvencies' (p. 85). The worst cases of financial panics, according to Meltzer, 'arose because the central bank did not follow Bagehotian principles.'[6]

Goodfriend–King and the Case for Open Market Operations

Goodfriend and King (1988) argue strongly for the exercise of the LLR function solely by the use of open market operations to augment the stock of high-powered money; they define this as monetary policy. Sterilized discount window lending to particular banks, which they refer to as banking policy, does not involve a change in high-powered money. They regard banking policy as redundant because they see sterilized discount window lending as similar to private provision of line-of-credit services; both require monitoring and supervision, and neither affects the

[6] Meltzer (1986) succinctly restates Bagehot's four principles:

'The central bank is the only lender of last resort in a monetary system such as ours.'

'To prevent illiquid banks from closing, the central bank should lend on any collateral that is marketable in the ordinary course of business when there is a panic . . .'

'Central bank loans, or advances, should be made in large amounts, on demand, at a rate of interest above the market rate.'

'The above three principles of central bank behavior should be stated in advance and followed in a crisis.' (Meltzer, 1986, p. 83)

stock of high-powered money.[7] Moreover, they argue that it is not clear that the Fed can provide such services at a lower cost than can the private sector. Goodfriend (1989) suggests that one reason the Fed may currently be able to extend credit at a lower cost is that it can make fully collateralized loans to banks, whereas private lenders cannot do so under current regulations. On the other hand, the availability of these fully collateralized discount window loans to offset funds withdrawals by uninsured depositors and others may on occasion permit delays in the closing of insolvent banks.[8] Goodfriend regards government-provided deposit insurance as basically a substitute for the portfolio diversification of a nationwide branch banking system. By itself, however, deposit insurance without a LLR commitment to provide high-powered money in times of stress is insufficient to protect the banking system as a whole from aggregate shock.

The Case for Central Bank Assistance to Insolvent Banks

Charles Goodhart (1985, 1987) advocates temporary central bank assistance to insolvent banks. He argues that the distinction between illiquidity and insolvency is a myth, since banks requiring LLR support because of 'illiquidity will in most cases already be under suspicion about . . . solvency.' Furthermore 'because of the difficulty of valuing [the distressed bank's] assets, a central bank will usually have to take a decision on last resort support to meet an immediate liquidity problem when it knows that there is a doubt about solvency, but does not know just how bad the latter position actually is' (Goodhart, 1985, p. 35).

He also argues that by withdrawing deposits from an insolvent bank in a flight to quality, a borrower severs the valuable relationship with his banker. Loss of this relationship, based both on trust and agent-specific information, adds to the cost of flight, making it less likely to occur. Replacing such a connection requires costly search, a process which imposes losses (and possible bankruptcy) on the borrowers. To protect borrowers, Goodhart would have the central bank recycle funds back to the troubled bank.

Solow (1982) also is sympathetic to assisting insolvent banks. According to him, the Fed is responsible for the stability of the whole financial system. He argues that any bank failure, especially a large one, reduces confidence in the whole system. To prevent a loss of confidence caused by a major bank failure from spreading to the rest of the banking system, the central bank should provide assistance to insolvent banks. However, such a policy creates a moral hazard, as banks respond with greater risk-taking and the public loses its incentive to monitor them.

[7] Like Goodfriend and King, Friedman (1960) earlier argued for use of open market operations exclusively and against the use of the discount window as an unnecessary form of discretion which 'involves special governmental assistance to a particular group of financial institutions' (p. 38). Also see Hirsch (1977) and Goodhart (1988) for the argument that Bagehot's rule was really designed for a closely knit/cartelized banking system such as the London clearing banks.

[8] Cagan (1988) in his comment on Goodfriend and King makes the case for retention of discount window lending in the case of 'a flight to quality'. In that case, the discount window can be used to provide support to particular sectors of the economy which have had banking services temporarily curtailed.

Free Banking: The Case against Any Public LLR

Proponents of free banking have denied the need for any government authority to serve as lender of last resort. They argue that the only reason for banking panics is legal restrictions on the banking system. In the absence of such restrictions, the free market would produce a panic-proof banking system.

According to Selgin (1988, 1990) two of the most important restrictions are the prohibition of nationwide branch banking in the U.S. and the prohibition everywhere of free currency issue by the commercial banking system. Nationwide branch banking would allow sufficient portfolio diversification to prevent relative price shocks from causing banks to fail. Free note issue would allow banks to supply whatever currency individuals may demand.

Free banking proponents also contend that contagious runs because of incomplete information would not occur because secondary markets in bank notes (note brokers, note detectors) would provide adequate information to note holders about the condition of all banks. True, such markets do not arise for demand deposits because of the agent-specific information involved in the demand deposit contract—it is costly to verify whether the depositor has funds backing his check. But, free banking advocates insist that clearing house associations can offset the information asymmetry involved in deposit banking.

According to Gorton (1985), and Gorton and Mullineaux (1987), clearing houses in the nineteenth century, by quickly organizing all member banks into a cartel-like structure, established a coinsurance scheme that made it difficult for the public to discern the weakness of an individual member bank. The clearing house could also allay a panic by issuing loan certificates which served as a close substitute for gold (assuming that the clearing house itself was financially sound). Finally, a restriction on convertibility of deposits into currency could end a panic. Dowd (1984) regards restrictions as a form of option clause.[9] In an alternative option (used in pre-1765 Scotland) banks had the legal right to defer redemption till a later date, with interest paid to compensate for the delay.

For Selgin and Dowd, the public LLR evolved because of a monopoly in the issue of currency. The Bank of England's currency monopoly within a 26-mile radius of London until 1826 and its extension to the whole country in 1844 made it more difficult than otherwise for depositors to satisfy their demand for currency in times of stress. This, in turn, created a need for the Bank, as sole provider of high-powered money, to serve as LLR.[10] In the U.S., bond-collateral restrictions on state banks before 1863 and on the national banks thereafter were responsible for the well-known problem of currency inelasticity. Selgin and Dowd do not discuss

[9] A restriction of convertibility itself could exacerbate a panic because the public, in anticipating such restriction, demands currency sooner.

[10] Selgin (1990) argues that the Bank Charter Act of 1844 exacerbated the problem of panics because it imposed tight constraints on the issue of bank notes by the Issue Department. However, the Banking Department surely could have discounted commercial paper from correspondent banks without requiring further note issue. That is one of Bagehot's main points in *Lombard Street*.

the case of a major aggregate shock that produces a widespread demand for high-powered money. In that situation, only the monetary authority will suffice.

In sum, the four views—classical, Goodfriend/King, Goodhart, and free banking—have considerably different implications for the role of a LLR. With these views as backdrop, the remaining paragraphs now examine evidence on banking panics and their resolution in the past.

IV. THE HISTORICAL RECORD

In this section, I present historical evidence for a number of countries on the incidence of banking panics, their likely causes, and the role of a LLR in their resolution. I then consider alternative institutional arrangements that served as surrogate LLRs in diverse countries at different times. Finally, I compare the historical experience with the more recent assistance to insolvent banks in the U.S., Great Britain, and Canada. This evidence is then used to shed light on the alternative views of the lender of last resort discussed in Section III.

Banking Panics and Their Resolution

The record for the past 200 years for at least 17 countries shows a large number of bank failures, fewer bank runs (but still a considerable number) and a relatively small number of banking panics. According to a chronology compiled by Anna Schwartz (1988), for the U.S. between 1790 and 1930, bank panics occurred in 14 years; Great Britain had the next highest number with panics occurring in 8 years between 1790 and 1866. France and Italy followed with 4 each.

An alternative chronology that I prepared (Bordo, 1986, Table 1) for 6 countries (the U.S., Great Britain, France, Germany, Sweden, and Canada) over the period 1870–1933 lists 16 banking crises (defined as bank runs and/or failures), and 4 banking panics (runs, failures, and suspensions of payments), all of which occurred in the U.S. It also lists 30 such crises, based on Kindleberger's definition of financial crises as comprising manias, panics, and crashes and 71 stock market crises, based on Morgenstern's (1959) definition.

The similar failure rates for banks and nonfinancial firms in many countries largely reflect that individual banks, like other firms, are susceptible to market vagaries and to mismanagement. Internal factors were important, as were the external factors of relative price changes, banking structure, and changes in the overall price level. The relatively few instances of banking panics in the past two centuries suggests that either (1) monetary authorities in time developed the procedures and expertise to supply the funds needed to meet depositors' demands for cash or (2) the problem of banking panics is exaggerated.

A comparison of the performances of Great Britain and the U.S. in the past century serves to illustrate the importance of the lender of last resort in preventing banking panics. In the first half of the nineteenth century, Great Britain experienced banking panics when the insolvency of an important financial institution precipitated runs on other banks, and a scramble for high-powered money ensued. In a number of instances, the reaction of the Bank of England to protect its own gold reserves worsened the panic. Eventually, the Bank supplied funds to the market, but often too late to prevent many unnecessary bank failures. The last such panic followed the failure of the Overend Gurney Company in 1866. Thereafter, the Bank accepted its responsibility as lender of last resort, observing Bagehot's Rule 'to lend freely but at a penalty rate'. It prevented incipient financial crises in 1878, 1890, and 1914 from developing into full-blown panics by timely announcements and action.

The United States in the antebellum period experienced 11 banking panics (according to Schwartz's chronology) of which the panics of 1837, 1839, and 1857 were most notable.[11] The First and Second Banks of the United States possessed some central banking powers in part of the period; some states developed early deposit insurance schemes (see Benston, 1983; Calomiris, 1989), and the New York Clearing House Association began issuing clearing house loan certificates in 1857. None of these arrangements sufficed to prevent the panics.

In the national banking era, the U.S. experienced three serious banking panics—1873, 1893, and 1907–08. In these episodes, the clearing houses of New York, Chicago, and other central reserve cities issued emergency reserve currency in the form of clearing house loan certificates collateralized by member banks' assets and even issued small denomination hand-to-hand currency. But these lender of last resort actions were ineffective. In contrast to successful intervention in 1884 and 1890, the issue of emergency currency was too little and too late to prevent panic from spreading. The panics ended upon the suspension of convertibility of deposits into currency. During suspension, both currency and deposits circulated freely at flexible exchange rates, thereby relieving the pressure on bank reserves. The panics of 1893 and especially 1907 precipitated a movement to establish an agency to satisfy the public's demand for currency in times of distrust of deposit convertibility. The interim Aldrich-Vreeland Act of 1908 allowed ten or more national banks to form national currency associations and issue emergency currency; it was successful in preventing a panic in 1914.

The Federal Reserve System was created in 1914 to serve as a lender of last resort. The U.S. did not experience a banking panic until 1930, but as Friedman and Schwartz point out, during the ensuing three years, a succession of nationwide banking panics accounted for the destruction of one-third of the money stock and the permanent closing of 40 percent of the nation's banks. Only with the establishment of federal deposit insurance in 1934 did the threat of banking panics recede.

Table I compares American and British evidence on factors commonly believed to be related to banking panics, as well as a chronology of banking panics and

[11] Selgin (1990), based on evidence by Rolnick and Weber (1985), argues that the episodes designated as panics in the antebellum Free Banking era are not comparable to those in the National Banking era because they did not involve contagion effects. Evidence to the contrary, however, is presented by Hasan and Dwyer (1988).

Table I. *Banking panics (1870–1933): Related factors, incidence, and resolution*

	Reference Cycle Peak	Reference Cycle Trough	Deviations from Trend of Average Annual Real Output Growth[a] (peak to trough) (%) **	Absolute Difference of Average Annual Rate of Price Level Change (trough to peak minus peak to trough) (%) *	Deviations from Trend of Average Annual Monetary Growth[b] (specific cycle peak to trough) (%) **	Change in Money due to Change in Deposit–Currency Ratio (specific cycle peak to trough) (%) **	Banking Crisis[c**]	Banking Panic[d**]	Existence of Clear and Credible LLR Policy***	Resolution***	Agency***
United States	1873	1879	0.5	−7.1	−4.7	2.7		8/73	No	Restriction of Payments	Clearing Houses/Treasury
	1882	1885	−3.2	−12.2	2.6	5.2	5/84		Yes	Successful LLR	Clearing Houses/Treasury
	1893	1894	−9.5	−9.0	−9.3	−4.3		7/93	No	Restriction of Payments	Clearing Houses/Treasury
	1907	1908	−14.7	−6.1	−1.7	−2.7		10/07	No	Restriction of Payments	Clearing Houses/Treasury
	1920	1921	−7.6	−56.7	−2.5	2.8			(?)		
	1929	1932	−16.7	−12.5	−11.7	−27.4	1930, 1931, 1932	1933	No	Unsuccessful LLR	Federal Reserve
Great Britain	1873	1879	0.9	−7.1	−3.1	5.2			Yes		
	1883	1886	−1.2	−5.4	−2.8	2.3			Yes		
	1890	1894	−0.2	−4.4	−2.5	−2.2	Baring Crisis 11/90		Yes	Successful	Bank of England
	1907	1908	−4.7	−13.6	−1.6	−1.0			Yes		
	1920	1921	−6.9	−68.0	−5.1	4.5			Yes		
	1929	1932	−3.7	−7.9	−4.3	−1.3			Yes		

Data sources: * See Data Appendix in Bordo (1981).
** See Data Appendix in Bordo (1986).
*** Judgmental, based on this paper and other research.

Notes: (a) The trend growth rates of real output were 3.22% for the U.S. (1870–1941) and 1.48% for Great Britain (1870–1933). Each was calculated as the difference between the natural logs of real output in terminal and initial years divided by the number of years.
(b) The trend monetary growth rates were 5.40% for the U.S. (1870–1941) and 2.71% for Great Britain (1870–1933). Each was calculated as in footnote (a).
(c) Banking crisis–runs and/or failures, Source Bordo (1986).
(d) Banking panic–runs, failures, suspension of payments. Ibid.

banking crises for severe NBER business cycle recessions (peak to trough) in the period 1870–1933.[12] The variables isolated include: deviations from trend of the average annual growth rate of real output; the absolute difference of the average annual rate of change in the price level during the preceding trough to peak and the current peak to trough as a measure of the effect of changes in the overall price level; deviations from trend of the average annual rate of monetary growth; and the percentage change in the money stock due to changes in the deposit-currency ratio.[13]

The table reveals some striking similarities in the behavior of variables often related to panics but a remarkable difference between the two countries in the incidence of panics. Virtually all six business cycle downturns designated by the NBER as severe were marked in both countries by significant declines in output, large price level reversals, and large declines in money-growth. Also, in both countries, falls in the deposit-currency ratio produced declines in the money stock in the three most severe downturns: 1893–94 (U.S.); 1890–94 (G.B.); 1907–08; and 1929–32.

However, the difference in the incidence of panics is striking—the U.S. had four while Britain had none. Both countries experienced frequent stock market crashes (see Bordo, 1986, Table 6.1). They were buffeted by the same international financial crises. Although Britain faced threats to the banking system in 1878, 1890, and 1914, the key difference between the two countries (see the last three columns of Table I) was successful LLR action by the British authorities in defusing incipient crises.

Similar evidence over the 1870–1933 period for France, Germany, Sweden, and Canada is available in Bordo (1986). In all four countries, the quantitative variables move similarly during severe recessions to those displayed here for the U.S. and Great Britain, yet there were no banking panics. In France, appropriate actions by the Bank of France in 1882, 1889, and 1930 prevented incipient banking crises from developing into panics. Similar behavior occurred in Germany in 1901 and 1931 and in Canada in 1907 and 1914.

One other key difference was that all five countries had nationwide branch banking whereas the U.S. had unit banking. That difference likely goes a long way to explain the larger number of bank failures in the U.S.

Alternative LLR Arrangements

In the traditional view, the LLR role is synonymous with that of a central bank. Goodhart's explanation for the evolution of central banking in England and other European countries is that the first central banks evolved from commercial banks which had the special privilege of being their governments' banks. Because of its

[12] For similar evidence for the remaining cyclical downturns in this period, see Bordo (1986, Table 6, 1A).

[13] In relating the change in the money stock to changes in the deposit-currency ratio, we hold constant the influence of the other two proximate determinants of the money supply: the deposit-reserve ratio and the stock of high-powered money. It is calculated using the formula developed in Friedman and Schwartz (1963), Appendix B.

sound reputation, position as holder of its nation's gold reserves, ability to obtain economies by pooling reserves through a correspondent banking system, and ability to provide extra cash by rediscounting, such a bank would evolve into a bankers' bank and lender of last resort in liquidity crises. Once such banks began to act as lenders of last resort, 'moral hazard' on the part of member banks (following riskier strategies than they would otherwise) provided a rationale for some form of supervision or legislation. Further, Goodhart argues that the conflict between the public duties of such an institution and its responsibilities to its shareholders made the transition from a competitive bank to a central bank lengthy and painful.

Though Goodhart (1985 Annex B) demonstrates that a number of central banks evolved in this fashion, the experiences of other countries suggests that alternative arrangements were possible. In the U.S. before the advent of the Fed, a variety of institutional arrangements were used on occasion in hopes of allaying banking panics, including:

- Deposit insurance schemes: relatively successful in a number of states before the Civil War (Benston, 1983; Calomiris, 1989);
- A variety of early twentieth century deposit insurance arrangements which were not successful (White, 1981);
- Clearing houses and the issue of clearing house loan certificates (Timberlake, 1984; Gorton, 1985);
- Restriction of convertibility of deposits into currency by the clearing house associations in the national banking era;
- Various U.S. Treasury operations between 1890 and 1907 (Timberlake, 1978);
- The Aldrich-Vreeland Act of 1908.

Two countries which managed successfully for long periods without central banks were Scotland and Canada. Scotland had a system of free banking from 1727 to 1844. The key features of this system were (a) free entry into banking and free issue of bank notes, (b) bank notes that were fully convertible into full-bodied coin, and (c) unlimited liability of bank shareholders.

Scotland's record under such a system was one of remarkable monetary stability. That country experienced very few bank failures and very few financial crises. One reason, according to White (1984), was the unlimited liability of bank stockholders and strict bankruptcy laws that instilled a sense of confidence in noteholders.[14] Indeed, the Scottish banks would take over at par the issue of failed banks (e.g. the Ayr bank, 1772) to increase their own business. A second reason was the absence of restrictions on bank capital and of other impediments to the development of extensive branching systems that allowed banks to diversify risk and withstand shocks.[15] Faced with a nationwide scramble for liquidity, however,

[14] Sweden from 1830 to 1902 had a system of competitive note issue and unlimited liability. According to Jonung (1985), there is evidence neither of overissue nor of bank runs.

[15] Switzerland also had a successful experience with free banks 1826–50 (Weber, 1988) but like Scotland's dependence on the Bank of England, she depended on the Bank of France as lender of last resort (Goodhart, 1985).

Scottish banks were always able to turn to the Bank of England as a lender of last resort (Goodhart, 1985).

Although Canada had a competitive fractional reserve banking system throughout the nineteenth century, no central bank evolved (Bordo and Redish, 1987). By the beginning of the twentieth century, though, virtually all the elements of traditional central banking were being undertaken either by private institutions or directly by the government.

By 1890, the chartered banks, with the compliance of the Government, had established an effective self-policing agency, the Canadian Bankers Association. Acting in the absence of a central bank, it succeeded in insulating the Canadian banks from the deleterious effects of the U.S. banking panics of 1893 and 1907. It did so by quickly arranging mergers between sound and failing banks, by encouraging cooperation between strong and weaker banks in times of stringency, and by establishing a reserve fund to be used to compensate note holders in the event of failure.

In addition, the nationwide branch system overcame the problem of seasonal liquidity crises that characterized the United States after the Civil War, thus lessening the need for a lender of last resort. However, the Bank of Montreal (founded in 1817) very early became the government's bank and performed many central bank functions.

Because Canadian banks kept most of their reserves on 'call' in the New York money market, they were able in this way to satisfy the public's demand for liquidity, again precluding the need for a central bank. On two occasions, 1907 and 1914, however, these reserves proved inadequate to prevent a liquidity crisis and the Government of Canada had to step in to supplement the reserves.

The Finance Act, passed in 1914 to facilitate wartime finance, provided the chartered banks with a liberal rediscounting facility. By pledging appropriate collateral (this was broadly defined) banks could borrow Dominion notes from the Treasury Board. The Finance Act clause, which was extended after the wartime emergency by the Amendment of 1923, provided a discount window/lender of last resort for the Canadian banking system.

In sum, though, Canada, Scotland, and several other countries did not have formal central banks serving as LLRs, all had access to a governmental authority which could provide high-powered money in the event of such a crisis.

LLR Assistance to Insolvent Banks

The classical prescription for LLR action is to lend freely but at a penalty rate to illiquid but solvent banks. Both Thornton and Bagehot advised strongly against assistance to insolvent financial institutions. They opposed them because they would encourage future risk-taking without even eradicating the threat of runs on other sound financial institutions. Bagehot also advocated lending at a penalty rate to discourage all but those truly in need from applying and to limit the expansion in liquidity to the minimum necessary to end the panic.

Between 1870 and 1970, European countries generally observed the classical strictures. In the Baring Crisis of 1890, the Bank of England successfully prevented panic. It arranged (with the Bank of France and the leading Clearing Banks) to advance the necessary sums to meet the Barings' immediate maturing liability. These other institutions effectively became part of a joint LLR by guaranteeing to cover losses sustained by the Bank of England in the process (Schwartz, 1986, p. 19). The German Reichs-bank in 1901 prevented panic by purchasing prime bills on the open market and expanding its excess note issue, but it did not intervene to prevent the failure of the Leipziger and other banks (Goodhart, 1985, p. 96). The Bank of France also followed classical precepts in crises in 1881 and 1889.

The Austrian National Bank, however, ignored the classical advice during the Credit Anstalt crisis of 1931 by providing liberal assistance to the Credit Anstalt at low interest rates (Schubert, 1987). Then, a run on the Credit Anstalt and other Viennese banks in May 1931 followed the disclosure of the Credit Anstalt's insolvency and a government financial rescue package. The run degenerated into a speculative attack on the fixed price of gold of the Austrian Schilling.

The U.S. record over the same period is less favorable than that of the major European countries. Before the advent of the Federal Reserve System and during the banking panics of the early 1930s, LLR action was insufficient to prevent panics. By contrast, over the past two decades, panics may have been prevented, but LLR assistance has been provided on a temporary basis to insolvent banks and, prior to the Continental Illinois crisis in 1984, no penalty rate was charged. In the U.S. on three notable occasions, the Fed (along with the FDIC) provided liberal assistance to major banks whose solvency was doubtful at the time of the assistance: Franklin National in 1974, First Pennsylvania in 1980, and Continental Illinois in 1984. Further, in the first case, loans were advanced at below-market rates (Garcia and Plautz, 1988). This Federal Reserve policy toward large banks of doubtful solvency differs significantly from the classical doctrine.

The Bank of England followed similar policies in the 1974 Fringe Bank rescue and the 1982 Johnson Matthey affair. In 1985, the Bank of Canada arranged for the major chartered banks to purchase the assets of two small insolvent Alberta banks and fully compensate all depositors. In contrast to the Anglo-Saxon experience, the German Bundesbank allowed the Herstatt Bank to be liquidated in 1974 but provided LLR assistance to the market. Thus, although the classical doctrine has been long understood and successfully applied, recent experience suggests that its basic message is no longer always adhered to.

V. CONCLUSION: SOME LESSONS FROM HISTORY

One can draw a number of conclusions from the historical record.

(1) Banking panics are rare events. They occurred more often in the U.S. than in other countries. They usually occurred during serious recessions associated with declines in the money supply and sharp price level reversals. The likelihood of their occurrence would be greatly diminished in a diversified nationwide branch banking system.

(2) Successful LLR actions prevented panics on numerous occasions. On those occasions when panics were not prevented, either the requisite institutions did not exist or the authorities did not understand the proper actions to take. Most countries developed an effective LLR mechanism by the last one-third of the nineteenth century. The U.S. was the principal exception.

(3) Some public authority must provide the lender of last resort function. The incidence of major international financial crises in 1837, 1857, 1873, 1890–93, 1907, 1914, 1930–33 suggests that in such episodes aggregate shocks can set in train a series of events leading to a nationwide scramble for high-powered money.

(4) Such an authority does not have to be a central bank. This is evident from the experience of Canada and other countries (including the U.S. experience under the Aldrich-Vreeland Act in 1914). In these cases, lender of last resort functions were provided by other forms of monetary authority, including the U.S. Treasury, Canadian Department of Finance, and foreign monetary authorities.

(5) The advent of federal deposit insurance in 1934 solved the problem of banking panics in the U.S. The absence of government deposit insurance in other countries that were panic-free before the 1960s and 1970s, however, suggests that such insurance is not required to prevent banking panics.

(6) Assistance to insolvent banks was the exception rather than the rule until the 1970s.[16] The monetary authorities in earlier times erred on the side of deficiency rather than excess. Goodhart's view is certainly not a description of past practice. The recent experience with assistance to insolvent banks is inconsistent with the classical prescription. Liberal assistance to insolvent banks, combined with deposit insurance which is not priced according to risk, encourages excessive risk-taking, creating the conditions for even greater assistance to insolvent banks in the future.

In sum, the historical record for a number of countries suggests that monetary authorities following the classical precepts of Thornton and Bagehot can prevent banking panics. Against the free banking view, the record suggests that such a role must be provided by a public authority. Moreover, contrary to Goodhart's view, successful LLR actions in the past did not require assistance to insolvent banks. Finally, the record suggests that the monetary authority's task would be eased considerably by allowing nationwide branch banking and by following a policy geared towards price level stability. Under such a regime, as Goodfriend and King argue, open marker operations would be sufficient to offset unexpected scrambles for liquidity.

REFERENCES

Bagehot, W. (1873). *Lombard Street: A Description of the Money Market*. London: H.S. King.

Benston, G. J. (1983). 'Deposit Insurance and Bank Failures.' Federal Reserve Bank of Atlanta *Economic Review*. (March), pp. 4–17.

[16] Although in the U.S., the policy of purchase and assumption carried out by the FDIC and FSLIC before that date incorporated elements of public subsidy.

Benston, G. J., *et al.* (1986). *Perspectives on Safe and Sound Banking: Past, Present, and Future.* Cambridge: MIT Press.

Bordo, M. D. (1981). 'The Classical Gold Standard: Some Lessons for Today.' Federal Reserve Bank of St. Louis *Review.* (May). 63: 2–17.

— (1986). 'Financial Crises, Banking Crises, Stock Market Crashes and the Money Supply: Some International Evidence, 1870–1933.' In F. Capie and G. E. Wood (eds.), *Financial Crises and the World Banking System.* London: MacMillan.

Bordo, M. D. and A. Redish (1987). 'Why did the Bank of Canada Emerge in 1935?' *Journal of Economic History.* (June), 47(2): 401–17.

Cagan, P. (1965). *Determinants and Effects of Changes in the Stock of Money,* 1875–1960. New York: Columbia University Press.

— (1988). 'Commentary.' In W. S. Haraf and R. M. Kushmeider, (eds.), *Restructuring Banking and Financial Services in America.* Washington: American Enterprise Institute.

Calomiris, C. (1989). 'Deposit Insurance: Lessons from the Record.' Federal Reserve Bank of Chicago *Economic Perspectives.* (May–June), pp. 10–30.

Cowen, T. and R. Kroszner (1989). 'Scottish Banking Before 1845: A Model for Laissez-Faire.' *Journal of Money, Credit and Banking.* (May), 21(2): 221–31.

Dowd, K. (1988). *Private Money: The Path to Monetary Stability.* Institute of Economic Affairs, Hobart Paper 112. London.

Friedman, M. (1960). *A Program for Monetary Stability.* New York: Fordham University Press.

Friedman, M. and A. J. Schwartz (1963). *A Monetary History of the United States.* Princeton: Princeton University Press.

Garcia, G. and E. Plautz (1988). *The Federal Reserve: Lender of Last Resort.* Cambridge: Ballinger Publishing Company.

Goodfriend, M. (1989). 'Money, Credit, Banking, and Payments System Policy.' In D. B. Humphrey (ed.), *The U.S. Payments Systems: Efficiency. Risk and the Role of the Federal Reserve.* Boston: Kluwer Academic Publishers.

Goodfriend, M. and R. A. King, (1988). 'Financial Deregulation, Monetary Policy, and Central Banking.' In W. S. Haraf and R. M. Kushmeider (eds.), *Restructuring Banking and Financial Services in America.* Washington: American Enterprise Institute.

Goodhart, C. A. E. (1985). *The Evolution of Central Banks.* London: London School of Economics and Political Science.

— (1987). 'Why Do Banks Need a Central Bank?' *Oxford Economic Papers.* (March), 39: 75–89.

Gorton, G. (1985). 'Clearing houses and the Origins of Central Banking in the U.S.' *Journal of Economic History.* (June), 45: 277–84.

Gorton, G. and D. J. Mullineaux (1987). 'Joint Production of Confidence: Endogenous Regulation and 19th Century Commercial Bank Clearinghouses.' *Journal of Money, Credit and Banking.* (November), 19(4): 457–68.

Hasan, I. and G. P. Dwyer, Jr. (1988). 'Contagious Bank Runs in the Free Banking Period.' (mimeo). Cliometrics Conference, Oxford, Ohio.

Hirsch, F. (1977). 'The Bagehot Problem.' *Manchester School of Economics and Social Studies.* (September), 45(3): 241–57.

Humphrey, T. (1975). 'The Classical Concept of the Lender of Last Resort.' Federal Reserve Bank of Richmond *Economic Review.* (January/February), 61: 2–9.

— (1989). 'Lender of Last Resort: The Concept in History.' Federal Reserve Bank of Richmond *Economic Review.* (March/April), 75: 8–16.

Jonung, L. (1985). 'The Economics of Private Money: the Experience of Private Notes in Sweden, 1831–1902.' (mimeo) Lund University.

Kaufman, G. G. (1988). 'The Truth about Bank Runs.' In C. England and T. Huerras (eds.), *The Financial Services Revolution*. Boston: Kluwer Academic Publishers.

Kindleberger, C. (1978). *Manias, Panics and Crashes*. London: MacMillan.

Meltzer, A. (1986). 'Financial Failures and Financial Policies.' In G. G. Kaufman and R. C. Kormendi (eds.), *Deregulating Financial Service: Public Policy in Flux*. Cambridge: Ballinger Publishing Company.

Morgenstern, O. (1959). *International Financial Transactions and Business Cycles*. Princeton: Princeton University Press.

Rockoff, H. (1986). 'Walter Bagehot and the Theory of Central Banking.' In F. Capie and G. E. Wood (eds.), *Financial Crises and the World Banking System*. London: MacMillan.

Rolnick, A. and W. Weber (1985). 'Inherent Instability in Banking: The Free Banking Experience.' *Cato Journal*, May.

Schubert, A. (1987). 'The Creditanstalt Crisis of 1931—A Financial Crisis Revisited.' *Journal of Economic History*. (June), 47(2).

Schwartz, A. J. (1988). 'Financial Stability and the Federal Safety Act.' In W. S. Haraf and R. M. Kushmeider (eds.), *Restructuring Banking and Financial Services in America*. Washington: American Enterprise Institute.

—(1986). 'Real and Pseudo—Financial Crises.' In F. Capic and G. E. Wood (eds.), *Financial Crises and the World Banking System*. London: MacMillan.

Selgin, G. A. (1988). *The Theory of Free Banking: Money Supply Under Competitive Note Issue*. Totowa, N. J.: Rowman and Littlefield.

—(1990). 'Legal Restrictions, Financial Weakening, and the Lender of Last Resort.' *Cato Journal*.

Solow, R. M. (1982). 'On the Lender of Last Resort.' In C. P. Kindleberger and J. P. Laffargue (eds.), *Financial Crises: Theory, History and Policy*. Cambridge: Cambridge University Press.

Thornton, H. (1802). *An Enquiry into the Nature and Effects of the Paper Credit of Great Britain*. Edited by F. A. Hayek. Fairfield: Augustus M. Kelley.

Timberlake, R., Jr. (1984). 'The Central Banking Role of Clearing House Associations.' *Journal of Money, Credit and Banking*. (February), 16: 1–5.

—(1978). *The Origins of Central Banking in the United States*. Cambridge: Harvard University Press.

Weber, E. J. (1988). 'Currency Competition in Switzerland, 1826–1850.' *Kyklas*. 41.4(3): 459–78.

White, E. N. (1981). 'State Sponsored Insurance of Bank Deposits in the United States, 1907–20.' *Journal of Economic History*. (March), 13(1): 33–42.

White, L. H. (1984). *Free Banking in Britain: Theory, Experience, and Debate 1800–1945*. Cambridge: Cambridge University Press.

Table 1. *Loan certificate issues and reserves of the New York clearinghouse banks: Selected dates*

Year	Date of First Issue	Aggregate Issue ($million)	Maximum Outstanding ($million)	Reserves of NYC National Banks
1860	November 23	7.38	6.86	
1861	September 19	22.6	22.0	
1863	November 6	11.5	9.61	
1864	March 7	17.7	16.4	
1873	September 22	26.6	22.4	46.9 (September 12)
1884	May 15	24.9	21.9	70.7 (June 20)
1890	November 12	16.6	15.2	92.5 (October 2)
1893	June 21	41.5	38.3	99.0 (July 12)
1907	October 26	101.0	88.4	181.0 (December 3)

Sources: Sprague (1910, pp. 432–3) and United States Comptroller of the Currency (1893, 1907).

Nonetheless, Andrew's account is scholarly and thorough. He reported that many state auditors and comptrollers had written to the banks under their jurisdiction encouraging them to restrict payments of legitimate cash and to pay out the various array of 'substitutes' in restricted amounts. This indulgence was only to be permitted to 'solvent' banks. But, wrote the Indiana State Auditor in a 'P.S.' to his letter circulated among Indiana banks, 'the question of your solvency is to be determined by yourselves upon an examination of your present condition' (p. 499). One can only imagine the soul-searching and painstaking self-study the banks engaged in prior to issuing their quasi-currencies!

Andrew's admittedly incomplete data revealed that in cities over 25,000 population, clearinghouse issues of all kinds totaled $330 million. The issues began in late October 1907, and the last of them was retired by late March 1908. Clearinghouses in at least 71 of 145 cities made such issues. For cities under 25,000 population, Andrew's data are even more fragmentary. He recorded $4.5 million clearinghouse issues, including some in places such as Willacoochee, Georgia, but he acknowledged that his accounting covered 'only a small fraction of what actually existed in the smaller localities' (p. 506). In the largest cities the amounts issued in 1907 were $3\frac{1}{2}$ times the amounts issued in 1893. In all cases, the note issues were secured by collateral which had $1\frac{1}{3}$ to 2 times the dollar value of the notes (p. 509).[5]

[5] Generally, the lower the denomination of the currency issues, the greater the collateral value of the securities supporting them.

7. SOME CONTEMPORARY VIEWS OF CLEARINGHOUSE CENTRAL BANKING

To a banker, such as James Cannon, who was intimately involved with clearinghouse operations, the issues were not only defensible but highly recommended. He denied that the loan certificates were a currency. Rather, he defined them as 'temporary loans,' and cited one Comptroller of the Currency who had called them 'due-bills.' In addition, Cannon argued, the courts in Pennsylvania had 'decided that [the issues] should not be regarded as money. A tax on them [the court decision read] would have been "a serious blow to one of the most effective and ingenious contrivances devised, [and] a direct violation of the spirit of the law"' (1910, p. 116). Cannon concluded that loan certificates were 'one of the finest examples the country has ever seen of the ability of the people when left to themselves to devise impromptu measures for their own relief' (p. 96).

One can endorse Cannon's conclusion without accepting his denial that the certificates were currency. Clearly, the small denomination items were media of exchange. They were used for transactions of all kinds by everyone, and they were reissuable. The clearinghouse loan certificates may not have seemed to be conventional currency, since they were not transacted by anyone except banks. They were on that account, however, the equivalent of bank reserves, that is, high-powered money, and therefore even more potent than the small-denomination items.

Horace White agreed with Cannon on the utility of the clearinghouse operations. Nonetheless, White, in contrast to Cannon, recognized that all the issues of 1907 were illegal: 'Some were engraved to resemble bank notes or government notes,' he stated, 'and these were doubly illegal; some were as small as twenty-five cents, and these were trebly illegal' (1935, p. 383).[6] Fritz Redlich remarked that where the initial clearinghouse loan certificates were 'extra-legal,' the various issues in 1907 were illegal, and presented 'new dangerous problems [unspecified].' Legalization of clearinghouse loan certificates, he claimed, would have been 'predicated on the incorporation of clearing houses under a federal law' (1951, pp. 167–8).

8. THE CHOICE BETWEEN THE CLEARINGHOUSE SYSTEM AND THE FEDERAL RESERVE SYSTEM

The widespread issues of clearinghouse currency associated with the panic of 1893 stimulated the only proposals for organizing the clearinghouse system on a legitimate and formal basis in the manner suggested by Redlich. Several plans appeared in the middle and late 1890s, the most comprehensive of which was one by Theodore Gilman (1898) of New York. Gilman noted that a reserve maintained

[6] White implied here that issues of currency were in violation of any or all of three laws: the Constitution, the national bank act, and the prohibition against private issues of fractional currency.

outside the commercial banking system might not ever be needed '[T]herefore, it should not be provided by capital [reserves] withdrawn from productive use. It will cost nothing and will be just as serviceable if it is provided by law as a power which may be used in case of need.' To provide this potential for the banking system, Gilman proposed what he termed a 'grade of banks higher than our ordinary commercial banks,' by which he meant a banking institution that would be one stage above commercial banks and able to furnish accommodation when needed (pp. 44–5).

His choice for this role was the clearinghouse association incorporated under federal law. A clearinghouse in each state would have the power to issue notes in much the same fashion as what was already being done in practice. The notes would have a maximum value of 75 percent of the security collateral on which they were based. They would be guaranteed, first by the bank issuing them, second, by the associated clearinghouse banks in their home state, and, third, by all the clearinghouses who would receive the notes at par. 'This protecting structure,' Gilman observed, 'would rise noiselessly over the heads of the people without the sound of axe or hammer' (pp. 46–7)[7]

He emphasized an additional safeguard in the clearinghouse system beyond the note and collateral guarantees. The clearinghouse loan committees would be 'conservative' in granting loans because of their 'pecuniary interest as stockholders in banks which they would endeavor to protect from loss on their contingent liability as guarantors' (pp. 71, 124). In short, the private clearinghouse 'central bank' would operate prudently because it would face a bottom line. 'The kind of currency [the clearinghouses] make for themselves,' he observed, '[should be] . . . good [enough] for the public' (p. 119).

Gilman also argued that the clearinghouse notes he envisioned would always be redeemed on demand at any clearinghouse and would therefore circulate at par (p. 126). He may have oversold his scheme with this pledge. It implied that no restrictions or suspensions would occur in the future. Or he may have meant only that if a note-holder were willing to go to the time and trouble of redeeming his note *at the clearinghouse*, he could do so.

Gilman saw the new currency as a temporizing device that would promote elasticity in the monetary system. It would allow time for goods to be sold, so that the clearinghouse currency would return to the banks as payment for liquidating the loans that gave rise to the original issues of notes. Gilman also felt that the interest charge of 6 percent to banks who took out clearinghouse currency 'would act as a check upon their issue, and they would not be taken so much for profit as for protection and necessity' (p. 157). Gilman's plan was introduced as a bill in the House of Representatives by Ben L. Fairchild (Rep. - N.Y.) in January 1896. It was then referred to the House Committee on Banking and Currency, but it never

[7] The clearinghouse agreements already in force called for sharing any resulting losses from the issues in proportion to the participating banks' capital and surplus or by the proportional amount of their clearings during the previous year.

appeared again, and no popular movement ever developed in support of his scheme.

One Treasury official who pointedly objected to the clearinghouse strategy was Leslie M. Shaw, Secretary of the Treasury from 1902 to 1907 (Timberlake 1978, pp. 171–85). The clearinghouse loan certificates, he stated in an address delivered in 1905, are a 'plea of guilty to an indictment charging bad management locally or bad legislation nationally' (Shaw 1908, p. 279). Yet, Shaw's prescription for appropriate policy during a panic logically supported the clearinghouse method. First, he wrote, the supplemental currency should be identical with the legitimate currency that already existed. Second, he continued, the relief should be capable of immediate and local application. Finally, he concluded, the additional currency should be retired promptly when 'the demand therefore ceases' (p. 293).

In point of fact, the clearinghouse issues fit Shaw's criteria reasonably well. Their use as currency was ubiquitous; they were issued in a multitude of localities on the perceptions and judgments of thousands of bankers, and the notes never stayed out more than a few months. Nevertheless, Shaw regarded them as undesirable because in his opinion they raised an alarm that something was wrong and thereby caused 'hoarding' (p. 294).[8]

The Comptroller of the Currency, James H. Eckels, in his *Report* for 1893 was more sympathetic. He lauded the clearinghouse associations for their actions during the previous summer. 'The service rendered by them,' he wrote 'was invaluable, . . . and to their timely issuance . . . is due the fact that the year's record of suspensions and failures is not greatly augmented' (U.S. Comptroller of the Currency 1893, p. 15). Eckels denied that the issues were currency; but he had tongue in cheek. 'If they had been used as currency,' he argued, 'the banks issuing them would have been fined' (p. 16). Since the banks were not fined by the government, the law must not have been violated. This syllogism is more reasonably viewed as pragmatic accommodation to events than logical defense of the law.

The comptroller in 1907, William Ridgely, proved to be more of a legal constructionist. He noted that the law, under Section 5192 of the Revised Statutes, declared that clearinghouse certificates *in the possession of any bank belonging to the clearinghouse association* were lawful money (U.S. Comptroller of the Currency 1907, p. 64). He begged the question of those issues that were used universally as media of exchange outside of banks.

Later in his *Report* he discussed the possibility of legalizing the clearinghouse issues as an 'emergency circulation.' He found 'merit' in this suggestion, but rejected it as a 'half-way measure.' The full development of the clearinghouse idea, he argued, 'should carry us further . . . to the inevitable and logical conclusion . . .,

[8] Further on in his article, Shaw contradicted his own implication that the government should oversee a supplemental, heavily taxed, national bank note currency. 'Government officials,' he stressed, are extremely cautious. The rejection of a proposition never causes trouble. Affirmative acts only are investigated and censured. Technical objections are as good as valid ones with the average bureau official' (p. 295). Given (his fact of bureaucratism, a government agency could hardly be expected to furnish relief for a typical crisis following the norms that Shaw had specified.

which is that we should have a national central bank of issue and reserve [acting under governmental authority].' This institution would be 'more systematic and efficient' and would have none of the 'disadvantages' of the clearinghouse system. Ridgely did not specify how or why the government central bank would be more systematic and efficient; he simply offered unsubstantiated assertions. For example, 'if we had had such a [government central] bank in operation in 1907, no such bank panic as we have had would have been possible' (p. 75). (Had Ridgely been able to witness the monetary and banking events of 1929–33, he might have experienced a fair amount of intellectual indigestion.) Most amazingly, his next paragraph is a description of how well the clearinghouse system generally operated.

9. RESTRICTION AND SUSPENSION OF CASH PAYMENTS

The most characteristic feature of a panic—the attempt to convert demand deposits into legal tender—stimulated the restriction of cash payments by the banks. Restriction took many forms: for example, limitation of cash payments to a nominal amount ($25 to $200) per transaction; or this amount per day or per customer. Often payments were 'discretionary' with the banks and therefore negotiable with the bank's managers. Its purpose was to induce as much friction as possible into any transaction that would provoke an 'internal drain' of bank reserves.

Sprague argued that the clearinghouse banks in New York assumed the indulgence of restriction too readily (1910, pp. 273–7). They faced reserve requirements of 25 percent and were prohibited from making new loans when reserve ratios reached this minimum. However, the law did not restrict them from paying out reserves even though they were in a reserve-deficit position.

In his article, William Dewald (1972) has reargued Sprague's analysis and found it valid. The New York banks, Dewald notes, 'had made a fetish out of their twenty-five percent reserve ratio and held closely to it. . . . Reserve deficits were small during crises, and New York banks in fact held enormous reserves on every occasion when they suspended payments. It was this policy that Sprague attacked and it was this policy that the legal authorization to issue clearing house "currency" promised to change' (p. 940). Sprague, Dewald notes, recommended that reserve banks be required to maintain payments as long as they held any reserves. This principle had been repeatedly urged as well by the Comptroller of the Currency (p. 939). The conclusion of the Sprague–Dewald thesis on restriction-of-payments policy is that, far from being complementary to the issue of clearinghouse currency, it increased uncertainty and generally upset the payments system. It witnessed the substitution of less efficient media for conventional money and also extended the period of disequilibrium (pp. 934, 941–2).[9]

[9] Sprague also favored the 'pooling' of reserves in order to reduce the too-ready tendency of the banks to restrict or suspend. Dewald apparently agrees (p. 941). However, this provision would have vitiated an important market constraint (see above). Sprague's principal remedy requiring banks to use their reserves, in conjunction with clearinghouse issues, would have been sufficient to stop any panic.

A contrary view on restriction comes from Friedman and Schwartz (1963), and also from Margaret Myers in her earlier study (1931, p. 143). Given a bank panic, Friedman and Schwartz argue, 'the fairly prompt restriction of payments was a therapeutic measure that almost surely kept the contraction from being even more severe and much more protracted than it was. . . . [T]he failure of one (unsound) bank did not set in train a chain reaction. Restriction of payments thus protected the banking system and gave time for the immediate panic to wear off, as well as for additional currency to be made available' (1963, pp. 163, 167). The alternative was for the fractional reserve banking system to experience a 'black hole' type of collapse in the face of the increased demand for money with the accompanying declines of prices, wages, income, and business activity (pp. 167–8).

Friedman and Schwartz correctly focus on the inherent instability of the fractional reserve banking system as the primary danger to the monetary system and the economy. Nonetheless, given that clearinghouse issues were already in progress, the *prompt* restriction of payments may have been ill-advised. Why not require the clearinghouse banks to run down their reserves to a very small minimum with graduated rate penalties on their reserve deficiencies? A law that provided explicitly for such an action would have countered the timidity of the banks and, in conjunction with the clearinghouse issues, encouraged them to maintain the level of their current portfolios as well as their cash payments. Ultimately, they might have been forced to suspend; but before they did so, their reserves would have been largely utilized in meeting internal and external demands for liquidity.

10. MONETARY REFORM LEGISLATION

The immediate legislative reaction to the events of 1907 was the Aldrich-Vreeland Act of 1908, which called for the grouping of ten or more national banks into a National Currency Association. The associations anticipated from this act were not to operate as clearinghouses, but were to issue 'emergency currency' just the way the clearinghouses had done in the past. The only difference was that the new institutions' currency issues were to be under the administration of the Secretary of the Treasury, who had some discretion in allocating the notes to different sections of the country. The currency outstanding was to be taxed at an annual rate of 5 percent during the first month, and at an additional 1 percent each month thereafter until the annual rate reached 10 percent (Friedman and Schwartz 1963, p. 170).

The Aldrich-Vreeland Act marked a critical turning point in United States of policy toward the monetary system. As Redlich observed, the act 'turned its back on the clearing-house loan certificate instead of legalizing it. . . . [The] subcommittee [Report] of the Committee of Banking and Currency declared the power to issue loan certificates dangerous as long as clearing-house associations were not under government control' (1951, p. 168).

The allegation of 'dangerous' flies in the face of the clearinghouse system's actual performance. The most extraordinary fact associated with the several clearinghouse episodes between 1857 and 1907 is that the losses from all the various note issues, spurious and otherwise, *were negligible!* The only loss reported in any of the accounts here considered was $170,000 in Philadelphia in 1890 out of an issue of $9.7 million—1.8 percent (Sprague 1910, p. 392). Few of the economists who analyzed clearinghouse operations even noted in passing this astonishing record, and none used it as an argument for continuing the system.

When the Federal Reserve Act was debated in Congress in 1913, the sentiment again reflected the notion that the government should have some control over the currency. In a typical statement, Congressman William A. Cullop of Indiana contrasted the new Federal Reserve Board with the clearinghouse executive committee: 'Every fair-minded man,' he declared, 'would prefer that the control over the currency be vested in seven men [on the Federal Reserve Board] selected from different parts of the country than to have it remain in the hands of the five managers of the New York clearing house. . . . To this self-constituted and unauthorized organization [the Federal Reserve Act] . . . deals a deadly blow in order to secure for us industrial and commercial freedom' (U.S. Congress 1913a, p. 332). Cullop's hyperbole demonstrated the decided influence populism still exerted in monetary affairs.

Hepburn's comment on the passage of the Federal Reserve Act was that this 'measure . . ., while open to criticism, is a vast improvement upon the old system and as good as could have been fairly expected under all the circumstances' (1924, p. 397). Margaret Myers was even more positive: 'The passage of the Federal Reserve Act,' she wrote, 'ended the long struggle with monetary problems which had harassed the New York money market and the rest of the country throughout history' (1931, p. 421).

11. RECAPITULATION

A fractional reserve banking system by its very nature contains an element of instability. An increased demand for currency can so deplete bank reserves that the supply of bank-created money (deposits) declines. This possible reaction means that the supply of money is at times unstable: an increased demand for one kind of money may result in a decline in the total quantity of money supplied. The banking industry recognized this problem at an early stage. Since both the money-supplying industry—the banks—and the users of money—firms and households—were harmed by the results of bank-aggravated crises, everyone had an interest in reducing or eliminating this structural instability.

The solution, arrived at through force of circumstances and some financial innovation, was clearinghouse creation of temporary currency. The banking industry simply reinstituted itself as an ad hoc central bank, and through its clearinghouse associations issued more currency. Since the laws proscribed private issues of money, clearinghouse currency had to be issued discreetly. It then worked so well that no one had any incentive to prosecute its issuers. It was the private-money-producing industry's answer to a pronounced need. It was, as well, constrained by market factors—interest rate charges on its issue, and the real stake the clearinghouse banks' directors had in seeing to it that the clearinghouse association did not make costly mistakes. In addition, the gold standard system regulated and constrained the monetary base. Bankers, who knew the rules of the gold standard game, realized that clearinghouse issues were only a temporizing device. They knew they had to restrain bank credit appropriately when their reserves were threatened.

Nonetheless, the issue of clearinghouse currency put the brakes on the development of an unstable bank credit contraction. It did not prevent the demise of inefficient banks; it only stopped the fractional reserve collapse that might otherwise have occurred.

One may then wonder why this system was rejected. Why was a government central bank superimposed on the banking industry when the clearinghouse method had proven so effective? The accounts of the times suggest several answers. First, the clearinghouse issues by 1907 had become recognizably illegal. This awareness could have meant simply that the laws were bad. Instead, the realization endowed the clearinghouse currency with a hucksterish quality. Because clearinghouse currency was illegal, it was makeshift funny money—never mind the logic of the laws prohibiting it. Second, since clearinghouse currency was market-regulated and because it was created and accepted voluntarily, many contemporary observers did not recognize its utility and integrity. They wanted an 'official' currency similar to national bank notes or greenbacks. Third, the clearinghouse currency seemed to arise out of nothing. Everyone could understand the principle of a quasi-public central bank standing by with a reserve obtained from contributions by participating banks and ready to be applied when a crisis threatened. But few could understand how a clearinghouse system could create emergency currency without seeming to have an emergency reserve on which to base it (Sprague 1910, p. 234). It was altogether too mystifying an operation for common understanding and acceptance. It smacked of Wall Street legerdemain. Last, the clearinghouse issues were associated with the restriction or suspension of cash payments. Sprague clearly demonstrated that the two actions were not at all necessarily related (1910, pp. 260–77). Nonetheless, the popular mind was only too willing to apply here the fallacy that correlation implies causation.

Many advocates of a central bank saw the Federal Reserve System as an evolutionary development of the clearinghouse associations. 'This bill, for the most part,' said Robert Owen, the sponsor of the Federal Reserve bill in the Senate,' is merely putting into legal shape that which hitherto has been illegally done' (U.S. Congress 1913b, p. 904; see also Willis 1922, p. 251).

The Federal Reserve alternative, however, was critically different from the clearinghouse system. It introduced a discretionary political element into monetary decision making and thereby divorced the authority for determining the system's behavior from those who had a self-interest in maintaining its integrity.

REFERENCES

Andrew, Abram Piatt. 'Hoarding in the Panic of 1907.' *Quarterly Journal of Economics* 22 (February 1908), 290–99 (a).

——.'Substitutes for Cash in the Panic of 1907.' *Quarterly Journal of Economics* 22 (August 1908), 497–516 (b).

Cannon, James Graham. *Clearing Houses, Senate Document Number 491.* 61st Congress, 2nd Session, National Monetary Commission, 1910.

Dewald, William G. 'The National Monetary Commission: A Look Back.' *Journal of Money, Credit, and Banking* 4 (November 1972), 930–56.

Frangul, Ramzi. Book Review of *Origins of Central Banking in the United States: Journal of Finance* 35 (March 1980), 212–14.

Friedman, Milton, and Anna J. Schwartz. *A Monetary History of The United States, 1867–1960.* Princeton: Princeton University Press for the National Bureau of Economic Research, 1963.

Gilman, Theodore. *A Graded Banking System.* Boston and New York: Houghton Mifflin, 1898.

Hayek, Freidrich A. *The De-Nationalization of Money,* 2nd ed. London: Institute of Economic Affairs, 1978.

Hepburn, Alonzo Barton. *History of Coinage and Currency in the United States and the Perennial Contest for Sound Money,* rev. ed. New York: Macmillan, 1924.

Klein, Benjamin. 'The Competitive Supply of Money.' *Journal of Money, Credit, and Banking* 6 (November 1974), 423–54.

Mints, Lloyd W. *A History of Banking Theory in Great Britain and the United States.* Chicago: University of Chicago Press, 1945.

Myers, Margaret. *The New York Money Market, Origins and Development,* Vol. I. New York: Columbia University Press, 1931.

Redlich, Fritz. *The Molding of American Banking, Men and Ideas, Part II, 1840–1910.* New York: Hafner, 1951.

Shaw, Leslie M. *Current Issues.* New York: Appleton, 1908.

Sprague, Oliver M. W. *History of Crises Under the National Banking System, Senate Document Number 538.* 61st Congress, 2nd Session, National Monetary Commission, 1910.

Timberlake, Richard H., Jr. *Origins of Central Banking in the United States.* Cambridge: Harvard University Press, 1978.

United States Comptroller of the Currency. *Annual Report.* Washington, D.C., 1893.

——. *Annual Report.* Washington, D.C., 1907.

United States Congress. *Congressional Record.* 63rd Congress, 1st Session, Appendix, 1913 (a).

——. *Congressional Record.* 63rd Congress, 2nd Session, 1913 (b).

White, Horace. *Money and Banking.* Revised and enlarged by Charles S. Tippetts and Lewis A. Froman. New York: Ginn, 1935.

Willis, Henry Parker. 'Federal Reserve Banks.' In *The Theory and History of Banking,* edited by Charles F. Dunbar. New York and London: G. P. Putnam's Sons, 1922.

PART II

CONTEMPORARY ANALYSIS

adjustment credit, seasonal credit, and extended or emergency credit assistance. Adjustment credit is temporarily employed by banks in good financial condition.[13] Seasonal credit is employed primarily by banks in agricultural areas. Its use is also rather routine. In contrast, emergency credit is longer-term borrowing by troubled banks.[14] The discount rates on adjustment and seasonal credit are lower than for emergency credit because the riskiness of a loan is generally lower on the former than the latter.

The riskiness of a discount window loan depends critically on the collateral. The Fed has considerable latitude as to what it will accept and the haircut it will take.[15] Fully collateralizing a loan with prime paper such as U.S. Treasury bills would make the value of a central bank's line of credit minimal, since a bank could acquire the funds by simply selling the bills in the private market. A central bank could still make its credit line attractive, however, by charging below market rates or taking less than a market haircut. Whatever a central bank might do in practice, the point of the current discussion is to analyze how a central bank providing line of credit services based on imperfect collateral would operate.

In addition to setting the terms on which a loan can be taken down, our discussion of private lines of credit emphasized the need for ongoing monitoring of potential borrowers by the lender. This is no less necessary for public provision of line of credit services by the Fed. A 1983 Federal Reserve position paper on financial regulation stated:

> Central banking responsibilities for financial stability are supported by discount window facilities—historically a key function of a central bank—through which the banking system, and in a crisis, the economy more generally, can be supported. But effective use of that critically important tool of crisis management is itself dependent on intimate familiarity with the operations of banks, and to a degree other financial institutions, of the kind that can only be derived from continuing the operational supervisory responsibilities. . . . ('Federal Reserve Position on Restructuring of Financial Regulation Responsibilities,' in U.S. Congress House. Committee on Government Operations, House of Representatives, 99th Congress, 1985, p. 235.)

the Federal Reserve prices line of credit services according to each bank's circumstances with respect to supervision cost, risk of insolvency, or collateral.

[13] Since the early 1960s, the Federal Reserve has allowed the Federal funds rate to move above the discount rate for long periods of time. To limit borrowing the Federal Reserve has imposed a noninterest cost, which rises with the level and the duration of borrowing. In practice, higher and longer duration borrowing increases the likelihood of costly Federal Reserve consultations with bank officials. See Goodfriend (1983, 1987) for discussions of how this means of administering the window has been employed in executing monetary policy.

[14] For example, Continental Illinois Bank borrowed extensively at the Federal Reserve discount window from May 1984 to February 1985. It was in the window for over 4 billion dollars during much of that period. See Benston *et al.*, pp. 120–4.

[15] Hackley (1973) documents the history of legal collateral requirements in discount window lending. Although the Federal Reserve has wide discretion in what it can take, it has generally required very good collateral on its loans.

A 'haircut' is a margin that is subtracted from the market or face value of a security for purposes of calculating its value as collateral in a loan transaction. For example, a 10 percent haircut off face value of a $100 security would value it as $90 for purposes of collateral.

We interpret the term 'effective use' in the above quotation to mean that the Fed must be able on short notice to discern the financial position of a bank requesting funds. Especially with respect to emergency credit assistance such information is necessary to price loans appropriately, and even more importantly, to determine that the borrower is still viable. If the Fed were too lax—in the sense of lending to excessively weak borrowers—it would risk supporting banks that should be dissolved. If it were too cautious, it would risk not supporting temporarily troubled but fundamentally sound banks, possibly allowing them to fail unnecessarily. Only by continually supervising banks to which it has credit commitments can the Fed hope to lend funds efficiently on short notice.[16]

Beyond setting lending terms and associated supervisory requirements, the Fed needs to set eligibility rules. Unlike a private firm, the Fed cannot simply choose its customers. The logic of the quotations presented above suggests that the Fed ought to provide line of credit services to the entire economy as well as to banks. To do so, however, would obviously require an enormous allocation of resources for regulation and supervision. Hence, the Fed and Congress have to limit that commitment rather arbitrarily. Currently, only Federal Reserve member banks, or depository institutions holding transaction accounts or nonpersonal time deposits, are entitled to basic discount window borrowing privileges. This group corresponds closely to the institutions holding reserves at Federal Reserve banks.

If this logic is carried one step further, we can better understand the concerns of some policymakers for maintaining a separation between banking on one hand, and finance and commerce on the other, and for limiting access to the payments system.[17] We interpret the argument as recognizing the need to limit the Fed's line of credit commitments, and the regulation and supervision that must accompany them, to a manageable subset of the economy, namely, depository institutions. Blurring the line, for example, between banking and commerce would make it difficult for the Fed to do so. Without a clear delineation, the Fed would tend to be drawn into additional implicit commitments that it could not keep. Further, without the regulatory and supervisory resources to safeguard its funds, the Fed might have to withdraw from providing line of credit services entirely.

The argument for limiting access to the payments system is similar. In the process of making payments over its electronic funds transfer network, the Federal Reserve grants intraday credit to depository institutions in the form of daylight overdrafts on their reserve accounts.[18] Because they are imperfectly collateralized,

[16] In fact, though Fed regulations apply to all banks, it directly supervises and examines only state-chartered Fed member banks and bank holding companies. The Comptroller of the Currency, for example, supervises and examines nationally chartered banks. The Federal Deposit Insurance Corporation does so for insured state-chartered non-Fed-member banks. Other agencies, however, make information available to the Fed. *Continental Illinois National Bank: Report of An Inquiry into its Federal Supervision and Assistance*, contains a good discussion of government supervision of banks.

[17] See Corrigan (1987).

[18] See Mengle, Humphrey, and Summers (1987) for a discussion of daylight overdrafts. They report total funds transfer daylight overdrafts of 76 billion dollars per day. This is an enormous number when one considers that total reserve balances with Reserve Banks are around 35 billion dollars. Daylight

contain any aggregate disturbances due to sudden sharp increases in currency demand, whether they result from banking problems or other difficulties.

We can make this point more concrete by using it to interpret Walter Bagehot's famous recommendation that a central bank should behave as a lender of last resort.[29] Bagehot's (1873) policy prescription—summarized as lend freely at a high rate—was to fix the discount rate at a level suitably above the normal range of market rates. The discount rate would then provide an interest rate ceiling, and therefore an asset price floor, which would allow banks, in the event of crises, to liquidate their assets while remaining solvent. The proposal amounts to providing a completely elastic supply of currency at the fixed ceiling rate. Put still another way, it amounts to a suggestion for smoothing nominal interest rates when market rates reach a certain height.

An important point about 'lender of last resort' policy in banking crises is that in our nomenclature it is not banking policy at all. It is monetary policy because it works by providing an elastic supply of high-powered money to accommodate precautionary demands to convert deposits into currency. Further, central bank lending, in the sense of advancing funds to particular institutions, is not essential to the policy since it can be executed by buying government securities outright.

One aspect of Bagehot's rule deserves additional comment. He argued that the last resort lending rate should be kept fixed above normal market rates, making central bank borrowing generally unprofitable, and minimizing any government subsidies that might accrue to individual banks. He counted on nominal interest rate spikes accompanying banking crises to hit the ceiling rate and thereby automatically trigger the injection of currency into the economy.

Bagehot's advice in this regard, has not been followed by the Fed. Rather, the Fed has chosen to regularly smooth interest rates. It has done so either by using a Federal funds rate policy instrument directly, or by using objectives for unsterilized borrowed reserves together with discount rate adjustments to achieve a desired Federal funds rate path.[30] In principle, regular interest rate smoothing could satisfy Bagehot's concerns. First, it could be free of subsidies to individual banks if carried out by purchases and sales of securities in the open market. Second, it provides lender of last resort services which are automatically triggered at the current central bank interest rate. Of course, routine seasonal and cyclical increases in currency demand are also accommodated at the same rate.

Thus, Federal Reserve lender of last resort policy and the routine provision of an elastic currency are functionally equivalent. Both are directed at insulating the nominal interest rate from disturbances to the demand for currency. Both can be executed by using open market operations to create and destroy high-powered money. Since both are monetary policy we may make the point that banking and financial regulations are neither necessary or sufficient for a central bank to pursue effective last resort lending.

[29] Humphrey and Keleher (1984) provide a historical perspective on the concept of the lender of last resort.

[30] See note 11.

3.3. Banking Policy and Credit Market Crises

In Section 2.3 we described how banking policy could provide line of credit services to enable illiquid but solvent banks to continue operating. Implicitly, we assumed that the source of the trouble was limited. At worst only a few banks were insolvent, so when line of credit services sorted the strong banks from the weak, there was a negligible effect on interest rates. We now ask whether banking policy has a role in general credit market crises when interest rates rise. If banking policy is to have a role it will be in response to real interest rate increases, since banking policy is clearly an inappropriate response to nominal interest rate increases caused by monetary disturbances.

The real rate is determined by macroeconomic conditions, including anticipated changes in the state of the economy and uncertainty in future prospects. It adjusts to equate aggregate supply and demand for output, or what is the same thing, to equate the aggregate supply and demand for credit. For example, an increase in future prospects which raises current consumption demand causes a rise in the real rate to induce consumers both to save more out of current income and to produce more, thereby restoring goods market equilibrium. Likewise, an increase in investment demand resulting from a perceived increased profit opportunity induces a real rate rise to maintain goods market equilibrium.

To investigate whether there is a role for banking policy in general credit market crises, we consider an unexpected rise in the real interest rate. Even a temporarily high real rate could cause previously profitable investment projects to become unprofitable.[31] This, in turn, would generate a rise in nonperforming bank loans, which could create insolvencies. The role for banking market intervention in such circumstances is usually formulated as 'lend only to illiquid but solvent banks,' as discussed in Section 2.3. But it was argued there that illiquidity arises only when financial markets cannot readily determine the status of a particular financial institution. However, unlike firm or bank-specific shocks a general increase in interest rates would be observable in financial markets. If all firms were alike on the one hand and all banks were alike on the other, the distinction between illiquidity and insolvency would surely be irrelevant for real interest rate shocks. A real interest rate spike per se could not make banks illiquid unless it also made them insolvent. In so far as its effects were distributed unevenly across firms and banks, of course, a real rate rise could cause some individual banks to be illiquid but solvent. Thus, aggregate disturbances can affect individual bank liquidity in addition to factors specific to a bank. But the fact that an aggregate disturbance is the source of the trouble does not alter the relative advantages of the central bank and private markets in providing liquidity. Central banks and private markets

[31] Many investment projects involve the purchase of inputs—fuel, intermediate goods, and labor—today, but only yield output in the future. Production is profitable if the current value of future output discounted back to the present at the real interest rate is greater than the current cost of inputs. By pushing the present discounted value of output below its cost of production, even a temporarily high real interest rate could cause a project to be shut down temporarily.

continue to face problems of screening strong from weak banks that we discussed in Section 2.3. Practically, the rule of thumb—lend only to illiquid but solvent banks—could rule out the use of banking policy entirely. But if banking policy did not respect this rule, then it could well have important negative effects by subsidizing risktaking.

We are somewhat uneasy about the implications of our result. While we think the familiar rule of thumb makes sense, we wonder whether discount window lending could be rationalized under a different criterion: to prevent the disruption costs of widespread insolvencies associated with temporary real interest rate spikes. If such aggregate disruption costs were large enough, temporary transfers to the banking system that could avoid such costs might be in society' interest. It should be pointed out, however, that a similar argument could be made for avoiding distruption costs of temporary insolvencies anywhere in the economy. Therefore, acceptance of the criterion for banking policy alone would need to be based on a demonstration that disruption costs are much larger in the banking sector than elsewhere.

In any case, because it would have no effect on goods supply or demand, banking policy could not reverse a real rate rise. Of course, a central bank's interest income could change as a result of banking policy, i.e., exchanging government securities for claims on private banks. But that fiscal effect, per se, would have no implications for the real interest rate.[32]

What banking policy could do is support otherwise insolvent banks by temporarily swapping government securities for nonperforming bank loans. If the disturbance were temporary, and the loans earned nothing for the central bank, then the size of the subsidy would be the lost interest on government securities that has been diverted to bank depositors. Alternatively, if the loans defaulted, the subsidy would be the entire face value of the loans purchased by the central bank. The Treasury, in turn, would have to finance the loss by cutting back goods purchases, raising current taxes, or borrowing, i.e., raising future taxes. Banking policy of this sort is clearly redistributive in nature, a contingent tax and transfer fiscal policy. It need not, however, represent a subsidy to the banking system as a whole if banks are taxed during normal times to finance any transfers during periods of high real rates. Importantly, to be effective at reducing insolvency risk, the tax and transfer policy would need supporting regulations. Otherwise banks might simply restore the risk of insolvency to its initially optimal level by reducing capital accordingly, or by restructuring contingent liabilities to offset the transfers.[33] Thus we have

[32] If a central bank's remittances to the Treasury changed as well, and the Treasury adjusted its goods purchases accordingly, then there could be a goods market effect. But this would involve more than banking policy.

[33] This argument is analogous to those that arise in consideration of the 'Ricardian Equivalence Proposition,' which states that under certain conditions a substitution of public debt for taxation will have no effects on prices or quantities. Robert Barro's *Macroeconomics* (1986) provides an accessible introduction to Ricardian analysis. Chan (1983) provides a proof of Ricardian neutrality under conditions of uncertainty, stressing the analogy to Modigliani–Miller propositions in finance.

another example of how banking policy needs supporting regulation and supervision to be effective.

It must be emphasized that we are by no means advocating the use of banking policy to rescue insolvent banks or, more generally, the use of tax and transfer policies to rescue insolvent firms in other industries. In fact, we think there are serious problems with such a policy. It requires costly regulation and supervision. It opens the door to bank rescues, which might be extremely difficult to limit in practice. It would be difficult to choose when to intervene. And there would be political pressure to abuse the policy. Moreover, it is far from clear that disruption costs associated with widespread temporary insolvencies are large. Last, the potentially perverse incentive effects of systematic banking policies are a matter of concern. Designed to promote financial market stability, they encourage risktaking and lead to the deterioration of private liquidity provision. Thus, they are likely to lead to more severe financial market crises, particularly if political conditions arise where the anticipated public provision of financial support does not materialize.

CONCLUSION

This paper has analyzed the need for financial regulations in the implementation of central bank policy. To do so, it has emphasized that a central bank serves two very different functions. First, central banks function as monetary authorities, managing high-powered money to influence the price level and real activity. Second, central banks engage in regular and emergency lending to private banks and other financial institutions. We have termed these functions monetary and banking policies. Our analytical procedure was to investigate how a minimally regulated system would operate and then to consider the consequences of various forms of public intervention. The analysis drew on contemporary economic knowledge in the areas of finance, monetary economics, and macroeconomics.

Our conclusions regarding the need for supporting financial regulation were radically different for monetary and banking policy, respectively. We emphasized that regulations were not essential for the execution of monetary policy. The reason is that high-powered money can be managed with open market operations in government bonds. By its very nature, however, banking policy involves a swap of government securities for claims on individual banks. Just as private lenders must restrict and monitor individual borrowers, a central bank must regulate and supervise the institutions that borrow from it.

The ineffectiveness of credit policy, of which banking policy is an example, is well-illustrated by the student loan program. Student loans need not result in increased expenditure on education. A loan may reduce the extent to which families draw down their own financial saving or sacrifice expenditure on other goods and services to pay for a student's education. Because loan funds are fungible, they cannot assure a net increase in expenditure in the targeted area. The targeted effect would require provisions in the program to prevent substitution for private outlays and to restrict access to other credit sources.

Virtually all economists agree that there is an important role for public authority in managing the nation's high-powered money. In contrast, there is little evidence that public lending to particular institutions is either necessary or appropriate. Banking policy has been rationalized as a source of funds for temporarily illiquid but solvent banks. To assess that rationale we developed the distinction between illiquidity and insolvency in some detail, showing the distinction to be meaningful precisely because information about the value of bank assets is incomplete and costly to obtain. Nevertheless, we saw that the costliness of information per se could not rationalize the public provision of line of credit services. Even if central bank lending served a useful purpose earlier in the century, today's financial markets provide a highly efficient means of allocating credit privately. On the basis of such considerations, we find it difficult to makes a case for central bank lending, either through the discount window or the payments system, and the regulatory and supervisory activities that support it.

Consideration of the use of monetary and banking policy in response to systemwide crises led us to modify our conclusion only slightly. We saw that monetary policy could play an important role in banking crises by managing the stock of high-powered money to smooth nominal interest rates. Moreover, it could do so without costly regulation and supervision. Banking policy, on the other hand, directly influences neither high-powered money nor the aggregate supply and demand for goods. So banking policy could not influence either nominal or real interest rates. We recognized, however, that a role for banking policy in preventing banking crises might arise in response to real interest rate spikes, which could cause widespread insolvencies against which monetary policy would be ineffective. Such banking policy actions could have social value if the temporary disruption costs associated with widespread insolvencies were large. But central bank transfers to troubled financial institutions redistribute wealth between different classes of citizens at best. And inappropriate incentives for risktaking and liquidity management might lead to more severe and frequent financial crises at worst. Hence, it is by no means clear that there is a beneficial role for banking policy even in this case.

REFERENCES

Bagehot, Walter. *Lombard Street* (1873). New York: Arno Press, 1978.

Barro, Robert J. *Macroeconomics* (2nd edition). New York: John Wiley, 1986.

Bennett, James and Thomas DiLorenzo. *The Underground Government: The Off-Budget Public Sector.* Washington, DC: Cato Institute, 1983.

Benston, George J., *et al. Perspectives on Safe and Sound Banking.* Cambridge, MA: MIT Press, 1986.

Benston, George and Clifford Smith. 'A Transaction Cost Approach to the Theory of Financial Intermediation.' *Journal of Finance* 31 (May 1976): 215–31.

Berlin, Mitchell. 'Loan Commitments: Insurance Contracts in a Risky World.' Federal Reserve Bank of Philadelphia *Business Review* (May/June 1986): 3–12.

Blueprint for Reform: The Report of the Task Group on Regulation of Financial Services. Washington, DC: Government Printing Office, 1984.

Board of Governors of the Federal Reserve System. *Federal Reserve Board Rules and Regulations.* Regulation A (12c FR 201). Washington, Board of Governors of the Federal Reserve System.

Boyd, John H. and Edward C. Prescott. 'Financial Intermediary Coalitions.' *Journal of Economic Theory* 38 (April 1986): 211–32.

Bulow, Jeremy I. and Kenneth Rogoff. 'A Constant Recontracting Model of Sovereign Debt.' The Hoover Institution, Stanford University, December 1986.

Cagan, Phillip. *Determinants and Effects of Changes in the Stock of Money 1875–1960.* Cambridge, MA: National Bureau of Economic Research, 1965.

Cannon, James G. *Clearing-Houses.* New York: D. Appleton and Company, 1908.

Chan, Louis. 'Uncertainty and the Neutrality of Government Financing Policy.' *Journal of Monetary Economics* 11 (May 1983): 351–72.

Continental Illinois National Bank: Report of An Inquiry into its Federal Supervision and Assistance. Staff Report to the Subcommittee on Financial Institutions Supervision, Regulation, and Insurance of the Committee on Banking, Finance and Urban Affairs. Washington, DC: Government Printing Office, 1985.

Cook, Timothy and Thomas Hahn. 'The Information Content of Discount Rate Announcements and Their Effect on Market Interest Rates.' Working Paper 86–5. Federal Reserve Bank of Richmond, September 1986.

Cook, Timothy Q. and Timothy D. Rowe, editors. *Instruments of the Money Market,* 6th ed. Richmond, VA: Federal Reserve Bank of Richmond, 1986.

Corrigan, E. Gerald. 'Financial Market Structure: A Longer View.' Federal Reserve Bank of New York *Annual Report,* February 1987.

Crane, Dwight B. *Managing Credit Lines and Commitments.* Chicago, IL: Association of Reserve City Bankers, 1973.

Cukierman, Alex and Allan H. Meltzer. 'A Theory of Ambiguity, Credibility, and Inflation Under Discretion and Asymmetric Information.' *Econometrica* 54 (September 1986): 1099–1128.

Diamond, Douglas. 'Financial Intermediation and Delegated Monitoring.' *Review of Economic Studies* 51 (July 1984): 393–414.

Fama, Eugene. 'What's Different About Banks?' *Journal of Monetary Economics* 15 (January 1985): 29–39.

Federal Deposit Insurance Corporation. *Annual Report,* 1940. Washington, DC: Federal Deposit Insurance Corporation, 1941.

Goodfriend, Marvin. 'Discount Window Borrowing, Monetary Policy, and the Post-October 1979 Federal Reserve Operating Procedure.' *Journal of Monetary Economics* 12 (September 1983): 343–56.

—. 'Monetary Mystique: Secrecy and Central Banking.' *Journal of Monetary Economics* 17 (January 1986): 63–92.

—. *Monetary Policy In Practice.* Richmond, VA: Federal Reserve Bank of Richmond, 1987.

Gorton, Gary and Donald J. Mullineaux. 'The Joint Production of Confidence: Endogenous Regulation and 19th Century Commercial-Bank Clearinghouses.' *Journal of Money, Credit, and Banking* 19 (November 1987): 457–68.

Gorton, Gary and Joseph Haubrich. 'Bank Deregulation, Credit Markets and the Control of Capital.' In *Bubbles and Other Essays.* Carnegie-Rochester Series on Public Policy, Vol. 26, edited by Karl Brunner and Allan Meltzer. Amsterdam: North Holland, 1987, pp. 289–334.

—. 'Loan Sales, Recourse, and Reputation: An Analysis of Secondary Loan Participations.' Department of Finance, University of Pennsylvania, May 1987.

Government Credit Allocation: Where Do We Go from Here? Center for Research in Government Policy and Business of the Graduate School of Management, The University of Rochester, November 1975. San Francisco, Institute for Contemporary Studies, 1975.

Hackley, Howard H. *Lending Functions of the Federal Reserve Banks: A History.* Washington, DC: Board of Governors of the Federal Reserve System, 1973.

Hanweck, Gerald A. 'Bank Loan Commitments.' In *Below the Bottom Line,* Staff Study, no 113. Washington, DC: Board of Governors of the Federal Reserve System, 1982, pp. 103–30.

Haubrich, Joseph. 'Financial Intermediation, Delegated Monitoring, and Long Term Relationship.' Wharton School, October 1986.

Hawkins, Gregory D. 'An Analysis of Revolving Credit Agreements.' *Journal of Financial Economics* 10 (March 1982): 59–81.

Hodgman, Donald R. *Selective Credit Controls in Western Europe.* Chicago, IL: Association of Reserve City Bankers, 1976.

Humphrey, Thomas M. and Robert E. Keleher. 'The Lender of Last Resort: A Historical Perspective.' *Cato Journal* 4 (Spring/Summer 1984): 275–318.

Kemmerer, E. W. *Seasonal Variations in the Relative Demand for Money and Capital in the United States.* Washington, DC: National Monetary Commission, 1910.

Lindow, Wesley. 'Bank Capital and Risk Assets.' *The National Banking Review,* Comptroller of the Currency, U.S. Treasury Department, September 1963, pp. 29–46.

Melnik, Arie and Steven E. Plaut. 'The Economics of Loan Commitment Contracts: Credit Pricing and Utilization.' *Journal of Banking and Finance* 10 (June 1986a): 267–80.

—. 'Loan Commitment Contracts, Terms of Lending, and Credit Allocations.' *Journal of Finance* 41 (June 1986b): 425–35.

Mengle, David L., David B. Humphrey, and Bruce J. Summers. 'Intraday Credit: Risk, Value, and Pricing.' Federal Reserve Bank of Richmond *Economic Review* (January/February 1987): 3–14.

Pavel, Christine. 'Securitization.' Federal Reserve Bank of Chicago *Economic Review* (July/August 1986): 16–31.

Pennacchi, George. 'Loan Sales and the Cost of Bank Capital.' Department of Finance, University of Pennsylvania, November 1986.

Reappraisal of the Federal Reserve Discount Mechanism. Volumes 1–3. Washington, DC: Board of Governors of the Federal Reserve System, 1971.

Rothschild, Michael and Joseph Stiglitz. 'Equilibrium in Competitive Insurance Markets: An Essay on the Economics of Imperfect Information.' *Quarterly Journal of Economics* 90 (November 1976): 629–50.

Smith, Clifford W., Jr. and Jerold B. Warner. 'On Financial Contracting: An Analysis of Bond Covenants.' *Journal of Financial Economics* 7 (June 1979): 117–61.

Sprague, Irvine H. *Bailout: An Insider's Account of Bank Failures and Rescues.* New York: Basic Books, 1986.

Sprague, O. M. W. *History of Crises Under the National Banking System.* Washington, DC: National Monetary Commission, 1910.

Summers, Bruce J. 'Loan Commitments to Business in United States Banking History.' Federal Reserve Bank of Richmond *Economic Review* (September/October 1975): 115–23.

Timberlake, Richard H. 'The Central Banking Role of Clearing Associations.' *Journal of Money, Credit, and Banking* 16 (February 1984): 1–15.

—. *The Origins of Central Banking in the United States.* Cambridge, MA: Harvard University Press, 1978.

Todd, Walker F. 'Outline of an Argument on Solvency.' Federal Reserve Bank of Cleveland, March 1987.

'The Tug-of-War Over "Float".' *The Morgan Guaranty Survey*, December 1983, pp. 11–14.

U.S. Congress. House. Subcommittee of the Committee on Government Operations. *Bush Task Group Report on Regulation of Financial Services Blueprint for Reform (Part 1).* Hearings before the Subcommittee of the Committee on Government Operations. 99th Congress, 1st session, 1985.

—. Subcommittee on Economic Stabilization of the Committee on Banking, Finance and Urban Affairs. *Federal Credit Activities.* Hearings before the Subcommittee on Economic Stabilization of the Committee on Banking, Finance and Urban Affairs. 98th Congress, 2nd session, 1984.

—. The Subcommittees of the Government Operations and Banking, Finance and Urban Affairs Committees. *The Role of the Federal Reserve in Check Clearing and the*

Nation's Payments System. Joint Hearings before Subcommittees of the Government Operations and Banking, Finance and Urban Affairs Committees. 98th Congress, 1st Session, 1983.

U.S. Department of Commerce. *Historical Statistics of the United States*. Washington, DC, 1975.

Young, John E. 'The Rise and Fall of Federal Reserve Float.' Federal Reserve Bank of Kansas City *Economic Review* (February 1986): 28–38.

9

Lender of Last Resort: A Contemporary Perspective

GEORGE G. KAUFMAN

Although much discussed in both the economic and banking literature, the lender of last resort (LLR) has always been a vague concept. Apparently first discussed by Sir Francis Baring in 1797 and refined by Henry Thornton (1802) and Walter Bagehot (1873), among others, the lender of last resort's function was to prevent financial panics and crises from being ignited by problems at individual institutions or markets. This has generally been interpreted as preventing the individual problem from causing a decline in the aggregate money supply. For example, Thomas Humphrey begins his recent historical review of the lender of last resort with the statement:

> Averting banking panics and crises is the job of the central bank. As lender of last resort (LLR), it has the responsibility of preventing panic-induced collapses of the money supply (Humphrey, 1989, p. 8).[1]

But concern over collapse of the money supply has not been very great, at least in the United States, since 1933. In part, this reflects the introduction of federal deposit insurance. Nevertheless, lender of last resort assistance has been provided by the Federal Reserve on a number of occasions, including the Penn Central Railroad failure in 1970, the Continental Illinois failure in 1984, the Bank of New York computer failure in 1985, the Ohio thrift crisis in 1986, the Texas bank failures in 1987–88, the Bank of New England failure in 1990, and the stock market crashes of October 1987 and October 1989. Of these, only the failure of the Continental Illinois Bank, primarily because it was the first failure of a money center bank in recent years and because our knowledge of the implications of runs on large banks was skimpy, should have been perceived by the Federal Reserve at the time to potentially impact the supply of money. The other events represented shocks that threatened the solvency of large banks or that imposed abrupt reductions in wealth in nonbank sectors directly involved and that were perceived to threaten similar wealth reductions in other sectors and thus threaten to reduce aggregate income in the economy. Thus, potential reductions in the aggregate money supply no longer appear to be the primary rationale for lender of last resort

[1] A similar view is expressed in Bordo (1990).

This article first appeared in the *Journal of Financial Services Research* 5, 1991.

intervention. This article reviews the theory of the lender of last resort, discusses its uses through time, and analyzes its applicability to current problems.

1. REVIEW OF THE THEORY

The theory of the lender of last resort was developed for economies in which the money supply was primarily specie or paper notes freely converted into specie. These economies were extremely sensitive to exogenous disturbances from internal and external sources. LLR operations were viewed as temporary with only short-term effects and were differentiated from continuing central bank operations to affect income, employment, and the price level in the longer term. To borrow current Federal Reserve terminology, LLR were 'defensive' operations rather than 'dynamic' operations.

When specie were drained from the system because of, say, an outflow to foreign countries (external source) or an outflow from the banks into private hands (internal source), a multiple contraction in note issue occurred. By restricting domestic trade, in the absence of sufficiently flexible prices, such contractions would have adverse effects on levels of real activity in all sectors of the economy. Thus, it would be efficient for a government agency, such as a central bank, to maintain a stock of specie sufficiently large to inject into the economy to prevent the contraction. The LLR was seen as ensuring that the aggregate economy was immunized from the adverse effects of the initial event causing the specie drain, at least as it would be transmitted through decreases in the money supply. According to Bagehot, external drains can be stopped primarily by raising interest rates sufficiently. On the other hand, domestic drains can be stopped by lending freely:

> A panic, in a word, is a species of neuralgia, and according to the rules of science you must not starve it. The holders of the cash reserve must be ready not only to keep it for their own liabilities, but to advance it most freely for the liabilities of others. They must lend to merchants, to minor bankers, to 'this man and that man,' whenever the security is good. In wild periods of alarm, one failure makes many, and the best way to prevent the derivative failures is to arrest the primary failure which causes them.... The problem of managing a panic must not be thought of as mainly a 'banking' problem. It is primarily a mercantile one....
>
> There should be a clear understanding between the Bank [of England] and the public ... that they [sic] will replenish it in times of foreign demand as fully, and lend it in times of internal panic as freely and readily, as plain principles of banking require. (Bagehot, 1894, pp. 53, 54, 73)

A number of observations follow from these statements. External and internal sources of disturbances have different implications. By reducing specie, external disturbances will of necessity reduce the money supply and need to be offset by an equal injection of specie into the economy by the LLR either directly or indirectly by increasing interest rates and attracting species from abroad in order to prevent spillover to the economy as a whole. Internal disturbances, however, may or may not result in an increase in the demand for specie and a decline in the money supply. Thus, maintenance of the money supply does not appear to be the sole objective. Rather, the LLR should inject whatever specie is necessary to relieve the panic and to prevent additional business failures. This injection can be through banks or in direct transactions with whomever has 'good' security. Good apparently refers to security whose equilibrium market value is not less than the assistance provided by the LLR, but whose instantaneous market value may be temporarily lower as a result of potential 'fire-sale' losses. That is, for internal shocks, the LLR should lend freely to curb short-run liquidity problems that are independent of underlying equilibrium solvency problems. This rule is considerably broader than preventing a collapse of the money supply per se and appears to focus more directly on preventing a temporary collapse of income regardless of how the shock is transmitted.[2]

Thus, the second sentence of Humphrey's statement limits the role of the LLR to a greater extent than envisioned by Bagehot. If this is so, and the quantity of money cannot be viewed as a criterion, what rules should guide LLR operations? The remainder of this article discusses such potential guidelines.

To analyze these guidelines, it is necessary to consider a number of questions:

1. What constitutes a panic or crisis?
2. How may individual shocks be transmitted into broader shocks representing crisis or panics?
3. How can the LLR interdict this transmission process or contagion?
4. What are the costs, if any, of such interdiction and how can the LLR evaluate whether assistance should be provided?
5. How should the LLR provide the necessary funding?

2. WHAT CONSTITUTES A PANIC OR CRISIS?

As Garcia and Plautz note, 'there is no general agreement on what constitutes a crisis' (Garcia and Plautz, 1988, p. 9). Webster's Dictionary defines crisis as a time 'at which the business organism is severely strained and forced liquidation occurs.' Likewise, a financial panic is defined as a 'sudden widespread fright concerning

[2] Bagehot does not differentiate clearly between lending on good security and lending to good borrowers. He notes that 'no advances indeed need be made by which the Bank will ultimately lose' (p. 200). But insolvent institutions generally do hold some good assets, or assets that have a positive equilibrium market value. A few lines later he states that 'the majority to be protected, are the "sound" people, the people who have good security to offer.' The Federal Reserve usually restricts its lending to banks that are not declared insolvent by their chartering authority. But, as demonstrated in the Continental Illinois, First Republic, and other large bank cases in recent years, *solvent* is an elastic term. Nearly all of these banks were insolvent on an economic or market value basis, although not on a book value basis, and thus were not declared insolvent by their chartering agency for some time. As discussed later in the article, the use of open market operations rather than the discount window permits the LLR to escape this dilemma.

During the Ohio S&L crisis of 1985, the Federal Reserve Bank of Cleveland did lend to book value insolvent institutions on a collateralized basis. The credit was extended 'for the purpose of facilitating an orderly closing or merger of the institution [and] . . . . the indebtedness [would] . . . . be assumed, or repaid, by a legal successor of the insolvent institution' (Federal Reserve Bank of Cleveland, 1985, p. 22).

financial affairs and resulting in a depression in values caused by . . . the sale of securities or other properties.' The key word in this definition is 'sudden.' This implies the potential for abrupt liquidations and temporary or fire-sale losses resulting in the destruction of real wealth that would not occur, or at least not to the same extent, if there was greater time. That is, a financial crisis or panic exists when there is a liquidity problem in one or more important sector of the economy.[3]

Correcting a liquidity problem does not imply that equilibrium asset prices may not decline, but only that market prices do not decline so abruptly that there is insufficient time to conduct an efficient search for the highest bidder. Thus, for example, although both are likely to produce fire-sale losses, the sudden appearance of an adverse rumor that is subsequentially identified as unfounded would not be expected to depress equilibrium asset values, while a sudden and unexpected military invasion or oil embargo might. Fire-sale reductions in asset prices are of concern to the LLR if they are sufficiently important in themselves to temporarily reduce aggregate real income significantly, even only temporarily, or if they threaten to spill over to other important sectors. How do widespread fire-sale losses arise?

Numerous types of shocks can cause a sudden reevaluation of asset prices either up or down. Some shocks are applicable to one or a very limited number of assets; others may impact prices of a broad array of assets. As discussed earlier, some shocks may cause only temporary equilibrium displacements of asset prices, and others, a more lasting shift in prices. In either case, in perfect markets, the assets to which the shock applies would attain their new postreevaluation prices immediately and without the need for any transactions (sales). But markets are not perfect, and some asset owners may want to sell their assets immediately upon observing the shock. The prices at which they can sell these assets depend on the liquidity of the particular market.

Liquidity may be related to the costs involved, including time, in searching out the potentially highest bidders and the underlying equilibrium price. The greater the costs, the less liquid the market. Liquidity varies with the characteristics of the asset traded. The more unique the asset, the smaller the volume outstanding, and smaller the daily trading volume, the less liquid the market and the greater and longer that fire-sale prices will be incurred. (Because prices and interest rates are inversely related, fire-sale prices imply upward interest rate spikes for these assets.) Thus, liquidity may be expected to differ across markets so that, for any given time interval after a shock, fire-sale losses will differ from market to market.

But even in the most liquid markets, sudden changes in perceived prices by a sufficiently large number of participants, because of, say, sudden new adverse

[3] Alternatively, Anna Schwartz has defined a financial crisis more restrictively as one:

> . . . fueled by fears that means of payment will be unobtainable at any price and . . . leads to a scramble for high-powered money, . . . is precipitated by actions of the public that suddenly squeeze the reserves in the banking systems, . . . [and] is short-lived, ending with a slackening of the public's demand for additional currency. (1986, p. 11)

information, can produce fire-sale losses.[4] In part, this reflects both technological restrictions on trade imposed by the extant mechanics of consummating trades on the particular market and the minimum amount of time necessary for market participants to reassess their strategies in consideration of the new information and place new buy or sell orders. These factors appear to have been the major causes of the fire-sale prices accompanying the breaks in the stock and derivative markets in October 1987 and 1989, among the most liquid of all markets.

Matching buyers and sellers and reassessing strategy require finite time, although both are greatly affected by the technology available. The more advanced the technology, the briefer the minimum time period required. Thus, liquidity is largely a technological characteristic and reflects the potential for a temporary mismatching of supply and demand in a particular market or across markets. For a given state of technology and liquidity, the greater the shock, the greater the expected resulting volume of transactions and the magnitude of fire-sale losses may be. LLR intervention cannot affect the state of technology but can offset its adverse implications by effectively providing additional time through stimulating demand.

Reassessing portfolio strategies by market participants in the wake of an adverse shock and new information is likely to be more difficult and time consuming for securities subject to default risk than for default-free securities, such as U.S. Treasury securities. In such times, there is also a likelihood of an immediate flight to quality as some market participants would rather be safe than sorry. This should worsen the liquidity problem for nondefault-free securities and improve them for default-free securities. Indeed, prices may even rise and interest rates decline for default-free securities.

It follows that the more liquid a market, the briefer fire-sale prices will be, the less wealth will be reduced in the sector, the less such prices are likely to affect other markets and sectors, and the less the need is for support from the LLR. The role of the LLR is thus to provide liquidity temporarily when market failure causes it to dry up. Both theory and evidence suggest that the LLR, or any other monetary assistance, cannot increase real income for extended periods of time and, therefore, should not be provided to attempt to offset lasting real income declines from the initial shocks.

As financial markets have become broader and the volume of transactions has increased, the mechanisms for providing liquidity have also improved so that fire-sale losses on particular markets from shocks of the same magnitude should be smaller and short-lived than earlier. Markets have become more efficient. However, at the same time innovations in computer and telecommunications technology have increased both the speed at which transactions may be consummated and the volume of transactions that may be conducted. This has increased the potential for abrupt price changes and fire-sale losses in response to shocks. That is,

[4] A theoretical model describing such behavior has recently been developed in Gennotte and Leland (1990).

there has been a race between advances in technology that have improved the mechanism for providing liquidity and advances in technology that have encouraged increases in transaction volume. The net effect on liquidity and the potential for the magnitude and length of fire-sale losses is uncertain.

3. THE TRANSMISSION OF SHOCKS

In evaluating whether a particular liquidity problem is sufficiently severe to warrant assistance, the LLR needs to consider whether the effects will be restricted to the particular sector directly impacted by the shock or will spill over to other sectors. This requires knowledge of the processes by which shocks may be transmitted from sector to sector.

Assume an initial exogenous shock that lowers some asset prices and thereby reduces wealth in a particular sector. The most obvious transmission linkage is through changes in the money supply. This channel is the focus of most analyses of LLR activities. However, in a modern economy without specie-based money, a collapse of the money supply for reasons other than central bank actions can come about only through an increase in currency from a run on the banking system as a whole. Runs or deposit outflows from individual banks in the pursuit of safety are likely only to reshuffle reserves and deposits within the banking system. The fleeing funds are likely to be redeposited at other, perceived safe banks either directly or indirectly through a flight-to-quality that first involves the purchase of non-bank, completely secure securities, such as Treasury securities, and then a redeposit of the proceeds by the seller of the securities, in a safe bank. No reserves or money supply are lost to the system as a whole in either scenario, even if deposits are transferred to banks overseas, and thus the cost of the runs is likely to be relatively minimal (Benston *et al.*, 1986, ch. 2; Kaufman, 1988; Schwartz, 1987).[5]

All runs will increase churning and uncertainty and, at least, temporarily disturb customer–bank relationships. But, money is highly fungible and, particularly in light of the easy entry into banking services in recent years, breaks in banking relationship should be less harmful to the real economy than breaks in many other industries: for example, automobile, steel, and construction. Except at times of massive government takeovers, such as in the current thrift crisis, most bank failures result in merger or sale in which only the name over the door and top management change. Loan files and loan officers remain in place. Moreover, surveys have shown that even households and small business firms tend to have more than one banking connection (Bennet, 1984; Elliehausen and Wolken, 1990). Maintaining insolvent banks in operation serves to prolong a misallocation of resources (Tussing, 1967).

Indirect redeposits do cause more important interest rate effects as rates on public securities are bid down and those on private securities are bid up, and direct redeposits possible exchange rate effects if deposits are transferred to

[5] For a contrary view, see Summers (1989).

banks overseas. However, only if neither the initial depositors nor the sellers of safe securities perceive any bank in the country or in other countries to be safe and want to hold currency outside the banking system is the aggregate supply of money affected. Such a run reduces aggregate bank reserves and, unless offset by an equal injection of reserves by the central bank, ignites a multiple contraction of money and credit.

The reduction in the aggregate money supply will cause the impact of the shock to spread out to other sectors of the economy and, if prices are not perfectly flexible, will reduce real as well as nominal income. But, as discussed earlier, in the presence of both federal deposit insurance that guarantees smaller depositors the full present value par value of their deposits, regardless of the financial solvency of their bank, and a well-informed central bank that may be assumed to have learned from its mistakes of the 1930s, when it failed to offset the effects of a currency outflow, it is highly unlikely that a shock will result in a currency run on the banking system and cause a reduction in aggregate money. (Larger depositors cannot conduct their operations efficiently with currency and are thus unlikely to convert from deposits to currency.) That is, federal deposit insurance has made the central bank as a LLR redundant for shocks transmitted through reductions in money supply.[6]

Runs on banks are widely viewed as the germs that spread contagion, and it was this fear that served as the basis for the Federal Reserve's discount window assistance to the Continental Illinois Bank in 1984 and subsequently to a number of other banks viewed as 'too large to fail.'[7] But historical evidence provides little support for bank runs leading to massive bank failures. A review of the causes of all national bank failures from 1865 through 1936, including the failures during the Great Depression, by J.F.T. O'Connor, who served as Comptroller of the Currency from 1933 through 1938, concluded that bank runs and loss of public confidence accounted for less than 10 percent of the total 4,449 causes cited for the 2,955 failures and less than 15 percent of the number of failures (O'Connor, 1938, p. 90). The same conclusion was reached in a study by the American Bankers Association in 1929 (Kaufman, 1989) and more recently by Anna Schwartz.[8] Thus, the likelihood that the run on the Continental Illinois or other large banks would have ignited a run on the banking system as a whole that would have led to massive bank failures was negligible. Indeed, the Federal Deposit Insurance Corporation (FDIC) implicitly

[6] A particularly interesting example of deposit insurance dominance of the central bank in providing LLR assistance is the Canadian experience of the 1930s. It is likely that all or nearly all Canadian commercial banks were economically insolvent in this period. Yet, there were no legal bank failures or bank runs into currency as there were in the United States. This appears to have been the result of an implicit but widely recognized 100 percent deposit guarantee by the federal government. Interestingly, there was neither explicit federal deposit insurance nor a central bank (Kryzanowski and Roberts, 1989).

[7] An expansion of this argument appears in Kaufman (forthcoming).

[8] Schwartz (1988) also notes that bank runs have been far less frequent in U.S. history than bank failures and that few runs have led to failures. The Comptroller of the Currency attributes only 16 of the 353 failures of national banks between 1921 and 1924 to runs.

acknowledged this when it began to impose pro-rata losses on creditors of insolvent large bank holding companies in 1986 after similar creditors had been protected completely in the earlier resolution of the Continental Illinois Bank.

But contagion may occur through channels other than the money supply. Shocks that reduce wealth in a particular sector by reducing asset prices in that sector, for example, sharp breaks in securities prices, may cause defaults by debtors in that sector, particularly where the debt is collateralized by assets whose prices have declined. Such defaults are most likely to occur in clearing payments for transactions on cash and options markets and on daily mark-to-market adjustments on futures positions (Bernanke, 1990; Brimmer, 1989). The defaults will cause a redistribution of wealth from creditors, who do not receive payments owed in full, to debtors, who do not make payments owed in full, but not a direct reduction in aggregate real wealth.[9] However, the defaults may ignite a chain of successive defaults as unpaid creditors may default on their debts to others, and so on, and may increase default risk premiums on bonds. As a result, the decline in asset prices may spread to other sectors.

The losses from defaults, however, may be expected to be substantially less than the value of the debt. They would only be equal to the difference between the amount owed and the fire-sale value of the underlying security. Moreover, the loss of primary concern to the LLR would be only the difference between the fire-sale value of the security and its new, lower equilibrium price. The LLR can assume either the full default loss from the initial shock or the fire-sale loss by purchasing the securities either at the last before-shock price or the estimated new equilibrium price, respectively, or by lending amounts equal to either price and holding the securities as collateral. These transactions may be with either the debtors or creditors directly or with the clearing facility.[10]

It is important to note that defaults do not necessarily decrease aggregate credit per se. If the creditor is a bank, a default would reduce its inflow of funds from other banks in repayment of the loan and its income and net worth. Therefore, the bank will be unable to replace the extinguished loan in part or in full. However, even if the bank were driven into insolvency as a result of the default, aggregate reserves in the banking system remain unchanged. The credit expansion potential is transferred to other solvent banks. If the initial shock reduced wealth sufficiently, the demand for credit may be reduced and aggregate credit will decline. But offsetting this reduction is outside the scope of LLR intervention.

The Federal Reserve has also provided extended LLR assistance through the discount window to large commercial banks experiencing more solvency problems than liquidity problems. Among others, these banks included the Franklin National Bank (1974), the Continental Illinois Bank (1984), the First Republic Bank

[9] Bernanke and Gertler argue that such a redistribution can directly impact real income adversely. See Gertler (1988).

[10] Direct temporary shocks to the clearing facility, due to technological or power breakdowns, such as in the Bank of New York computer failure (1985), can be analyzed in a similar framework.

(1987), MCorp (1988), the Bank of New England, and the National Bank of Washington (1990). All subsequently failed.[11] The justification for such lending is more difficult to classify. Although officially justified each time by the 'too-large-to-fail' doctrine, only the Continental Illinois Bank failure may reasonably have been perceived capable, at the time, of igniting a currency run on the banking system and a progressive series of defaults from losses to correspondent banks (Kaufman, 1990).[12] The Continental was the eighth largest bank in the United States and a true money center bank with interbank deposits from throughout the world. In 1984, inherited wisdom on the implications of runs on large banks was still based on the perceived experience of the Great Depression. Although possibly known before 1929, the taxonomy of deposit runs reviewed earlier in this article had not been analyzed since, and systemic risk was viewed as a real concern. Ex post, the fear was not justified. Nor were the shocks to the banks so sudden that they caused massive fire-sale losses nor so large that they directly reduced wealth sufficiently to impact aggregate income or increase risk premiums on healthy banks and cause fire-sale losses there.

It appears that such LLR assistance was motivated jointly by an atmosphere of camaraderie with fellow 'bankers,' desire to 'buy' time to work out a solution, knowledge that the loans are fully collateralized by someone else—the FDIC, and/or failure to understand fully the nature of the problem. In the words of Anna Schwartz, the Fed has confused 'financial distress' with 'financial crisis' (Schwartz, 1986).[13] In such assistance, the Federal Reserve has effectively made discount window lending part of the safety net under too-large-to-fail institutions.[14] There

[11] Technically, because its assets were only $2 billion and it was only about the 250th largest bank in the country, the National Bank of Washington could not be considered too large to fail. But since it was located in Washington, D.C., and the controlling shareholders in its parent Washington Bancorp appear to have close political connections, the bank may be classified in a new category of 'too political to fail.' Nevertheless, it failed shortly after borrowing nearly $500 million from the Federal Reserve Bank of Richmond with losses to the FDIC of about the same magnitude.

[12] See also Kaufman (1985) and Meltzer (1986). For a defense of assisting insolvent banks, see Goodhart (1985). A description of Federal Reserve assistance to the Franklin National Bank (New York) in 1974 is provided in Garcia and Plautz (1988, 213–32).

[13] For similar reasons, the U.S. Treasury, acting as a LLR, provided assistance to (bailed out) Lockheed (1971), New York City (1975), and Chrysler (1979). See also Bordo (1989) and Todd (1988, pp. 533–77).

The practice of providing LLR assistance to insolvent banks is not limited to the Federal Reserve and the United States. Similar behavior has been followed by the Bank of Canada (Dowd, 1989, pp. 113–28). Interestingly, the Federal Reserve did not provide LLR assistance to Drexel Burnham during the final days of its demise. In part, this may have been motivated by the dislike of policy makers for the firm. The *Wall Street Journal* reported that

> Drexel was getting its comeuppance and that didn't seem to bother many in the regulatory establishment. 'The old Drexel Burnham Lambert that everyone knew and hated for the last 10 years is gone,' said one Bush administration official. The same article also quoted FDIC Chairman William Seidman as saying that 'if the market floats through all this, then we have greater stability than we had hoped'. (Murray and Salwer, 1990, p. A6)

[14] Indeed, the Federal Reserve lent to numerous small insolvent banks. A recent study by the U.S. House Banking Committee concluded that 90 percent of the 418 banks that had received extended or

is neither precedent for such assistance in the LLR literature nor even a discussion of it in published Federal Reserve materials. Indeed, in his testimony before Congress on the Drexel Burnham failure, Federal Reserve Chairman Alan Greenspan stated that:

> Then, as now, our concern was not with the fortune of a particular firm; rather it was and remains the orderly operation of the financial markets, because that is a prerequisite for the orderly functioning of the economy (1990, pp. 301–2).

When the Fed provides assistance directly to an economic insolvent or near insolvent but open institution, it provides time for uninsured depositors to withdraw their funds at full face value. Because the Fed collateralizes its loans fully, it will not experience losses if and when the institution fails. Rather, the losses are passed on to the FDIC, as was the case with all loans made to banks considered too large to fail.

In sum, LLR assistance appears appropriate to offset shocks that (1) threaten to reduce aggregate money supply and (2) in the absence of a potential reduction in the money supply, ignite temporary liquidity problems that are likely to produce significant fire-sale losses that may be expected to reduce aggregate income and wealth temporarily below equilibrium levels or the levels that would exist if the markets were perfectly efficient. What constitutes a sufficient severe liquidity problem to warrant intervention is difficult to define precisely and, as is argued later in the article, requires a careful and publicly verifiable cost-benefit analysis. Also, for reasons discussed later, there is a strong tendency for the LLR to view crises as more severe than they actually are and the costs of intervention as smaller than they actually are.

4. WHAT IS THE COST OF LLR ASSISTANCE?

Lender of last resort assistance, no matter how apparent the immediate need or by whom provided, is not costless. Any government assistance that reduces losses below those that would occur as a result of market forces in the absence of such assistance incurs the danger of discouraging action by private participants to protect themselves from future market shocks. Thus, unless priced correctly, LLR assistance induces moral hazard problems by encouraging market participants to alter their behavior in a way that shifts risks to the LLR and government. This potential hazard has been described succinctly by Charles Kindleberger as follows:

> Markets generally work, but occasionally they break down. When they do, they require government intervention to provide the public good of stability... [But] if the markets know in advance that help is forthcoming under generous dispensations, they break down more frequently and function less effectively. . . . This paradox is equivalent to the prisoner's

LLR credit from the Federal Reserve subsequently failed (U.S. House of Representatives 1991). Some cynics might argue that the best early indicator of a large bank's economic insolvency is extended emergency borrowing from the Federal Reserve. For an expansion of the LLR's role in the federal safety net, see Kaufman (forthcoming).

dilemma. Central banks should act one way (lending freely) to halt the panic, but another (leave the market to its own devices) to improve the chances of preventing future panics (1978, pp. 6, 163).

Indeed, the potential for moral hazard was noted as early as by Thornton, who wrote:

> It is by no means intended to imply that it would become the Bank of England to relieve every distress which the rashness of country banks may bring upon them: the bank, by doing this, might encourage their improvidence. There seems to be a medium at which a public bank should aim in granting aid to inferior establishments, and which it must often find very difficult to be observed. The relief should neither be so prompt and liberal as to exempt those who misconduct their business from all the natural consequences of their fault, nor so scanty and slow as deeply to involve the general interests. These interests, nevertheless, are sure to be pleaded by every distressed person whose affairs are large, however indifferent or even ruinous may be their state (1939, p. 188).

The decision whether to provide LLR assistance and at what price involves an economic cost-benefit analysis. The benefits have been described earlier and are both immediate and obvious. The costs are delayed and thus more likely both not to be perceived to be associated with the earlier and removed LLR action and to be more diffuse and difficult to measure.[15] For example, LLR provision of liquidity to prevent fire-sale losses in a particular sector at a price below that which the private market would charge is unlikely to encourage market participants in that sector to improve the mechanisms for achieving increased liquidity through private means. As a result, the LLR is more likely to be required to provide assistance again in the future, and the sector is effectively being subsidized by being permitted to operate less efficiently than otherwise. Moreover, in the process, participants are encouraged to assume greater risk exposure with likely greater losses in the future than they would if they had to absorb the full share of the current losses.

Similarly, assistance to economically insolvent banks encourages the banks to increase their own risk exposures as they have little if any of their own shareholder funds at risk, discourages other banks from reducing their risk exposures, and frequently provides sufficient time for uninsured depositors to shift their funds elsewhere at full par value before the bank is declared legally insolvent and the value of their deposits is reduced. Any loss from such resolution is borne by the FDIC or the taxpayer. Thus, the potential future costs of current LLR intervention are substantially larger than the benefits of the current intervention. But the discount rate used by policy makers, who are under considerable political pressure to optimize economic performance in the short-term and whose terms of office are relatively short and not guaranteed to last until the next crisis, is likely to be overestimated. As a result, the present value of the current benefits of intervention are likely to be found greater than the present value of the future costs, and the benefit of any doubts will be resolved in favor of current intervention. In the words of

[15] For an attempt to measure the benefits and costs of LLR actions, see Garcia and Plautz (1988, pp. 197–211).

Kindleberger, 'Actuality inevitably dominates contingency. Today wins over tomorrow' (1978, p. 163).

5. HOW SHOULD LLR INTERVENTION BE PROVIDED AND PRICED?

Lender of last resort intervention by the central bank may be provided in either of two ways: (1) through the discount window and (2) through open market operations. The discount window has been the traditional means of providing LLR assistance, both because it was the major tool of central banking before the development of broad financial markets that permitted open market operations to be conducted and because it could direct the assistance more precisely to the particular sector under pressure (Hackley, 1973). As financial markets developed in breadth and resiliency, not only did open market operations preempt the discount window as the major tool of monetary policy but they reduced the need for the central bank to direct its actions at particular sectors since the market could not direct funds made available anywhere in the system to the affected sector efficiently. The Federal Reserve appears to have recognized these changes in its 'Reappraisal of the Federal Reserve Discount Mechanism' study when it concluded that:

> Under present conditions, sophisticated open market operations enable the System to head off general liquidity crisis, but such operations are less appropriate when the System is confronted with serious financial strains among individual firms or specialized groups of institutions . . . . It is in connection with these limited crisis that the discount window can play an effective role as 'lender of last resort'. (Board of Governors of the Federal Reserve System, 1968, p. 17)

Recent Federal Reserve operations that may be classified as LLR intervention appear to have been divided between open market and discount window assistance in line with the Fed's statement. Assistance was provided primarily through the discount window in the Franklin National Bank (1974), the Continental Illinois Bank (1984), the Texas bank (1987–89) and the Bank of New England (1990) failures, and through open market operations in the October 1987 and 1989 stock market breaks.[16] This division may have been determined at least in part by a recognition of the probable insolvency of the banks in question and the unlikelihood that funds would be directed to them by the private market. Unlike the FDIC, the Federal Reserve is in an enviable position as a LLR. As noted earlier, because it requires full market value collateralization of its discount window loans, it can lend freely to economically insolvent banks, if it so wishes, without fear of suffering losses.[17] Any loss is shifted to the FDIC and, if sufficiently large, to the

[16] In the Penn Central failure (1971) the Fed announced its intentions to provide liquidity through the discount window if necessary, but apparently did not have to do so to a great extent. It did remove the ceilings on deposit rates on large, short-term certificates of deposit to make it easier for large commercial banks to accommodate customers who experienced difficulties in raising funds through commercial paper as a result of the deterioration in the market. This policy is consistent with Bagehot's strategy.

[17] An 'insider's' account of the conflict between the Fed and the FDIC caused by full collateralization appears in Sprague (1986, pp. 88–92).

taxpayer. This moral hazard problem can be reduced by requiring the Fed to obtain permission from the FDIC before extending emergency assistance through the discount window or by not permitting it to collateralize fully its loans to institutions (Benston *et al.*, 1986, ch. 5).

Reliance on open market operations to provide assistance reduces the political pressures on the LLR to assist all entities in financial distress—in particular, financially weak but politically strong entities directly through the discount window: for example, commercial banks and savings and loan associations. The private market is less likely to direct additional funds provided by open market operations to such entities. Indeed, there is little reason to apply different standards to banks than to other firms experiencing possible funding problems in the market.

Only if the central bank had superior or more timely information about the nature of the crisis or the solvency of the participants involved than the market does, should providing assistance through the discount window dominate open market operations. Because it is unlikely that the Federal Reserve has such knowledge at all or even most of the time, providing LLR assistance through the discount window should be limited to rare occasions. Moreover, the LLR may not find it easy, particularly on short notice, to differentiate between good and bad security or solvent and insolvent banks. In this, as in many other areas, the cost of government failure may be expected to be at least as great as the cost of market failure.

Lastly, open market operations eliminate the need to price LLR assistance correctly. By definition, if markets are considered efficient, funds provided through open market operations are priced at the current market rate for the particular securities involved. In contrast, funds provided through the discount window need to be priced administratively and, if priced incorrectly, may reduce the effectiveness of the assistance. If the discount rate charged is too low, too much assistance is likely to be provided with resulting subsidies and encouragement to risk taking. If the discount rate is too high, insufficient assistance is likely to be provided. Identifying the correct price is, however, not an easy task and is unlikely to be achieved at all times.[18] Since Bagehot, students of LLR intervention have suggested that the assistance be provided at a 'penalty' rate to avoid underpricing, discourage undue use, and compensate for the risk premium that the market assigns to such funding (Meltzer, 1986, pp. 85–9). But an administered penalty rate is by necessity an imprecise concept that is as likely to be mispriced as priced correctly. This reduces the usefulness of Bagehot's rule to lend freely, but a high (penalty) rate. Thus, by making it less necessary to worry about either the correct rate to charge or the correct borrowers to whom to lend, particularly about providing assistance to those experiencing the initial shock who may be expected to exert the greatest pressures on the LLR, open market operations appear to be a more efficient way of providing LLR assistance.[19]

[18] For an expansion of the problems in pricing assistance provided through the discount window, see Goodfriend and King (1988).

[19] The Swiss National Bank (SNB) appears to conduct its lender of last resort operations in conformity with this principal. Two of its research economists have recently described the Bank's

6. SUMMARY AND CONCLUSION

This article has argued that the concept of LLR intervention has changed substantially since its original development in the early 1800s. In large part, this change has reflected the changes in the economic structure in the intervening years. Protection of macro-liquidity has shifted from protection of the aggregate money supply to protection of equilibrium asset prices from sudden adverse shocks that cause markets to temporarily overadjust and impose unnecessary fire-sale losses. This change in the appropriate role for the LLR has not been fully appreciated in the LLR literature. The justification for LLR intervention has always been to minimize, if not prevent, the effects of financial crises on real income and levels of economic activity. LLR intervention was and is viewed as temporary and separate from central bank operations to influence income, employment, and price through time.

In the early days, adverse shocks to the economy were likely to spill over to initially unaffected sectors and potentially the economy as a whole through reduction in the money supply. Thus, early analysts gave heavy weight in justifying LLR intervention to the protection of the money supply. But since the abandonment of specie-based money and later the introduction of federal deposit insurance, collapses of the money supply have become highly unlikely.

The second reason for LLR intervention was to offset temporary liquidity strains from adverse shocks that induced large number of market participants to reassess quickly their asset portfolios and sell some assets without a concurrent threat to the money supply. If the trading mechanics of the particular market were not sufficiently efficient, fire-sale losses would be incurred that would temporarily depress aggregate real income and serve no lasting social or economic purpose. As Bagehot noted long ago, the LLR could prevent these by providing additional funds freely. This reason remains valid today and justifies LLR assistance such as was provided in response to the October 1987 stock market break. However, the LLR should attempt to offset only the potential fire-sale losses associated with an adverse shock, not the adverse income effects of the shock itself. As is well

operations as follows:

[T]he Swiss National Bank is obliged to act as lender of last resort to the banking system. It has traditionally interpreted its lender-of-last-resort role restrictively. As a rule, the SNB is only prepared to provide liquidity assistance in exceptional circumstances. It is willing to intervene in the event of major liquidity problems that may threaten the stability of the domestic financial system. In the SNB's view, liquidity problems arising from the interbank payments system do not call for central bank action, at least not in normal circumstances. The banks should maintain sufficiently high case reserves in order to be able to absorb normal fluctuations in their payments flows. Should the SNB be compelled to intervene, it prefers to provide liquidity assistance to the market as a whole, rather than to individual banks. Its reluctance to deal with individual banks derives from two observations. First, if caught in a liquidity squeeze, a solvent bank should always be able to get the required funds on the money market provided the aggregate supply of liquidity is adequate. Second, owing to the rapid development of financial activities outside the banking system, liquidity problems may erupt increasingly in the nonbank sectors of the economy. Therefore, the SNB should not direct its liquidity assistance exclusively at the bank (Bircher and Rich, forthcoming).

recognized, monetary actions can at best affect real income only marginally and temporarily. Likewise, assistance to insolvent banks and other individual entities directly is inappropriate and inefficient. Solvency problems should not be hidden under the cloak of liquidity problems.

To reduce problems of correctly pricing the assistance, providing assistance to equilibrium insolvent institutions, and succumbing to political pressures to direct assistance to special institutions, LLR assistance, if provided by the Federal Reserve, should be provided through open market operations.[20] Only in the exceptional instances when the Federal Reserve can clearly demonstrate that it has superior information than the market should assistance be provided through the discount window and then only either without full collateralization or after receiving permission from the FDIC, the ultimate bearer of any losses, to reduce the moral hazard problem.

LLR assistance to offset liquidity strains cannot be justified solely on the basis of an actual or perceived crisis. It is an integral part of the federal safety net. If it is not priced correctly, such assistance can cause the same kinds of moral hazard problems as federal deposit insurance has in recent years with similar high costs to society. The beneficiaries of the assistance may be encouraged not to improve the efficiency of the market to avoid similar future liquidity crisis, rather than to protect themselves from suffering fire-sale losses. Indeed, they are likely to assume greater risk since any losses will be borne primarily by others. In the case of insolvent banks, the assistance also provides time for uninsured depositors to flee unscathed. Thus, LLR assistance either through open market operations or the discount window should be required to be justified by a comprehensive and reproducible benefit-cost analysis before it is provided, possibly reviewed for approval by an independent body, such as the General Accounting Office.

Because shocks generally do not announce themselves in advance, contingency analyses for different types of shocks should be prepared and approved beforehand. LLR assistance would then be limited to instances where the present value benefits of intervention outweighs the present value costs. To the extent that cost-benefit analysis presently is more an art than a science, the justification for the timing and magnitude of LLR intervention may be expected to remain relatively imprecise even with the above safeguards. But it is in the best longer-run interests of both the LLR and the economy if the rules could be specified as precisely as possible, maintained at all times, and publicized widely.

REFERENCES

Bagehot, Walter. *Lombard Street*, 11th ed. London: Kegan, Paul, Trench, Truber & Co., 1984.

Bennett, Veronica. 'Consumer Demand For Product Deregulation.' *Economic Review*, Federal Reserve Bank of Atlanta (May 1984), 28–37.

[20] Limiting LLR to open market operations was recommended by Milton Friedman more than 30 years ago in his *Program for Monetary Stability* (1959, pp. 50–1).

Benston, George J., Eisenbeis, Robert A., Horvitz, Paul M., Kane, Edward J., and Kaufman, George G., *Perspectives on Safe and Sound Banking*. Cambridge, MA: MIT Press, 1986.

Bernanke, Ben. 'Clearing and Settlement During the Crash.' *Review of Financial Studies* 3,1(1990). 133–151.

Bircher, Urs, and Rich, Georg. 'Switzerland.' In: George G. Kaufman, ed., *Banking Structures in Major Countries*. Boston: Kluwer, forthcoming.

Board of Governors of the Federal Reserve System. *Reappraisal of the Federal Reserve Discount Mechanism: Report of a System Committee*. Washington, DC, 1968.

Bordo, Michael D. 'The Lender of Last Resort: Some Historical Insights.' Working Paper No. 3011, National Bureau of Economic Research, June 1989.

—. 'The Lender of Last Resort: Alternative Views and Historical Experience.' *Economic Review*, Federal Reserve Bank of Richmond (January/February 1990), 18–29.

Brimmer, Andrew F. 'Central Banking and Systematic Risk.' *Journal of Economic Perspectives* (Spring 1989), 3–16.

Dowd, Kevin. 'Some Lessons From the Recent Canadian Bank Failures.' In: George G. Kaufman, ed., *Research in Financial Services: Private and Public Policies*. Greenwich, CT: JAI Press, 1989.

Elliehausen, Gregory, and Wolken, John. 'Banking Markets and the Use of Financial Services by Small and Medium Sized Businesses.' Staff Study 160, Washington, DC: Board of Governors of the Federal Reserve System, September 1990.

Federal Reserve Bank of Cleveland. *Annual Report, 1985*. Cleveland, 1985.

Friedman, Milton. *A Program for Monetary Stability*. New York: Fordham University Press, 1959.

Garcia, Gillian, and Plautz, Elizabeth. *The Federal Reserve: Lender of Last Resort*. Cambridge, MA: Ballinger, 1988.

Gennotte, Gerard, and Leland, Hayne. 'Market Liquidity, Hedging and Crashes.' *American Economic Review* (December 1990), 999–1021.

Gertler, Mark. 'Financial Structure and Economic Activity: An Overview.' *Journal of Money, Credit and Banking* (August 1988, Pt. 2), 559–588.

Goodfriend, Marvin, and King, Robert G. 'Financial Deregulation, Monetary Policy, and Central Banking.' *Economic Review*, Federal Reserve Bank of Richmond (May/June 1988), 3–22.

Goodhart, Charles. *The Evolution of Central Banks*. London: London School of Economics and Political Science, 1985.

Greenspan, Alan. 'Statement before the Subcommittee on Economic and Commercial Law, Committee on the Judiciary, March 1, 1990.' *Federal Reserve Bulletin* (May 1990), 301–304.

Hackley, Howard H. *Lending Functions of the Federal Reserve Banks: A History*. Washington, DC: Board of Governors of the Federal Reserve System, May 1973.

Humphrey, Thomas M. 'Lender of Last Resort: The Concept in History.' *Economic Review*, Federal Reserve Bank of Richmond (March/April 1989), 8–16.

Kaufman, George G. 'Implications of Large Bank Problems and Insolvencies for the Banking System and Economic Policy.' *Staff Memoranda*, 85-3. Chicago: Federal Reserve Bank of Chicago, 1985.

—. 'Bank Runs: Causes, Benefits and Costs.' *CATO Journal* (Winter 1988), 559–588.

— 'Banking Risk in Historical Perspective.' In: George G. Kaufman, ed., *Research in Financial Services: Private and Public Policies*. Greenwich, CT: JAI Press, 1989.

—. 'Are Some Banks Too Large to Fail? Myth and Reality.' *Contemporary Policy Issues* (October 1990), 1–14.

—. 'Lender of Last Resort, Too Large to Fail, and Deposit Insurance Reform.' In: James Barth and Dan Brumbaugh, eds., *Reform of Deposit Insurance and the Regulation of Depository Institutions in the 1990s*. Cambridge, MA: Ballinger, forthcoming.

Kindleberger, Charles P. *Manias, Panics and Crashes*. New York: Basic Books, 1978.

Kryzanowski, Lawrence, and Roberts, Gordon S. 'The Performance of Canadian Banking System: 1920–1940.' *Banking System Risk: Chartering a New Course*, Federal Reserve Bank of Chicago (1989), 221–232.

Meltzer, Allan H. 'Financial Failures and Financial Policies.' in George G. Kaufman and Roger C. Kormendi, eds., *Deregulating Financial Services*. Cambridge, MA: Ballinger, 1986.

Murray, Alan and Salwen, Kevin G. 'Fed, SEC Officials Decided Hands-Off Policy Was Best.' *Wall Street Journal* (February 14, 1990).

O'Connor, J. F. T. *The Banking Crisis and Recovery Under the Roosevelt Administration*. Chicago: Callaghan and Co., 1938.

Schwartz, Anna J. 'Real and Pseudo-Financial Crises.' In: Forrest Capie and Geoffrey E. Wood, eds, *Financial Crises and the World Banking System*. New York: St. Martin's Press, 1986.

—. 'The Lender of Last Resort and the Federal Safety Net.' *Journal of Financial Services Research* (September 1987), 1–18.

—. 'Financial Stability and the Federal Safety Net.' In: William Haraf and Rose Marie Kushmeider, eds., *Restructuring Banking and Financial Services in America*. Washington, DC: American Enterprise Institute, 1988.

Selgin, George A. 'Legal Restrictions, Financial Weakening, and the Lender of Last Resort.' *CATO Journal* (Fall 1989), 429–495.

Sprague, Irvine. *Bailout: An Insider's Account of Bank Failures and Rescues*. New York: Basic Books, 1986.

Summers, Lawrence H. 'Planning for the Next Financial Crisis.' Working Paper, Harvard University and National Bureau of Economic Research, October 17, 1989.

Thornton, Henry. *An Enquiry into the Nature and Effects of the Paper Credit of Great Britain (1802)*. New York: Farrar and Rinehart, 1939.

Todd, Walker F. 'Lessons of the Past and Prospects for the Future in Lender of Last Resort Theory.' In: *The Financial Services Industry in the Year 2000: Risk and Efficiency*. Chicago: Federal Reserve Bank of Chicago, 1988, pp. 533–578.

Tussing, Dale. 'The Case for Bank Failures.' *Journal of Law and Economics* (October 1967), 129–148.

U.S. House of Representatives, Committee on Banking, Finance and Urban Affairs. 'An Analysis of Federal Reserve Discount Window Loans to Failed Institutions.' June, 1991.

10

The Bagehot Problem

FRED HIRSCH

I

Under the lead of Friedman and Johnson, monetary analysis in the past two decades has been largely transformed. The previous institutional approach has been replaced by the application of micro-economic analysis; banking has been treated as an industry in which the size and pattern of output, and the remuneration of factor inputs, are determined by the standard market influences. Normatively, particular characteristics of banking have been recognised as justifying some minimum of official regulation. But such regulation is itself to be exercised with the minimum administrative discretion and the minimum social control. Thus, the major normative implication of the analysis is that competition in banking is to be maximised, and administrative intervention minimised, subject only to the constraints stemming from the technical monopoly characteristics embodied in banking.[1]

The application of standard microeconomic analysis to banking has yielded obvious and now well known insights. But an important limitation of the approach has been the neglect of one general characteristic of banking: the prevalence of imperfection of information, and of associated asymmetries in information. This omission, which is part of a more general neglect by financial analysts of the implications of imperfect information for the working of financial markets, suggests the need to extend the standard microeconomic analysis to embrace the wider set of factors, including externalities, that determine social optima in market conditions of this kind.

This article focuses on one consequence of informational imperfection, on the relationship between the banks and the regulatory authorities, and the resulting

[1] The characteristics of banking that modern monetary theorists have regarded as justifying official regulation have been (1) the position of currency issue and supply of aggregate money as a technical monopoly if infinite inflationary escalation is to be avoided, (2) the need to prevent fraud and the reneging on promises to pay, i.e., to enforce contracts, (3) the externalities endemic in the destruction and creation of money, and (4) general banking economies of scale. See Friedman (1959, pp. 4–8) and Johnson (1968).

This article originally appeared in *The Manchester School Journal* 45 (1977).

influence on banking stability.[2] This approach qualifies the Friedman–Johnson normative prescription of maximum competition combined with minimum administrative discretion, although it yields no dominant alternative prescription.

The problem of banking stability came into sudden prominence in 1974 as an international phenomenon. A succession of failures of medium-sized banks in Germany, the United States and Switzerland, following the collapse of the 'fringe' banks in the United Kingdom, threatened the international credit structure with repercussive effects on the illiquidity or insolvency of banks with important connections in the international system. The problem was indeed an old one—it was what the nineteenth century knew as a financial crisis; but many analysts, the present author included, had assumed this class of problem to have been left behind with the Credit-Anstalt in 1931. Thus, the issue found no place in the extensive academic literature and official documentation of the previous fifteen years; it is absent from the literature comprehensively surveyed by Williamson (1973).[3]

This omission reflected the belief that banking stability had been ensured by the greater responsibilities and improved regulations adopted by central banks in the wake of the Great Depression. The doctrine expounded by Walter Bagehot in *Lombard Street*, in 1873, that the bankers' bank had a duty to lend freely when no other lenders would, had become the orthodoxy, even among those who resisted active counter cyclical policy of the Keynesian type. But the form in which this Bagehot function of lender of last resort is to be performed, and reconciled with operation of the economy according to anonymous market forces, has remained curiously vague and ambiguous. The join between macrostability and microefficiency here is an awkward corner, to use the terminology of Joan Robinson. When central banks lend, they need to take a specific view about the quality of the assets they are acquiring. Moreover, at a time of banking panic, the need is to prevent the failure of specific banks. How can these things be done consistently with maintaining the normal market incentives for prudence and good management?

This article suggests that these issues are related to a more general problem of a market economy. This is the dependence of well functioning markets on certain individual behavioural characteristics, such as telling the truth and keeping one's word, which because of limitations and asymmetries of information, can be regarded as collective intermediate goods. That is to say, these goods and the final output dependent upon them, will not be 'produced' in socially optimal quantity by maximisation of individual welfare without implicit or explicit co-operation (see Arrow, 1972; Sen, 1973a; Hirsch, 1977, chapter 10). But such co-operation is

[2] The need to invoke asymmetries of information to justify government intervention in the supply of money is also discussed by Klein (1974). Klein points out that if future divergences in the supply of different private currencies could be perfectly anticipated, along with the likelihood of fulfilment of contractual obligations, the private incentive for over-issue of such currencies would disappear. The crucial role of the informational assumptions, and their obvious non-fulfilment in any conceivable real world, is ignored by Hayek (1976) in his advocacy of *Choice in Currency*.

[3] I refer here to official documentation in the context of international monetary reform, as distinct from particular operational or policy issues.

technically easier to organise in a small group of like-minded individuals and institutions than in an open group.

Competition and free entry in themselves tend to impede the supply of intermediate collective goods. In industries or markets where these factors are significant, there will therefore be some offset to the beneficial effects of competition and free entry on optimality of final output and on internal or X-efficiency (see Leibenstein, 1966). Restriction of competition will still involve allocative distortions in the mix of output, e.g. providing bank buildings rather than bank services. But the standard depressive effect on total output then runs together with an expansionary effect from the support given to collective intermediate goods. This article suggests that banking can fruitfully be regarded as an industry subject to such ambivalence in the net impact of competition. This view suggests a positive explanation for the worldwide phenomenon of cartelisation and/or oligopoly in commercial banking, and for the exercise of central banking functions by public agencies making use of administrative discretion and informal influence.

II

Central banking was pioneered in the British banking system, and in that system it embodied an informal control mechanism. The Bank of England grew into its responsibility for the stability of the London money market as a natural outcome of its position as the dominant bank, and as the bank endowed with privileges of note issue and banker to the government. Acceptance by the Bank of England of the function of lender of last resort gave it leverage over the institutions that enjoyed direct or indirect access to this facility, and enabled it to influence their normal operation and management. Exertion of this leverage was helped by the closely knit social connections between the leading City institutions.[4] But the influence also ran the other way, with the Bank's paternalism reinforcing the existing club and keeping newcomers out. The closely knit social pattern of the British financial system was traditionally seen as a factor of stability and strength, e.g. in the 1931 crisis (see, e.g., Truptil, 1936).[5]

In the 1950s and 1960s the growth ethos turned attention to the nether side of institutional stability, now seen as a potential impediment to efficiency and innovation. The social connections permeating the British financial system were exposed to prominent public view in the evidence of the Parker Tribunal (1957)

[4] Leading merchant banking families such as the Barings and the Normans participated in the management of the Bank of England as directors and as governors; professional management was introduced only in the 1930s and became dominant only in the 1960s.

[5] Truptil emphasised the importance of Oxbridge connections as well as family ties in the development of trust and the exchange of information, and the collective concern felt for safeguarding the reputation of the City. He cites with approval an encomium in the *Financial News* that 'A city which for six months on end can obey a sanctionless ordinance to refrain from issuing foreign loans . . . is no mere agglomeration of banks and brokers, but an organism knit together by bonds of a finer fibre than the common desire to make money'. *Op. cit.*, p. 197.

and the Radcliffe Committee (1959), and became a target of criticism (see in particular Lupton and Wilson, 1959; Devons, 1959; Artis, 1965). A growing chorus called for British banking to be opened to competition by downgrading informal and administrative controls, which were seen as protecting existing institutions. Academic analysts in Britain, less concerned than their predecessors with institutional arrangements, increasingly argued that the basis of official regulation should be switched to a general and in principle anonymous control over the supply of money and/or credit. They were backed part of the way by official agencies concerned with competition rather than financial regulation (see Griffiths, 1970; NBPI, 1967; Johnson, 1967; Monopolies Commission, 1968; Artis, 1968). The new approach was partially accepted by the British authorities in 1971,[6] when the political pendulum as well as economic fashion had swung in favour. In conjunction with an expansionary monetary policy, the liberalisation of banking regulation produced a major credit boom, and ensuing inflation of stock exchange and property values. The subsequent collapse of this boom in turn brought illiquidity, and in a number of cases consequential insolvency, to the new banks that had played a big part in fuelling it.

To check the contagion, the Bank of England reverted to traditional habits. The established 'primary' banks were organised to mount a collective rescue operation, ensuring that no depositors in British banks lost money. Foreign parent companies of subsidiaries and consortium banks in London were obliged to take responsibility for any losses incurred by their British offshoots. The significant characteristic of a bank again became its standing with the Bank of England. Banking stability was preserved at its core, but only by closing the ring. The Bagehot function was again associated with paternalism and informal control within a close knit group.

III

The question arises: are there any general factors, unconnected with the historical legacy of particular institutional arrangements and habits, that impede the efficient exercise of a comprehensive backstop function for commercial banking on the basis of arm's length operations, such as would leave the banks to pursue their own direct profit-oriented interests, as constrained only by formalised statutory regulations? One such important general factor can be derived from the economics of imperfect information. The insurance element in central banking—i.e. the insurance provided to both commercial banks and the economy as a whole against illiquidity—can be seen as part of a more general class of problems that has been associated by economic theorists in recent years with imperfect information: and

[6] As enunciated in 'Competition and Credit Control', *Bank of England Quarterly Bulletin*, 1971, pp. 189–93, and address by Governor of the Bank of England, *ibid*, pp. 195–8. Continued concern with protection of the existing institutional structure, and notably of the discount houses, was evident in the selection of bank assets eligible for the reserve base; by including commercial bills and call loans to the London money market which could be backed by government securities, the authorities weakened their control over the money supply. See the critique by Lomax (1971).

more specifically with unequal information in the possession of the two parties to a market transaction.

A pioneering exposition of the effect of asymmetrical information on commercial transactions was provided by Akerlof (1970) in his analysis of the used car market as 'The Market for "Lemons"'. Because I know more about the true condition of the car I have been using than you as a potential buyer can expect to know about it, the price you will be prudently willing to pay will be what it seems to be worth to your eye *less* some discount estimated to represent the deficiencies in quality you may have missed. Obviously, therefore, if my car really is as good as it looks, I will gain by not selling it but continuing to use it myself. Because the market must assume used cars to be lemons, they mostly are: the market for used cars is sub-optimal, and the market for good used cars may be non-existent.

The insurance literature has long recognised the phenomena of adverse selection based on unequal information between buyer and seller (disproportionately many sick people try to get insurance and disproportionately many healthy people self-insure) and of moral hazard (when the insurance pays the bill, you let it run up more than if you paid outright) (see Grubel, 1971). Arrow (1963) has shown that the health insurance market is sub-optimal in total size, and non-existent for those most in need of it.[7] This produces a case for public health insurance on allocational as well as on equity grounds. Yet, institutions of public insurance established as a corrective must be expected, as long as moral hazard is present, to overshoot in the other direction, by the standard criterion of equating consumers' marginal rates of substitution with producers' marginal rates of transformation; as well as needing to find a substitute for the stimulus given by competition to internal or X-efficiency.

This is the economic dilemma in the health industry. But in the case of health, the problem is somewhat mitigated by the existence of time costs and other consumption deterrents (having operations is not pleasant in itself, for most of us); in addition, availability of health services at normal or zero cost to those in greatest physical need (i.e. the unhealthy) can be counted as a distributional benefit in itself,[8] as can substitution of time costs for money costs which encourages consumption by the worse off (see Nichols *et al.*, 1971). These considerations probably explain why in practice we have a state health service, but not a state used car exchange. But we do have a state central bank.

Imperfections in capital and credit markets have long been noted, being most apparent in the phenomenon of credit rationing, but they have usually been

[7] Pauly has contested the appellation 'moral hazard' in this context, on the grounds that an increase in consumption stimulated by a zero price implies individual economic rationality, with no moral connotations. Arrow points out that moral standards of behaviour to reinforce trust (in this case, trust that individuals who seek to insure risks associated with a particular pattern of behaviour will not change that behaviour when they get the insurance), is one means to an efficient solution that may otherwise be unattainable. See Pauly (1968, pp. 531–7) and Arrow (*ibid*, pp. 537–8). In the same vein, Sen (1973a, *op. cit.*) has argued that individualistic preferences, in 'prisoners' dilemma' situations, can be most efficiently met only by non-individualistic behaviour.

[8] This is strongly argued by Sen (1973b, p. 79): 'The national health service has a built-in system of attempting to match payments to needs . . .'.

attributed to institutional imperfections. A different interpretation has recently been put forward by Arrow (1974). He suggests that imperfections are inherent in the characteristics of loan transactions, because they necessitate enforcement of a contract in the uncertain future, which weakens the self-enforcing element. This element of uncertainty makes it especially desirable for the lender to have as much information about the borrower as possible, which can be obtained only by a 'very individualised information-seeking relation which is quite far removed from the arm's length impersonal model of a market.' People who are known and trusted can buy all the banking services they are prepared to pay for; others cannot. Banking and other forms of financial intermediation, we may infer, are less extensively developed than they would be if the information and unenforceability problems did not exist. This leads to familiar gaps and discontinuities in the capital market, some of which are countered by public intervention (small loan agencies, etc.).[9]

The absence of banking services involves associated welfare losses, but no obvious external diseconomies. But the same is not true at the higher level of banking for bankers, as embodied in the lender of last resort function of central banks. A deficiency of 'output' here, in the form of denial of facilities to the risky borrower, may threaten national output as a whole, if it leads to panic and general collapse.

The commercial market institutions that performed some of the functions of a bankers' bank before the emergence of the fully fledged central banking function were inclined to essentially the same dysfunctional selectiveness that has been diagnosed for the purely commercial health insurance agency. That is to say, they preferred to avoid the risks that most needed to be covered and to withdraw altogether in the face of a threatened crisis in the system, involving uncertainty of a kind that commercial insurance cannot allow for.[10] Hence Bagehot's behest to the Bank of England to reverse the banker's normal instinct in a crisis and to lend more freely rather than less. But provision of banking reinsurance beyond the scope forthcoming on a commercial basis would itself tend to induce distortions of the kind

[9] The non-existence of markets in future contingencies, including markets in forward exchange for more than six or twelve months, is a more familiar example of the influence discussed in this paragraph. For Friedman and his school, the failure of such markets to develop is explained by the intrusion of arbitrary intervention of governments and central banks, and anticipation of such intervention. The Arrow approach suggests rather that only government can be expected to create or under-write such markets, either because the social risks involved are less than the sum of individual risks, or because government decides to shoulder uncertainty that market institutions shun. The same line of thought gives a rationale for official exchange market intervention in general (Fred Hirsch, *Comment*, IMF conference on The New International Monetary System, 1977, forthcoming).

[10] This inclination towards a *sauve qui peut* strategy—i.e. action that is individually optimal but collectively second best and perhaps disastrous—admittedly tends to be checked in an oligopolistic structure, in which the small-numbers characteristic allows the collective good of mutual credit support to be produced on a voluntary basis. However, this basis is inherently uncertain, and thereby lacking in assurance. Moreover, oligopolies may choose to renounce possible short term gains from stabilising action in the expectation of strengthening or protecting their market dominance over a longer term, i.e. they may let outside or otherwise disfavoured competition go to the wall and reckon on riding out the consequences themselves. The collapse of the Bank of the United States in 1930 may be interpreted in this light (see footnote 12).

noted in the case of public health insurance—viz. encouraging extravagance or carelessness (moral hazard) and consequential excess 'output' of banking services for the public.

A familiar example of this phenomenon on the international plane is the granting of commercial credits and other short term loans to governments and other borrowers beyond their prospective capacity to repay, in the expectation that the commercial lenders will be baled out by their own authorities, whether through specific credit insurance cover or in the context of a negotiated debt re-scheduling. Moral hazard virtually rules out insurance of loans on a commercial basis.

The extra-market facility accordingly demands an extra-market control mechanism. In England this developed in a natural way, and completely consistently with Bagehot's pragmatic and eclectic approach, as informal control exercised through paternalistic and moral leadership within a small-numbers group.[11]

A striking recent manifestation of this tendency was seen in Britain in 1973–74 with the virtual collapse of the 'fringe banks' (i.e. banking newcomers: the appellation exactly captures the implicit presumption of an established banking fraternity). This new sector of British banking was laid low by a panic of pre-Bagehotian severity. When the first such banks ran into difficulties in December 1973, and it became clear that the fire break was to be drawn around the newcomer banks rather than among them, new deposits were immediately switched to established banks; and all banks outside the protected circle experienced large attempted withdrawals of deposits, so that their fate was sealed. The underlying cause was an erosion of asset values through the collapse of the property market in which these banks had been heavily involved. The resulting threat to solvency set off a consequential liquidity drain in deposit withdrawals.

A banking name in Britain has always had a special cash value deriving from rules of access to facilities at the Bank of England, notably the requirement that commercial bills eligible for re-discount at the Bank must bear two approved British names, normally of members of the Accepting Houses Association. In the past this made the most practicable means of breaking into British banking the acquisition of an existing but tired merchant bank as a 'shell'. This route has never been available for injection of competition into deposit banking, which has now

[11] Bagehot, as one of his few hostile critics has indelicately pointed out, was through his family bank of Stuckey's a not uninterested party: 'He was recommending *other people* to lend freely, in time of panic, as a way of saving Bagehot.' (Sisson, 1972, p. 97) Bagehot made clear that he would have preferred the responsibility for maintaining the 'ultimate banking reserve' to have been spread among a number of comparably sized leading banks, and was merely recognising the accomplished fact of the Bank of England's dominance (*Op. cit.*, pp. 65–70). This passage has sometimes been regarded as an aberration in which Bagehot failed to understand Bagehot, since the concept of a spontaneous joint effort to fulfil the reserve function misses the potential conflict between private and collective interest in reserve banking for a bank other than one dominant in size. But the anomaly appears rather less if the banks are assumed to be not pure individual profit maximisers but institutions imbued with a felt responsibility for doing their part to preserve order in the system. Bagehot, like John Stuart Mill, took it for granted that private behaviour was substantially permeated by collective norms, so it is not surprising that the collective good 'problem' seen by modern economists was less obtrusive.

become largely divided between a four member oligopoly. The established banks were effectively required, through the informal network, to commit their resources through the 'lifeboat committee' to avoiding losses to depositors of the fringe banks. Some banks indicated their displeasure at the imposition. The complaint detracted attention from the main significance of the episode for the British banking structure. For individual banks, the tying up of funds in a joint support operation is an irritant. For the established banks collectively, the rescue operation marks the removal of a source of competition, at least compared with the *status quo ante* and a situation in which central bank support was available to all banks.

The informal controls and established patterns of behaviour which underpin official regulation of the banking structure in Britain constitute a mechanism closer to the understanding of the sociologist than of the modern neo-classical economist thinking in terms of optimisation subject to a budget, but not social, constraint. It is significant that while Friedman cites Bagehot with approval, he strongly favours the downgrading of re-discounting and its substitution by the more impersonal mechanism of open market operations. In this approach, controls against abuse of central bank facilities would be limited to explicit statutory regulations, such as reserve requirements—possibly at 100 per cent—which might eliminate the need for compulsory deposit insurance (see Friedman, 1959, *op. cit.*; Friedman and Schwartz, 1963, especially chapter 7; also the review of the former work by Lerner, 1962).

But appropriate general regulations are notoriously difficult to lay down. Balance sheet ratios have well known weaknesses as a control device. In Revell's (1974) recent assessment: 'What the supervisory authorities must aim at is being able to put themselves in the position of the management of each bank . . . no set rule-of-thumb ratios can substitute for this vicarious participation in the management process.' The various overlapping banking authorities in the United States attempt in principle a comprehensive and detached review which fits the category of Revell's vicarious management (see Pesek and Saving, 1968, chapter II; and Kaufman, 1973, pp. 86–8).

IV

Resistance to this degree of intervention by public authorities requires a readiness to endure the failure of particular banks, relying on the support given to the aggregate money supply through open market operations to maintain stability. The adequacy of this approach has never been tested, and Friedman himself does not push it to its limits.[12] The Federal Reserve in 1969 gave serious consideration to

[12] Witness Friedman's emphasis on the especial importance of the failure of the Bank of the United States in December 1930. The refusal by the leading New York banks to respond to appeals from the New York Federal Reserve to rescue this bank with predominantly Jewish connections, a refusal which Friedman has associated with anti-Semitism, illustrates how dependent any private substitute for the Bagehot function is on social affinity and eventual solidarity (Friedman and Schwartz, *op. cit.*, pp. 308–11).

supporting the paper of Penn Central (see Maisel, 1973, pp. 41–5 and 122). In 1974 the New York Federal Reserve Bank gave massive support to the Franklin National Bank, in the view that failure of the bank would have serious adverse consequences for its depositors and creditors and would have 'jeopardised the stability of the United States banking system, with further serious repercussions for domestic and international financial markets in general' (see Federal Reserve Bank of New York, 1974). To be sure, the Federal Reserve like other central banks attempts to draw lines between depositors, other creditors, management and equity shareholders. Maximum protection for depositors,[13] combined with full exposure for the equity and risk of dismissal for management, would serve the insurance function while retaining some restraints against moral hazard in the form of excessive risk taking by bank managements. But a distinction of this kind, even if successfully applied, is not sufficient to prevent contingent support for depositors from encouraging banking concentration. To maintain the balance between banks of different size, it would be necessary in addition for the public to be persuaded that the central bank is prepared to allow the largest banks to go under as readily as smaller banks.

In the nervous atmosphere caused by a small crop of bank failures in the third quarter of 1974, placements of large money market deposits both nationally and internationally immediately became more selective; and the dominating principle of selection was a bank that was sure of having its central bank behind it. Marked differentials developed in rates on certificates of deposits of different banks, with size and preeminence being taken as the main general criterion. The largest international banks such as the Chase Manhattan and the First National City were widely believed to be overwhelmed with offers of very large deposits in this period, and consequently shaded down their offered rates on such deposits—a reversal of the normal premium on deposit size.[14]

This tendency exposed a continuing dilemma faced by central banks anxious to prevent their support of banking stability from weakening banking competition and long term banking efficiency. The central bank has to find a means of checking moral hazard. It can take the 'English' route of informal controls and inculcation of a club spirit among the commercial banks to play the game according to the

[13] Deposit insurance in the United States by the Federal Deposit Insurance Corporation is limited to small deposits up to a limit recently raised from $20,000 to $40,000; this still leaves one third of deposit volume uncovered.

[14] In the London market for dollar certificates of deposits, the list of issuer names acceptable to the majority of institutional buyers was described by a market participant as having become very narrow indeed—'perhaps as few as seven names being universally acceptable' (Clark, 1975, p. 43). Between end-April and July 1974, banks with total deposits of $500 million or more accounted for nearly 90 per cent of the increase in large time deposits issued to individuals, partnerships and corporations, increasing their share of the total from 74.2 to 75.9 per cent. The Federal Reserve Board had earlier referred to 'an increased preference by some investors for the liabilities of a small number of the largest commercial banks' in an atmosphere of 'heightened public concern about the stability of financial institutions' in the third quarter of 1974 (*Federal Reserve Bulletin*, January 1975, p. 13, and November 1974, p. 748).

established conventions which are seen to be in the interests of all participants.[15] In return for the insurance premium of responsible behaviour, insurance cover is comprehensive and assured. Participation in such an arrangement must obviously be limited to those who can be trusted to be responsible—call them gentlemen. This will mean excluding those not known to be gentlemen; and they will be those not known to existing gentlemen. So entry will be socially controlled, and competition discouraged.[16]

The alternative strategy is for the central bank to attempt to exert its counterforce to moral hazard through a continued market discipline which makes no demands on commercial banks to depart from their individual profit orientation but confronts them with a contingent risk of failure. Insurance here is less than comprehensive and available only along with significant self insurance (e.g. of the equity and of large deposits, which are in effect 'deductibles' from the insured risk).[17] This may be categorised as the German and to the lesser extent the American approach to the lender of last resort function. The difficulty with this approach is that it appears unlikely in practice to be applied evenly to banks of different size, because failure of big banks is generally, and surely correctly, regarded as more disruptive to the financial system than failure of small ones. Consequently, the greater the perceived risk of particular banks being allowed to go under, the greater will be the tendency for bank depositors to seek shelter in the banks considered too large for the authorities to subject to such therapy, and the greater the tendency towards banking concentration. It is significant in this context that the country in which the Bagehot function is perhaps least entrenched, Germany, is also the country in which the large banks are especially dominant, not only within banking but in ownership and control of industry.

The general point can be put as follows. In principle, the regulatory authorities may aim to preserve the sanctions against bank equity and management to maintain solvency, while relieving the mass of bank depositors and the banking system as a whole of the risk of illiquidity. In practice, solvency and liquidity are not fully separable, since insolvency is often exposed only under liquidity stress. Enforced liquidation itself usually depresses the value of assets. Large banks that can count on the confidence of the public, based ultimately on the unwillingness of the authorities to face the repercussions of the bank's default to even large depositors and perhaps also other creditors, thereby enjoy a cushion against careless bank management that is denied to smaller banks.

Thus, informal controls lead to cartelisation; 'market' controls to oligopoly. Whichever strategy the central banking authorities choose, their ultimate support

[15] Informal controls play an important role also in a number of continental European countries, notably Switzerland.

[16] Entry of new participants will tend to be further restricted by the general tendency for informal agreements to become more difficult to enforce as the size of the group increases. This is well established in the literature on collective goods. See for example Olson (1965).

[17] Henry C. Wallich, a governor of the Federal Reserve Board, has referred to bank capital as self-insurance and deposit insurance as pooled insurance. ('Some Thoughts on Capital Adequacy', Speech at a Management Seminar, Washington, D.C., February 28, 1975, mimeograph.)

for banking stability tends to discourage banking competition. Neither strategy, therefore, is dominant as a means of promoting internal efficiency. In addition, non-market controls are needed to attain the allocation that a market with perfect information would reach, and to give individuals the benefit of the transactions they will relinquish if they take advantage of their opportunity to 'cheat' (i.e. alter their behaviour) in response to market opportunity (see also footnote 7). As Arrow (1968, *op. cit.*) has emphasised, truth and trust are preconditions of well functioning markets; yet the habits of truth and trust cannot be expected to result from individual optimisation, except perhaps in small and immobile communities where any benefit from transgressions is relinquished by the future costs imposed by the damage to reputation. Therefore: 'Non-market controls, whether internalised as moral principles or externally imposed, are to some extent essential for efficiency.' The non-market controls that permeate banking systems underpin efficient banking, as well as often undermining it.

V

An unresolved question hovering over the international financial system is how the huge continuing surpluses of most of the oil exporting countries will be channelled through that system: and, specifically, whether it will continue to be sound and feasible for the bulk of the funds to be channelled, as they have been since 1974, through the private sector and predominantly through the banks in unmanaged market processes. In a continuing refrain, what is so special about this problem that the market, left to itself, cannot handle it? The answer to this refrain should probably be: that it is a banking problem, which the market left to itself has never been able to handle, for solid but neglected reasons of economic theory.

The difficulty is that the means of public intervention that can themselves make good the market deficiency involve unwanted side effects that can bring new distortions. Domestically, in the development of the stabilising and insurance functions of central banking and bank supervision, these objectives have conflicted in some part with the objective of maximum competition and arm's length controls free of paternalism and of subjective official judgments about banking business. It remains uncertain whether the full Bagehot function can be fulfilled in a system in which the key banks extend further than the length of a Lombard Street, in social space as distinct from geographical space. This poses an obvious obstacle to the international extension of the Bagehot function. But the pressure for such extension has undoubtedly been increased by the large additions to the funds seeking placement through the international banking system as disposition of the oil surpluses. This suggests that some of the same side effects of central banking that have encouraged banking concentration at the national level may now be extended internationally.

Nor is it fanciful to envisage as a concomitant the international extension of informal controls and élite groups. The arena for such socialisation has existed for some time in the growing contact between top commercial bankers and financial officials of other countries, contacts that are formalised at annual gatherings such as those of the American Bankers' Association, and at the inner core of the annual meetings of the International Monetary Fund. The chairman of the Federal Reserve Board, Dr. Arthur Burns, has recently proposed more formal coordination, under which commercial banks would align their loan terms with the IMF and would be given partial access to its information.[18]

The support in financial circles for a wider role for international official financing has stemmed in large part from the over-exposure of commercial banks operating in a competitive environment. Yet, it is difficult to foresee on the international plane more than a minimal degree of cohesion and informal controls by the standards prevailing in the parish of the Bank of England. To this extent the potentiality for international extension of the Bagehot function remains ambiguous, reflecting the same ambiguity as exists in the scope for a lender of last resort in a domestic banking system regulated only at arm's length.

REFERENCES

Akerlof, G. A. (1970). 'The Market for "Lemons": Qualitative Uncertainty and the Market Mechanism', *Quarterly Journal of Economics*, Vol. LXXXIV, No. 3, pp. 488–500.

Arrow, K. J. (1963). 'Uncertainty and the Welfare Economics of Medical Care', *American Economic Review*, Vol. LIII, No. 5, pp. 941–73.

— (1968). 'The Economics of Moral Hazard: Further Comment', *American Economic Review*, Vol. LVIII, No. 3, Part I, pp. 537–80.

— (1972). 'Gifts and Exchanges', *Philosophy & Public Affairs*, Vol. I, No. 4, pp. 343–63.

— (1974). 'Limited Knowledge and Economic Analysis', *American Economic Review*, Vol. LXIV, No. I, pp. 1–10.

Artis, M. J. (1965). *Foundations of British Monetary Policy*, Oxford, Oxford University Institute of Economics and Statistics Monograph 9.

—. (1968). 'The Monopolies Commission Report', *Bankers' Magazine*, Vol. 206, No. 1494, pp. 128–135; reprinted in Johnson, H. G. (ed.), *Readings in British Monetary Economics*, Oxford, Clarendon Press, 1972.

Bagehot, W. (1915). *Lombard Street* (14th edition), London, John Murray.

Bank of England (1971). 'Competition and Credit Control', *Bank of England Quarterly Bulletin*, Vol. 11, No. 2.

Clark, J. B. (1975). 'Top Seven Only Please', *Euromoney*, February, p. 43.

Devons, E. (1959). 'An Economist's View of the Bank Rate Tribunal Evidence', *The Manchester School*, Vol. XXVII, No. 1, pp. 1–16.

Federal Reserve Bank of New York (1974). *Annual Report*, New York, Federal Reserve Bank.

Federal Reserve Board (1974). 'Financial Developments in the Third Quarter of 1974', *Federal Reserve Bulletin*, Vol. 60, No. 11, p. 748.

— (1975). 'Changes in Time and Savings Deposits at Commercial Banks, April–July 1974', *Federal Reserve Bulletin*, Vol. 61, No. 1, p. 13.

[18] Speech in New York reported in the *Financial Times*, April 14, 1977.

Friedman, M. (1959). *A Program for Monetary Stability*, New York, Fordham University Press.

— and Schwartz, A. (1963). *A Monetary History of the U.S., 1867–1960*, Princeton, Princeton University Press.

Griffiths, B. (1970). *Competition in Banking* (Hobart Paper 51), London, The Institute of Economic Affairs.

Grubel, H. G. (1971). 'Risk, Uncertainty and Moral Hazard', *Journal of Risk and Insurance*, Vol. 38, No. 1, pp. 99–106.

Hayek, F. A. (1976). *Choice in Currency* (Occasional Paper 48), London, The Institute of Economic Affairs.

Hirsch, F. (1977). *Social Limits to Growth*, London, Routledge & Kegan Paul.

Johnson, H. G. (1967). 'The Report on Bank Charges', *Bankers' Magazine*, Vol. 204, No. 1481, pp. 64–8; reprinted in Johnson, H. G. (ed.), *Readings in British Monetary Economics*, Oxford, Clarendon Press, 1972.

Johnson, H. G. (1968). 'Problems of Efficiency in Monetary Management', *Journal of Political Economy*, Vol. 76, No. 5, pp. 971–90; reprinted in Johnson, H. G. (ed.), *op. cit.*

Kaufman, G. F. (1973). *Money, the Financial System and the Economy*, London, Rand McNally.

Klein, B. (1974). 'The Competitive Supply of Money', *Journal of Money, Credit and Banking*, Vol. VI, No. 4, pp. 423–53.

Leibenstein, H. (1966). 'Allocative Efficiency Versus X-Efficiency', *American Economic Review*, Vol. LVI, No. 3, pp. 392–415.

Lerner, A. P. (1962). 'Review of Milton Friedman, *A Program for Monetary Stability*', *American Statistical Association Journal*, Vol. 57, pp. 211–20; reprinted in Mittra, S. (ed.), *Money and Banking*, New York, Random House, 1970.

Lomax, D. F.(1971). 'The New Credit Controls', *The Banker*, Vol. 121, No. 548, pp. 1160–5.

Lupton, T. and Wilson, C. S. (1959). 'The Social Background and Connections of "Top Decision Makers"', *The Manchester School*, Vol. XXVII, No. 1, pp. 30–51.

Maisel, S. J. (1973). *Managing the Dollar*, New York, Norton.

Monopolies Commission (1968). *Report on Proposed Bank Merger*, London, H.M.S.O.

National Board for Prices & Incomes (1967). *Bank Charges*, Report No. 34, Cmnd. 3292, London, H.M.S.O.

Nichols, D., Smolensky, E. and Tideman, T. N. (1971). 'Discrimination in Waiting Time by Merit Goods', *American Economic Review*, Vol. LXI, No. 3, Part 1, pp. 312–23.

Olson, M. (1965). *The Logic of Collective Action*, Cambridge, Mass., Harvard University Press.

Parker Tribunal (1957). *Tribunal to Inquire into Allegations of Improper Disclosure of Information Relating to the Raising of Bank Rate, Report and Proceedings*, London, H.M.S.O.

Pauly, M. V. (1968). 'The Economics of Moral Hazard: Comment', *American Economic Review*, Vol. LVIII, No. 3, Part 1, pp. 531–7.

Pesek, B. and Saving, T. R. (1968). *The Foundations of Money and Banking*, New York, Macmillan & Co.

Radcliffe Committee (1959). *Committee on the Working of the Monetary System, Report*, Cmnd. 827, and *Minutes of Evidence* (1960), London, H.M.S.O.

Revell, J. (1974). 'The Solvency of Banks', *The Banker*, Vol. 124, No. 575, pp. 29–31.

Sen, A. (1973a). 'Behaviour and the Concept of Preference', *Economica*, Vol. XL, No. 159, pp. 241–59.

Sen, A. (1973b). *On Economic Inequality*, Oxford, Clarendon Press.
Sisson, C. H. (1972). *The Case of Walter Bagehot*, London, Faber & Faber.
Truptil, R. J. (1936). *British Banks and the London Money Market*, London, Jonathan Cape.
Williamson, J. (1973). 'International Liquidity: A Survey', *Economic Journal*, Vol. 83, No. 331, pp. 685–746.

11

On the Lender of Last Resort

ROBERT M. SOLOW

I. INTRODUCTION

In this chapter I must try to walk a narrow line. My task is to discuss the role of the lender of last resort from the point of view of a theorist interested in economic policy. That seems to be the natural role for the theorist of last resort. Everyone at this conference knows more than I do about the historical and institutional texture of lenders of last resort, and most know more about the history of economic thought on the subject. That very fact suggests that no one at this conference wants to see real (or even nominal) theorist's theorizing, complete with hard mathematical models. So I shall aim for a compromise. My goal is to indicate in a general way what economic theory has to say on the two main analytical questions that generally arise in discussions of this subject.

The first question seems to be this: Is there a case for having a lender of last resort? In terms of the domestic economy, the only candidate in practice is the central bank. Should it stand ready, under well-defined circumstances, presumably including but not limited to situations of general credit stringency, to lend freely to private financial institutions, perhaps suspending the normal standards of credit-worthiness? In terms of the international economy, the same question can be asked, but if there is to be a lender of last resort it might have to be an institution yet to be created, and its potential borrowers might well include national central banks. In any case, because I owe to C. P. Kindleberger, the guiding spirit of this conference, the dictum that 'We don't pay Solow to think about international economics,' I shall think mostly about a national lender of last resort; but the issues I intend to take up are general enough so that the context is almost unimportant.

The second question to be discussed follows naturally: Does a serious problem of 'moral hazard' arise whenever there is an effective lender of last resort? Does the existence of a credible commitment by the central bank to lend freely in time of trouble lead to the assumption of excessive risk by private banks in exactly the same way in which a family that is insured against theft may be excessively careless about locking up a house or a car before leaving it? The force of the term *excessive* here is not merely that banks or families may exercise less than socially optimal amounts of care because with insurance the net marginal social value of care exceeds its net marginal private value. In both the instances mentioned the existence of insurance may have the particularly perverse effect of increasing the incidence of the contingency being insured against—bank failures in one case and burglaries in the other. The answer to this second question is pretty obviously 'Yes.' The point of putting so easy a question is that the process of answering it will suggest what sorts of rules or devices might be expected to mitigate the consequences of moral hazard. I shall have a few words to say on that subject.

II. THE NEED FOR A LENDER OF LAST RESORT

Any fractional-reserve banking system is in principle vulnerable to runs. There is no guarantee that runs will occur, or occur often, but the possibility is there. If a run does occur, there is always a chance that it will cumulate, because any bank failure diminishes confidence in the whole system and brings stronger banks under increased pressure. The consequences of a banking crisis are likely to extend beyond the banking system into the 'real' economy. Any developed capitalist economy supports a network of interrelated debtor–creditor relations. Inability of *A* to meet obligations to *B* may impair *B*'s ability to meet obligations to *C*, and production may suffer as a result. The function of the lender of last resort is to stop such a chain reaction in its earliest stages, before it has a chance to cumulate, by visibly providing ample credit to keep the weaker links from giving way. This protection need not extend to the weakest links.

In the English-language literature the classic case for aggressive emergency use of its lending power by the central bank was, of course, Walter Bagehot's *Lombard Street* (1873). Actually, as early as 1802 the remarkable Henry Thornton argued quite forcefully that the Bank of England should use its reserves early and strongly to meet an internal drain of cash from the banks. Thornton understood clearly the role of the lender of last resort; witness this recent exegesis from *Paper Credit* (Reisman, 1971, p. 82): 'In Thornton's model the Bank should be at its freest in loans to the banks and the public precisely when risk and need are greatest and the Bank's gold is least, if only so that the total quantity of money in circulation does not decrease. . . . The Bank should not relieve those banks whose difficulties arise from "improvidence" or "misconduct" [although] the alternative to relief would be letting the bank fail, and this would shatter that very confidence in the credit system which is so necessary for the pyramiding of claims.'

John Hicks, in his essay on Thornton (1967. p. 187), elaborates on what he describes as an 'essential idea of Thornton's':

> Every economy is liable to unexpected shocks—of which the harvest failures, that are Thornton's principal example, are of course no more than an example. One of the things which we should require of economic organization is that its institutions should be such that it can stand up to shocks; that it should have cushions against them, so that their secondary repercussions are minimized, not intensified by the fears and alarms that they so easily engender. But there are few cushions that will drop into place automatically; the most that is usually possible is that there should be reserves which can be used, if there are people who have the skill and courage to use them, at the right and not at the wrong time.

> A developed credit system . . . has the advantage over a pure hard money system, in that its reserves are in places where they can more readily be used, if there is the intelligence and the strength of will to use them. It is, of course, only too true that these essential qualities may not be there. But to fall back on rules, making the monetary system mechanical, is a confession of failure.

Bagehot, by the way, also commented that 'the practical difficulties of life cannot be met by simple rules,' and he would no doubt have applied this piece of wisdom to central banking. I mention this bit about rules only to remind everyone that there is another point of view. In *A Program for Monetary Stability* (1960, pp. 37–8), Milton Friedman takes the opposite position on central-bank emergency lending. At the beginning, 'The Reserve System was to be a "lender of last resort," ready to provide liquidity in a time of crisis to satisfy a widespread demand for currency that otherwise would produce either suspension of payments or a substantial decline in the stock of money.' After the passage of the Federal Deposit Insurance Act, however, depositors have no reason to fear that their deposits might become inconvertible into currency. 'A liquidity crisis involving such runs on a widespread scale is now almost inconceivable. The need for rediscounting in order for the Reserve System to serve as "a lender of last resort" has therefore become obsolete, not because the function has been taken over by someone else but because it no longer needs to be performed.'

If Friedman is anti-Thornton, let me quote Harry Johnson as anti-Bagehot: 'At least in the presence of a well-developed capital market, and on the assumption of intelligent and responsible monetary management by the central bank, the commercial banks should be able to manage their own reserve positions without the need for the central bank to function as "lender of last resort".'

The proviso about intelligent and responsible monetary management is pretty sweeping. It comes close to saying that if central banks are smart enough to avoid liquidity crises they will not need to do the things they are supposed to do in liquidity crises. Both Johnson and Friedman seem to pay too little attention to nonbank financial institutions and their stability, and this failure is consistent with the normal monetarist fixation on M_1 as means of payment. Others would at least ask whether or not the central bank, or some other arm of the government, ought to be prepared to act as lender of last resort directly or indirectly to a wider class of financial institutions to avoid instability in the financial mechanism defined a little more broadly than currency and demand deposits. I do not think the answer is open-and-shut, but the question can be asked. It should be mentioned that Friedman has supported a 100% reserve requirement for checking accounts. This would sever the maintenance of the payments mechanism from any connection with the credit market. One might still want deposit insurance as protection against embezzlement, but there would be no way for bad debts to infect the payments mechanism or vice versa. Then, as Friedman could correctly point out, the lender of last resort would be a lot like the buyer of agricultural commodities of last resort, and the desirability of having one would be suddenly more problematical.

I am not sure that theory has much to contribute to this issue. There is, of course, an inevitable pure-externality aspect associated with the interlocking debt structure.

My bank may go under, and I may suffer a loss, because we are at the far end of a chain reaction launched by the inability of some other debtor to pay a creditor who . . . . But one expects bank depositors, like other lenders, to look into the soundness of their banks. The capital market will and should offer a range of risk–yield combinations, and those who choose to live dangerously have to expect to take a tumble now and then. That does not call for a rescue operation. Lenders and depositors can legitimately be expected to know something about the asset structure they are buying into, but it may be asking too much to expect them to see through the thrice-removed financial interrelationships that might ultimately cause trouble. If that argument is accepted, there is clearly a case for intervention, and the lender of last resort seems like a good form for the intervention to take.

The cumulative chain reaction is an important part of this argument. My goose-down business may suffer because of some events involving labor relations in the industry manufacturing the cables that carry ski lifts, but hardly anyone would regard that complicated story as a case for indemnifying wholesalers of goose down. The difference appears to be that the Ski Lift Story is expected to damp quickly; the process is effectively stable, self-limiting. The financial panic is an unstable system; small differences in initial conditions lead to vast differences in the final outcome.

That, at least, seems to be the logic of the argument. Its empirical truth or falsity is another matter. How far would the waves and ripples have traveled if the Franklin National had simply been allowed to fail? Does anyone know? Did the rescue operation stage-managed by the Fed head off a panic, even a minipanic, or did it simply bail out a few big shots? One could argue that merely to count noses, after allowance for deposit insurance, is an inadequate measure of the potential damage, because any blow to confidence in the banking system may later prove highly destabilizing. On the other hand, it is inadequate to rest on the fact that financial panics do happen; the optimal flood-control system will not necessarily reduce the probability of overflow to zero. All the theorist can say is that there is a potentially sound argument that rests on the unstable propagation of disturbance through the financial system, beyond the bounds of what ordinary prudence can be expected to cope with. For the very same reason, private insurance cannot be expected to meet the system's needs, because what needs to be insured against is a crisis on a scale too large for any private lender. But it is not obvious, especially in the presence of deposit insurance, that the instability is really there.

Throughout its history the Federal Deposit Insurance Corporation has had an upper limit on the coverage provided on any one account (that maximum is now $40,000). The logic of this limit presumably has been that the small depositor cannot be expected to judge the ultimate soundness of his bank. One consequence of this limit has been that the FDIC has been generally unwilling to let a major bank fail and trigger the payment of insurance, because a substantial fraction of aggregate deposits would go uncovered. In the case of the U.S. National Bank of San Diego in 1973, with almost a billion dollars in deposits, only about three-quarters of aggregate deposit liabilities would have been covered by deposit insurance.

In this case of the Franklin National Bank, pretty clearly a case of poor management, only about half of the $1.7 billion in deposit liabilities would have been covered. The FDIC has generally tried, in such cases, to arrange a takeover of the weak bank by a solvent one, perhaps with the help of an infusion of FDIC funds. The argument has been that partial payoff of insurance would not be enough to maintain confidence in the banking system as a whole. On FDIC policy, see the work of Varvel (1976).

All this suggests a slightly different way to describe the role of the lender of last resort in terms of the categories of economic theory. One could argue, with some justice, that a confidence-worthy and confidence-inspiring monetary-financial system is a public good. Exactly like the standard textbook examples—national defense, the cop on the beat—it necessarily spreads its benefits over those who contribute to it and those who do not. The advantages of a well-functioning monetary-financial system are not divided up, like coffee, but shared, like peace. As with any public good, the problem of the free rider intrudes. It may profit any individual to do things that undermine the stability of the monetary-financial system, so long as everyone else plays the game. Everyone is then a potential free rider. If the stability of the monetary-financial system is not looked after by a public body, it will be inadequately looked after, perhaps not at all.

I think that is a sound argument. I have tried to call attention to the one important weakness in it by using the awkward phrase 'the monetary-financial system.' Reasonable people could differ about the size of the umbrella that should be provided. At the core, I suppose everyone would include the payments mechanism; a drift toward barter is bound to be inefficient. But 100% reserve banking or deposit insurance is probably enough to prevent a breakdown of the payments mechanism. At the other extreme, hardly anyone would wish the lender of last resort to provide backstop credit for even fundamentally solvent mutual funds. Somewhere there is a line to be drawn, and I tend to side with Thornton and Bagehot that it is better to rely on sometimes fallible judgment than to try to draw the line once for all times and occasions.

Neither mode of operation is without its problems, as pointed out by Fred Hirsch (1977). Any informal system that leaves a lot to the discretion of the central bank is open to refined corruption. The authorities will have to protect the system from exploitation by those who would naturally like to pocket the profits from successful ventures and pass the losses from unsuccessful ones to the lender of last resort. Some sort of code of good behavior is required; the central bank can extend the rescue net only to those who can be trusted not to abuse the privilege. You can trust only those whom you know. The situation is ripe for the emergence of a club of insiders, old-timers, gentlemen, and for the exclusion of newcomers, unknowns, and aggressively competitive upstarts.

The alternative is a system of objective criteria and formal rules. As Hirsch remarks, any such system is bound to provide more complete coverage for large banks than for small ones, and for defensible reasons: If the purpose of the system is to protect the monetary-financial system against socially destructive disturbance, then the failure of a large bank is clearly socially more costly than the failure of a small one. But this provides an incentive for risk-averse depositors to shift from small to large banks and confers a clear competitive advantage on large size. So a formal system can be expected to promote concentration in banking. This can perhaps be regarded as a manifestation of a species of increasing returns to scale; it will be reinforced by the normal advantage that the law of large numbers confers on any large pooler of risks.

It does not follow from this difficulty that the function of lender of last resort costs more than it is worth. If the analogy to increasing returns to scale is acceptable, then the corresponding element of natural monopoly needs to be offset or corrected by regulation. Obviously the regulatory process is itself vulnerable to corruption through the club of insiders, but that problem is common to all regulated industries, not special to the lender of last resort.

III. THE PROBLEM OF MORAL HAZARD

The existence of a credible lender of last resort must reduce the private cost of risk taking. It can hardly be doubted that, in consequence, more risk will be taken. The portfolios of insured financial institutions will be less conservative and their average yields will be higher.

All insurance schemes face this problem, and in that context it is called the problem of moral hazard. I have already mentioned the obvious examples: All of us would be more careful about fire prevention if our houses were not insured against damage from fires. Evidently, then, the availability of fire insurance probably increases the number of fires. The social advantage of fire insurance is that by reducing individual uncertainty in a risk-averse population, it creates benefits that presumably outweigh the extra fire damage that occurs because the insured are less careful than they would otherwise be.

Moral hazard, however, is not confined to ordinary insurance situations. It has been argued recently that the building of levees or dikes may increase the amount of flood damage. The mechanism is similar: In the absence of levees, no one would dare to build in the flood plain. There would be many floods, but little damage each time. When levees are built, people crowd closer to the river. Floods occur very rarely, but cause much more damage when they do occur. This case differs from fire insurance in one respect; there the availability of insurance can be expected to increase the incidence of fires, whereas here the physical incidence of floods decreases, but the damage per incident rises.

The effect of the lender of last resort is something of a mixture. The number of bad debts will rise, like the number of fires. But the number of financial crises will be reduced, like the number of floods. It might be possible, in principle, to build dikes so high and so strong that no flood will ever occur, and therefore no flood losses. But the cost of complete security could easily be so great that it would be preferable to limit the amount of building near the river, either by direct regulation or by other means to be discussed in due course. Financial crises do not have the nice statistical properties of flood crests; I take it for granted that a national (and perhaps an international) lender of last resort would be instructed to permit no panic that it was able to prevent.

Here, I shall digress briefly. No one has a kind word to say in favor of fires and floods. There may, however, be something to be said for risky assets. One can imagine a situation in which it is felt that lenders are too conservative, perhaps because the private cost associated with default exceeds social cost. In that case, at least part of the moral hazard accompanying the introduction of an insurance scheme might be a good thing. The question would then turn on whether or not the increase in portfolio risk goes too far. Thus, for instance, when Governor Zolotas of the Bank in Greece proposes an international loan-insurance scheme (1979, pp. 34–46), his explicit purpose is to encourage the flow of international lending to developing countries despite its riskiness. The motivation in this case is primarily redistribution rather than efficiency, but the point is the same. I do not intend to consider this issue further. It may be important, but it is off the main theoretical track.

Where does the main theoretical track lead? The standard model is an abstraction of the fire-insurance situation; an excellent example is provided by Shavell (1979). A risk-averse consumer can buy an insurance policy against a contingency whose probability of occurrence is known, but it is known as a function of the amount of 'care' taken by the customer himself. The customer pays a premium, which may perhaps be a function of the amount of care taken. If the adverse event happens, the consumer receives an indemnity that may also be a function of the amount of care taken. In the fire-insurance context, care includes such acts as fire-proofing, the installation of alarm systems, the avoidance of certain dangerous activities, and so on. In the context we are concerned with here, care would relate primarily to the characteristics of the assets acquired and the liabilities issued by a financial institution. The relation between the probability of loss and the amount of care is a fact of nature. But the relation between premium and care, or between indemnity and care, is a characteristic of the insurance policy. Taking care is costly to the consumer, in terms of current cash costs or foregone earnings.

Given the terms of the insurance policy, one naturally assumes that the consumer chooses the amount of insurance and the amount of care that maximize the expected value of a utility function. I have already stipulated that the consumer is supposed to be risk-averse (the utility function exhibits diminishing marginal utility of wealth), because otherwise there is no point in insurance. The insurance company or central bank, on the other hand, is quite naturally supposed to pool a lot of relatively small risks; it is therefore risk-neutral and is concerned only with the difference between its premium inflow and its average indemnity outflow. In designing an insurance policy, the insuror (in our case, the lender of last resort) must take account of the fact that consumers will react to the terms of the policy offered by choosing how much care to exercise, and choosing in their own best interest.

If it were not for moral hazard, the problem would be easy. Suppose the contingency in question were a pure act of nature, and care were entirely irrelevant. Then obviously the optimal insurance scheme is full coverage at an actuarially fair premium. With full indemnification in case of loss, everyone is completely relieved of uncertainty, and the law of large numbers guarantees that the insurance company breaks even. In practice, of course, there are administrative costs to be covered, but let us suppose them to be trivial.

The possibility of costly care and the consequent inducement of moral hazard make the problem more difficult. One can ask: What is the socially best insurance policy, taking account of the amount of risk that will actually be borne by the individual consumer and the amount of resources that will be used up in care, given that the insuror must break even (or meet some other specified budget constraint)? The precise answer depends on the precise formulation, but there are some general propositions that would seem to apply to a wide variety of circumstances.

First of all, let us suppose that the degree of care is unobservable by the insuror. That is to say, the lender of last resort cannot discover, ex ante or ex post, the quality of the assets acquired by insured banks and other institutions. Then neither the premium nor the indemnity can depend on the actions of the insured banks. Theory suggests, first of all, that some degree of insurance coverage is desirable, for standard risk-pooling reasons. The first little bit of insurance must gain more social utility by spreading risk than it loses by reducing the amount of care taken. But theory also suggests that insurance coverage should only be partial. A policyholder should be indemnified only for part of any loss suffered, so that some marginal incentive to take care remains. The optimal degree of coverage depends on the cost of care. If care is very expensive, then the policy should offer almost full coverage; the socially optimal amount of care will be small anyhow, and so the risk-sharing motive predominates. If the cost of care is very low, then once again the policy should offer almost full coverage; there will be few losses anyway. In between, partial coverage—coinsurance—is the rule.

An alternative form of coinsurance would be randomization. The contract could specify that a valid claim will be indemnified fully with probability q and partially (or not at all) with probability $1 - q$. Analogous schemes have appeared in the theory of optimal taxation. In principle, the introduction of another degree of freedom in the description of the insurance policy cannot be disadvantageous. But neither does randomization appear to be a practical possibility. Besides, because the object of insurance is the reduction of individual risk, the deliberate creation of additional risk in the insurance contract seems to be an unlikely form of coinsurance.

Now suppose that the insuror can observe the amount of care exercised by the insured. There are two cross-cutting distinctions to be made. The first is between ex ante observation, made at the time the policy is written, and ex post observation, made when a claim is filed. This distinction, which may be important in the ordinary insurance context, is almost empty in the application to financial institutions. Credit-worthiness standards can be stipulated ex ante, but the quality of loans actually made can be verified only ex post. Periodic bank examination is a compromise, though rather more like ex ante observation. The second distinction is between accurate observation and inaccurate observation. The usual theoretical assumption is that a standard of care is imposed in the insurance contract. In the case of ex post observation, the insuror studies each claim that is presented; indemnity is paid if and only if the standard of care has been met. If the observation is noisy, there is a risk that the insured will be judged falsely to have taken inadequate care and deprived unjustly of indemnity.

Suppose observation is accurate. The socially optimal degree of care depends on the cost and effectiveness of care and on the population's degree of risk aversion. Once the right degree of care has been calculated, the correct form of policy imposes that degree of care and then offers full coverage if the standard is met. Ex post observation is presumably cheaper and therefore appropriate. The rationale here is that accurate observation permits the optimal degree of care to be imposed. The danger of moral hazard is effectively eliminated, and risk aversion then calls for the complete elimination of uncertainty.

Even noisy observation is useful in the sense that it permits the design of a better insurance policy. There is some advantage to ex ante observation, because then the premium can be made to depend on the level of care. In the ordinary insurance context, a window-dressing problem may arise. Construction standards can be verified when a policy is issued and a premium agreed, but ongoing items of care (proper waste disposal, day-to-day safety precautions) can be allowed to lapse once the policy is in force. In the banking context, ex ante observation presumably means at least a continuing spot check on the credit-worthiness of accepted borrowers; I leave it to others to judge whether or not this degree of surveillance is reasonable and likely to be achieved.

When observation is imperfect, either in the nature of the case or because it is very costly, the best form of insurance policy is likely to call for partial coverage. Some incentive to take adequate care has to be provided for the insured, and this incentive is self-administered if the insured must share in any loss.

IV. APPLICABILITY TO BANKING

How well does this insurance-inspired theory apply to the situation of the lender of last resort? Imperfectly, I think, but not trivially.

The important difference is in the source of the social value of insurance in the first place. In the context of accident insurance, for which the theory is designed, there need be no important externality. (I emphasize 'need be'—Mrs O'Leary's cow provides the counterexample.) Insurance is desirable because individuals are risk-averse, and everyone gains when risk is shared. There are some intrinsic difficulties with insurance markets, but, in general, one can imagine that the best policies will be generated by competitive insurance companies.

The lender of last resort is bound to be a public body, for several reasons. The most obvious one is scale; for credibility, the lender of last resort needs access to greater resources than any private lender can have. The more important reason is that the primary function of the lender of last resort is not to share default risks among private financial institutions. Banking is a business, not a religion; default risk belongs with stockholders just as fashion risk belongs with clothing manufacturers. The job of the lender of last resort is not to preserve individual banks from failure but to preserve the monetary-financial system from being forced into undesirable deflationary pressure by epidemic loss of confidence in its soundness.

The desirable degree of coverage is likely to be higher for that reason. To take an extreme case, if full or nearly full coverage were required to generate the necessary confidence, then presumably the lender of last resort would offer full indemnification and hope to combat the resulting deterioration of credit standards by other means. Bagehot's insistence that the Bank of England should lend freely but at a penalty rate fits in here. His explanation was that only 'fundamentally sound' banks should be rescued, and a fundamentally sound bank would eventually be able to pay off, with interest. In our language, the fundamentally sound bank is one that has not allowed the availability of insurance to undermine its credit standard. Thus, the penalty rate is a way of reducing moral hazard. It is a form of coinsurance.

Unless there is strong evidence to the contrary, I think one should presume that complete coverage is not necessary for the safety of the monetary-financial system. The theoretical presumption in favor of partial coverage should certainly be the starting point for the design of a lender of last resort.

This impression (it hardly rises to the level of a conclusion) rests also on casual empiricism about the quality of observation. The theory suggests that if observation is cheap and accurate, standards of care should be imposed, and then full coverage offered. That suggestion would be strengthened by the public-good objective of safeguarding the financial system. I doubt that a central bank (or, a fortiori, an international agency) can judge accurately enough the quality of the credit issued by each insured bank. And even if it could, I doubt that it would, partly because of the tendency of regulatory bodies to be co-opted by the regulated via the 'club' mechanism, and partly because there would arise issues of invasion of privacy and national pride.

I suggest that there should indeed be standards, but they will need to be reinforced by some degree of coinsurance. There is a tradeoff: The more stringent the standards, the nearer one can come to full insurance. In choosing a point on that tradeoff schedule, one should keep in mind that the object of the lender of last resort is stabilization of the monetary system, not the protection of bank managements from their own errors of judgment.

REFERENCES

Bagehot (1873) (reprinted 1962). *Lombard Street*. Homewood, Ill.: R. D. Irwin.

Friedman, M. (1960). *A Program for Monetary Stability*. New York: Fordham University Press.

Hicks, J. (1967). *Critical Essays in Monetary Theory*. Oxford: Clarendon Press.

Hirsch (1977). 'The Bagehot Problem.' *Manchester School* 45:241–57.

Reisman, D. A. (1971). 'Henry Thornton and Classical Monetary Economics.' *Oxford Economic Papers* 23:70–89.

Shavell, S. (1979). 'On Moral Hazard and Insurance.' *Quarterly Journal of Economics* 93:541–62.

Thornton, H. (1802) (reprinted 1962). *An Enquiry into the Nature and Effects of the Paper Credit of Great Britain.* London: F. Cass.

Varvel, W. A. (1976). 'FDIC Policy toward Bank Failures.' *Federal Reserve Bank of Richmond Economic Review* September/October, pp. 3–12.

Zolotas, X. (1979). *The Dollar Crisis and Other Papers.* Bank of Greece Papers and Lectures No. 41. Athens: Bank of Greece.

12

Financial Crises, Payment System Problems, and Discount Window Lending (*excerpts*)

MARK J. FLANNERY

A developed economy's basic infrastructure must include a cheap, reliable payment system to facilitate the mutually profitable exchanges required for agents to exploit economies of specialization. A better payment system permits risks to be spread more efficiently, makes prices more informative, and enhances the allocation of real resources. If payments cannot be effected cheaply and reliably, social welfare is constrained to a lower level. Modern economies possess complex payment systems that successfully transmit numerous daily payments, totaling a large fraction of the typical country's GDP. A staggering velocity of monetary claims can be attained in these systems, largely because institutional arrangements have evolved that substitute credit exposures for the immediate payment of 'good money' (Goodfriend 1991).[1] The payment system's credit component constitutes its (potential) Achilles' heel: if traders lose faith in their counterparties' abilities to pay as promised, the costs of transacting within a credit-based system can rise dramatically. The close interconnection of many financial institutions through the payment system has raised public concerns that one firm's failure could jeopardize the solvency of many others.[2] Because the payment system is so crucial to a modern economy's functioning, its potential failure—'payment system risk'—elicits great concern: 'without doubt the most important public policy issue of global application is the containment or elimination of payment system risk' (Morris 1994, p. 18). The proper role of a government lender of last resort (LLR) in producing payment system stability has become an increasingly relevant and important question in recent years.

Many writers contend that the government or central bank must sometimes act as a lender of last resort (LLR), standing ready to provide liquidity to individual banks which cannot fund themselves in private markets. Goodhart (1988, ch. 7) bases this conclusion on the fact that banking firms specialize in financing assets

Section I from the original published version of this article has been removed in order to save space.

[1] The annual transactions velocity of demand deposit balances in major NYC banks has risen from 503 in 1977 to 4,481 in 1995 (Federal Reserve *Bulletin*, various issues).

[2] McAndrews and Wasilyew (1995) provide a recent example.

This article first appeared in complete form in the *Journal of Money, Credit and Banking* 28 (4), 1996, published by Ohio State University Press.

which are intrinsically hard to value. An illiquid bank may have trouble convincing private lenders of its solvency, giving rise to the common prescription that the LLR should lend to 'solvent, but illiquid' banks. The difficulty, of course, lies in determining which illiquid banks are solvent. If the government has better information about banks' solvency than market investors do, the optimal social policy might be for the central bank to lend directly to illiquid institutions. However, if private lenders possess (or, absent a government LLR, *could* possess) more accurate estimates of bank solvency, the argument for direct LLR loans becomes less tenable.

Open market operations can always provide liquidity to the financial system, but how should that liquidity be allocated to individual firms in a crisis? Goodfriend and King (1988) contend that the monetary authority *should never lend to individual banks* because private lenders can best identify solvent-but-illiquid institutions. Kaufman (1991) and Schwartz (1992) enthusiastically endorse this view that a central bank should limit its 'lender of last resort' activities to providing general market liquidity through open market operations. According to these authors, the main danger (social cost) of extending LLR credit to individual banks is that the central bank will be inclined to support insolvent institutions, thus blunting market discipline and producing riskier, less-efficient banks. (Rochet and Tirole (1996) evaluate a similar problem.) In the context of payment system stability, direct government lending (for example, daylight overdrafts) subsidizes payments made via the central bank's large-dollar payment system, blunting private initiatives to produce safer payment arrangements.

This paper evaluates whether private credit markets can, in fact, be relied upon to channel liquidity to the appropriate banking firms during a 'financial crisis.' I begin by defining two main features of a 'financial crisis' in a developed economy. First, at least a few large banks (and/or perhaps many small ones) experience a liquidity shock, most likely because bank creditors suddenly become concerned that some banks may be insolvent. Aharoney and Swary (1983), Swary (1986), and Musumeci and Sinkey (1990) demonstrate that a negative surprise about one bank's condition depresses equity prices at other banks with similar credit risk exposures.[3] Informed depositors should similarly revise their assessments of the same banks, and a sufficiently large shock could set off substantial withdrawals from the exposed banks. The second essential feature of a financial crisis is that the initial liquidity shock makes private lenders uncertain about the accuracy (appropriateness) of their traditional underwriting techniques and judgments. Just when some banks require credit from new sources on short notice, potential lenders become uncertain about how to identify borrower solvency. Section 1 presents a simple model in which information costs during a 'financial crisis' prevent private lenders from redistributing aggregate liquidity to firms that truly deserve it. *In this model open market operations cannot replace direct LLR lending to specific institutions.*

[3] In Flannery (1994), I argue that these findings support the market's rational ability to separate banks that are affected by the news from those that are not. Such discrimination bodes well for the market's ability to evaluate and discipline risky banks during 'normal' times.

Although my model could be applied to any type of firm, I evaluate the efficacy of direct discount window lending in the context of a payment system crisis because private credit arrangements seem most likely to falter in this situation. During a payment system crisis, troubled institutions' liquidity problems must be resolved within (at most) a few hours. Arguably, many private lenders will be unable to gather and evaluate appropriate credit information in such a short interval. If the payment problems occur in the context of a financial crisis, aggregate liquidity may not flow to the appropriate banks—even if it would do so in 'normal' times. Confronted with a private credit market failure, there may be a positive role for government in assuring payment system stability.[4]

The paper proceeds as follows. Section 1 presents a simple model of private credit extensions under asymmetric information. The model is applied to a payment system liquidity crisis in the following section, which develops policies to govern the Federal Reserve's discount window operations. Section 3 concludes by summarizing the paper's main points.

1. A MODEL OF COMPETITIVE LENDING WITH INFORMATION ASYMMETRY

Open market operations constitute a sufficient policy response to all instances of financial illiquidity (Goodfriend and King 1988; Kaufman 1991; Schwartz 1992) *only if* private loan markets continue to function well, even during a crisis. But the assertion that private credit markets function better at some times than others is quite common:

> Financial markets function most efficiently when market participants have sufficient information about risks and returns to make informed investment and trading decisions. However, the evolution of financial trading and risk management practices has moved ahead of the public disclosures that most firms make of information that is relevant for such decisions. . . . This asymmetry of information can cause a misallocation of capital among firms and *can also amplify market disturbances. During episodes of market stress, this lack of transparency can contribute to an environment in which rumours alone can cause a firm's market access and funding to be impaired.* (BIS 1994, p. 1, emphasis added)

> Even though the interbank market operates quite well during normal times among most banks, it cannot necessarily be relied upon to protect the banking system from panics. (Calomiris 1994, p. 34)

> The August 1995 paralysis of the banking system was caused by the practices of Russian bankers, likely aggravated by a change in monetary policy in early 1995. . . . A lack of truthful, publicly available information made it impossible to tell strong banks from weak. The banks themselves became nervous about their large exposures in the interbank market; the crisis erupted as banks, with no good way to judge counterparty risk, reacted to mild signs of illiquidity by simply refusing to transact. (Jaffee and Levonian 1995, p. 3)

[4] The primary motive for government interventions in the private sector should be that intervention improves on market solution.

The necessary condition for government intervention in credit markets is not that private markets are doing a poor job, but that the government could do better. Unless the government possesses superior information about individual banks' solvency, it is difficult to defend the proposition that a government LLR should displace private credit decisions and assessments during a crisis. Indeed, many critics of direct LLR loans contend that the advantages of private lending are greatest when lenders must make informed judgments about illiquid firms' solvency during turbulent times. Justification for direct government lending to illiquid banks must therefore rest on an argument that the government can sometimes lend on more socially appropriate terms than the private sector would. This section presents a model of private lending that illustrates one mechanism by which asymmetric information can 'amplify market disturbances' and prevent legitimate credit needs from being fulfilled.[5]

Consider a one-period economy with many potential borrowers, of whom some are 'Good' and others are 'Bad.' At the end of the period, Good loan applicants will be worth V_G, which is sufficient to repay loans *provided* that the contract rate is not too high. Bad applicants will be worth only V_B ($<< V_G$) and will be unable to repay any loans they may obtain. The number of borrowers and their quality are fixed exogenously: the proportion of Good firms is δ_G, while the proportion of Bad firms is δ_B ($= (1 - \delta_G)$).[6] There are two lenders, each of which has a costless[7] technology for assessing the creditworthiness of loan applicants. Specifically, the lender i observes a signal of the kth borrower's quality such that

$$\text{if} \quad \hat{V}_k = 1 \quad \text{then } \Pr(V_k = V_G) = p_i \text{ and } \Pr(V_k = V_B) = (1 - p_i)$$

and

$$\text{if} \quad \hat{V}_k = 0 \quad \text{then } \Pr(V_k = V_B) = p_i \text{ and } \Pr(V_k = V_G) = (1 - p_i).$$

Informative credit quality signals increase the probability of identifying an applicant's true quality. Credit signals used to make loan decisions must therefore have $p_i > \max[\delta_B, \delta_G]$. Within this range, a higher p_i is preferred. For simplicity, assume that a borrower who cannot repay in full repays nothing, that the riskless market rate of interest is zero, and that the loan signals obtained for the same applicant by competing lenders are independent of one another.

Suppose that $p_1 > p_2$, and that each lender knows its relative underwriting accuracy. Then the loan pricing problem is simple if applicants randomly apply to

[5] This model was inspired by Calomiris' (1994) intriguing (but nontechnical) analysis of the Fed's discount window response to the Penn Central crisis.

[6] I conjecture that an endogenous supply of Bad applicants would make it more difficult for the LLR to add value to the private sector's allocational equilibrium, unless the government were at least as good an underwriter as the private sector is.

[7] One could imagine that a costly test of creditworthiness could generate private credit market failures similar to those derived below.

only one lender. The ith lender will charge a Good-looking applicant a loan rate (R_i) given by

$$1 \leq (1 + R_i)\, p_i + 0(1 - p_i)$$

The contract rate, which will be paid with probability p_i, must compensate for the probability ($1 - p_i$) that nothing will be repaid. A lender therefore charges

$$R_i \geq \frac{1}{p_i} - 1. \tag{1}$$

Analogously, an applicant who appears to be Bad will be charged a loan rate that reflects the possibility that the credit quality signal is incorrect:

$$1 \leq (1 + R_i)(1 - p_i) + 0(p_i)$$

or

$$R_i \geq \frac{1}{1 - p_i} - 1 \tag{2}$$

For simplicity, I assume that the loan rate implied by (2) is so large that even a Good firm could not repay the loan, and subsequently ignore the possibility that any lender would extend credit to a firm showing a Bad credit signal.

If borrowers can apply to *both* lenders and accept the lowest available rate, the less-accurate lender cannot price according to (1) and expect to break even. (Broecker (1990) presents a related model.) If a borrower is truly Good, the more-accurate lender is likely to have offered her a loan. Lender 2 will be repaid only if the borrower is truly Good (which happens with probability p_2) *and* the more accurate lender has mistakenly assessed the borrower's quality as Bad (which happens with probability ($1 - p_1$) if the borrower is truly Good). Accordingly, the less-accurate lender's break-even loan rate satisfies

$$1 \leq (1 + R_2)\, p_2\, (1 - p_1) + 0$$

or

$$R_2 \geq \frac{1}{p_2(1 - p_1)} - 1 \tag{3}$$

Equation (3) illustrates three important features of the less-accurate lender's pricing and portfolio risk exposure. First, competing with a stronger underwriter (that is, one with a larger p_1) raises a lender's break-even loan rate. Second, the value of the less-accurate lender's loan portfolio depends on the *accuracy* of its assessment about the competitor's underwriting ability. If Lender 2 underestimates p_1, its loan contract rates will be too low. Finally, and most important, this competitive risk is *not* diversifiable across loans. Regardless of the number of individual loans in its portfolio, Lender 2 bears more portfolio risk the greater is its uncertainty about Lender 1's underwriting ability.

That private financial markets function well in normal times strongly implies that the winner's curse in (3) is generally manageable. Perhaps lenders know enough about their usual customers that another lender's opinion does not materially influence their probability of securing the loan business. (See, e.g., Nakamura (1995).) However, when a large shock impacts the financial system, normal lending relationships may become insufficient to provide all the funds required for an illiquid firm's continued operations. If banks must turn to new potential lenders at just the time when it is feared (or known) that many have been substantially weakened, a lender's assessment of its own underwriting abilities *and that of its competitors* may become much less certain. Lenders must innovate new information evaluation systems to interpret credit quality. Even banks that are normally the most accurate lenders could become uncertain about their relative underwriting ability during a crisis. The winner's curse has a more substantial effect on break-even loan rates when lenders are uncertain about their relative underwriting abilities.

To see this effect, assume that in a financial crisis each lender believes that there is a fifty-fifty chance that it is the more accurate underwriter. While each lender is confident about the quality (p_i) of its own creditworthiness test, it is unsure about the rival's test quality (p_j). For Lender i (who competes only with Lender j), the break-even loan rate is then given by

$$1 \leq (1 + R_i)[0.5(p_i) + 0.5(p_i(1 - p_j))].$$

Lender i believes that it is the better underwriter with probability 0.5, in which case it would get the loan business of any applicant who appears to be Good, and p_i of these borrowers will repay. But there is also a 50 percent chance that Lender i is the *less*-accurate underwriter, in which case it will attract a truly Good loan applicant only if Lender j mistakenly believes the borrower is Bad. Solving for the break-even loan rate yields

$$R_i \geq \frac{1}{p_i(1 - 0.5p_j)} - 1. \tag{4}$$

Both lenders now confront the *non-diversifiable* risk that their loan offers will be subject to a winner's curse. By contrast, this risk was absent (or, at least, smaller) during 'normal' times, when relative underwriting abilities were better understood.[8]

The model thus implies that equilibrium loan rates will rise during a financial crisis, as documented by Mishkin (1991).[9] If the winner's curse effect is sufficiently large, the break-even loan rate (4) might become so high that even Good borrowers cannot repay the promised amount and the private loan market would collapse

[8] My model generates a discrete shift in loan-pricing behavior in response to an exogenous credit quality shock. Romer (1993) presents a related model in which equity prices change discretely when traders learn something about other traders' beliefs.

[9] The model's loan rates rise even if the underlying distribution of borrower qualities remain unchanged. A deterioration in average borrower quality during a crisis would raise equilibrium loan rates even further.

as in Akerlof (1970). The interbank loan market may also fail if aversion to the nondiversifiable winner's curse causes lenders to withdraw from the new loan market. This could occur for either (or both) of two reasons. First, if a lender's solvency depends on the repayment of new loans made during a financial crisis, a poor outcome would expose the firm to financial distress costs.[10] Less-confident underwriters may rationally confine their investments to the Treasury market, in which they have no information disadvantage. Second, if obtaining an applicant's quality signal is costly, lenders will incur the cost only if there is a reasonable chance of obtaining an apparently Good borrower's loan business. When a lender is unsure of its relative underwriting ability, it may choose to forego investing in credit quality signals until the crisis has passed.

To summarize, the model implies that private loan markets can fail not because the average borrower's credit quality deteriorates, but because lenders become less certain about how to identify risks. When lenders become uncertain about the accuracy of their own or competitors' underwriting abilities, break-even loan rates can rise sharply and the loan market can fail. In addition, lenders must accept nondiversifiable risk exposures in order to satisfy new loan demands. Rather than bear these risks, lenders may decide to protect their charter value by withdrawing from the interbank market during a crisis. If so, some illiquid banks will be unable to obtain funds, regardless of their solvency or of the aggregate state of financial sector liquidity. This private market equilibrium entails socially wasteful distress costs for the illiquid-but-solvent banks.

I now consider whether a government lender of last resort can mitigate the dead-weight costs of a financial crisis.

2. MODEL IMPLICATIONS: HOW CAN THE DISCOUNT WINDOW SUPPORT A STABLE PAYMENT SYSTEM?

When a bank encounters settlement difficulties near the end of a business day, it must either borrow or convert assets to good funds in order to make settlement. The salient question is how a needy bank can obtain other banks' excess funds, on short notice. In normal times, the banks with excess funds may confidently lend to the needy banks. If the liquid banks are unfamiliar with the needy bank, they can lend to other (familiar) banks which are, in turn, willing to lend to the illiquid institution. During a financial crisis, however, the banks with excess funds may not be confident that they properly understand the condition of other banks in the system. The situation may be exacerbated by the fact that illiquid banks tend to approach new potential lenders in a crisis because their usual loan providers are also short of funds. Given the time pressures associated with settlement, it might be rational for banks with excess liquidity to seek refuge in riskless investments

[10] This loss of value could arise from a nonmarketable charter value (as in Marcus (1984)), or if large fluctuations in the lender's cash flows reduce its ability to finance attractive investment projects (as in Froot, Sharfstein, and Stein (1993)).

rather than extending loans to distressed firms. This market equilibrium would entail deadweight bankruptcy costs for the illiquid banks, and perhaps also for their counterparties.

The 'winner's curse' equilibrium occurs because no bank has sufficient resources to lend to *all* the illiquid banks. If the banks with excess liquidity could form a consortium or mutual fund, however, they could lend to all troubled banks knowing that δ_G are Good and $(1-\delta_G)$ are Bad (Calomiris 1994). The break-even loan rate (R^*) would be

$$1 = (1 + R^*)\delta_G + 0(1 - \delta_G)$$

or

$$R^* = \frac{1}{\delta_G}.$$

Is this sort of cooperative private solution likely to suffice? Three problems seem obvious. First, private-sector coordination costs may prevent formation of the loan consortium. Second, even if a consortium were formed in anticipation of a crisis, individual members may refuse to perform. (Sometimes, it seems cheaper to take one's chances in the courts than to lay out large amounts in an uncertain environment.) Finally, a payments problem requires action within a very short time frame, and coordinated action may not occur quickly enough to avert a settlement failure.

Another potential solution to the private lending problem described in Section 1 would be for illiquid banks to provide security for new loans. Goodfriend (1991, p. 16 and footnote 37) explains that banks may not pledge any assets, except Treasury and agency bonds, as security for loans. This restriction means that most private loans to distressed banks must be made on an unsecured basis, though the Federal Reserve may accept any marketable collateral as security for its advances. Under present federal statutes, the discount window therefore constitutes a unique mechanism for providing secured funding to a distressed institution on short notice. Should we protect payment system stability by revising these statutes to permit secured interbank lending? This is a complex issue. A banking firm's decision to pledge collateral or sell assets can materially affect its *unsecured* creditors' ability to obtain repayment if the firm defaults. Attaining payment system stability through this mechanism would therefore generate higher unsecured debt rates, which may depress banking firms' values in other ways. We cannot discuss pledging or discount window collateralization without regard for the impact of these devices on banks' other credit arrangements. It seems unlikely that a general equilibrium analysis would imply that banks should be permitted to pledge assets without limit in order to render the payment system more secure.

What, then, can a government LLR do to ameliorate a payment system crisis? Putting aside the (unlikely?) possibility that the government's supervisory responsibilities provide it with better information about illiquid banks' true condition, the government has two advantages over private lenders: its size and its immunity to bankruptcy. A government LLR can (uniquely) finance the entire banking sector's liquidity needs, and it can do so quickly, with no coordination problems. Moreover, in order to protect itself against adverse selection, the government can afford to lend at a rate below any (potential) private lender's. If all private lenders withdraw from the market, the Fed simply charges R^* and breaks even on its advances. However, if some private lenders remain sufficiently confident of their underwriting abilities that they 'skim off' a disproportionate share of Good borrowers, the Fed's break-even loan rate may exceed the rate which Good banks could afford to repay. The Fed should therefore evaluate whether lending at a loss entails lower social costs than those associated with letting Good firms bear distress costs.

It is very important to contrast this view of the appropriate Fed discount rate with Bagehot's classical view that in a crisis the central bank should lend *freely, but at a penalty rate.* If the Fed sets a penalty rate on loans during my type of financial crisis, it may suffer a winner's curse vis-à-vis private lenders, potentially increasing its cost of intervention. In a crisis, the Federal Reserve must stand ready to *subsidize* credit in order to avoid the winner's curse that governs private loan pricing decisions.[11]

A. Discount Window Loans During 'Normal' Times

My model provides no justification for LLR advances to an *individual* firm with an *idiosyncratic* liquidity problem. Indeed, during normal times there are several reasons for the Fed to avoid all loans:

(1) If private lenders are better underwriters, the Fed will tend to attract the weaker credits, imposing losses on taxpayers.
(2) Access to cheap Fed credit will subsidize bank risk-taking, contributing to riskier payment and financial systems.
(3) Cheap Fed credit will inhibit the development of private mechanisms for providing quick access to liquidity.

During normal times, private markets should be able to assess the distressed firm's condition at least as well as the LLR can. Once the Fed has provided sufficient aggregate liquidity through open market operations, it should rely on private lending to channel funds to solvent but illiquid firms.

Some will argue that the Fed should support a troubled institution if its failure would impose large credit losses on other banks. Rochet and Tirole (1996) point out that the bad incentive effects of this 'too big to fail' policy can be avoided by subsidizing the troubled institution's counterparties instead of bailing out the troubled firm itself.

[11] In an important sense, this is a tautology: if the Fed lent only on the same terms which the market would set, it cannot improve upon private market outcomes.

B. Collateral and Discount Window Lending

The Fed presently lends on both secured and unsecured bases. Regulation A requires that overnight discount window advances be fully collateralized, while Fedwire DO are generally unsecured. Unsubsidized, collateralized discount window loans can add no social value except to the extent that they constitute a means of circumventing securities trading deadlines or statutory restrictions on pledging assets to private lenders.[12] Without meaning to minimize the value of these services, I wish to concentrate on unsecured lending—where the Fed can most dramatically influence social allocations. The model in Section 1 implies that the Fed can best mitigate social deadweight costs by lending on an unsecured basis to any illiquid bank, perhaps at a subsidized rate.

C. Discount Loans' Maturity

I have discussed discount window lending in the context of a payment system crisis because such crises must be resolved within a very short time. Private efforts to coordinate emergency lending cannot be relied upon to occur quickly enough to avoid an important settlement failure. At the same time, my confidence in private investors' ingenuity suggests that discount window loans should be very short term, *even* in a financial crisis. The Fed's value lies in carrying banks over the period of market uncertainty, until they can sell securities (which should be possible on the next business day) or demonstrate their solvency to liquid outsiders (which may take longer when asset prices are more volatile). It is hard to imagine situations in which widespread Fed lending would be appropriate for more than a few business days.

D. Comparing the Costs and Benefits of Discount Window Lending

So far, I have tried to define the circumstances under which direct LLR lending *could* supplement open market operations as a means of enhancing social welfare during a crisis. While these circumstances are quite limited, we should not dismiss the discount window as obviously unnecessary. At the same time, however, almost any government activity entails inefficiencies and costs as well as the benefits identified here. Assessing whether such lending *is truly* appropriate requires a comparison between the deadweight costs of a settlement failure and the (ex ante and ex post) costs of inefficient risk bearing in the financial system. These latter social costs *do not* include the Fed's direct credit losses (which are only a transfer payment), but rather the effects of distorted risk-taking incentives induced by a

[12] The Fed's current practice, making *secured* loans to individual firms in normal times, tends to reduce the value of unsecured creditors' claims, should the bank eventually go bankrupt. No strong justification for this type of loan springs immediately to mind.

policy of lending broadly to banks, regardless of their credit condition. Provided that very short-term discount window loans are extended only during a broad financial crisis, the potential benefits of LLR loans far outweigh the likely damage to the banking system's risk-taking incentives.

3. SUMMARY AND CONCLUSIONS

Substantial amounts of public and private credit underlie modern large-dollar payment systems. A number of institutional arrangements make it possible to reduce the amount of credit required to effect payments, but each has costs as well as benefits. During 'normal' times, in which private lenders can assess one another's financial conditions with reasonable accuracy, a payment system that entails substantial private credit exposures is efficient and appropriate. However, any credit-based payment system incorporates the potential for 'systemic risk,' by which one firm's failure to settle can make other firms also unable to settle. We must consider the appropriate role for a government LLR when one or more banks cannot fulfill their payment system obligations.

Unless we believe that private banks and investors routinely make poor credit quality evaluations, there is little need for unsecured discount window loans during 'normal' times. When credit markets are functioning well, the LLR's only advantage lies in its ability to provide good funds more quickly than the distressed bank could raise them by asset sales or private borrowing. However, such advances must be kept very short term (perhaps extending no longer than a single business day), after which a solvent bank should be able to sell assets or secure funding from private lenders. Unless the discount window administrator is assumed to know more about a bank's true condition than the market does, there is no reason to extend loans for very long.

The discount window's unique value arises when disarray strikes private financial markets. If lenders cannot confidently assess other firms' conditions, they may rationally withdraw from the interbank loan market, leaving solvent but illiquid firms unable to fund themselves. Private lenders seeking to fill this gap would confront a nondiversifiable adverse selection bias (winner's curse), which the discount window need not experience. In response to this sort of financial crisis, government may need to do more than assure adequate aggregate liquidity through open market operations. Broad, short-term discount window lending, unsecured and at (perhaps) subsidized rates, may constitute the least-cost means of resolving some types of widespread financial uncertainties, including those affecting payment systems settlement.

REFERENCES

Baer, Herbert L., Virginia G. France, and James T. Moser. 'Opportunity Cost and Prudentiality: An Analysis of Futures Clearinghouse Behavior.' The World Bank, Policy Research Working paper 1340, August 1994.

Bank for International Settlements. *Payments Systems in the Group of Ten Countries*. Basle, December 1993.

—. 'Public Disclosure of Market and Credit Risks by Financial Intermediaries.' Mimeo, September 1994.

—. 'Prudential Supervision of Banks' Derivatives Activities.' Mimeo, December 1994.

—. 'Public Disclosure of the Trading and Derivatives Activities of Banks and Securities Firms.' Mimeo, November 1995.

Benston, George J., and George C. Kaufman. *Risk and Solvency Regulation of Depository Institutions: Past Policies and Current Options*. Salomon Brothers Center, Graduate School of Business, New York University, 1988.

Berger, Allen N., Diana Hancock, and Jeffrey Marquardt. 'Introduction.' *Journal of Money, Credit and Banking* 28 (November 1996, Part 2).

Borio, C. E. V., and P. Van den Bergh. 'The Nature and Management of Payment System Risks: An International Perspective.' *BIS Economic Paper*, no. 35, February 1993.

Calomiris, Charles W., and Charles M. Kahn, 'The Efficiency of Self-Regulated Payment Systems: Learning from the Suffolk System.' *Journal of Money, Credit, and Banking* 28 (November 1996, Part 2).

Cody, Brian J. 'Reducing the Costs and Risks of Trading Foreign Exchange.' Federal Reserve Bank of Philadelphia *Business Review* (November/December 1990), 13–23.

Cohen, Hugh, and William Roberds. 'Toward the Systematic Measurement of Systemic Risk.' Federal Reserve Bank of Atlanta Working Paper Series, WP-93-14, October 1993.

Emmons, William R. 'The Payments System, Delegated Monitoring, and Banking Safety Nets.' Working paper, Dartmouth College, November 1994.

Federal Reserve Bank of New York. 'The Clearinghouse Interbank Payments System.' January 1991.

Flannery, Mark J. 'Payments System Risk and Public Policy.' In *Restructuring Banking and Financial Services in America*, edited by William S. Haraf and Rose Marie Kushmeider, pp. 261–87. Washington, D.C.: American Enterprise Institute for Public Policy Research, 1988.

—. 'Regulatory Responses to the Potential for Systemic Risk in the Financial Sector.' In *Research in Financial Services: Private and Public Policy*, edited by George G. Kaufman, pp. 323–36. Greenwich: JAI Press, 1995.

George, Eddie. 'International Banking, Payment Systems, and Financial Crises.' In *Symposium Proceedings: International Symposium on Banking and Payment Services*, Board of Governors of the Federal Reserve System, December 1994.

Gilbert, R. Alton. 'Payments System Risk: What Is It and What Will Happen If We Try to Reduce It?' Federal Reserve Bank of St. Louis *Review* (January/February 1989), 3–17.

—. 'Implications of Netting Arrangements for Bank Risk in Foreign Exchange Transactions.' Federal Reserve Bank of St. Louis *Review* (January/February 1992), 3–16.

Goldstein, Morris. 'International Aspects of Systemic Risk.' Working paper, Office of the Comptroller of the Currency, December 1994.

Gorton, Gary. 'Clearing Houses and the Origin of Central Banking in the U.S.' *Journal of Economic History* 45(2) (1985), 277–83.

Guynn, Randall D. 'Modernizing Securities Ownership, Transfer and Pledging Laws: A Discussion Paper on the Need for International Harmonization.' Mimeo, May 1995.

Hancock, Diana, and James A. Wilcox. 'Intraday Bank Reserve Management: The Effects of Caps and Fees on Daylight Overdrafts.' *Journal of Money, Credit, and Banking* 28 (November 1996, Part 2).

Hanley, William J., Karen McCann, and James T. Moser. 'Public Benefits and Public Concerns: An Economic Analysis of Regulatory Standards for Clearing Facilities.' Federal Reserve Bank of Chicago Working Paper Series (WP-95-12), September 1995.

Humphrey, David B. 'Payments System Risk, Market Failure, and Public Policy.' In *Electronic Funds Transfers and Payments: The Public Policy Issues*, edited by Elinor Harris Solomon, pp. 83–110. Boston: Kluwer-Nijhoff Publishing, 1987.

McAndrews, James, and William Roberds. 'Banks, Payments, and Coordination.' Working paper. Federal Reserve Banks of Philadelphia and Atlanta, August 1994.

Mengle, David L. 'Legal and Regulatory Reform in Electronic Payments: An Evaluation of Payment Finality Rules.' In *The U.S. Payment System: Efficiency, Risk and the Role of the Federal Reserve*, edited by David B. Humphrey, pp. 145–95. Boston: Kluwer Academic Publishers, 1990.

Merton, Robert C. 'Financial Innovation and the Management and Regulation of Financial Institutions.' *Journal of Banking and Finance* (July 1995), 461–82.

Petzel, Todd E. 'Managing Collateral On Exchanges and Off: A New Perspective.' *The Journal of Derivatives* (Spring 1995), 64–72.

Schoenmaker, Dirk. 'A Comparison of Net and Gross Settlement.' London School of Economics Financial Markets Group Special Paper, May 1994.

Stehm, Jeff. 'Clearance and Settlement of Mortgage-Backed Securities through the Participants Trust Company.' Finance and Economic Discussion Series #214, Board of Governors of the Federal Reserve System, November 1992.

Stigum, Marcia. *After the Trade*. Homewood: Dow Jones-Irwin, 1988.

Van den Bergh, Paul. 'Operational and Financial Structure of the Payment System.' In *The Payment System: Design, Management and Supervision*, edited by Bruce J. Summers. Washington: The International Monetary Fund, 1994.

13

Myths about the Lender of Last Resort

CHARLES GOODHART

I. INTRODUCTION

There are few issues so subject to myth, sometimes unhelpful myths that tend to obscure rather than to illuminate real issues, as is the subject of whether a central bank (or an international financial institution (IFI) such as the International Monetary Fund (IMF)), should act as a lender of last resort (LOLR).

Perhaps the very first myth is that the fount of all wisdom, the *fons et origo*, on this subject is to be found in Bagehot's great book *Lombard Street* (1873). In fact, most of the key policy proposals set out there were anticipated by Henry Thornton in his outstanding study *The Paper Credit of Great Britain* (1802), the greatest treatise on the conduct of monetary operations ever written, though Bagehot gave little credit to any prior writers on the subject in his own book. The main proposals outlined by Bagehot (1873, pp. 196–7) are:

1. Lend freely.
2. At a high rate of interest.
3. On good banking securities.

Let me demonstrate how Thornton dealt with these same questions. First, he wrote on lending freely, as follows:

> The directors [of the Bank], therefore, must seem to themselves to act with extraordinary liberality towards those who apply to them for discounts, [during a season of consternation] . . . . The liberality in lending which they must exercise, if, when the gold is low, they even augment their paper, must be very extended indeed. (Thornton 1802, p. 116)

On Bagehot's second two principles of lending on good security at a high rate of interest, Thornton wrote:

> It is by no means intended to imply, that it would become the Bank of England to relieve every distress which the rashness of country banks may bring upon them: the bank, by doing this, might encourage their improvidence. . . . The relief should neither be so prompt and liberal as to exempt those who misconduct their business from all the natural consequences of their fault, nor so scanty and slow as deeply to involve the general interest. (Thornton 1802, p. 121)

This article first appeared in *International Finance* 2 (3), 1999.

And again:

That the bills which the bank discounts are, generally speaking, so safe, that the security either of goods, or stocks, or land. . . . may be considered as nearly superfluous. A very small proportion of the five per cent discount, gained upon the bills turned into ready money at the bank, has compensated, as I believe, for the whole of the loss upon them, even in the years of the greatest commercial failures which have yet been known. (Thornton 1802, pp. 119–20)

Bagehot only goes further than Thornton in placing more emphasis on the need to raise interest rates to deter unnecessary domestic borrowing, for both Thornton and Bagehot were aware of the need to raise interest rates to check a foreign drain of gold from the bank. But Thornton's lack of emphasis on this point may well have been due to the continuing effect of the usury laws, in force until the 1830s, capping (formal) interest rates at 5% and preventing the bank from using this instrument aggressively in a crisis.

But this emphasis in Bagehot on the need for 'high' interest rates for LOLR has led some commentators (e.g. Keleher and Humphrey 1984)[1] to go further and claim that Bagehot proposed that LOLR should always be at a 'penalty' rate; that is, at a rate *higher* than that available in the market place. This is not so.[2] Certainly the rate should be above that in effect in the market prior to the panic, but not necessarily above the contemporaneous market rate.[3] Bagehot was very concerned that, unless the Bank of England was prepared to lend on the basis of what was normally regarded as good security, no one else would do so at all. The penalty rate would then be infinite. Bagehot wrote:

If it is known that the Bank of England is freely advancing on what in ordinary times is reckoned a good security—on what is then commonly pledged and easily convertible—the alarm of the solvent merchants and bankers will be stayed. But if securities, really good and usually convertible, are refused by the Bank, the alarm will not abate, the other loans made

[1] They describe the policy prescription for simultaneously meeting external and internal drains as being to 'lend freely at a high (penalty) rate' (p. 200), with those words in quotes, as presumably coming from a separate authority, e.g. Thornton or Bagehot. But no source, or page numbers, are given, and I have not been able to find such a reference, or indeed *any* reference to a 'penalty' rate in either Thornton or Bagehot.

[2] I asked a research assistant to check for any references in *Lombard Street* to 'penalty' or 'penal'. There are four. One, at the start of Chapter 13 (p. 329), notes that the Bank of England is 'under no effectual penalty of failure'. A second (Chapter 7, p. 175), commends the Bank for not over-issuing during the suspension of the Gold Standard when there was 'no present penalty on it'. The other two references are in Chapter 4, describing the penalty individual banks might suffer for over-lending in a 'natural' system without a central bank.

[3] The key reference in Bagehot (p. 197) reads as follows: 'The end is to stay the panic; and the advances should, if possible, stay the panic. And for this purpose there are two rules: First. That these loans should only be made at a very high rate of interest. This will operate as a heavy fine on unreasonable timidity, and will prevent the greatest number of applications by persons who do not require it. The rate should be raised early in the panic, so that the fine may be paid early; that no one may borrow out of idle precaution without paying well for it; then the banking reserve may be protected as far as possible. Secondly. That at this rate these advances should be made on all good banking securities, and as largely as the public ask for them. The reason is plain. The object is to stay alarm, and nothing therefore should be done to cause alarm.'

will fail in obtaining their end, and the panic will become worse and worse. (Bagehot 1873, pp. 198–9)

The levels to which bank rates were raised during the period of the Gold Standard were mild[4] by the standards of our current age, with its bouts of inflation and currency crises. When Bagehot remarked that LOLR 'loans should only be made at a very high rate of interest', he would have it in mind that a bank rate of 6 or 7% was very high, and 10% extraordinarily high. It was then said that '7% would draw gold from the moon'.[5]

An even more pervasive interpretation of the teaching of these early scholars is that they advocated that LOLR lending could, and should, be adjusted to distinguish between the illiquid and the insolvent. Indeed, the first of the main myths that I shall discuss is that it is generally possible for a central bank to distinguish between illiquidity and insolvency, and should then confine its LOLR loans solely to the former. Thereafter I want to deal with three other views, which I also hold to be mistaken. These are:

1. That national central bank LOLR capacities are unrestricted, whereas international bodies, or IFIs such as the IMF, cannot function as an ILOLR.
2. That moral hazard is everywhere and at all times a predominant consideration.
3. That it might be possible to dispense with an LOLR altogether.

II. MYTH 1

The first myth is that it is generally possible to distinguish between illiquidity and insolvency.

The possibility of large shocks—for example, large jumps in asset prices, especially in crises when such a jump is downwards—means that there may be multiple equilibria, to use the current jargon. Panic conditions can lead to circumstances where firms that would be viable during normal times become insolvent, though perhaps only temporarily. This syndrome may be especially serious in

[4] They were certainly so in nominal terms in comparison to today. Given medium-term expectations of price stability, 7% nominal is quite high in real terms, but it was not expected to last long, as can be inferred by the remarkable stability (again as compared to today) of Consol prices. It is difficult to compare these real rates with those applied in modern crises, since the forward-looking expectations of future inflation are less well anchored. Even so, the rates introduced in Sweden, and the 15% bank rate briefly attempted in the UK during the EMS crises, and several occasions of official rates during the East Asian crises, e.g. in Korea and Hong Kong, produced real rates well above those in nineteenth-century crises. Moreover, these latter real rates failed to restore confidence and bring in foreign exchange inflows from abroad, perhaps because they were perceived as 'too high'.

[5] David Kynaston quotes this in his history of the City of London (Volume II, p. 453), where he writes, 'It was probably at this time [1907] that the tag was coined in the London money market that "7% brings gold from the moon".' The problem nowadays is that, with less of a firm anchor for exchange rate expectations, during crises the minimum level of interest rates necessary to maintain or restore foreign confidence may be perilously close to the maximum that the domestic economy can meet without instigating a financial collapse.

commercial banks, because of their interconnectedness (Allen and Gale 1998, 1999). Bagehot[6] and Thornton[7] were well aware of this; Bagehot remarked approvingly of the Bank's operations in 1825 when the Bank made advances 'by every possible means consistent with the safety of the Bank, and we were not on some occasions over-nice' (p. 52).

In Bagehot's time, the money market operated almost entirely through the discount of bills of exchange. If the bill was 'good' in the sense that the initial drawer of the bill would certainly pay on maturity, a central bank that rediscounted the bill would be repaid in due course, whatever happened to the (bank) intermediary from which it had rediscounted in the meantime.

Bagehot's test of whether a central bank should lend during a crisis did not depend on the individual borrower, but on the security; thus 'advances should be made on all good banking securities and as largely as the public ask for them' (p. 197). But this test has really nothing to do with the question of whether (on best mark-to-market accounting principles) the applicant borrower (commercial bank) had a capital value below some lower limit (e.g. zero or insolvency). Indeed, then as now, a central bank faced with an application for LOLR had, and has, no quick or accurate way of ascertaining this. Instead, Bagehot's proposal related simply to the collateral that the applicant could offer, and the effect of this rule in practice was to distinguish, in part, between those loans on which the central bank might expect with some considerable probability to make a loss (bad bills and collateral) and those on which little, or no, loss should eventuate.

Such discounting of bills was simultaneously the standard way in Bagehot's time both for injecting cash into the market as a whole and for lending to individual banks. This changed thereafter in the UK towards the end of the nineteenth century, because the Bank of England became increasingly unhappy about regular direct bilateral negotiations with the joint stock commercial banks, since the amalgamation process was causing the latter to become much larger in size than the Bank itself. Instead, from the latter part of the nineteenth century right through to the final decade of the twentieth century, the Bank would carry out its general liquidity operations through the discount houses, a group of small intra-market subsidiaries which the Bank actively fostered. Meanwhile direct, last resort support for individual commercial banks, as in the Baring crisis (1890), was separately organized, as we shall discuss below.

This distinction between generalized control of systemic liquidity via open market operations, determining the rate of growth of the monetary base, and LOLR

[6] 'A panic, in a word, is a species of neuralgia, and according to the rules of science you must not starve it. The holders of the cash reserve must be ready not only to keep it for their own liabilities, but to advance it most freely for the liabilities of others. They must lend to merchants, to minor bankers, to "this man and that man", wherever the security is good. In wild periods of alarm, one failure makes many, and the best way to prevent the derivative failures is to arrest the primary failure which caused them' (Bagehot 1873, pp. 51–2).

[7] 'If any one bank fails, a general run upon the neighbouring ones is apt to take place, which, if not checked in the beginning by pouring into the circulation a large quantity of gold leads to very extensive mischief' (Thornton 1802, p. 113).

transactions with individual financial institutions, (normally banks) has been taken further today. With the development of broad and deep money markets, e.g. repo markets, the CB operates to determine interest rates (and by those same actions to adjust the monetary base) by open market operation (OMO), undertaken through general market operations, and not in bilateral negotiation with any individual institution.

Among the factors influencing the CB in its conduct of OMO will be issues such as the degree of confidence/risk aversion in markets (e.g. as measured by the pattern of spreads), the demand for cash or measures of public confidence in the banking system. Some writers on this subject have described injections of high-powered money, open market purchases, undertaken to calm actual, or potential, losses of confidence in the financial system as a whole (that is, systemic problems), as LOLR operations. In my view it is wrong to do so. One main reason is that it is practically impossible then to distinguish LOLR-OMO from non-LOLR-OMO. For example, the Bank of Japan has at times in recent years aggressively increased the monetary base. Which actions, and how much of this increase, could be designated as LOLR? It is not possible, except in rare circumstances[8] to make such a distinction. Hence the concept is effectively non-operational. By contrast, the distinction between lending by the CB to an individual institution and OMO dealing with the market as a whole is simple, practical and self-evidently justifiable. In my view only the former should be described as LOLR, and that is what will be done henceforth.

Individual banks nowadays adjust their own liquidity through these same wholesale money markets. Banks will much prefer, under normal conditions, to do so than to borrow directly, and bilaterally, from the CB, whether collateralized or not. There is a potential reputational cost from being observed to borrow directly from the CB (at least this is so in most countries). Again in most countries, bilateral direct borrowing from the CB will be more expensive (a penalty rate) than the market rate. There will be times when the wholesale market rate is driven up to the CB's penalty (Lombard) rate, or when the CB's discount rate is commonly below the market rate (as in the US), when lending to individual banks becomes both commonplace and constrained by other (reputational) factors.

Except in such instances, an individual bank will only go to a CB for direct bilateral LOLR assistance when it *cannot* meet its liquidity needs on the wholesale interbank money markets. Almost by definition this must be because it is running out of good security for collateralized loans *and* other (bank) lenders will not lend to it on an unsecured basis in the quantities required (at acceptable rates). Again, almost by definition, this latter must be because there is some question about its ultimate solvency. The greater the insistence of the CB on charging a 'penalty' rate on its own LOLR loans, the greater the endeavour of commercial banks to use their existing good collateral to borrow in the market place first.

[8] One such occasion was the announcement by the Federal Reserve after the 1987 stock market crash that it would make additional liquidity available to the financial system both via OMO and through easy access to the discount window.

There are some exceptions to this rule, that nowadays illiquidity implies at least a *suspicion* of insolvency. But such exceptions tend to prove the rule. One of the most famous LOLR occasions of recent decades was the massive lending on one overnight occasion (20 November 1985) by the Federal Reserve Bank of New York to the Bank of New York. The Bank of New York had had a computer malfunction. It was a leading participant in the US Treasury bond market; the computer had paid out good funds for Treasury bonds bought, but would not accept cash in-payments for Treasury bonds sold. As a major player in the market with a huge gross turnover, this rapidly led to a ballooning cash deficit. The bank was still, of course, patently solvent; moreover its cash deficit was matched by surpluses spread amongst the other banks, mostly in New York. Nevertheless, the private market could not cope with recycling the money back to the Bank of New York, at least not quickly enough. The size of the liquidity deficit was so huge that no one single bank could possibly have been the counterpart lender, since it would have both exhausted its own liquidity and broken through its various (internal) controls on large exposures. Thus a coordinated, syndicated response would have been necessary, and the arrangement of such coordination is time-consuming, somewhat expensive and subject to free rider problems. It was just far easier to let the FRBNY manage the temporary problem.

So, as a generality, whenever an individual commercial bank approaches the CB for direct bilateral loans (LOLR) (unless interest rate relativities make that profitable for the commercial bank), the CB must/should suspect that the failure of the bank to adjust its liquidity on the open market means that there is at least a whiff of suspicion of insolvency. It is not, however, possible for the CB, at least within the relevant timescale, to ascertain whether such suspicions are valid or not; and if valid, what the extent of the solvency problem is.[9] Of course, a CB, or the associated bank supervisory agency, will, or should, have a good knowledge of the prior reputation of a bank seeking assistance, and *may* be able to obtain a quick reading of the market value of its trading book. I emphasize 'may' because in a crisis situation liquidity can disappear and values become very volatile; moreover, the true value of a complex position in derivatives markets can be far from easy to ascertain.

There certainly will be cases where the CB has such concern about the solvency, and prior inappropriate banking behaviour of a suppliant bank borrower, that the request for LOLR can, and should, be turned down flat. The fact that there is often a murky area where illiquidity and insolvency cannot be distinguished does not mean that this is so in every case of requests for LOLR.

For many 'liberal' commentators the argument that bilateral LOLR generally occurs only when there is a suspicion of insolvency is a good reason why a CB should eschew any such LOLR actions, but confine itself only to OMO. They claim (e.g. Humphrey and Keleher 1984) that this course of action is consistent with the

[9] Moreover, as Freixas (1999) has noted, the franchise value of a bank as a going concern may often exceed its mark-to-market accounting value, so the franchise value may be positive while at the same time the accounting value is negative; that is, the bank is insolvent.

Bagehot principles.[10] I do not believe that this is so. The rules proposed by Bagehot were intended both to prevent the CB suffering any significant loss on its LOLR loans and to prevent an excessive expansion of the money stock. When the CB discounted 'good bills' for a financial intermediary, it did not and could not at the same time estimate the borrower's solvency. It had no good measure of the borrower's balance sheet.

An LOLR loan by a CB is like any other loan, in that it may be repaid (plus interest) or alternatively will be subject to default and some potential loss. That loss would impair the capital of the CB. When the CB was private, as in most cases in the nineteenth century, the capital strength of the CB was as important and relevant an issue as it was to any other private institution. From a CB's viewpoint, Bagehot's concern that no CB should lend in a manner that might expose it to undue loss resonated with good sense.

How far does this concern alter, if at all, when the CB becomes explicitly a public sector body, via outright nationalization or otherwise? Not necessarily that much. For example, in the case of the Bank of England there used to be an implicit distinction between those aspects of its business that were the affairs of the Bank and those that were the affairs of the government.[11] The Bank of England's own retained capital still gave it some leeway and freedom to act at its own independent volition, and it prized that margin of freedom. Most crisis management continued to be done under the aegis of the Bank, *qua* Bank, with its independent capacity for action. This capacity remained, in some large part though not entirely, bounded by its capital. In Japan, for example, Okina (1999) has noted that the Bank of Japan is concerned whether further purchases of assets, in order to increase the monetary base, might bring about losses. This could be so even for purchases of government bonds, JGBs (see Okina 1999, pp. 18–21). In so far as a CB acts independently but subsequently is forced by events to go directly to the government for financial support in one guise or another, it will lose reputation and independence, as in the case of the Bank of England and Johnson Matthey Bankers in 1984.

Under the Gold Standard, CB loans, whether to maintain market liquidity, to protect the financial system or to support the government's wartime aims, could lead to a drastic reduction of its gold reserves (and in some cases also to an impairment of its capital strength). In such cases the government would step in to declare the Bank's liabilities to be legal tender. Such '*cours forcé*', as this was known in the nineteenth century, was always perceived as a sign of the fundamental weakness of the CB. Such weakness, of course, became generalized in the First

[10] Thus they write: 'Conspicuously absent is any mention of the need to channel aid to specific institutions, as would be implied by bail-out operations. Bagehot's emphasis is clearly on aid to the market rather than to the initially distressed bank. He obviously did not think it necessary to prevent the initial failure at all costs' (Humphrey and Keleher 1984, p. 300).

[11] See the Radcliffe Committee's (1959) discussion of 'The Bank's Relationship with the Central Government' (paragraphs 760–75), and the associated Minutes of the session of the Committee with C. F. Cobbold (Governor), H. C. B. Mynors (Deputy Governor) and A. W. C. Dascombe (Secretary of the Bank) (pp. 892–900).

World War, and thereafter with the breakdown of the Gold Standard in the inter-war period. Although usually emitted notionally by the CB,[12] fiat money depended not on the (capital) strength of the CB, but on the strength and taxing power of the government behind it. Does this mean that Bagehot's limits for the potential capital loss to the CB no longer had much, or any, force?

The answer, to some extent and in some countries, is 'yes', as Max Fry (1997) has shown. CBs in some countries, mainly in Latin America, have actually become technically insolvent (using generally accepted accounting principles) as a result of losses incurred on loans in support of the domestic financial system. But such insolvency does not make much difference because what stands behind the liabilities of the CB is *not* the capital of the CB but the strength and taxing power of the State.[13]

What does this tell us about the handling of systemic problems within a country? Unless such problems involve only a small potentiality for loss, so that the CB can handle it on its own books, such systemic problems will nowadays require joint management and resolution by the supervisory body, the CB and the government. As emphasized in Goodhart and Schoenmaker (1993), he who pays the piper calls the tunes. In large-scale, systemic domestic cases the government pays the piper, so it will be the government which ultimately will decide how the crisis is handled and who bears the losses.

III. MYTH 2

The second myth is that a national CB's LOLR capacities are unrestricted (even without support from its own government), whereas international bodies, or IFIs such as the IMF, cannot function as an ILOLR.

The gist of my thesis so far has been that the key factor determining the scope and scale of a CB's LOLR functions has been its ability to absorb losses. As this has waned, relative to the scale of financial losses involved in systemic problems, as in Japan and Scandinavia recently, the responsibility for handling such crises has, willy-nilly, passed to the governments involved.

[12] Usually, but not always. The ten shilling and one pound notes issued in the UK in 1914 after the start of the First World War were the liabilities of H. M. Treasury.

[13] Both Thornton and Bagehot were well aware of this. Thornton, for example, noted (pp. 31–3) that the 1793 financial crisis was resolved, absent sufficient resolve by the Bank of England, by direct LOLR support from Parliament. Bagehot noted that the experience of 1797, and the subsequent suspension of the 1844 Bank of England Act, 'confirmed the public conviction that the Government is close behind the Bank, and will help it when wanted'. The complete passage reads as follows: 'But no one in London ever dreams of questioning the credit of the Bank, and the Bank never dreams that its own credit is in danger. Somehow everybody feels the Bank is sure to come right. In 1797, when it had scarcely any money left, the Government said not only that it need not pay away what remained, but that it *must* not. The "effect of letters of licence" to break Peel's Act has confirmed the popular conviction that the Government is close behind the Bank, and will help it when wanted. Neither the Bank nor the Banking Department have ever had an idea of being put "into liquidation"; most men would think as soon of "winding up" the English nation' (p. 40).

But such governments only have domestic, not (almost by definition) international powers. They can require domestic taxes be paid, and internal debts be settled, in their own fiat money. But they cannot create foreign currency,[14] and they cannot force foreign creditors to accept payment in domestic liabilities, if the contract specifies otherwise. Moreover, if the domestic authorities create additional domestic fiat money to buy the requisite foreign currency in the open market, this would usually be largely or entirely offset by depreciation in the international value of the domestic currency.

So, just as commercial banks will turn to their CB when they cannot borrow additional high-powered money on acceptable terms in money markets, these national governments and CBs will want to turn to an international LOLR when they, or their private sector, cannot borrow foreign currency on acceptable terms in the international money market. Step forward the IMF. How does the IMF's position as an ILOLR compare with that of a domestic CB's position as an LOLR? In several respects the IMF is much *better* able to act as ILOLR than a CB to act as LOLR within the domestic context. The IMF has more capital, and could sustain larger losses. Moreover, the IMF always has the most senior ranking as creditor, so losses are perhaps even less likely than in the case of a domestic CB. Historically, the IMF has suffered very little actual loss on its loans, although quite a large number of countries, almost all heavily indebted poor countries, such as the Sudan, have been in arrears in repayment. Few countries, other than 'basket cases', are likely voluntarily to remain in 'arrears to the IMF', since it carries such a high penalty. Such a country cannot get access to private funds or other public funds (other than concessional funds, e.g. from the World Bank), no matter how desperate it may be.

Nevertheless, as is well known, the IMF's resources and capital are limited, exactly as those of a domestic CB are limited.[15] As a result CBs have eked out their own scarce resources by involving the private sector and by acting as crisis manager in arranging the disposition of funds from a much wider range of private sector institutions. The Fund has done exactly the same. CBs have often sought to

[14] Kevin Dowd has raised the question with me, in personal correspondence, of whether governments could not also require taxes to be paid in foreign currency. This would happen naturally in a country that 'dollarized'. Even in the absence of dollarization, in certain emerging countries where access to the international capital market is restricted, serious thought has been given to the possibility of requiring multinationals operating in that country to make (tax) payments in US dollars to the government.

[15] Moreover, the class of recipient of both the IMF's and domestic CBs' LOLR loans are limited. The IMF can only lend to member governments; the CB (by convention) to domestic commercial banks. In both cases this is primarily because the key reserves, foreign currency in the case of the IMF, high-powered money in the case of the CBs, are centralized in the recipient bodies. But there are subsidiary reasons in both cases, relating to trying to economize on monitoring efforts, to limit the scale and scope of 'safety nets', to concerns about the use of power, etc. The dividing lines between commercial banks and other financial intermediaries and between domestic and multinational banks are becoming blurred, and this may cause some difficulties on this front to domestic CBs. There may be some analogues for the IMF; for example, if there were, as an unlikely event, a foreign currency crisis in Euroland, to whom would the IMF lend? Again, could the IMF lend to a subsidiary government with a different currency from the federal government, as in the case of Hong Kong. No doubt Fund lawyers have thought about all such cases.

resolve crises by acting as guarantors, rather than putting up their own money up front, and by giving their seal of approval to the affairs of the distressed borrower. The Fund does so even more. In these respects, as Fischer (1999) has noted in his paper on the IMF as an ILOLR, the IMF acts in exactly the same way as a CB.

The IMF differs from national CBs in two main respects. First, it cannot buy/sell assets in open financial markets using its own currency liability (the Special Drawing Right, or SDR). Indeed, the conditions under which, and how, the issue of SDRs may be made are strictly controlled and constrained; consequently no issue has been made since 1981; and the issues actually made between the first issues, at the start of the 1970s, and 1981 had relatively little impact on world liquidity. Without the ability to issue its own liabilities at will, the IMF has virtually no capacity to undertake open market operations,[16] e.g. in order to influence world liquidity conditions. Of course, given free international capital mobility, no domestic CB, apart from the US Federal Reserve Board, can do much to influence the level of real interest rates, and/or the risk spreads, in its own country.[17] So in that sense the IMF is not at such a disadvantage in comparison to the capacities of most national CBs.

Nevertheless, it is generally the level of nominal, rather than real, interest rates that is important for the resolution of (systemic) financial difficulties.[18] Indeed, it is the fear that national CBs may lower short-term interest rates too far, for the maintenance of price stability, in the pursuit of systemic stability, that lies behind the argument that a CB with both price and stability objectives could occasionally face a conflict of interest (see Goodhart and Schoenmaker 1993). Whether, or not, such conflicts may be common and problematical, this is clearly a power which the IMF cannot use *directly*. In practice, however, the IMF can influence borrowing governments to vary interest rates as part of 'conditionality'. In the Asian crisis the main criticism of the IMF was that it put pressure on the countries involved to raise interest rates *too much*.

Where the IMF is, however, at a crucial disadvantage compared with national CBs is that it does not have a single (world?) government standing behind it, with international powers and taxing authority (note also that the first difference

[16] For some economists writing on this subject (e.g. Capie 1998; Keleher 1999), the central, possibly sole, function of a proper, effective LOLR is to use OMO to offset generalized liquidity crises. For them, no OMO capacity implies, virtually by definition, no LOLR capacity. I have been trying to explain throughout this paper why I disagree.

[17] Robert Keleher, in his role of Chief Macroeconomist to the Joint Economic Committee, has seized on this difference to argue that the Federal Reserve, rather than the IMF, could, and perhaps should, act as an ILOLR. Thus his conclusions (Keleher 1999, p. 10) are: 'Under existing institutional arrangements, the IMF cannot serve as a genuine LOLR. Specifically, the IMF cannot create reserves, cannot make quick decisions, and does not act in a transparent manner in order to qualify as an authentic international LOLR. The Federal Reserve, however, does meet the essential requirements of an international LOLR. It can quickly create international reserves and money, although it has not openly embraced international LOLR responsibilities. The Federal Reserve can easily implement this function by employing several readily available market price indicators and global measures.'

[18] It is sometimes argued that the Federal Reserve helped to relieve US financial difficulties at the end of the 1980s and outset of the 1990s by keeping short rates low, relative to long rates.

above, the inability freely to issue its own fiat liabilities, follows logically from this second and much more fundamental difference). Consequently the IMF can neither issue fiat money freely nor—and this is vastly more important for ILOLR concerns—expect any loss that impairs its available capital resources to be absorbed by its member governments, or not at least without such a row as would imperil the IMF's own position. The fundamental issue is about decision-taking and burden-sharing in national and international government forums. No CB can cope with a large financial crisis on its own, but it can usually expect to obtain a clear and reasonably quick decision on how to proceed and how the burdens are to be shared from its own national government. As, I would hope, the exception that proves the rule, the failure of the Japanese government to reach any such clear, quick decisions has been a major cause of the long drawn-out difficulties in the financial system there. By contrast, the problems that the IMF would face in getting its disparate governing body to agree to a clear, quick decision on crisis handling and burden sharing are obvious.[19]

This view of LOLR emphasizes the potentiality for loss involved, and hence the need for decisions on burden sharing. After all, if there was no such prospective loss, why could not the market handle any such problem on its own? If such losses may be large, the ability of a CB to absorb them on its own will be stretched beyond its limit; hence the need to involve government. A national CB has one national government with which to cooperate and jointly to come to a decision. This process *should* be much easier than that facing an international body, such as the IMF, with many national representatives on its governing body.

What this analysis also indicates is that the crucial features of the organization of Euroland are such that the European Central Bank (ECB) has much more in common with the IMF, effectively operating as an ILOLR, than with national CBs operating as domestic LOLRs. The central EU government is weak, with strictly limited taxing powers. If the ESCB should find that a rescue operation stretched its own capital position unduly, it could not look for executive action, financial support and decisions on burden sharing from the Commission, the European Parliament and the EU Budget. It would have to appeal for support to the European Council and the Parliaments and budgets of the member states. The 'political' difficulties of that course are all too clear.

Since national governments still maintain the bulk of fiscal power in Europe, the retention of LOLR activities within the euro zone in the hands of NCBs and national governments would seem the best course for the time being. The problem is that, once financial systems across the euro zone become more integrated, NCBs and

[19] Keleher (1999, p. 6) emphasizes this point as follows: '*The IMF cannot act quickly enough to serve as a LOLR*. Genuine LOLR decisions often must be made very quickly, sometimes within hours (as in a banking liquidity crisis). Under current practices, however, IMF decision-making is ordinarily quite slow and cumbersome. For example, in providing money to a borrowing country, the IMF conducts lengthy negotiations involving reform programs and related conditionalities. Letters of intent and memoranda of understandings are drawn up. IMF executive board decisions are subject to the votes of executive directors who often consult their national authorities. All of this takes a good deal of time.'

national Parliaments will become increasingly unwilling to resolve, and pick up the tab for, problems that may have largely originated elsewhere within the EU.

For the time being the considerable (and even surprising) extent of segmentation in national financial systems within Europe will enable the present system of crisis resolution being centred on national institutions to continue (with the ECB playing a consultative, overseeing and advisory role). Once the European financial system becomes more integrated, the disjunction between a centralized, federal monetary system and decentralized national fiscal powers will become more difficult to reconcile. It will be interesting to observe how this disjunction will be resolved in future.

IV. MYTH 3

The third myth is that moral hazard is everywhere and at all times a major consideration.

The market can be expected to provide loans on its own to banks short of liquidity when no loss is to be expected. So LOLR is, almost always, only sought, or needed, when there is some potentiality for loss, in some cases a very large potential loss. If LOLR is then provided, this raises the possibility, often the likelihood, that such losses will fall on those providing the support funds (with CBs nowadays being public sector bodies, this effectively means the tax-payer, whether the loss is absorbed on the books of the CB or not).

This means that some part of the loss will generally fall on those who have had no responsibility for the decisions that led to the loss. This shifting of the burden from those closer to the source of the loss-making decisions to those further away, tax-payers, may cause the decision-makers to take riskier decisions for well known reasons—that is, moral hazard. Many liberal economists and commentators claim that moral hazard is so serious and pervasive that LOLR, as contrasted with standard OMO for liquidity control reasons, should be eschewed altogether.

Even if moral hazard is so pervasive, there remains the question of the possible extent of loss, should there be a (contagious) systemic panic, if the CB refuses LOLR. The CB has to weigh the benefits of preventing panic now against the costs of inducing riskier activity later. Liberal economists claim that any such panic can be checked and prevented by OMO rather than LOLR. But Goodhart and Huang (1999) reply that the uncertainty, dismay and panic engendered by the newsworthy failure of a (large) bank make it that much more difficult to calibrate the necessary extent of LOLR with any accuracy. Again, Okina (1999, pp. 23–4) argues against base money targetry on the grounds that financial instability made the public's demand for currency unstable and unpredictable.

The danger of moral hazard affecting those *closest* to decision-making has always been recognized. There is an apocryphal story of the CEO of a large money-centre bank in the US coming to the then Chairman of the Federal Reserve, Paul Volcker, and asking how he, Volcker, would react if the CEO was to come to him with a request for a rescue injection of liquid funds. Volcker is reputed[20] to have replied that he would be happy to discuss the issue with the CEO's successor. The need to ensure that those whose actual executive decisions have led the commercial bank, or financial institution, into a mess do not benefit from CB LOLR, or rescue, operations is well known and widely understood. It was the failure to remove the executives of LTCM from their positions that caused much of the public disquiet about that episode, even given that no public Federal Reserve money was at stake in this rescue.

While the principle is clear, it is sometimes honoured in the breach. In particular, the current executives have a certain monopoly of inside information, and at times of crisis that information may have particular value. For such reasons some of the executives of Barings (1995), and the top management of LTCM (1998), were allowed to continue in post.

In the case of ILOLR operations carried out by the IMF, the policy measures required to be implemented under the conditionality agreements have been so severely restrictive in recent cases that no one can regard calling in the Fund as a 'soft option'. Indeed, the reverse is probably the greater danger–that is, that the Fund's required terms are perceived as likely to be so onerous that calling for Fund assistance is delayed too long,[21] by which time foreign exchange reserves are depleted, the financial system is weakened, wealth eroded, foreign capital in full flight, etc. (see, for example, Lissakers 1999).[22]

Besides the decision-taking executives, the terms and nature of the equity contract imply that shareholders should also be required to face the responsibility and the adverse consequences of failure, loss and insolvency until their positive asset valuation is eliminated. Shareholders, with their downside protected by limited liability, and being the recipients of any upside potential, have some incentive to encourage (bank) executives into riskier action. (Note that the question of whether shareholders, whether in banks, financial intermediaries or elsewhere, should *not* enjoy the full protection of limited liability is too complex to discuss here.) One proposal recently put forward at a joint meeting of Shadow Regulatory Committees (June 1999) is to require banks also to hold a tranche of subordinated debt as part of their capital. Without any share in upside profit potential, and unprotected from loss of their stake following insolvency, such debt holders could

[20] Alas the story is apocryphal. When I checked with him, he wrote back, 'I wish the story were true. In spirit, it is true.' Private correspondence.

[21] Dr Lastra has reminded me that, in order to counter this syndrome, conditionality has been relaxed in certain respects over recent years, through new facilities (with 'softer' conditions) and through accelerated procedures to disburse money.

[22] McKinnon, in personal correspondence, has, however, pointed out that the two-step procedure whereby the IMF lends to a government, and then the domestic monetary authorities lend to commercial banks can lead to a double jeopardy in moral hazard. 'Because the IMF must lend through national governments who in turn bail out national banks, limiting moral hazard involved faces double jeopardy. To be effective, IMF conditionality imposed on governments must sanction them from misbehaving in the future. But this is only effective if the government receiving the loans is not undermined by (undetected) undue risk taking by its own banks.'

be expected to be acutely sensitive to risk. One benefit could be that the yield on such debt might be a good measure of perceived risk. If so, it would need to be understood that support by the authorities, whether resulting from LOLR activities or otherwise, did not temper any losses to such debt-holders associated with a fall in the distressed bank's capital values.

The problem of where the burden of loss should fall becomes more difficult and complex the further away one moves from the central locus of decision-making. How far, if at all, should a failing bank's losses, beyond those already absorbed by equity and bond holders, fall on its other creditors, especially but not only its interbank creditors? The principle has been broadly accepted that it would be socially wasteful to require ordinary small depositors to monitor their bank, and that some considerable (though preferably *not* 100%) deposit insurance for such depositors is justified. There is no need to re-open that issue here. One hundred per cent deposit insurance may, indeed at times certainly does, lead to moral hazard in the sense that depositors do not monitor their bankers, and instead shift their funds to institutions offering the highest interest rates irrespective of reputation or apparent probity. This can be contained by partial insurance, or co-insurance. Meanwhile, the polar opposite of zero insurance is just too inequitable and socially wasteful to be acceptable. The absence of any (partial) deposit insurance is, therefore, likely to enhance the implicit guarantee of full protection to all depositors, since the political alternative is just too horrible to contemplate.

The more immediate question is what to do about the nexus of interbank connections, both domestically and internationally. It is above all such connections that are feared to lead to contagion and systemic problems, as was demonstrated in the Continental Illinois case and has been modelled theoretically by Allen and Gale (1999) and by Aghion *et al.* (1999). On the other hand, banks ought to be in a better position to monitor their fellow-banks than anyone else, (apart from the official supervisors). Moreover, interest rate terms and spreads are set in bank-dominated wholesale financial markets. If interbank lenders are (thought to be) protected from loss by the operation of domestic and international LOLRs, will not then the pattern of relative interest rates fail properly to reflect true risk, and hence the allocation of capital become distorted?

This is, perhaps, now the focus of most concern, certainly internationally, and to a rather lesser extent nationally. How far does LOLR primarily benefit other bank creditors? If so, should this be allowed to continue? When banks have lent to financial intermediaries, such as the Juzen in Japan, what should be the balance of burden absorption between the banks and the tax-payers? On the one hand, placing the burden on the banks would weaken them further at a time of fragility and hence cause more danger of contagion. On the other hand, the banks *should* have known the risks, and it is unfair (besides incurring moral hazard) to shift the burden to the tax-payer.

The same argument runs in the international sphere. There are several schemes for 'bailing-in' the international bank lenders. The 'U-drop' proposal by Buiter and Sibert (1999) is one, among several other, such. As in the domestic arena, a response of the banks is that any such prospective restriction/penalty would make contagion (between countries) more likely and more immediate, and that it could further worsen the volatility of both spreads and flows, as well as raising the average level of spreads faced by emerging countries.

Any supportive action by the authorities represents a form of insurance, and any form of insurance involves moral hazard. But that does not mean that insurance must never be undertaken. There is a need to be careful about the resulting incentive structure. Within this field of LOLR, and financial support actions more generally, the main need—though often not honoured—is to avoid any protection of the position of the main executive decision-makers. Thereafter, there is a consensus that equity and bond holders should suffer the full 'hit', up to the extent implied by limited liability at least, but that ordinary (retail) depositors should be largely (though not necessarily) protected. The current battle-ground, both domestically and internationally—but especially the latter—is what should be the status of interbank creditors of failing institutions. That will no doubt continue to be a main focus for discussion.

V. MYTH 4

The fourth myth is that it is possible to dispense with LOLR altogether.

Being caught in a financial crisis is highly unpleasant. The history of capitalism is littered with such episodes. If the public sector authorities are not in a position to help to prevent the worst effects of such crises, those involved will try to establish private sector alternatives.

Of course, central banking was not the only model, and more oligopolistic systems, as in the US and Canada, had other self-help mechanisms, concentrating in the US around the institution of the clearing house. In the American crises of the late nineteenth century, the (New York) clearing house provided LOLR after a fashion to its members (Timberlake 1978, 1984). But both this mechanism and the underlying problems of moderating (seasonal) fluctuations in liquidity in a system without a central bank were perceived as inherently unsatisfactory after the 1907 crisis. A mammoth official comparative study, the National Monetary Commission (1910–11), indicated that the alternative central bank model was superior; hence the advent of the Federal Reserve.

Given our history, it is unthinkable that any government or central bank would now stand idly by and watch the closure of any of its major banks, the realization of large-scale losses on the bank deposits of its citizens and the collapse of its financial markets, if the authorities could avoid such events. And they could avoid them by judicious LOLR. It is all very well for academic liberals to claim that the best long-term course for the economy would be for the authorities to allow *any* bank to close its doors, while restricting their assistance to generalized OMO. Even if the externalities generated by the resultant panic were not so severe as to make this line of action socially wasteful, it would not be politically acceptable, in the sense that a government doing so would suffer extreme unpopularity.

There is an important question of what *exactly* we mean when we talk about a bank 'failing', and/or about a bank being 'rescued' or 'bailed out'. If the current management of a bank is removed, and the shareholders lose their equity, but the bank is allowed to continue in operation, does that count as a 'rescue' or a 'bail-out'? If we mean by 'failure' the removal of ownership from existing shareholders and of control from existing management, then this can be done, effectively by (temporary) nationalization. This has happened in Japan and Scandinavia, for example. If we mean by failure the closure and liquidation of all positions, then the economic, social and political consequences would become much more extreme.

There *may* be other ways of providing mutual insurance within the banking system with a much larger role for the private sector, e.g. the cross-guarantee scheme advocated by Bert Ely (for example, 1995). There are certainly ways of trying to lessen the potential burden on the tax-payer, e.g. via prompt corrective action, otherwise known as Structured Early Intervention and Resolution, suggested by Benston and Kaufman (1994a, b), and partially incorporated in the Federal Deposit Insurance Corporation Improvement Act, or FDICIA (1991). The approach taken by New Zealand of requiring all directors, each year as a condition of continued appointment, to sign a letter indicating that they have personally checked, and are happy with, internal risk control mechanisms, thereby leaving themselves open to legal suit if something goes badly wrong, is another highly promising innovation (see Mayes 1997; Shirakawa 1997).

There is much that can be done around the edges, for example, to improve the incentives facing bank executives and to encourage bank supervisors to intervene earlier. But such measures, highly desirable though they may be, do not lessen the crucial economic verity, that the domestic monetary authorities, the government and central bank, will be held responsible by the electorate for the maintenance of systemic financial stability. This cannot be abrogated in a fit of extreme *laissez-faire*, and any attempt to pre-commit to do so would run into the most patent time-inconsistency.

The domestic monetary authorities have many powers. They can create fiat money, force errant bank managers to step down, recapitalize, merge or nationalize financial intermediaries, etc. But, by definition, they cannot create foreign currency, and they cannot by their own actions normally relieve foreign currency indebtedness within their own countries, except by encouraging or facilitating various forms of default (the pros and cons of which take us beyond the range of this paper).

Since a shortage of foreign currency, and an associated potential shortfall in imports and trade finance for exports (in its other guise a collapsing foreign value of the domestic currency), will disrupt the domestic economy, weak countries in such crises will seek financial support from their stronger neighbours. Just as weaker, smaller banks sought financial help from a larger, more central bank within a country, so smaller countries will seek out a larger protector in case of need.

If the IMF should be abolished, it would *not* lead to a cessation of intercountry support actions and 'bail-outs'. Instead of an international financial intermediary, we could then expect arrangements to develop whereby certain groupings of states attempt to arrange their own mutual insurance, perhaps around a hegemon, perhaps not. In Latin America, the abolition of the IMF would simply transfer more responsibility and involvement to the US Treasury. It is arguable that the main moral hazard in international lending came from the view that friends of the US would always be bailed out, rather than anything that the IMF, in so far as it could act independently of the US, would do. Circumscribing the role of the IMF in such circumstances would be akin to shooting the messenger, but failing to understand the message. In Asia, perceived limitations of the IMF in dealing with the recent crisis have led to proposals for an Asian Monetary Fund under Japanese leadership. In the absence of effective IMF ILOLR, the euro zone would play a similar role in Eastern Europe and Africa (and possibly elsewhere).

If the IMF were abolished, or so circumscribed in its resources and functions that it could not play an effective ILOLR role, the alternative would not be the restoration of a perfectly free market, in which each country stood, or fell, on the basis of its own individual failures or successes. There would, instead, develop an *ad hoc* system of regional (self-help) systems centred on a major currency, and a major power. The implications of that are not, on this view, welcome. Dividing the world into regional spheres of major powers would not be an advance on a truly international solution. Proponents of pure international *laissez-faire* should be aware that the political realities suggest that the result of curtailing the IMF would be a descent into a murkier world of regional major-power groupings, and not a system of pure free markets.

Financial crises are all too common, painful and potentially contagious. Faced with such dangers, all agents will try to insure against it. The weak will look to the strong for support. The question is not whether to have a lender of last resort, either nationally or internationally, because it is vain to think that such a mechanism can be abolished on the altar of free-market doctrine. The more relevant and interesting question is how best to organize the LOLR function that will continue to exist both nationally and internationally.

REFERENCES

Aghion, P., P. Bolton and M. Dewatripont (1999), 'Contagious Bank Failures', preliminary draft paper (March).

Allen F., and D. Gale (1998), 'Optimal Financial Crises', *Journal of Finance*, 53, 1245–84.

—. (1999), 'Financial Contagion', draft paper (March).

Bagehot, W. (1873), *Lombard Street: A Description of the Money Market*, revised edition with a foreword by Peter Bernstein. New York: Wiley (1999).

Benston, G. J., and G. G. Kaufman (1994a). 'The Intellectual History of the Federal Deposit Insurance Corporation Improvement Act of 1991', in G. G. Kaufman, ed., *Reforming Financial Institutions and Markets in the United States*. Dordrecht: Kluwer Academic Publishers.

Benston, G. J., and G. G. Kaufman (1994b), 'Improving the FDIC Improvement Act: What Was Done and What Still Needs to Be Done to Fix the Deposit Insurance Problem', in G. G. Kaufman, ed., *Reforming Financial Institutions and Markets in the United States.* Dordrecht: Kluwer Academic Publishers.

Buiter, W., and A. Sibert (1999), 'UDROP: A Contribution to the New International Financial Architecture', *International Finance*, 2(2), 227–48.

Calomiris, D. (1999), 'Moral Hazard is Avoidable', in W. L. Hunter, G. G. Kaufman and T. H. Krueger, eds., *The Asian Financial Crisis: Origins, Implications and Solutions.* Dordrecht: Kluwer Academic Publishers.

Capie, F. M. (1998), 'Can There Be an International Lender-of-last-resort?', *International Finance*, 1(2), 311–25.

Ely, B. (1995), 'Bringing Market-driven Regulation to European Banking: A Proposal for 100 Per Cent Cross-guarantees', Centre for the Study of Financial Innovation, Paper 16, July.

Fischer, S. (1999), 'On the Need for an International Lender of Last Resort', paper presented at CFS Research Conference, Frankfurt, 11 June.

Freixas, X. (1999), 'Optimal Bail Out Policy, Conditionality and Creative Ambiguity', paper presented at the Financial Markets Group conference on 'The Lender of Last Resort', London School of Economics, 13 July.

Fry, M. J. (1997), 'The Fiscal Abuse of Central Banks', in M. I. Blejer and T. Ter-Minassian, eds., *Macroeconomic Dimensions of Public Finance: Essays in Honour of Vito Tanzi.* London: Routledge, pp. 337–59.

Goodfriend, M., and R. G. King (1988), 'Financial Deregulation, Monetary Policy, and Central Banking', *Federal Reserve Bank of Richmond Economic Review*, May/June, 3–22.

Goodhart, C. A. E., and H. Huang (1999), 'A Model of the Lender of Last Resort', IMF Working Paper, WP/99/39, March.

Goodhart, C. A. E., and D. Schoenmaker (1993), 'Institutional Separation between Supervisory and Monetary Agencies', in F. Bruni, ed., *Prudential Regulation, Supervision and Monetary Policy.* Centro di Economia Monetaria e Finanziaria 'Paolo Baffi', Università Commerciale Luigi Bocconi.

Humphrey, T. M., and R. E. Keleher (1984), 'The Lender of Last Resort: A Historical Perspective', *Cato Journal*, 4(1), 275–317.

Keleher, R. (1999), 'An International Lender of Last Resort, the IMF, and the Federal Reserve', Joint Economic Committee Report of the US Congress, February.

Kynaston, D. (1995), *The City of London. Volume 2, Golden Years, 1890–1914.* London: Chatto & Windus.

Lissakers, K. (1999), 'The IMF and the Asian Crisis: A View from the Executive Board', in W. L. Hunter, G. G. Kaufman and T. H. Krueger, eds., *The Asian Financial Crisis: Origins, Implications and Solutions.* Dordrecht: Kluwer Academic Publishers.

Lindgren, C. J. (1999), 'Commentary on 'What's Wrong with the IMF' and 'Containing the Risk' ', in W. L. Hunter, G. G. Kaufman and T. H. Krueger, eds., *The Asian Financial Crisis: Origins, Implications and Solutions.* Dordrecht: Kluwer Academic Publishers.

Mayes, D. G. (1997), 'Incentives for Bank Directors and Management: The New Zealand Approach', paper presented at the Bank of England Conference on 'Regulatory Incentives', 13–14 November.

National Monetary Commission (1910–11), *Series of Volumes Presented to the US 61st Congress as Senate Documents.* Washington, DC.

Okina, K. (1999), 'Monetary Policy under Zero Inflation: A Response to Criticisms and Questions Regarding Monetary Policy', Institute for Monetary and Economic Studies, Bank of Japan, IMES Discussion Paper Series, no. 99-E-20.

Radcliffe Committee (1959), *Committee on the Working of the Monetary System: Report*, Cmnd 827, and *Minutes of Evidence to the Committee* (1960). London: HMSO.

Shirakawa, M. (1997), 'Reflections on the "New Zealand Approach" to Banking Supervision', paper presented at the Bank of England Conference on 'Regulatory Incentives', 13–14 November.

Thornton, H. (1802), *An Enquiry into the Nature and Effects of the Paper Credit of Great Britain*. London: Hatchard.

Timberlake, R. H. Jr (1978), *The Origins of Central Banking in the United States*. Cambridge, MA: Harvard University Press.

—. (1984), 'The Central Banking Role of Clearinghouse Associations', *Journal of Money, Credit and Banking*, 16(1), 1–15.

PART III

BANK RUNS AND CONTAGION

14

Systemic Risk in Banking: A Survey

OLIVIER DE BANDT AND PHILIPP HARTMANN

1. INTRODUCTION

In the last couple of years significant concerns about the stability of national and international financial systems have been raised. These concerns are reflected in a series of official summits and reports, private initiatives and academic papers,[1] and they have been underlined by the recent crises in East-Asia, Russia and Brazil. Fears exist that in an environment of relatively free international capital markets such events are becoming more frequent and that such developments may easily spill over to other countries. Although the increase in theoretical, empirical and policy analyses of financial instability has been substantial, we make two observations: First, while 'systemic risk' is now widely accepted as a fundamental underlying concept for the study of financial instability and possible policy responses, most work so far tackles one or several aspects of that risk, and there is no clear understanding of the *overall* concept of systemic risk. Second, we are not aware of any comprehensive survey of the substantial recent theoretical and empirical work on systemic risk in banking.

In this paper we attempt to provide a more comprehensive analysis of systemic risk, as the primary ingredient to understand financial crises and as the

The authors wish to thank, without implication, Ivo Arnold, Lorenzo Bini-Smaghi, Frank Browne, Elena Carletti, Pietro Catte, E.P. Davis, Kevin Dowd, Mark Flannery, Charles Goodhart, Mauro Grande, Gerhard Illing, Jeff Lacker, Tim Montgomery, María Nieto, Rafael Repullo, Daniela Russo, Benjamin Sahel, the participants of the ECB research seminar, the Tinbergen Institute economics seminar in Rotterdam, the Banking Supervisory Sub-Committee, the Second Joint Central Bank Conference on 'Risk Measurement and Systemic Risk', hosted by the Bank of Japan in Tokyo, and the Center for Financial Studies Conference on 'Systemic Risk and Lender of Last Resort Facilities' in Frankfurt for their comments on an earlier draft of the paper. Any views expressed in this paper are the authors' own and do not necessarily reflect those of the European Central Bank, the Banque de France or the Eurosystem.

[1] Financial stability issues have recently been addressed on the G-7 1995 Halifax, 1996 Lyon and 1997 Denver summits. Among the reports and papers are Cole and Kehoe (2000), Committee on Payments and Settlements Systems (1996), Federal Reserve Bank of Kansas City (1998), Goodhart *et al.* (1998), Group of Thirty (1997), International Organization of Securities Commissions (1998), Kaminsky and Reinhart (1998), Lindgren, Garcia and Saal (1996), Peek and Rosengren (1997), Working Party on Financial Stability in Emerging Markets (1997), Hunter, Kaufman and Krueger (1999), Agénor *et al.* (2000) and Shiller (2000). During the preparation of this paper, the G-7 countries also adopted a plan by former Bundesbank President Hans Tietmeyer to establish a Financial Stability Forum (FSF), gathering national and international authorities in charge of ensuring financial stability to further improve international co-operation in financial market supervision and surveillance (Tietmeyer 1999). The FSF, chaired by BIS general manager Andrew Crockett, published various reports of its working groups during the year 2000 (Financial Stability Forum 2000a–d).

main rationale for banking regulation, prudential supervision and crisis management. In a first step, we bring together the most important analytical elements of systemic risk and integrate them into a coherent working concept, which could be used as a baseline for monetary and prudential policy decisions to preserve the stability of financial systems.

While the 'special' character of banks plays a major role, we stress that systemic risk goes beyond the traditional view of single banks' vulnerability to depositor runs. At the heart of the concept is the notion of 'contagion', a particularly strong propagation of failures from one institution or system to another. Especially nowadays the way in which wholesale interbank markets function and large-value payment systems are set up can play an important role in the way shocks may propagate through the bank system and the financial system as a whole. Although searching for an ultimate definition of systemic risk may be futile due to the ever changing financial markets and institutions, it may still be useful to give some general structure to our thinking in this area in order to help avoid piecemeal policy making.

In a second step we review the existing theoretical and empirical literature about systemic risk in the light of the previously developed general concept, in order to identify areas in which future research is needed. More specifically, the survey of the empirical evidence on systemic effects tries to clarify their practical relevance. Our preference for reviewing the quantitative literature is so that we can focus on the work formulating and testing very specific hypotheses with the most advanced techniques.[2] However, this should not be interpreted as meaning that we consider the more descriptive literature of particular crisis periods in history as not being important.

When we started studying systemic risk more than two years ago the literature appeared to be very incomplete, especially when considering the issues raised by actual crisis situations. It is for this reason that we try to set out, first, what we think is important for understanding systemic risk and, second, examine where satisfactory answers have and have not been given. However, due to the rapid development of the theoretical work on bank contagion during the second half of the 1990s many of the gaps we discovered in our early work have now been filled, although many are still present in both the empirical and theoretical literature. First, theoretical studies of large-value payment systems have not yet addressed the risks in 'hybrid' systems, which mix the characteristics of net and gross systems and which are often encountered in practice. Second, empirical analyses of contagion effects in payment systems seem to be limited to net systems, widely ignoring 'network externalities' potentially resulting from 'gridlock' situations in real-time gross payment systems. Third, the overwhelming part of econometric

[2] The only other large literature surveys in the area of systemic risk we are aware of have been written by Kaufman (1994) and Davis (1995). However, the former is narrower in scope than ours, focusing on bank contagion alone, mainly but not exclusively taking an empirical perspective. The latter is broader than this, building its case from the basics of the debt contract, but it does not interpret the literature within one coherent concept of systemic risk. Both cannot consider the more recent developments. Bartholomew and Kaufman (1995) contains a useful selection of non-technical essays about various aspects of systemic risk. Freixas and Rochet (1997, chapter 7) give a thorough theoretical exhibition of a selection of key models in the bank run literature, which are also surveyed in Bhattacharya and Thakor (1993). Dowd (1992a) reviews this literature critically.

tests for bank contagion effects is limited to data for the United States. Event studies of bank equity returns, debt risk premiums, deposit flows or physical exposures for European or Japanese data are rare or virtually absent. Fourth, and perhaps most importantly, it appears to be hard to disentangle empirically information-based revisions of bank depositor expectations from 'pure' (sunspot-type) contagion, 'efficient' from 'inefficient' crises and contagion from macro shocks. This difficulty has implications for the policy debate about the lender of last resort.

The paper is intended to provide readers with a concise review of the literature on systemic risk and also to help stimulate additional research efforts aimed at filling the remaining gaps. This future research should further improve our understanding of specific banking crises and thereby help conduct better policies to prevent or alleviate future crises. However, we only briefly discuss policy issues, such as optimal crisis prevention and management.

The remainder of the paper is organized as follows. Section 2 contains the general conceptual discussion. It provides the framework within which the theoretical and empirical literature will be interpreted in the subsequent parts and briefly discusses its relevance for economic policy. Section 3 gives a detailed account of systemic risks in banking markets and payment systems, surveying theoretical models explaining them and adding theoretical considerations where no model is available. Section 4 surveys a large number of econometric tests and some other quantitative assessments of the various facets of systemic risk described before, focussing particularly on bank contagion but also on joint crises. Section 5 concludes.

2. THE CONCEPT OF SYSTEMIC RISK

Systemic risk in a very general sense is by no way a phenomenon limited to economics or the financial system. Maybe the most natural illustration of the concept is in the area of health and epidemic diseases. In severe cases (e.g. the Great Plague in the Middle Ages) widespread contamination with a disease may wipe out a significant portion of a population. In the area of economics it has been argued that systemic risk is a special feature of financial systems, in particular the banking system. While contamination effects may also occur in other sectors of the economy, the likelihood and severity in financial systems is often regarded as being considerably higher.[3] A full systemic crisis in the financial system may then have strong adverse consequences for the real economy and general economic welfare.

The objective of this section is to provide a framework for the economic analysis of systemic risk. We start out by proposing a specific terminology, clarifying some important ideas involved in systemic risk and develop a general working

[3] However, see for example, Lang and Stulz (1992) for a study of stock market value spillovers among non-financial firms. One challenge to the existence of systemic risk is provocatively summarized by Sheldon and Maurer (1998, p. 685): 'Systemic risks are for financial market participants what Nessie, the monster of Loch Ness, is for the Scots (and not only for them): Everyone knows and is aware of the danger. Everyone can accurately describe the threat. Nessie, like systemic risk, is omnipresent, but nobody knows when and where it might strike. There is no proof that anyone has really encountered it, but there is no doubt that it exists.'

definition. Then the reasons why financial systems can be regarded as being more vulnerable to systemic risk than other parts of economic systems are discussed. Since information asymmetries can play a crucial role we proceed in the next section by distinguishing between self-fulfilling systemic events and those that can be regarded as individually rational responses to the revelation of new information between agents. Finally, the relevance of systemic risk in banking for public policy is briefly examined together with opposing arguments from the free banking school.

2.1. Systemic Events

In order to reach a definition of systemic risk in bank systems, we first clarify a number of concepts—illustrated in Table 1—needed for that definition. We define a *systemic event* in the *narrow* sense as an event, where the release of 'bad news' about a bank, or even its failure, leads in a sequential fashion to considerable adverse effects on one or several other banks, for example, their failure. The shaded area in Table 1 encompasses these systemic events in the narrow sense. Essential is the 'domino effect' from one institution to the other or from one system to the other emanating from a limited ('idiosyncratic') shock.[4] On the other hand, systemic events in the *broad* sense, shown by ticks in both shaded and non

Table 1. *Systemic events in banking systems*

Type of initial shock	Single systemic events (affect only one bank in the second round effect)		Wide systemic events (affect many banks in the second round effect)	
	Weak (no failure)	Strong (failure of one bank)	Weak (no failure)	Strong (failures of many banks)
Narrow shock that propagates				
• Idiosyncratic shock	✔	✔ contagion	✔	✔ contagion leading to a systemic crisis
• Limited systematic shock	✔	✔ contagion	✔	✔ contagion leading to a systemic crisis
Wide systematic shock			✔	✔ systemic crisis

Note: ✔ means that the combination of events defined by the cell is a systemic event. The shaded area describes cases of systemic events in the narrow sense. Systemic events in the broad sense *also* include the cells with ✔ in the last row.

[4] Notice that such systemic events do not include, for example, the failure of a *single* financial institution as a consequence of a wild decline of some asset value. Failures confined to single institutions lack the systemic element. See also Calomiris and Gorton (1991) and Bhattacharya and Thakor (1993).

shaded areas of Table 1, include not only the events described above but *also* simultaneous adverse effects on a large number of banks as a consequence of severe and widespread ('systematic') shocks. The union of the shaded and non-shaded ticked areas in Table 1 describes systemic events in the broad sense. Therefore, this category also includes the widespread and simultaneous effects on banks that may arise from the release of new information ('signals').

A systemic event in the narrow sense is *strong*, if the institution(s) affected in the second round or later actually fail as a consequence of the initial shock, although they have been fundamentally solvent ex ante. We denote these strong instances of systemic events in the narrow sense as *contagion*. Otherwise, that is, if the external effect is less than a failure, we denote a systemic event in the narrow sense as weak. Similarly, systemic events related to systematic shocks are strong (weak), if a significant part of the banks simultaneously affected by them (do not) actually fail.

Following the terminology of financial theory, *shocks* are defined as idiosyncratic or systematic. In an extreme sense *idiosyncratic* shocks are those which initially affect only the health of a single financial institution, while *systematic* (or widespread) shocks can affect the whole economy, for example, all financial institutions together at the same time.[5] An example of an idiosyncratic shock to a national bank system is the failure of a single regional bank, say, as a result of internal fraud. Systematic shocks to national bank systems can include general business cycle fluctuations or a sudden increase in the inflation rate. Stock market crashes can also act as a type of systematic shock on most financial institutions, even though due to different exposures they will usually not be affected uniformly. Of course, there is a continuum of intermediate types of shocks (e.g. sector-wide or regional) between the theoretical extremes of idiosyncratic and wide systematic shocks. Idiosyncratic shocks that do not propagate widely are 'insurable', in the sense that an investor can protect herself against them via diversification, whereas wide systematic shocks are often 'uninsurable' or non-diversifiable. Negative systematic shocks, such as a severe recession, will—when they reach a certain strength—always adversely affect a wide range of banks, so that their consequences have been included in the broad concept of systemic risk.

Based on this terminology a *systemic crisis* (in the narrow and broad sense) can be defined as a systemic event that affects a considerable number of banks in a strong sense, thereby severely impairing the general functioning of a major part of the financial system, in which case the effectiveness and efficiency of the financial system to direct savings into real investments is compromised. For example, a systemic financial crisis can lead to extreme credit rationing of the real sector ('credit

[5] Since it is widely used in finance, we prefer the term 'systematic' for wide shocks. A systematic shock may imply a systemic event (in the 'broad' sense), as explained above, but a systemic event does not need to originate in a systematic shock (e.g. in the case of contagion). Therefore, the two terms have to be distinguished.

crunch').[6] The distinction between the narrow and the broad concept of systemic events and crises is important, since crisis management measures, tackling the source of the problem, might be different in the case of an idiosyncratic shock that risks causing contagion compared to the case of a systematic shock that might have a broad simultaneous destabilization effect (see Section 2.4). However, in practical crisis situations both aggregate shocks and contagious failures may sometimes become intertwined, since macroeconomic downturns might weaken banks, making contagion of single failures more likely. Similarly, it might be necessary for contagion effects to materialize so that the initial shock impairs more than just one bank (Chen 1999).

Systemic risk (in the narrow and broad sense) can then be defined as the risk of experiencing systemic events in the strong sense.[7] In principle, the spectrum of systemic risk ranges from the second-round effect on a single bank (column 'single systemic events' in Table 1) to the risk of having a systemic crisis affecting most, or even the whole of the banking system (column 'wide systemic events' in Table 1).[8] The geographical reach of systemic risk can be regional, national or international.

As well as the source of the systemic event, idiosyncratic or systematic shocks, a key element in the narrow sense of systemic events is the mechanism through which shocks propagate from one bank to another. In our view, this lies at the very heart of systemic risk. Note that systematic shocks are equally important for the non-financial sectors in the economy. Therefore, the propagation of shocks within the financial system, manifesting themselves through physical bank exposures or information effects/potential losses of confidence, must be characteristically different. In what follows we shall look at the various propagation chains in banking in much detail. However, from a conceptual point of view it is important that the *transmission* of shocks is a natural part of the self-stabilizing adjustments of the market system to a new equilibrium. What one has in mind with the concept of systemic risk, in the narrow sense, is propagation that is not incorporated in market prices ex ante or can lead to general destabilisation. Such propagation may show particularly 'violent' features, such as cumulative reinforcement ('non-linearities') and price 'jumps' ('discontinuities'), for example through abrupt changes in expectations.

A systemic event caused by a simultaneous systematic shock may often involve a macroeconomic propagation that includes interactions between real and financial variables. For example, a cyclical downturn may trigger a wave of failures

[6] Other accompanying factors of a systemic crisis may include severe liquidity shortages in various financial markets, major inefficiencies in the allocation of risks and severe misalignments of asset prices.

[7] Bartholomew and Whalen (1995) as well as Goldstein (1995) review various definitions of systemic risk. We think that this definition, derived from our conceptual framework, encompasses most other definitions explicitly or implicitly used so far. See also Aglietta and Moutot (1993) and Davis (1995).

[8] However, as pointed out by Kaufman (1988), due to 'flight to quality' it is unlikely in practice that, for example, all banks of a country face a deposit run at the same time. For a discussion of the 'flight to quality' phenomenon in the context of bank runs, see Benston *et al.* (1986, chapter 2) and Saunders and Wilson (1996).

by corporate firms, not only rendering many loans by all types of banks non-performing due to possible default, but also inducing them to cut lending further. This in turn can deepen the cyclical downturn. When considering banks, the widely observed non-indexation of their liabilities, that is, their deposits, to the value of their assets which can fluctuate after macroeconomic shocks has been mentioned as one major reason why banking crises in the form of simultaneous failures are often associated with severe macroeconomic fluctuations (Gorton 1988; Hellwig 1998).

Obviously, both the occurrence of shocks as well as the subsequent propagation is uncertain. So the importance of systemic risk has two dimensions, the severity of systemic events as well as the likelihood of their occurrence. Strong systemic events, in particular systemic crises, are low probability events, which might lead some to consider them as less of a concern. However, once a crisis strikes the consequences could be very severe. In particular, systemic events occurring in the financial sector might have considerable impacts on the real sector, that is, on output and general welfare. One may distinguish a *horizontal* view on the concept of systemic risk, in which the focus is limited to events in the financial sector alone (particularly through the bankruptcy of banks), from a *vertical* view on systemic risk, where the impact of a systemic event on output can proxy the severity of such an event.[9] In many of the papers discussed below real effects play some role. However, in order to keep the scope of the paper manageable we concentrate the discussion on the horizontal dimension.[10]

It is straightforward to apply this definition and conceptual discussion also to the case of financial market crashes.[11] The sequential spillover of a crash in one market to one or more other markets would constitute contagion, whereas the simultaneous crash of two or more markets as a consequence of a systematic shock would be included in the case of a 'broad' financial market event. However, the issue whether contagious or joint crashes of asset markets constitute instances of 'systemic risk', similar to the case of bank systems, has proven to be controversial in the literature. In fact, Anna Schwartz, among others, argued that financial market crashes alone are only 'pseudo' financial crises (or if they cluster constitute only 'pseudo' systemic risk) and not 'real' ones, unless they affect the stability of the banking system and thereby endanger the availability of a means of payment (see Schwartz 1986; Bordo, Mizrach and Schwartz 1995). Behind this view must be the assumption that, similar to the events described by Friedman and Schwartz

[9] We would like to thank Lorenzo Bini-Smaghi, who suggested this distinction and terminology.

[10] See Lindgren, Garcia and Saal (1996) for a synthesis of the output effects of a large number of bank crisis situations. As is evident from systematic shocks as one potential source of systemic crises (Table 1), the relationship between the performance of the real and financial sectors can go in both directions (see e.g. Section 3.1.2.1).

[11] A market crash can be defined as an unusually large general price fall. In statistical terms this fall can be made more precise by relating it to the extreme percentiles of the respective market's empirical return distribution. For example, cases where a representative price index decreases by a higher percentage than the 1 or 5 percentile of the historical return distribution (i.e. the extreme left tail of the distribution) could be defined as crashes (Jansen and de Vries 1991).

(1963) for the Great Depression, banking crises and related monetary contractions correspond much more with severe real effects than just the losses of wealth associated with financial market crashes. A discussion of contagious and joint asset market crashes and a survey of the related literature is provided in a companion paper (Hartmann and De Bandt 2001).

2.2. The Financial Fragility Hypothesis

Why is it then that systemic risk, in particular potential contagion effects, are of special concern in the financial system? There are three interrelated features of financial systems that can provide a basis for this 'financial fragility hypothesis': (i) the structure of banks, (ii) the interconnection of financial institutions through direct exposures and settlement systems and (iii) the information intensity of financial contracts and related credibility problems.

(i) Traditionally, commercial banks take fixed-value deposits that can be withdrawn (unconditionally and at fixed value) at very short notice and lend long-term to industrial companies (Bryant 1980; Diamond and Dybvig 1983). Normally, that is, when the law of large numbers applies, only a small fraction of assets needs to be held in liquid reserves to meet deposit withdrawals. This fractional reserve holding can lead to illiquidity and even default, when exceptionally high withdrawals occur and long-term loans cannot be liquidated, although the bank might be fundamentally solvent in the long run.[12] Moreover, single bank loans do not have an 'objective' market price. Since, usually the lending bank alone has most information about the real investments funded, they are largely non-tradable. (However, this statement should be qualified in that (the risk incorporated in) single loans to certain types of borrowers can be bundled and traded via securitization techniques (or credit derivatives). See for example, Goodhart *et al.* 1998, chapter 5. So, the health of a bank not only depends on its success in picking profitable investment projects for lending but also on the *confidence* of depositors in the value of the loan book and, most importantly, in their confidence that *other* depositors will not run on the bank. Notice that this 'special' character of banks does not apply to most other financial intermediaries, such as insurance companies, securities houses and the like (see e.g. Goodhart *et al.* 1998, chapter 1).[13] However, if banks and other intermediaries belong to the same financial entity, as is now more often the case, non-bank intermediaries' problems might still become a source of bank fragility. Obviously, the more depositors are protected through some deposit insurance, as exists now in most industrialized countries, the less likely it is that confidence crises occur.[14]

12 Diamond and Rajan (2000a,b) argue that this fragility in the structure of banks is a necessary side-effect of an efficient performance of their role as liquidity providers to the economy. See Section 3.1.1.1.

13 The speciality of banks and their vulnerability to runs is widely recognized in the economic literature, which will be surveyed in detail in Section 3.1.1.1.

14 The problems associated with deposit insurance and their relationship to systemic risk are addressed in Section 2.4.

(ii) There is a complex network of exposures among banks (and potentially some other financial intermediaries) through the interbank money market and the large-value (wholesale) payment and security settlement systems (Humphrey 1986; Folkerts-Landau 1991; Committee on Payment and Settlement Systems 1992, 1996). In fact, banks tend to play a key role in wholesale and retail payment and settlement systems. At certain points during the business day, these exposures can be very large, so that the failure of one bank to meet payment obligations can have an immediate impact on the ability of other banks to meet their own payment obligations. Even worse, a crisis situation can trigger difficulties in the technical completion of the different steps of the payment and settlement process, which would amplify effective exposures and 'domino' effects. Various techniques used in securities and derivatives markets, such as margin requirements and portfolio insurance, although intended to limit risk ex ante can also account for large and immediate payments needs by banks and other intermediaries ex post, namely in times of large asset price changes. Since financial conglomerates include banks and other financial intermediaries it is possible that securities or insurance subsidiaries can play a role in these interlinkages. Various special risk management measures are usually applied to limit the potential of contagion in payment and settlement systems.[15]

(iii) The third feature is, more generally, the information and control intensity of financial contracts (e.g. Stiglitz 1993). Decisions regarding the intertemporal allocation of consumption are based on expectations of what the value of various assets are going to be in the future or whether the future cash flows promised in a financial contract are going to be met. (The use of deposit contracts described in (i) provides a specific example.) Hence, when uncertainty increases or the credibility of a financial commitment starts to be questioned, market expectations may shift substantially and in an 'individually rational' way in short periods of time leading to equally volatile investment and disinvestment decisions. For example, credibility issues can lead to large asset price fluctuations, whose sizes and directions are virtually impossible to explain through 'fundamental' analysis alone (Shiller 1989).[16]

These three features taken together seem to be the principal sources for the potentially higher vulnerability of financial systems to systemic risk than other sectors of the economy.

2.3. 'Efficient' Versus Self-Fulfilling Systemic Events

General uncertainty and agents' awareness of potential asymmetries of information highlight the role that expectations can play in systemic events. In fact, systemic events driven by expectations can be individually rational but not socially

[15] Financial intermediaries' interconnection through payment systems is further studied in Section 3.2.

[16] Fundamental analysis attempts to explain or predict asset price changes through the factors influencing the 'intrinsic' values of assets. For example, 'fundamentals' influencing shares are companies' earnings, 'fundamentals' influencing exchange rates include inflation rates.

optimal. It is useful to distinguish between three potential causes of narrow systemic events related to asymmetric information and expectations. (i) The full revelation of new information about the health of banks to the public, (ii) the release of a 'noisy signal' about the health of banks to the public and (iii) the occurrence of a signal which co-ordinates the expectations of the public without being actually related to the health of banks ('sunspot'; Cass and Shell 1983).

(i) Suppose that, hidden from depositors, a bank has made a number of loans that turn bad, so that it is basically insolvent but continues to survive for some time since it can roll over debts in the interbank market. Suppose further that other banks—having neglected to monitor their counterparties properly—develop substantial solvency threatening exposures to it. If the information about these facts were then released in full, it would be individually rational for depositors to withdraw their funds and force those banks into liquidation. *Ceteris paribus* such an outcome, which can be denoted as a 'fully revealing' equilibrium, would also be 'efficient', as opposed to a scenario where the banks continue to accumulate losses.[17]

(ii) Suppose that the information about bad loans and interbank exposures is not revealed in full but that depositors only receive imperfect information (a 'noisy' signal) from some outside source, which from their point of view increases the likelihood of the bank's adverse position. In such a situation it might still be rational for them to try and withdraw their funds early and thereby force the default of those banks. Whether the signal has been 'right' or 'wrong' would determine, *ceteris paribus*, whether this outcome is 'efficient' or not. As it is triggered by imperfect information on fundamentals, this type of contagion could be denoted as 'information-based'.[18]

(iii) Suppose that the level of deposit withdrawals in itself provides an imperfect signal for all depositors about the health of their own banks and the respective banks' interbank counterparties. This involves 'endogenous uncertainty' and can cause depositors to behave in a way that results in multiple equilibria. In these circumstances, even if all the banks have been healthy ex ante, any event that coordinates depositors' expectations about the withdrawal behaviour of other depositors might induce them to rush to withdraw even from different banks and force those banks into liquidation. The related systemic event might still have been 'individually rational' ex ante, while the outcome of a self-fulfilling panic or 'pure' contagion is inefficient, since depositors lose the benefits from financial intermediation (and might also incur capital losses if the liquidation leads to asset values declining below the 'normal', non-crisis market levels).

[17] The efficiency holds under the assumption that there would not be any subsequent problems in the payment system amplifying the problem beyond the group of unsound banks. In a somewhat related vein, Kaufman (1988) points to a 'benefit' of bank crises, forcing governments to step in and close all insolvent banks so that asymmetric information between the public and bank managers is removed.

[18] Gorton (1985) provides a model of fully revealing equilibria and information-based depositor runs without interbank contagion.

The asymmetric information problems also illustrate how banking problems can build up over an extended period of time before an 'efficient' or 'inefficient' crisis occurs. In other words, the systemic event is only the manifestation of a more fundamental underlying problem, for example reckless lending and bad loans, which has been hidden from policy makers or the general public for some time. Hence, before we turn to potential policy responses to inefficient systemic events, it needs to be stressed that ex ante policies, i.e. measures trying to prevent a fundamental problem from actually arising (such as financial regulation and supervision or measures allowing market forces to be more effective), should always be the primary line of defence, so that the use of ex post policies in the form of crisis management is limited as much as possible.

2.4. Systemic Risk and Public Policy

An assessment of how relevant extent systemic risk is when considering economic and financial policies can now be undertaken. Musgrave and Musgrave (1973) have introduced the 'classical' distinction of three functions for public policies: the allocation function, the stabilization function and the distribution function. First, consider allocation policies. Strong systemic events, such as contagious failures, may involve external effects; that is, the private costs of the initial failure can be lower than the social costs. As a consequence, individually rational bank management may lead to a higher level of systemic risk than would be socially optimal. This is one, may be even the fundamental rationale for the regulation and supervision of banks; an ex ante (or pre-emptive) policy to avoid the emergence of systemic problems (in contrast to ex post policies, i.e. crisis management). Notice that in this sense, the socially optimal probability of bank failures is *not* zero. However, for a socially optimal outcome, the probability of 'pure' contagion (a self-fulfilling systemic event as described above) and certain cases of 'information-based' contagion will be zero. Apart from investor protection considerations, this point is sometimes also brought forward as a rationale for the introduction of deposit insurance. Another element of the safety net and of crisis management that has been widely debated is emergency liquidity assistance by the central bank to *individual financial institutions* in distress, the default of which may trigger contagion effects. Moreover, since *any* systemic event might involve payment and settlement system problems, which exacerbate any externalities, it also provides a rationale for ex ante policies to ensure the safety of those systems (oversight, collateral requirements, position caps etc.).

Second, a systemic crisis affecting a large number of banks can—via a 'credit crunch' or 'debt deflation'—lead to a recession or even to a depression. In such situations macroeconomic stabilization policies, such as monetary or fiscal expansions, may be used to maintain an adequate level of liquidity in the *banking system as a whole* ('lending to the market' by the central bank) and dampen the recessionary impact on the real economy. Interestingly, in the case of systemic risk, allocation and stabilization problems can be closely intertwined. If contagion is very strong, then the microeconomic risk allocation problem can degenerate to a macroeconomic destabilization. So, the ex ante (regulation and supervision) and ex post (crisis management) policies described in the previous paragraph can both be seen as stabilization policies.[19]

The concept of systemic risk developed above is also relevant to the debate about the role a central bank can take on as 'lender of last resort'. When taking on this role, the central bank can either implement a general monetary policy expansion and lend to the market. This can be done in response to an aggregate shock that affects many banks simultaneously. By definition, 'lending to the market' is not sterilized, but any monetary impulse could normally be taken out of the economy at a later stage, when the crisis is over, through a more contractionary monetary policy stance.[20] Or the central bank can provide emergency liquidity assistance to individual banks, so preventing individual failures that, in the absence of such emergency lending, have a high likelihood of causing contagion (systemic risk in the 'narrow' sense). Individual emergency loans can be sterilized through opposite monetary policy transactions *vis-à-vis* the market as a whole. For various reasons, the literature about the lender of last resort showed much more controversy regarding this second type of activity than about the first one (see Goodfriend and King (1988, reprinted in this volume) and Goodhart and Huang (1999) for two opposite views). This is one main motivation for developing a more complete concept of systemic risk, for distinguishing between a 'narrow' and a 'broad' type of systemic risk and for putting considerable emphasis on the empirical evidence of contagion in Section 4 of this paper.

It is now widely recognized that public and private safety nets, whether they take the form of deposit insurance or lender of last resort facilities, bear the risk of creating moral hazard. For example, if deposit insurance premiums do not reflect the banks' relative portfolio risks, then the protection may incite the insured to take on higher risks (Merton 1976, 1978). Moreover, market expectations could be created that large banks with substantial clearing, market and settlement links with many other players in the financial system are 'too big to fail' or 'too sophisticated to fail'. Such effects may be countered by very effective financial regulation and prudential supervision, as for example shown by Kareken and Wallace (1978), Buser, Chen and Kane (1981) and Furlong and Keeley (1989) for the case of deposit insurance. They also create a case for 'constructive ambiguity' *vis-à-vis* the potential use of public emergency lending. However, if the measures to control moral hazard are not successful, then the insured institutions could become more

[19] In principle, systemic crisis can also have distribution effects. Since less wealthy people will have a higher share of their, relatively small, savings invested in relatively simple bank deposits etc., and not in physical property for example, and since they might be even less able to judge the health of a bank, they are particularly exposed to lose out. In virtually all industrialized countries at present this problem is dealt with in the form of a deposit insurance schemes.

[20] For example, Friedman and Schwartz (1963) argued that a more expansionary monetary policy by the Fed during the Great Depression could have prevented banking panics and reduced the severity of the real contraction.

vulnerable to adverse shocks, so that the likelihood of propagation across institutions may rise as well. This latter scenario would imply a higher level of systemic risk through inadequate safety net provisions or, in other words, high costs of maintaining the safety net.

When considering different policies to contain systemic risk, the issue of market-oriented approaches to deal with banking instabilities is also raised. There is an ongoing academic debate about whether 'free banking' or private payment arrangements could be equally stable and yet more efficient than current regulated banking systems with partly public payment systems in industrial countries. 'Free bankers' point to the disciplinary effects of demandable bank deposits (Calomiris and Kahn 1991), which can also be relevant in interbank markets. Also, historical episodes of relatively unregulated and publicly unprotected banking systems in various countries suggested that such liberal structures were at least as stable as their more regulated counterparts (see e.g. White 1984; Rolnick and Weber 1986; Dowd 1992b, 1996, chapter 7).[21] Apart from the ex ante disciplinary effects of greater market forces, the conceived success of the examples discussed in this literature is also seen as a result of private and self-regulated safety provisions against financial instabilities, such as clearing houses (Gorton and Mullineaux 1987; Calomiris and Kahn 1996; Rolnick, Smith and Weber 1999). An opposing view points to the risk of non-competitive practices by private 'bankers clubs' or monopolies in charge of these provisions (Goodhart 1988; Rolnick, Smith and Weber 1998). It also highlights the 'inherent instability' of free banking, as evidenced by frequent bank failures and historical episodes of systemic crises in free banking systems, and the difficulty of a private and heterogeneous club to decisively intervene in a crisis situation (Goodhart 1969, 1988).

Whereas historical analogies bear the risk of neglecting the considerable differences between today's and former bank systems, many industrialized countries have market-oriented elements in their safety net provisions; for example, the 'solidarité de place' for failing banks in the 1984 French banking law and 'life boat' arrangements in the UK or the Liquiditätskonsortialbank fulfilling the function of a semi-private 'lender of penultimate resort' in Germany.[22] A few industrialized countries have also established deposit insurance arrangements on a largely private basis (see Kyei 1995, for a survey). Such arrangements aim at imposing the cost of bank crises on the banking sector itself, thereby helping to prevent moral

[21] Historical episodes chosen in this literature include the US free banking period (1837–63), the Scottish free banking period (late eighteenth, early nineteenth centuries), Australia (early 1890s) and Canada (late nineteenth, early twentieth centuries). White (1984), for example, argues that the English bank instabilities in the early nineteenth century did not affect Scottish free banks, and Rolnick and Weber (1986) do not find evidence that regional (intrastate) clusters of bank failures in the US free banking era spilled over across state borders.

[22] Two thirds of the Liko bank's capital are held by private and public banks domiciled in Germany and the rest by the Deutsche Bundesbank. The publicly co-ordinated but privately financed bail-out of Long-Term Capital Management in September 1998 provides an example of private sector involvement of the 'life boat' type.

hazard. However, the existence of public crisis prevention and crisis management provisions in today's financial systems make it difficult to assess systemic risk in private banking markets, since one can never be certain about the outcome of systemic events in the absence of such public provisions. In this sense the historical experience with 'free banking' episodes has some value for the formulation of today's policies.

3. THEORETICAL MODELS OF SYSTEMIC RISK IN BANKING

We now consider in greater detail the forms that systemic risk may take, distinguishing between risks in banking markets and risks in the interbank payment infrastructure. Payment systems are treated separately since settlement of transactions involves technical peculiarities, which are quite different from the underlying retail deposit taking and interbank trading activities. The theoretical literature on systemic risk in banking is surveyed in the light of the concept discussed in the previous section.

3.1. Systemic Risk in Banking Markets

As has been observed numerous times in the past, banks may, in the absence of a safety net, be prone to runs. At some occasions, individual runs may spill over to other parts of the banking sector, potentially leading to a full-scale panic. While the theory of individual runs is well developed, the same did *not*—until very recently—apply to bank contagion, which incorporates the *systemic* component. One can distinguish two main channels through which contagion in banking markets can work: the 'real' or exposure channel and the informational channel.[23] The former relates to the potential for 'domino effects' through real exposures in the interbank markets and/or in payment systems. The information channel relates to contagious withdrawals when depositors are imperfectly informed about the type of shocks hitting banks (idiosyncratic or systematic) and about their physical exposures to each other (asymmetric information). In principle, these two fundamental channels can work in conjunction as well as quite independently. More elaborate theories of bank contagion, which explicitly model these channels, starting with Flannery (1996, reprinted in this volume) and Rochet and Tirole (1996a), have only recently begun to be developed. Traditionally, many systemic banking panics have been associated with recessions and macroeconomic shocks (systemic risk in the 'broad' sense; see e.g. Gorton 1988), but formal theories beyond individual bank run models have been scarce. We start in the next section with the classical bank run literature to juxtapose it with the more recent bank contagion literature. Then we discuss the small literature taking the traditional view of systemic banking panics as a consequence of macroeconomic shocks and lending booms.

[23] See, for example, Saunders (1987, pp. 205f.).

3.1.1. Bank Runs Versus Bank Contagion

The banking literature in the last 20 years has developed sophisticated models of *single* banks' fragility (see also point (i) in Section 2.2). However, regarding systemic risk the speciality of 'the bank contract' is only part of the story. The other part of it are interbank linkages through direct exposures and payment systems, which can only be studied in a model of a multiple bank system (point (ii) in Section 2.2). In other words, one should distinguish between a 'run' which involves only a single bank and a 'banking panic' where more than one bank is affected (Calomiris and Gorton 1991; Bhattacharya and Thakor 1993). We continue by reviewing the traditional bank run literature before covering the more recent models of contagion in multiple bank systems. The latter encompass models applying the logic of the single bank run literature to multiple bank systems, models of physical interbank exposures and extensions of the credit rationing literature to the interbank case.

3.1.1.1. The Classical Bank Run Models. The first class of models, following Diamond and Dybvig (1983, reprinted in this volume), was designed to address the issue of the instability of single banks with fractional reserve holdings. Banks transform short-term deposits into long-term investments, with a liquidity premium, while depositors face a pay-off externality due to a 'sequential service constraint' (when depositors withdraw their deposits, a first-come-first-served rule applies) and there is no market for investment or bank shares. A fraction of bank customers experience a liquidity shock and wish to withdraw their deposits 'early'. The crucial element is that the fear of 'early' withdrawals by a too large number of depositors may trigger a run on the bank in the form of a self-fulfilling prophecy ('sunspot').[24] Due to the stochastic nature of 'early' withdrawals, the model has been interpreted as suggesting that bank runs are a random phenomenon. Whereas in the Diamond and Dybvig model banks are seen as providers of insurance for depositors against liquidity shocks, Waldo (1985) sees them as a mechanism for small savers to indirectly access primary securities markets at rates equal to their expected yields. In this model runs can also occur as self-fulfilling prophecies as a consequence of the sequential service constraint, but when they occur they imply fire sales of primary long-term securities that lead to interest rate increases and declines in the deposit-currency ratio.

In the second class of models depositor runs are caused by the release of new information about the viability of bank investments, such as a leading business cycle indicator. Gorton (1985) shows how, under complete information, rational and efficient depositor runs can occur. Under incomplete information the noisy signal can sometimes trigger rational but inefficient ('information based') runs. The author shows that within his model this problem can be resolved by adding a suspension of convertibility on the deposit contract, so that banks can signal the mutually beneficial continuation of investments and thereby approximate the complete information world. (No sequential service constraint is imposed.) In

[24] Both 'run' as well as 'no run' are possible Nash equilibria.

another model of 'information based' or 'efficient' bank runs by Jacklin and Bhattacharya (1988), some informed depositors receive an imperfect signal that the risky investment made by the bank may yield a lower than expected payoff. They may therefore decide to withdraw their deposits (facing a sequential service constraint), forcing the bank to liquidate its assets prematurely. In this model a trade-off arises in that equity contracts are vulnerable to asymmetric information but not runs (since they are conditional on the performance of bank assets) whereas (unconditional) deposit contracts are vulnerable to runs but not so much to asymmetric information.[25]

As indicated by Chari and Jagannathan (1988), agents can only identify the real performance of a bank ex post. In their model, which incorporates both approaches (but without a sequential service constraint), some agents receive information about the performance of the bank's assets. Although the other agents can observe the length of the 'queue at the bank's door', they are not informed about the actual proportion of informed withdrawers, having received a negative signal about the bank's assets, as compared to agents simply experiencing a liquidity shock. The related signal-extraction problem can lead to uninformed depositors running on the bank when the queue is too long, even if informed depositors had not received any negative signal.

If interbank competition is imperfect, Calomiris and Kahn (1991) point to the benefits of the demandability of deposit contracts as a disciplining tool against moral hazard by bank managers. However, Carletti (1999a) shows that there is a trade-off between the role of demand deposits as a disciplinary tool and as a source of bank runs, since uninformed depositors might erroneously run in response to liquidity problems (and informed depositors might follow suit) or not run in spite of solvency problems. Hence, she argues that the risk of runs might be an inefficient disciplinary tool. The beneficial role of demandable debt is also analysed by Diamond and Rajan (2000a,b), who consider a case without asymmetric information and loan liquidation costs. They show that deposit contracts enable banks, in spite of their relationship-related power in loan collection skills, to commit to liquidity creation by satisfying depositors' withdrawal needs while at the same time isolating banks' long-term borrowers from these shocks. In other words, in their framework liability-side fragility is a necessary condition for efficient credit provision in the economy.

3.1.1.2. Extensions of the Classical Bank Run Models to Multiple Bank Systems. Garber and Grilli (1989) extend the model by Waldo (1985) to a two-country open economy environment. They show that—with fixed exchange rates or a gold standard—a bank run in one country will lead to fire sales of long-term securities to the other country, which will also experience higher interest rates there. If the income

[25] In general share contracts are superior to deposit contracts in the model. However, when the underlying asset is not too risky, a deposit contract, even with possible runs, may be welfare superior to a share contract.

effect of the increased securities holdings abroad is larger than the substitution effect, then the subsequent increase in foreign consumption can lead to a run abroad as well.[26] Smith (1991) extends Diamond and Dybvig's model to correspondent banking in the US during the National Banking Era. In his model, local correspondent banks may run the money centre banks following a local shock. De Bandt (1995) extends Jacklin and Bhattacharya's (1988) model to a multiple banking system and considers how an aggregate and an idiosyncratic shock affect the return on banks' assets. If depositors in one bank are the first to be informed about the difficulties experienced by their bank, depositors in other banks will then revise their expectations about the aggregate shock, and hence also the return on deposits in their own bank. This creates a channel for the propagation of bank failures. Temzelides (1997) develops a repeated version of the Diamond and Dybvig model where agents adjust their choices over time after learning about the state of the banking system from past experience. One of the two Nash equilibria of panic/no panic is selected and learning introduces some state-persistence. The author also introduces a multiple banking system, where depositors observe bank failures in their own region and may shift to the panic equilibrium for the next period. In this specific framework, more concentrated banking systems are less sensitive to idiosyncratic shocks and are therefore less prone to contagious panics.

3.1.1.3. The Modern Bank Contagion Literature. In a recent contribution, Chen (1999, reprinted in this volume) combines an extension of the bank run models to a multiple banking system with the rational herding approach mentioned in Section 3.1.2.2 (Bikhchandani, Hirshleifer and Welsh 1992). In period 0 consumers decide whether or not they deposit their endowments in banks and the banks invest the funds they receive in uncertain long-term projects. At the start of period 1 depositors at a subset of banks simultaneously learn about liquidity shocks and about their banks' exact long-term investment outcome ('bank-specific information'). They then decide whether to withdraw. As a result a subset of these banks might be run on and subsequently fail. Then depositors of the remaining banks learn how many of these banks failed, update their expectations in a Bayesian fashion about the likelihood that investment projects succeed in general and decide whether to withdraw or not. In the next step, still in period 1, the liquidity shocks and information about these banks are revealed and depositors can withdraw, if a panic has not yet taken place. At the end of this period, all banks that are not liquidated can invest their funds in a speculative short-term project ('gamble for resurrection'). In period 2 all remaining (long- and short-term) projects mature and remaining depositors are reimbursed.

[26] Paroush (1988) already modelled bank contagion by *assuming* that the failure of any single bank entails a chain reaction of many failing banks. He focuses on the conflict between the public's and private banks' differential interests in taking such externalities into account, and draws some policy conclusions. We focus here more on *why* such external consequences of individual banks' failures may occur in the first place.

There are two externalities in this model that cause contagious bank runs, a pay-off externality through the first-come, first-served rule for servicing withdrawing depositors and an information externality through the Bayesian updating of beliefs about the macroeconomic situation as a function of observed failures. So the model is also linked to the broad sense of systemic risk (see Section 3.1.2). In this framework Chen shows that, even when depositors choose the Pareto-dominant equilibrium, there is a critical number of early failures above which a run on the remaining banks in the system will always be triggered. This critical number is decreasing both in the a priori probability for low investment returns in the economy and the pay-off for early deposit withdrawals and (weakly) decreasing in the pay-off for late withdrawals. Finally, Chen shows that even if the deposit contract is designed to maximize depositors' welfare, there are cases in which systemic crises occur with positive probability in equilibrium, but there also exists a deposit insurance scheme that could eliminate any contagious bank runs in this model.

A further important step are models of the *interbank market* and direct exposures. Rochet and Tirole (1996a) present a model of the interbank market, where peer monitoring among banks in this market solves the *moral hazard* problem between bank debt holders and bank shareholder-managers, but also induces contagion risk. In period 0 banks decide upon liquid reserves and invest available assets in risky projects ('commercial loans'). In period 1 they are hit by a liquidity shock, which—if exceeding reserves—has to be met by raising debt from outside agents. If additional debt cannot be raised, the projects have to be liquidated with zero return, which can lead to banks failing. Otherwise the project is executed in period 2 and, if successful, a positive return is realized and shared between shareholder-managers and debt holders. The moral hazard problem arises since debt holders cannot force the shareholder-managers to put in sufficient effort at the time the projects are undertaken.

By assumption, under 'period-1' peer monitoring among the banks the private benefits from making a low effort ('shirking') become less important relative to the private costs of proper peer project monitoring, giving the right incentives against moral hazard.[27] However, economies of scope between interbank monitoring and the effort in commercial lending causes the profitability (and therefore closure) of the monitoring peers to be closely related to the profitability and closure of the monitored banks. For example, the authors show that for any two banks the greater the size of the liquidity shock hitting one of them, the greater is the likelihood of the other being liquidated. This is the case even when a Pareto optimal contractual arrangement is in force between all debt holders and shareholder-managers. More dramatically, for certain parameter values of the model, a small increase in the size of the liquidity shock hitting any of the banks can lead to the closing down of the entire banking system, a particularly severe case of contagion.

[27] The authors also analyse the case of 'period 0' peer monitoring for two banks, which focuses on the precautions against liquidity shocks. Interlinkages between monitoring and monitored banks also occur in this case, but only in one direction (failure of the monitored bank impairing the situation of the monitoring bank).

Allen and Gale's (2000a, reprinted in this volume) model of bank contagion also addresses the role of interbank lending, although not by focusing on peer monitoring. Instead they focus on the physical exposures of banks in four different regions and on the 'real' linkages between regions, as represented by the correlation of liquidity needs of the respective depositors. Since only symmetric equilibria are analysed by the authors, each of the four regions considered can be characterized by one representative bank, taking in period 0 retail deposits (insuring depositors against liquidity shocks), lending or borrowing in the interbank market and investing in (non-risky) short- or long-term projects of outside firms ('loans'). In period 1 depositors whose region faces a negative liquidity shock withdraw. The bank can meet the withdrawals from maturing short-term investments, by liquidating interbank deposits it made earlier in other regions (if it is long in the interbank market), or as a last resort by liquidating long-term projects. In period 2 long-term projects mature and interbank and retail deposits are reimbursed, except for those banks that became bankrupt after a large liquidity shock in period 1 resulted in an inability to serve all withdrawals.

Normally, in this model, liquidity shocks across regions fluctuate randomly, with aggregate liquidity staying constant. Banks know in period 0 the different states of nature and their probabilities, but not the effective realization of liquidity needs, which are observed only in period 1. In this situation the interbank market serves as an insurance mechanism among banks of different regions, leading to the efficient sharing of liquidity risks and no bank failures, irrespective of the particular structure of interbank lending. However, in a 'special', unexpected state of the world, to which all agents assign a probability of zero in period 0, one region (A) faces additional withdrawals, so that aggregate liquidity is not sufficient to serve all depositors.[28] The authors show that inter-regional contagion of bank failures can occur, depending on how much liquid assets the bank in A has available and how much banks in other regions contingent on bank A withdrawing its interbank deposits. Whether and how much propagation occurs depends on the parameter values. For example, for a circular lending structure (region A lends to B, B to C, C to D and D back to A; 'incomplete' markets), they prove within the model chosen that for certain parameter values the unexpected liquidity perturbation can lead to the failure of the banks in all regions. They show that for more 'complete' markets (each bank has lending relationships with two other regions) the system is likely to be more stable.

In a related paper Freixas, Parigi and Rochet (2000, reprinted in this volume) discuss physical interbank lending exposures as a consequence of depositors' uncertain geographical consumption decisions.[29] In period 0 depositors give their endowment to their local bank, which invests it long-term or stores it (*N* regions

[28] Allen and Gale (2000a) use an example to argue that their main results are not sensitive to the zero probability assumption regarding this special shock.

[29] This paper is also closely related to the authors' earlier work on interbank payment systems (Freixas and Parigi 1998), discussed further below. In fact, it could also be interpreted as a payment system contagion paper.

with one bank in each). In period 1 a fraction of all depositors learn that they have to consume in a different location in period 2, and they either withdraw their endowment to transport it themselves or request a bank transfer. To minimize liquidation of long-term investments and foregone investment returns, banks execute these transfers via credit lines to each other, resulting in the exposure being eliminated in period 2. Then long-term investments mature and depositors consume.

In the case where all banks are solvent and only the liquidity shocks through geographical preferences occur (given some parameter constraints), two pure strategy equilibria are possible. In the 'credit line equilibrium' efficient interbank lending takes place, all obligations are honoured and no contagious runs occur. In the 'gridlock equilibrium' depositors cause inefficient and contagious bank runs for fear of insufficient reserves in the system. Consequently, all investments are liquidated, although credit lines are honoured up to the total of period 2 resources. For the cases of one failing insolvent bank and of liquidity shocks, the authors discuss three scenarios of interbank exposures through credit lines: a 'credit chain' scenario (analogous to the circular, 'incomplete' case in Allen and Gale (2000a) above), a 'diversified' lending scenario (credit lines between any two banks exist) and a money centre scenario (one bank is central, since the other two only have interbank lending with it and not directly with each other). Contagious failures occur more easily in the 'credit chain' scenario than in the 'diversified' lending case, although in the 'diversified' case withdrawals can occur more easily.

Aghion, Bolton and Dewatripont (2000) focus again on the trade-off related to interbank lending, namely that the advantage of insurance against liquidity shocks from the interbank market (resulting in fewer individual failures) comes at the price of systemic risk (contagious character of bank failures). In the model banks invest in partly illiquid projects and are subject to uncertain depositor withdrawals in periods 1, 2 and 3. If withdrawals exceed the liquid project returns, then banks can either liquidate the remaining project at a discount or enter the interbank market. If the availability of liquid funds is sufficient, then no failures occur since interbank loans by other banks save those facing problems. However, if a single bank cannot acquire the liquidity from the interbank market and fails, then contagious runs can lead to the closure of the entire banking system, because other depositors interpret the failure of an institution as a signal of general illiquidity in the system.

Mishkin (1991) suggested that the classical *adverse selection* model (Akerlof 1970) and its application to rationing phenomena in credit markets (Stiglitz and Weiss 1981) are useful tools in explaining financial crises in history. Davis (1995) suggested extending the credit rationing ideas to interbank markets. If banks face a demand for credit by other banks of ex ante unknown quality, to avoid the proportion of bad risks increasing with interest rates, lenders may decide to ration the amount of credit rather than raising interest rates. In the same vein, Flannery (1996, reprinted in this volume) suggests a model of adverse selection in the interbank market. It is assumed that banks receive imperfect signals about the quality of prospective borrowers. In this simple model, banks only lend when they receive a 'good' signal. However, following a large shock in the financial system, banks may become uncertain about the borrowing banks' credit quality. As they feel less able to distinguish between 'good' and 'bad' banks, lenders raise interest rates across the board. If the loan rate becomes too high, 'good' banks might not be able to repay their interbank loans any more, so that illiquid but solvent banks may go bankrupt.

Interbank market crises which result from adverse selection problems can be related to the structure of project financing in the economy. This, together with the implications for the interbank market are studied by Huang and Xu (2000). They compare the possibility of crises in the case of single-bank financing (one bank finances a project) and multiple-bank financing (two banks finance a project). It turns out that multiple-bank financing systems are more stable, because—as shown in the corporate finance literature (Bolton and Scharfstein 1996)—decentralized multiple-lender debt structures can function as a commitment device where insolvent banks cannot mimic solvent banks. Since under these circumstances only solvent banks can borrow in the interbank market, idiosyncratic shocks will never lead to a crisis beyond the insolvent banks. Under single-bank financing renegotiation costs and so restructuring is favoured over liquidation. Good and bad projects will be pooled and an idiosyncratic shock can lead to a collapse of the interbank market, if quality differences between projects are large enough.

3.1.2. Macroeconomic Fluctuations, Aggregate Shocks and Lending Booms

3.1.2.1. Aggregate Shocks to the Bank Sector. It has been observed that many banking crises have occurred in conjunction with cyclical downturns or other aggregate shocks, such as interest rate increases, stock market crashes or exchange rate devaluations (see e.g. Gorton 1988; Lindgren, Garcia and Saal 1996; and also Section 4.1.2). Why is it that banks simultaneously get into trouble in those events (included in the concept of systemic risk in the 'broad' sense according to the terminology of Section 2.1), even in the absence of direct interbank contagion, and why are the prudent banks not better protected than the imprudent ones? One answer could be given on the basis of the individual bank run models discussed in Section 3.1.1.1. News about a cyclical downturn, for example, could provide the negative signal about the bank's loans to all or a subset of depositors. To the extent that the banking system is competitive, the behaviour of a single bank can be interpreted as representing the banking sector as a whole. In a similar vein, Cukierman (1991) provides a macroeconomic model in which an unexpected decline in the supply of deposits occurs after long-term loan contracts have been made, inciting banks to increase their deposit rates to attract new depositors. This suggests that interest rate changes and bank profits are inversely correlated. He derives from this fact a rationale for the US Federal Reserve to smooth interest rates in attempts to stabilize the financial system.

Hellwig (1994) studies the efficient allocation of *interest rate risk* induced by technology shocks and argues that part of it should be borne by agents with urgent liquidity needs, that is, early withdrawing depositors. Of course, this opens the question why the market mechanism does not generate state contingent bank deposit contracts like this in practice. Allen and Gale (1998 and 2000b) take issue with the interpretation of bank runs as random phenomena, because of their historical association with severe *business cycle fluctuations*. They model the occurrence of runs on a representative bank resulting from aggregate asset risk, as a function of say the realization of a leading business cycle indicator, without resorting to a 'sequential service constraint' for (fixed-value) deposits. They argue that in this framework if depositors make their withdrawal decisions based on the leading indicator, the first-best outcome can occur in spite of the non-contingent character of the deposit contract. However, the result breaks down when early withdrawals are costly, in which case a public intervention is necessary to restore the first-best outcome. Finally, Chen (1999) shows within his model that an adverse macroeconomic shock will also increase the likelihood of contagion.[30]

Another source of systematic shocks to the banking sector can be *financial market crashes* or *market liquidity crises*, in particular when they concern any of the major markets (stocks, government bonds, foreign exchange etc.) and when they are contagious across markets (see e.g. Morgenstern 1959; King and Wadhwani 1990; Hartmann, Straetmans and de Vries 2000; Hartmann and De Bandt 2001). Recently, former 'commercial' banks have become more and more involved in financial market trading (as opposed to traditional lending). Their larger trading books potentially lead to larger exposures to shocks originating in those markets. This implies that the structurally higher systemic risk in banking markets due to fixed value deposits and cross-exposures, as described in Sections 2.2 and 3.1, will be more dependent on financial market fluctuations than has previously been the case. For example, Miller (1996) develops a model where if deposits are used for currency speculation and banks are 'loaned-up' then a speculative currency attack can give rise to a banking crisis. Similarly, the health of banks have become more dependent on the safety of the security and foreign exchange settlement process (Brimmer 1989; Bernanke 1990). The same applies to banks' participation in financial conglomerates where other units are involved in securities activities.

Investment banks, securities houses, hedge funds etc. are generally more risky than traditional commercial banks (e.g. in terms of earnings volatility), but they are less vulnerable to the type of contagion we have considered.[31] However, the

[30] Of course, there can also be the reverse causality. Restrictions in bank lending due to financial fragility may affect the business cycle, thereby creating adverse acceleration or feedback effects. See, in particular, Bernanke (1983), Bernanke and Gertler (1990) as well as Mishkin (1991). However, the introduction of a banking sector in 'financial accelerator' models is still a task for future research (Bernanke, Gertler and Gilchrist 1999).

[31] One study investigates the effect of the announcement of OTC derivative losses by four clients of Bankers Trusts on other investment banks' stock prices during the first 9 months of 1994 (Clark and Perfect 1996). The results tend to indicate that capital markets discriminate between derivative dealers on the basis of their exposure levels.

more investment banks and the like are involved in interbank money market borrowing the more likely it is that their failure caused by a large shock originating from market crashes may still spill over to the banking system (see Section 3.1.1.3).

Alternatively, various events in financial markets (such as the failure of a large institution or a significant price fall) may increase uncertainty about the ability and willingness to trade by the main participant in these markets, in particular among market makers (Davis 1994). Somewhat analogous to the case of the interbank money market discussed above, liquidity in the respective financial instruments traded may dry up through adverse selection (Flannery 1996). For example, market makers might increase bid-ask spreads to reduce the likelihood of being hit by a transaction (price rationing) or even 'refuse' to trade at all (quantity rationing). Such a liquidity 'freeze' could involve a systematic shock on all those banks and non-bank financial institutions, whose risk management strategies depend on the ability to trade in these markets.[32]

3.1.2.2. Bank Lending Booms. An issue related to the real macroeconomic shocks discussed above is why banks expand so much credit, implying risks that can bring them all into trouble at business cycle turning points, even though they know they cannot pass on the risk to depositors. The lending boom literature has addressed this question. Minsky (1977, 1982) believed that the post-World War II free market economy has a natural tendency towards financial instability on the aggregate level. In good times agents consume and invest, generating more income. As *euphoria* and *gregarious behaviour* pick up, more speculative or even 'Ponzi finance' is undertaken, as opposed to safer 'hedging finance'. The boom is fed by an over-expansion of bank credit until some exogenous outside shock to the macroeconomic systems ('displacement') brings it to an end. Kindleberger (1978/1996) shares the basic model, although perhaps being more moderate in pointing out that the market system 'occasionally' faces such bubbles leading to financial crises. In contrast to most of the more recent literature, these early writers emphasized the role of uncertainty (of the 'Knightian' type, where agents even have no information about the probability distribution of asset returns) as opposed to risk and the inability of banks to take the appropriate decisions in some circumstances. For example, Guttentag and Herring (1984) develop a simple model of credit expansion and discuss the consequences of 'Knightian' uncertainty about catastrophic shocks on investment returns and default risk premiums. On the basis of results from psychology they also argue that the subjective probabilities attached to catastrophic events will decline as time elapses after the realization of such an event. This 'disaster myopia' will lead to a widespread underestimation of the likelihood of extreme events that could question the health of banks.

Related explanations for credit over-expansion and lending booms can be found in the more recent rational expectations literature on *herding* in investment

[32] A recent event that has raised these issues in practice is the privately financed bail-out of Long-Term Capital Management (LTCM), a large hedge fund, in September 1998.

and loan decisions. Banerjee (1992), Bikhchandani, Hirshleifer and Welsh (1992) and Avery and Zemsky (1998) introduce formal models of information externalities that can lead to herding. Each agent only observes the actions of other agents and uses Bayesian updating to derive his or her own subjective probabilities of future returns on his investment decisions.[33] Scharfstein and Stein (1990) model managers' incentives to mimic others in investment or loan decisions, when their own evaluation and reputation depends on their performance relative to the rest of the market. They quote Gwynne's (1986) description of a typical credit analyst's behaviour in lending decisions to less developed countries (LDCs): 'His job would never be measured on how correct his country risk analysis was. At the very least, Herrick was simply doing what hundreds of other large international banks had already done, and any ultimate blame for poor forecasting would be shared by tens of thousands of bankers around the globe; this was one of the curious benefits of following the herd'.

This literature and also the writings by Minsky, Kindleberger and others address the issue of systemic risk in an indirect way. Banks' herding and credit overexpansion to specific sectors, regions etc. will result in simultaneous problems for a large number of banks once a negative aggregate shock (or a signal of it) will make the non-sustainability of this sector's or this region's growth apparent. However, a problem of this literature is that it does not give clear explanations as to which events can start a herding wave and when it breaks down. It is also not clear why herding should be more of a concern in banking than in other sectors often regarded less fragile.

A further branch of the literature attributes excessive or excessively risky lending by banks to *moral hazard* (see also Section 2.4). These writings refer to features of banking markets that normally do *not* exist for other industries. For example, Merton (1976, 1978) develops a model showing how fixed-rate deposit insurance premiums that are insensitive to banks' portfolio risks (as observed in many countries) may lead them to increase risk-taking in order to maximize the put-option value on the insurance corporation's funds. Boot and Thakor (1993) further argue that such deposit insurance can lead to an inefficiently low level of monitoring, under certain assumptions on the form of the costs. Applying modern corporate finance models of firms' capital structures to the case of banks, Dewatripont and Tirole (1993) argue that banks' excessive reliance on debt financing (partly related to their provision of retail payment services to a large number of small and relatively uninformed depositors) can also lead to more risk-taking in lending. Due to the existence of explicit or implicit government guarantees for financial institutions, the issue of moral hazard has also been raised in the context of the US savings and loans crisis (Kane 1989) or more recently regarding the lending boom that partly led to the East Asian crisis (Krugman 1998). However, in a recent paper Goodhart and Huang (1999) show that a positive level of moral hazard resulting from safety net provisions, such as lending of last resort, might be unavoidable or even optimal to contain the systemic costs or monetary disturbances associated with financial crises.

[33] In Kindleberger's (1996, p. 13) words, 'monkey see, monkey do'.

This lending boom literature also relates to the potentially slow build up of structural problems in the financial sector. These structural problems can increase the likelihood as well as the severity of systemic events.

3.2. Systemic Risk in Interbank Payment Systems

By providing the technical infrastructure through which wholesale bank market transactions are settled, large-value payment systems determine the physical exposures among financial institutions. In a way, looking at payment systems is like looking at the network of interbank exposures with a magnifying glass. Hence, depending on their internal organization they also determine how shocks may propagate through the financial system, in particular how severe bank contagion can be. However, the analytical literature on systemic risk has only recently considered the importance of payment systems. The fundamental underlying risks in these systems are similar to those encountered by financial institutions in general: operational risk (such as the failure of a computer, as for the Bank of New York in 1985), liquidity risk (reception of final or 'good' funds, not being realized at the desired time but at an unspecified time in the future), credit risk (failure of an insolvent participant with a subsequent loss of principal). Nevertheless, as the settlement process in these systems reshuffles the effective exposures between banks over time according to the technical specifications of the respective payment system, it makes sense to treat them separately from the retail depositor and the wholesale trading side discussed in the previous section (although in practice obviously all these aspects can be interrelated).

There are three main types of interbank payment systems: net settlement systems, gross settlement systems and correspondent banking. In what follows we shall first describe 'prototypes' of these systems and then refer to the most important practical deviations from these types. In *net settlement systems* payments among members are collected over a certain period of time, for example, a whole day or several hours, and at the settlement time the gross payments between members are netted against each other, so that only the net balances have to be settled. With bilateral net settlement the members effectively remain the only counterparties to each other, while in multilateral net settlement systems debit and credit positions are accumulated *vis-à-vis* a central counterparty (usually a clearing house) until they are offset at the settlement time. Net settlement systems involve relatively low costs, because actual settlement is relatively rare—normally occurring only once at the end of the day (and in some cases twice a day)—and thus liquidity costs are low. Due to the limited number of direct counterparties, these cost savings are usually more pronounced in multilateral systems than in bilateral netting. The netting off between institutions can considerably reduce the effective debit positions, and thereby systemic risk, as compared to pure gross settlement undertaken at the same time scale, where incoming and outgoing payments are settled independently. However, without additional provisions, net settlement systems are comparatively vulnerable to systemic risk, since gross exposures accumulating between settlement times can become very large.

In *real-time gross settlement systems* (RTGS) payment finality is virtually immediate for every transaction, so that the systemic risk from unsettled claims appears at first sight to be very limited. Due to the high costs of intra-day liquidity management (in order to have always enough liquid funds available during the day) it is comparatively costly for member banks. Moreover, banks' ability to pay out may depend on the timing of incoming payments, but counterparties may sometimes have incentives to delay making payments. Therefore, RTGS can be characterized by relatively frequent queuing phenomena, which can lead to widespread liquidity ('network') externalities or even system 'gridlock' when participants economize on their intra-day liquidity or default. This shows that even RTGS may not be totally free of systemic risk, at least not in the 'weak' sense (see Section 2.1).

Most real-life systems have specific additional institutional features in order to reduce systemic risk or liquidity costs (and gridlock risk) in both net and gross systems, so that both types can become quite similar. For example, net settlement systems often introduce caps on the exposures between settlement times and loss-sharing arrangements between members for cases of default. 'Decentralized' multilateral net systems though are to be distinguished from 'centralized' systems, where the central counterparty takes over the risks and can, therefore, default itself. Also, legally binding netting-arrangements can apply for the periods between settlement times or the number of settlement times during the day could be increased.[34] In order to reduce the liquidity costs of real-time gross systems the possibility of intra-day overdrafts are now often allowed. Since they are a potential source of systemic risk, these overdrafts are either secured through collateral requirements, as is the case for the Trans-European Automated Real-time Gross Settlement Express Transfer System (TARGET) and the connected national RTGS, or through daylight overdraft fees, as in the case of Fedwire in the United States. Alternatively, routine queuing facilities can be established, which however imply similar risks as net settlement systems.

Correspondent banking relationships appear to be very diverse. Correspondent banks provide payment services for groups of usually smaller or foreign banks, which do not have cost-effective access to the domestic net or gross systems. Each of the latter groups of banks settle bilaterally with the correspondent via debits and credits on nostro and loro accounts, whereby gross exposures can be netted against each other.[35] Therefore, the failure of an important correspondent bank can directly affect a large number of those institutions. Moreover, correspondent banking is used by large credit institutions for international transactions. In this respect, it could become one of the major channels for the transmission of the so-called Herstatt risk (see the next section).[36]

[34] The legal enforcement of these netting arrangements can be particularly difficult for international transactions. For example, in some jurisdictions a liquidator may be able to engage in 'cherry picking' favouring the domestic creditors of a failed institution (BIS 1990).

[35] In a way correspondent banking can be seen as a step from bilateral net settlement towards multilateral net settlement, although happening at a smaller scale.

[36] For other reviews of practical payment system arrangements and the risks involved, see Folkerts-Landau (1991), Borio and Van den Bergh (1993), Summers (1994), Berger, Hancock and Marquardt (1996), Rochet and Tirole (1996a or b), Schoenmaker (1996b), Kobayakawa (1997) and Rossi (1997).

The development of theoretical models describing the risks of different payment systems is in its early stages. Angelini (1998) models profit-maximizing banks' behaviour in an RTGS where intraday liquidity is available from the central bank for a fee proportional to the size of the overdraft. (Following the example of the US Fedwire system, overdrafts are not collateralized.) Delaying payments has also a cost in terms of customer dissatisfaction. In this framework, Angelini shows that the competitive (Nash) equilibrium is not welfare optimal, since the cost of intra-day credit induces banks to delay payments rather than to draw on the overdraft facility. These payment delays result in network externalities, since payees attempt to free ride on other banks' reserves, thereby reducing overall liquidity. (However, the author does not address explicitly the question whether a 'gridlock' equilibrium can exist, in which payment activity comes to a standstill; a stronger form of a systemic event). He concludes that in RTGS intra-day overdrafts (by the central bank) must be made cheap enough so as to remain lower than banks' customer dissatisfaction costs from delaying payments. Moreover, he suggests that banks could be induced to pay earlier during the day via variable overdraft fees, which penalize late payments. In contrast, Humphrey (1989) has argued that payment delays in gross systems with uncollateralized overdraft facilities may be desirable to reduce the actual overdrafts and therefore systemic risk (or the costs for the system guarantor).

Schoenmaker (1995) compares multilateral net settlement systems (à la US CHIPS) and collateralized RTGS systems both theoretically and through the simulation of average costs with real transactions and historical bank default data. It turns out that the average costs through settlement failures (defined as historical failure rates times maximum open intraday positions) are higher in the net than in the gross system, but those through settlement delays (or gridlock) and collateral requirements are lower in the net systems. This might explain why central banks often prefer 'safer' gross systems while market participants favour 'less costly' net systems, and it also reflects the trade-off between risks and costs described in Berger, Hancock and Marquardt (1996). In particular, Schoenmaker explicitly derives the potential occurrence of systemic events in the form of gridlock in the RTGS variant.

Elaborating on Schoenmaker's comparative approach and using a theoretical framework similar to that of Angelini, Kobayakawa (1997) provides a broad analysis of multilateral net settlement and both types of RTGS, with full collateralization of intraday overdrafts ('EU type') and with fees on uncollateralized overdrafts ('US type'). However, he focuses on their relative efficiency and (apart from externalities through payment delays) does not derive any firm conclusions on 'strong' systemic events.

In contrast, a careful theoretical study of foreign exchange netting by Yamazaki (1996) focuses entirely on the relative importance of systemic exposures in bilateral net settlement as compared to multilateral net settlement (decentralized with loss-sharing among participants and without a clearing house). He establishes that for single failures multilateral netting reduces other banks' exposures as compared to bilateral netting, if the initial loss is not 'extreme'. However, when a chain reaction of failures occurs, he shows that there are plausible cases in which the systemic event under multilateral netting (which has moral hazard implications) is more severe than under bilateral netting.

In a more elaborate model, Freixas and Parigi (1998) (building on McAndrews and Roberds 1995) introduce geographical consumption preferences in a Diamond–Dybvig-type model, which lead to 'interbank payments' between two regions. 'Gross settlement' imposes relatively high opportunity cost through foregone interest on liquidated investments but is free from contagion in this framework. With 'net settlement' the banks can extend credit lines to each other in order to finance future consumption of 'foreign' consumers. The 'net system' exhibits systemic risk and potential welfare losses in so far as inefficient banks may stay open for longer. Holthausen and Rønde (2000) study the implications of co-existing international gross and net settlement systems for cross-border systemic risk, when bank supervisory information is only generated at the national level.

4. EMPIRICAL EVIDENCE ON SYSTEMIC RISK IN BANKING

In this section we survey the existing empirical evidence on systemic events and systemic bank crises in the light of the concepts developed in Section 2 and the theoretical literature in Section 3, mainly focusing on rigorous empirical analyses of contagion. The objective is to identify how much we know about how pervasive the different elements of systemic risk are in different national and international contexts. Another objective is to detect those areas of systemic risk, which have not received enough attention yet in order to stimulate future research efforts.

4.1. Evidence on Bank Contagion and Joint Banking Crises

As has been pointed out in Section 3, the risk of contagious bank failures may be viewed as the 'classical' case of systemic risk. Testing for bank contagion amounts to testing whether 'bad news' or the failure of a specific bank (or group of banks) adversely affects the health of other banks. On the other side, systemic risk in banking markets in the 'broad' sense also includes simultaneous bank failures (widespread panics without necessarily the occurrence of contagion), for example, as a consequence of macroeconomic shocks. In this section we will first address the large number of econometric papers that attempt to identify contagion effects and then the few econometric papers dealing with joint crises and aggregate fluctuations.

4.1.1. Bank Contagion

The empirical literature that developed around this theme can be separated into several groups. One group of papers tries to link bank failures with subsequent other bank failures directly by measuring autocorrelation. A second approach tests whether the survival time of banks decreases during historically identified episodes of panics or through failures of other banks. Many studies also estimate the relationship between bank failures or 'news' and either stock market values of other banks or the reaction of depositors. Another group analyses the effect of 'news' or failures on the *probability* of other banks' defaults, shown by risk premiums in interbank lending. Finally, one can measure the physical exposures among operating banks (or between those and banks which have been 'bailed out' by the government) to evaluate whether a default would render other banks insolvent. We proceed in successive order.

4.1.1.1. Intertemporal Correlation of Bank Failures. The common ground of this first branch of the bank contagion literature is a test for autocorrelation in bank failures. Basically, the rate of bank failures in a period t is regressed on the rate in the previous period $(t-1)$ and a number of macroeconomic control variables. Provided that all macroeconomic shocks are effectively covered by the control variables a positive and significant autocorrelation coefficient indicates that bank failures and periods of tranquility cluster over time, which is consistent with the contagion hypothesis. Since the safety net provisions in modern financial systems, such as deposit insurance and lender-of-last-resort facilities tend to prevent a single bank failure from leading to contagion, these tests have to be undertaken for historical periods in countries without strong (public) safety nets.

Grossman (1993) finds with an instrumental variable regression analysis of quarterly US data for the period between 1875 and 1914 (i.e. before the establishment of the Federal Reserve System) that a 1 per cent increase in failures in a given quarter led on average to a 0.26 per cent increase in the following quarter. Hasan and Dwyer (1994) and Schoenmaker (1996a or b) have substantially refined this approach and provide more evidence of intertemporal failure clustering in 'free banking' markets. Hasan and Dwyer apply a probit analysis to data from the US Free Banking Era (1837 through 1863). They find some evidence compatible with contagion, depending on the type of crisis and region considered. By applying an autoregressive Poisson (count data) model to the number of bank failures, Schoenmaker (1996a or b) finds strong results for a sample of monthly data covering the second half of the US National Banking System and the early years of the Fed (1880 through 1936). The autoregressive parameters are strongly significant up to a lag of 3 months and they increase in size and significance for the subsample encompassing the Great Depression, while macroeconomic factors appear to become less informative for the prediction of failures.

In sum, this approach seems to have been relatively successful in supporting the contagion hypothesis. However, the main disadvantages of this approach are that, first, autocorrelated macroeconomic factors that have been omitted would cloud any 'evidence' of contagion and, second, it can only detect intertemporal contagion at the frequencies at which macroeconomic data is published.

4.1.1.2. Duration of Bank Survival Unexplained by Fundamentals. In a new study of US banking crises during the Great Depression, Calomiris and Mason (2000) have estimated the average survival time of several thousand Fed member banks between January 1930 and March 1933. They apply a microeconometric duration model in which bank survival is explained by a host of economic fundamentals (such as individual bank balance sheet items, regional and national macroeconomic variables) and some proxies of contagion, panics or liquidity crises. These proxies include a series of dummy variables, denoting the 'panic' episodes identified in the historical works of Friedman and Schwartz (1963), Wicker (1996) and others, and the level of deposits in other banks that failed in the same county (measuring regional contagion effects).

Grosso modo it turns out that bank level micro fundamentals as well as regional and national aggregate fundamentals are able to explain a large part of the variation in the duration of bank survival during the Depression (see also Section 4.1.2). However, apart from a highly significant time trend, regional aggregates seem to explain bank survival time much better than national aggregate fundamentals. The historical panic dummies provide some support for the occurrence of the regional bank panics during 1930 and 1931 described by Wicker (1996), but less support for the national panics during 1930 and 1931 described by Friedman and Schwartz (1963). Dummies for the 1932 Chicago bank panic and the January and February 1933 national panics appear very significant, but the authors caution that according to their earlier paper (Calomiris and Mason 1997; discussed below) only banks that were already unhealthy before actually failed during the Chicago episode and that a good deal of the 'flight to currency' in early 1933 might rather have been related to the anticipated departure from the gold standard. Finally, the regional contagion coefficient is highly significant in all specifications tested, but the inclusion or not of this variable does not have a very large effect on the aggregate duration of bank survival.

In sum, this study seems to indicate the presence of some bank contagion effects in specific episodes during the Great Depression, but also that in most of these episodes they seem to have been rather contained, namely limited to a specific region of the US. The authors also point out that some of the reductions in survival duration they observed might still be related to some unobservable regional or national fundamentals.

4.1.1.3. Event Studies on Stock Price Reactions. The most popular approach to test for contagion effects are event studies of bank stock price reactions in response to 'bad news', such as the announcement of an unexpected increase in loan-loss reserves or the failure of a commercial bank or even of a country to service its debt. The presence of contagion is usually tested by comparing the 'normal' return of a bank stock, as predicted by a standard capital market equilibrium model (such as the CAPM) estimated with historical data, to the actually observed returns at the announcement date or during a window around this date. 'Bad news' for a bank i leading to significantly negative 'abnormal' returns on the stock of bank j is interpreted as evidence in favour of contagion.

The forerunners in applying this approach were Aharony and Swary (1983) who studied the effects of the three largest bank failures in the United States before 1980: United States National Bank of San Diego (1973), Franklin National Bank of

New York (1974) and the Hamilton National Bank of Chattanooga (1976). Each of these three failures appears to have originated from idiosyncratic sources, related to in-house fraud, illegal real-estate loans or foreign exchange losses. The failure of the Franklin National bank, the 12th largest US bank at the time, caused substantial negative abnormal returns in money-centre, medium-size and small banks, whereas no negative external effects of the other two cases occurred.[37]

Swary (1986) applies the same approach to the Continental Illinois National Bank failure in 1983–84, the 8th largest bank in the United States. The failure was larger than Franklin National but there were less idiosyncratic problems (bad domestic and international loans). As such, the negative abnormal returns of 67 other US banks turned out to be weaker and somewhat proportional to their own pre-crisis solvency situations. Wall and Peterson (1990) find that part of these negative stock market reactions can also be explained by more general 'bad news' arriving about the Latin American debt crisis. Jayanti and Whyte (1996) show that stock market values of British and Canadian banks with significant LDC debt exposures were also adversely affected by Continental's failure but not those British banks which were unexposed to debt crisis countries. Also Peavy and Hempel (1988) show that the Penn Square Bank failure of Oklahoma in 1982 had only regional repercussions.

In a similar vein, Madura and McDaniel (1989) analyse the effect of the 3 billion-dollar loan-loss reserve announcement of Citicorp in 1987 on the stock prices of the 11 other US money-centre banks, which also issued loan-loss announcements later that year. Their results indicate that most of the losses had already been anticipated by the market. Docking, Hirschey and Jones (1997) study the effects of 188 loan-loss reserve announcements by nine leading money-centre banks and 390 announcements by 102 regional banks in the United States from 1985 to 1990. It turns out that there is little impact of money-centre bank announcements on the stocks of other money-centre banks, but regional banks' announcements can have detrimental effects on other regional or money-centre banks. These results are compatible with the hypothesis that investors better anticipate unfavourable announcements from the large and 'visible' money-centre banks than from regional banks. Slovin, Sushka and Polonchek (1999) undertake yet another event study of bank stock price reactions in response to 'bad news', but the conditioning events are taken to be 62 announcements of reduced dividends and 61 announcements of regulatory enforcement for a sample of US money-centre and regional banks between 1975 and 1992. In contrast to the evidence on loan-loss reserve announcements, the authors find that for money-centre banks there are large negative effects of reduced dividends on many other money-centre and regional banks. Regulatory enforcement actions against money-centre banks do not cause any negative bank-industry effects, whereas all announcements (regulatory or reduced dividends) generate positive competition effects among regional banks within the same area.

[37] However, Aharony and Swary caution that there were a number of other banks which faced foreign exchange losses similar to those of Franklin National Bank of New York shortly after the switch to floating exchange rates (notably Germany's Herstatt bank).

The early results of adverse 'external' stock market reactions to 'bad news' triggered a debate about whether they can be interpreted as evidence of 'pure' contagion effects or whether they rather reflect rational investor choices in response to the revelation of new information. In a series of papers the strength of abnormal returns during the international debt crisis of the 1980s was linked to banks' own exposures to problem countries. Cornell and Shapiro (1986) undertook cross-sectional regressions for 43 US bank stocks and for various sub-periods during 1982 and 1983 and Smirlock and Kaufold (1987) used seemingly unrelated regressions for 23 exposed and 37 non-exposed US banks around the 1982 Mexican debt moratorium. Musumeci and Sinkey (1990) and Karafiath, Mynatt and Smith (1991) study the effects of the 1987 Brazilian debt moratorium on US bank stocks. The former use an OLS cross-section regression for 25 banks, the latter a Generalized Least Squares (GLS) cross-section regression for 46 bank holding companies. Madura, Whyte and McDaniel (1991) assess the impact of Citicorp's announcement of substantial loan-loss reserves on the share prices of 13 large British banks. The general result of this debate was that abnormal returns varied in proportion to banks' exposures to problem countries, which is consistent with the hypothesis of rational investor choice.[38]

Since most of these results are found for US data, an interesting question to ask is whether they carry over to other financial systems. Unfortunately, not much seems to have been published for other countries. An exception is Gay, Timme and Yung (1991) who chose to examine bank failures in Hong Kong during the 1980s. These cases are interesting, because first Hong Kong did not have an explicit deposit insurance scheme (which could have dampened any contagion effects) and second at least two of the three failures studied (Hang Lung Bank in 1982 and Overseas Trust Bank in 1985) seem to have had rather idiosyncratic sources, such as management misconduct and embezzlement, while the third (Ka Wah Bank in 1985) appears related to the failures of Overseas Trust Bank and of a specific foreign borrower. In the first two cases strong negative abnormal returns occurred for locally listed bank stocks, but the evidence on investor reactions being proportional to exposures is inconclusive.

In terms of the concepts developed above this literature considers *weak* systemic events, since stock price fluctuations do not imply failures. However, many of the systemic events studied seem to have been 'efficient', that is, in proportion to actual exposures (see Section 2.3). Also, several of the cases studied rather represent systemic repercussions in the 'broad' sense, since, for example, events related to the LDC debt crisis could be regarded as caused by an aggregate shock.

[38] However, there is one early study, Schoder and Vankudre (1986), that challenges the market efficiency hypothesis. These authors examine the stock price behaviour of 169 US banks around the August 1982 Mexican debt crisis. They estimate a two-factor (market and industry) stock return model and find that the average return of the 45 banks with exposures to Mexico was abnormally negative when rumours about Mexico spread on 19 August, whereas it was not for the whole sample of banks. However, the individual returns, net of market and industry factors, did not discriminate between banks according to the relative size of their (with one exception unpublished) Mexico exposures.

4.1.1.4. Analyses of Deposit Flows. Another test of contagion measures the reaction of depositors (wholesale and retail) to 'bad news'. If in response to problems revealed about bank *i* (or a group of banks) depositors also withdraw funds from bank *j*, then there is evidence of a contagious bank run.

Saunders (1987) examines whether two key announcements about the shape of Continental Illinois Bank in April and May 1984 had any discernible effect on other banks' US or overseas deposits. The announcement on 18 April of a US $400 million increase in Continental's problem loans seemed to have no effect on US deposits, while the May 10th 'denial of rumours' announcement by the US Office of the Comptroller of the Currency (OCC) seems to have triggered 'flight to quality' (i.e. shifts to safer banks and more secure deposits) by large US banks but not a general run. The total of non-sterling deposits at either American, Japanese or other overseas banks in London did not decline in April or May (but risk premiums on these deposits generally increased, see Section 4.1.1.5).

Saunders and Wilson (1996) study the annual deposit flows of 163 failed national banks and 229 surviving banks (of similar size and location) in the United States during the Great Depression (1929 through 1933). They look at the deposit movements for each group in each year of the Depression and compare them to the movement in the other group and to the movements in the three previous years. It turns out that for the years 1929 and 1933 withdrawals at failed banks are associated with *deposit increases* at non-failing banks. However, for the subperiod 1930–32 accelerations of deposit withdrawals at failing banks are associated with significantly *higher withdrawals* at non-failing banks. The authors point out that their evidence is consistent with panic-type 'pure' (regional) contagion effects between 1930 and 1932 and with 'flight-to-quality' (non-panic) phenomena in 1929 and 1933. However, they also observe that the level of withdrawals at failing banks was always significantly higher than at non-failing banks, which could be interpreted as higher levels of 'informed' withdrawals at unhealthy banks as compared to 'uninformed'/'purely contagious' withdrawals at banks that in the end turned out to be healthy. Again, in our terminology this approach can only address the occurrence of ('narrow') systemic events in the 'weak' sense. However, the possibility that some of the failing banks considered in this paper collapsed as a consequence of 'uninformed' withdrawals, while being fundamentally solvent, cannot be excluded.

Calomiris and Mason (1997) examine the June 1932 Chicago bank panic during the Great Depression to study whether some ex ante healthy banks collapsed during this episode. They group their sample of 114 banks into 3 categories: non-panic failures, panic failures and survivors. Statistically significant deposit withdrawals from the 62 survivors, which are only weakly smaller than those from the 28 panic failures, indicate the presence of systemic events in the narrow sense due to asymmetric information regarding individual banks' solvency situation. The authors ask whether these contagious withdrawals led to contagious failures or whether the failures observed were rather those of relatively weak banks in the face of a common asset price decline. To that end they apply a logit estimation of 'ex-ante' failure probabilities (based on balance-sheet data) for these groups, either including panic failures or excluding them. Since in both cases panic failures received a higher *predicted* failure probability than survivors, the authors conclude that only weaker banks ex ante actually failed during the panic, which is consistent with the hypothesis that 'pure' contagious *failures*, or 'strong' systemic events (in the 'narrow' sense), did not occur. They explain this finding with the existence of private co-operative arrangements among banks. In a section of their paper about the whole Great Depression, discussed in Section 4.1.1.2. (Calomiris and Mason 2000), they show that the regional 1930 bank panic identified by Wicker (1996) was associated with greater deposit withdrawals than could have been predicted from bank level micro data, regional and national fundamentals, but they question the notion that uniform withdrawals, unexplained by fundamentals, have happened on the national level before 1933.

4.1.1.5. Examinations of Bank Debt Risk Premiums. A little bit of work has been done to see whether contagion effects can be detected in the market prices of bank debt instruments. Carron (1982, table 1) shows that the Franklin National failure in New York (and perhaps also the Herstatt failure in Germany) in mid-1974 led to an increase in the quarterly average spread between US 'jumbo' certificates of deposits (CDs) and 3-month Treasury bills by a factor of at least six, which is consistent with systemic events via risk premiums. Saunders (1986) computes correlations of interbank rate risk premium indices for three different country groups before and after the start of the 1982 debt crisis. He observes statistically significant increases of the correlation of risk premiums between industrial countries and middle-income LDCs and between middle income and low-income LDCs, which he considers to be consistent with contagion between those two groups of countries. However, in a follow-up study (Saunders 1987) he finds that the correlation of risk premiums between industrial countries, non-oil exporting LDCs and countries with debt re-scheduling was actually *lower* in the 'crisis period' 1974 through 1978 than in the 'non-crisis period' 1979 through 1983, so that 'there appears to be no evidence of contagion in the crisis period' (p. 215). In any case, the simple correlation approach cannot distinguish between systematic shocks and contagion, as defined in Section 2.

Karafiath, Mynatt and Smith (1991) undertake an event study of the effect of the 1987 Brazilian debt moratorium on bond prices of 22 US bank holding companies (all with country exposures to Brazil). In contrast to the equity price reactions reported in the previous section, the cross section of weekly bond yields in excess of Treasury note yields were far from being significantly abnormal. One interpretation of their differing results between equity and bond returns is that the market expected that those banks would earn lower profits (and therefore pay less dividends) due to the debt crisis, but that none of the bank holding companies would actually default on its debt. Cooperman, Lee and Wolfe (1992) examine the effect of the 1985 Ohio Deposit Insurance crisis on the pricing of retail (insured) six-month certificates of deposits (CDs) for a sample of 69 federally-insured Ohio banks and savings and loans. The results indicate a significant unexpected rise in weekly CD prices for less solvent Ohio depository institutions (lasting approximately seven weeks), which is consistent with risk-based pricing as suggested by Kane's (1989) contingent insurance guarantee hypothesis. Finally, Jayanti and White (1996) estimate statistically significant increases in the average CD rates relative to Treasury bill, for both UK and Canadian banks after the Continental Illinois failure in the United States in May 1984. In their case this result is consistent with the international contagion effect visible in equity returns mentioned previously. Saunders (1987, fn. 28) also acknowledges that the average spread between 3-month Euro-dollar deposits and T-Bills doubled during the Continental Illinois problem months of April and May, which again is consistent with international systemic risk in the 'weak' sense. An even stronger effect was visible in the average monthly domestic risk premium, as measured by the difference between 3-month CD rates and 3 month T-Bill rates, which more than tripled during April and May (Saunders 1987, fn. 27).

The evaluation of the event study approach applied to risk premiums in debt rates, as a test for contagion effects is, of course, similar to the application to equity returns. Usually, it cannot show the occurrence of systemic events in the 'strong' sense and occasionally it is not clear whether the measured effects originate from an aggregate shock (potentially revealed by a specific event) or are a reflection of propagation effects.

4.1.1.6. Measurement of Effective Exposures. A last approach is to measure whether exposures to certain (potentially or effectively failing) banks are larger than capital. While prudential rules limiting large exposures should usually prevent banks from lending more than a small share of their capital to a single borrower, very large exposures can occur temporarily *vis-à-vis* 'core institutions', namely large clearing banks.

Kaufman (1994) reports some results from the US inquiry into the Continental Illinois case, one of the 'core institutions' at the time. Shortly before the failure, 65 financial institutions had uninsured exposures to the bank in excess of their capital. It was estimated by the Congressional study that, if Continental's losses were 60 per cent (i.e. creditors would lose 60 cents of every dollar lent), then 27 banks would have been legally insolvent and 56 banks would have suffered losses above 50 per cent of their capital. The actual losses of Continental finally amounted to below 5 per cent, so that none of its correspondents suffered solvency-threatening losses. Michael (1998) reports some effective exposures from London interbank markets.

This approach is strongly linked to empirical research on the impact of failures in payment systems, which we survey in Section 4.2. However, it cannot show the actual occurrence of systemic events but it can tell us something about the ex ante risks that such events might materialize in the future.[39]

[39] Benston *et al.* (1986, chapter 2) review a number of older and non-quantitative studies, discussing the banking crises in US history between 1873 and 1933, as well as quote a number of contemporaneous observers. They argue (on p. 70) that 'systemwide contagious bank runs were not a frequent occurrence in U.S. history (probably occurring at most only in 1878, 1893, 1908, and 1931–1933 and doing

4.1.2. Banking Crises, Aggregate Fluctuations and Lending Booms

Whereas there are numerous descriptive accounts of banking crises referring to macroeconomic fluctuations, the number of econometric papers is much more scarce.[40] In the paper by Gorton (1988) the case is made that during the US National Banking Era (1865–1914) widespread banking panics did not occur as random events à la Diamond and Dybvig (1983) or Waldo (1985), but rather as 'normal' widespread reactions of depositors to severe cyclical downturns. In contrast, during the Great Depression panics appeared to be much more special events. The former result is derived with the help of a non-linear non-parametric estimation of the determinants of the aggregate deposit-currency ratio in the US economy (notably time trends, the predictable rate of return on deposits and the predictable co-variability between aggregate consumption and capital losses on deposits). When this model is estimated for the National Banking Era, an additional dummy variable indicating panic times is not significant, suggesting that the regular explanatory variables are sufficient to explain widespread deposit withdrawals both in normal *and* in crisis times. For the period following the establishment of the Fed (1914–1934), the relationship between explanatory variables and deposit-currency ratio breaks down. However, the relationship between non-predictable changes in the liabilities of failed businesses and the proportion of banks that fail is more stable over time. Exploiting this relationship Gorton argues that bank failures and losses were many times greater during the 1930s than could have been expected from the model estimated over the National Banking Era. The author therefore concludes that the banking panics in US history were not generally random 'sunspots', but that many of them can be explained by regular consumer/depositor behaviour over the business cycle.

Gonzalez-Hermosillo, Pazarbaşioğlu and Billings (1997) and Gonzalez-Hermosillo (1999) estimate fixed effect logit models for various panels of banks to study the determinants of bank 'distress' in various episodes in the United States (Southwest 1986–92; Northeast 1991–92; California 1992–93), Colombia (1982–87)

major damage probably only in 1893 and 1931–1933), and that fear of widespread ripple effects did not appear to be of major concern to most students of U.S. banking before 1932'. And they conclude (on p. 77) that 'U.S. history suggests that runs on individual banks or groups of banks only rarely spread to other banks that are not subject to the same conditions that started the runs, and that most bank runs have been contained by *appropriate action*, with only minimal or short-lived effects on national financial stability and economic activity. Generally, the instability of individual banks or groups of banks has not translated into instability in the banking system as a whole. The major exception was the run on all banks in late 1932 through early 1933, which caused the banking system to grind to almost a complete halt and substantially reinforced the economic crisis at the time. Although an exception, this event was so traumatic that it has coloured analysis of bank runs and failures ever since.' See also Park (1991) and Wicker (1996 and 2000) for broad studies of banking crises in the history of the United States.

[40] There is, of course, a fairly broad literature about early warning indicator systems to predict individual bank failures and banking system crises for micro- and macro-prudential purposes. The indicators identified in this literature are obviously related to the factors explaining banking crises, but for reasons of space we abstain from reviewing it systematically in the present paper.

and Mexico (1994–95). 'Distress' is measured by the 'coverage ratio', the ratio of capital equity and loan reserves minus non-performing loans to total assets, exceeding a certain threshold. It turns out that market and liquidity risk factors played a role in explaining 'distress', whereas the role of credit risk and moral hazard is more case specific. However, the introduction of aggregate variables, such as macroeconomic fundamentals and regional variables, significantly improved the predictive power of the models tested, providing evidence in favour of the macro explanation of systemic bank difficulties in the 'broad' sense.

Demirgüç-Kunt and Detragiache (1998) study the macroeconomic and structural determinants of banking crises in 45 to 60 developing and industrial countries between 1980 and 1994. With the help of a multivariate logit model they estimate the impact of a set of macroeconomic, financial and institutional fundamentals, such as GDP growth, real interest rates, inflation, private credit growth, the liquidity position of the banking sector, the existence of an explicit deposit insurance scheme and some law and order indexes, pooling the data for all countries.[41] Consistent with the business-cycle hypothesis for bank crises, in all specifications GDP growth is a highly significant explanatory variable. The same applies to real interest rates and inflation rates. However, private sector credit growth, whether contemporaneous or lagged, has only explanatory power in some specifications, providing only mixed evidence in favour of the lending boom hypothesis. In contrast, the evidence in favour of the moral-hazard hypothesis regarding explicit deposit insurance schemes is stronger. Since data for crises and non-crises times are pooled, this study can claim to isolate the factors causing full-scale banking crises from those only causing a gradual increase in financial fragility or single bank failures.

Gourinchas, Valdés and Landerretche (1999) examine more narrowly the properties of lending booms in a sample of 91 industrial and developing countries between 1960 and 1996 and link them to the likelihood of banking and currency crises. In fact, the unconditional probability of banking crises directly *after* lending boom periods is higher than during tranquil periods. However, only few robust results are found when specific characteristics of boom periods are related to crises. For example, the size of the boom seems to increase the probability of a bank crisis, whereas the occurrence of high real investment during a lending boom decreases the probability. Somewhat contrary to conventional wisdom Gourinchas, Valdés and Landerretche also find that the build-up and ending phases of booms are fairly symmetric, so that on average abrupt and crash-type ends are not consistent with their data.

[41] The presence or not of a banking crisis is not measured by a strong systemic event in the broad sense but rather as a situation in which at least one of a list of four criteria is met. These criteria include threshold shares of total non-performing loans, the costs of any rescue operations, the occurrence of widespread bank runs or large-scale bank nationalizations and the implementation of emergency measures. Because of the occurrence of crisis management operations, concentrating only on the number or size of bank failures would have run the risk of underestimating the systemic breadth of a crisis in the absence of policy responses.

4.2. Evidence on Contagion in Interbank Payment Systems

Published empirical studies about the importance of systemic risk in payment systems are very rare. To our knowledge, there are only three rigorous analyses of it, all of which use simulations to examine the scope of contagion effects in large-value interbank net payment systems.

Humphrey (1986) simulates the potential effects of a major participant's failure in the US CHIPS by 'unwinding' all the transactions involving such a participant on two randomly selected business days in January 1983. When this event rendered another bank's net debit position larger than its capital this bank's transactions were also cancelled due to 'insolvency', and so on. This simulation suggested that a large share of all CHIPS participants could default (around 37 percent). Also, Humphrey finds that the institutions affected by the initial failure were quite different between the two days examined.

In a very careful study, Angelini, Maresca and Russo (1996) apply a substantially generalized simulation exercise to the Italian net settlement system, considering end-of-day bilateral net balances for all 288 participants during January 1992. Basically, the authors generate frequency distributions of defaults, eliminated payments etc., by letting each system member alone fail once per business day. From these simulations, the systemic risk in the Italian settlement system seems to be lower than that for CHIPS (when compared with Humphrey's (1986) results). Recorded chain defaults involved on average less than 1 per cent of system participants and never more than 7 banks. The share of participants potentially triggering a systemic crisis amounted to 4 per cent of the total, and the 'suspects' did not change a lot over time (many of them being foreign banks).[42]

McAndrews and Wasilyew (1995) undertake a similar study of systemic risk in net systems with unwinding provisions based entirely on Monte Carlo simulations. In each run the number of system participants and their bilateral payments are drawn from random distributions. Then the participant with the largest overall net debit position is made to fail on all its payment obligations. It turns out that system-wide repercussions of such a failure increase with the average size of bilateral payments, the number of system participants and with the degree of 'connectedness' between the participants (as measured by the likelihood that any two banks exchange payments).

Closely connected to the 'measurement of effective exposures' approach in Section 4.1.1.6, Furfine (1999) examines interbank positions resulting from 719 commercial banks' US fed funds transactions settled through the Fedwire real-time gross settlement system during February and March 1998. (Notice that Fedwire intra-day overdrafts are priced but not collateralized, so that the entirety of the bilateral positions from these transactions can be regarded as credit exposures at any point in time for the lifetime of the contract.) He assesses the contagion risk through these exposures by making assumptions about which banks fail and how

[42] The largest individual worsening of a net position was 18.5 times capital (as compared to 32.4 times capital in Humphrey, 1986).

large the recovery rate of the failure is likely to be. These parameters determine the effective losses of other banks and conditional on the capital of these other banks, whether any further failures will be caused. The author shows that the degree of systemic risk depends dramatically on the recovery rate. If only 60 percent of the failing bank's (banks') exposure(s) can be recovered, then the failure of the most significant bank alone would cause between 2 and 4 other banks to fail (depending on the date of the initial failure). Whereas the joint failure of the two most significant banks would raise the direct contagion effect to between 4 and 8 other banks in the sample. Interestingly enough, it also turns out that second-round failures appear to be extremely rare (only at isolated dates 1 bank fails as a consequence of a second round effect, but never more). If the recovery rate is 95 percent (a figure close to the effective recovery rate experienced in the Continental Illinois case of 1983–84; see Kaufman 1994), then simulated contagion even vanishes almost entirely in this study. In none of the scenarios or dates considered more than 1 bank would ever fail in the first round, and second-round failures disappear entirely. However, Furfine also cautions that since the concentration on Fedwire and overnight contracts alone ignores many other sources of interbank exposures his estimates should be regarded as 'a reliable lower bound on the risk of contagion'.

One advantage of this type of simulation approach to payment system risk is the quantitative measurement of the extent of contagion and its very practical implications, in particular when real payments data are considered. An objection to this approach is that it does not allow for reactions of other payment system participants to initial failures and might therefore either overstate contagion risk (if banks manage to undertake hedging transactions quickly) or understate contagion risk (if adverse selection phenomena in relation to banks' health in a crisis situation would lead market participants to hold back payments). Moreover, nowadays many net payment systems reduced or removed potential unwinding of transactions for exactly the reason that they might enhance systemic risk. Most other evidence of systemic problems in payment (and settlement) systems seem to be rather anecdotal in nature, such as that describing the 1987 stock market crash (see e.g. Brimmer 1989, and Bernanke 1990).

To conclude the empirical part on systemic risk in the banking sector, it appears fairly clear that many banking crises in history have been related to macroeconomic fluctuations and other aggregate or regional shocks. However, the interpretation of the results on the importance of bank contagion is less straightforward. Whereas, there seem to be episodes of strong autocorrelation in the number of bank failures, of strong co-movements in bank equity and debt prices and of cross-bank deposit withdrawals, many of the results do not state clearly whether these constitute contagion phenomena or rather represent cases of joint exposures to aggregate shocks. In fact, the evidence from capital markets seems to suggest that equity and bond price reactions to bank problems in the US may have been 'efficient' responses to the arrival of new information. The studies surveyed also illustrate a general difficulty to distinguish empirically between 'information-based' contagion and 'pure' contagion of the sunspot type. Finally, while various simulation studies illustrate the risk of bank contagion through large-value payment systems, there is less econometric evidence of such risks actually materializing. The available evidence in this regard is then rather anecdotal. In sum, on the basis of the available information it seems to be very hard to resolve one of the main policy debates in the area of banking crisis management (see Section 2.4), namely whether emergency liquidity assistance to individual banks should sometimes be provided by central banks or whether lending to the market is an efficient answer (Goodfriend and King 1988, reprinted in this volume). This remains a major issue to be addressed in future research efforts.

5. CONCLUSIONS

In this paper we discussed the various elements of systemic risk in banking, which are essential for the understanding of financial crises. The overall concept developed can be used as a baseline for financial and monetary policies when attempting to maintain stable banking systems. We argue that a comprehensive view of systemic risk has to consider bank failure contagion, financial markets spillover effects and payment and settlement risks. However, for reasons of space we deal with the issue of financial market and security settlement system contagion in a companion paper (Hartmann and De Bandt 2001). At the heart of systemic risk (in the narrow sense) is the notion of contagion—often a strong form of external effect—working from one institution or system to another. In a broad sense the concept also includes wide systematic shocks which by themselves adversely affect many banks at the same time. In this sense, systemic risk goes much beyond the vulnerability of single banks to runs in a fractional reserve system.

We reviewed the quantitative literature in the light of our concept of systemic risk. Some important new theoretical contributions have appeared in this literature in the last couple of years. First of all, and probably most importantly, a considerable number of theoretical studies have now directly addressed the issue of contagion through interbank markets. Although a generally accepted paradigm has not yet emerged, these models have greatly enhanced our understanding of the potential propagation of problems in the banking system. Second, further theoretical work has now also illustrated the greater scope for bank contagion in net settlement systems as compared to real-time gross settlement systems. However, the theoretical literature has not yet tackled the issues raised by 'hybrid' systems often encountered in practice.

On the empirical side a few valuable developments on the explanation of banking crises across countries have recently taken place, but insights into payment system contagion remain scarce, particularly outside the US and on systems that do not work on net settlement. Whereas the empirical literature has provided some evidence of the existence of systemic risk (as defined in Section 2), in particular in the 'broad' sense, it is more puzzling that many tests for bank contagion do not control for all the macroeconomic factors that might be behind the observation of joint bank failures in history. These difficulties in empirically identifying the importance of contagion as opposed to joint banking crises as consequences of macro shocks is not innocuous, since it has some implications for crisis management policies. Bank crises emerging from contagion could be stopped at an early stage at the individual bank level through emergency liquidity assistance—if identified in a timely manner—, whereas macro problems would normally be addressed through more standard stabilization policies, such as open market operations. In other words, the current empirical literature cannot resolve the old policy debate about emergency lending to individual institutions versus lending to the market. Moreover, most traditional tests for bank contagion are not conclusive about whether spillovers are 'information-based' or 'pure' sunspot phenomena, and whether the former constitute efficient or inefficient systemic events. Finally, the overwhelming part of existing econometric tests for bank contagion effects is still limited to data for the United States. Event studies of bank equity returns, debt risk premiums, deposit flows or physical exposures for European, Japanese or emerging market countries are rare or virtually absent. Clearly, more empirical research is needed about the actual importance and character of bank contagion, but this agenda will not be easy to fulfil due to data constraints and the presence of safety nets in many countries.

Overall, we feel that the recent financial crises (Nordic banking crises, Mexico, East Asia, Japanese banking crisis, Russia etc.) sufficiently underline the importance of understanding systemic risk in banking systems as a tool in designing policies and encouraging market initiatives aimed at financial stability. It was not our objective to explain any of these crises in itself. If we succeeded in convincing some researchers to try filling some of the remaining gaps we identified in the systemic risk literature, which could be used to help explain and prevent real crisis situations, then we have achieved what we could hope for.

REFERENCES

Agénor, P.R., M. Miller, D. Vines and A.A. Weber (eds.), 1999, 'The Asian Financial crisis: Causes, Contagion and Consequences' (Cambridge, UK: Cambridge University Press).

Aghion, P., P. Bolton and M. Dewatripont, 2000, 'Contagious Bank Failures', paper presented at the Center for Financial Studies Conference, 'Systemic Risk and Lender of Last Resort Facilities', 11–12 June, Frankfurt.

Aglietta, M. and P. Moutot, 1993, 'Le risque de système et sa prévention', Cahiers Economiques et Monétaires (Banque de France), 41, 21–53.

Aharony, J. and I. Swary, 1983, 'Contagion Effects of Bank Failures: Evidence from Capital Markets', Journal of Business, 56(3), 305–17.

Akerlof, G., 1970, 'The Market for Lemons: Quality Uncertainty and the Market Mechanism, Quarterly Journal of Economics, 84, 488–500.

Allen, F. and D. Gale, 1998, 'Optimal Financial Crises', Journal of Finance, 53(4), 1245–84.

—, 2000a, 'Financial Contagion', Journal of Political Economy, 108(1), 1–33.

—, 2000b, 'Bubbles and Crises', Economic Journal, 110(460), 236–55.

Angelini, P., 1998, 'An Analysis of Competitive Externalities in Gross Settlement Systems', Journal of Banking and Finance, 22, 1–18.

—, G. Maresca and D. Russo, 1996, 'Systemic Risk in the Netting System', Journal of Banking and Finance, 20, 853–68.

Avery, C. and P. Zemsky, 1998, 'Multidimensional Uncertainty and Herd Behaviour', American Economic Review, 88(4), 724–48.

Banerjee, A.V., 1992, 'A Simple Model of Herd Behaviour', Quarterly Journal of Economics, 107(3), 797–811.

Bank for International Settlements, 1990, Report of the Committee on Interbank Netting Schemes of the Central Banks of the Group of Ten Countries, 'Lamfalussy Report' (Basel: BIS, November).

Bank of Japan, 1998 (ed.), 'Risk Measurement and Systemic Risk. Proceedings of the Second Joint Central Bank Research Conference' (Tokyo: BoJ, November).

Bartholomew, P.F. and G.G. Kaufman, (eds.), 1995, 'Banking, Financial Markets and Systemic Risk', Research in Financial Services: Private and Public Policy, 7 (Greenwich, CN: JAI Press).

—, and G.W. Whalen, 1995, 'Fundamentals of Systemic Risk', in Banking, Financial Markets and Systemic Risk, Research in Financial Services: Private and Public Policy, 7 (Greenwich, CN: JAI Press), 3–17.

Benston, G.J., R. Eisenbeis, P. Horvitz, E. Kane and G. Kaufman, 1986, 'Perspectives on Safe and Sound Banking: Past, Present and Future' (Cambridge, MA: MIT Press).

Berger, A.N., D. Hancock and J.C. Marquardt, 1996, 'A Framework for Analyzing Efficiency, Risks, Costs, and Innovations in the Payment System', Journal of Money, Credit, and Banking, 28(4), 696–732.

Bernanke, B.S., 1983, 'Nonmonetary Effects of the Financial Crisis in the Propagation of the Great Depression', American Economic Review, 73(3), 257–76.

—, 1990, 'Clearing and Settlement during the Crash', Review of Financial Studies, 3(1), 133–51.

— and M. Gertler, 1990, 'Financial Fragility and Economic Performance', Quarterly Journal of Economics, 105(1), 87–114.

Bernanke, B.S., M. Gertler and S. Gilchrist, 1999, 'The Financial Accelerator in a Quantitative Business Cycle Framework', in Handbook of Macroeconomics, I, ed. by J.B. Taylor and M. Woodford (Amsterdam: Elsevier).

Bhattacharya, S. and A. Thakor, 1993, 'Contemporary Banking Theory', Journal of Financial Intermediation, 3, 2–50.

Bikhchandani, S., D. Hirshleifer and I. Welsh, 1992, 'A Theory of Fads, Fashions, Customs and Cultural Changes as Informational Cascade', Journal of Political Economy, 100, 992–1026.

Bolton, P. and D.S. Scharfstein, 1996, 'Optimal Debt Structure and the Number of Creditors', Journal of Political Economy, 104(1), 1–25.

Boot, A. and A. Thakor, 1993, 'Bank Regulation, Reputation and Rents: Theory and Policy', in Capital Markets and Financial Intermediation, ed. by C. Mayer and X. Vives (Cambridge: Cambridge University Press).

Bordo, M.D., 1990, 'The Lender of Last Resort: Alternative Views and Historical Experience', Federal Reserve Bank of Richmond Economic Review, 76(1), 18–29.

—, B. Mizrach and A.J. Schwartz, 1995, 'Real versus Pseudo-international Systemic Risk: Lessons from History', NBER Working Paper, no. 5371 (Cambridge, MA: National Bureau of Economic Research, December).

Borio, C.E.V. and P. Van den Bergh, 1993, 'The Nature and Management of Payment System Risks: An International Perspective', BIS Economic Papers, no. 36 (Basel: Bank for International Settlements, February).

Brimmer, A.F., 1989, 'Distinguished Lecture on Economics in Government: Central Banking and Systemic Risks in Capital Markets', Journal of Economic Perspectives, 3, 3–16.

Bryant, J., 1980, 'A Model of Reserves, Bank Runs, and Deposit Insurance', Journal of Banking and Finance, 4, 335–44.

Buser, S.A., A.H. Chen and E.J. Kane, 1981, 'Federal Deposit Insurance, Regulatory Policy, and Optimal Bank Capital', Journal of Finance, 35(1), 51–60.

Calomiris, C.W. and G. Gorton, 1991, 'The Origins of Banking Panics: Models, Facts, and Bank Regulation', in Financial Markets and Financial Crises, ed. by G. Hubbard (Chicago, IL: The University of Chicago Press), 109–73.

— and C.M. Kahn, 1991, 'The Role of Demandable Debt in Structuring Optimal Banking Arrangements', American Economic Review, 81(3), 497–513.

— and C.M. Kahn, 1996, 'The Efficiency of Self-regulated Payments Systems: Learning from the Suffolk System', Journal of Money, Credit, and Banking, 28(4), 767–97.

— and J.R. Mason, 1997, 'Contagion and Bank Failures During the Great Depression: The June 1932 Chicago Banking Panic', American Economic Review, 87(5), 863–83.

— and J.R. Mason, 2000, 'Causes of U.S. Bank Distress During the Depression', NBER Working Paper, no. 7919 (Cambridge, MA: National Bureau of Economic Research, September).

Carletti, E., 1999a, 'Bank Moral Hazard and Market Discipline', L.S.E Financial Markets Group Discussion Paper, no. 326 (London: London School of Economics and Political Science, May).

—, 1999b, 'Competition, Regulation and Stability', mimeo., Financial Markets Group, London School of Economics and Political Science, October.

Carron, A.S., 1982, 'Financial Crises: Recent Experience in U.S. and International Markets', Brookings Papers on Economic Activity, no. 2, 395–418.

Cass, D. and K. Shell, 1983, 'Do Sunspots Matter?', Journal of Political Economy, 91, 193–227.

Chari, V.V. and R. Jagannathan, 1988, 'Banking Panics, Information, and Rational Expectations Equilibrium', Journal of Finance, 43, 749–61.

Chen, Y., 1999, 'Banking Panics: The Role of the First-come, First-served Rule and Information Externalities', Journal of Political Economy, 107(5), 946–68.

Clark, J.A. and S.B. Perfect, 1996, 'The Economic Effects of Client Losses on OTC Bank Derivative Dealers: Evidence from the Capital Markets', Journal of Money, Credit, and Banking, 28(3), 527–45.

Cole, H.L. and T.J. Kehoe, 2000, 'Self-fulfilling Debt Crises', Review of Economic Studies, 67(1), 91–116.

Committee on Payment and Settlement Systems, 1992, 'Delivery versus Payment in Securities Settlement Systems' (Basel: Bank for International Settlements, September).

— , 1996, 'Settlement Risk in Foreign Exchange Transactions', Allsopp Report (Basel: Bank for International Settlements, March).

Cooperman, E.S., W.B. Lee and G.A. Wolfe, 1992, 'The 1985 Ohio Thrift Crisis, the FSLIC's Solvency, and Rate Contagion for Retail CDs', Journal of Finance, 47(3), 919–41.

Cornell, B. and A.C. Shapiro, 1986, 'The Reaction of Bank Stock Prices to the International Debt Crisis', Journal of Banking and Finance, 10, 55–73.

Cukierman, A., 1991, 'Why Does the Fed Smooth Interest Rates?', in Monetary Policy on the 75th Anniversary of the Federal Reserve System: Proceedings of the Fourteenth Annual

Economic Policy Conference of the Federal Reserve Bank of St. Louis, ed. by M.T. Belongia (Dordrecht: Kluwer Academic), 111–47.

Davis, E.P., 1994, 'Market Liquidity Risk', in The Competitiveness of Financial Institutions and Centres in Europe, ed. by D. Fair (Dordrecht: Kluwer Academic Publishers).

—, 1995 (2nd ed.), 'Debt, Financial Fragility and Systemic Risk' (Oxford: Clarendon Press).

De Bandt, O., 1995, 'Competition among Financial Intermediaries and the Risk of Contagious Failures', Notes d'Etudes et de Recherche, no. 30 (Paris: Banque de France).

—, 1996, 'Risque de panique et liquidité interbancaire', Revue d'Economie Politique, 106(4), 705–26.

Demirgüç-Kunt, A. and E. Detragiache, 1998, 'The Determinants of Banking Crises in Developing and Developed Countries', IMF Staff Papers, 45, 81–109.

Dewatripont, M. and J. Tirole, 1994, 'The Prudential Regulation of Banks', Walrus–Pareto Lecture, Translation (Cambridge: MIT Press).

Diamond, D.V. and P. Dybvig, 1983, 'Bank Runs, Deposit Insurance, and Liquidity', Journal of Political Economy, 91(3), 401–19.

— and R.R. Rajan, 2000a, 'Liquidity Risk, Liquidity Creation and Financial Fragility: A Theory of Banking', mimeo., University of Chicago, August.

— and R.R. Rajan, 2000b, 'Banks, Short Term Debt and Financial Crises: Theory, Policy Implications and Applications', Paper presented at the Center for Financial Studies Conference 'Liquidity Risk: Rethinking Risk Management', 30 June–1 July 2000, Frankfurt.

Docking, D.S., M. Hirschey and E. Jones, 1997, 'Information and Contagion Effects of Bank Loan-loss Reserve Announcements', Journal of Financial Economics, 43(2), 219–40.

Dowd, K., 1992a, 'Models of Banking Instability: A Partial Review', Journal of Economic Surveys, 6(2), 107–32.

—, (ed.), 1992b, 'The Experience of Free Banking' (London: Routledge).

—, 1996, 'Competition and Finance' (London: Macmillan).

Drees, B. and C. Pazarbaşioğlu, 1995, 'The Nordic Banking Crises: Pitfalls in Financial Liberalization?', IMF Working Paper, WP/95/61 (Washington, DC: International Monetary Fund).

Federal Reserve Bank of Kansas City, 1998, 'Maintaining Financial Stability in a Global Economy', Proceedings of the 1997 Jackson Hole Symposium, August 28–30 (Jackson Hole, WY: Kansas City Fed).

Financial Stability Forum, 2000a, 'Report of the Working Group on Capital Flows' (Basel: FSF, April).

—, 2000b, 'Report of the Working Group on Highly Leveraged Institutions' (Basel: FSF, April).

—, 2000c, 'Report of the Working Group on Offshore Financial Centres' (Basel: FSF, April).

—, 2000d, 'International Guidance on Deposit Insurance: A Consultative Process' (Basel: FSF, June).

Fischer, I., 1933, 'The Debt Deflation Theory of Great Depressions', Econometrica, 1, 337–57.

Flannery, M., 1996, 'Financial Crises, Payment System Problems, and Discount Window Lending', Journal of Money, Credit, and Banking, 28(4), 804–24.

Folkerts-Landau, D., 1991, 'Systemic Financial Risk in Payment Systems, in: Determinants and Systemic Consequences of International Capital Flows', IMF Occasional Paper, no. 77 (Washington, DC: IMF, March), 46–67.

Folkerts-Landau, D., P. Garber and D. Schoenmaker, 1996, 'The Reform of Wholesale Payment Systems and its Impact on Financial Markets', Group of Thirty Occasional Paper, no. 21 (Washington, DC: Group of Thirty).

Freixas, X. and B. Parigi, 1998, 'Contagion and Efficiency in Gross and Net Interbank Payment Systems', Journal of Financial Intermediation, 7(1), 3–31.

— and J.-C. Rochet, 1997, 'Microeconomics of Banking' (Cambridge, MA: MIT Press).

—, B. Parigi and J.-C. Rochet, 2000, 'Systemic Risk, Interbank Relations and Liquidity Provision by the Central Bank', Journal of Money, Credit, and Banking, 32(3/2), 611–40.

—, C. Giannini, G. Hoggarth and F. Soussa, 1999, 'Lender of Last Resort: A Review of the Literature', Financial Stability Review, 7, November, 151–67.

Friedman, M. and A.J. Schwartz, 1963, 'A Monetary History of the United States' (Princeton, NJ: Princeton University Press).

Furfine, C.H., 1999, 'Interbank Exposures: Quantifying the Risk of Contagion', BIS Working Papers, no.70 (Basel: Bank for International Settlements, June).

Furlong, F.T. and M.C. Keeley, 1989, 'Capital Regulation and Bank Risk-Taking: A Note', Journal of Banking and Finance, 13, 883–91.

Garber, P.M., V.U. Grilli, 1989, 'Bank Runs in Open Economies and the International Transmission of Panics', Journal of International Economics, 27, 165–75.

Gay, G.D., S.G. Timme and K. Yung, 1991, 'Bank Failure and Contagion Effects: Evidence from Hong Kong', Journal of Financial Services Research, 14(2), 153–65.

Goldstein, M., 1995, 'International Financial Markets and Systemic Risk', mimeo., Institute of International Economics, Washington (DC), December.

González-Hermosillo, B., 1999, 'Determinants of Ex-ante Banking System Distress: A Macro-Micro Empirical Exploration of Some Recent Episodes', IMF Working Paper, WP/99/33 (Washington, DC: International Monetary Fund, March).

—, C. Pazarbaşioğlu and R. Billings, 1997, 'Banking System Fragility: Likelihood Versus Timing of Failure–An Application to the Mexican Financial Crisis', IMF Staff Papers, 44(3), 295–314.

Goodfriend, M. and R. King, 1988, 'Financial Deregulation, Monetary Policy, and Central Banking', in Restructuring Banking and Financial Services in America, AEI Studies, no. 481 (Washington, DC: American Enterprise Institute for Public Policy Research), 216–53.

Goodhart, C.A.E., 1969, 'The New York Money Market and the Finance of Trade, 1900–1913' (Cambridge, MA: Harvard University Press).

—, 1988, 'The Evolution of Central Banks' (Cambridge, MA: MIT Press).

—, and H. Huang, 1999, 'A Model of the Lender of Last Resort', L.S.E. Financial Markets Group Discussion Paper, no. 313 (London: London School of Economics, January).

—, P. Hartmann, D.T. Llewellyn, L. Rojas-Suarez and S.R. Weisbrod, 1998, 'Financial Regulation: Why, How and Where Now?', Monograph prepared for the Bank of England Central Bank Governors' Symposium 1997 (London: Routledge).

Gorton, G., 1985, 'Bank Suspension of Convertibility', Journal of Monetary Economics, 15, 177–193.

—, 1988, 'Banking Panics and Business Cycles', Oxford Economic Papers, 40, 751–81.

— and D.J. Mullineaux, 1987, 'The Joint Production of Confidence: Endogenous Regulation and Nineteenth Century Commercial-bank Clearinghouses', Journal of Money, Credit, and Banking, 19(4), 457–68.

Gourinchas, P.-O., R. Valdés and O. Landerretche, 1999, 'Lending Booms: Some Stylized Facts', mimeo., Princeton University, October.

Grossman, R., 1993, 'The Macroeconomic Consequences of Bank Failures under the National Banking System', Explorations in Economic History, 30, 294–320.

Group of Thirty, 1997, 'Global Institutions, National Supervision and Systemic Risk' (Washington, DC: G 30).

Guttentag, J. and R. Herring, 1984, 'Credit Rationing and Financial Disorder', Journal of Finance, 39(5), 1359–82.

Gwynne, S., 1986, 'Selling Money' (New York: Weidenfeld and Nicholson).

Hartmann, P. and O. De Bandt 2001, 'A Review of the Literature on Financial Market Contagion', mimeo., ECB and Banque de France.

Hartmann, P., S.T.M. Straetmans and C.G. de Vries, 2000, 'Asset Market Linkages in Crisis Periods', ECB Working Paper no. 71 (Frankfurt: European Central Bank, July).

Hasan, I. and G. Dwyer, 1994, 'Bank Runs in the Free Banking Period', Journal of Money, Credit, and Banking, 26, 271–88.

Hellwig, M., 1994, 'Liquidity Provision, Banking, and the Allocation of Interest Rate Risk', European Economic Review, 38(7), 1363–89.

—, 1998, 'Systemische Risiken im Finanzsektor', Zeitschrift für Wirtschafts- und Sozialwissenschaften, Beiheft 7, 123–51.

Holthausen, C. and T. Rønde, 2000, 'Regulating Access to International Large-value Payment Systems', ECB Working Papers, no. 22 (Frankfurt: European Central Bank, June).

Huang, H. and C. Xu, 2000, 'Financial Institutions, Financial Contagion, and Financial Crises', IMF Working Paper, WP/00/92 (Washington, DC: International Monetary Fund, May).

Humphrey, D.B, 1986, 'Payments Finality and Risk of Settlement Failure', in Technology and the Regulation of Financial Markets: Securities, Futures, and Banking, ed. by Anthony Saunders and Lawrence J. White, 97–120 (Lexington, MA: Lexington Books).

—,1989, 'Market Responses to Pricing Fedwire Daylight Overdrafts', Federal Reserve Bank of Richmond, Economic Review, 75, 23–34.

Hunter, W.C., G.G. Kaufman and T.H. Krueger (eds.), 1999, 'The Asian Financial Crisis: Origins, Implications and Solutions', Proceedings of a joint Fed Chicago/IMF conference (Boston, MA: Kluwer Academic Publishers).

International Organization of Securities Commissions, 1998, 'Risk Management and Control Guidance for Securities Firms and their Supervisors' (Montreal: IOSCO, March).

Jacklin, C. and S. Bhattacharya, 1988, 'Distinguishing Panics and Information-based Runs: Welfare and Policy Implications', Journal of Political Economy, 96(3), 568–92.

Jansen, D.W. and C.G. de Vries, 1991, 'On the Frequency of Large Stock Returns: Putting Booms and Busts into Perspective', Review of Economics and Statistics, 73, 18–24.

Jayanti, S.V. and A.M. Whyte, 1996, 'Global Contagion Effects of the Continental Illinois Failure', Journal of International Financial Markets, Institutions and Money, 6(1), 87–99.

Kaminsky, G.I. and C.M. Reinhart, 1998, 'The Twin Crisis: The Causes of Banking and Balance-of-Payments Problems', American Economic Review, 89(3), 473–500.

Kane, E.J., 1985, 'The Gathering Crisis in Federal Deposit Insurance' (Cambridge, MA: MIT Press).

—, 1989, 'The S&L Mess: How Did it Happen?' (Washington, DC: Urban Institute Press).

Karafiath, I., R. Mynatt and K.L. Smith, 1991, 'The Brazilian Default Announcement and the Contagion Effect Hypothesis', Journal of Banking and Finance, 15, 699–716.

Kareken, J.H. and N. Wallace, 1978, 'Deposit Insurance and Bank Regulation: A Partial-Equilibrium Exposition', Journal of Business, 51(3), 413–38.

Kaufman, G.G., 1988, 'Bank Runs: Causes, Benefits and Costs', Cato Journal, 7, 559–87.

—, 1994, 'Bank Contagion: A Review of the Theory and Evidence', Journal of Financial Services Research, 7, 123–150.

Kindleberger, C.P., 1978/1996 (3rd ed.), 'Manias, Panics and Crashes. A History of Financial Crises' (London: Macmillan).

Kindleberger, C.P., 1986 (2nd ed.), 'The World in Depression, 1929–1939' (Berkeley, CA: University of California Press).

King, M. and S. Wadhwani, 1990, 'Transmission of Volatility between Stock Markets', Review of Financial Studies, 3(1), 5–35.

Kobayakawa, S., 1997, 'The Comparative Analysis of Settlement Systems, CEPR Discussion Paper, no. 1667 (London: Centre for Economic Policy Research, July).

Krugman, P., 1998, 'What happened to Asia?', mimeo., Massachusetts Institute of Technology, January.

Kyei, A., 1995, 'Deposit Protection Arrangements: A Survey', IMF Working Paper, WP/95/134 (Washington, DC: International Monetary Fund).

Lang, L.H.P. and R.M. Stulz, 1992, 'Contagion and Competitive Intra-industry Effects of Bankruptcy Announcements', Journal of Financial Economics, 32, 45–60.

Lindgren, C.-J., G. Garcia and M.I. Saal, 1996, 'Bank Soundness and Macroeconomic Policy' (Washington, DC: International Monetary Fund).

Madura, J. and W.R. McDaniel, 1989, 'Market Reactions to Increased Loan Loss Reserves at Money-Center Banks', Journal of Financial Services Research, 3141, 359–69.

—, A.M. Whyte and W.R. McDaniel, 1991, 'Reaction of British Bank Share Prices to Citicorp's announced $3 Billion Increase in Loan-loss Reserves', Journal of Banking and Finance, 15, 151–63.

McAndrews, J.J. and W. Roberds, 1995, 'Banks, Payments, and Coordination', Journal of Financial Intermediation, 4, 305–27.

— and G. Wasilyew, 1995, 'Simulations of Failure in a Payment System', Working Paper, no. 95-19 (Philadelphia, PA: Federal Reserve Bank of Atlanta, June).

Merton, R.C., 1976, 'An Analytical Derivation of the Cost of Deposit Insurance and Loan Guarantees: An Application of Modern Option Pricing Theory', Journal of Banking and Finance, 1(1), 3–11.

—, 1978, 'On the Cost of Deposit Insurance When There Are Surveillance Costs', Journal of Business, 51(3), 439–52.

Michael, I., 1998, 'Financial Interlinkages and Systemic Risk', Financial Stability Review, 4, Spring, 26–33.

Miller, V., 1996, 'Speculative Currency Attacks with Endogenously Induced Commercial Bank Crises', Journal of International Money and Finance, 15(3), 383–403.

Minsky, H.P., 1977, 'A Theory of Systemic Fragility', in Financial Crises, ed. by E.I. Altman and A.W. Sametz (New York, NY: Wiley).

—, 1982: 'The Financial-instability Hypothesis: Capitalist Processes and the Behaviour of the Economy', in Financial Crises: Theory, History, and Policy, ed. by C.P. Kindleberger and J.-P. Laffargue (Cambridge, UK: Cambridge University Press), 13–39.

Mishkin, F.S., 1991, 'Asymmetric Information and Financial Crises: A Historical Perspective' in Financial Markets and Financial Crises, ed. by G. Hubbard (Chicago, IL: The University of Chicago Press).

—, 1997, 'The Causes and Propagation of Financial Instability: Lessons for Policy Makers', in Maintaining Financial Stability in a Global Economy (Jackson Hole, WY: Federal Reserve Bank of Kansas City).

Morgenstern, O., 1959, 'International Financial Transactions and the Business Cycle' (Princeton, NJ: Princeton University Press, National Bureau of Economic Research Studies in Business Cycles).

Musgrave, R.A. and P.B. Musgrave 1973 (2nd ed.), 'Public Finance in Theory and Practice', (New York, NY: McGraw-Hill).

Musumeci, J.J. and J.F. Sinkey, 1990, 'The International Debt Crisis, Investor Contagion, and Bank Security Returns in 1987: The Brazilian Experience', Journal of Money, Credit, and Banking, 22(2), 210–33.

Park, S., 1991, 'Bank Failure Contagion in Historical Perspective', Journal of Monetary Economics, 28, 271–86.

Paroush, J., 1988, 'The Domino Effect and the Supervision of the Banking System', Journal of Finance, 43(5), 1207–18.

Peavy, J.W. and G.H. Hempel, 1988, 'The Penn Square Bank Failure: Effect on Commercial Bank Security Returns—A Note', Journal of Banking and Finance, 12, 141–50.

Peek, J. and E.S. Rosengren, 1997, 'The International Transmission of Financial Shocks: The Case of Japan', American Economic Review, 87(4), 495–505.

Portes, R. and A.K. Swoboda, eds. 1987, 'Threats to International Financial Stability' (New York, NY: Cambridge University Press).

Rochet, J.-C. and J. Tirole, 1996a, 'Interbank Lending and Systemic Risk', Journal of Money, Credit, and Banking, 28(4), 733–62.

——, 1996b, 'Controlling Risk in Payment Systems', Journal of Money, Credit, and Banking, 28(4), 832–62.

Rolnick, A.J. and W.E. Weber, 1986, 'Inherent Instability in Banking: The Free Banking Experience', Cato Journal, 5(3), 877–90.

—, B.D. Smith and W.E. Weber, 1998, 'Lessons From a Laissez-faire Payments System: The Suffolk Banking System (1825–58)', Federal Reserve Bank of Minneapolis Quarterly Review, 22(3), 11–21.

———, 1999, 'The Suffolk Bank and the Panic of 1837: How a Private Bank Acted as a Lender of Last Resort', in Risk Measurement and Systemic Risk, Proceedings of the Second Joint Central Bank Research Conference (Tokyo: Bank of Japan), 483–505.

Rossi, M., 1997, 'Payment Systems in the Financial Markets: Real-time Gross Settlement Systems and the Provision of Intraday Liquidity' (New York: St. Martin Press).

Saunders, A., 1986, 'An Examination of the Contagion Effect in the International Loan Market', Studies in Banking and Finance, 3, 219–47.

—, 1987, 'The Inter-bank Market, Contagion Effects and International Financial Crises', in Threats to International Financial Stability, ed. by R. Portes and A.K. Swoboda (New York, NY: Cambridge University Press), 196–232.

— and B. Wilson, 1996, 'Contagious Bank Runs: Evidence from the 1929–33 Period', Journal of Financial Intermediation, 5(4), 409–23.

Scharfstein, D.S. and J.C. Stein, 1990, 'Herd Behaviour and Investment', American Economic Review, 80(3), 465–79.

Schoder, S. and P. Vankudre, 1986, 'The Market for Bank Stocks and Banks' Disclosure of Cross-border Exposure', Studies in Banking and Finance, 3, 179–202.

Schoenmaker, D., 1995, 'A Comparison of Alternative Interbank Settlement Systems', L.S.E. Financial Markets Group Discussion Paper, no. 204 (London: London School of Economics).

—, 1996a, 'Contagion Risk in Banking', L.S.E. Financial Markets Group Discussion Paper, no. 239 (London: London School of Economics, March).

—, 1996b, 'Central Banking and Financial Stability: The Central Bank's Role in Banking Supervision and Payment Systems', unpublished Ph.D. thesis (London: London School of Economics and Political Science, May).

Schwartz, A.J., 1986, 'Real and Pseudo-financial Crises', in Financial Crises and the World Banking System, ed. by F. Capie and G.E. Wood (London: Macmillan), 11–31.

Sheldon, G. and M. Maurer, 1998, 'Interbank Lending and Systemic Risk: An Empirical Analysis for Switzerland', Swiss Journal of Economics and Statistics, 134(2), 685–704.

Shiller, R.J., 1989, 'Market Volatility' (Cambridge, MA: MIT Press).

—, 2000, 'Irrational Exuberance' (Princeton, NJ: Princeton University Press).

Slovin, M.B., M.E. Sushka and J.A. Polonchek 1999, 'An Analysis of Contagion and Competitive Effects at Commercial Banks', Journal of Financial Economics, 54, 197–225.

Smirlock, M. and H. Kaufold, 1987, 'Bank Foreign Lending, Mandatory Disclosure Rules, and the Reaction of Bank Stock Prices to the Mexican Debt Crisis', Journal of Business, 60(3), 347–64.

Smith, B.D., 1991, 'Bank Panics, Suspensions and Geography: Some Notes on the Contagion of Fear in Banking', Economic Inquiry, 29(2), 230–48.

Sprague, O.M.W., 1910, 'A History of Crises under the National Banking System' (Washington, DC: US Government Printing Office).

Staub, M., 1998, 'Inter-Banken-Kredite und systemisches Risiko', Schweizerische Zeitschrift für Volkswirtschaft und Statistik, 134(2), 193–230.

Stiglitz, J.E., 1993, 'The Role of the State in Financial Markets', paper presented to the Annual Bank Conference on Development Economics (Washington, DC: World Bank).

— and A. Weiss, 1981, 'Credit Rationing in Markets with Imperfect Information', American Economic Review, 71, 393–410.

Summers, B.J., (ed.), 1994, 'The Payment System: Design, Management and Supervision' (Washington, DC: International Monetary Fund).

Swary, I., 1986, 'Stock Market Reaction to Regulatory Action in the Continental Illinois Crisis', Journal of Business, 59(3), 451–73.

Temzelides, T., 1997, 'Evolution, Co-ordination and Banking Panics', Journal of Monetary Economics, 40, 163–83.

Tietmeyer, H., 1999, 'International Cooperation and Coordination in the Area of Financial Market Supervision and Surveillance,' Report to the G-7 Finance Ministers and Central Bank Governors Meeting in Bonn, 20 February 1999.

Waldo, D.G., 1985, 'Bank Runs, the Deposit Currency Ratio and the Interest Rate', Journal of Monetary Economics, 15, 269–77.

Wall, L.D. and D.R. Peterson, 1990, 'The Effect of Continental Illinois Failure on the Financial Performance of Other Banks', Journal of Monetary Economics, 26, 77–99.

White, L.H., 1984, 'Free Banking in Britain: Theory, Experience, and Debate', 1800–1845' (Cambridge, UK: Cambridge University Press).

Wicker, E., 1996, 'The Banking Panics of the Great Depression' (Cambridge, UK: Cambridge University Press).

Wicker, E., 2000, 'Banking Panics of the Gilded Age' (Cambridge, UK: Cambridge University Press).

Working Party on Financial Stability in Emerging Markets, 1997, 'Financial Stability in Emerging Markets' (Basel: Bank for International Settlements, Secretariat of the Group of Ten, April).

Yamazaki, A., 1996, 'Foreign Exchange Netting and Systemic Risk', IMES Discussion Paper Series, no. 96-E-23 (Tokyo: Bank of Japan, June).

15

Bank Runs, Deposit Insurance, and Liquidity

DOUGLAS W. DIAMOND AND PHILIP H. DYBVIG

I. INTRODUCTION

Bank runs are a common feature of the extreme crises that have played a prominent role in monetary history. During a bank run, depositors rush to withdraw their deposits because they expect the bank to fail. In fact, the sudden withdrawals can force the bank to liquidate many of its assets at a loss and to fail. In a panic with many bank failures, there is a disruption of the monetary system and a reduction in production.

Institutions in place since the Great Depression have successfully prevented bank runs in the United States since the 1930s. Nonetheless, current deregulation and the dire financial condition of savings and loans make bank runs and institutions to prevent them a current policy issue, as shown by recent aborted runs.[1] (Internationally, Eurodollar deposits tend to be uninsured and are therefore subject to runs, and this is true in the United States as well for deposits above the insured amount.) It is good that deregulation will leave banking more competitive, but we must ensure that banks will not be left vulnerable to runs.

Through careful description and analysis, Friedman and Schwartz (1963) have provided substantial insight into the properties of past bank runs in the United States. Existing theoretical analysis has neglected to explain why bank contracts are less stable than other types of financial contracts or to investigate the strategic decisions that depositors face. The model we present has an explicit economic role for banks to perform: the transformation of illiquid assets into liquid liabilities. The analyses of Patinkin (1965, chap. 5), Tobin (1965), and Niehans (1978) provide insights into characterizing the liquidity of assets. This paper gives the first explicit analysis of the demand for liquidity and the 'transformation' service provided by banks. Uninsured demand deposit contracts are able to provide liquidity but leave

[1] The aborted runs on Hartford Federal Savings and Loan (Hartford, Conn., February 1982) and on Abilene National Bank (Abilene, Texas, July 1982) are two recent examples. The large amounts of uninsured deposits in the recently failed Penn Square Bank (Oklahoma City, July 1982) and its repercussions are another symptom of banks' current problems.

This article first appeared in the *Journal of Political Economy* 91(3), 1983.

banks vulnerable to runs. This vulnerability occurs because there are multiple equilibria with differing levels of confidence.

Our model demonstrates three important points. First, banks issuing demand deposits can improve on a competitive market by providing better risk sharing among people who need to consume at different random times. Second, the demand deposit contract providing this improvement has an undesirable equilibrium (a bank run) in which all depositors panic and withdraw immediately, including even those who would prefer to leave their deposits in if they were not concerned about the bank failing. Third, bank runs cause real economic problems because even 'healthy' banks can fail, causing the recall of loans and the termination of productive investment. In addition, our model provides a suitable framework for analysis of the devices traditionally used to stop or prevent bank runs, namely, suspension of convertibility and demand deposit insurance (which works similarly to a central bank serving as 'lender of last resort').

The illiquidity of assets enters our model through the economy's riskless production activity. The technology provides low levels of output per unit of input if operated for a single period but high levels of output if operated for two periods. The analysis would be the same if the asset were illiquid because of selling costs: one receives a low return if unexpectedly forced to 'liquidate' early. In fact, this illiquidity is a property of the financial assets in the economy in our model, even though they are traded in competitive markets with no transaction costs. Agents will be concerned about the cost of being forced into early liquidation of these assets and will write contracts which reflect this cost. Investors face private risks which are not directly insurable because they are not publicly verifiable. Under optimal risk sharing, this private risk implies that agents have different time patterns of return in different private information states and that agents want to allocate wealth unequally across private information states. Because only the agent ever observes the private information state, it is impossible to write insurance contracts in which the payoff depends directly on private information, without an explicit mechanism for information flow. Therefore, simple competitive markets cannot provide this liquidity insurance.

Banks are able to transform illiquid assets by offering liabilities with a different, smoother pattern of returns over time than the illiquid assets offer. These contracts have multiple equilibria. If confidence is maintained, there can be efficient risk sharing, because in that equilibrium a withdrawal will indicate that a depositor should withdraw under optimal risk sharing. If agents panic, there is a bank run and incentives are distorted. In that equilibrium, everyone rushes in to withdraw their deposits before the bank gives out all of its assets. The bank must liquidate all its assets, even if not all depositors withdraw, because liquidated assets are sold at a loss.

Illiquidity of assets provides the rationale both for the existence of banks and for their vulnerability to runs. An important property of our model of banks and bank runs is that runs are costly and reduce social welfare by interrupting production (when loans are called) and by destroying optimal risk sharing among depositors.

Runs in many banks would cause economy-wide economic problems. This is consistent with the Friedman and Schwartz (1963) observation of large costs imposed on the U.S. economy by the bank runs in the 1930s, although they attribute the real damage from bank runs as occurring through the money supply.

Another contrast with our view of how bank runs do economic damage is discussed by Fisher (1911, p. 64).[2] In this view, a run occurs because the bank's assets, which are liquid but risky, no longer cover the nominally fixed liability (demand deposits), so depositors withdraw quickly to cut their losses. The real losses are indirect, through the loss of collateral caused by falling prices. In contrast, a bank run in our model is caused by a shift in expectations, which could depend on almost anything, consistent with the apparently irrational observed behavior of people running on banks.

We analyze bank contracts that can prevent runs and examine their optimality. We show that there is a feasible contract that allows banks both to prevent runs and to provide optimal risk sharing by converting illiquid assets. The contract corresponds to suspension of convertibility of deposits (to currency), a weapon banks have historically used against runs. Under other conditions, the best contract that banks can offer (roughly, the suspension-of-convertibility contract) does not achieve optimal risk sharing. However, in this more general case there is a contract which achieves the unconstrained optimum when government deposit insurance is available. Deposit insurance is shown to be able to rule out runs without reducing the ability of banks to transform assets. What is crucial is that deposit insurance frees the asset liquidation policy from strict dependence on the volume of withdrawals. Other institutions such as the discount window ('lender of last resort') may serve a similar function; however, we do not model this here. The taxation authority of the government makes it a natural provider of the insurance, although there may be a competitive fringe of private insurance.

Government deposit insurance can improve on the best allocations that private markets provide. Most of the existing literature on deposit insurance assumes away any real service from deposit insurance, concentrating instead on the question of pricing the insurance, taking as given the likelihood of failure (see, e.g., Merton 1977, 1978; Kareken and Wallace 1978; Dothan and Williams 1980).

Our results have far-reaching policy implications, because they imply that the real damage from bank runs is primarily from the direct damage occurring when recalling loans interrupts production. This implies that much of the economic damage in the Great Depression was *caused* directly by bank runs. A study by Bernanke (in press) supports our thesis, as it shows that bank runs give a better predictor of economic distress than money supply.

The paper proceeds as follows. In the next section, we analyze a simple economy which shows that banks can improve the risk sharing of simple competitive markets by transforming illiquid assets. We show that such banks are always vulnerable to runs. In Section III, we analyze the optimal bank contracts that prevent runs.

[2] Bryant (1980) also takes this view.

In Section IV, we analyze bank contracts, dropping the previous assumption that the volume of withdrawals is deterministic. Deposit insurance is analyzed in Section V. Section VI concludes the paper.

II. THE BANK'S ROLE IN PROVIDING LIQUIDITY

Banks have issued demand deposits throughout their history, and economists have long had the intuition that demand deposits are a vehicle through which banks fulfill their role of turning illiquid assets into liquid assets. In this role, banks can be viewed as providing insurance that allows agents to consume when they need to most. Our simple model shows that asymmetric information lies at the root of liquidity demand, a point not explicitly noted in the previous literature.

The model has three periods ($T = 0, 1, 2$) and a single homogeneous good. The productive technology yields $R > 1$ units of output in period 2 for each unit of input in period 0. If production is interrupted in period 1, the salvage value is just the initial investment. Therefore, the productive technology is represented by

$$\begin{array}{ccc} T=0 & T=1 & T=2 \\ & & \\ -1 & \begin{cases} 0 \\ 1 \end{cases} & \begin{array}{c} R \\ 0, \end{array} \end{array}$$

where the choice between $(0, R)$ and $(1, 0)$ is made in period 1. (Of course, constant returns to scale implies that a fraction can be done in each option.)

One interpretation of the technology is that long-term capital investments are somewhat irreversible, which appears to be a reasonable characterization. The results would be reinforced (or can be alternatively motivated) by any type of transaction cost associated with selling a bank's assets before maturity. See Diamond (1980) for a model of the costly monitoring of loan contracts by banks, which implies such a cost.

All consumers are identical as of period 0. Each faces a privately observed, uninsurable risk of being of type 1 or of type 2. In period 1, each agent (consumer) learns his type. Type 1 agents care only about consumption in period 1 and type 2 agents care only about consumption in period 2. In addition, all agents can privately store (or 'hoard') consumption goods at no cost. This storage is not publicly observable. No one would store between $T = 0$ and $T = 1$, because the productive technology does at least as well (and better if held until $T = 2$). If an agent of type 2 obtains consumption goods at $T = 1$, he will store them until $T = 2$ to consume them. Let c_T represent goods 'received' (to store or consume) by an agent at period T. The privately observed consumption at $T = 2$ of a type 2 agent is then what he stores from $T = 1$ plus what he obtains at $T = 2$, or $c_1 + c_2$. In terms of this publicly observed variable c_T the discussion above implies that each agent has a state-dependent utility function (with the state private information), which we assume has the form

$$U(c_1, c_2; \Theta) = \begin{cases} u(c_1) & \text{if } j \text{ is of type 1 in state } \Theta \\ \rho u(c_1 + c_2) & \text{if } j \text{ is of type 2 in state } \Theta, \end{cases}$$

where $1 \geq \rho > R^{-1}$ and $u: R_{++} \to R$ is twice continuously differentiable, increasing, strictly concave, and satisfies Inada conditions $u'(0) = \infty$ and $u'(\infty) = 0$. Also, we assume that the relative risk-aversion coefficient $-cu''(c)/u'(c) > 1$ everywhere. Agents maximize expected utility, $E[u(c_1, c_2; \Theta)]$, conditional on their information (if any).

A fraction $t \in (0, 1)$ of the continuum of agents are of type 1 and, conditional on t, each agent has an equal and independent chance of being of type 1. Later sections will allow t to be random (in which case, at period 1, consumers know their own type but not t), but for now we take t to be constant.

To complete the model, we give each consumer an endowment of 1 unit in period 0 (and none at other times). We consider first the competitive solution where agents hold the assets directly, and in each period there is a competitive market in claims on future goods. It is easy to show that because of the constant returns technology, prices are determined: the period 0 price of period 1 consumption is 1, and the period 0 and 1 prices of period 2 consumption are R^{-1}. This is because agents can write only uncontingent contracts as there is no public information on which to condition. Contracting in period $T = 0$, all agents (who are then identical) will establish the same trades and each will invest his endowment in the production technology. Given this identical position of each agent at $T = 0$, there will be trade in claims on goods for consumption at $T = 1$ and at $T = 2$. Each has access to the same technology and each can choose any positive linear combination of $c_1 = 1$ and $c_2 = R$. Each individual's production set is proportional to the aggregate set, and for there to be positive production of both c_1 and c_2, the period $T = 1$ price of c_2 must be R^{-1}. Given these prices, there is never any trade, and agents can do no better or worse than if they produced only for their own consumption. Letting c_k^i be consumption in period k of an agent who is of type i, the agents choose $c_1^1 = 1$, $c_2^1 = c_1^2 = 0$, and $c_2^2 = R$, since type 1's always interrupt production but type 2's never do.

By comparison, if types were *publicly* observable as of period 1, it would be possible to write optimal insurance contracts that give the ex ante (as of period 0) optimal sharing of output between type 1 and type 2 agents. The optimal consumption $\{c_k^{i*}\}$ satisfies

$$c_1^{2*} = c_2^{1*} = 0 \tag{1a}$$

(those who can, delay consumption),

$$u'(c_1^{1*}) = \rho R u'(c_2^{2*}) \tag{1b}$$

(marginal utility in line with marginal productivity), and

$$tc_1^{1*} + [(1 - t)c_2^{2*}/R] = 1 \tag{1c}$$

(the resource constraint).

By assumption, $\rho R > 1$, and since relative risk aversion always exceeds unity, equation (1) implies that the optimal consumption levels satisfy $c_1^{1*} > 1$ and

$c_2^{2*} < R$.[3] Therefore, there is room for improvement on the competitive outcome ($c_1^1 = 1$ and $c_2^2 = R$). Also, note that $c_2^{2*} > c_1^{1*}$ by equation (1b), since $\rho R > 1$.

The optimal insurance contract just described would allow agents to insure against the unlucky outcome of being a type 1 agent. This contract is not available in the simple contingent-claims market. Also, the lack of observability of agents' types rules out a complete market of Arrow–Debreu state-contingent claims, because this market would require claims that depend on the nonverifiable private information. Fortunately, it is potentially possible to achieve the optimal insurance contract, since the optimal contract satisfies the self-selection constraints.[4] We argue that banks can provide this insurance: by providing liquidity, banks guarantee a reasonable return when the investor cashes in before maturity, as is required for optimal risk sharing. To illustrate how banks provide this insurance, we first examine the traditional demand deposit contract, which is of particular interest because of its ubiquitous use by banks. Studying the demand deposit contract in our framework also indicates why banks are susceptible to runs.

In our model, the demand deposit contract gives each agent withdrawing in period 1 a fixed claim of r_1 per unit deposited at time 0. Withdrawal tenders are served sequentially in random order until the bank runs out of assets. This approach allows us to capture the flavor of continuous time (in which depositors deposit and withdraw at different random times) in a discrete model. Note that the demand deposit contract satisfies a *sequential service constraint*, which specifies that a bank's payoff to any agent can depend only on the agent's place in line and not on future information about agents behind him in line.

[3] The proof of this is as follows:

$$\rho R u'(R) < R u'(R) = 1 \cdot u'(1) + \int_{\gamma=1}^{R} \frac{\partial}{\partial \gamma}[\gamma u'(\gamma)]d\gamma$$

$$= u'(1) + \int_{\gamma=1}^{R} [u'(\gamma) + u''(\gamma)]d\gamma$$

$$< u'(1),$$

as $u' > 0$ and $(\forall \gamma)\ -u''(\gamma)\gamma/u'(\gamma) > 1$. Because $u'(\cdot)$ is decreasing and the resource constraint (1c) trades off c_1^{1*} against c_2^{2*}, the solution to (1) must have $c_1^{1*} > 1$ and $c_2^{2*} < R$.

[4] The self-selection constraints state that no agent envies the treatment by the market of other indistinguishable agents. In our model, agents' utilities depend on only their consumption vectors across time and all have identical endowments. Therefore, the self-selection constraints are satisfied if no agent envies the consumption bundle of any other agent. This can be shown for optimal risk sharing using the properties described after (1). Because $c_1^{1*} > 1$ and $c_1^{2*} = 0$, type 1 agents do not envy type 2 agents. Furthermore, because $c_1^{2*} + c_2^{2*} = c_2^{2*} > c_1^{1*} = c_1^{1*} + c_2^{1*}$, type 2 agents do not envy type 1 agents. Because the optimal contract satisfies the self-selection constraints there is necessarily a contract structure which implements it as a Nash equilibrium—the ordinary demand deposit is a contract which will work. However, the optimal allocation is not the unique Nash equilibrium under the ordinary demand deposit contract. Another inferior equilibrium is what we identify as a bank run. Our model gives a real-world example of a situation in which the distinction between implementation as a Nash equilibrium and implementation as a *unique* Nash equilibrium is crucial (see also Dybvig and Spatt, in press, and Dybvig and Jaynes, 1980).

We are assuming throughout this paper that the bank is mutually owned (a 'mutual') and liquidated in period 2, so that agents not withdrawing in period 1 get a pro rata share of the bank's assets in period 2. Let V_1 be the period 1 payoff per unit deposit withdrawn which depends on one's place in line at $T = 1$, and let V_2 be the period 2 payoff per unit deposit not withdrawn at $T = 2$, which depends on total withdrawals at $T = 1$. These are given by

$$V_1(f_j, r_1) = \begin{cases} r_1 & \text{if } f_j < r_1^{-1} \\ 0 & \text{if } f_j \geq r_1^{-1} \end{cases} \tag{2}$$

and

$$V_2(f, r_1) = \max\{[R(1 - r_1 f)/(1 - f)], 0\}, \tag{3}$$

where f_j is the number of withdrawers' deposits serviced before agent j as a fraction of total demand deposits; f is the total number of demand deposits withdrawn. Let w_j be the fraction of agent j's deposits that he attempts to withdraw at $T = 1$. The consumption from deposit proceeds, per unit of deposit of a type 1 agent, is thus given by $w_j V_1(f_j, r_1)$, while the total consumption, from deposit proceeds, per unit of deposit of a type 2 agent is given by $w_j V_1(f_j, r_1) + (1 - w_j) V_2(f, r_1)$.

Equilibrium Decisions

The demand deposit contract can achieve the full-information optimal risk sharing as an equilibrium. (By equilibrium, we will always refer to pure strategy Nash equilibrium[5]—and for now we will assume all agents are required to deposit initially.) This occurs when $r_1 = c_1^{1*}$, that is, when the fixed payment per dollar of deposits withdrawn at $T = 1$ is equal to the optimal consumption of a type 1 agent given full information. If this contract is in place, it is an equilibrium for type 1 agents to withdraw at $T = 1$ and for type 2 agents to wait, provided this is what is anticipated. This 'good' equilibrium achieves optimal risk sharing.[6]

Another equilibrium (a bank run) has all agents panicking and trying to withdraw their deposits at $T = 1$: if this is anticipated, all agents will prefer to withdraw at $T = 1$. This is because the face value of deposits is larger than the liquidation value of the bank's assets.

It is precisely the 'transformation' of illiquid assets into liquid assets that is responsible both for the liquidity service provided by banks and for their susceptibility to runs. For all $r_1 > 1$, runs are an equilibrium.[7] If $r_1 = 1$, a bank would not

[5] This assumption rules out a mixed strategy equilibrium which is not economically meaningful.

[6] To verify this, substitute $f = t$ and $r_1 = c_1^{1*}$ into (2) and (3), noting that this leads to $V_1(\cdot) = c_1^{1*}$ and $V_2(\cdot) = c_2^{2*}$. Because $c_2^{2*} > c_1^{1*}$, all type 2's prefer to wait until time 2 while type I's withdraw at 1, implying that $f = t$ is an equilibrium.

[7] The value $r_1 = 1$ is the value which rules out runs and mimics the competitive market because that is the per unit $T = 1$ liquidating value of the technology. If that liquidating value were $\Theta < 1$, then $r_1 = \Theta$ would have this property. It has nothing directly to do with the zero rate of interest on deposits.

be susceptible to runs because $V_1(f_j, 1) < V_2(f, 1)$ for all values of $0 \le f_i \le f$; but if $r_1 = 1$, the bank simply mimics direct holding of the assets and is therefore no improvement on simple competitive claims markets. A demand deposit contract which is not subject to runs provides no liquidity services.

The bank run equilibrium provides allocations that are worse for all agents than they would have obtained without the bank (trading in the competitive claims market). In the bank run equilibrium, everyone receives a risky return that has a mean one. Holding assets directly provides a riskless return that is at least one (and equal to $R > 1$ if an agent becomes a type 2). Bank runs ruin the risk sharing between agents and take a toll on the efficiency of production because all production is interrupted at $T = 1$ when it is optimal for some to continue until $T = 2$.

If we take the position that outcomes must match anticipations, the inferiority of bank runs seems to rule out observed runs, since no one would deposit anticipating a run. However, agents will choose to deposit at least some of their wealth in the bank even if they anticipate a positive probability of a run, provided that the probability is small enough, because the good equilibrium dominates holding assets directly. This could happen if the selection between the bank run equilibrium and the good equilibrium depended on some commonly observed random variable in the economy. This could be a bad earnings report, a commonly observed run at some other bank, a negative government forecast, or even sunspots.[8] It need not be anything fundamental about the bank's condition. The problem is that once they have deposited, anything that causes them to anticipate a run will lead to a run. This implies that banks with pure demand deposit contracts will be very concerned about maintaining confidence because they realize that the good equilibrium is very fragile.

The pure demand deposit contract is feasible, and we have seen that it can attract deposits even if the perceived probability of a run is positive. This explains why the contract has actually been used by banks in spite of the danger of runs. Next, we examine a closely related contract that can help to eliminate the problem of runs.

III. IMPROVING ON DEMAND DEPOSITS: SUSPENSION OF CONVERTIBILITY

The pure demand deposit contract has a good equilibrium that achieves the full-information optimum when t is not stochastic. However, in its bank run equilibrium, it is worse than direct ownership of assets. It is illuminating to begin the analysis of optimal bank contracts by demonstrating that there is a simple variation on the demand deposit contract which gives banks a defense against runs: suspension of allowing withdrawal of deposits, referred to as suspension of convertibility (of deposits to cash). Our results are consistent with the claim by Friedman and Schwartz (1963) that the newly organized Federal Reserve Board

[8] Analysis of this point in a general setting is given in Azariadis (1980) and Cass and Shell (1983).

may have made runs in the 1930s worse by preventing banks from suspending convertibility: the total week-long banking 'holiday' that followed was more severe than any of the previous suspensions.

If banks can suspend convertibility when withdrawals are too numerous at $T = 1$, anticipation of this policy prevents runs by removing the incentive of type 2 agents to withdraw early. The following contract is identical to the pure demand deposit contract described in (2) and (3), except that it states that any agent will receive nothing at $T = 1$ if he attempts to withdraw at $T = 1$ after a fraction $\hat{f} < r_1^{-1}$ of all deposits have already been withdrawn—note that we redefine $V_1(\cdot)$ and $V_2(\cdot)$,

$$V_1(f_j, r_1) = \begin{cases} r_1 & \text{if } f_j \le \hat{f} \\ 0 & \text{if } f_j > \hat{f} \end{cases}$$

$$V_2(f, r_1) = \max\left\{\frac{(1 - fr_1)R}{1 - f}, \frac{(1 - \hat{f}r_1)R}{1 - \hat{f}}\right\},$$

where the expression for V_2 assumes that $1 - \hat{f}r_1 > 0$.

Convertibility is suspended when $f_j = \hat{f}$, and then no one else 'in line' is allowed to withdraw at $T = 1$. To demonstrate that this contract can achieve the optimal allocation, let $r_1 = c_1^{1*}$ and choose any $\hat{f} \in \{t, [(R - r_1)/r_1(R - 1)]\}$. Given this contract, no type 2 agent will withdraw at $T = 1$ because no matter what he anticipates about others' withdrawals, he receives higher proceeds by waiting until $T = 2$ to withdraw; that is, for all f and $f_j \le f$, $V_2(\cdot) > V_1(\cdot)$. All of the type 1's will withdraw everything at period 1 because period 2 consumption is worthless to them. Therefore, there is a unique Nash equilibrium which has $f = t$. In fact, this is a dominant strategy equilibrium, because each agent will choose his equilibrium action even if he anticipates that other agents will choose nonequilibrium or even irrational actions. This makes this contract very 'stable.' This equilibrium is essentially the good demand deposit equilibrium that achieves optimal risk sharing.

A policy of suspension of convertibility at $\hat{f}$ guarantees that it will never be profitable to participate in a bank run because the liquidation of the bank's assets is terminated while type 2's still have an incentive not to withdraw. This contract works perfectly only in the case where the normal volume of withdrawals, t, is known and not stochastic. The more general case, where t can vary, is analyzed next.

IV. OPTIMAL CONTRACTS WITH STOCHASTIC WITHDRAWALS

The suspension of convertibility contract achieves optimal risk sharing when t is known ex ante because suspension never occurs in equilibrium and the bank can follow the optimal asset liquidation policy. This is possible because the bank knows exactly how many withdrawals will occur when confidence is maintained. We now allow the fraction of type 1's to be an unobserved random variable, $\tilde{t}$. We consider a general class of bank contracts where payments to those who withdraw at $T = 1$ are any function of f_j and payments to those who withdraw at $T = 2$ are any function of f. Analyzing this general class will show the shortcomings of suspension of convertibility.

The full-information optimal risk sharing is the same as before, except that in equation (1) the actual realization of $\hat{t} = t$ is used in place of the fixed t. As no single agent has information crucial to learning the value of t, the arguments of footnote 3 still show that optimal risk sharing is consistent with self-selection, so there must be some mechanism which has optimal risk sharing as a Nash equilibrium. We now explore whether banks (which are subject to the constraint of sequential service) can do this too.

From equation (1) we obtain full-information optimal consumption levels, given the realization of $\hat{t} = t$, of $c_1^{1*}(t)$ and $c_2^{2*}(t)$. Recall that $c_2^{1*}(t) = c_1^{2*}(t) = 0$. At the optimum, consumption is equal for all agents of a given type and depends on the realization of t. This implies a unique optimal asset liquidation policy given $\hat{t} = t$. This turns out to imply that uninsured bank deposit contracts cannot achieve optimal risk sharing.

Proposition 1. *Bank contracts (which must obey the sequential service constraint) cannot achieve optimal risk sharing when t is stochastic and has a nondegenerate distribution.*

Proposition 1 holds for all equilibria of uninsured bank contracts of the general form $V_1(f_j)$ and $V_2(f)$, where these can be any function. It obviously remains true that uninsured pure demand deposit contracts are subject to runs. Any run equilibrium does not achieve optimal risk sharing, because both types of agents receive the same consumption. Consider the good equilibrium for any feasible contract. We prove that no bank contract can attain the full-information optimal risk sharing. The proof is straightforward, a two-part proof by contradiction. Recall that the 'place in line' f_j is uniformly distributed over $[0, t]$ if only type 1 agents withdraw at $T = 1$. First, suppose that the payments to those who withdraw at $T = 1$ is a nonconstant function of f_j over feasible values of t: for two possible values of $\hat{t}$, t_1 and t_2, the value of a period 1 withdrawal varies, that is, $V_1(t_1) \neq V_1(t_2)$. This immediately implies that there is a positive probability of different consumption levels by two type 1 agents who will withdraw at $T = 1$, and this contradicts an unconstrained optimum. Second, assume the contrary: that for all possible realizations of $\hat{t} = t$, $V_1(f_j)$ is constant for all $f_j \in [0, \underline{t}]$. This implies that $c_1^1(t)$ is a constant independent of the realization of t, while the budget constraint, equation (1c), shows that $c_2^2(t)$ will vary with t (unless $r_1 = 1$, which is itself inconsistent with optimal risk sharing). Constant $c_1^1(t)$ and varying $c_2^2(t)$ contradict optimal risk sharing, equation (1b). Thus, optimal risk sharing is inconsistent with sequential service.

Proposition 1 implies that no bank contract, including suspension convertibility, can achieve the full-information optimum. Nonetheless, suspension can generally improve on the uninsured demand deposit contract by preventing runs. The main problem occurs when convertibility is suspended in equilibrium, that is, when the point $\hat{f}$ where suspension occurs is less than the largest possible realization of $\hat{t}$

In that case, some type 1 agents cannot withdraw, which is inefficient ex post. This can be desirable ex ante, however, because the threat of suspension prevents runs and allows a relatively high value of r_1. This result is consistent with contemporary views about suspension in the United States in the period before deposit insurance. Although suspensions served to short-circuit runs, they were 'regarded as anything but a satisfactory solution by those who experienced them, which is why they produced so much strong pressure for monetary and banking reform' (Friedman and Schwartz 1963, p. 329). The most important reform that followed was federal deposit insurance. Its impact is analyzed in Section V.

V. GOVERNMENT DEPOSIT INSURANCE

Deposit insurance provided by the government allows bank contracts that can dominate the best that can be offered without insurance and never do worse. We need to introduce deposit insurance into the analysis in a way that keeps the model closed and assures that no aggregate resource constraints are violated. Deposit insurance guarantees that the promised return will be paid to all who withdraw. If this is a guarantee of a real value, the amount that can be guaranteed is constrained: the government must impose real taxes to honor a deposit guarantee. If the deposit guarantee is nominal, the tax is the (inflation) tax on nominal assets caused by money creation. (Such taxation occurs even if no inflation results; in any case the price level is higher than it would have been otherwise, so some nominally denominated wealth is appropriated.) Because a private insurance company is constrained by its reserves in the scale of unconditional guarantees which it can offer, we argue that deposit insurance probably ought to be governmental for this reason. Of course, the deposit guarantee could be made by a private organization with some authority to tax or create money to pay deposit insurance claims, although we would usually think of such an organization as being a branch of government. However, there can be a small competitive fringe of commercially insured deposits, limited by the amount of private collateral.

The government is assumed to be able to levy any tax that charges every agent in the economy the same amount. In particular, it can tax those agents who withdrew 'early' in period $T = 1$, namely, those with low values of f_j. How much tax must be raised depends on how many deposits are withdrawn at $T = 1$ and what amount r_1 was promised to them. For example, if every deposit of one dollar were withdrawn at $T = 1$ (implying $f = 1$) and $r_1 = 2$ were promised, a tax of at least one per capita would need to be raised because totally liquidating the bank's assets will raise at most one per capita at $T = 1$. As the government can impose a tax on an agent *after* he or she has withdrawn, the government can base its tax on f, the realized total value of $T = 1$ withdrawals. This is in marked contrast to a bank, which must provide sequential service and cannot reduce the amount of a withdrawal after it has been made. This asymmetry allows a potential benefit from government intervention. The realistic sequential-service constraint represents some services that a bank provides but which we do not explicitly model. With deposit insurance we will see that imposing this constraint does not reduce social welfare.

Agents are concerned with the after-tax value of the proceeds from their withdrawals because that is the amount that they can consume. A very strong result (which may be too strong) about the optimality of deposit insurance will illuminate the more general reasons why it is desirable. We argue in the conclusion that deposit insurance and the Federal Reserve discount window provide nearly identical services in the context of our model but confine current discussion to deposit insurance.

Proposition 2. *Demand deposit contracts with government deposit insurance achieve the unconstrained optimum as a unique Nash equilibrium (in fact, a dominant strategies equilibrium) if the government imposes an optimal tax to finance the deposit insurance.*

Proposition 2 follows from the ability of tax-financed deposit insurance to duplicate the optimal consumptions $c_1^1(t) = c_1^{1*}(t)$, $c_2^2(t) = c_2^{2*}(t)$, $c_2^1(t) = 0$, $c_1^2(t) = 0$ from the optimal risk sharing characterized in equation (1). Let the government impose a tax on all wealth held at the beginning of period $T = 1$, which is payable either in goods or in deposits. Let deposits be accepted for taxes at the pretax amount of goods which could be obtained if withdrawn at $T = 1$. The amount of tax that must be raised at $T = 1$ depends on the number of withdrawals then and the asset liquidation policy. Consider the proportionate tax as a function of f, τ: $[0, 1] \rightarrow [0, 1]$ given by

$$\tau(f) = \begin{cases} 1 - \dfrac{c_1^{1*}(f)}{r_1} & \text{if } f \leq \bar{t} \\ 1 - r_1^{-1} & \text{if } f > \bar{t}, \end{cases}$$

where $\bar{t}$ is the greatest possible realization of $\hat{t}$.

The after-tax proceeds, per dollar of initial deposit, of a withdrawal at $T = 1$ depend on f through the tax payment and are identical for all $f_j \leq f$. Denote these after-tax proceeds by $\hat{V}_1(f)$, given by

$$\hat{V}_1(f) = \begin{cases} c_1^{1*}(f) & \text{if } f \leq \bar{t} \\ 1 & \text{if } f > \bar{t}. \end{cases}$$

The net payments to those who withdraw at $T = 1$ determine the asset liquidation policy and the after-tax value a withdrawal at $T = 2$. Any tax collected in excess of that needed to meet withdrawals at $T = 1$ is plowed back into the bank (to minimize the fraction of assets liquidated). This implies that the after-tax proceeds, per dollar of initial deposit, of a withdrawal at $T = 2$, denoted by $\hat{V}_2(f)$, are given by

$$\hat{V}_2(f) = \begin{cases} \dfrac{R\{1 - [c_1^{1*}(f)f]\}}{1 - f} = c_2^{2*}(f) & \text{if } f \leq \bar{t} \\ \dfrac{R(1 - f)}{1 - f} = R & \text{if } f > \bar{t}. \end{cases}$$

Notice that $\hat{V}_1(f) < \hat{V}_2(f)$ for all $f \in [0, 1]$, implying that no type 2 agents will withdraw at $T = 1$ no matter what they expect others to do. For all $f \in [0, 1]$, $\hat{V}_1(f) > 0$, implying that all type I agents will withdraw at $T = 1$. Therefore, the unique dominant strategy equilibrium is $f = t$, the realization of $\tilde{t}$. Evaluated at a realization t,

$$\hat{V}_1(f = t) = c_1^{1*}(t)$$

and

$$\hat{V}_2(f = t) = \frac{[1 - tc_1^{1*}(t)]R}{1 - t} = c_2^{2*}(t),$$

and the optimum is achieved.

Proposition 2 highlights the key social benefit of government deposit insurance. It allows the bank to follow a desirable asset liquidation policy, which can be separated from the cash-flow constraint imposed directly by withdrawals. Furthermore, it prevents runs because, for all possible anticipated withdrawal policies of other agents, it never pays to participate in a bank run. As a result, no strategic issues of confidence arise. This is a general result of many deposit insurance schemes. The proposition may be too strong, as it allows the government to follow an unconstrained tax policy. If a nonoptimal tax must be imposed, then when t is stochastic there will be some tax distortions and resource costs associated with government deposit insurance. If a sufficiently perverse tax provided the revenues for insurance, social welfare could be higher without the insurance.

Deposit insurance can be provided costlessly in the simpler case where t is nonstochastic, for the same reason that there need not be a suspension of convertibility in equilibrium. The deposit insurance guarantees that type 2 agents will never participate in a run; without runs, withdrawals are deterministic and this feature is never used. In particular, so long as the government can impose *some* tax to finance the insurance, no matter how distortionary, there will be no runs and the distorting tax need never be imposed. This feature is shared by a model of adoption externalities (see Dybvig and Spatt, in press) in which a Pareto-inferior equilibrium can be averted by an insurance policy which is costless in equilibrium. In both models, the credible promise to provide the insurance means that the promise will not need to be fulfilled. This is in contrast to privately provided deposit insurance. Because insurance companies do not have the power of taxation, they must hold reserves to make their promise credible. This illustrates a reason why the government may have a natural advantage in providing deposit insurance. The role of government policy in our model focuses on providing an institution to prevent a bad equilibrium rather than a policy to move an existing equilibrium. Generally, such a policy need not cause distortion.

VI. CONCLUSIONS AND IMPLICATIONS

The model serves as a useful framework for analyzing the economics of banking and associated policy issues. It is interesting that the problems of runs and the differing effects of suspension of convertibility and deposit insurance manifest themselves in a model which does not introduce currency or risky technology. This demonstrates that many of the important problems in banking are not necessarily related to those factors, although a general model will require their introduction.

We analyze an economy with a single bank. The interpretation is that it represents the financial intermediary industry, and withdrawals represent net withdrawals from the system. If many banks were introduced into the model, then there would be a role for liquidity risk sharing between banks, and phenomena such as the Federal Funds market or the impact of 'bank-specific risk' on deposit insurance could be analyzed.

The result that deposit insurance dominates contracts which the bank alone can enforce shows that there is a potential benefit from government intervention into banking markets. In contrast to common tax and subsidy schemes, the intervention we are recommending provides an institutional framework under which banks can operate smoothly, much as enforcement of contracts does more generally.

The riskless technology used in the model isolates the rationale for deposit insurance, but in addition it abstracts from the choice of bank loan portfolio risk. If the risk of bank portfolios could be selected by a bank manager, unobserved by outsiders (to some extent), then a moral hazard problem would exist. In this case there is a trade-off between optimal risk sharing and proper incentives for portfolio choice, and introducing deposit insurance can influence the portfolio choice. The moral hazard problem has been analyzed in complete market settings where deposit insurance is redundant and can provide no social improvement (see Kareken and Wallace 1978; Dothan and Williams 1980), but of course in this case there is no trade-off. Introducing risky assets and moral hazard would be an interesting extension of our model. It appears likely that some form of government deposit insurance could again be desirable but that it would be accompanied by some sort of bank regulation. Such bank regulation would serve a function similar to restrictive covenants in bond indentures. Interesting but hard to model are questions of regulator 'discretion' which then arise.

The Federal Reserve discount window can, as a lender of last resort, provide a service similar to deposit insurance. It would buy bank assets with (money creation) tax revenues at $T = 1$ for prices greater than their liquidating value. If the taxes and transfers were set to be identical to that of the optimal deposit insurance, it would have the same effect. The identity of deposit insurance and discount window services occurs because the technology is riskless.

If the technology is risky, the lender of last resort can no longer be as credible as deposit insurance. If the lender of last resort were *always* required to bail out banks with liquidity problems, there would be perverse incentives for banks to take on risk, even if bailouts occurred only when many banks fail together. For instance, if a bailout is anticipated, all banks have an incentive to take on interest rate risk by mismatching maturities of assets and liabilities, because they will all be bailed out together.

If the lender of last resort is not required to bail out banks unconditionally, a bank run can occur in response to changes in depositor expectations about the bank's credit worthiness. A run can even occur in response to expectations about the general willingness of the lender of last resort to rescue failing banks, as illustrated by the unfortunate experience of the 1930s when the Federal Reserve misused its discretion and did not allow much discounting. In contrast, deposit insurance is a binding commitment which can be structured to retain punishment of the bank's owners, board of directors, and officers in the case of a failure.

The potential for multiple equilibria when a firm's liabilities are more liquid than its assets applies more generally, not simply to banks. Consider a firm with illiquid technology which issues very short-term bonds as a large part of its capital structure. Suppose one lender expects all other lenders to refuse to roll over their loans to the firm. Then, it may be his best response to refuse to roll over his loans even if the firm would be solvent if all loans were rolled over. Such liquidity crises are similar to bank runs. The protection from creditors provided by the bankruptcy laws serves a function similar to the suspension of convertibility. The firm which is viable but illiquid is guaranteed survival. This suggests that the 'transformation' could be carried out directly by firms rather than by financial intermediaries. Our focus on intermediaries is supported by the fact that banks directly hold a substantial fraction of the short-term debt of corporations. Also, there is frequently a requirement (or custom) that a firm issuing short-term commercial paper obtain a bank line of credit sufficient to pay off the issue if it cannot 'roll it over.' A bank with deposit insurance can provide 'liquidity insurance' to a firm, which can prevent a liquidity crisis for a firm with short-term debt and limit the firm's need to use bankruptcy to stop such crises. This suggests that most of the aggregate liquidity risk in the U.S. economy is channeled through its insured financial intermediaries, to the extent that lines of credit represent binding commitments.

We hope that this model will prove to be useful in understanding issues in banking and corporate finance.

REFERENCES

Azariadis, Costas. 'Self-fulfilling Prophecies.' *J. Econ. Theory* 25 (December 1980): 380–96.

Bernanke, Ben. 'Nonmonetary Effects of the Financial Crisis in the Propagation of the Great Depression.' *A.E.R.* (in press).

Bryant, John. 'A Model of Reserves, Bank Runs, and Deposit Insurance.' *J. Banking and Finance* 4 (1980): 335–44.

Cass, David, and Shell, Karl. 'Do Sunspots Matter?' *J.P.E.* 91 (April 1983): 193–227.

Diamond, Douglas W. 'Financial Intermediation and Delegated Monitoring.' Working Paper, Graduate School Bus., Univ. Chicago, 1980.

Dothan, U. and Williams, J. 'Banks, Bankruptcy and Public Regulations.' *J. Banking and Finance* 4 (March 1980): 65–87.

Dybvig, Philip H., and Jaynes, G. 'Microfoundations of Wage Rigidity.' Working Paper, Yale Univ., 1980.

Dybvig, Philip H., and Spatt, Chester S. 'Adoption Externalities as Public Goods.' *J. Public Econ.* (in press).

Fisher, Irving. *The Purchasing Power of Money: Its Determination and Relation to Credit, Interest and Crises.* New York: Macmillan, 1911.

Friedman, Milton, and Schwartz, Anna J. *A Monetary History of the United States, 1867–1960.* Princeton, N.J.: Princeton Univ. Press (for Nat. Bur. Econ. Res.), 1963.

Kareken, John H., and Wallace, Neil. 'Deposit Insurance and Bank Regulation: A Partial-Equilibrium Exposition.' *J. Bus.* 51 (July 1978): 413–38.

Merton, Robert C. 'An Analytic Derivation of the Cost of Deposit Insurance and Loan Guarantees: An Application of Modern Option Pricing Theory.' *J. Banking and Finance* 1 (June 1977): 3–11.

—. 'On the Cost of Deposit Insurance When There Are Surveillance Costs.' *J. Bus.* 51 (July 1978): 439–52.

Niehans, Jürg. *The Theory of Money.* Baltimore: Johns Hopkins Univ. Press, 1978.

Patinkin, Don. *Money, Interest, and Prices: An Integration of Monetary and Value Theory.* 2nd ed. New York: Harper & Row, 1965.

Tobin, James. 'The Theory of Portfolio Selection.' In *The Theory of Interest Rates*, edited by Frank H. Hahn and F. P. R. Brechling. London: Macmillan, 1965.

16

Optimal Currency Crises

FRANKLIN ALLEN AND DOUGLAS GALE

1. INTRODUCTION

The large movements in exchange rates that occurred in many South East Asian countries in 1997 have revived interest in the topic of currency crises. In many of the early models of currency crises, such as Krugman (1979), currency crises occur because of inconsistent and unsustainable government policies (see Flood and Marion (1998) for a survey of the literature on currency crises). These models were designed to explain the problems experienced by a number of Latin American countries in the 1970s and early 1980s. In the recent South East Asian crises, by contrast, many of the countries which experienced problems had pursued macroeconomic policies that were consistent and sustainable. This characteristic of the recent crises has prompted a re-examination of theoretical models of currency crises.

The other characteristic of the South East Asian crises that has received considerable attention is that the banking systems of these countries also experienced crises. In an important paper, Kaminsky and Reinhart (1999) have investigated the relationship between banking crises and currency crises. They find that in the 1970s, when financial systems were highly regulated in many countries, currency crises were not accompanied by banking crises. However, after the financial liberalization that occurred during the 1980s, currency crises and banking crises became intertwined. The usual sequence of events is that initial problems in the banking sector are followed by a currency crisis and this in turn exacerbates and deepens the banking crisis. Although banking crises typically precede currency crises, the common cause of both is usually a fall in asset values due to a recession or a weak economy. Often the fall is part of a boom–bust cycle that follows financial liberalization. It appears to be rare that banking and currency crises occur when economic fundamentals are sound.

Despite the apparent inter-relationship between currency crises and banking crises in recent episodes, the literatures on the two topics have for the most part

This paper is reprinted from *Carnegie Rochester Series on Public Policy*, vol. 53, 2000, pp. 177–230, with permission from Elsevier Science. It was prepared for the November 1999 Carnegie-Rochester Conference on Public Policy. We are grateful to our discussant Nancy Marion and other participants in the conference. We also thank Paolo Pesenti, Anjan Thakor, and participants at seminars and presentations at the Federal Reserve Bank of New York, New York University, Indiana University, the University of Frankfurt, and the University of Pennsylvania for helpful comments. Financial support from the Wharton Financial Institutions Center, the C.V. Starr Center for Applied Economics at NYU, and the NSF is gratefully acknowledged.

developed separately. Important exceptions are Chang and Velasco (1998a,b). The first paper develops a model of currency and banking crises based on the Diamond and Dybvig (1983) model of bank runs. Chang and Velasco introduce money as an argument in the utility function. A central bank controls the ratio of currency to consumption. Different exchange rate regimes correspond to different rules for regulating the currency-consumption ratio. There is no aggregate uncertainty in these models: banking and currency crises are 'sunspot' phenomena. In other words, there are at least two equilibria, a 'good' equilibrium in which early consumers receive the proceeds from short-term assets and late consumers receive the proceeds from long-term assets and a 'bad' equilibrium in which everybody believes a crisis will occur and these beliefs are self-fulfilling. Chang and Velasco (1998a) show that the existence of the bad equilibrium depends on the exchange rate regime in force. In some regimes, only the good equilibrium exists; in other regimes there exists a bad equilibrium in addition to the good equilibrium. The selection of the good or the bad equilibrium is not modeled. In Chang and Velasco (1998b) a similar model is used to consider recent crises in emerging markets. Again there is no aggregate uncertainty and crises are sunspot phenomena.

A number of other recent papers have focused on the possibility of multiple equilibria. These include Flood and Garber (1984), Obstfeld (1986, 1994) and Calvo (1988). In these models governments are unable to commit to policies and this lack of commitment can give rise to multiple equilibria, at least one of which is a self-fulfilling crisis. Again, the selection of equilibrium is problematic. An exception is Morris and Shin (1998) who show that traders' lack of common knowledge about the state of the economy can lead to a unique equilibrium selection.

Kaminsky and Reinhart's (1999) finding that crises are related to economic fundamentals is consistent with work on US financial crises in the nineteenth and early twentieth centuries. Gorton (1988) and Calomiris and Gorton (1991) argue that the evidence is consistent with the hypothesis that banking crises are an essential part of the business cycle rather than a sunspot phenomenon. Allen and Gale (1998) develop a model in which banking crises are generated by aggregate uncertainty about asset returns. Moreover, although equilibrium is not necessarily unique, it can be shown that crises are a feature of all equilibria of the model when asset returns are low.[1]

In the Allen–Gale model, crises can improve risk sharing but they also involve deadweight costs if they cause projects to be prematurely liquidated. A central bank can avoid these deadweight costs and implement an optimal allocation of resources through an appropriate monetary policy. By creating fiat money and lending it to banks, the central bank can prevent the inefficient liquidation of investments while at the same time allowing optimal sharing of risks.

In this paper we extend the model of Allen and Gale (1998) to an international context and study the relationship between banking and currency crises. Section 2 begins by describing a simple one-country version of the model with three dates

[1] For a discussion of other banking papers with aggregate uncertainty and how they relate see Allen and Gale (1998).

and two assets. As in Allen and Gale (1998), there is a large number of ex ante identical agents who discover at the intermediate date whether they require liquidity immediately or at the final date. There are two assets, a safe, short-term asset represented by a storage technology and a risky, long-term asset that pays off at the final date. At the intermediate date a leading economic indicator reveals the true return to the risky asset. If the long-term asset is liquidated at the intermediate date, there is a liquidation cost. The optimal allocation is characterized as a planner's problem with state contingent contracts.

Section 3 analyses risk sharing in a banking system in which banks use a non-contingent nominal deposit contract and the central bank controls the price level through its monetary policy. By adopting an appropriate monetary policy, the central bank makes the real value of the deposit contract state-contingent and the banking system uses this state-contingent contract to achieve the first-best allocation. Depositors bear risk, but it is allocated optimally between early consumers and late consumers.

Section 4 extends the model by introducing an international bond market in which the domestic country can borrow and lend at a fixed rate. The domestic country is assumed to be small relative to the rest of the world and therefore has no impact on foreign prices and interest rates. Also, since the domestic country is small relative to the global market, lenders are risk neutral.

We begin by studying the optimal allocation implemented by a planner who is allowed to trade state-contingent contracts on the international market. Since the market is risk neutral, the optimal allocation requires the (risk-averse) domestic depositors to bear no risk. Instead, all the risk is borne by the international capital market.

Next, we consider a market equilibrium in which banks issue debt denominated in the domestic currency on the international bond market. Both domestic-currency debt and the domestic deposit contracts promise a fixed amount of the domestic currency. However, the central bank controls the real value of these securities, through its control of the price level. Once again, an appropriate monetary policy introduces the right amount of state-contingency into the real contracts. This allows the banking system to achieve optimal risk sharing. In this case, access to the international market allows the banking system to eliminate all risk for domestic depositors. Banks issue a large amount of bonds denominated in the domestic currency and invest the money in bonds denominated in foreign currency. Variations in the price level cause variations in the relative value of bonds denominated in the domestic and foreign currencies, respectively. These state-contingent variations in the relative values of the bonds allow the banking system to export all the risk to the international market.

In order to achieve optimal risk sharing, banks acquire large offsetting positions in domestic-currency bonds and foreign-currency bonds. This is consistent with the observation that the volume of trading in foreign exchange markets is much higher than can be justified by the needs of world trade.

It is also shown that the use of short-term debt is optimal if the yield curve in the international bond market is flat or upward sloping. Providing liquidity at the intermediate date by rolling over debt is at least as good as borrowing long-term in these circumstances. This may help to rationalize the otherwise puzzling use of unhedged short-term debt in many emerging markets.

The use of domestic-currency debt presents a risk to investors in the domestic country. After the contracts with foreign bondholders are written, the country has an incentive to inflate its currency and effectively expropriate the bondholders. For this reason, lenders may be reluctant to hold debt denominated in the domestic currency. Instead, they may demand debt denominated in terms of a foreign (reserve) currency which is not subject to inflation risk. Section 5 considers two variants of the model in which debt denominated in foreign currency is used. The first represents a dollarized economy in which bonds and deposit contracts are denominated in foreign currency. In certain circumstances, it is still possible to shift risk to the international market. In this case, it is the possibility of default that makes domestic debt and deposit contracts state contingent. In the limit, domestic depositors bear no risk but costly liquidation cannot be avoided. It is generally true that banks can eliminate all risk for domestic depositors by acquiring large offsetting positions in (risky) domestic and (safe) foreign debt. However, it is typically sub-optimal to eliminate all risk because of the costly liquidation this entails.

In the second variant of the model, a central bank is introduced. By writing nominal contracts in domestic currency, the amount of bankruptcy caused by the foreign denominated debt can be reduced for a given portfolio of bank assets and a given amount of real liabilities. Although risk sharing between early and late consumers is improved, risk sharing between depositors and the international bond market is eliminated. Given these trade-offs, the existence of a central bank and a domestic monetary system may or may not improve welfare when international debt is denominated in foreign currency.

Section 6 discusses the policy implications of the model for the role of the International Monetary Fund (IMF).

2. OPTIMAL RISK SHARING

In this section, we define the risk sharing problem for a closed economy. Later the model will be 'opened' to include an international bond market.

The basic structure of the model is drawn from Allen and Gale (1998). There are three dates $t = 0, 1, 2$. At each date, there is a single good that can be used for consumption and investment. There are two kinds of asset in the domestic economy, a safe asset and a risky asset. The safe asset is modeled as a storage technology: one unit of the good invested at date t produces one unit of the good at date $t + 1$, for $t = 0, 1$. The risky asset takes two periods to mature: x units of the good invested at date 0 yields $Rh(x)$ units of the good at date 2 where $h(x)$ is a neoclassical, decreasing-returns-to-scale production function (increasing, strictly concave, twice continuously differentiable). The random variable R has realization r and a support $[r_0, r_1]$, where $0 \leq r_0 < r_1 < \infty$. The cumulative distribution function $F(r)$ is assumed to be continuous and increasing on the support $[r_0, r_1]$. At date 1 agents observe a signal, which can be thought of as a leading economic indicator. For simplicity, it is assumed that this signal predicts with perfect accuracy the value of r that will be realized at date 2. We begin by considering the planner's problem, in which the optimal allocation is contingent on r. In subsequent sections we consider the case where it is impossible to write explicit contracts contingent on r.

There is a continuum of ex ante identical agents. Each agent has an endowment of one unit of the good at date 0 and none at dates 1 and 2. Agents are subject to a time-preference shock at date 1. A fraction of them become *early consumers*, who only value consumption at date 1 and the remainder of them become *late consumers*, who only value consumption at date 2. For simplicity, we assume that there are equal numbers of early and late consumers and that each consumer has an equal chance of belonging to each group. The size of each group is normalized to one. Thus, the agent's utility function can be written as

$$U(c_1, c_2) = u(c_1) + u(c_2)$$

where $c_t \geq 0$ is the agent's consumption at date $t = 1, 2$ and $u(\cdot)$ is a neoclassical utility function (increasing, strictly concave, twice continuously differentiable).

At date 0 all agents hold the same beliefs about the future asset returns. Uncertainty is resolved at the beginning of date 1: individual agents learn whether they are early or late consumers and the returns to the risky asset are revealed. A consumer's type is not observable, so late consumers can always imitate early consumers. Therefore, contracts explicitly contingent on this characteristic are not feasible.

Suppose that a planner were given the task of choosing an optimal risk-sharing arrangement. Since all agents are ex ante identical, it is natural for the planner to treat all agents alike and maximize their ex ante expected utility. The optimal consumption allocation will depend only on the aggregate wealth of the economy. Let (x, y) denote the optimal portfolio, where x is the investment in the risky asset and y is the investment in the safe asset. Let $(c_1(r), c_2(r))$ denote the optimal consumption allocation, where $c_t(r)$ is the consumption at date $t = 1, 2$ when r is the realization of the risky return.

The planner's problem can be defined as follows:

$$\begin{aligned} \max \quad & E_R[u(c_1(r)) + u(c_2(r))] \\ \text{s.t.} \quad & x + y \leq 2 \\ & c_1(r) \leq y \\ & c_2(r) \leq rh(x) + y - c_1(r) \\ & c_1(r) \leq c_2(r). \end{aligned} \tag{1}$$

The first constraint is the budget constraint at date 0, which says that the investment in safe and risky assets must be less than or equal to the endowment. The second constraint is the budget constraint at date 1, which says that consumption at date 1 must be less than or equal to the amount of the safe asset held over from date 0. The third constraint is the budget constraint at date 2, which says that consumption at date 2 must be less than the return from the risky asset $rh(x)$ plus the amount of the safe asset $y - c_1(r)$ left over from date 1. The final constraint is the incentive constraint, which says that the late consumers (weakly) prefer their own allocation to that of the early consumers. If this constraint were violated, the late consumers would pretend to be early consumers, receive $c_1(r)$ at date 1, save it in the form of the safe asset until date 2, and then consume it.

The preferences and technology are assumed to satisfy the inequalities

$$E[r]h'(0) > 1 \tag{2}$$

and

$$u'(0) > E[u'(rh(2))rh'(2)]. \tag{3}$$

The first inequality ensures that a positive amount of the risky asset is held while the second ensures a positive amount of the safe asset is held.

In solving the planner's problem, it turns out that we can ignore the incentive constraint. To see this, we drop the constraint and solve the unconstrained problem. From the first-order conditions, we see that a necessary condition for an optimum is that the consumption of the early and late consumers be equal, unless the budget constraint $c_1(r) \leq y$ is binding, in which case it follows from the first-order conditions that $c_1(r) = y \leq c_2(r)$. Thus, the incentive constraint will always be satisfied if we optimize subject to the first three constraints only and the solution to the planner's problem is in fact the first-best allocation.

Proposition 1. *The solution $(x, y, c_1(.), c_2(.))$ to the planner's problem is uniquely characterized by the following conditions:*

$$c_1(r) = c_2(r) = \frac{rh(x) + y}{2} \quad \text{if } y \geq rh(x),$$
$$c_1(r) = y,\ c_2(r) = rh(x) \quad \text{if } y \leq rh(x),$$
$$x + y = 2$$

and

$$E[u'(c_1(r))] = E[u'(c_2(r))rh'(x)].$$

Under the maintained assumptions, the optimal portfolio must satisfy $x > 0$ and $y > 0$. The allocation is first-best efficient.

Proof. See the Appendix.

The optimal allocation is illustrated by Figure 1, which plots consumption at each of the two dates against r. At date 0, the portfolio (x, y) is chosen to equate the expected marginal utilities of early and late consumers. Suppose that at date 1 it is found out that $r = 0$. The optimal allocation divides the available output y between the early and late consumers. As r increases, both early and late consumers receive equal but higher consumption levels. Eventually, asset returns reach a level $\bar{r}$ such that $\bar{r}h(x) = y$. For $r > \bar{r}$, it is no longer possible to equate consumption at the two dates. Most of the output is now produced at date 2 instead of date 1. Whereas it is

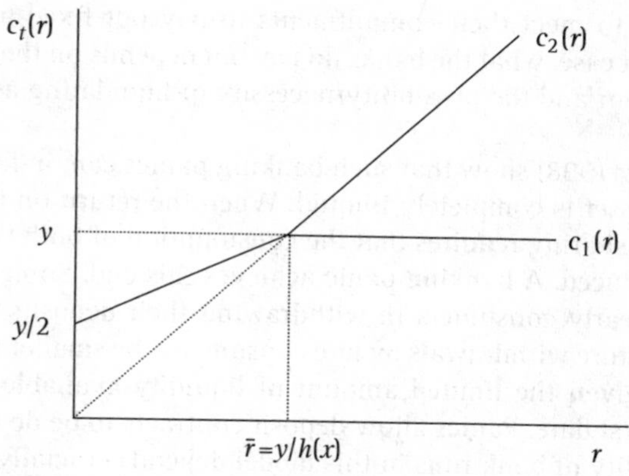

Figure 1. *The efficient allocation in a closed economy*

technologically feasible to carry output forward through time, it is not physically possible to do the reverse. The best that can be done is to give all the output available at date 1, that is, y to the early consumers. The late consumers receive everything produced at date 2, that is, $rh(x)$.

It is a well-known result that the allocation achieved by a classical stock market is inefficient (Jacklin 1987) in a model with individual liquidity shocks. In such a market, agents invest their individual endowments in the long and short assets to provide for consumption at dates 1 and 2, but this provides no insurance against the intertemporal preference shock. If they invest in the short asset to provide consumption at date 1, they miss out on the higher returns from the long asset. If they invest in the long asset to provide consumption at date 2, they run the risk of having to sell the asset at a low price to provide consumption at date 1. The absence of an effective market for insuring individual preference shocks means that the first-best cannot be implemented using the stock market alone.

3. BANKING

We next consider the risk sharing that can be achieved through a competitive banking system, in which individual banks purchase assets to provide for the future consumption of depositors. The country is assumed to have a large number (continuum) of banks. Competition among banks leads them to maximize the expected utility of the typical depositor subject to a zero-profit (feasibility) constraint. Agents who live in the country only have access to domestic banks.

Banks are assumed to take deposits from agents at date 0 and offer them a deposit contract specified in real terms promising $d_1 \geq 0$ units of consumption at date 1 and $d_2 \geq 0$ units of consumption at date 2. It is crucial here, as in all the literature on bank runs, that the deposit contract is not explicitly contingent on the returns to the risky assets. When the returns to the risky assets are low, the banks may not be able to meet their commitments to pay out fixed amounts to their depositors. In that case, what the banks do pay out depends on the rules governing the banks' behavior and the possibility/necessity of liquidating assets. A banking panic may result.

Allen and Gale (1998) show that such banking panics can, in fact, be beneficial when the risky asset is completely illiquid. When the return on the risky asset is low, optimal risk sharing requires that the consumption of both the early and late consumers be reduced. A banking panic achieves this end. Some of the late consumers join the early consumers in withdrawing their deposits. The greater the number of premature withdrawals by late consumers, the smaller the amount each agent receives, given the limited amount of liquidity available for those withdrawing at the first date. Panics allow deposit contracts to be de facto contingent on r. The optimality of bank runs in this model depends crucially on the assumption that assets cannot be liquidated prematurely. When liquidation is possible and costly, things are not quite so simple.

Suppose that the risky asset can be liquidated at date 1 and that this premature liquidation is costly. Here we simplify the analysis by assuming that premature liquidation costs are a fixed proportion of the return at maturity.[2] More precisely, if the return on the risky asset is r at date 2, x units of the asset can be liquidated at date 1 for a return of $\gamma rh(x)$, where $0 < \gamma < 1$. Note that we are assuming that all or none of the risky asset is liquidated.

If the costs of liquidation are small, it may sometimes be optimal to use the liquidation technology to provide liquidity, rather than holding the short asset. We rule out this possibility by assuming that

$$u(c_1(r)) + u(c_2(r)) > 2u\left(\frac{y + \gamma rh(x)}{2}\right), \quad \forall r \in [r_0, r_1]. \tag{4}$$

where (x, y) is the optimal portfolio from the planner's problem and $(c_1(r), c_2(r))$ is the optimal consumption allocation.

Next, we specify the bankruptcy rules that govern the bank's behaviour if it cannot meet its obligations. If it can pay d_1 to depositors demanding withdrawal at date 1 it must do so, even if that means liquidating its holding of the risky asset at a loss; if it cannot pay d_1 to all the depositors demanding withdrawal at date 1, it must liquidate all its assets and pay out the liquidated value to the depositors at date 1. Obviously, in this last case, there will be nothing left for depositors at date 2, so all depositors, whether early or late consumers, will withdraw at date 1. In other words, there will be a run on the bank.

The assets remaining in the bank at date 2 are paid out to the remaining depositors. Hence, it is optimal for the bank to choose d_2 large enough so that nothing is left over after the late consumers have been paid. Since only premature liquidation

[2] In Allen and Gale (1998), we show how liquidation values can be endogenized by introducing a market for the risky asset at date 1. The return on the liquidated asset is then determined by the price at which it can be sold at short notice on the asset market.

is costly there are no deadweight losses from insolvency at date 2. In what follows we assume without loss of generality that $d_2 \equiv \infty$ and write d in place of d_1.

As a result of these assumptions, there will be a critical value of r at which the bank is just able to avoid a run. To avoid a run, it must be possible to give both early and late consumers d units of consumption. Given (4) it will never be optimal for the bank to choose $d > y$. It would be better for the bank to increase y and avoid the need to liquidate the long asset. Thus, in equilibrium we have $d \leq y$, that is, liquidation only occurs when there is a run.

The consumption of late consumers in the absence of a run is

$$c_2(r) = rh(x) + y - d.$$

Let r^* denote the critical value of r defined by the condition $c_2(r) = d$. Then r^* is implicitly defined by

$$d = r^*h(x) + y - d.$$

For $r \geq r^*$, the early consumers receive d and the late consumers receive

$$c_2(r) = rh(x) + y - d.$$

For $r < r^*$, all consumers receive an equal share of the liquidated value of the assets at date 1:

$$c_1(r) = c_2(r) = \frac{\gamma rh(x) + y}{2}.$$

With these assumptions, the bank's decision problem can be written as follows:

$$\begin{aligned}
\max \quad & E_R[u(c_1(r)) + u(c_2(r))] \\
\text{s.t.} \quad & x + y \leq 2 \\
& c_1(r) = d, \quad \forall r \geq r^* \\
& c_2(r) = rh(x) + y - d, \quad \forall r \geq r^* \\
& c_1(r) = c_2(r) = \tfrac{1}{2}(\gamma rh(x) + y), \quad \forall r < r^* \\
& r^* = (2d - y)/h(x).
\end{aligned}$$

Assuming that (4) is satisfied, so the planner does not want to use the liquidation technology at the optimum, we can compare the solution of the planner's problem directly with the solution of the typical banker's problem and conclude that the two are different if there is a positive probability of liquidation.

Proposition 2. *Let $(x, y, c_1(r), c_2(r))$ be the solution to the planner's problem and let $(\hat{x}, \hat{y}, \hat{c}_1(r), \hat{c}_2(r))$ be the solution to the bank's problem above. If condition (4) is satisfied, the solution to the planner's problem does not require premature liquidation of the long asset. If $\Pr[r < r^*] > 0$ then the solution to the bank's problem yields depositors a lower ex ante expected utility than they obtain in the first-best allocation.*

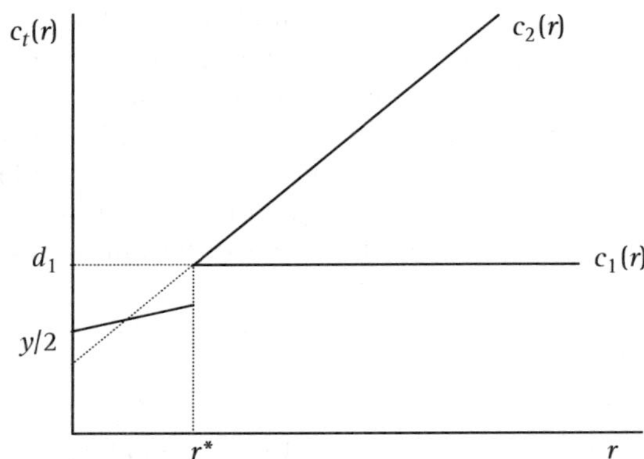

Figure 2. *Banking equilibrium without a central bank in a closed economy*

Figure 2 illustrates the allocation provided by a banking system using real deposit contracts. The optimal consumption allocation has the same general form as in Figure 1 with one important difference. When $r < r^*$ there is costly liquidation of the risky asset, resulting in a discontinuity at r^*. The portfolio (x, y) chosen by the bank may also be different. A positive probability of liquidation reduces the marginal returns to investment in the risky asset, so the amount invested by the bank may be lower. It is also possible that the bank will choose $y > d$. This 'buffer stock' of the safe asset reduces r^* and hence reduces liquidation costs.

3.1. Optimal Monetary Policy

The inefficiency of equilibrium with bank runs arises from the fact that liquidating the risky assets at date 1 is costly. Costly liquidation can be avoided if the deposit contract is specified in nominal terms and the central bank adopts a monetary policy that has the effect of making the price level contingent on the state of nature. In the previous version of our model, banks are restricted to use a deposit contract that promises a constant amount of *consumption* in every state of nature (except in states where the bank defaults). Now we assume that a deposit contract promises a constant amount of the *domestic currency* in every state of nature. The real value of this deposit contract will depend on the price level and since the price level is contingent on the state of nature, so is the real value of the deposit contract. In short, we have replaced a deposit contract that is non-contingent in real terms with a deposit contract that is non-contingent in nominal terms and contingent in real terms. If the central bank chooses its monetary policy appropriately, that is, if it introduces the appropriate variation in the price level, the banks can use the deposit contract to avoid costly bank runs and achieve efficient risk sharing.

Formally, a deposit contract promises the depositor D_1 units of money if she withdraws in the middle period and D_2 if she withdraws in the final period.

(Nominal amounts are denoted by upper case variables.) As before, there is no loss of generality in assuming that D_2 is chosen large enough that the depositors receive whatever assets the representative bank has left in the final period. In the sequel, we set $D_2 \equiv \infty$ and write D for D_1.

Let $p_t(r)$ denote the price level at date $t = 1, 2$ when the return on the risky asset is r. In what follows, it simplifies matters to note that

$$p_1(r) = p_2(r) = p(r).$$

This follows from a no-arbitrage argument. Note that when $p_1(r) = p_2(r)$, the return on holding money between date 1 and date 2 is the same as the return on the safe asset. By contrast, if $p_1(r) > p_2(r)$ then banks will only be willing to hold money while if $p_1(r) < p_2(r)$ they will only be willing to hold the short asset (store goods).

Let $(x, y, c_1(\cdot), c_2(\cdot))$ denote the solution to the planner's problem in Section 2 and suppose that at date 0 the representative bank chooses the portfolio (x, y). The central bank determines the price level $p(r)$ by promising to exchange money for goods at a ratio of $p(r)$. Since r is publicly observable, the central bank is able to implement such a policy. The individual banks take $p(r)$ as given. If $p(r)$ is chosen to be inversely proportional to $c_1(r)$, then the banks will choose D so that

$$\frac{D}{p(r)} = c_1(r). \tag{5}$$

For example, we could choose the deposit contract so that $D = y$. The price level that implements the first-best allocation is

$$p(r) = \begin{cases} 1 & \text{for } r \geq \bar{r} \\ \dfrac{2D}{rh(x) + y} & \text{for } r < \bar{r}. \end{cases}$$

This is illustrated in Figure 3. For $r \geq \bar{r}$, the central bank fixes the price level at 1 by promising to exchange money for goods at this ratio. For $r < \bar{r}$, the central bank sets the price level equal to the ratio of the nominal claims on the banking system $2D$ to the real output from the banking system's assets $rh(x) + y$.

To show that (x, y, D) is optimal for the bank's decision problem, we simply appeal to the fact that $(x, y, c_1(r), c_2(r))$ solves the planner's problem. Thus, there is no better allocation $(x, y, c_1(r), c_2(r))$ satisfying the constraints of the planner's problem. It is easy to show that anything that is feasible for the bank must also satisfy the planner's constraints. Thus, it cannot do better than the solution to the planner's problem.

Proposition 3. *If the central bank chooses the appropriate monetary policy (one that makes the price level contingent on the state of nature) and banks use nominal deposit contracts, the solution to the bank's decision problem implements the first-best allocation.*

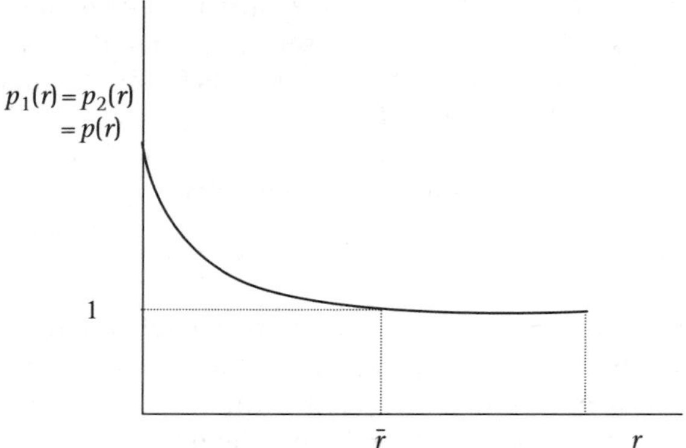

Figure 3. *The price level in a closed economy*

4. INTERNATIONAL FINANCE

The closed economy can be 'opened' by assuming the existence of an international bond market. The economy is assumed to be small relative to the rest of the world so the value of foreign currency is fixed in terms of the consumption good and interest rates are also fixed. For simplicity one unit of the foreign currency is normalized so that it purchases one unit of the consumption good. Initially, we assume that short-term bonds are used in the international bond market. The introduction of long-term bonds is considered later. The risk-free return on the short-term bonds is fixed at $\rho \geq 1$. This means that one unit of the good at date t can be exchanged for ρ units at date $t + 1$ for $t = 0, 1$. Of course, the risk of default will be reflected in the face value of any debt that is issued by the banks of the small country. We assume that because the country is small, the international bond market is risk netural in the sense that, when there is a risk of default, the loan is priced so that the expected return is ρ. The banks of the small country can also invest in the international bond market. International bonds now replace the storage technology as the safe asset.

To guarantee there is positive investment in the risky asset, it is necessary that (2) be replaced by

$$E[r]h'(0) > \rho^2.$$

In the closed-economy version of the model condition (3) ensures that banks invest some of the deposits in the short asset. This condition is no longer imposed.

Access to international capital markets is then potentially valuable for three reasons.

- First, because the return on bonds is lower than the expected return on the risky asset, banks can make a profit for their depositors by borrowing short in the international market and investing the proceeds in the risky asset at date 0.

- Second, it means that when r is high, liquidity can be obtained for early consumers by borrowing in the international market at date 1.
- Third, it may be possible to transfer the small country's asset return risk to lenders in the international bond market.

It is important to note that individuals also have access to the international bond market. In the closed-economy version, we assumed that individuals had access to the storage technology. Here they can buy or sell bonds, that is, they can lend or borrow at the rate ρ.

4.1. Optimal Risk Sharing

As usual, we start by characterizing the first-best allocation assuming the planner can use contracts which are contingent on r. If a planner in the small country can write state-contingent contracts with the international capital market, he can transfer all risk to the foreigners and give depositors a constant amount of consumption, independent of r, at each date. Let $I(r)$ be the transfer from the international capital market contingent on r. The planner's problem is

$$\begin{aligned}
\max \quad & E_R[u(c_1(r)) + u(c_2(r))] \\
\text{s.t.} \quad & x + y \le 2 \\
& c_1(r) + c_2(r)/\rho \le rh(x)/\rho + \rho y + I(r) \\
& \int_\infty^0 I(r)\mathrm{d}F = 0 \\
& \rho c_1(r) \le c_2(r).
\end{aligned}$$

The first constraint is the familiar budget constraint at date 0. The second is the present-value budget constraint covering dates 1 and 2: for each value of r, the present value of consumption must be less than or equal to the present value of asset returns plus the state contingent transfer from the international capital market. The third constraint ensures that the expected state contingent transfer is zero. The final constraint is the incentive constraint. Since all consumers have access to the international capital market, the late consumers can withdraw $c_1(r)$ at date 1, invest it in the international bond market, and consume $\rho c_1(r)$ at date 2. We assume that early consumers cannot imitate late consumers, borrowing against an anticipated future withdrawal at date 2.

Since consumption must be non-negative, a feasible transfer function $I(r)$ must satisfy

$$rh(x)/\rho + \rho y + I(r) \ge 0.$$

It will be seen that this condition is automatically satisfied by the solution to the planner's problem. The first-order conditions for this problem are

$$u'(c_1(r)) \ge \rho u'(c_2(r)), \quad \forall r$$

with equality if $\rho c_1(r) < c_2(r)$,

$$\int_{\infty}^{0} u'(c_1(r))\left(\frac{r}{\rho}h'(x) - \rho\right)dF = 0$$

and

$$u'(c_1(r)) = \lambda, \quad \forall r,$$

where λ is the Lagrange multiplier on the third constraint.

The third condition implies that $c_1(r)$ is a constant, independently of r. The following result then follows directly.

Proposition 4. *The incentive-efficient allocation with access to complete, risk-neutral international capital markets has a consumption allocation*

$$(c_1(r), c_2(r)) = (\bar{c}_1, \bar{c}_2)$$

where the ordered pair $(\bar{c}_1, \bar{c}_2)$ *solves the problem*

$$\begin{aligned} \max \quad & u(\bar{c}_1) + u(\bar{c}_2) \\ \text{s.t.} \quad & \bar{c}_1 + \bar{c}_2/\rho = E[r]h(\bar{x})/\rho + \rho(2 - \bar{x}) \\ & \rho\bar{c}_1 \leq \bar{c}_2 \end{aligned}$$

and the amount $\bar{x} > 0$ *invested in the risky asset satisfies*

$$E[r]h'(\bar{x}) = \rho^2.$$

Since the international capital market is risk neutral and domestic depositors are risk averse, the optimal allocation imposes no risk on domestic consumers when the planner can enter into state-contingent contracts. The international capital market bears all the risk. The investment in the risky asset equates the expected marginal product to the opportunity cost of funds.

In Section 3 the incentive constraint does not bind. Because the return to the short asset is 1 the first-order condition for an optimal consumption allocation implies that $c_1(r) \leq c_2(r)$ and the incentive constraint is automatically satisfied. When the return on the short asset is $\rho > 1$ the incentive may or may not bind, depending on the curvature of the utility function. The consumption allocation $(\bar{c}_1, \bar{c}_2)$ that solves the planner's problem satisfies a Kuhn–Tucker condition

$$u'(\bar{c}_1) \geq \rho u'(\bar{c}_2)$$

and this holds as an equation when the incentive constraint does not bind, that is, when $\rho\bar{c}_1 \leq \bar{c}_2$. So whether the incentive constraint binds depends on whether the solution of the first-order condition

$$u'(\bar{c}_1) = \rho u'(\bar{c}_2) \tag{6}$$

is consistent with the incentive constraint. Suppose that $u(\cdot)$ has constant relative risk aversion:

$$u(c) = c^{1-a}/(1-a).$$

Then a solution to the first-order condition (6) satisfies

$$\rho^{1/a}\bar{c}_1 = \bar{c}_2,$$

which implies that $\rho\bar{c}_1 \lesseqgtr \bar{c}_2$ as $a \lesseqgtr 1$. Intuitively, the first-order condition (6) requires the ratio of the marginal utilities $u'(\bar{c}_1)/u'(\bar{c}_2)$ to be ρ whereas the incentive constraint requires the ratio of consumption $\bar{c}_2/\bar{c}_1$ to be at least ρ. When the marginal utility is elastic, the first-order condition (6) implies that the ratio of consumption $\bar{c}_2/\bar{c}_1$ will be less than ρ, thus violating the incentive constraint. So the incentive constraint binds when marginal utility is elastic and does not bind when marginal utility is inelastic.

4.2. Domestic Currency Debt

We next consider the allocation of resources when the international capital market is a debt market and there is a domestic banking system that issues deposits denominated in the domestic currency. For the moment we assume that domestic banks can issue debt denominated in the domestic currency on the international capital market. A bond issued at date 0 promises one unit of the domestic currency to the holder at date 1. Let q denote the price of one domestic currency bond and let B denote the number of bonds issued at date 0. The benefits of borrowing at a low rate in the international bond market are passed on to the depositors in the form of a more attractive deposit contract $(c_1(r), c_2(r))$. We assume, as before, that competition in the banking sector ensures that each bank seeks to maximize the expected utility of the typical depositor.

For simplicity, we assume that the nominal domestic interest rate is 0. Arbitrage between foreign-currency bonds and domestic currency ensures that

$$p_1(r) = \rho p_2(r) \tag{7}$$

for every value of r, where $p_t(r)$ is the domestic price level at date $t = 1, 2$. In what follows we write $p(r)$ for the price level at date 1 and set $p_2(r) \equiv p(r)/\rho$.[3]

Suppose the representative bank chooses a portfolio (x, y) at date 0, where x is the investment in the risky asset and y is the investment in the safe asset (debt denominated in the international reserve currency). The bank takes in a deposit of 1 from each of the consumers and in return gives each a nominal claim of D_1 at date 1 and D_2 at date 2. As usual, we can assume without loss of generality that D_2 is chosen so large that the late withdrawers get whatever assets are left over at date 2. In what follows, we write D in place of D_1 and assume that $D_2 = \infty$.

The bank borrows qB of the consumption good on the international capital market so the budget constraint at date 0 is

$$x + y \leq 2 + qB. \tag{8}$$

[3] With the domestic interest rate normalized to 0, the domestic price level must fall between date 1 and date 2 in order to satisfy the covered interest arbitrage condition (7). A different normalization would imply a different rate of inflation. For example, if we set the domestic interest rate equal to $\rho - 1$ then the domestic inflation rate would be 0.

At date 1, r is observed and investors learn whether they are early or late consumers. The bank has promised early withdrawers D units of the domestic currency and the international bondholders B. The real values of these claims are $D/p(r)$ and $B/p(r)$, respectively. Since the bank can borrow and lend at the rate ρ (now that uncertainty has been resolved) the present value budget constraint at dates 1 and 2 can be written as

$$c_1(r) + \frac{c_2(r)}{\rho} + \frac{B}{p(r)} = \frac{rh(x)}{\rho} + \rho y.$$

The bank must also satisfy the incentive constraint

$$\rho c_1(r) \leq c_2(r).$$

Otherwise, late consumers can withdraw D units of currency at date 1 and spend it on $D/p_2(r) = \rho D/p(r) = \rho c_1(r)$ units of goods at date 2, thus increasing their utility. Using the definition of $c_1(r){=}D/p(r)$ and the budget constraint, we can rewrite the incentive constraint as

$$\frac{D}{p(r)} \leq \frac{c_2(r)}{\rho} = \frac{rh(x)}{\rho} + \rho y - \frac{D + B}{p(r)}$$

or

$$\frac{2D + B}{p(r)} \leq \frac{rh(x)}{\rho} + \rho y. \tag{9}$$

Conversely, if this constraint is satisfied, then the budget constraint and the incentive constraint can also be satisfied with $c_1(r){=}D/p(r)$.

If it is possible to satisfy all of these constraints at date 1, then the bank is solvent and there is no need to liquidate the risky asset. (We are assuming that runs do not occur unnecessarily—if there exists an equilibrium without runs we assume that such an equilibrium obtains). However, if (9) is not satisfied, then it is impossible to satisfy the budget constraint and the incentive constraint simultaneously. The real value of claims on the bank is greater than the value of its assets and the bank must declare bankruptcy. All assets are liquidated to meet the claims of the domestic depositors and the international bondholders. The liquidated value of the assets is distributed in proportion to the creditors' claims. The depositors each receive a fraction $D/(2D + B)$ of the asset value and the international bondholders receive the rest. Then

$$c_1(r) = c_2(r)/\rho = \frac{D}{2D + B}(\gamma rh(x) + y).$$

Note that, although early and late consumers receive equal shares of the liquidated assets of the bank, the late consumers can invest in the international bond market, so their share of the liquidated assets yields them a higher consumption level at date 2.

The bank takes prices as given and chooses a portfolio (x, y, B) and a deposit contract D to maximize the expected utility of the typical depositor. Thus, the bank's decision problem is

$$\begin{array}{ll} \max & E_R[u(c_1(r)) + u(c_2(r))] \\ \text{s.t.} & x + y \leq 2 + qB \\ & \rho c_1(r) \leq c_2(r), \quad \forall r, \end{array} \tag{10}$$

where the consumption functions of the early and late consumers are given by the equations

$$c_1(r) = \begin{cases} \dfrac{D}{p(r)} & \text{if } \dfrac{2D+B}{p(r)} \leq \dfrac{rh(x)}{\rho} + \rho y \\ \dfrac{D}{2D+B}(\gamma rh(x) + y) & \text{otherwise.} \end{cases} \tag{11}$$

and

$$\frac{c_2(r)}{\rho} = \begin{cases} rh(x)/\rho + \rho y - \dfrac{D+B}{p(r)} & \text{if } \dfrac{2D+B}{p(r)} \leq \dfrac{rh(x)}{\rho} + \rho y \\ \dfrac{D}{2D+B}(\gamma rh(x) + y) & \text{otherwise,} \end{cases} \tag{12}$$

respectively.

4.3. Optimal Exchange Rate Policy

In the closed economy of Section 3.1, the central bank makes the real value of deposits contingent on the state of nature by controlling the price level. Using this contingent deposit contract, the banking system avoids financial crises and achieves optimal risk sharing between early and late consumers.

In the open economy, the central bank is assumed to control the exchange rate $e(r) \equiv 1/p(r)$ (i.e. foreign currency per unit of domestic currency). The central bank's exchange rate policy makes the real values of the deposit contract and the domestic-currency bond contingent on the state of nature at date 1. The state-contingent variation in the real value of domestic debt allows the banks to shift risk to the international market. Banks borrow from the international market by issuing domestic-currency bonds and invest the proceeds in foreign-currency bonds. Because of the state-contingent exchange rate policy, domestic-currency bonds and foreign-currency bonds have different state-contingent real returns. Domestic banks, by holding an optimal portfolio of the two kinds of bonds, share risk between the domestic depositors and the international capital market.

Exactly how optimal risk sharing is achieved is a complicated story. We begin by exploring the possibilities for sharing risk from the point of view of an individual bank. A single bank, taking as given the central bank's policy and the behaviour of other banks, can eliminate risk for its depositors by simultaneously issuing domestic-currency debt and buying foreign-currency debt. This cannot be achieved in equilibrium, however, because each bank wants to issue more debt than each of the others. To analyse the equilibrium possibilities for risk sharing, we assume a bank's access to the international market is artificially constrained. In the artificially constrained equilibrium, banks choose to borrow the maximum amount. As the borrowing constraint is relaxed, the banks increase their borrowing and, in the limit, achieve perfect risk sharing.

To gain some insight into the structure of equilibrium, consider the following situation. Suppose the representative bank chooses $(x, y, \overline{B}, D)$. The incentive constraint is binding for all values of r. Rearranging (9) with an equality and using the date 0 budget constraint gives

$$\frac{1}{p(r)} = \frac{(rh(x)/\rho) + \rho(2 + q\overline{B} - x)}{2D + \overline{B}}. \tag{13}$$

The central bank implements this exchange rate, which is simply the ratio of the representative bank's (real) asset returns to the nominal claims on it.

The equilibrium price q at which domestic-currency bonds promising to repay 1 unit of domestic currency are issued must on average allow the lenders to recoup ρq on each bond. Since there is no risk of default if (13) holds, the fair-pricing condition is

$$q = \frac{1}{\rho}\int_0^\infty \frac{1}{p(r)}\,\mathrm{d}F. \tag{14}$$

From (11), (12) and (13) each bank choosing $(x, y, \overline{B}, D)$ is able to give its depositors a consumption allocation

$$c_1(r) = \frac{c_2(r)}{\rho} = \frac{D}{2D + \overline{B}}\left(\frac{rh(x)}{\rho} + \rho(2 + q\overline{B} - x)\right).$$

It can be seen that the exchange rate is positively correlated with consumption. This suggests that by issuing domestic-currency bonds and putting the proceeds in foreign-currency bonds a bank can create a portfolio which is negatively correlated with consumption. This is illustrated in Figure 4. Suppose at date 0 the bank issues a bond promising to pay 1 unit of domestic currency at date 1. This will raise q units of consumption which can be invested in foreign-currency bonds to give ρq units of foreign currency at date 1. At date 1 the bank will owe 1 unit of domestic currency which is equivalent to $1/p(r)$ units of foreign currency. The net payoff on the portfolio is $\rho q - 1/p(r)$. There is a profit when r is low and a loss when r is high. Since bonds are fairly priced the expected payoff on the portfolio is zero and its only effect is to transfer funds from high payoff states to low payoff states. Since anything left over at date 2 is consumed by the late consumers, using this portfolio in addition to $(x, y, \overline{B}, D)$ will allow the bank to improve their welfare and hence ex ante expected utility by reducing the variability of their consumption.

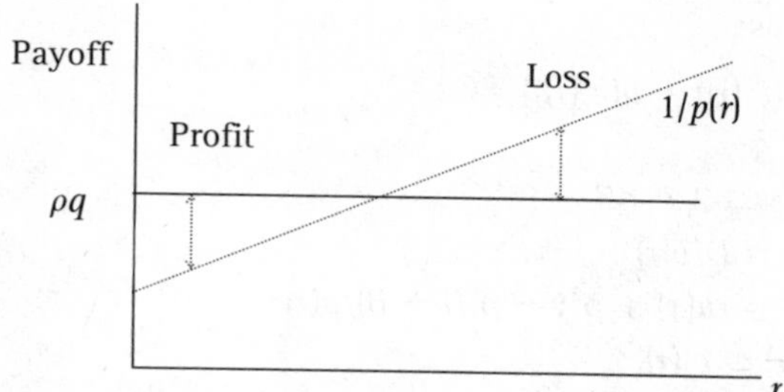

Figure 4. *The payoff $\rho q - 1/p(r)$ from issuing domestic-currency bonds and investing in foreign-currency bonds*

In fact, since in this particular case $1/p(r)$ and $c_2(r)$ are both linear in r it is possible for the bank to eliminate all risk in $c_2(r)$. To see this, suppose the bank chooses x and D the same as other banks but borrows B in domestic currency and invests $2+qB - x$ in foreign bonds. Using (12) and (13) gives

$$\frac{c_2(r)}{\rho} = \frac{D + \overline{B} - B}{2D + \overline{B}}\left(\frac{rh(x)}{\rho} + \rho(2 - x)\right) + \rho q D\frac{2B - \overline{B}}{2D + \overline{B}}$$

By setting

$$B = \overline{B} + D, \tag{15}$$

it is possible to eliminate all risk for the late consumers and

$$\frac{c_2(r)}{\rho} = \rho q D = E_R[c_1(r)],$$

where the second equality follows from (11) and (14). Since D is held constant this means that the ex ante expected utility of depositors is raised.

In general, it is not possible for banks collectively to hedge all the risk in this way. First, the incentive-constraint may not be binding for some or all values of r, in which case the real returns to the domestic-currency bonds will not be a linear function of r. In that case, shorting domestic-currency bonds will not provide a perfect hedge for this risk. Secondly, (15) shows that in order to hedge the risk perfectly, each bank has to issue more bonds than the other banks. This alerts us to the fact that existence of equilibrium may be problematical, unless we find some way to limit the issue of domestic currency bonds.

We adopt the following strategy for analysing 'equilibrium' in the limiting case where B becomes very large. We restrict the borrowing of the representative bank so that $B \leq \overline{B}$, where $\overline{B}$ is an exogenously imposed bound on borrowing in terms of the domestic currency. The representative bank chooses (x, y, B, D) taking the exchange rate policy of the central bank as given. For the moment, we restrict banks to choose (x, y, B, D) so that runs do not occur. Then the banks' modified decision problem is:

$$\begin{aligned} \max \quad & E_R[u(c_1(r)) + u(c_2(r))] \\ \text{s.t.} \quad & B \leq \overline{B} \\ & x + y \leq 2 + qB \\ & c_1(r) = D/p(r) \\ & c_2(r) = rh(x) + \rho^2 y - \rho(D + B)/p(r) \\ & \rho c_1(r) \leq c_2(r). \end{aligned} \tag{16}$$

This problem has a concave objective function and a convex feasible set for any price function $p(r)$.

Define a *pseudo-equilibrium* to be an array $(x, y, B, D, q, p(\cdot))$ such that (x, y, B, D) solves the problem (16) for the given values of $(q, p(\cdot))$ and q satisfies the fair-pricing condition (14). Condition (14) is the appropriate condition since runs are not allowed in a pseudo-equilibrium. The representative bank is maximizing the expected utility of the investors, as required in an ordinary equilibrium, subject to two additional constraints, one being the limit on domestic-currency borrowing and the other being the no-runs condition. The first of these we can treat as a regulatory requirement for the moment. The no-runs condition will later be shown to be optimal when the borrowing limit $\overline{B}$ is sufficiently large.

First, we note that a pseudo-equilibrium exists for each possible borrowing limit $\overline{B} > 0$.

Proposition 5. *For any value of $\overline{B} > 0$, there exists a pseudo-equilibrium $(x, y, B, D, q, p(\cdot))$ such that $B = \overline{B}$, $D = 1$, and for each value of r the consumption allocation $(c_1(r), c_2(r))$ solves the problem:*

$$\begin{aligned} \max \quad & u(c_1(r)) + u(c_2(r)) \\ \text{s.t.} \quad & c_1(r) + c_2(r)/\rho = rh(x)/\rho + \rho(2 + qB - x) - B/p(r) \\ & \rho c_1(r) \leq c_2(r). \end{aligned}$$

Proof. See the appendix.

The pseudo-equilibrium described in Proposition 5 has three special features:

- the consumption allocation satisfies the conditions analogous to those in Proposition 4;
- the nominal value of a deposit is normalized to 1;
- every bank borrows the maximum on the international bond market.

The fact that the consumption allocation satisfies necessary conditions for incentive-efficiency, given the other choices of the bank, reflects the way in which prices are chosen, that is, the exchange rate policy attributed to the central bank. In order for a feasible (incentive-compatible) consumption allocation $(c_1(r), c_2(r))$ to solve the maximization problem in the proposition, the following conditions are necessary and sufficient:

$$u'(c_1(r)) \geq \rho u'(c_2(r)),$$

and

$$u'(c_1(r)) = \rho u'(c_2(r)) \quad \text{if } \rho c_1(r) < c_2(r).$$

As in Proposition 4, the fact that the incentive constraint may or may not be binding complicates the analysis. Another way of expressing the conditions is to say that

$$c_2(r) = \max\{\rho c_1(r), \varphi(c_1(r))\},$$

where $\varphi(\cdot)$ is defined implicitly by the equation $u'(z)=\rho u'(\varphi(z))$. To ensure that these conditions are satisfied in equilibrium, we choose the price function $p(r)$ so that

$$\max\left\{\rho\frac{D}{p(r)}, \varphi\left(\frac{D}{p(r)}\right)\right\} = rh(x) + \rho^2(2 + q\bar{B} - x) - \rho\frac{1 + \bar{B}}{p(r)}. \tag{17}$$

This equation determines the price function $p(r)$ uniquely for any values of x and q.

This policy is not necessarily optimal and it is certainly not the only policy that the central bank could have chosen. We adopt it here because it is salient (suggested by Proposition 4) and because it is consistent with an incentive-efficient outcome in the limit, as the next proposition shows.

Normalizing the face value of the deposit to 1 is equivalent to normalizing prices. It ensures that the nominal constraint $B \leq \bar{B}$ on borrowing is a real constraint (equi-proportionate changes in D, B, and $p(\cdot)$ leave the pseudo-equilibrium conditions unchanged). As a result, the fact that banks borrow the maximum amount $B = \bar{B}$ has real content: banks want to shift the maximum amount of risk to the international market and in fact would like to borrow more if they were allowed to do so.

The next proposition shows that, as the borrowing limit $\bar{B}$ increases, all risk is shifted from the domestic economy to the international capital market.

Proposition 6. *Let $\{\bar{B}^k\}$ be an increasing sequence of bounds such that $\bar{B}^k \to \infty$ and let $\{(x^k, y^k, 1, \bar{B}^k, q^k, p^k(\cdot))\}$ be the corresponding sequence of pseudo-equilibria described in Proposition 5. Then for all values of r,*

$$\bar{p} = \lim_{k\to\infty} p^k(r),$$

$$(\bar{c}_1, \bar{c}_2) = \lim_{k\to\infty} (c_1^k(r), c_2^k(r)),$$

$$\bar{x} = \lim_{k\to\infty} x^k,$$

where $(\bar{c}_1, \bar{c}_2)$ is the incentive-efficient consumption allocation from Proposition 4 and $\bar{x}$ is the efficient investment in the risky asset.

Proof. See the appendix.

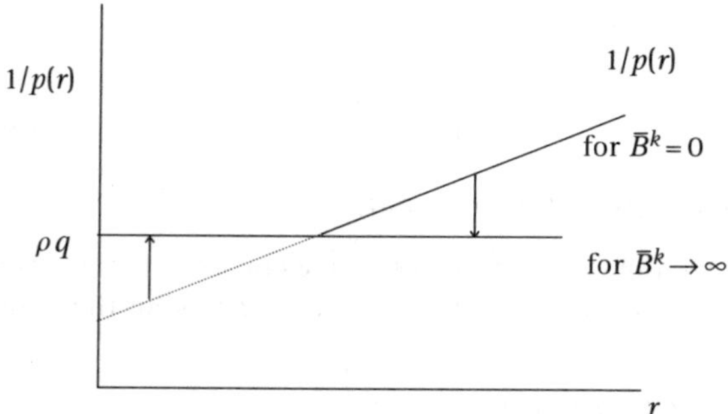

Figure 5. *The exchange rate $1/p(r)$ as $\overline{B}^k$ increases from 0 to ∞*

The proposition can be illustrated for the case where the incentive constraint binds for all r. In that case, it can be seen from (13) that

$$\overline{p} = \lim_{k\to\infty} p^k(r) = \frac{1}{\rho q}.$$

The change in the exchange rate policy $e(r) = 1/p(r)$ as $\overline{B}^k \to \infty$ is illustrated in Figure 5.

In effect, what is happening is that the individual banks construct portfolios consisting of a large investment in riskless foreign-currency debt y^k and a small investment x^k in the risky asset. Most of this portfolio is 'owned' by the foreign bondholders, who hold the outstanding domestic-currency bonds $\overline{B}^k$, so the domestic investors receive a relatively small share of the returns. As a result, they bear a relatively small share of the risk generated by the returns from the risky asset.

The mechanism by which risk is transferred is rather subtle. In the limit, prices are constant at $\overline{p}$ and so the domestic-currency debt is riskless: it pays $1/\overline{p}$ for every r. However, if the banks were to issue a real bond, that is, a bond denominated in the foreign currency, none of the risk could be transferred to the international market. In order to transfer risk, the real returns to the two assets, domestic-currency bonds and foreign-currency bonds, must be different. This requires variability in the exchange rate $e(r) = 1/p(r)$. For each value of k, the early consumers who receive $c_1^k(r) = D/p^k(r)$ bear some risk. As $\overline{B}^k \to \infty$, the degree of exchange-rate variability needed to transfer the risk to the international market shrinks. In the limit, the exchange rate becomes constant and the early consumers bear no risk. There are thus two reasons why borrowing using domestic-currency bonds must be limited. One is to ensure existence of a pseudo-equilibrium and the other is to ensure enough variability in the real value of domestic bonds to transfer risk to the international market.

There is a similarity between this problem and the non-existence of equilibrium with incomplete markets studied by Hart (1975). Hart gives an example of an economy with two states of nature, two goods, and two assets with returns represented by a fixed basket of goods. When markets are complete, the returns to the two assets in terms of the numeraire are collinear and the assets cannot be used to span the entire commodity space. When markets are incomplete, the returns to the two assets in terms of the numeraire are not collinear and the assets can be used to span the entire commodity space. Thus, markets can neither be complete nor incomplete: an equilibrium does not exist. Placing an arbitrary bound on trades in the two assets can resolve the non-existence problem. As the bound is relaxed, the returns of the two assets will become more nearly collinear and, in order to span the entire commodity space, the trades in the two assets will grow larger as well. In the limit, even infinite trades in the assets will not suffice to make markets complete because the asset returns have become perfectly collinear. While Hart's example suffices to give substance to the non-existence problem, we are not aware of any practical application before now.[4]

It has been noted that Hart's example, which relies on an exogenously specified matrix of asset returns, is non-generic (see Duffie and Schaefer 1985, 1986). The asset returns in our model are endogenous so the issue of genericity does not arise.

The role of the central bank in maintaining an optimal exchange rate rule is critical. If the central bank did not choose the price function $p^k(r)$ in the manner prescribed, the banks would not necessarily choose $B^k = \overline{B}^k$, and the risk borne by the domestic investors would not necessarily disappear even in the limit as $\overline{B}^k \to \infty$.

So far we have only considered pseudo-equilibria, in which banks are constrained to choose their portfolios and deposit contracts so that runs do not occur. However, for $\overline{B}^k$ sufficiently large, we can show that this is in fact an optimal choice. A pseudo-equilibrium $(x, y, B, D, q, p(\cdot))$ is called an *equilibrium relative to the borrowing constraint* $\overline{B}$ if (x, y, B, D) solves the maximization problem

$$
\begin{aligned}
\max \quad & E_R[u(c_1(r)) + u(c_2(r))] \\
\text{s.t.} \quad & B \leq \overline{B} \\
& x + y \leq 2 + qB \\
& \rho c_1(r) \leq c_2(r), \quad \forall r.
\end{aligned}
$$

This is just the maximization problem (10) with the added borrowing constraint $B \leq \overline{B}$.

Proposition 7. *For all k sufficiently large, the pseudo-equilibrium* $(x^k, y^k, \overline{B}^k, 1, q^k, p^k(\cdot))$ *described in Proposition 6 is an equilibrium relative to the bound* $\overline{B}^k$.

Proof. The one condition that needs to be checked is whether the bank will want to violate the no bankruptcy condition for large k. Violating the no-bankruptcy constraint involves a loss of output and a possible distortion in the allocation of

[4] Gale (1990) identifies a similar problem in the design of optimal government debt in an overlapping generations economy. In order to achieve optimal intergenerational risk sharing, it is necessary to make the returns to government securities contingent on the state of nature. While it is possible to get close to the first best by introducing state-contingent government securities, the first-best is unattainable. In order to span the states of nature the returns of government securities have to be unbounded.

consumption, but may improve risk sharing. Because the consumption allocations and prices are becoming approximately constant as $k \to \infty$ (Proposition 4), the gain from risk sharing vanishes as $k \to \infty$. For k sufficiently large, the costs of bankruptcy must outweigh the benefits.

It is interesting to note that, when implementing the first-best allocation, the representative bank must simultaneously borrow large amounts in domestic currency and then invest in foreign bonds. This is consistent with the puzzling observation that the volume of trade in foreign exchange is many times the magnitude needed to finance world trade.

4.4. Long-Term Versus Short-Term Debt

We have considered short-term debt and have so far excluded the case of long-term debt. Suppose next that instead of borrowing qB at date 0 and repaying B at date 1 the representative bank borrows $q_L L$ at date 0 and repays L at date 2. The opportunity cost in real terms for lenders in the international bond market between dates 0 and 1 is ρ_{2L}. Thus the counterpart to (14) is

$$q_L = \frac{1}{\rho_{2L}} \int_0^\infty \frac{1}{p_2(r)} \, dF. \tag{18}$$

The other changes are that the date 0 budget constraint becomes

$$x + y \leq 2 + q_L L$$

and the date 1 budget constraint becomes

$$c_1(r) + \frac{c_2(r)}{\rho} + \frac{L}{\rho p_2(r)} = \frac{rh(x)}{\rho} + \rho y.$$

It is easiest to start by considering the case with a flat yield curve so that

$$\rho_{2L} = \rho^2.$$

Substituting this into (18) and using the fact that $\rho p_2(r) = p(r)$ it can be seen that $q_L = q$. Then the two budget constraints are identical to before since we can choose $L = B$. Hence, it does not matter whether short- or long-term debt is used. This is not very surprising given that all uncertainty is resolved at date 1. It does not matter whether debt is rolled over or repaid at the final date.

If $\rho_{2L} > \rho^2$ so that the yield curve is upward sloping then clearly long-term borrowing will be undesirable relative to short-term debt, other things equal, because it is more expensive. Of course, if the yield curve is downward sloping so $\rho_{2L} < \rho^2$, long-term debt will be superior but this is not often the empirically relevant case. This gives the following result.

Proposition 8. *When the yield curve is flat there is no difference between long-term borrowing and short-term borrowing. When it is upward (downward) sloping short-term debt is strictly preferred (inferior) to long-term borrowing.*

5. FOREIGN CURRENCY DEBT

The analysis in the previous section suggests that the combination of a flexible exchange rate and international debt denominated in domestic currency can lead to a first-best allocation of resources. In the advanced industrial countries such as the US, UK, Japan, Germany and France it is possible for banks to borrow in the domestic currency and invest in foreign currency bonds. The results in the previous section may be applicable to these countries. In contrast, in emerging economies foreign debt is usually denominated in dollars (i.e. in real terms) rather than in domestic currency. How can this be understood in the context of the current model? The problem in emerging economies is that large amounts of domestic-currency debt held by foreigners create a temptation for the government to adopt inflationary policies after debt contracts have been signed. This 'inflation tax' has the effect of reallocating resources to the government from the domestic depositors and foreign bondholders. The government may be able to return some of these resources to the domestic depositors so that the net effect of such inflation is to expropriate foreign bondholders. If political constraints or the desire to create a reputation for fiscal rectitude limit inflationary policies then the foreign lenders' expectations may be reflected in a lower interest rate. If political constraints are lax or the desire to form a reputation is low, then the 'inflation premium' foreign lenders demand may be substantial. Also, they will only be willing to lend short term because this reduces their exposure to inflation risk. In extreme cases foreign lenders may not be willing to lend in the country's domestic currency at all. Banks will find it preferable to borrow using debt denominated in a foreign currency, that is, in real terms.

Denominating international debt in terms of foreign currency avoids the inflation premium but it introduces other problems. The ability to avoid costly liquidation can be lost and the degree of risk sharing that can be obtained may also be reduced. The benefits that the central bank can generate are reduced. We start by considering what happens in the absence of a central bank that issues domestic currency and then consider what benefits the central bank can bring.

5.1. The Dollarized Economy

The dollarized economy is essentially a real economy. It is closed apart from access to the international bond market. There is no interaction between the banks. The rate at which each bank can borrow on the international market depends on the amount that it borrows and the portfolio of bonds and risky investments it chooses. Each bank has a distinct contracting problem and each bank's decisions can be analysed separately from the behaviour of other banks. We focus on short-term debt. A result similar to Proposition 8 concerning long-term debt can also be proved in this context. Since uncertainty is resolved at date 1 there is essentially no difference between short-term and long-term debt except possibly for a different interest rate.

To simplify the analysis, we assume that the random variable R has a two-point support $\{r_L, r_H\}$, where $0 < r_L < r_H < \infty$. Let $0 < \pi_i < 1$ denote the probability that $R = r_i$ for $i = L, H$. The analysis of the representative bank's decision problem can be broken down into three cases.

5.1.1. *No Default*

The bank chooses a consumption allocation $\{c_1(r_i), c_2(r_i)\}$ that is determined by a portfolio (x,y), a level of borrowing b, and a deposit contract d. Because there is no risk of default, the price of the bank's debt is $q = 1/\rho$. The bank's decision problem is

$$
\begin{aligned}
\max \quad & \sum_i \pi_i \{u(c_1(r_i)) + u(c_2(r_i))\} \\
\text{s.t.} \quad & x + y \leq 2 + (b/\rho) \\
& c_1(r_i) = d, \quad i = L, H \\
& c_2(r_i) \leq r_i h(x) - \rho(d + b), \quad i = L, H \\
& \rho c_1(r_i) \leq c_2(r_i), \quad i = L, H.
\end{aligned}
$$

The first three constraints are budget constraints corresponding to dates 0, 1, and 2, respectively and the last is the incentive constraint. Also, notice that if the incentive constraint is satisfied for r_L it is automatically satisfied for r_H.

Since domestic debt and international debt are perfect substitutes, there is no essential loss of generality in assuming that the bank will not simultaneously borrow and lend on the international market. The case in which we are interested is the one in which the bank borrows in the international market ($b > 0$) and does not invest in international bonds ($y = 0$). Here the investment in the domestic risky asset is greater than the endowment and the welfare of depositors is greater than in the closed economy.

The avoidance of default is costly in several ways. First, depositors bear the entire risk of the returns on the long asset. Secondly, there will be an intertemporal distortion because the early consumers do not bear any of the risk and receive a low average consumption. It will be optimal to avoid default in both states when uncertainty is low, the risk aversion of depositors is low and the costs of premature liquidation are high.

5.1.2. *Default in One State*

Suppose that bankruptcy occurs only when asset returns are low at r_L. The international bondholders receive the face value of the debt b if asset returns are high and a fraction $\beta \equiv b/(2d + b)$ of the bank's assets if asset returns are low. The maximum amount the bank can borrow at date 0 is the expected present value of this stream:

$$
qb = \frac{1}{\rho}\{\pi_L \beta(\gamma r_L h(x) + \rho y) + \pi_H b\}.
$$

Substituting this into the first-period budget constraint, we get

$$x + y = 2 + \frac{1}{\rho}\{\pi_L\beta(\gamma r_L h(x) + \rho y) + \pi_H b\}.$$

The bank's maximization problem can be written as follows

$$\begin{aligned}
\max \quad & \sum_i \pi_i\{u(c_1(r_i)) + u(c_2(r_i))\} \\
\text{s.t.} \quad & x + y \leq 2 + \frac{1}{\rho}\{\pi_L\beta(\gamma r_L h(x) + \rho y) + \pi_H b\} \\
& c_1(r_L) = c_2(r_L)/\rho = \beta(\gamma r_L h(x) + \rho y) \\
& c_1(r_H) = d \\
& c_2(r_H)/\rho \leq r_H h(x)/\rho + \rho y - (d + b) \\
& \rho c_1(r_H) \leq c_2(r_H).
\end{aligned} \tag{19}$$

Unfortunately, this problem turns out to have no solution. The 'optimum' requires unbounded values of b and y. Rather than analyse the problem (19) directly, we adopt a two-step strategy. First, we set up an artificial problem in order to define a benchmark consumption allocation. The artificial problem has the same objective function as the original problem (19). The constraints are such that any solution to the original problem is also a solution to the artificial problem. Thus, the solution to the artificial problem (the benchmark consumption allocation), must be at least as good as the solution to the original problem. The second step is to show that the benchmark can be approximated by a choice of (b, d, x, y) that satisfies the feasibility constraints of the original problem (19). As the amount borrowed and invested in the international bond market becomes larger, so $b \to \infty$, $y \to \infty$, and the feasible consumption allocation from the original problem (19) converges to the benchmark. This is the sense in which the 'solution' to the original problem (19) is achieved in the limit as $b \to \infty$.

The artificial problem is defined as follows:

$$\begin{aligned}
\max \quad & \sum_i \pi_i\{u(c_1(r_i)) + u(c_2(r_i))\} \\
\text{s.t.} \quad & \sum_i \pi_i(c_1(r_i) + c_2(r_i)/\rho) \leq \rho(2 - x) + (\pi_L\gamma r_L + \pi_H r_H/\rho)h(x) \\
& c_1(r_L) = c_2(r_L)/\rho \\
& c_1(r_H) \leq c_2(r_H)/\rho \\
& c_1(r_L) \leq c_1(r_H).
\end{aligned} \tag{20}$$

The first constraint is a present value budget constraint in terms of consumption, endowments, and profits. The second and third constraints are incentive constraints. The final constraint is added because the rules for bankruptcy imply that $c_1(r_L) \leq c_1(r_H)$. It is straightforward to check that a solution of (19) must satisfy the constraints of (20). Hence, the solution to (20) must be at least as good as the solution to (19).

Proposition 9. *Suppose that* $(\{c_1(r_i), c_2(r_i)\}, b, d, x, y)$ *satisfies the feasibility constraints associated with the problem* (19). *Then* $(\{c_1(r_i), c_2(r_i)\}, x)$ *satisfies the feasibility constraints associated with the problem* (20).

Proof. See the appendix.

The proof proceeds by showing that the budget constraints for date 1 and date 2 from (19) imply that $(\{c_1(r_i), c_2(r_i)\}, x)$ satisfies the budget constraint for (20). The incentive constraints are the same in both problems and the final constraint in (20) follows from the fact that there is bankruptcy in state r_L. Since the objective functions are the same the solution to (20) must be at least as good as the solution to (19).

The next step is to characterize the solution to (20) and show that borrowing and lending large amounts allows the benchmark solution to be approximated.

Proposition 10. *Suppose that* $(\{\hat{c}_1(r_i), \hat{c}_2(r_i)\}, \hat{x})$ *is a solution to the artificial problem* (20). *Then*

$$\hat{c}_1(r_L) = \hat{c}_1(r_H),$$

$$\hat{c}_2(r_L) = \rho\hat{c}_1(r_L)$$

and

$$\hat{c}_2(r_H) = \max\{\rho\hat{c}_1(r_H), \phi(\hat{c}_1(r_H))\},$$

where $\phi(c)$ *is defined implicitly by the equation*

$$(\pi_L + \pi_H)u'(c) + \pi_L\rho u'(\rho c) \equiv (2\pi_L + \pi_H)\rho u'(\phi(c)), \quad \forall c.$$

For any $\varepsilon > 0$ *we can find a feasible choice* $(\{c_1(r_i), c_2(r_i)\}, x, y, b, d)$ *for the original problem* (19) *such that*

$$\sum_i \pi_i\{u(c_1(r_i)) + u(c_2(r_i))\} \geq \sum_i \pi_i\{u(\hat{c}_1(r_i)) + u(\hat{c}_2(r_i))\} - \epsilon.$$

Proof. See the appendix.

In the previous section the variation in the exchange rate $e(r)$ makes the real value of domestic-currency debt state contingent and this allows risk to be transferred to the international market. Here, even though domestic banks issue bonds denominated in the foreign reserve currency, the possibility of default makes the real value of domestically issued debt contingent on the state of nature. By issuing risky bonds and investing some of the proceeds in risk-free bonds, domestic banks can shift all of the domestic risk to the international market. Note that it is important for this result that we have two securities (domestic debt and foreign debt) and two states of nature.

As in the previous section, as the amount borrowed and re-invested in the international market increases without bound, the riskiness of the banks' portfolio becomes relatively small. Since the depositors own a progressively smaller amount of it, the risk they bear eventually becomes negligible. Hence there is efficient risk sharing in the bankrupt state.

Improved risk sharing comes at the price of default in one state. There is a trade-off between the state-contingency of domestically issued debt and costly liquidation of assets.

5.1.3. Default in Both States

Bankruptcy in both states implies that

$$c_1(r_i) = \frac{c_2(r_i)}{\rho} = \frac{1}{2}(1 - \beta)(\gamma r_i h(x) + \rho y) \tag{21}$$

for $i = H, L$ where $\beta \equiv b/(2d + b)$ and the first-period budget constraint can be written

$$x + y \leq 2 + \frac{\beta}{\rho}\{\gamma E[r]h(x) + \rho y\}. \tag{22}$$

The problem is solved by choosing β, x and y to maximize the usual objective function subject to the budget constraint.

Re-arranging the budget constraint (22), we can calculate that

$$(1 - \beta)y = 2 - x + \frac{\beta}{\rho}\gamma E[r]h(x).$$

Substituting this into the consumption equation (21) we get

$$c_1(r_i) = \frac{c_2(r_i)}{\rho} = \frac{1}{2}(1 - \beta)\gamma r_i h(x) + 2 - x + \frac{\beta}{\rho}\gamma E[r]h(x).$$

From inspection of this equation, it is clear that the expected value of consumption is independent of β, for a fixed value of x. Further, all uncertainty is eliminated as $b \to \infty$ and so $\beta \to 1$. Thus, a risk averse consumer would strictly prefer increasing β to the limit.

We have shown that the optimum policy for the bank, given that it goes bankrupt in both states, is to eliminate all risk by issuing an unlimited amount of risky debt and investing in an unlimited amount of risk-free debt. Since the bank is bankrupt with probability one, an increase in borrowing and lending does not increase the probability of bankruptcy and hence does not increase liquidation costs.

5.1.4. Bankruptcy and Risk Elimination

This last argument also applies with a continuum of states. If bankruptcy occurs in every state then it is optimal to eliminate all risk. The argument is essentially the same as that given above. From the budget constraints, we see that

$$c_1(r) = \frac{c_2(r)}{\rho} = \frac{1}{2}(1 - \beta)\gamma r h(x) + 2 - x + \frac{\beta}{\rho}\gamma E[r]h(x).$$

Again, the expected value of consumption is independent of β whereas the variance of consumption converges to 0 as β converges to 1. So once again, conditional on bankruptcy occurring with probability 1, it is optimal to eliminate all the risk by borrowing and lending an unbounded amount in the international market.

Of course, typically it is sub-optimal to have bankruptcy with probability one. If the probability of bankruptcy is less than one, then there is a trade-off between risk sharing and liquidation costs. Issuing more risky domestic debt to invest in safe international debt improves risk sharing, but increases the probability of default and hence liquidation costs.

There is one case where bankruptcy always occurs with probability 1 and that is the case where liquidation costs are zero because $\gamma = 1/\rho$. If $\gamma = 1/\rho$ there is no loss of generality in assuming that all assets are liquidated at date 1. Let $\{\bar{c}_1, \bar{c}_2\}$ denote the first-best consumption allocation and let $x = \bar{x}$ be the first best investment in the risky asset. If the incentive constraint is binding for every value of r, then the first best can be approximated by setting $\beta \approx 1$.

One point worth noting is that when default does occur with probability one, both the domestic depositors and international bondholders are essentially holding shares in the domestic bank. When bankruptcy is costly, default is something to be avoided. In that case, the use of equity contracts can avoid default while allowing some beneficial risk sharing.

5.2. Foreign-Currency Loans and Domestic-Currency Deposits

In the dollarized economy, there is no role for the central bank. All contracts are specified in real terms. Even though the possibility of bankruptcy makes domestic debt contracts risky, there is nothing the central bank can do to alter the probability of bankruptcy or the realized returns on domestic debt.

We turn now to the case where bank deposits are denominated in terms of the domestic currency. Domestic depositors are effectively holding domestic currency debt, since a bank deposit promises a fixed amount of the domestic currency at each date. International bondholders are holding dollar-denominated debt. In this case, the central bank can alter the real value of the domestic-currency debt, so it can alter the returns received by domestic depositors and indirectly the returns received by international bondholders. For example, by reducing the exchange rate (raising the domestic price level) the central bank reduces the real value of domestic deposits, thus making it easier for the banks to repay the foreign bondholders. In this way, the central bank can prevent some inefficient liquidation. It cannot entirely eliminate the risk of bankruptcy, however. Since the foreign held debt is denominated in dollars, it may be impossible to repay the foreign debt in full for very low realizations of asset returns, even if the domestic depositors receive nothing.

In addition to reducing inefficient liquidation, the introduction of debt instruments denominated in domestic currency may allow risk sharing between early and late consumers.

Banks now face two quite different types of creditors in the event of bankruptcy, foreigners who hold reserve-currency debt and domestic depositors who hold domestic-currency debt. It is not obvious what the rule for dividing the assets between the two different classes of creditors should be. We begin by considering an extreme case, in which the foreign debtholders are assumed to have absolute priority. Other possibilities are discussed below.

The analysis of the equilibrium at date 1 is similar to the previous section. Let qb be the amount borrowed at date 0 and b be the amount repaid at date 1. The bank will go bankrupt when the output available is insufficient to pay the foreign debt. Hence r^* is given by

$$\frac{r^*h(x)}{\rho} + \rho y = b. \tag{23}$$

The value of q will be set so that the foreign bondholders obtain their opportunity cost,

$$\int_0^{r^*} (\gamma rh(x) + \rho y)\, dF + \int_{r^*}^{\infty} b\, \mathrm{d}F = \rho qb. \tag{24}$$

For simplicity we again focus on the case where the incentive constraint $\rho c_1(r) \leq c_2(r)$ binds. For $r < r^*$ the foreign bondholders receive everything at date 1 and the domestic depositors receive nothing. For $r \geq r^*$ the price level is given by the ratio of nominal claims to output when the incentive constraint binds

$$p_1(r) = \rho p_2(r) = \frac{2D}{rh(x)/\rho + \rho(2 - x) + (\rho q - 1)b}$$

$$c_1(r) = \frac{c_2(r)}{\rho} = \frac{1}{2}\left(\frac{rh(x)}{\rho + \rho(2 - x) + (\rho q - 1)b}\right). \tag{25}$$

If the counterpart of (3) is satisfied so that

$$u'(0)\rho^2 > E[u'(rh(2))rh'(2)], \tag{26}$$

an interior solution in the sense that $x < 2$ is assured. Now if $r^* \leq r_0$, then $\rho q = 1$ and the level of b is irrelevant. If $r^* > r_0$, then $\rho q < 1$ and the representative bank's optimal choice given its objective is to maximize the expected utility of the representative consumer involves $b = 0$.

Although there will be no borrowing at date 0 there will of course be borrowing at date 1 to smooth consumption between periods. Apart from that the outcome is similar to the case where there is no international finance. In particular there will be no bankruptcy or inefficient liquidation.

It can be seen that the introduction of a central bank is a mixed blessing. It does allow risk sharing between the early and late consumers for all values of r. However, there is no risk sharing with the international bond market. As demonstrated above, when there is no central bank so all contracts are in foreign currency terms there can be risk sharing with the international bond market. It is therefore not immediate whether a central bank and independent monetary policy is desirable. It will depend on the parameter values. For $\gamma = 1/\rho$, using foreign currency denominated debt and deposits will be optimal since in that case $r^* = r_1$ and the first best can be implemented. At the other extreme if γ is very small and $E[r]$ is sufficiently large, a system with a central bank will do better.

It follows from (23) and (25) that $c_1(r^*) = c_2(r^*) = 0$. As more and more of the economy's output goes to pay the foreign debtholders, less is left for domestic depositors and the domestic price level becomes very high. In fact, as $r \to r^*$, $p_1(r) \to \infty$. For $r < r^*$ the domestic price level is not well defined. We return to this problem below.

So far, we have assumed that the foreign debtholders have priority in the event of bankruptcy. Given this extreme assumption, it is optimal not to borrow at date 0. With different priorities, this may no longer be the case.

In the (opposite) extreme, where domestic depositors have absolute priority in bankruptcy, the analysis is similar. The main difference will be that in (24) there will be no term for $r < r^*$. As a result the interest rate charged will be higher. Given that the international bond market is risk neutral and depositors are risk averse, the effective transfer from high income states to low income states that a higher interest rate involves will lead to an increase in welfare compared to the case where foreign bondholders receive the liquidation proceeds.

Giving priority to domestic depositors raises a problem, however. We noted above that $c_1(r^*) = c_2(r^*) = 0$. If depositors receive anything from bankruptcy, then there will be an incentive for the bank to declare bankruptcy even though it is in fact solvent. This makes the administration of anything other than full priority to foreign bondholders problematic. However, the lenders can take into account this aspect and adjust the interest rate on the debt appropriately.

In addition to the two extremes of absolute priority, there are many intermediate cases where both parties receive some portion of the liquidated assets. The problem with analysing these cases is to specify the precise way in which the liquidation proceeds are split between the two groups. One possibility is to rely on ex post bargaining. Another is to base the priority rules on the proportionate claims at date 0. The problem here is that some claims are denominated in dollars and some in the domestic currency. Until the exchange rate is determined, it is not clear what the relative shares of domestic depositors and foreign bondholders should be. If the priority rules are specified as a proportion of the liquidation proceeds, independently of the real values of the respective claims, then the analysis is determinate and can be undertaken as in the case of absolute priority. Clearly, the range of possibilities is large.

6. POLICY IMPLICATIONS

The events in South East Asia in recent years have sparked a debate about the role of the IMF in dealing with international crises. One part of the debate revolves around the appropriateness of IMF actions in particular countries (see Corsetti,

Pesenti and Roubini (1998a,b, 1999) for a detailed discussion of these issues). Another part of the debate focuses on the broader issue of whether the IMF has a role to play in such crises and if so what the rationale for such intervention is.

There is widespread acceptance of the need for a lender of last resort (LOLR) in a domestic context. Krugman (1998), Fischer (1999), and others have argued by analogy with the domestic role for a LOLR, that the IMF should act as an international LOLR.

At the other end of the spectrum, Friedman (1998) and Schwartz (1998) have argued that when the IMF intervenes it distorts markets and leads to inefficiency. They argue that by bailing out imprudent investors, the IMF encourages lenders to invest without due care and attention. If the lenders knew that the IMF would not intervene, they would take more care to investigate projects and invest only where the risk was justified by the expected return.

A number of authors, such as Sachs (1995) and Feldstein (1998), have taken a middle course, suggesting that the IMF has a role to play, but criticizing many of its actions. Sachs argues for the need for an international bankruptcy court while Feldstein emphasizes that the IMF's actions should be more closely related to overcoming market failures.

Chari and Kehoe (1999) have suggested that the role of the IMF should be limited to cases where there is a clear problem of collective action. They argue that, in recent international crises, liquidity has been adequately provided by the US Federal Reserve and other major central banks, which suggests that a problem of collective action between the central banks does not exist. Chari and Kehoe do suggest that there are important collective action problems with regard to creditor coordination. In the domestic context, bankruptcy laws and institutions are designed to overcome these problems but in an international context there is no equivalent. They argue that the IMF has an important role to play as an international bankruptcy court. One of the major activities the IMF currently undertakes is the provision of information about the economic situation in member countries. Chari and Kehoe suggest that this is a valuable function and should continue. Finally, they argue that the IMF could provide a currency to which member countries could peg their exchange rate.

This paper does not resolve the debates about the proper role of the IMF, but it does provide a framework for understanding the different perspectives on the global financial system and the conditions under which each might be valid. In some situations it appears that an international organization has little role to play. In others, however, it may be able to prevent the costly liquidation and contagion associated with financial crises and improve the allocation of resources. Speaking very broadly, we may distinguish two different situations.

- The first case is applicable to advanced industrial economies. These countries have flexible exchange rates and can issue debt denominated in terms of their own domestic currency. The analysis in Section 4 shows that a combination of appropriate exchange rate policy and borrowing and lending by banks in the

international capital market leads to optimal risk sharing and avoids the costly liquidation associated with bankruptcy.
- The second case is applicable to emerging markets. Here, problems of commitment to financial discipline mean that international lenders are unwilling to buy bonds denominated in the domestic currency. As a result, foreign lending takes the form of dollar loans. In the versions of the model analysed in Section 5, domestic financial intermediaries issue bonds denominated in the foreign reserve currency. In this case, banking crises with inefficient liquidation can occur. Given that bankruptcy occurs with positive probability, it may or may not be optimal to eliminate the risk borne by the domestic depositors. Even if it is technically possible, shifting the risk to the international market may increase the probability of bankruptcy and the associated costs of inefficient liquidation.

From the point of view of monetary policy, the difference between these two situations is that, in the former, which we have identified with advanced industrial economies, the domestic central bank controls the supply of the domestic currency and consequently has the ability, together with an optimally functioning international capital market and domestic financial system, to adjust the foreign claims on the domestic economy in a way that promotes risk sharing and investment and avoids financial crises. In what we identify as the emerging markets case, the central bank has lost much of its control over foreign claims on the economy because they are denominated in the foreign currency.

It is tempting to think that some kind of intervention by the US Federal Reserve or by the IMF could somehow achieve optimal risk sharing and investment in the case of emerging markets. We have not analysed this possibility, but the analysis of Section 4 suggests some obstacles. In principle, some combination of the Fed and the IMF could transfer dollars to the emerging markets to prevent inefficient liquidation of banks. However, the political feasibility of making real transfers to foreign countries may be questioned. One thinks here of the opposition in the US to the Mexican bailout.

Another possibility would be to vary the real value of the dollar to make the real value of the debt issued in emerging markets state-contingent. This would give emerging markets the same opportunity as the advanced industrial economies to avoid inefficient liquidation and transfer risk to the international market. There are several problems with this kind of policy. First, there are many emerging economies and only one reserve currency (many targets, one instrument), so it is not clear that we could replicate the results in Section 4.3 by varying the value of the dollar. Secondly, by using the value of the dollar to support optimal risk sharing in emerging economies, the Fed would lose the ability to vary the price level for domestic reasons. Concerns about inflation are likely to discourage the Fed from accommodating this policy. Finally, any variations in the real value of the dollar would again imply real transfers between the developed and emerging economies, which are likely to lead to objections ex post. So the prospects of an international agency like the IMF—or a domestic agency like the Fed—playing this particular role may founder on the shoals of political reality.

Another aspect of currency crises, not considered in this paper is the possibility of financial contagion. Our analysis of optimal risk sharing demonstrates the need for financial linkages between countries. These are the conditions under which the possibility of financial contagion becomes an issue. Allen and Gale (2000) show that contagion allows a shock in one region to propagate throughout a network of interlinked regions. In their model, liquidity is a public good that is subject to a free-rider problem. Contagion can be prevented if the banks in all the countries coordinate to provide a small amount of liquidity. However, each country has an incentive to let the other countries supply the liquidity. The result can be a 'meltdown' in which all countries' financial systems are adversely affected and forced to liquidate assets inefficiently. In this kind of situation, there is a role for an agency like the IMF to solve the coordination problem by forcing each country to play its part in providing liquidity.

In summary, the IMF may have an important role to play. Whether it can effectively play this role—and what the optimal policy would be—are subjects for future research.

Appendix

Proof of Proposition 1. If we ignore the incentive constraint, the risk-sharing problem described in (1) becomes:

$$\begin{aligned} \max \quad & E_R[u(c_1(r)) + u(c_2(r))] \\ \text{s.t.} \quad & x + y \leq 2 \\ & c_1(r) \leq y, \quad \forall r \\ & c_2(r) \leq rh(x) + y - c_1(r), \quad \forall r. \end{aligned} \tag{27}$$

A necessary condition for a solution to (27) is that, for each value of r, the consumption levels $c_1(r)$ and $c_2(r)$ solve the problem

$$\begin{aligned} \max \quad & u(c_1(r)) + u(c_2(r)) \\ \text{s.t.} \quad & c_1(r) \leq y \\ & c_2(r) \leq rh(x) + y - c_1(r). \end{aligned}$$

The necessary Kuhn–Tucker conditions imply that

$$u'(c_1(r)) \geq u'(c_2(r)),$$

with strict equality if $c_1(r) < y$. In other words, $c_1(r) \leq c_2(r)$ so the incentive constraint is satisfied automatically. Thus, a solution to (27) is also a solution to the original problem (1).

The Kuhn–Tucker condition implies that $c_1(r) = c_2(r)$ whenever $c_1(r) < y$, so there are two regimes to be considered. Either $c_1(r) = y$ and (hence) $c_2(r) = rh(x)$

or $c_1(r) = c_2(r) = \frac{1}{2}(rh(x) + y)$. The first case arises if $y \leq rh(x)$, so the optimal consumption allocation must satisfy

$$c_1(r) = c_2(r) = \frac{1}{2}(rh(x) + y) \quad \text{if } y \geq rh(x),$$

and

$$c_1(r) = y, \qquad c_2(r) = rh(x) \quad \text{if } y \leq rh(x).$$

This allows us to write the risk-sharing problem more compactly as follows:

$$\max \quad \int_0^{\bar{r}} 2\mathrm{u}\left(\frac{\mathrm{rh(x) + y}}{2}\right)\mathrm{d}F + \int_{\bar{r}}^{\infty} (u(y) + u(rh(x)))\mathrm{d}F$$

$$\text{s.t.} \quad x + y \leq 2,$$

where $\bar{r} \equiv y/h(x)$ is the critical value of R at which the liquidity constraint begins to bind. Note that so far we have not established that the critical value of $\bar{r}$ belongs to the support of R.

It remains to characterize the optimal portfolio. We first rule out two extreme cases. Suppose that $x = 0$. Then it is clear that $c_1(r) = c_2(r) = 1$ and $\bar{r} = \infty$. This will be optimal only if $y = 2$ maximizes

$$u(y/2) + E[u(rh(2 - y)) + y/2)],$$

and the first-order condition for this is

$$u'(2/2)/2 + u'(2/2)\left(\frac{1}{2} - E[r]h'(2 - 2)\right) \geq 0,$$

which implies $E[r]h'(0) \leq 1$, contradicting one of our maintained assumptions.

Next, suppose that $y = 0$. Then $c_1(r) = 0 \leq c_2(r) = rh(2)$. For this to be an optimal choice, it must be the case that $x = 2$ maximizes

$$u(2 - x) + E[u(rh(x))],$$

and the necessary first-order condition for this is

$$u'(0) \leq E[u'(h(r2))rh'(2)],$$

which contradicts another of our maintained assumptions. Thus, any optimal portfolio must satisfy $y > 0$ and $x > 0$.

Returning to the compact form of the risk-sharing problem above, we see that necessary conditions for an interior solution are:

$$\int u'(c_1(r))\mathrm{d}F = \lambda$$

and

$$\int u'(c_2(r))rh'(x)\mathrm{d}F = \lambda,$$

where λ is the Lagrange multiplier of the constraint $x + y = 2$. Under the strict concavity of $u(\cdot)$, these first-order conditions uniquely determine the optimal values of y and x, which in turn determine $\bar{r}$, $c_1(r)$, and $c_2(r)$ through the relationships described above.

Proof of Proposition 5. Set $B = \bar{B}$ and $D = 1$. From the date 1 budget constraint we have

$$c_1(r) = \frac{1}{p(r)}. \tag{28}$$

Use the date 0 budget constraint $y = 2 + q\bar{B} - x$ to eliminate y from the date 2 budget constraint:

$$c_2(r) = rh(x) + \rho^2(2 + q\bar{B} - x) - \rho(1 + \bar{B})c_1(r). \tag{29}$$

Thus, consumption at each date is expressed in terms of the parameters x, q, and $c_1(r)$. In order for the consumption allocation $(c_1(r), c_2(r))$ to solve the maximization problem in the proposition, it is necessary and sufficient that $u'(c_1(r)) \geq \rho u'(c_2(r))$, $\rho c_1(r) \leq c_2(r)$, and $u'(c_1(r)) = \rho u'(c_2(r))$ if $\rho c_1(r) < c_2(r)$. Another way of expressing this is to say that

$$c_2(r) = \max\{\rho c_1(r), \varphi(c_1(r))\} \tag{30}$$

where $\varphi(\cdot)$ is defined implicitly by the equation $u'(z) = \rho u'(\varphi(z))$.

Substituting (28) and (29) into (30), we obtain the following:

$$\max\{\rho c_1(r), \varphi(c_1(r))\} = rh(x) + \rho^2(2 + q\bar{B} - x) - \rho(1 + \bar{B})c_1(r). \tag{31}$$

This equation determines the consumption function $c_1(r)$ uniquely in terms of x and q. To ensure that these conditions are satisfied in equilibrium, we choose the consumption function $c_1(r)$ to satisfy (31). More precisely, let $\bar{q}$ be some large but arbitrary finite value and

$$K \equiv \{(q, x) \in \mathbf{R}_+ \times \mathbf{R}_+ \mid q \leq \bar{q},\ r_0 h(x) + \rho^2(2 + q\bar{B} - x) \geq 0\}.$$

Lemma 11. *For every* $(q, x) \in K$ *there exists a function* $\Phi(\cdot; q, x)\colon \mathbf{R}_+ \to \mathbf{R}_{++}$ *such that* $\Phi(r; q, x)$ *satisfies equation* (31) *for every value of* r. *Moreover,* Φ *is continuous.*

Proof. To see that $\Phi\ (\cdot; q, r)$ is well defined, note that φ is an increasing function. Thus, the left-hand side of (31) is an increasing function of $c_1(r)$. The right-hand side of (31) is a decreasing function of $c_1(r)$ so there is at most one solution $c_1(r)$ for any pair (q, x). To see that a solution exists, note that both sides are continuous in $c_1(r)$. The left-hand side approaches 0 as $c_1(r) \to 0$ and ∞ as $c_1(r) \to \infty$. The right-hand side approaches $rh(x) + \rho^2 (2 + q\overline{B} - x) \geq 0$ as $c_1(r) \to 0$ and $-\infty$ as $c_1(r) \to \infty$. Thus, there must be at least one value $c_1(r)$ that satisfies the equation.

By the same argument, the solution value of $c_1(r)$ must be finite and non-negative. Continuity of Φ follows from the implicit function theorem.

Construct a mapping from the set K to itself as follows. Given (q, x), the consumption function $c_1(r) = \Phi(r; q, x)$ is well defined, and we can define q' by putting

$$q' = \min\left\{\overline{q}\int_{r0}^{r1}\frac{\Phi(r; q, x)}{\rho}\,\mathrm{d}F\right\}.$$

We choose x' to maximize

$$E[u(rh(x') + \rho^2(2 + q'\overline{B} - x') - \rho(1 + \overline{B})\Phi(r; q, x))]$$

subject to the non-negativity constraint $r_0 h(x') + \rho^2(2 + q'\overline{B} - x') \geq 0$. The set of values of x' that solve the maximization problem is convex and non-empty. Let $Z(q, x) \in K$ denote the set of points (q', x') constructed in this way. Standard arguments suffice to show that Z has a closed graph, so by the Kakutani theorem Z has a fixed point $(q^*, x^*) \in Z(q^*, x^*)$.

We claim that (q^*, x^*) defines the desired pseudo-equilibrium. By construction, the consumption allocations corresponding to (q^*, x^*) solve the maximization problem in the proposition and q^* satisfies the pricing equation (14) as long as $\overline{q}$ is chosen large enough. To see this, it is enough to show that $E[c_1(r)]$ is bounded. From (31) we have

$$\rho c_1(r) = rh(x) + \rho^2(2 + q\overline{B} - x) - \rho(1 + \overline{B})c_1(r)$$

and by construction $\rho q \leq E[c_1(r)]$ so taking expectations and substituting

$$E[\rho c_1(r)] \leq E[rh(x) + \rho^2(2 - x) - \rho c_1(r)],$$

or

$$E[2\rho c_1(r)] \leq E[rh(x) + \rho^2(2 - x)].$$

This shows that $E[c_1(r)]$ is bounded independently of $\overline{q}$ and $\overline{B}$, so choosing $\overline{q}$ large enough, we will have $q^* = E[c_1(r)/\rho] < \overline{q}$ at the fixed point.

Since the bank's maximization problem (16) is a convex problem, it is sufficient to show that the Kuhn–Tucker first-order conditions are satisfied. This must be true by construction for all the variables except D and B, since they are chosen optimally. To show that $D = 1$ and $B = \overline{B}$ are optimal for the bank, we have to show that the first-order conditions for the decision problem are satisfied. From (16) we can see that the first-order condition for D is

$$E_R\left[\frac{u'(c_1(r))}{p(r)} - \frac{\rho u'(c_2(r))}{p(r)}\right] \geq 0$$

because we cannot increase D if the incentive constraints bind within the support of R. This condition must be satisfied because we know that $u'(c_1(r)) \geq \rho u'(c_2(r))$ for all r, with strict equality if the incentive constraint is not binding.

Similarly, the first-order condition for B is

$$E_R\left[u'(c_2(r))\left(\rho^2 q - \frac{\rho}{p(r)}\right)\right] \geq 0$$

because the constraint $B \leq \overline{B}$ is binding. Then substituting the condition for q from (14) gives us

$$E_R\left[u'(c_2(r))\left(E_R\left[\frac{\rho}{p(r)}\right] - \frac{\rho}{p(r)}\right)\right] \geq 0.$$

Since $u'(c_2(r))$ is decreasing in r and $p(r)$ is decreasing in r

$$E_R\left[u'(c_2(r))\left(E_R\left[\frac{\rho}{p(r)}\right] - \frac{\rho}{p(r)}\right)\right] \geq E_R[u'(c_2(r))]\, E_R\left(E_R\left[\frac{\rho}{p(r)}\right] - \frac{\rho}{p(r)}\right) = 0,$$

as required.

Proof of Proposition 6. From equation (31), for a fixed but arbitrary r and for each k,

$$\max\{\rho c_1^k(r), \varphi\,(c_1^k(r))\} = rh(x^k) + \rho^2(2 + q^k\,\overline{B}^k - x^k) - \rho(1 + \overline{B}^k)c_1^k(r_1).$$

The left-hand side is non-negative, so

$$r_1 h(x^k) + \rho^2(2 + q^k\,\overline{B}^k - x^k) - \rho(1 + \overline{B}^k)c_1^k(r_1) \geq 0, \tag{32}$$

for all k. From the pricing equation (14) we know that $\rho q^k = E[c_1^k(r)]$, and (31) implies that $c_1^k(r)$ is non-decreasing in r, so $\rho q^k \leq c_1^k(r_1)$. Then (32) implies that the sequence $\{(\rho q^k - c_1^k(r_1))\,\overline{B}^k\}$ is bounded below, which implies that

$$\lim_{k\to\infty} pq^k - c_1^k\,(r_1) \to 0. \tag{33}$$

The pricing equation (14) together with (33) implies that $c_1^k(r)$ converges to a constant almost surely. Then $(c^k(r), c_2^k(r))$ converges to $(\overline{c}_1, \overline{c}_2)$, say, almost surely and the first-order condition for x^k

$$E_R\,[u'(c_2^k(r))(rh'(x^k) - \rho^2)] \geq 0$$

becomes

$$E_R[(rh'(\overline{x}) - \rho^2)] = 0$$

in the limit (assuming the bankruptcy constraint is not binding because $\overline{c} = \lim_k c_1^k(r)$ is positive).

Proof of Proposition 9
Using the budget constraints for date 1 and date 2 from (19),

$$\begin{aligned}&\pi_L\left\{c_1(r_L)+\frac{c_2(r_L)}{\rho}\right\}+\pi_H\left\{c_1(r_H)+\frac{c_2(r_H)}{\rho}\right\}\\&\leq \pi_L\{(1-\beta)\,(\gamma r_L h(x)+\rho y)\}+\pi_H\{r_H h(x)/\rho+\rho y-b\}\\&=\pi_L(\gamma r_L h(x)+\rho y)+\pi_H\,(r_H h(x)/\rho+\rho y)\\&\quad-\pi_L\beta(\gamma r_L h(x)+\rho y)-\pi_H b.\end{aligned}$$

From the first-period budget constraint in (19),

$$\rho(x+y-2)=\pi_L\beta\,(\gamma r_L h(x)+\rho y)-\pi_H b,$$

so

$$\begin{aligned}&\pi_L\left\{c_1(r_L)+\frac{c_2(r_L)}{\rho}\right\}+\pi_H\left\{c_1(r_H)+\frac{c_2(r_H)}{\rho}\right\}\\&=\pi_L\,(\gamma r_L h(x)+\rho y)+\pi_H\,(r_H h(x)/\rho+\rho y)-\rho(x+y-2)\\&=\pi_L\gamma r_L h(x)+\pi_H r_H h(x)/\rho-\rho(x-2).\end{aligned}$$

So $(\{c_1(r_i), c_2(r_i)\}, x)$ satisfies the budget constraint in (20).

The incentive constraints are the same in both problems, so it remains to show that $c_1(r_L)\leq c_1(r_H)$. But this follows from the fact that there is bankruptcy in state r_L, which requires that

$$2d+b>\gamma r_L h(x)+\rho y,$$

so

$$c_1(r_L)=\frac{d}{2d+b}(\gamma r_L h(x)+\rho y)<d=c_1(r_H).$$

Since the objective functions for the two problems are the same and any feasible solution of the original problem is feasible for the artificial problem the solution to the artificial problem must be at least as good as the solution to the original problem.

Proof of Proposition 10. The first part of the proposition characterizes the consumption allocation $\{\hat{c}_1(r_i), \hat{c}_2(r_i)\}$ that solves (20). Since bankruptcy in state r_L implies $c_2(r_L)=\rho c_1(r_L)$, any solution to the problem (20) must solve

$$\begin{aligned}\max\quad & \pi_L\,(u(c_1(r_L))+u(\rho c_1(r_L)))+\pi_H\,(u(c_1(r_H))+u(c_2(r_H)))\\ \text{s.t.}\quad & 2\pi_L c_1(r_L)+\pi_H\,(c_1(r_H)+c_2(r_H)/\rho)\leq\hat{w}\\ & c_1(r_L)\leq c_1(r_H)\leq c_2(r_H)/\rho,\end{aligned}$$

where

$$\hat{w}=\pi_L\,(\hat{c}_1(r_L)+\hat{c}_2(r_L)/\rho)+\pi_H\,(\hat{c}_1(r_H)+\hat{c}_2(r_H)/\rho)$$

is the expected present value of the consumption allocation $\{\hat{c}_1(r_i), \hat{c}_2(r_i)\}$.

Suppose that $c_1(r_L) < c_1(r_H)$. From the first-order conditions,

$$u'(c_1(r_L)) + \rho u'(\rho c_1(r_L)) = \lambda$$
$$u(c_1(r_H)) = \lambda + \mu$$
$$u(c_2(r_H)) = (\lambda + \mu)/\rho.$$

But $c_1(r_L) < c_1(r_H)$ implies that $c_2(r_H) \geq \rho c_1(r_H) > \rho c_1(r_L)$, so

$$u'(c_1(r_L)) + \rho u'\ (\rho c_1(r_L)) > u'(c_1(r_H)) + \rho u'(c_2(r_H)),$$

contradicting the first-order conditions. This shows that $c_1(r_L) = c_1(r_H)$, as claimed.

Then any solution to the problem (20) must solve

$$\begin{aligned} \max \quad & (\pi_L + \pi_H)u(c_1 r_L)) + \pi_L u(\rho c_1(r_L)) + \pi_H u(c_2(r_H)) \\ \text{s.t.} \quad & (2\pi_L + \pi_H)c_1(r_L) + \pi_H c_2(r_H)/\rho \leq \hat{w} \\ & c_1(r_H) \leq c_2(r_H)/\rho. \end{aligned}$$

The first-order conditions are

$$(\pi_L + \pi_H)u'(c_1(r_L)) + \pi_L \rho u'(\rho c_1(r_L)) \geq \lambda(2\pi_L + \pi_H)$$
$$u'(c_2(r_H)) \leq \lambda/\rho$$

with strict equality if $\hat{c}_1(r_H) < \rho\hat{c}_2(r_H)$. On the one hand, if the incentive constraint is binding, that is, $\hat{c}_2(r_H) = \rho\hat{c}_1(r_H) = \rho\hat{c}_1(r_L)$, then

$$\pi_L \rho u'(\rho\hat{c}_1(r_L)) \leq \lambda\pi_L.$$

Substituting this into the first-order conditions implies that

$$u'(c_1(r_L)) \geq \lambda \geq \rho u'(c_2(r_H)).$$

On the other hand, if the incentive constraint is not binding then

$$(\pi_L + \pi_H)u'(c_1(r_L)) + \pi_L \rho u'(\rho c_1(r_L)) = \rho u'(c_2(r_H))(2\pi_L + \pi_H).$$

In either case,

$$\hat{c}_2(r_H) = \max\ \{\rho\hat{c}_1(r_H), \phi(\hat{c}_1(r_H))\},$$

as claimed.

The second part of the proposition states that the consumption allocation in the benchmark problem (20) can be approximated by a feasible allocation in the original problem (19). Let $x = \bar{x}$. There are two cases to consider.

Case 1. If the incentive constraint is binding in the state r_H, then the bondholders and depositors receive a constant fraction of the total value of the bank's assets in each state. Let β denote the fraction going to the bondholders. Then from the first-period budget constraint, we can calculate that

$$\hat{x} + y = 2 + \frac{\beta}{\rho}\left\{\pi_L \gamma r_L h(\hat{x}) + \frac{\pi_H r_H}{\rho} h(\hat{x}) + \rho y\right\}$$

or

$$y(1-\beta) = 2 - \hat{x} + \frac{\beta}{\rho}\left\{\pi_L \gamma r_L + \frac{\pi_H r_H}{\rho}\right\} h(\hat{x}).$$

So for each value of β we can calculate a feasible value of y. Then set

$$c_1(r_H) = \frac{c_2(r_H)}{\rho} = d = \frac{(1-\beta)}{2}\left\{\frac{r_H h(\hat{x})}{\rho} + \rho y\right\},$$

$$c_1(r_L) = \frac{c_2(r_L)}{\rho} = \frac{d}{2d+b}\{\gamma r_L h(\hat{x}) + \rho y\}$$

and

$$b = \beta\left\{\frac{r_H h(\hat{x})}{\rho} + \rho y\right\}$$

and we have determined a feasible set of choices for each value of β. Now let $\beta \to 1$ and observe that $(2d + b)$ equals $r_H h(\hat{x})/\rho + \rho y$ so

$$\begin{aligned}\frac{c_1(r_L)}{c_1(r_H)} &= \frac{\gamma r_L h(\hat{x}) + \rho y}{2d+b} \\ &= \frac{\gamma r_L h(\hat{x}) + \rho y}{r_H h(\hat{x})/\rho + \rho y}\end{aligned}$$

converges to 1 as $y \to \infty$. Then the budget constraint ensures that $\{c_1(r_i), c_2(r_i)\} \to \{\hat{c}_1(r_i), \hat{c}_2(r_i)\}$ as $b \to \infty$.

Case 2. In the case where the incentive constraint is not binding in state $R = r_H$, put $x = \hat{x}$, $d = \hat{c}_1(r_H)$ and choose b arbitrarily. Then, as before, the first-period budget constraint tells us that

$$y = 2 - x + \frac{1}{\rho}\left\{\pi_L \frac{d}{2d+b}(\gamma r_L h(\hat{x}) + \rho y) + \pi_H b\right\}$$

or

$$y = \left(1 - \frac{\pi_L b}{2d+b}\right)^{-1}\left\{(2-x) + \frac{1}{\rho}\left(\pi_L \frac{b}{2d+b}\gamma r_L h(\hat{x}) + \pi_H b\right)\right\}.$$

This shows that y is uniquely determined by our choice of x, b, and d. Then the consumption allocation is determined by the budget constraints at dates 1 and 2:

$$\begin{aligned}c_1(r_H) &= d \\ c_2(r_H) &= r_H h(x) + \rho^2 y - \rho(b+d) \\ c_1(r_L) &= c_2(r_L)/\rho = \frac{d}{2d+b}(\gamma r_L h(x) + \rho y).\end{aligned}$$

As $b \to \infty$ we have $y \to \infty$ and $b/(2d + b) \to 1$. From the first-period budget constraint, we have

$$\frac{y}{b} = \left(1 - \frac{\pi_L b}{2d + b}\right)^{-1} \left\{\frac{(2 - x)}{b} + \frac{1}{\rho}\left(\pi_L \frac{1}{2d + b}\gamma r_L h(\hat{x}) + \pi_H\right)\right\}$$

$$\to (1 - \pi_L)^{-1}\left\{\frac{1}{\rho}(\pi_H)\right\} = \frac{1}{\rho}.$$

Thus, from the definition of the consumption allocation above,

$$\frac{c_1(r_L)}{c_1(r_H)} = \frac{1}{2d + b}(\gamma r_L h(x) + \rho y)$$

$$\to 1.$$

Thus, in the limit as $b \to \infty$, the consumption of early consumers is equalized between the two states, and then the budget constraint implies that $c_2(r_H) \to \hat{c}_2(r_H)$. Thus, $\{c_1(r_i), c_2(r_i)\} \to \{\hat{c}_1(r_i), \hat{c}_2(r_i)\}$ as $b \to \infty$ and this in turn implies that for sufficiently large values of b the consumption level $c_2(r_H)$ defined above is non-negative and satisfies the incentive constraint.

This completes the proof that $\{\hat{c}_1(r_i), \hat{c}_2(r_i)\}$ can be approximated by some feasible choice of $(\{c_1(r_i), c_2(r_i)\}, b, d, x, y)$ in the original problem (19).

REFERENCES

Allen, F. and D. Gale (1998). 'Optimal Financial Crises', *Journal of Finance* 53, 1245–84.

Allen, F. and D. Gale (2000). 'Financial Contagion', *Journal of Political Economy* 108, 1–33.

Calomiris, C. and G. Gorton (1991). 'The Origins of Banking Panics, Models, Facts, and Bank Regulation,' in G. Hubbard, ed., *Financial Markets and Financial Crises* (University of Chicago Press, Chicago, IL).

Calvo, G. (1988). 'Servicing the Public Debt: The Role of Expectations,' *American Economic Review* 78, 1411–28.

Chang, R. and A. Velasco (1998a). 'Financial Fragility and the Exchange Rate Regime,' working paper, New York University.

Chang, R. and A. Velasco (1998b). 'Financial Crises in Emerging Markets: A Canonical Model,' working paper, New York University.

Chari, V. and P. Kehoe, (1999). *Asking the Right Questions About the IMF*, Federal Reserve Bank of Minneapolis, 1998 Annual Report, Volume 13, May 1999.

Corsetti, G., P. Pesenti and N. Roubini (1998a). 'What Caused the Asian Currency and Financial Crisis? Part I: A Macroeconomic Overview,' NBER Working Paper 6833.

Corsetti, G., P. Pesenti and N. Roubini (1998b). 'What Caused the Asian Currency and Financial Crisis? Part II: The Policy Debate,' NBER Working Paper 6834.

Corsetti, G., P. Pesenti and N. Roubini (1999). 'Paper Tigers? A Model of the Asian Crisis,' *European Economic Review* 43, 1211–36.

Diamond, D. and P. Dybvig (1983). 'Bank Runs, Deposit Insurance, and Liquidity,' *Journal of Political Economy* 91, 401–19.

Duffie, D. and W. Shaefer (1985). 'Equilibrium in Incomplete Markets: I-A Basic Model of Generic Existence,' *Journal of Mathematical Economics* 14, 285–300.

Duffie, D. and W. Shaefer (1986). 'Equilibrium in Incomplete Markets: II-Generic Existence in Stochastic Economies,' *Journal of Mathematical Economics* 15, 199–216.

Feldstein, M. (1998). 'Refocusing the IMF,' *Foreign Affairs* 77(March/April), 20–33.

Fischer, S. (1999). 'On the Need for an International Lender of Last Resort,' working paper, International Monetary Fund.

Friedman, M. (1998). 'Markets to the Rescue,' *The Wall Street Journal*, October 13.

Flood, R. and P. Garber (1984). 'Gold Monetization and Gold Discipline,' *Journal of Political Economy* 92, 90–107.

Flood, R. and N. Marion (1998). 'Perspectives on the Recent Currency Crisis Literature,' Working Paper 98/130, Research Department, International Monetary Fund.

Gale, D. (1990). 'The Efficient Design of Public Debt,' in M. Draghi and R. Dornbusch, eds., *Public Debt Management: Theory and History*. Cambridge: Cambridge University Press.

Gorton, G. (1988). 'Banking Panics and Business Cycles,' *Oxford Economic Papers* 40, 751–81.

Hart, O. (1975). 'On the Optimality of Equilibrium when the Market Structure is Incomplete,' *Journal of Economic Theory* 11, 418–43.

Jacklin, C. (1987). 'Demand Deposits, Trading Restrictions, and Risk Sharing,' in E. Prescott and N. Wallace, eds., *Contractual Arrangements for Intertemporal Trade* (University of Minnesota Press, Minneapolis, MN).

Kaminsky, G. and C. Reinhart (1999). 'The Twin Crises: The Causes of Banking and Balance-of-Payments Problems,' *American Economic Review* 89, 473–500.

Krugman, P. (1979). 'A Model of Balance-of-Payments Crises,' *Journal of Money Credit and Banking* 11, 311–25.

Krugman, P. (1998). 'The Indispensable IMF,' *The New York Times*, May 15.

Morris, S. and H. Shin (1998). 'Unique Equilibrium in a Model of Self-Fulfilling Currency Attacks,' *American Economic Review* 88, 587–97.

Obstfeld, M. (1986). 'Rational and Self-Fulfilling Balance of Payments Crises,' *American Economic Review* 76, 72–81.

Obstfeld, M. (1994). 'The Logic of Currency Crises,' *Cahiers Economiques et Monetaires*, Bank of France 43, 189–213.

Sachs, J. (1995). 'Do We Need an International Lender of Last Resort?' Lecture delivered at Princeton University, Princeton, N.J., April 20.

Schwartz, A. (1998). 'Time to Terminate the ESF and IMF,' working paper, New York University.

17

Banking Panics: The Role of the First-Come, First-Served Rule and Information Externalities

YEHNING CHEN

I. INTRODUCTION

Moral hazard is always an important factor contributing to banking crises. The savings and loan crisis of the United States demonstrated that distressed financial institutions with negative equity values have a strong incentive to pursue high risks. Imprudent bank lending is also cited as a major cause of banking problems happening to Mexico, Japan, and Southeast Asian countries in the 1990s. Moreover, the huge losses some banks suffer from their positions in financial derivatives show that there are highly risky investment opportunities that banks can gamble on. These facts imply that the threat of moral hazard is real and serious in the banking industry.

One way to alleviate moral hazard problems in the banking system is to impose market discipline, that is, to have depositors or other creditors of banks share the responsibility of monitoring banks. For example, if depositors have to lose part of their deposits when their banks fail, they will withdraw from banks pursuing unsound risks. The threat of a bank run will force banks to reduce their portfolio risk. However, whether market discipline can efficiently control moral hazard problems is still under debate. The experiences of the United States during the national banking era show that bank runs are contagious. Runs on a few banks may trigger runs on other banks, and a large scale of contagious runs may even result in the collapse of the whole financial system. If the contagious feature cannot be removed from bank runs, then requiring depositors to monitor banks may incur huge social costs. A better understanding of the nature of bank runs can help regulators evaluate various proposals for enforcing market discipline.

In this paper, I set up a model to demonstrate how failures of a few banks may cause runs on other banks. The intuition of the model is as follows. At a bank, some depositors may be better informed than others about the value of bank assets. The informed depositors enjoy an advantage over the uninformed by being able to withdraw earlier in bad states in which the bank cannot fully repay all depositors.

This article first appeared in the *Journal of Political Economy* 107(5), 1999.

Facing this informational disadvantage, the uninformed depositors have an incentive to respond to other sources of information before the value of bank assets is revealed. Failures of other banks can be one such information source. If banks' returns are positively correlated, a high bank failure rate implies that returns of the remaining banks are likely to be low. Although information contained in bank failures is very noisy, the uninformed depositors may still respond to it and withdraw. Knowing that the uninformed depositors will withdraw early, the informed are forced to withdraw early too even if more precise information will soon become available. Therefore, bank runs can be contagious. That is, failures of a few banks may trigger runs on other banks. In this paper, I shall call contagious runs 'panic' for two reasons. First, during contagious runs, depositors are compelled to respond to early information. Their behavior looks as though they are panicking. Second, because a contagious run is based on noisier information, it incurs higher social costs than a run triggered by more precise information about banks.

My paper is closely related to several papers in the literature. Diamond and Dybvig (1983) show how the first-come, first-served rule imposed in the deposit contract can cause a bank run to happen. In their model, the sequential service constraint creates a negative payoff externality[1] among depositors and results in two equilibria. A bank run is the Pareto-dominated one. My paper shares a common feature with Diamond and Dybvig in that the payoff externality is important in causing inefficient bank runs. In contrast to the model in Diamond and Dybvig, the results in my model do not rely on the multiple equilibria scenario. It is shown that contagious runs occur even if depositors choose the Pareto-dominant equilibrium when there are multiple equilibria. What I emphasize in this paper is how the negative payoff externality affects the way depositors respond to information, not how it creates multiple equilibria.

Chari and Jagannathan (1988) provide an information-based story to explain bank panics. In their model, a panic run is the phenomenon that uninformed depositors misinterpret liquidity withdrawal shocks as withdrawals caused by pessimistic information about bank assets. In my paper, bank runs are also triggered by information, but the mechanism by which information causes panic is different from theirs. While Chari and Jagannathan define panic as the ex post mistake depositors make during their information updating process, I explain panic as the result that depositors respond to early noisy information because of the payoff externality imposed in the deposit contract.

In terms of whether bank runs are an efficient mechanism for monitoring banks, Calomiris and Kahn (1991) argue that a debt contract together with the sequential service constraint is an optimal banking arrangement.[2] My model reaches a

[1] The negative payoff externality refers to the phenomenon that the withdrawal of a depositor reduces the expected payoff for depositors who have not yet withdrawn. In Diamond and Dybvig, given the optimal deposit contract, some depositors will lose their deposits if all depositors try to withdraw early. Therefore, there is a negative payoff externality among depositors in their model.

[2] In their model, the informed depositors who observe pessimistic information start a run, which results in liquidation of the bank. The run has the merit of controlling the bank manager's moral hazard problem.

conclusion different from theirs. In their model, disciplining banks by bank runs is efficient because runs are always triggered by precise information about bank assets. I show that when failures of other banks can be observed, the uninformed depositors may start a run before more precise information arrives, so bank runs can be inefficient in disciplining banks.

In the way contagious runs happen, my model is similar to the cascade model in Bikhchandani, Hirshleifer, and Welch (1992). In both papers, some agents' actions generate an information externality, inducing other agents to discard their own information and follow suit.[3] In addition to an information externality, my model also includes the negative payoff externality, which is not discussed in Bikhchandani *et al.* Complementing the cascade model, my paper provides another example that results in herd behavior.

This model can be used to evaluate proposals for reforming the Federal Deposit Insurance Corporation (FDIC). In this paper, I propose a deposit insurance system that can eliminate panic runs and can induce depositors to respond to more precise information. This system fully protects uninformed depositors and induces informed depositors to monitor banks. Moreover, in this system the informed depositors' deposits are not insured, and their claims are junior to the claim of the deposit insurer. This system shares several common features with the subordinated-debt requirements proposed by Calomiris (1997).[4] Both proposals suggest that banks should be disciplined by informed parties and the informed parties' claims should be junior. The results in this paper imply that subordinated debt can be an efficient mechanism for disciplining banks.

The rest of the paper is organized as follows. Section II presents the model. Section III shows the equilibrium and demonstrates the importance of the negative payoff externality and sequential information arrival. The optimal deposit contract is discussed in Section IV. A proposal for reforming the FDIC is studied in Section V. Section VI contains discussions and concluding remarks.

II. A MODEL OF CONTAGIOUS BANK RUNS

This is a three-date model (dates 0, 1, and 2). There are N banks and numerous depositors. Each bank is owned and managed by a risk-neutral banker. Banks do not have capital; they collect deposits from depositors to make investments. Depositors are atomistic. Each depositor receives an endowment of one dollar at date 0. A depositor can either deposit her endowment at a bank or costlessly store the endowment.[5] Depositors face liquidity shocks. A fraction α of depositors die at date 1, and the remaining depositors die at date 2. As in Diamond and Dybvig

[3] In my model, when a panic run occurs, the informed depositors give up the information they will receive in the near future.

[4] I am grateful to an anonymous referee for pointing out the similarities between the subordinated-debt proposal and the deposit insurance system that I propose.

[5] I assume that a depositor cannot deposit at more than one bank. Also, in contrast to Diamond and Dybvig (1983), in my model depositors cannot invest in long-term projects themselves.

(1983), I shall call depositors who die at date 1 early diers and depositors who die at date 2 late diers. Early diers have to consume at date 1, and late diers can defer their consumption to date 2. The utility function of a depositor is

$$U(c_1, c_2) = \begin{cases} u(c_1) & \text{if she dies early} \\ u(c_1 + c_2) & \text{if she dies late,} \end{cases}$$

where c_1 and c_2 are, respectively, the nonnegative consumption levels of the depositor at dates 1 and 2, and u is a utility function with $u' > 0 > u''$. By the strict concavity of u, depositors are risk-averse. Liquidity shocks are realized at date 1. At date 0, a depositor does not know whether she will become an early dier or a late dier.

At date 0, if depositors make deposits, then each bank invests the proceeds in a long-term project.[6] The investment is divisible and will mature at date 2. Different banks choose different projects, but the expected returns on all long-term projects are the same. For each project, the date 2 cash flow generated by one dollar invested at date 0 is either R or r, $R > 1 > r \geq 0$. I shall call R the good outcome and r the bad outcome. For each long-term project, the probability of a bad outcome is a, and the probability of a good outcome is $1 - a$, where a is a random variable whose value depends on the prospects of the banking industry. Assume that a is equal to a_g if the prospects of the banking industry are favorable and is equal to a_b if the prospects are unfavorable $(1 > a_b > a_g > 0)$. Given the realized value of a, the outcomes of two different long-term projects are independent. Let η_0 denote the prior probability of unfavorable banking industry prospects, and let a_0 denote the expected value of a at date 0. We thus have

$$a_0 \equiv \eta_0 a_b + (1 - \eta_0) a_g.$$

Although long-term projects mature at date 2, they can be liquidated earlier. Assume that, whatever the date 2 outcome would be, early liquidation releases one dollar for each dollar invested at date 0.

After a bank invests in a long-term project at date 0, at date 1 the banker receives perfect information about the outcome of the investment. There exists a moral hazard problem between bankers and depositors. At date 1, a banker can liquidate the long-term project and invest in an inefficient short-term project. For the short-term project, the investment of one dollar generates either $\overline{R}$ or nothing at date 2, $\overline{R} > R$. The probability of the outcome $\overline{R}$ is ϵ and $\epsilon\overline{R} < 1$, which implies that the expected return on the short-term project is negative. I assume that a banker does not speculate on the inefficient short-term project if he feels indifferent between speculating and not speculating.

At each bank, a fraction β of depositors also receive perfect information about the bank's long-term investment at date 1. These depositors are called informed

[6] For simplicity, the possibility that a bank may diversify its risks by investing in many long-term projects is not considered. If this assumption is relaxed, the main results in this paper still hold as long as banks cannot perfectly diversify risks and returns of different banks' assets are not perfectly correlated.

depositors. Depositors who do not receive information are called uninformed depositors. At date 0, depositors know whether they are informed or not. An informed depositor's chance of becoming an early dier is the same as that of an uninformed depositor. Information about banks and depositors' liquidity shocks are revealed at the same time. This makes it impossible to distinguish informational withdrawals from liquidity withdrawals. Under these assumptions, early diers (both informed and uninformed) always withdraw at date 1 after liquidity shocks are realized. The informed and uninformed late diers may withdraw at either date 1 or date 2.

For most parts of the paper, the deposit contract is assumed to be exogenous. The issue of the optimal deposit contract will be discussed in Section IV. Assume that all banks offer depositors the same deposit contract, which is a debt contract. For each dollar deposited, banks promise to pay a depositor y if she withdraws at date 1 and x if she withdraws at date 2.[7] Withdrawals by depositors are observable to other depositors. When serving customers, banks adopt the first-come, first-served rule, so depositors arriving first can withdraw earlier. If several depositors withdraw at the same time, the order in which they are served is randomly assigned. Convertibility suspension is not allowed: a bank has to be open if it still has money. A bank is liquidated at date 1 if it is out of money. Define

$$\bar{x}(y) \equiv \frac{R - \epsilon\bar{R}}{1-\epsilon}\frac{1 - \alpha y}{1 - \alpha}. \tag{1}$$

I assume that the deposit contract (y, x) satisfies

$$x = \bar{x}(y) > y > 1. \tag{2}$$

In Section IV, I shall show that under some circumstances the optimal deposit contract maximizing depositor welfare does satisfy condition (2). The condition $x > y$ is necessary for depositors to make deposits at date 0. If $y \geq x$, all depositors will prefer to withdraw at date 1. The condition $y > 1$ is not a trivial assumption. It will be shown that this assumption creates payoff externalities among depositors and causes panic runs.

The function $\bar{x}(y)$ is the largest return a bank can promise to late withdrawers without causing the moral hazard problem in the good state. This can be seen as follows. Suppose that none of the late diers withdraw at date 1. If the outcome of the bank's long-term investment is good, then to prevent a banker from speculating, the deposit contract must satisfy

$$(1 - \alpha y)R - (1 - \alpha)x \geq \epsilon[(1 - \alpha y)\bar{R} - (1 - \alpha)x]. \tag{3}$$

The left-hand side of (3) is a bank's profit if the outcome is good and the banker does not speculate on the short-term project; the right-hand side is his expected

[7] Since long-term projects are divisible, at date 1, banks liquidate part of their long-term projects to pay off withdrawing depositors.

profit if he speculates. It can be verified that (3) is equivalent to $x \leq \bar{x}(y)$. On the other hand, when the outcome is bad, a banker will speculate on the short-term project if

$$\epsilon[(1-\alpha y)\bar{R} - (1-\alpha)x] > 0. \tag{4}$$

It can be shown that (4) is satisfied when $x = \bar{x}(y)$. Therefore, when $x = \bar{x}(y)$ and none of the late diers withdraw at date 1, a banker will speculate on the inefficient short-term project if and only if the outcome of the bank's investment is bad.

Although liquidity shocks and information about the long-term projects of all banks are revealed at date 1, I assume that the timing of revelation is different for different banks. At date 1, N_1 banks are randomly picked, where N_1 is a constant smaller than N. Liquidity shocks and information of these N_1 banks are revealed first; liquidity shocks and information of the remaining $N - N_1$ banks are revealed later. Depositors learn whether their banks are among the first N_1 banks at date 1 before information and liquidity shocks are revealed.

Information revelation may result in bank failures. Let K_1 denote the number of failed banks among the first N_1 banks. Since bank failures are usually public information, I assume that all depositors at the remaining $N - N_1$ banks learn K_1 at the same time. A large K_1 implies that the prospects of the banking industry are likely to be pessimistic. To distinguish the information contained in K_1 from the information that bankers and informed depositors receive, I shall call the latter 'bank-specific information.' The timetable of the model is shown in Table 1. Finally, I assume that $\beta < 0.5$ and that

$$\alpha + (1-\alpha)\beta < \frac{1}{R}. \tag{5}$$

Table 1. *Timetable*

Date	Events
Date 0	Depositors decide whether to deposit. If they make deposits, banks invest the proceeds in long-term projects
Date 1	(1) Depositors learn whether their banks are among the first N_1 banks. Depositors then decide whether to withdraw (2) Information and liquidity shocks of the first N_1 banks are revealed. Depositors at these banks decide whether to withdraw (3) Depositors at the remaining $N - N_1$ banks observe K_1, which is the number of failures among the first N_1 banks. According to K_1, depositors at the remaining banks decide whether to withdraw (4) Informatin and liquidity shocks of the remaining $N - N_1$ banks are revealed. If a panic run has not yet occurred, depositors at the remaining banks decide whether to withdraw (5) For each bank that has not been liquidated, the banker decides whether to speculate on an inefficient short-term project
Date 2	Investment projects mature. If a bank is still open, its depositors who have not yet withdrawn withdraw

The assumption that $\beta < 0.5$ means that the proportion of informed depositors is not large. Condition (5) guarantees that all the informed depositors can successfully withdraw at date 1 if a run is triggered by bank-specific information.[8]

III. THE EQUILIBRIUM

The model is solved backward. I shall first study depositors' date 1 withdrawal decisions under the assumption that they have made deposits at date 0. I shall then discuss the conditions under which depositors prefer depositing to self-storing at date 0. Throughout this section, I assume that depositors choose the Pareto-dominant equilibrium when three are multiple equilibria. The reasons for making this assumption will be explained in Section VI. Also, only symmetric, pure-strategy, subgame-perfect Nash equilibria are studied. For simplicity, depositors are assumed not to withdraw when they feel indifferent between withdrawing and not withdrawing.

Suppose that depositors make deposits at date 0 and none of them withdraw after they learn they learn whether their banks are among the first N_1 banks. For each of the first N_1 banks, if the outcome of the bank's long-term investment is good, the informed late diers will not withdraw.[9] Having observed that the fraction of depositors who withdraw early is α, the uninformed late diers will not withdraw either. On the other hand, if the informed late diers learn that the investment outcome is bad, they will withdraw immediately.[10] When the uninformed late diers observe that the fraction of depositors who withdraw early exceeds α, they realize that the investment outcome must be bad, and they will withdraw too. The bank fails in this case.

As mentioned, depositors at the remaining $N - N_1$ banks can observe K_1, which is the number of bank failures among the first N_1 banks. Given K_1, depositors at the remaining banks update the probability that the prospects of the banking industry are unfavorable. Information contained in bank failures is especially valuable for the uninformed depositors. Under the assumption that $\alpha + (1 - \alpha)\beta < 1/R$, informed depositors can always withdraw successfully when a run is triggered by bank-specific information. In contrast, the uninformed may be unable to get their money back if they wait until bank-specific information arrives and the outcome

[8] When a run is triggered by bank-specific information, the ratio of deposits withdrawn by the informed depositors and early diers to the total date 0 deposits is $[\alpha + (1 - \alpha)\beta]y$. Given the assumptions that $y < R$ and $\alpha + (1 - \alpha)\beta < 1/R$, this ratio is strictly smaller than one, which implies that all the informed depositors can successfully withdraw at date 1.

[9] For each for the first N_1 banks, when the outcome of the long-term investment is good, obviously 'no late diers withdraw at date 1' is a Nash equilibrium and it Pareto-dominates all the other equilibria. Therefore, if depositors choose the Pareto-dominant equilibrium, the informed late diers will not withdraw in this case.

[10] Given a bad investment outcome, the expected utility of an informed late dier for not withdrawing at date 1 is no larger than $u(1)$, which is strictly smaller than $u(y)$.

of the long-term investment turns out to be bad. Because of this informational disadvantage, uninformed depositors have a strong incentive to respond to K_1.

Let η_1 denote the posterior probability that the prospects of the banking industry are unfavorable given K_1. Term η_1 can be written as

$$\eta_1(K_1) \equiv \frac{\eta_0 a_b^{K_1}(1 - a_b)^{N_1 - K_1}}{(1 - \eta_0)a_g^{K_1}(1 - a_g)^{N_1 - K_1} + \eta_0 a_b^{K_1}(1 - a_b)^{N_1 - K_1}}. \tag{6}$$

From η_1, depositors calculate a_1, the probability of a bad investment outcome given K_1, where

$$a_1(K_1) \equiv \eta_1(K_1)a_b + [1 - \eta_1(K_1)]a_g. \tag{7}$$

Depositors at the remaining banks use a_1 to decide whether to withdraw in response to K_1. The condition under which depositors will respond to K_1 is shown in Proposition 1 below. Lemmas 1 and 2 provide the results necessary for the proof of Proposition 1. The proof of Lemma 2 is in the Appendix. The proof of Lemma 1 will be discussed below.

Lemma 1. *For each of the remaining $N - N_1$ banks, when K_1 arrives, 'no depositors withdraw in response to K_1' can be supported as an equilibrium if and only if*

$$\frac{a_1(K_1)}{1 - a_1(K_1)} \leq z(y, x) \equiv \frac{(1 - \alpha)(1 - \beta)y}{y - 1}\frac{u(x) - u(y)}{u(y) - u(0)}. \tag{8}$$

Lemma 2. *For each of the remaining $N - N_1$ banks when K_1 arrives, if both 'all depositors withdraw in response to K_1' and 'no depositors withdraw in response to K_1' are equilibria, the latter always Pareto-dominates the former.*

Since only symmetric pure-strategy equilibria are studied, there are only two possible equilibria when K_1 arrives: all depositors withdraw responding to K_1, and no depositors withdraw.[11] As mentioned in the Introduction, I shall call the former a panic run. When $y > 1$, a panic run is always an equilibrium. Lemma 1 states that 'no depositors withdraw in response to K_1' can be sustained as a Nash equilibrium when the posterior probability of a bad investment outcome is small. Lemma 2 shows that

[11] Given K_1, there are two other equilibrium candidates. One is that all the informed depositors withdraw and none of the uninformed depositors do. The other is that all the uninformed depositors withdraw and none of the informed depositors do. The former is never an equilibrium because the uninformed depositors have stronger incentives to respond to K_1 than the informed. As to the latter, when $\beta < 0.5$, if it can be sustained as an equilibrium, then it is always Pareto-dominated by the equilibrium in which no depositors withdraw in response to K_1 (the proof of this result is available from the author on request). Therefore, we need not consider this equilibrium candidate when $\beta < 0.5$ and the Pareto-dominance criterion is imposed.

the panic run equilibrium is always Pareto-dominated by the no-withdrawal equilibrium when both are equilibria. Therefore, if we assume that depositors choose the Pareto-dominant equilibrium when there are multiple equilibria, a panic run will occur if and only if (8) is violated.

The intuition behind Lemma 1 can be explained as follows. 'No depositors respond to K_1' can be supported as an equilibrium if, under the belief that no others respond to K_1, no depositors want to withdraw when K_1 is revealed. Since uninformed depositors have a stronger incentive to respond to K_1, the no-withdrawal equilibrium can be sustained if none of the uninformed depositors have the incentive to respond to K_1.

Consider the withdrawal decision of an uninformed depositor who believes that no other depositors at her bank will respond to K_1. If she withdraws in response to K_1, her utility is $u(y)$. On the other hand, if she waits until liquidity shocks and information about her bank are revealed, her expected utility is

$$u_g(y, x) \equiv \alpha u(y) + (1 - \alpha) u(x) \tag{9}$$

if the bank's investment outcome is good and is[12]

$$u_b(y) \equiv \alpha u(y) + (1 - \alpha)\left\{\frac{1 - [\alpha + (1 - \alpha)\beta]y}{(1 - \alpha)(1 - \beta)y} u(y) + \frac{y - 1}{(1 - \alpha)(1 - \beta)y} u(0)\right\}$$

$$= \frac{1 - \beta y}{(1 - \beta)y} u(y) + \frac{y - 1}{(1 - \beta)y} u(0) \tag{10}$$

if the bank's investment outcome is bad. Given K_1, the depositor's expected utility for not withdrawing is

$$a_1(K_1) u_b(y) + [1 - a_1(K_1)] u_g(y, x). \tag{11}$$

The uninformed depositor will not respond to K_1 if and only if (11) is no less than $u(y)$. It can be shown that this condition is equivalent to (8) in Lemma 1.

Let K_1^* denote the lowest K_1 that will induce all depositors at the remaining $N - N_1$ banks to withdraw early. If $a_g/(1 - a_g) > z(y, x)$, then, from Lemma 1, depositors at the remaining banks always respond to K_1 for whatever K_1 is, so $K_1^* = 0$.[13] On the other hand, if $a_b/(1 - a_b) \leq z(y, x)$, from Lemma 1, depositors at

[12] Suppose that the realized outcome of the bank investment is bad. IF the depositor becomes an early dier, she can always successfully withdraw, so her utility is $u(y)$. On the other hand, if she becomes a late dier, her expected utility is

$$\frac{1 - [\alpha + (1 - \alpha)\beta]y}{(1 - \alpha)(1 - \beta)y} u(y) + \frac{y - 1}{(1 - \alpha)(1 - \beta)y} u(0).$$

In this expression, $\{1 - [\alpha + (1 - \alpha)\beta]y\}/[(1 - \alpha)(1 - \beta)]$ is the probability that the uninformed late dier can successfully withdraw at date 1 given the bad outcome.

[13] Note that $a_1(K_1)/[1 - a_1(K_1)]$ is increasing in $a_1(K_1)$ and $a_g \leq a_1(K_1) \leq a_b$.

the remaining banks never respond to K_1, so $K_1^* = N_1 + 1$. If $a_g/(1-a_g) \leq z(y,x) < a_b/(1-a_b)$, then using equations (6) and (7) to rearrange condition (8), we can show that K_1^* is the minimum K_1 that satisfies

$$K_1 > \frac{\log\left(\frac{1-\eta_0}{\eta_0}\right) + \log\left(\frac{1-a_g}{1-a_b}\right) + \log\left[\frac{z(y,x) - \frac{a_g}{1-a_g}}{\frac{a_b}{1-a_b} - z(y,x)}\right]}{\log\left[\frac{a_b(1-a_g)}{a_g(1-a_b)}\right]} + \frac{\log\left(\frac{1-a_g}{1-a_b}\right)}{\log\left[\frac{a_b(1-a_g)}{a_g(1-a_b)}\right]} N_1. \tag{12}$$

Proposition 1 summarizes depositors' behavior. The Proof of Proposition 1 is in the Appendix.

Proposition 1. *Assume that depositors choose the Pareto-dominant equilibrium when there are multiple equilibria. Having observed the behavior of depositors at the N_1 banks on which information is revealed early, depositors at the remaining $N - N_1$ banks will start a panic run if and only if $K_1 \geq K_1^*$. Moreover, K_1^* is weakly decreasing in η_0 and y and is weakly increasing in x.*

Proposition 1 states that, even if bank-specific information will be available and depositors choose the Pareto-dominant equilibrium, contagious runs can still be triggered by failures of other banks. Both payoff externalities and information externalities are important in causing panic runs. If $y = 1$, there are no payoff externalities among depositors, so depositors always wait until bank-specific information is revealed.[14] On the other hand, if information about all banks arrives at the same time, depositors have no chance to respond to failures of other banks, so contagious runs never happen.

Proposition 1 also shows the conditions under which a panic run is more likely to occur. The probability of a panic run is higher when the prospects of the banking industry are more likely to be unfavorable. That is, K_1^* is decreasing in η_0. This is consistent with the empirical evidence that large-scale bank runs followed pessimistic macro-economic information (see Gorton 1988; Calomiris and Gorton 1991). Also, panic runs are more likely to occur if either an early withdrawer gets more (the larger the y) or a late withdrawer gets less (the smaller the x). A larger y or a smaller x makes early withdrawals less costly for depositors and thus increases the possibility of a panic run. This result implies that one way to eliminate the threat of panic runs is to adjust the deposit contract. This issue will be discussed in the next section.

[14] Note that $z(1, x)$ approaches infinity, which is always larger than $a_b/(1-a_b)$. So $K_1^* = N_1 + 1$ in this case.

At date 1, depositors may have an incentive to withdraw when they learn whether their banks are among the first N_1 banks.[15] To find the condition under which they will not do so, let p_b^p *and* p_g^p denote the probabilities that a panic run will occur when the prospects of the banking industry are unfavorable and favorable, respectively. If $K_1^* > N_1$, a panic run never occurs, so $p_b^p = p_g^p = 0$. If $K_1^* \leq 0$, a panic run always occurs, so $p_b^p = p_g^p = 1$. If $1 \leq K_1^* \leq N_1$, we have

$$p_b^p \equiv \sum_{i=K_1^*}^{N_1} \binom{N_1}{i} a_b^i (1 - a_b)^{N_1 - i} \tag{13}$$

$$p_g^p \equiv \sum_{i=K_1^*}^{N_1} \binom{N_1}{i} a_g^i (1 - a_g)^{N_1 - i}. \tag{14}$$

Using p_b^p and p_g^p, we can calculate depositors' expected utilities. Let $\overline{U}_{u1}$ denote the expected utility of an uninformed depositor at the first N_1 banks and let $\overline{U}_{u2}$ denote the expected utility of an uninformed depositor at the remaining banks.[16] The expressions for $\overline{U}_{u1}$ and $\overline{U}_{u2}$ are in the Appendix. When depositors learn whether their banks are among the first N_1 banks, no depositors will withdraw if and only if[17]

$$\min\{\overline{U}_{u1}, \overline{U}_{u2}\} \geq u(y). \tag{15}$$

Now we go back to date 0, when depositors determine whether to make deposits. Let $\overline{U}_i$ and $\overline{U}_u$ denote the date 0 expected utilities of the informed and uninformed depositors, respectively. The expression for $\overline{U}_i$ is in the Appendix, and $\overline{U}_u$ can be written as

$$\overline{U}_u \equiv \frac{N_1}{N}\overline{U}_{u1} + \frac{N - N_1}{N}\overline{U}_{u2}. \tag{16}$$

Obviously $\overline{U}_i > \overline{U}_u$. Because the informed depositors enjoy an informational advantage over the uninformed, their expected utility from making deposits is higher. From the definition of $\overline{U}_u$ and the assumption that $y > 1$, $\overline{U}_u \geq u(y) > u(1)$ if (15) is satisfied. Therefore, all depositors will choose to deposit at date 0 if (15) holds.[18]

[15] The reason is that at date 1 depositors' expected utilities depend on whether their banks are among the first N_1 banks.

[16] Note that $\overline{U}_{u1}$ and $\overline{U}_{u2}$ are uninformed depositors' expected utilities after depositors learn whether their banks are among the first N_1 banks and before liquidity shocks and bank-specific information are revealed.

[17] Because the uninformed depositors have a stronger incentive to withdraw than the informed, the informed will not withdraw if the uninformed will not withdraw.

[18] Note that depositors may still deposit at date 0 when (15) is violated. It can be shown that if $\overline{U}_{u1} < u(y)$, then depositors never make deposits at date 0. However, if $\overline{U}_{u1} > u(y) > \overline{U}_{u2}$, then depositors will deposit at date 0 if and only if

$$\frac{N_1}{N}\overline{U}_{u1} + \frac{N - N_1}{N}\left[\frac{1}{y}u(y) + \frac{y-1}{y}u(0)\right] \geq u(1).$$

IV. THE OPTIMAL DEPOSIT CONTRACT

It has been shown in the previous section that failures of a few banks may trigger panic runs on other banks. Proposition 1 implies that one way to eliminate panic runs is to increase x or decrease y. A natural question follows: If the deposit contract can be endogenously determined, will panic runs still occur in equilibrium? It might always be optimal to choose a deposit contract under which panic runs never happen. The scenario in this paper would become less convincing if this were true.

To answer this question, I modify the model. Instead of assuming that the deposit contract is exogenously given, I assume that the deposit contract maximizes depositor welfare, and every depositor has the same weight when welfare is calculated.

Let a_2 denote the probability that a bank will be liquidated at date 1. We have[19]

$$a_2 \equiv \frac{N_1}{N}a_0 + \frac{N - N_1}{N}\{\eta_0[p_b^p + (1 - p_b^p)a_b] + (1 - \eta_0)[p_g^p + (1 - p_g^p)a_g]\}. \tag{17}$$

The optimization problem is

$$\max_{(y,x)} a_2\left[\frac{1}{y}u(y) + \left(1 - \frac{1}{y}\right)u(0)\right] + (1 - a_2)\,u_g(y, x) \tag{18}$$

subject to (15) and

$$\bar{x}(y) \geq x > y \geq 0. \tag{19}$$

The objective function in (18) can be explained as follows. With probability a_2, a bank is liquidated at date 1. In this case, a depositor's utility is $u(y)$ if she withdraws successfully and is $u(0)$ if she loses her deposits. The probabilities of these two events are $1/y$ and $1 - (1/y)$, respectively. With probability $1 - a_2$, a bank is not liquidated at date 1. In this case, the utility of an early dier is $u(y)$ and the utility of a late dier is $u(x)$.[20] Condition (15) guarantees that all depositors prefer to

When this condition holds and $\overline{U}_{u1} > u(y) > \overline{U}_{u2}$, all the depositors at the remaining $N - N_1$ banks withdraw at date 1 once they realize that their banks are not among the first N_1 banks. In this case, a panic run occurs before any information about bank assets is revealed. In the rest of the paper, I shall discuss only the case in which (15) is satisfied.

[19] Equation (17) can be explained as follows. If a bank is among the first N_1 banks, then the probability that it will be liquidated at date 1 is a_0. If a bank is among the remaining banks, it will be liquidated at date 1 either because of a panic run or because of an informed run. If the prospects of the banking industry are unfavorable, the probability of a panic run is p_b^p and the probability of an informed run is $(1-p_b^p)\,a_b$. Term η_0 is the prior probability of unfavorable banking industry prospects. The case in which the prospects of the banking industry are favorable can be explained in a similar way.

[20] Since informed depositors receive perfect information about their banks, the outcome of a bank's investment must be good if the bank is not liquidated at date 1. Also, because every depositor has the same weight when depositor welfare is calculated, in the objective function there is no need to distinguish between the informed and the uninformed depositors.

make deposits at date 0 and no depositors withdraw when they learn whether their banks are among the first N_1 banks. As to condition (19), $x > y$ is necessary since all depositors will prefer to withdraw at date 1 if $y \geq x$; $\bar{x}(y) \geq x$ makes sure that a banker will not speculate on the short-term project when the outcome of the bank's long-term investment is good.

Although a_2 is a function of x and y, it is not differentiable with respect to x and y. This makes solving the optimal (y, x) very difficult. Here I shall briefly discuss the basic trade-offs in determining the optimal deposit contract. Since the contract maximizes depositor welfare, it is obvious that x should be equal to $\bar{x}(y)$.[21] Note that $\bar{x}(y)$ is decreasing in y. To eliminate panic runs, y should be set small and x should be set large so that depositors have more incentive to wait. However, doing so may weaken the merit of the deposit contract in insuring depositors' liquidity risks. As Diamond and Dybvig (1983) show, risk sharing among depositors can be improved if early diers are allowed to consume more.

Intuitively, panic runs would be allowed to happen in equilibrium if (i) risk sharing among depositors is important, (ii) the threat of panic runs is not serious at date 0, and (iii) a large K_1 dramatically raises the posterior probability that the remaining banks are in a bad state.[22] These conditions together reflect a situation in which the major concern for designing the deposit contract is risk sharing rather than the prevention of panic runs, and a large K_1 makes depositors pessimistic about the prospects of the banking industry. Proposition 2 states that numerical examples in which panic runs occur in equilibrium do exist.

Proposition 2. *Assume that depositors choose the Pareto-dominant equilibrium when there are multiple equilibria. Even if the deposit contract is designed to maximize depositor welfare, there are cases in which panic runs occur with positive probability in equilibrium.*

The following is a numerical example. Assume that $\alpha = 0.3$, $\beta = 0.1$, $R = 1.2$, $\epsilon = 0.1$, $\bar{R} = 1.6$, $a_g = 0.0001$, $a_b = 0.1$, $\eta_0 = 0.005$, $N = 1{,}000$, $N_1 = 1$, and $u(c) = 1 - \exp(-5c)$. The optimal deposit contract (y^*, x^*) is (1.0653, 1.1232) and $K_1^* = 1$. It can be verified that the largest y that will not cause panic runs is 1.02016 (the corresponding x is 1.14557). However, setting y equal to 1.0202 is dominated by setting y equal to 1.0653.

V. POLICY IMPLICATIONS FOR REFORMING THE FDIC

This paper proposes that bank runs are depositors' rational response to information rather than mysterious panic. However, this claim does not necessarily imply that bank runs can efficiently discipline banks. Because of the negative payoff

[21] If $x < \bar{x}(y)$, an increase in x will raise depositor welfare by reducing the probability of a panic run and by increasing the late diers' payoff when a panic run does not happen.

[22] The first condition is satisfied if the depositors' utility function meets certain requirements. For example, Diamond and Dybvig (1983) require that the measure of relative risk aversion $-cu''(c)/u'(c)$ be larger than one. The second condition is satisfied when both η_0 and a_g are small. The third condition is satisfied when a_b is large.

externalities in the deposit contract, bank runs can be triggered by very noisy information. To enforce market discipline, there should be a mechanism that can induce depositors to be more patient in responding to information.

In this section, I show that there is a deposit insurance system that can eliminate panic runs and can induce depositors to respond to bank-specific information. The basic idea behind this system is simple. Because uninformed depositors have a stronger incentive to start a panic run, they should enjoy more insurance coverage. One way to do so is to fully insure the uninformed depositors and offer no insurance to the informed depositors. The fully protected uninformed depositors need not withdraw early unless they have liquidity needs. The uninsured informed depositors at a bank still have to withdraw early when the outcome of the bank's long-term investment is bad. However, because the uninformed never start the run, the informed depositors can always wait until bank-specific information is revealed. It is shown that this system can be incentive compatible. That is, even if the deposit insurer cannot distinguish between the informed and the uninformed, the uninformed depositors will voluntarily buy deposit insurance, whereas the informed will not.

For simplicity, assume that the insurer is the government. Given a deposit contract described in Section II,[23] the insurer offers the following deposit insurance system. (i) An insured depositor receives y if she withdraws at date 1 and receives $x - \pi$ if she withdraws at date 2, where π is the insurance premium charged by the insurer.[24] (ii) A bank is closed by the insurer at date 1 if the fraction of depositors who withdraw early reaches $\alpha + (1 - \alpha)\beta$. (iii) If a bank is closed by the insurer at date 1, the uninsured depositors who have not yet withdrawn lose all their deposits. In other situations, the uninsured depositors at a bank are paid by the bank according to the deposit contract and the amount of money left at the bank. (iv) If a bank's realized fraction of depositors who withdraw early is between α and $\alpha + (1 - \alpha)\beta$, the insurer subsidizes the bank so that the banker will not speculate on the short-term project.[25]

The following proposition documents the result that the proposed deposit insurance system can eliminate panic runs. Its proof is in the Appendix.

Proposition 3. *Suppose that (i) the deposit contract is (y, x), where $x = \bar{x}(y) > y > 1$, and (ii) without deposit insurance, panic runs occur with positive probability. There exists a deposit insurance system with the following properties. (a) In this*

[23] The purpose of this section is not to find the optimal combination of the deposit contract and the deposit insurance system, but to show how a deposit insurance system may improve welfare given a deposit contract described in Section II.

[24] If an insured depositor is not fully paid by her bank, the insurer gives the depositor the difference.

[25] Assume that the subsidy can be given to the bank before the banker decides whether to speculate. It can be shown that the ratio of the required subsidy to the bank's total date 0 deposits is

$$\frac{(y - 1)(R - \epsilon\bar{R})(t - \alpha)}{(1 - \alpha)(1 - \epsilon)},$$

where t is the fraction of depositors who withdraw.

system, all the uninformed depositors buy deposit insurance and no informed depositors do. (b) In this system, panic runs never occur, and a bank is liquidated at date 1 if and only if the outcome of its long-term investment is bad. (c) Bankers, informed depositors, and uninformed depositors are better off than in the case without deposit insurance. Moreover, in this system the insurer's expected profit may be positive.

As Proposition 3 shows, in the deposit insurance system, panic runs are eliminated. Bank runs are efficient because they are based on bank-specific information. Moreover, it is possible that the welfare of all parties, including depositors, bankers, and the deposit insurer, is improved. The success of the proposed system in enforcing market discipline without triggering panic runs can be attributed to the following features of the system. First, banks are monitored only by their informed depositors. By fully protecting the uninformed depositors, this system allows the informed depositors to be more patient in responding to information. Second, the claims of the uninsured depositors are junior to the claim of the deposit insurer.[26] Because of this feature, an uninformed depositor who does not buy insurance will lose all of her deposits once a run is triggered by bank-specific information.[27] This gives uninformed depositors a strong incentive to buy deposit insurance. Third, the system requires the insurer to subsidize sound banks suffering liquidity problems. The subsidy prevents bankers with good investment outcomes from speculating on inefficient short-term projects. Knowing this, an informed depositor need not panic even if she believes that all the other informed depositors will withdraw at date 1. Therefore, there is only one subgame-perfect Nash equilibrium in this system, which implies that it is no longer necessary to assume that depositors choose the Pareto-dominant equilibrium.

In addition to the merits that have been mentioned, the proposed deposit insurance system may have others. For example, consider the case in which information collection is costly and whether a depositor is informed is endogenously determined. In this case, requiring uninsured depositors' claims to be junior gives these depositors a strong incentive to acquire information and monitor banks. Moreover, inducing only uninsured depositors to monitor banks can avoid duplication of efforts expended on information acquisition.

A problem with this deposit insurance system is that it relies on the strong assumption that α and β are constants. If α and β are random variables, the design of the deposit insurance system would become much more complicated. However, the insights provided in the analysis above—that banks should be monitored by informed depositors with junior claims and that the deposit insurer should subsidize sound banks suffering liquidity problems—will be robust to the change of assumptions.

[26] This feature is implied by the requirement that uninsured depositors lose all their deposits when banks are closed by the insurer.

[27] Note that a bank is closed when the fraction of depositors who withdraw early reaches $\alpha + (1 - \alpha)\beta$. When an uninformed depositor finds that the outcome of the bank's investment is poor, it is too late for her to withdraw.

One thing worth mentioning is that the deposit insurance system discussed in this section shares several common features with the subordinated-debt requirements proposed by Calomiris (1997). Calomiris suggests that commercial banks should be required to finance a minimal fraction of their total nonreserve assets with subordinated debt earning a yield no greater than 50 basis points above the riskless rate. Under this proposal, banks have to reduce their portfolio risk so that investors are willing to hold their subordinated debts. Moreover, subordinated-debt holders of a bank have a strong incentive to monitor the bank because they are likely to receive nothing if the bank fails. The role of subordinated-debt holders in Calomiris's proposal is similar to that of informed depositors in the deposit insurance system I propose. Both proposals suggest that banks should be monitored by informed parties and the informed parties' claims should be junior. A policy implication of this paper is that, for enforcing market discipline in the banking industry, the subordinated-debt approach has advantages over the fractional-insurance approach. Under a fractional-insurance reform proposal, deposits are fractionally insured. In this case, all depositors have incentives to acquire information about banks, and all depositors have incentives to withdraw in response to various sources of information. From discussions in this section, it should be obvious that both the probability of a panic run and the social costs incurred in monitoring banks will be lower under the subordinated-debt proposal than under a fractional-insurance proposal.

VI. DISCUSSION AND CONCLUDING REMARKS

In this paper, I set up a model with multiple banks to study the contagious nature of bank runs. The model suggests that both payoff and information externalities are important in causing inefficient runs. This paper also discusses a plausible proposal for reforming the FDIC. I show that there is an incentive-compatible deposit insurance system that can make bank runs an efficient mechanism for disciplining banks.

In most parts of this paper, I assume that depositors choose the Pareto-dominant equilibrium when there are multiple equilibria. The reasons for adopting this Pareto-dominance criterion can be explained as follows. First, the results I get under this assumption are consistent with the empirical evidence that bank runs are triggered by pessimistic information about banks. Second, by making this assumption, I can concentrate on how the negative payoff externality affects depositors' incentives in responding to information rather than how it creates multiple equilibria. Third, one purpose of this paper is to demonstrate that bank runs may not be an efficient mechanism for monitoring banks. If it can be shown that a panic run can occur even if depositors choose the Pareto-dominant equilibrium, panic runs will occur more frequently when depositors may choose a Pareto-dominated equilibrium. Finally, there is evidence that under some circumstances the behavior of economic agents does converge to what is predicted by the Pareto-dominant equilibrium (see, e.g., Harrison and Hirshleifer 1989). I conjecture that most of the results in this paper will hold if the Pareto-dominance criterion is replaced by the assumption that depositors are more likely to withdraw when the posterior probability of a bad investment outcome is higher.

In addition to the equilibrium selection criterion, the assumptions about the information structure also deserve discussion. I assume that bank-specific information always exists, so depositors can always receive better information if they do not respond to failures of other banks. I also assume that no costs are incurred between the information release of the first group of banks and that of the remaining banks. These assumptions imply that depositors should wait until bank-specific information arrives to decide whether to withdraw. If failures of other banks were the only information available to depositors or if banks would suffer great losses supposing that depositors did not respond immediately to failures of other banks, then panic runs might be socially efficient. The assumptions in the model are justified by the following arguments. First, during the bank panics in U.S. history, the authorities or clearinghouse associations always played the role of verifying the states of banks. In general, the process of information revelation took about one month. Therefore, if depositors were patient, bank-specific information would be available. Second, according to Gilbert (1990), most empirical studies show that the stock price of an individual bank accurately reflects the risk assumed by the bank, which implies that bank-specific information exists. Third, the span of a panic was always shorter than three months. It is not plausible that large losses could be incurred in such a short time.

There are several directions to extend the present model. One is to assume that information collection is costly and depositors' information acquisition decisions are endogenously determined. Since depositors' incentives to collect information may be different under different reform proposals, this extension can offer new insights into reform of the FDIC. Another direction of extending this paper is to study the case in which the proportions of early diers and informed depositors are random variables rather than constants. The information-updating process of the uninformed depositors will become more complicated. Issues discussed in Chari and Jagannathan (1988), such as depositors' misinterpretation of liquidity withdrawals as informational withdrawals, can then be studied. Finally, the model in this paper can also be used to investigate the feasibility of mutual insurance among banks. As suggested by Calomiris (1990), banks can form a coalition to monitor and insure one another. Because banks are usually better informed than depositors, monitoring of banks by other banks may be more efficient. The mutual insurance arrangement gives banks a strong incentive to monitor one another. Moreover, once the coalition is formed, depositors care about the health of the coalition rather than that of individual banks. It is interesting to see whether mutual insurance among banks can provide an effective mechanism for disciplining banks.[28]

Appendix

Proof of Lemma 2. There are three groups of agents in this model: bankers, informed depositors, and uninformed depositors. Bankers obviously prefer the no-withdrawal

[28] For more discussion on this proposal, see Calomiris (1990) and Chen (1994, chap. 2).

equilibrium since a bank's expected profit is positive in the no-withdrawal equilibrium and is zero in the panic run equilibrium. Note that a depositor's expected utility in the panic run equilibrium is

$$\frac{1}{y}u(y) + \left(1 - \frac{1}{y}\right)u(0),$$

which is less than $u(y)$. In the no-withdrawal equilibrium, the informed depositors' expected utility is strictly larger than $u(y)$ since they can always successfully withdraw. From the analysis in Section III, the uninformed depositors' expected utility in the no-withdrawal equilibrium is also larger than $u(y)$. Therefore, all parties prefer the no-withdrawal equilibrium to the panic run equilibrium. □

Proof of Proposition 1. To show (12) from (8), note that

$$\frac{a_1(K_1)}{1 - a_1(K_1)} = \frac{\eta_0 a_b^{K_1+1}(1 - a_b)^{N_1-K_1} + (1 - \eta_0)a_g^{K_1+1}(1 - a_g)^{N_1-K_1}}{\eta_0 a_b^{K_1}(1 - a_b)^{N_1-K_1+1} + (1 - \eta_0)a_g^{K_1}(1 - a_g)^{N_1-K_1+1}}.$$

Condition (8) can then be written as

$$\eta_0 a_b^{K_1}(1 - a_b)^{N_1-K_1+1}\left[\frac{a_b}{1 - a_b} - z(y, x)\right]$$
$$\leq (1 - \eta_0)\, a_g^{K_1}(1 - a_g)^{N_1-K_1+1}\left[z(y, x) - \frac{a_g}{1 - a_g}\right].$$

Taking the log of both sides and rearranging the expression, we get (12). The result that K_1^* is decreasing in η_0 is obvious from (12). Other parts of the comparative statics can be proved using the facts that the right-hand side of (12) is increasing in $z(y, x)$, and $z(y, x)$ is increasing in x and is decreasing in y. □

Expressions for $\overline{U}_{u1}$, $\overline{U}_{u2}$, *and* $\overline{U}_i$

$$\overline{U}_{u1} \equiv a_0 u_b(y) + (1 - a_0)\, u_g(y, x),$$
$$\overline{U}_{u2} \equiv \eta_0\{(1 - p_b^p)\,[a_b u_b(y) + (1 - a_b)u_g(y, x)] + p_b^p u_p(y)\}$$
$$+ (1 - \eta_0)\{(1 - p_g^p)[a_g u_b(y) + (1 - a_g)u_g(y, x)] + p_g^p u_p(y)\},$$
$$\overline{U}_i \equiv \frac{N_1}{N}[a_0 u(y) + (1 - a_0)u_g(y, x)] + \frac{N - N_1}{N}$$
$$\cdot\,(\eta_0\{(1 - p_b^p)\,[a_b u(y) + (1 - a_b)u_g(y, x)] + p_b^p u_p(y)\}$$
$$+ (1 - \eta_0)\{(1 - p_g^p)\,[a_g u(y) + (1 - a_g)u_g(y, x)] + p_g^p u_p(y)\}),$$

where

$$u_p(y) \equiv \frac{1}{y}u(y) + \left(1 - \frac{1}{y}\right)u(0).$$

Proof of Proposition 3. I first show that there exists a $\pi > 0$ such that parts *a–c* hold given this π. In the deposit insurance system, at date 1 a banker will try to speculate on the short-term project if and only if the outcome of the long-term project is adverse. The date 0 expected utility of a depositor who buys deposit insurance is

$$\overline{U}'_u \equiv \alpha u(y) + (1-\alpha)u(x-\pi).$$

Given the proposed equilibrium, the expected utility of an informed depositor who does not buy deposit insurance is

$$\overline{U}'_i \equiv \alpha u(y) + (1-\alpha)[a_0 u(y) + (1-a_0)u(x)].$$

Given the belief that all the other uninformed buy deposit insurance, the expected utility of the uninformed depositor who does not buy deposit insurance is

$$\overline{U}_d \equiv \frac{N_1}{N}(\alpha u(y) + (1-\alpha)\max\{u(y), a_0 u(0) + (1-a_0)u(x)\})$$

$$+ \frac{N-N_1}{N}\Bigg(\alpha u(y) + (1-\alpha)\sum_{i=0}^{N_1}\text{prob}(K_1 = i)$$

$$\cdot \max\{u(y), a_1(i)u(0) + [1-a_1(i)]u(x)\}\Bigg),$$

where $\text{prob}(K_1 = i)$ is the probability that $K_1 = i$. The deviating uninformed depositor can use K_1 to decide whether to withdraw at date 1, so given K_1, her expected utility is

$$\alpha u(y) + (1-\alpha)\max\{u(y), a_1(K_1)u(0) + [1-a_1(K_1)]u(x)\}.$$

Note that $\overline{U}'_i > \max\{\overline{U}_u, \overline{U}_d\} > u(y)$, $\overline{U}'_i > \overline{U}_i$, $\overline{U}'_u > \overline{U}'_i$ when $\pi = 0$, and $\overline{U}'_u = u(y)$ when $\pi = x - y$. Therefore, we can find a $\pi \in (0, x-y)$ such that, given this π,

$$\overline{U}'_i > \overline{U}'_u > \max\{\overline{U}_u, \overline{U}_d\}.$$

The expression above implies that, given this π, 'all the uninformed buy deposit insurance and none of the informed do' can be supported as an equilibrium. Moreover, since the uninformed depositors have more incentive to buy deposit insurance than the informed and a depositor's incentive to buy deposit insurance is decreasing in the number of depositors who buy deposit insurance, the proposed equilibrium is in fact the unique equilibrium. It is obvious that part *b* holds in this equilibrium. As to part *c*, bankers and the informed depositors are better off when the deposit insurance system is imposed. The uninformed depositors also prefer deposit insurance since $\overline{U}'_u > \overline{U}_u$. Therefore, part *c* also holds. To show that it is possible that the insurer's expected profit is positive, let π^* denote the fairly priced insurance premium. It can be verified that

$$\pi^* = a_0\left\{\bar{x} - \frac{1 - [\alpha + (1-\alpha)\beta]y}{(1-\alpha)(1-\beta)}\right\}.$$

The insurer's expected profit is positive if

$$\bar{U}_i' > \bar{U}_u' > \max\{\bar{U}_u, \bar{U}_d\}$$

when $\pi = \pi^*$. This condition is satisfied for the numerical example discussed in Section IV. Therefore, the insurer's expected profit in the proposed deposit insurance system that satisfies parts *a*–*c* can be positive. □

REFERENCES

Bikhchandani, Sushil; Hirshleifer, David; and Welch, Ivo. 'A Theory of Fads, Fashion, Custom, and Cultural Change as Informational Cascades.' *J.P.E.* 100 (October 1992): 992–1026.

Calomiris, Charles W. 'Is Deposit Insurance Necessary? A Historical Perspective.' *J. Econ. Hist.* 50 (June 1990): 283–95.

—. *The Postmodern Bank Safety Net: Lessons from Developed and Developing Economies.* Washington: American Enterprise Inst. Press, 1997.

Calomiris, Charles W., and Gorton, Gary. 'The Origins of Banking Panics: Models, Facts, and Bank Regulation.' In *Financial Markets and Financial Crises*, edited by R. Glenn Hubbard. Chicago: Univ. Chicago Press (for NBER), 1991.

Calomiris, Charles W., and Kahn, Charles M. 'The Role of Demandable Debt in Structuring Optimal Banking Arrangements.' *A.E.R.* 81 (June 1991): 497–513.

Chari, V. V., and Jagannathan, Ravi. 'Banking Panics, Information, and Rational Expectations Equilibrium.' *J. Finance* 43 (July 1988): 749–61.

Chen, Yehning. 'The Role of Information Externalities in Bank Runs.' Ph.D. dissertation, Univ. California, Los Angeles, 1994.

Diamond, Douglas W., and Dybvig, Philip H. 'Bank Runs, Deposit Insurance, and Liquidity.' *J.P.E.* 91 (June 1983): 401–19.

Gilbert, R. Alton. 'Market Discipline of Bank Risk: Theory and Evidence.' *Fed. Reserve Bank St. Louis Rev.* 72 (January/February 1990): 3–18.

Gorton, Gary. 'Banking Panics and Business Cycles.' *Oxford Econ. Papers* 40 (December 1988): 751–81.

Harrison, Glenn W., and Hirshleifer, Jack. 'An Experimental Evaluation of Weakest Link/Best Shot Models of Public Goods.' *J.P.E.* 97 (February 1989): 201–25.

18

Financial Contagion

FRANKLIN ALLEN AND DOUGLAS GALE

1. INTRODUCTION

There is a long tradition of regarding dislocation in the financial sector as a cause of economic fluctuations (Friedman and Schwartz 1963; Bernanke 1983; Bernanke and Gertler 1989). According to this view, financial crises are important because they raise the costs of intermediation and restrict credit, which in turn restrain the level of activity in the real sector and ultimately can lead to periods of low growth and recession.

The prevalence of financial crises has led many to conclude that the financial sector is unusually susceptible to shocks. One theory is that small shocks, which initially affect only a few institutions or a particular region of the economy, spread by contagion to the rest of the financial sector and then infect the larger economy. In this paper, we focus on one channel of contagion, the overlapping claims that different regions or sectors of the banking system have on one another. When one region suffers a bank crisis, the other regions suffer a loss because their claims on the troubled region fall in value. If this spillover effect is strong enough, it can cause a crisis in the adjacent regions. In extreme cases, the crisis passes from region to region and becomes a contagion.

In order to focus on the role of one particular channel for financial contagion, we exclude other propagation mechanisms that may be important for a fuller understanding of financial contagion. In particular, we assume that agents have complete information about their environment. Incomplete information may create another channel for contagion. If a shock in one region serves as a signal predicting a shock in another region, then a crisis in one region may create a self-fulfilling expectation of a crisis in another region.

We also exclude the effect of international currency markets in the propagation of financial crises from one country to another. Currency crises have been extensively studied, and Calvo (1995) and Chang and Velasco (1998), among others, have studied the interaction of the banking system and currency markets in a crisis; but the role of currency markets in financial contagion is left as a subject for future research.

The central aim of this paper is to provide some microeconomic foundations for financial contagion. Although the analysis may have some relevance to the recent

This article first appeared in the *Journal of Political Economy* 108(1), 2000.

Asian financial crisis, the model developed in this paper is not intended to be a description of any particular episode. If it does resemble any historical episode, it would be the banking crises in the United States in the late nineteenth and early twentieth centuries (Hicks 1989).

We take as our starting point the model presented in Allen and Gale (1998). The basic assumptions about technology and preferences have become the standard in the literature since the appearance of the Diamond and Dybvig (1983) model. There are three dates $t = 0, 1, 2$ and a large number of identical consumers, each of whom is endowed with one unit of a homogeneous consumption good. At date 1, the consumers learn whether they are early consumers, who value consumption only at date 1, or late consumers, who value consumption only at date 2. Uncertainty about their preferences creates a demand for liquidity.

Banks have a comparative advantage in providing liquidity. At the first date, consumers deposit their endowments in the banks, which invest them on behalf of the depositors. In exchange, depositors are promised a fixed amount of consumption at each subsequent date, depending on when they choose to withdraw. The bank can invest in two assets. There is a short-term asset that pays a return of one unit after one period and there is a long-term asset that pays a return $r < 1$ after one period or $R > 1$ after two periods. The long asset has a higher return if held to maturity, but liquidating it in the middle period is costly, so it is not very useful for providing consumption to early consumers. The banking sector is perfectly competitive, so banks offer risk-sharing contracts that maximize depositors' ex ante expected utility, subject to a zero-profit constraint.

Using this framework, we are interested in constructing a model in which small shocks lead to large effects by means of contagion, more precisely, in which a shock within a single sector can spread to other sectors and lead to an economy-wide financial crisis. One view is that financial crises are purely random events, unrelated to changes in the real economy (Kindleberger 1978). The modern version of this view, developed by Diamond and Dybvig (1983) and others, is that bank runs are self-fulfilling prophecies. An alternative view is that financial crises are an inherent part of the business cycle (Mitchell 1941; Gorton 1988; Allen and Gale 1998). The disadvantage of treating contagion as a 'sunspot' phenomenon is that, without some real connection between different regions, any pattern of correlations is possible. So sunspot theories are equally consistent with contagion and the absence of contagion. We are interested in establishing a stronger result, that under certain circumstances every equilibrium of the model must be characterized by contagion. This form of contagion must be driven by real shocks and real linkages between regions.

The economy consists of a number of regions. The number of early and late consumers in each region fluctuates randomly, but the aggregate demand for liquidity is constant. This allows for interregional insurance as regions with liquidity surpluses provide liquidity for regions with liquidity shortages. The provision of insurance can be organized through an interbank market in deposits. Suppose that region A has a large number of early consumers when region B has a low number of early consumers, and vice versa. Since regions A and B are otherwise identical, their deposits are perfect substitutes. The banks exchange deposits at the first date before they observe the liquidity shocks. If region A has a higher than average number of early consumers at date 1, then banks in region A can meet their obligations by liquidating some of their deposits in the banks of region B. Region B is happy to oblige because it has an excess supply of liquidity in the form of the short asset. At the final date the process is reversed, as banks in region B liquidate the deposits they hold in region A to meet the above-average demand from late consumers in region B.

Interregional cross holdings of deposits work well as long as there is enough liquidity in the banking system as a whole. If there is an excess demand for liquidity, however, the financial linkages caused by these cross holdings can turn out to be a disaster. While cross holdings of deposits are useful for reallocating liquidity within the banking system, they cannot increase the total amount of liquidity. If the economywide demand from consumers is greater than the stock of the short asset, the only way to provide more consumption is to liquidate the long asset. This is very costly (see Shleifer and Vishny [1992] and Allen and Gale [1998] for a discussion of the costs of premature liquidation), so banks try to avoid liquidating the long asset whenever possible. In this case, they can avoid liquidating the long asset by liquidating their claims on other regions instead. This mutual liquidation of claims does not create any additional liquidity, however. It merely denies liquidity to the troubled region, and bank runs and bankruptcy may be the result. What begins as a financial crisis in one region can then spread by contagion to other regions because of the cross holdings of deposits.

The interbank market works quite differently from the retail market. In the latter, runs occur because deposit contracts commit banks to a fixed payment and banks must begin liquidating the long asset when they cannot meet liquidity demand from the short asset. In the interbank market the initial problem is caused by the fact that banks with an excess demand for liquidity cannot get anything from banks in other regions. This is the opposite of the problem in the retail market and, in contrast, cannot be solved by making the contracts discretionary or contingent since whatever their form they cancel each other out. Instead of being caused by the nature of interbank claims, spillovers and contagion result just from the fall in the value of bank assets in adjacent regions.

Whether the financial crisis does spread depends crucially on the pattern of interconnectedness generated by the cross holdings of deposits. If the interbank market is *complete* and each region is connected to all the other regions, the initial impact of a financial crisis in one region may be attenuated. On the other hand, if the interbank market is *incomplete*, each region is connected with a small number of other regions. The initial impact of the financial crisis may be felt very strongly in those neighboring regions, with the result that they too succumb to a crisis. As each region is affected by the crisis, it prompts premature liquidation of the long asset, with a consequent loss of value, so that previously unaffected regions find that they too are affected because their claims on the region in crisis have fallen in value.

It is important to note the role of the free-rider problem in explaining the difference between a complete and an incomplete interbank market. There is a natural pecking order among different sources for liquidity. A bank will meet withdrawals first from the short asset and then from holdings in other regions, and only in the last resort will it choose to liquidate the long asset. Cross holdings are useful for redistributing liquidity, but they do not create liquidity; so when there is a global shortage of liquidity (withdrawals exceed short assets), the only solution is to liquidate long assets. If every region takes a small hit (liquidates a small amount of the long asset), there may be no need for a global crisis. This is what happens with complete markets: banks in the troubled region have direct claims on banks in every other region, and there is no way to avoid paying one's share. With incomplete markets, banks in the troubled region have a direct claim only on the banks in adjacent regions. The banks in other regions pursue their own interests and refuse to liquidate the long asset until they find themselves on the front line of the contagion.

The notion of a region is intended as a metaphor for categories of banks that may differ along several dimensions. For example, some banks may be better at raising funds whereas other banks are better at lending them. Or it might be that banks focus on lending to different industries or in different regions and as a result have lending opportunities that are not perfectly correlated with their deposit base. In either case, an interbank market plays an important role in redistributing the funds efficiently. However, the existence of claims between different categories of banks opens up the possibility of contagion when one category is hit by a sudden demand for liquidity.

Our paper is related to a number of others. Perhaps the closest is that by Lagunoff and Schreft (1998), which studies the spread of crises in a probabilistic model. Financial linkages are modeled by assuming that each project requires two participants and each participant requires two projects. When the probability that one's partner will withdraw becomes too large, all participants simultaneously withdraw; this is interpreted as a financial crisis. The banking system plays no role in Lagunoff and Schreft's analysis. Rochet and Tirole (1996) use monitoring as a means of triggering correlated crises: if one bank fails, it is assumed that other banks have not been properly monitored and a general collapse occurs. Financial multipliers are modeled by Kiyotaki and Moore (1998). In their model, the impact of illiquidity at one link in the credit chain travels down the chain. Models of crises based on multiple equilibria are contained in Cole and Kehoe (1996) and Cooper and Corbae (1997). For a survey of recent work on crises, see Calomiris (1995).

The rest of the paper is organized as follows. In Section II, we present a model of liquidity preference based on Diamond and Dybvig (1983) and Allen and Gale (1998). In Section III, we characterize optimal risk sharing in terms of a planning problem subject to incentive constraints and show that the incentive-efficient allocation is in fact the same as the first-best. Section IV shows how the first-best allocation can be decentralized through a competitive banking system with an interbank market in deposits. Several different market structures are described, and each turns out to be consistent with the first-best. The robustness of this schema is tested in the next three sections. We do this by perturbing the model to allow for an (aggregate) excess demand for liquidity in some states of nature. In Section V, it is shown that with an incomplete interbank market and a high degree of interconnectedness, a liquidity shock that causes a crisis in one region will spread by contagion to others. In Section VI, we consider a complete interbank market and an even higher degree of connectedness. It is shown that, with the same size shock and the same model parameters, there is no contagion. In Section VII, it is shown that with an incomplete interbank market and a low degree of connectedness, there is again no contagion. So the interaction of connectedness and incompleteness appears to be conducive to contagion. Section VIII considers alternatives to an interbank deposit market for sharing risk between regions. Finally, Section IX considers extensions of the basic framework.

II. LIQUIDITY PREFERENCE

In this section we describe a simple model in which stochastic liquidity preference provides a motive for risk sharing. The framework is based on Diamond and Dybvig (1983) and Allen and Gale (1998), with some significant differences.

There are three dates, $t=0$, 1, 2. There is a single consumption good that serves as the numeraire. This good can also be invested in assets to produce future consumption. There are two types of assets, a liquid asset and an illiquid asset. The liquid asset is represented by a storage technology. One unit of the consumption good invested in the storage technology at date t produces one unit of the consumption good at date $t+1$. Because the returns to this asset are available one period later, we refer to it as the *short asset*. The illiquid asset has a higher return but requires more time to mature. For this reason we call it the *long asset*. Investment in the long asset can take place only in the first period, and one unit of the consumption good invested in the long asset at the first date produces $R>1$ units of output at the final date.

The long asset is not completely illiquid. Each unit of the long asset can be prematurely liquidated to produce $0<r<1$ units of the consumption good at the middle date. Here we assume that liquidation takes the form of physical depreciation of the asset, and the liquidation value is treated as a technological constant, the 'scrap value.' In practice, it is more likely that assets are liquidated by being sold, in which case the liquidation value is determined by the market price. Introducing a secondary market on which assets can be sold would complicate the analysis without changing the qualitative features of the model. Allen and Gale (1998) incorporate an asset market and endogenize the liquidation values of assets. Their analysis confirms that the liquidation value will be low for appropriate parameter values.

The economy is divided into four ex ante identical regions, labeled A, B, C, and D. The regional structure is a spatial metaphor that can be interpreted in a variety of ways. The important thing for the analysis is that different regions receive

Table 1. *Regional liquidity shocks*

	A	B	C	D
S_1	ω_H	ω_L	ω_H	ω_L
S_2	ω_L	ω_H	ω_L	ω_H

different liquidity shocks. Any story that motivates different shocks for different (groups of) banks is a possible interpretation of the regional structure. So a region can correspond to a single bank, a geographical region within a country, or an entire country; it can also correspond to a specialized sector within the banking industry.

Each region contains a continuum of ex ante identical consumers (depositors). A consumer has an endowment equal to one unit of the consumption good at date 0 and nothing at dates 1 and 2. Consumers are assumed to have the usual Diamond–Dybvig preferences: with probability ω they are early consumers and value consumption only at date 1; with probability $1 - \omega$ they are late consumers and value consumption only at date 2. Then the preferences of the individual consumer are given by

$$U(c_1, c_2) = \begin{cases} u(c_1) \text{ with probability } \omega \\ u(c_2) \text{ with probability } 1 - \omega, \end{cases}$$

where c_t denotes consumption at date $t = 1, 2$. The period utility functions $u(\cdot)$ are assumed to be twice continuously differentiable, increasing, and strictly concave.

The probability ω varies from region to region. Let ω_i denote the probability of being an early consumer in region i. There are two possible values of ω_i, a high value and a low value, denoted ω_H and ω_L, where $0 < \omega_L < \omega_H < 1$. The realization of these random variables depends on the state of nature. There are two equally likely states S_1 and S_2, and the corresponding realizations of the liquidity preference shocks are given in Table 1. Note that, ex ante, each region has the same probability of having a high liquidity preference shock. Also, the aggregate demand for liquidity is the same in each state: half the regions have a high liquidity preference and half have a low liquidity preference.

All uncertainty is resolved at date 1 when the state of nature S_1 or S_2 is revealed and each consumer learns whether he is an early or late consumer. A consumer's type is not observable, so late consumers can always imitate early consumers.

Before we introduce the banking sector into our story, it will be convenient to characterize the optimal allocation of risk.

III. OPTIMAL RISK SHARING

In this section we characterize optimal risk sharing as the solution to a planning problem. Since consumers are ex ante identical, it is natural to treat consumers symmetrically. For this reason, the planner is assumed to make all the investment and consumption decisions to maximize the unweighted sum of consumer's expected utility.

We begin by describing the planner's problem under the assumption that the planner can identify early and late consumers. The symmetry and concavity of the objective function and the convexity of the constraints simplify the problem considerably. (1) Since there is no aggregate uncertainty, the optimal consumption allocation will be independent of the state. (2) Since the consumers in one region are ex ante identical to consumers in another region, all consumers will be treated alike. Without loss of generality, then, we can assume that every early consumer receives consumption c_1 and every late consumer receives c_2, independently of the region and state of nature. At the first date, the planner chooses a portfolio $(x, y) \geq 0$ subject to the feasibility constraint

$$x + y \leq 1, \tag{1}$$

where x and y are the per capita amounts invested in the long and short assets, respectively. (3) Since the total amount of consumption provided in each period is a constant, it is optimal to provide for consumption at date 1 by holding the short asset and to provide for consumption at date 2 by holding the long asset. Let the average fraction of early consumers be denoted by $\gamma = (\omega_H + \omega_L)/2$. Then the feasibility constraint at date 1 is

$$\gamma c_1 \leq y \tag{2}$$

and the feasibility constraint at date 2 is

$$(1 - \gamma)\, c_2 \leq Rx. \tag{3}$$

At date 0, each consumer has an equal probability of being an early or a late consumer, so the ex ante expected utility is

$$\gamma u(c_1) + (1 - \gamma)\, u(c_2), \tag{4}$$

and this is what the planner seeks to maximize, subject to the constraints (1), (2), and (3). The unique solution to this unconstrained problem is called the *first-best allocation.*

The first-best allocation satisfies the first-order condition $u'(c_1) \geq u'(c_2)$. Otherwise, the objective function could be increased by using the short asset to shift some consumption from early to late consumers. Thus the first-best allocation automatically satisfies the *incentive constraint*

$$c_1 \leq c_2, \tag{5}$$

which says that late consumers find it weakly optimal to reveal their true type rather than pretend to be early consumers. The *incentive-efficient allocation* maximizes the objective function (4) subject to the feasibility constraints (1), (2), and (3) and the incentive constraint (5). What we have shown is that the incentive-efficient allocation is the same as the first-best allocation.

Proposition 1. *The first-best allocation (x, y, c_1, c_2) is equivalent to the incentive-efficient allocation, so the first-best can be achieved even if the planner cannot observe the consumers' types.*

In order to achieve the first-best, the planner has to transfer resources among the different regions. In state S_1, for example, there are ω_H early consumers in regions A and C and ω_L early consumers in regions B and D. Each region has γc_1 units of the short asset, which provide γc_1 units of consumption. So regions A and C each have an excess demand for $(\omega_H - \gamma)c_1$ units of consumption and regions B and D each have an excess supply of $(\gamma - \omega_L)c_1 = (\omega_H - \gamma)c_2$ units of consumption. By reallocating this consumption, the planner can satisfy every region's needs. At date 2, the transfers flow in the opposite direction because regions B and D have an excess demand of $(\omega_H - \gamma)c_2$ units each and regions A and C have an excess supply of $(\omega_H - \gamma)c_2$ units each.

IV. DECENTRALIZATION

In this section we describe how the first-best allocation can be decentralized by a competitive banking sector. There are two reasons for focusing on the first-best. One is technical: it turns out that it is much easier to characterize the equilibrium conditions when the allocation is the first-best. The second reason is that, as usual, we are interested in knowing under what conditions the market 'works.' For the moment, we are concerned only with the feasibility of decentralization. The optimality of the banks' behavior is discussed in Section IXA.

The role of banks is to make investments on behalf of consumers and to insure them against liquidity shocks. We assume that only banks invest in the long asset. This gives the bank two advantages over consumers. First, the banks can hold a portfolio consisting of both types of assets, which will typically be preferred to a portfolio consisting of the short asset alone. Second, by pooling the assets of a large number of consumers, the bank can offer insurance to consumers against their uncertain liquidity demands, giving the early consumers some of the benefits of the high-yielding long asset without subjecting them to the high costs of liquidating the long asset prematurely at the second date.

In each region there is a continuum of identical banks. We focus on a symmetric equilibrium in which all banks adopt the same behavior. Thus we can describe the decentralized allocation in terms of the behavior of a representative bank in each region.

Without loss of generality, we can assume that each consumer deposits his endowment of one unit of the consumption good in the representative bank in his region. The bank invests the deposit in a portfolio $(x^i, y^i) \geq 0$ and, in exchange, offers a deposit contract (c_1^i, c_2^i) that allows the depositor to withdraw either c_1^i units of consumption at date 1 or c_2^i units of consumption at date 2. Note that the deposit contract is not contingent on the liquidity shock in region i. In order to achieve the first-best through a decentralized banking sector, we need to put $(x^i, y^i) = (x, y)$ and $(c_1^i, c_2^i) = (c_1, c_2)$, where (x, y, c_1, c_2) is the first-best allocation.

The problem with this approach is that, while the investment portfolio satisfies the bank's budget constraint $x + y \leq 1$ at the first date, it will not satisfy the budget constraint at the second date. The planner can move consumption between regions, so he needs to satisfy only the average constraint $\gamma c_1 \leq y$. The representative bank, on the other hand, has to face the possibility that the fraction of early consumers in its region may be above average, $\omega_H > \gamma$, in which case it will need more than y to satisfy the demands of the early consumers. It can meet this excess demand by liquidating some of the long asset, but then it will not have enough consumption to meet the demands of the late consumers at date 2. In fact, if r is small enough, the bank may not be able to pay the late consumers even c_1. Then the late consumers will prefer to withdraw at date 1 and store the consumption good until date 2, thus causing a bank run.

There is no overall shortage of liquidity, it is just badly distributed. One way to allow the banks to overcome the maldistribution of the liquidity is to introduce an interbank market in deposits.

A. The Interbank Deposit Market

Suppose that banks are allowed to exchange deposits at the first date. This case of complete markets is illustrated in Figure 1. Each region is negatively correlated with two other regions. We therefore assume that every bank in region i holds $z^i = (\omega_H - \gamma)/2 > 0$ deposits in each of the regions $j \neq i$. Since bank deposits are identical and worth one unit each at the first date, the representative bank's budget constraint will still be satisfied at date 0. At the beginning of the second period the state of nature S is observed, and the banks have to adjust their portfolios to satisfy their budget constraints. If the region has a high demand for liquidity, $\omega^i = \omega_H$, it liquidates all its deposits in other regions. On the other hand, if it has a low demand for liquidity, $\omega^i = \omega_L$, it retains the deposits it holds in the other regions until the final date.

Consider the budget constraint of a bank in a region with a high demand for liquidity. It must pay c_1 to the fraction ω_H of early consumers in its own region and

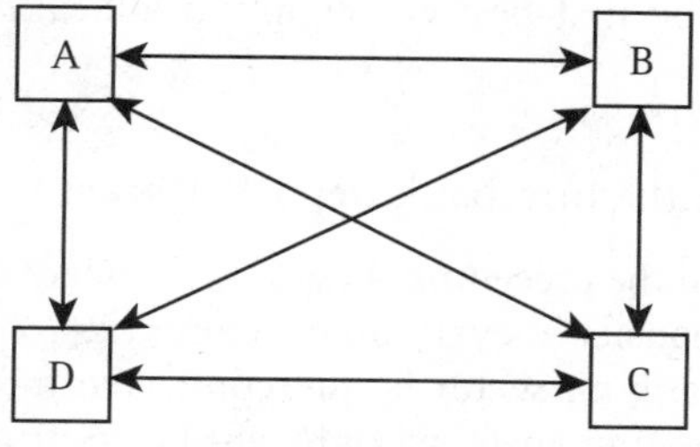

Figure 1. *Complete market structure*

also redeem the $z^j = (\omega_H - \gamma)/2$ deposits of the other high-demand region. So the total demand for repayment is $\{\omega_H + [(\omega_H - \gamma)/2]\}c_1$. On the other side of the ledger, it has y units of the short asset and claims to $3z^i = 3(\omega_H - \gamma)/2$ deposits in the other three regions. Thus, the budget constraint that must be satisfied is

$$\left(\omega_H + \frac{\omega_H - \gamma}{2}\right)c_1 = y + \frac{3(\omega_H - \gamma)}{2},$$

which simplifies to the planner's constraint $\gamma c_1 = y$. A bank in a region with low liquidity demand must pay c_1 to a fraction ω_L of its own depositors and redeem $2z^i = \omega_H - \gamma$ deposits from the banks in the regions with high liquidity demand. It has y units of the short asset to meet these demands, so the budget constraint that must be satisfied is

$$[\omega_L + (\omega_H - \gamma)]c_1 = y.$$

Since $\omega_H - \gamma = \gamma - \omega_L$, this equation simplifies to the planner's constraint $\gamma c_1 = y$. In both cases, the cross holdings of deposits allow the banks to meet the demands of their depositors without liquidating the long asset.

At the last date, all the banks liquidate their remaining assets, and it is easy to show that if the budget constraints at the second date are satisfied, the budget constraints at the third date are automatically satisfied too. For example, the budget constraint at date 2 for a region that had high liquidity preference at date 1 will be

$$[(1 - \omega_H) + (\omega_H - \gamma)]c_2 = Rx,$$

where the left-hand side is the demand for withdrawals, comprising the demand of the late consumers in the region $1 - \omega_H$ plus the demand from the two regions with low liquidity preference, $2z^j = \omega_H - \gamma$. On the right-hand side, we have the liquidation value of the long asset Rx. This simplifies to the planner's constraint $(1 - \gamma)c_2 = Rx$. The same is true of the budget constraint for the regions with a low liquidity shock:

$$\left[(1 - \omega_L) + \frac{\omega_H - \gamma}{2}\right]c_2 = Rx + 3\left(\frac{\omega_H - \gamma}{2}\right)c_2.$$

Thus, by shuffling deposits among the different regions, banks are able to satisfy their budget constraints in each state S and at each date $t = 0, 1, 2$ while providing their depositors with the first-best consumption allocation through a standard deposit contract.

B. Incompleteness in the Interbank Deposit Market

The interbank market in the preceding section is complete in the sense that a bank in region i can hold deposits in every other region $j \neq i$. In some cases, this may not be realistic. The banking sector is interconnected in a variety of ways, but transaction and information costs may prevent banks from acquiring claims on banks in remote regions. To the extent that banks specialize in particular areas of

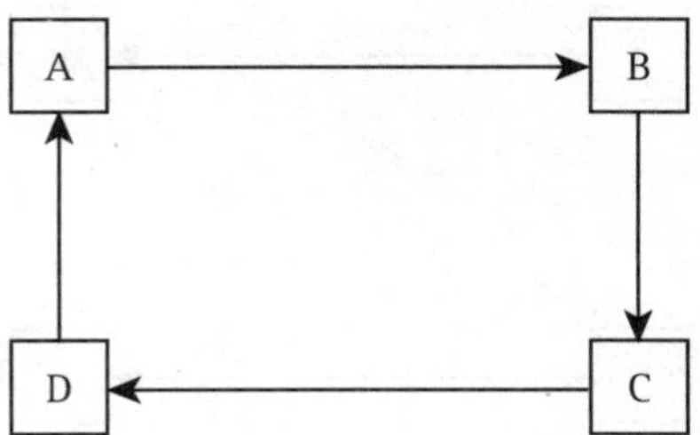

Figure 2. *Incomplete market structure*

business or have closer connections with banks that operate in the same geographical or political unit, deposits may tend to be concentrated in 'neighboring' banks. To capture this effect, which is crucial in the sequel, we introduce the notion of incompleteness in the interbank market by assuming that banks in region i are allowed to hold deposits in some but not all of the other regions. For concreteness we assume that banks in each region hold deposits only in one adjacent region, as shown in Figure 2. It can be seen that banks in region A can hold deposits in region B, banks in region B can hold deposits in region C, and so on.

As before we suppose that the representative bank in region i holds an investment portfolio $(x^i, y^i) = (x, y)$ and offers a deposit contract $(c_1^i, c_2^i) = (c_1, c_2)$. We also assume that the bank holds $z^i = \omega_H - \gamma$ deposits in the adjacent region at the first date; that is, the bank in region A holds $\omega_H - \gamma$ deposits in region B, and so on. The first-period budget constraint is satisfied as before because the exchanges of deposits, having the same values, cancel out, leaving the budget constraint $x + y \leq 1$.

At date 1 the aggregate state is observed, and banks and consumers learn the liquidity shock in each region. As before, we need only to distinguish regions according to whether they have high or low demands for liquidity. Regions with the high liquidity shock ω_H liquidate their deposits in other banks at the second date whereas banks with the low liquidity shock ω_L do not. The market structure that is assumed here has the property that every region with a high liquidity shock has deposits in a region with a low liquidity shock, and vice versa. The budget constraint of a region with high liquidity shocks is

$$\omega_H c_1 = y + (\omega_H - \gamma)c_1,$$

and the budget constraint of a region with low liquidity shocks is

$$[\omega_L + (\omega_H - \gamma)]c_1 = y.$$

Substituting $\omega_H - \gamma = \gamma - \omega_L$ and simplifying, we see that both constraints are equivalent to the planner's constraint $\gamma c_1 = y$. Likewise, at the final date the budget constraints for the regions with high and low liquidity shocks are, respectively,

$$[(1 - \omega_H) + (\omega_H - \gamma)]c_2 = Rx$$

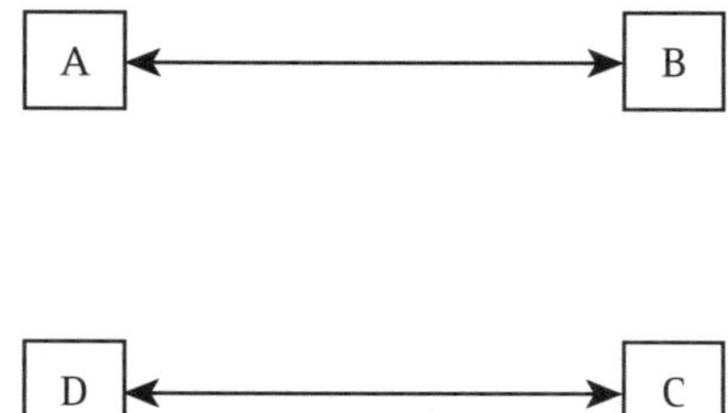

Figure 3. *Disconnected incomplete market structure*

and

$$(1 - \omega_L)c_2 = Rx + (\omega_H - \gamma)c_2,$$

and both are equivalent to the planner's constraint $(1 - \gamma)c_2 = Rx$.

So even if the interbank deposit market is incomplete, it is possible to satisfy the budget constraints by shuffling deposits through the interbank market. However, although it is possible to achieve the first-best with either complete or incomplete markets, we shall see that the implications for financial fragility are very different in the two cases.

One interesting feature of the market structure in Figure 2 is that, although each region is relying on just its neighbor for liquidity, the entire economy is connected. Region A holds deposits in region B, which holds deposits in region C, and so on. In fact, this is unavoidable given the market structure assumed. Consider the alternative market structure shown in Figure 3. Region A holds deposits in region B and region B holds deposits in region A. Likewise, region C holds one unit of deposits in region D and region D holds one unit of deposits in region C. This market structure is more incomplete than the one in Figure 2, and the pattern of holdings in Figure 2 is incompatible with it. However, it is possible to achieve the first-best through the pattern of holdings in Figure 3. This is true even though the economy is disconnected, since regions A and B trade with each other but not with regions C and D and regions C and D trade with each other but not with regions A and B. Again, these patterns do not seem to have any significance as far as achieving the first-best is concerned; but they turn out to have striking differences for financial fragility.

V. FRAGILITY

To illustrate the *financial fragility* of the optimal risk-sharing allocation, we use the decentralization results from Section IV. Then we perturb the model to allow for the occurrence of a state S in which the aggregate demand for liquidity is greater than the system's ability to supply liquidity and show that this can lead to an economywide crisis.

The market structure is assumed to be given by Figure 2. The corresponding allocation requires each bank to hold an initial portfolio of investments (x, y) and

Table 2. *Regional liquidity shocks with perturbation*

	A	B	C	D
S_1	ω_H	ω_L	ω_H	ω_L
S_2	ω_L	ω_H	ω_L	ω_H
$\bar{S}$	$\gamma + \epsilon$	γ	γ	γ

offer a deposit contract (c_1, c_2), where (x, y, c_1, c_2) is the first-best allocation. In order to make this deposit contract feasible, the representative bank in each region holds $z = \omega_H - \gamma$ deposits in the adjacent region. Note that z is the minimal amount that is needed to satisfy the budget constraints. It will become apparent that larger cross holdings of deposits, while consistent with the first-best in Section IV, would make the contagion problem worse.

Now, let us take the allocation as given and consider what happens when we 'perturb' the model. By a perturbation we mean the realization of a state $\bar{S}$ that was assigned zero probability at date 0 and has a demand for liquidity that is very close to that of the states that do occur with positive probability. Specifically, the liquidity shocks are given in Table 2. In state $\bar{S}$, every region has the previous average demand for liquidity γ except for region A, where the demand for liquidity is somewhat higher at $\gamma + \epsilon$ The important fact is that the average demand for liquidity across all four regions is slightly higher than in the normal states S_1 and S_2. Since the abnormal state $\bar{S}$ occurs with zero probability, it will not change the allocation at date 0. In states S_1 and S_2 the continuation equilibrium will be the same as before at date 1; in state $\bar{S}$ the continuation equilibrium will be different.

In the continuation equilibrium beginning at date 1, consumers will optimally decide whether to withdraw their deposits at date 1 or date 2, and banks will liquidate their assets in an attempt to meet the demands of their depositors. Early consumers always withdraw at date 1; late consumers will withdraw at date 1 or date 2 depending on which gives them the larger amount of consumption. Because we want to focus on essential bank crises, we assume that late consumers will always withdraw their deposits at date 2 if it is (weakly) optimal for them to do so. Banks are required to meet their promise to pay c_1 units of consumption to each depositor who demands withdrawal at date 1. If they cannot do so, they must liquidate all their assets at date 1. As in Allen and Gale (1998), the proceeds of the liquidation are split pro rata among depositors (i.e., we do *not* assume first come, first served). If the bank can meet its obligations at date 1, then the remaining assets are liquidated at date 2 and given to the depositors who have waited until date 2 to withdraw. In the rest of this section, we describe the continuation equilibrium at date 1 in state $\bar{S}$, assuming the actions consistent with the first-best at date 0.

A. The Liquidation 'Pecking Order'

At date 1 a bank can find itself in one of three conditions. A bank is said to be *solvent* if it can meet the demands of every depositor who wants to withdraw (including banks in other regions) by using only its liquid assets, that is, the short asset and the deposits in other regions. The bank is said to be *insolvent* if it can meet the demands of its deposits but only by liquidating some of the long asset. Finally, the bank is said to be *bankrupt* if it cannot meet the demands of its depositors by liquidating all its assets.

These definitions are motivated by the assumption that banks will always find it preferable to liquidate assets in a particular order at date 1. We call this the 'pecking order' for liquidating assets, and it goes as follows: first, the bank liquidates the short asset, then it liquidates deposits, and finally it liquidates the long asset. To ensure that the long asset is liquidated last, we need an additional assumption,

$$\frac{R}{r} > \frac{c_2}{c_1}, \tag{6}$$

which is maintained in the sequel. Since the first-best consumption allocation (c_1, c_2) is independent of r (this variable does not appear in the first-best problem in Section III), we can always ensure that condition (6) is satisfied by choosing r sufficiently small.

Each of the three assets offers a different cost of obtaining current (date 1) consumption in terms of future (date 2) consumption. The cheapest is the short asset. One unit of the short asset is worth one unit of consumption today, and if reinvested in the short asset, it is worth one unit of consumption tomorrow. So the cost of obtaining liquidity by liquidating the short asset is one. Similarly, by liquidating one unit of deposits, the bank gives up c_2 units of future consumption and obtains c_1 units of present consumption. So the cost of obtaining liquidity by liquidating deposits is c_2/c_1. From the first-order condition $u'(c_1) = Ru'(c_2)$, we know that $c_2/c_1 > 1$. Finally, by liquidating one unit of the long asset, the bank gives up R units of future consumption and obtains r units of present consumption. So the cost of obtaining liquidity by liquidating the long asset is R/r. Thus we have derived the pecking order, short assets, deposits, long assets:

$$1 < \frac{c_2}{c_1} < \frac{R}{r}.$$

In order to maximize the interests of depositors, the bank must liquidate the short asset before it liquidates deposits in other regions before it liquidates the long asset.

The preceding argument assumes that the banks in other regions are not bankrupt. The bankruptcy rules require all assets to be liquidated immediately, so all deposit holders in a bankrupt institution will want to liquidate their deposits immediately regardless of their own condition.

B. Liquidation Values

The value of a deposit at date 1 is c_1 if the bank is not bankrupt, and it is equal to the liquidation value of all the bank's assets if the bank is bankrupt. Let q^i denote the value of the representative bank's deposits in region i at date 1. If $q^i < c_1$, then all the depositors will withdraw as much as they can at date 1. In particular, the banks in other regions will be seeking to withdraw their claims on the bank at the same time the bank is trying to redeem its claims on them. *All depositors must be treated equally*; that is, every depositor gets q^i from the bank for each unit invested at the first date, whether the depositor is a consumer or a bank from another region. Then the values of q^i must be determined simultaneously. Consider the representative bank in region A, for example. If all the depositors withdraw, the total demands will be $1 + z$, since the banks in region D hold z deposits and the consumers in region A hold one deposit. The liabilities of the bank are valued at $(1 + z)q^A$. The assets consist of y units of the short asset, x units of the long asset, and z deposits in region B. The assets are valued at $y + rx + zq^B$. The equilibrium values of q^A must equate the value of assets and liabilities:

$$q^A = \frac{y + rx + zq^B}{1 + z}. \tag{7}$$

A similar equation must hold for any region i in which $q^i < c_1$.

If $q^B = c_1$, then we can use this equation to calculate the value of q^A; but if $q^B < c_1$, then we need another equation to determine q^B; this equation will include the value of q^C, and so on.

C. Buffers and Bank Runs

Suppose that a bank is insolvent and has to liquidate some of the long asset. For the moment, we assume that the late consumers wait until the last date, and we ignore the role of banks in other regions. How much can the bank afford to give the consumers at the first date? The bank must give the late consumers at least c_1 at date 2; otherwise they would be better off withdrawing at date 1. So a bank with a fraction ω of early consumers must keep at least $(1 - \omega)c_1/R$ units of the long asset to satisfy the late consumers at date 2. Then the amount of the long asset that can be liquidated at date 1 is $x - [(1 - \omega)c_1/R]$, and the amount of consumption that can be obtained by liquidating the long asset without causing a run is

$$b(\omega) = r\left[x - \frac{(1 - \omega)\, c_1}{R}\right].$$

We call $b(\omega)$ the bank's buffer.

In region A, the bank has $y = \gamma c_1$ units of the short asset. The fraction of early consumers is $\gamma + \epsilon$ in state $\bar{S}$, so in order to pay each early consumer c_1 units of consumption, the bank will have to get ϵc_1 units of consumption by liquidating the long asset. This is feasible, without any help from the banks in other regions, if and only if the increased demand for liquidity ϵc_1 is less than the buffer:

$$\epsilon c_1 \leq b(y + \epsilon). \tag{8}$$

In most of what follows, we assume that condition (8) is violated. In other words, if region A had to remain self-sufficient, it would be bankrupt because there is no way it can feasibly offer its late consumers c_1 at date 2 (to prevent a run) and meet the demands of its early consumers for c_1 at date 1.

When $\epsilon > 0$ is small enough to satisfy the inequality (8), the banks in region A are insolvent, but there are no repercussions for the banks in other regions. The late consumers in region A are worse off because the premature liquidation of the long asset at date 1 prevents the bank from paying c_2 to depositors at date 2. (The pecking order implies that the banks in regions B, C, and D will liquidate their deposits in regions C, D, and A, respectively, rather than liquidate the long asset.)

When ϵ is large enough to violate condition (8), banks in region A will be bankrupt. Although they have deposits in region B, these deposits are of no use as long as the value of deposits in region A is $q^A = c_1$. Other regions will liquidate their deposits in order to avoid liquidating the long asset. As long as all the deposits have the same value, the mutual withdrawals simply cancel out. Once the banks in region A are bankrupt, there will be a spillover effect to region D. A deposit in region D is worth $q^D = c_1$ and a deposit in region A is worth $q^A < c_1$, so banks in region D suffer a loss when cross holdings of deposits are liquidated. If ε is not too large, this spillover effect will make region D banks insolvent but will not force them into bankruptcy.

Once bankruptcy has occurred in region A, all consumers are withdrawing at date 1 and the distinction between early and late consumers is immaterial. A further increase in ε will have no effect. The spillover effect to region D may be larger or smaller than region D's buffer. If the spillover is smaller than the buffer, the banks in region D will lose part of their buffer but the contagion will spread no further. If the spillover is larger than the buffer in region D, then region D banks will be bankrupt too.

The size of the spillover will depend on a number of parameters, especially the size of the liquidation value r. If r is small, then the loss of asset value in region A is large and the spillover effect is large. A small value of r also makes the buffer in each region smaller. Thus there are two ways in which a small liquidation value r makes it more likely that the spillover will exceed the buffer in region D.

The liquidation of region D's long assets will cause a loss to banks in region C, and this time the accumulated spillover effect is already large enough that region C too will be bankrupt. As we go from region to region the spillover gets larger and larger, because more regions are in bankruptcy and more losses have accumulated from liquidating the long asset. So once region D goes bankrupt, all the regions go bankrupt. This result is summarized in proposition 2 below.

As this informal discussion suggests, two conditions must be satisfied in order for the initial shock to region A to spread to all the other regions. First, the liquidity preference shock in region A must exceed the buffer in region A:

$$\epsilon c_1 > b(\gamma + \epsilon). \tag{9}$$

Second, the spillover effect to region D must exceed the buffer in region D. A lower bound for the spillover effect is $z(c_1 - \bar{q}^A)$, where z is the amount of deposits held and $\bar{q}^A$ is an upper bound on the value of the deposits in region A under bankruptcy. To derive the upper bound $\bar{q}^A$, we use equation (7) and assume that $q^B = c_1$:

$$q^A \leq \bar{q}^A = \frac{y + rx + zc_1}{1 + z}. \tag{10}$$

Then a sufficient condition for the spillover to exceed the buffer in region D is

$$z(c_1 - \bar{q}^A) > b(\gamma). \tag{11}$$

The term zc_1 is the amount promised to the banks in region C, and $z\bar{q}^A$ is the upper bound on the value of deposits in region A. Hence the left-hand side of the condition is the difference between liabilities and the upper bound on assets in the interbank deposit market for region D. If this exceeds region D's buffer, the spillover will force region D banks into bankruptcy.

Proposition 2. *Consider the model with market structure described in Figure 2 and perturb it by the addition of the zero probability state $\bar{S}$. Suppose that each bank chooses an investment portfolio (x, y, z) and offers a deposit contract (c_1, c_2), where (x, y) is the first-best investment portfolio, (c_1, c_2) is the first-best consumption allocation, and $z = \omega_H - \gamma$. Suppose that conditions (9) and (11) are satisfied. Then, in any continuation equilibrium, the banks in all regions must go bankrupt at date 1 in state $\bar{S}$.*

Proof. The proof requires several steps.

Step 1. We first suppose that there is a continuation equilibrium in which $q^i = c_1$ in every region i and show that this leads to a contradiction. The demand for deposits from early consumers is $\gamma + \epsilon$ in region A and γ in regions B, C, and D. The stock of the short asset is $y = \gamma c_1$, so there is an aggregate excess demand for liquidity that can be met only by liquidating the long asset in some region. To avoid liquidating the long asset, banks must redeem at least as many deposits as are withdrawn by banks from other regions. Since no bank wants to liquidate the long asset if it can be avoided, the only equilibrium is one in which all banks simultaneously withdraw their deposits in banks in other regions at date 1. These mutual withdrawals offset each other, so each region is forced to be self-sufficient; that is, no region is able to get extra liquidity from the other regions.

We have already seen that self-sufficiency implies that the banks in region A are bankrupt. Thus we have a contradiction that implies that the banks in some region must be bankrupt. In fact, the banks in region A must be bankrupt. By the earlier argument, $q^i < c_1$ for some i implies that all banks will withdraw their deposits in other regions. Then either $q^B = c_1$ and region A receives no net inflows from the interbank market or $q^B < c_1$ and the situation is even worse because region A loses money on its deposits in region B. In either case, $q^A = c_1$ is impossible because of condition (9).

Step 2. Having established that banks in region A must be bankrupt, we next show that the financial crisis must extend to other regions. Consider region D first. For the reasons explained above, all banks will be liquidating their deposits in other regions in any continuation equilibrium in state $\bar{S}$. An upper bound on the liquidation value q^A of the deposits in region A is obtained by assuming that $q^B = c_1$, that is, $q^A \leq \bar{q}^A$. If banks in region D are not bankrupt, the liabilities of the banks in region D are $(\gamma + z)c_1$, because a fraction γ of consumers withdraw early, the banks in region C withdraw z deposits, and each deposit is worth c_1. The liquid assets of the bank are worth $y + zq^A$, and the buffer $b(\gamma)$ is the most that can be obtained from liquidating the long asset without violating the incentive constraint. So, to avoid bankruptcy, it must be the case that

$$\begin{aligned}(\gamma + z)c_1 &\leq y + b(\gamma) + zq^A \\ &\leq y + b(\gamma) + z\bar{q}^A.\end{aligned}$$

Since $\gamma c_1 = y$, this inequality implies that $z(c_1 - \bar{q}^A) \leq b(\gamma)$, contradicting condition (11). Thus the banks in region D must be bankrupt also.

Step 3. The argument from step 2 can be continued by induction. In fact, since we know that $\bar{q}^A < c_1$, we must have $q^D < \bar{q}^A$. Then it is easier to violate the nonbankruptcy condition in region C than it was in region D, and this shows that $q^C < \bar{q}^A$. Then using the same argument, we have $q^i < \bar{q}^A$ for every region i. All regions are in bankruptcy, and the only possible continuation equilibrium is one in which $q^i = y + rx < c_1$ for $i =$ A, B, C, D. □

VI. ROBUSTNESS

The incompleteness of markets in figure 2 is essential to the contagion result in the following sense. There exist parameter values for which any equilibrium with incomplete markets involves runs in state $\bar{S}$ (this is the set of parameter values characterized in section V). For the same parameter values, we can find an equilibrium with complete markets that does not involve runs in state $\bar{S}$.

To see this, we go back to the complete markets equilibrium in Section IV. The values of the investment portfolio (x, y) and the deposit contract (c_1, c_2) are the same; but to make the first-best allocation feasible at dates 1 and 2, the representative bank holds $z/2 = (\omega_H - \gamma)/2$ deposits in each of the other regions. The claim on any one region is smaller than in the equilibrium in Section V, but the total claim $3z/2$ is larger. Again, $z/2$ is the smallest amount of deposits consistent with feasibility.

Consider now what happens in a continuation equilibrium at date 1 when state $\bar{S}$ occurs, assuming that the actions at date 0 have not changed. We assume, of course, that the conditions of proposition 2 continue to hold. Using exactly the same argument as before, we can show that banks in region A are bankrupt: there is an aggregate excess demand for liquidity, the other regions will not provide liquidity, and because condition (8) is violated the banks in region A cannot meet their depositors' demands. The question is whether this requires that the other regions should also experience bankruptcy.

To address this question, we have to calculate the liquidation value of the deposits in region A. Assuming that none of the other regions is bankrupt, we observe that the assets are valued at $y + rx + 3(z/2)c_1$ and the liabilities are valued at $[1 + (3z/2)]q^{\mathrm{A}}$, so

$$\bar{q}^{\mathrm{A}*} = \frac{y + rx + 3(z/2)c_1}{1 + (3z/2)}. \tag{12}$$

The loss to each bank in regions $j \neq \mathrm{A}$ because of the collapse of banks in region A is $(z/2)\,(c_1 - \bar{q}^{\mathrm{A}*})$, and since the bank's holding of the short asset y is just enough to satisfy its own early consumers, the bank will be insolvent, but not bankrupt, if and only if this amount is less than or equal to the buffer:

$$\left(\frac{z}{2}\right)(c_1 - \bar{q}^{\mathrm{A}*}) \leq b(\gamma). \tag{13}$$

Condition (13) can be satisfied even though conditions (8) and (11) are violated because the financial interdependence, measured by $z/2$, is smaller.

The special nature of the incompleteness of markets in figure 2 is discussed in the following section.

VII. CONTAINMENT

The critical ingredient in the example of contagion analyzed in Section V is that any two regions are connected by a chain of overlapping bank liabilities. Banks in region A have claims on banks in region B, which in turn have claims on banks in region C, and so on. If we could cut this chain at some point, the contagion that begins with a small shock in region A would be contained in a subset of the set of regions.

Consider the incomplete market structure in Figure 3 and the allocation that implements the first-best, which was described in Section IV. The allocation requires banks in regions A and B to have claims on each other and banks in regions C and D to have claims on each other, but there is no connection between the region {A, B} and the region {C, D}. If state $\bar{S}$ occurs, the excess demand for liquidity will cause bankruptcies in region A, and they may under certain conditions spread to region B; but there is no reason why they should spread any further. Banks in regions C and D are simply not connected to the troubled banks in regions A and B.

Comparing the three market structures we have considered so far—complete markets in Figure 1, incomplete markets in Figure 2, and the disconnected market structure in Figure 3—we can see that there is a nonmonotonic relationship between completeness or incompleteness of markets and the extent of the financial crisis in state $\overline{S}$. With the complete markets structure of Figure 1 the crisis is restricted to region A, with the market structure in Figure 2 the crisis extends to all regions, and with the market structure in Figure 3 the crisis is restricted to regions A and B.

It could be argued that the market structures are not monotonically ordered: the complete markets network does contain the other two, but the paths in the network in Figure 3 are not a subset of the network in Figure 2. This could be changed by adding paths to Figure 2, but then the equilibrium of Figure 3 would also be an equilibrium of Figure 2. This raises an obvious but important point: that contagion depends on the *endogenous* pattern of financial claims. An incomplete market structure like the one in Figure 2 may preclude a complete pattern of financial connectedness and thus encourage financial contagion; but a complete market structure does not imply the opposite: even with complete markets, there may be an endogenous choice of overlapping claims that causes contagion. In fact, the three equilibria considered so far are all consistent with the complete market structure. There are additional equilibria for the economy with the complete market structure. Like the three considered so far, they achieve the first-best in states S_1 and S_2 but have different degrees of financial fragility in the unexpected state $\overline{S}$, depending on the patterns of interregional deposit holding.

What is important about the market structure in Figure 2, then, is that the pattern of interregional cross holdings of deposits that promotes the possibility of contagion is the only one consistent with this market structure. Since we are interested in contagion as an essential phenomenon, this market structure has a special role. The complete markets economy, by contrast, has equilibria with and without contagion and provides a weaker case for the likelihood of contagion.

VIII. ALTERNATIVE INTERBANK MARKETS

In our analysis of contagion, interbank deposits play an important role. Without the interlinkages they provide, the financial crisis would not spread between regions. An important issue is whether there exist alternatives to interbank deposits that achieve risk sharing in states S_1 and S_2 but avoid contagion in state $\overline{S}$. In the context of banks' interactions with ordinary depositors in the retail market, it is well known from the work of Diamond and Dybvig (1983) and before that the combination of liquid liabilities (in the form of demand deposits) and illiquid assets is essential to the theory of bank runs. Runs can be prevented by making the amount paid out contingent on asset returns or by 'suspending convertibility.' The rationale for standard deposit contracts is not entirely clear, though some attempts have been made (see, e.g., Calomiris and Kahn 1991); but at least there is clear empirical evidence that deposit contracts are used. However, in the context of interbank markets, where deposit contracts are not as widely used, it is natural to ask whether there are feasible alternatives that would prevent runs.

Once we accept that consumers hold demand deposits, it is inevitable that banks in region A will come under pressure in state $\overline{S}$. What leads to contagion is the fact that (a) banks have an incentive to hoard liquidity when there is an excess demand for it and that (b) once bankruptcies have occurred in one or more regions, spillovers result from the ex ante claims that banks hold on each other. The crucial property of the claims traded on the interbank market is not that they are noncontingent. Rather, it is the fact that banks, by simultaneously liquidating their claims on each other, can effectively cancel them until at least one region goes bankrupt. Once banks in one region are bankrupt, the claims on that region have lower value and a spillover to its creditors follows.

Making the interbank claims contingent would not change the operation of the contagion. A similar result holds if the security traded on the interbank market is contingent on the state or on the level of demand for liquidity. As long as the holdings are symmetric across regions and the liquidation of cross holdings nets out to zero, so that region A has to find additional liquidity on its own, there will be contagion when the shock in region A is sufficiently large and the conditions of Proposition 2 are satisfied.

This argument shows us that the use of demand deposits in the interbank market is not analogous to the use of demand deposits in the retail market. The two markets operate in very different ways. In the retail market, it is generally accepted that suspension of convertibility would prevent a bank run. The opposite is true in the interbank market. To illustrate this idea, suppose that interbank deposits are not payable on demand. Instead, banks can refuse payment at their own discretion. This kind of contract in the interbank market will support the first-best allocation (when the probability of $\overline{S}$ is zero), but it clearly will not prevent contagion in state $\overline{S}$. The reason is that banks will invoke their right to delay payment whenever they would otherwise have to liquidate the long asset. The option to delay payment is no different from using claims on other regions to cancel out the claims of those regions in the earlier analysis. The result in both cases is that banks in region A will have to satisfy the extra demand ϵ from ordinary depositors in state $\overline{S}$ from their own resources. This entails liquidating the long asset, and when their buffer is exhausted, it entails bankruptcy.

This argument shows that provided that there are ex ante contracts between banks that are signed at date 0, a contagion will occur even if contracts are not demand deposits. However, if liquidity was provided on an ex post basis, there would be no possibility of contagion. Suppose, for example, that instead of an interbank market for deposits at the first date, there is an interbank market for one-period loans at the second date. Then a bank that finds it has an excess demand for liquidity at date 1 has no preexisting claim on banks in other regions, but it can borrow from banks in regions with an excess suppley of liquidity. In states like S_1 and S_2, this mechanism will be enough to achieve the first-best. If the lending rate is ρ, then the markets will clear if $1 + \rho = c_2/c_1$. In state $\overline{S}$, however, there will be an economywide shortage of liquidity. The fraction of early consumers is $\gamma+\epsilon$ in region A and γ in the other regions; but there is only enough of the short asset in the economy to provide for a fraction γ of early consumers. The only way in which more liquidity can be provided to the banks in region A is for the long asset to be liquidated. The other regions will be willing to do this only if the rate of interest on loans compensates for the cost of liquidation: $1+\rho=R/r$. At this rate, the cost of borrowing is too high to be of any help to the banks in region A. It is just like liquidating more of the long asset, and we have already assumed that the bank is liquidating as much as it can, subject to the incentive constraint.

So the interbank loan market turns out to be of no use in state $\overline{S}$, where there is an economywide shortage of liquidity. It protects other regions from contagion but does nothing to stop the crisis in the affected region.

Although ex post markets allow banks to meet their liquidity needs at date 1, given the first-best choices at date 0, this arrangement is not an equilibrium. If banks expect to be able to borrow and lend at the rate ρ, they will not make the first-best choices at date 0. Thus, if the probability of contagion is very small, there will be a welfare loss associated with ex post markets. In richer models, ex post markets to provide liquidity will have problems associated with them. In particular, there can be a *lemons* problem if banks that have low asset values are more likely to use the ex post loan market than banks that have high asset values. Then it will be difficult for lenders to distinguish between banks that are in trouble because of poor loan performance and banks whose depositors have higher than average liquidity needs. The lemons problem may lead to extremely high interest rates on the ex post interbank market or even to a breakdown of the ex post interbank market. An alternative would be to negotiate a risk-sharing arrangement ex ante, when information is symmetric, and thus avoid the lemons problem altogether.

Another problem with ex post interbank markets arises when lenders have some *monopoly* power. Banks with excess liquidity can exploit banks with insufficient liquidity. Anticipating the possibility of a 'holdup,' banks will prefer to enter into an ex ante risk-sharing arrangement that fixes the price of liquidity at the risk of contagion.

We have argued that ex post markets can provide liquidity, without risk of contagion, when the uncertainty arises only from liquidity shocks. When uncertainty arises from other sources, however, ex post markets may not be feasible. Consider, for example, the case in which the liquidity shock ω_i is nonstochastic but the return to the long asset in region i is a random variable R_i. If the returns are not perfectly correlated across regions, there will be gains from sharing risks, and this will lead banks to hold claims on each other. For appropriately specified contracts, the first-best can be achieved through an ex ante interbank market. Ex post, however, there will be no possibility of risk sharing once the values of the random variables $\{R_i\}$ are known. We chose not to examine this case formally here because of the complexity of the analysis and because the specification of the bankruptcy rules becomes somewhat arbitrary, but it is clear that ex post arrangements will not work in this case. The implications of asset risk are discussed further in Section IXD.

An interesting question is what kinds of arrangements banks will choose to set up, given the trade-off between the individual benefits of access to liquidity and the social costs of contagion. This is an important topic for further study.

IX. DISCUSSION

A. Equilibrium

In the preceding sections we have discussed the continuation equilibrium at dates 1 and 2 but not said anything about the equilibrium behavior at date 0. It is clear that it is optimal for consumers at date 0 to deposit their endowment with the banks because they could not achieve the same level of expected utility in autarky, even if they were able to invest in both the short and the long assets. What is less obvious is whether the behavior of the banks is optimal in some sense.

The bank has to choose an investment portfolio, a deposit contract, and a position in the interbank deposit market to maximize the consumers' expected utility at date 0. The tricky part is choosing how much to trade on the interbank market. In order to finance deposists in other regions, it will have to sell its own deposits to other banks. But the value of its deposits will depend on the choice of the investment portfolio and the deposit contract and the withdrawal decisions made by depositors at the second and third dates. We can finesse the complex calculation of the banks' optimal behavior by noting that since all trade is voluntary, anything the bank does to make its own consumers better off cannot make anyone else worse off (since a single bank is negligible, the rest of the economy gets zero surplus from trading with it). Then the fact that the allocation at the second and third dates if first-best optimal implies that there is no deviation that the bank would prefer.

When the probability of a bank crisis is positive, things become much more complicated. The absence of aggregate uncertainty is necessary for the achievement of the first-best. When the probability of a crisis is positive, the first-best is no longer achieved at date 0, and as a result, markets for individual risk sharing are incomplete. As is well known, when markets are incomplete the valuation of assets may vary from individual to individual, there may be a lack of unanimity about the proper objective function for a bank, and the feasible actions for a bank are difficult to characterize.

However, although we have not extended the theory to the more general case, we do not believe that our results are dependent on the assumption that the probability of a crisis is exactly zero. As an illustration, consider the model described in Section V, but make it symmetric by assuming that each of the four regions has an equal probability of being the one with an excess demand for liquidity. The shocks are described in Table 3, where each of the special states $S_A, \ldots, S_D$ occurs

Table 3. *Regional liquidity shocks with symmetric perturbation*

	A	B	C	D
S_1	ω_H	ω_L	ω_H	ω_L
S_2	ω_L	ω_H	ω_L	ω_H
S_A	$\gamma+\epsilon$	γ	γ	γ
S_B	γ	$\gamma+\epsilon$	γ	γ
S_C	γ	γ	$\gamma+\epsilon$	γ
S_D	γ	γ	γ	$\gamma+\epsilon$

with probability $\delta>0$ and states S_1 and S_2 occur with probabilities $1/2 - 2\delta$. At date 0 each of the regions is ex ante identical.

Now suppose that risk sharing is to be achieved through a decentralized banking system of the kind described in Section V, but assume that all decisions at date 0 are made by a central planner. The planner will seek to maximize the ex ante expected utility of the representative agent at date 0. He can make any feasible decisions he likes at date 0, but he is constrained to work through the decentralized banking system at dates 1 and 2. In particular, he must use demand deposits to provide risk sharing for individuals and banks. Considerations of continuity imply that when δ is small, he must be able to get close to the first-best for the limiting economy with $\delta=0$. If (c_1^δ, c_2^δ) is the optimal demand deposit and (x^δ, y^δ) is the optimal portfolio for $\delta>0$, then $(c_1^\delta, c_2^\delta)\rightarrow(c_1, c_2)$ and $(x^\delta, y^\delta)\rightarrow(x, y)$ as $\delta\rightarrow 0$, where (c_1, c_2) is the optimal allocation and (x, y) the optimal portfolio from the planner's problem in Section III. This follows from continuity and the uniqueness of the planner's optimum. But then the arguments that we have used in Section V imply that in states $S_A, \ldots, S_D$ there must be contagion under the conditions given in Section V when δ is sufficiently small. So even if a planner were coordinating the choices made at date 0, there will still be contagion at date 1 in a decentralized banking system.

The reason for this can readily be seen. The way to prevent contagion is to hold a discrete amount more of the liquid asset to meet the extra liquidity demand in states $S_A, \ldots, S_D$. However, holding more of the liquid asset means that less of the illiquid asset is held and output is lower at date 2 in states S_1 and S_2. When δ is sufficiently small, this trade-off is not worthwhile. It is better to simply allow the possibility of contagion.

The fact that the allocation at the second and third dates is constrained efficient rather than first-best efficient for $\delta>0$ means that decentralized banks may not make even approximately the same choices as the planner at date 0. Such behavior would yield an ϵ-Nash equilibrium, but the action profile of an ϵ-Nash equilibrium does not have to be close in any sense to the action profile of a Nash equilibrium, however small ε becomes. Even though everyone would be better off if every bank made the same choices as a planner, they may all find it in their interests (in equilibrium) to behave in a very different way. It may even be true that this date 0 behavior is inconsistent with contagion at date 1; but although this is a theoretical possibility, we cannot think of any reason why it should occur and in fact are quite dubious that it would occur. This is an important topic for future research, but it lies outside the scope of this paper.

B. Many States and Regions

The arguments developed in this paper extend easily to the case of many regions and many states of nature. Suppose that there are n regions and suppose that the liquidity shocks ω^i are finite-valued and exchangeable. If the economywide fraction of early consumers is a constant, then the first-best allocation (x, y, c_1, c_2) is nonstochastic and independent of the consumer's region.

A market structure is characterized by a family of neighborhoods: for each region i the neighborhood N^i is the set of regions in which a bank in region i can hold deposits. The market structure is *connected* if for any regions i and j there is a finite chain of regions, beginning with i and ending with j such that, for each adjacent pair, banks in the first region can hold deposits in the second. As long as the market structure is connected and the maintained assumptions hold, the first-best can be decentralized by a competitive banking sector using standard deposit contracts.

A market structure is complete if banks in regions i can hold deposits in every other region $j \neq i$; otherwise it is incomplete. The degree of completeness and connectedness is crucial for determining the inevitability of contagion. When markets are complete, increasing the number of regions eventually eliminates the necessity of contagion for any fixed set of parameter values. The reason is that the initial impact of a liquidity shortage in a single region becomes negligible as the number of regions becomes unboundedly large. In this sense, the banking system is robust against any shock to a single region when the economy is sufficiently large and markets are complete.

On the other hand, when markets are incomplete and the economy is large, small shocks can have extremely large effects. In the example of Section V, a liquidity shortage in one region can lead to crises in all four regions. The same argument works with any number of regions. In fact, as contagion 'spreads' from one region to another, the spillovers become larger and it is easier to keep the contagion going. In the general case, contagion can spread from a single region to an arbitrarily large number n of regions.

In this sense, the results for the example of Section V are quite strong and are easily extended to large, complex economies.

C. Sunspot Equilibria

This paper focuses on financial contagion as an essential feature of equilibrium. We do not rely on arguments involving multiple equilibria. The aim is instead to show that under certain conditions every continuation equilibrium at date 1 exhibits financial contagion. Nonetheless, there are multiple equilibria in the model, and if one is so disposed one can use the multiplicity of equilibria to tell a story about financial contagion as a sunspot phenomenon.

To illustrate the multiplicity as simply as possible, suppose that markets are complete and the fraction of early consumers in each region is nonstochastic and equal to γ. There are no interregional cross holdings of deposits at date 0. If every consumer in every bank chooses to withdraw his deposit at date 1, regardless of the size of the liquidity shock, then the banks will all be bankrupt because $c_1 > y + rx$. This outcome is an equilibrium because it is optimal for each individual depositor to withdraw assuming that all other depositors withdraw. Of course, there also exists an equilibrium in which late consumers choose not to withdraw until date 2 and the bank's portfolio (x, y) allows the first-best to be achieved.

The low-probability event $\bar{S}$ is now a 'sunspot.' It represents extraneous uncertainty that does not change the demand for liquidity but simply triggers the self-fulfilling prophecy that a bank run will occur. The outcome in terms of the pattern of bank runs in state $\bar{S}$ is the same as in Section V. Whether one wants to call this a contagion is a matter of taste.

D. Risky Assets

For simplicity, we have assumed that the long asset has a nonstochastic return, but it would be more realistic to assume that the long asset is risky. In Allen and Gale (1998), the long asset is risky and bank runs are triggered by negative information about future asset returns. In the present framework, uncertainty about long asset returns could be used both to motivate interregional cross holdings of deposits and to provoke insolvency or bankruptcy. The results should be similar. What is crucial for the results is that the financial interconnectedness between the regions takes the form of claims held by banks in one region on banks in another region.

If, instead of holding claims on banks in other regions, banks were to invest directly in the long assets of that region, there would be a spillover effect, but it would be much weaker. To see this, suppose that banks in region A hold some of the long asset in region B. If asset returns are low in region B, then the depositors in region A must accept a reduction in consumption, but that is all. As long as the banks in region A are not bankrupt, they can afford to wait until date 2 to get the higher return $R > r$. Banks in region B, which hold a large proportion of their assets in region B, are forced to liquidate their assets at date 1 and therefore suffer a much greater loss because $r < R$.

On the other hand, if the banks in region A had invested in the banks in region B, then they would suffer a larger loss when the banks in region B liquidate their assets.

Another way in which banks can invest indirectly in risky assets is to lend to investors. If banks cannot observe the investment portfolio chosen by the investors, the investors will engage in risk shifting. Allen and Gale (2000) show that this kind of behavior can lead to bubbles in asset prices and increase the probability of a banking crisis (general default).

E. Alternative Market Structures

Figures 1–3 do not exhaust the possible range of market structures that could exist given the four regions A, B, C, and D. There are two more structures that are substantively different (we ignore the switching of identical regions, such as A for C or B for D). The first alternative is like Figure 2, but with regions B and C interchanged. In this case, region A's and region B's deposits are made with positively correlated regions rather than with negatively correlated regions as in Figure 2. This does not prevent the achievement of the first-best. However, the size of deposits banks must hold if the first-best allocation is doubled. Depending on the state and date, regions will be required to satisfy not only their own liquidity needs but that of the region next to them. In order to do this they must hold twice the deposits they did with Figure 2's market structure, where they had to satisfy only their own region's shortfall. The higher the level of deposits, the higher the amount of the spillover and hence the more likely there is contagion.

The second remaining market structure is like that in Figure 1 but without any deposits in positively correlated regions (i.e., there are no cross links between regions A and C or regions B and D). The first-best can again be achieved. The difference is that in state $\overline{S}$ the amount of spillover and hence contagion is different. The amount of A's deposits spread between other regions is smaller than in Figure 1 but larger than in Figure 2. As a result, the spillover is larger and the contagion more likely than in Figure 1; the reverse is true compared to Figure 2.

So far we have not mentioned the central bank. The analysis of contagion suggests that one way of thinking about the role of a central bank is to complete markets. In the market structure with a central bank, all banks have a link to it. By intervening appropriately, the central bank can ensure that the inefficient liquidation associated with contagion can be avoided.

REFERENCES

Allen, Franklin, and Gale, Douglas. 'Optimal Financial Crises.' *J. Finance* 53 (August 1998): 1245–84.

—. 'Bubbles and Crises.' *Econ. J.* 110 (January 2000): 1–20.

Bernanke, Ben S. 'Nonmonetary Effects of the Financial Crisis in Propagation of the Great Depression.' *A.E.R.* 73 (June 1983): 257–76.

— and Gertler, Mark. 'Agency Costs, Net Worth, and Business Fluctuations.' *A.E.R.* 79 (March 1989): 14–31.

Calomiris, Charles W. 'Financial Fragility: Issues and Policy Implications.' *J. Financial Services Res.* 9 (December 1995): 241–57.

— and Kahn, Charles M. 'The Role of Demandable Debt in Structuring Optimal Banking Arrangements.' *A.E.R.* 81 (June 1991): 497–513.

Calvo, Guillermo. 'Varieties of Capital Market Crises.' Manuscript. College Park: Univ. Maryland, Center Internat. Econ., 1995.

Chang, Roberto, and Velasco, Andres. 'Financial Fragility and the Exchange Rate Regime.' Manuscript. New York: New York Univ., Dept. Econ., 1998.

Cole, Harold, and Kehoe, Timothy, 'Self-Fulfilling Debt Crises.' Manuscript. Minneapolis: Fed. Reserve Bank, Res. Dept., 1996.

Cooper, Russell, and Corbae, Dean. 'Financial Fragility and the Great Depression.' Manuscript. Cambridge, Mass.: NBER, 1997.

Diamond, Douglas W., and Dybvig, Philip H. 'Bank Runs, Deposit Insurance, and Liquidity.' *J.P.E.* 91 (June 1983): 401–19.

Friedman, Milton, and Schwartz, Anna Jacobson. *A Monetary History of the United States, 1867–1960*. Princeton, N.J.: Princeton Univ. Press (for NBER), 1963.

Gorton, Gary. 'Banking Panics and Business Cycles.' *Oxford Econ. Papers* 40 (December 1988): 751–81.

Hicks, John R. *A Market Theory of Money*. Oxford: Clarendon, 1989.

Kindleberger, Charles P. *Manias, Panics, and Crashes: A History of Financial Crises*. New York: Basic Books, 1978.

Kiyotaki, Nobuhiro, and Moore, John. 'Credit Chains.' Manuscript. London: London School Econ., Dept. Econ., 1998.

Lagunoff, Roger, and Schreft, Stacy. 'A Model of Financial Fragility.' Manuscript. Washington: Georgetown Univ., Dept. Econ., 1998.

Mitchell, Wesley Clair. *Business Cycles and Their Causes*. Berkeley: Univ. California Press, 1941.

Rochet, Jean-Charles, and Tirole, Jean. 'Interbank Lending and Systemic Risk.' *J. Money, Credit and Banking* 28, no. 4, pt. 2 (November 1996): 733–62.

Shleifer, Andrei, and Vishny, Robert W. 'Liquidation Values and Debt Capacity: A Market Equilibrium Approach.' *J. Finance* 47 (September 1992): 1343–66.

19

Systemic Risk, Interbank Relations, and Liquidity Provision by the Central Bank

XAVIER FREIXAS, BRUNO M. PARIGI, AND JEAN-CHARLES ROCHET

The possibility of a systemic crisis affecting the major financial markets has raised regulatory concern all over the world. Whatever the origin of a financial crisis, it is the responsibility of the regulatory body to provide adequate fire walls for the crisis not to spill over other institutions. In this paper we explore the possibilities of contagion from one institution to another that can stem from the existence of a network of financial contracts. These contracts are essentially generated from three types of operations: the payments system, the interbank market, and the market for derivatives.[1] Since these contracts are essential to the financial intermediaries' function of providing liquidity and risk sharing to their clients, the regulating authorities have to set patterns for central bank intervention when confronted with a systemic shock. In recent years, the 1987 stock market crash, the Saving and Loans crisis, the Mexican, Asian, and Russian crises and the crisis of the Long-Term Capital Management hedge fund have all shown the importance of the intervention of the central banks and of the international financial institutions in affecting the extent, contagion, patterns, and consequences of the crises.[2]

[1] There is ample empirical evidence on financial contagion. For a survey see de Bandt and Hartmann (1998). Kaufman (1994) reviews empirical studies that measure the adverse effects on banks' equity returns of default of a major bank and of a sovereign borrower or unexpected increases in loan-loss provisions announced by major banks. Others have studied contagion through the flow of deposits (Saunders and Wilson 1996), and using historical data (Gorton 1988; Schoenmaker 1996; and Calomiris and Mason 1997). Whatever the methodology, these studies support the view that pure panic contagion is rare. Far more common is contagion through perceived correlations in bank asset returns (particularly among banks of similar size and/or geographical location).

[2] A well-known episode of near financial gridlock where a coordinating role was played by the central bank is represented by the series of events the day after the stock crash of 1987. Brimmer (1989, pp. 14–15) writes that 'On the morning of October 20, 1987, when stock and commodity markets opened, dozens of brokerage firms and their banks had extended credit on behalf of customers to meet margin calls, and they had not received balancing payments through the clearing and settlement systems.... As margin calls mounted, money center banks (especially those in New York, Chicago, and San Francisco) were faced with greatly increased demand for loans by securities firms. With an eye on their capital ratios and given their diminished taste for risk, a number of these banks became increasingly reluctant

This article first appeared in the *Journal of Money, Credit and Banking* 32(3), 2000 published by Ohio State University Press. The proceedings were originally from the JMCB Conference entitled 'What Should Central Banks Do?', which was sponsored by the Federal Reserve Bank of Cleveland.

In contrast to the importance of these issues, theory has not succeeded yet in providing a convenient framework to analyze systemic risk so as to derive how the interbank markets and the payments system should be structured and what the lender of last resort (LOLR) role should be.

A good illustration of the wedge between theory and reality is provided by the deposits shift that followed the distress of Bank of Credit and Commerce International (BCCI). In July 1991, the closure of BCCI in the United Kingdom made depositors with smaller banks switch their funds to the safe haven of the big banks, the so-called 'flight to quality' (Reid 1991). Theoretically this should not have had any effect because big banks should have immediately lent again these funds in the interbank market and the small banks could have borrowed them. Yet, the reality was different: the Bank of England had to step in to encourage the large clearers to help those hit by the trend. Some packages had to be agreed upon (as the £200 million to the National Home Loans mortgage lender), thus supplementing the failing invisible hand of the market. So far theory has not been able to explain why the intervention of the LOLR in this type of events was important.

Our motivation to analyze a model of systemic risk stems from both the lack of a theoretical setup, and the lack of consensus on the way the LOLR should intervene. In this paper we analyze interbank networks, focusing on possible liquidity shortages and on the coordinating role of the financial authorities—which we refer to as the central bank for short—in avoiding and solving them. To do so we construct a model of the payment flows that allows us to capture in a simple fashion the propagation of financial crises in an environment where both liquidity shocks and solvency shocks affect financial intermediaries that fund long-term investments with demand deposits.

We introduce liquidity demand endogenously by assuming that depositors are uncertain about where they have to consume. This provides the need for a payments system or an interbank market.[3] In this way we extend the model of Freixas and Parigi (1998) to more than two banks, to different specifications of travel patterns and consumers' preferences. The focus of the two papers is different. Freixas and Parigi consider the trade-off between gross and net payments systems. In the current paper we concentrate instead on system-wide financial fragility and central bank policy issues. This paper is also related to Freeman (1996a,b). In Freeman, demand for liquidity is driven by the mismatch between supply and demand of goods by spatially separated agents that want to consume the good of

to lend, even to clearly creditworthy individual investors and brokerage firms. . . . To forestall a freeze in the clearing and settlement systems, Federal Reserve officials (particularly those from the Board and the Federal Reserve Bank of New York) urged key money center banks to maintain and to expand loans to their creditworthy brokerage firm customers.'

[3] Payment needs arising from agents' spatial separation with limited commitment and default possibilities were first analyzed in Townsend (1987). For the main theoretical issues related to systemic risk in payment systems see Berger, Hancock, and Marquardt (1996) and Flannery (1996), for an analysis of peer monitoring on the interbank market see Rochet and Tirole (1996), and for an analysis of the main institutional aspects see Summers (1994).

the other location, at different times. If agents' travel patterns are not perfectly synchronized, a centrally accessible institution (for example, a clearinghouse) may arise to provide means of payments. This allows the clearing of the debt issued by the agents to back their demand. In our paper, instead, liquidity demand arises from the strategies of agents with respect to the coordination of their actions.

Our main findings are, first, that, under normal conditions, a system of interbank credit lines reduces the cost of holding liquid assets. However, the combination of interbank credit and the payments system makes the banking system prone to experience (speculative) gridlocks, even if all banks are solvent. If the depositors in one location, wishing to consume in other locations, believe that there will not be enough resources for their consumption at the location of destination, their best response is to withdraw their deposits at the home location. This triggers the early liquidation of the investment at the home location, which, by backward induction, makes it optimal for the depositors in other locations to do the same.

Second, the structure of financial flows affects the stability of the banking system with respect to solvency shocks. On one hand, interbank connections enhance the 'resiliency' of the system to withstand the insolvency of a particular bank, because a proportion of the losses on one bank's portfolio is transferred to other banks through the interbank agreements. On the other hand, this network of cross-liabilities may allow an insolvent bank to continue operating through the implicit subsidy generated by the interbank credit lines, thus weakening the incentives to close inefficient banks.

Third, the central bank has a role to play as a 'crisis manager.' When all banks are solvent, the central bank's role of preventing a speculative gridlock is simply to act as a coordinating device. By guaranteeing the credit lines of all banks, the central bank eliminates any incentive for early liquidation. This entails no cost for the central bank since its guarantees are never used in equilibrium. When instead one bank is insolvent because of poor returns on its investment, the central bank has a role in the orderly closure of this bank. When a bank is to be liquidated, the central bank has to organize the bypass of this defaulting bank in the payment network and provide liquidity to the banks that depend on this defaulting bank. Furthermore, since the interbank market may loosen market discipline, there is a role for supervision, with the regulatory agency having the right to close down a bank even if this bank is not confronted with any liquidity problem.

Fourth, when depositors have asymmetric payment needs across space, the role of the locations where many depositors want to access their wealth (money center locations) becomes crucial for the stability of the entire banking system. We characterize the too-big-to-fail (TBTF) approach often followed by central banks in dealing with the financial distress of money center banks, that is, banks occupying key positions in the interbank network system.

The results of our paper are closely related to those of Allen and Gale (1998) where financial connections arise endogenously between banks located in different regions. In our work interregional financial connections arise because depositors face uncertainty about the location where they need to consume. In Allen and

Gale, instead, financial connections arise as a form of insurance: when liquidity preference shocks are imperfectly correlated across regions, cross-holdings of deposits by banks redistribute the liquidity in the economy. These links, however, expose the system to the possibility of a small liquidity shock in one location spreading to the rest of the economy. Despite the apparent similarities between the two models and the related conclusions pointing at the relevance of the structure of financial flows, it is worth noticing that in our paper instead we focus on the implications for the stability of the system when one bank may be insolvent.

This paper is organized as follows. In Section 1 we set up our basic model of an interbank network. In Section 2 we describe the coordination problems that may arise even when all banks are solvent. In Section 3 we analyze the 'resiliency' of the system when one bank is insolvent. In Section 4 we investigate whether the closure of one bank triggers the liquidation of others, and we show under which conditions the intervention of the central bank is needed to prevent a domino or contagion effect. Section 5 provides an example of asymmetric travel patterns and its implications for central bank intervention. Section 6 discusses the policy implications, offers some concluding remarks and points to possible extensions.

1. THE MODEL

1.1. Basic Setup

We consider an economy with one good and N locations with exactly one bank[4] in each location. There is a continuum of risk-neutral consumers of equal mass (normalized to one) in each location. There are three periods: $t = 0, 1, 2$. The good can be either stored from one period to the next or invested. Each consumer is endowed with one unit of the good at $t = 0$. Consumers cannot invest directly but must deposit their endowment in the bank of their location, which stores it or invests it for future consumption. Consumption takes place at $t = 2$ only. The storage technology yields the riskless interest rate which we normalize at 0. The investment of bank i yields a gross return R_i at $t = 2$, for each unit invested at $t = 0$, and not liquidated at $t = 1$. At $t = 0$ the bank optimally chooses the fraction of deposits to store or invest. The deposits contract specifies the amount c_1 received by depositors if they withdraw at $t = 1$, and their bank is solvent. At $t = 2$ remaining depositors equally share the returns of the remaining assets. To finance withdrawals at $t = 1$ the bank uses the stored good, and for the part in excess, liquidates a fraction of the investment. Each unit of investment liquidated at $t = 1$ gives only α units of the good (with $\alpha \leq 1$).

We extend this model by introducing a spatial dimension: a fraction $\lambda > 0$ of the depositors (we call them the *travelers*) must consume at $t = 2$ in other locations. The remaining $(1 - \lambda)$ depositors (the *nontravelers*) consume at $t = 2$ in the home

[4] This unique bank can be interpreted as a mutual bank, in the sense that it does not have any capital and acts in the best interest of its customers.

location. So in our model, consumers are uncertain about *where* they need to consume.

Our model is in the spirit of Diamond and Dybvig (1983) (hereafter D–D) but with a different interpretation. In D–D, risk-averse consumers are subject to a preference shock as to *when* they need to consume. The bank provides insurance by allowing them to withdraw at $t = 1$ but exposes itself to the risk of bank runs since it funds an illiquid investment with demand deposits. Our model corresponds to a simplified version of D–D where the patient consumers must consume at home or in the other location(s) and the proportion of impatient consumers is arbitrarily small. This allows us to concentrate on the issue of payments across locations without analyzing intertemporal insurance. Our focus is on the coordination of the consumers of the various locations, and not on the time-coordination of the consumers at the same location.[5]

Since we analyze interbank credit, the good should be interpreted as cash (that is, central bank money). Cash is a liability of the central bank that can be moved at no cost, but only by the central bank.[6]

If we interpret our model in terms of payment systems the sequence of events takes place within a twenty-four-hour period. Then we could interpret $t = 0$ as the beginning of the day, $t = 1$ as intraday, $t = 2$ as overnight, and the liquidation cost $(1 - \alpha)$ as the cost of (fire) selling monetary instruments in an illiquid intraday market.[7]

We assume that R_i is publicly observable at $t = 1$. In a multiperiod version of our model, R_i would be interpreted as a signal on bank i's solvency that could provoke withdrawals by depositors or liquidation by the central bank at $t = 1$ (intraday). For simplicity, we adopt a two-period model, and we assume here that the bank is liquidated anyway, either at $t = 1$ or at $t = 2$. Notice that even if R_i is publicly observed at $t = 1$ (we make this assumption to abstract from asymmetric information problems) it is not verifiable by a third party at $t = 1$ (only ex post, at $t = 2$). Therefore the deposit contract cannot be fully conditioned on R_i. More specifically, the amount c_1 received for a withdrawal at $t = 1$ can just depend on the only verifiable

[5] The demandable deposit feature of the contract in this model does not rely necessarily on intertemporal insurance but may have alternative rationales. For example, Calomiris and Kahn (1991) suggest that the right to withdraw on demand, accompanied by a sequential service constraint, gives informed depositors a credible threat in case of misuse of funds by the bank.

[6] Models in the tradition of Diamond–Dybvig have typically left the characteristics of the one good in the economy in the mist. This is all right in a microeconomic setup, but the model has monetary implications that lead to a different interpretation depending on the fact that the good is money or not. In particular, if the good is not money but, for example, wheat, then Wallace's (1988) criticism applies. In other words, if the good was interpreted as wheat we would have to justify why the central bank was endowed with a superior transportation technology. As we assume the good to be money, it is the fact that commercial banks use central bank money to settle their transactions that gives the central bank the monopoly of issuing cash. Therefore, the possibility to transfer money from one location to another corresponds to the ability to create and destroy money. Notice also that interpreting the good as cash implies that currency crises, which are often associated with systemic risk, are left out of our analysis. This is so because 'cash' is then limited by the level of reserves of the central bank.

[7] Since banks specialize in lending to information-sensitive customers, $1 - \alpha$ can also be interpreted as the cost of selling loans in the presence of a lemons' problem.

information at $t = 1$, namely, the closure decision. We denote by D_0 this contractual amount[8] in the case where the bank is not closed at $t = 1$. On the other hand, whenever the bank is closed (whether at $t = 1$ or at $t = 2$) its depositors equally share its assets (see Assumptions 1 and 2 below).

In order to be more explicit it is worth examining the characteristics of the optimal deposit contract in the D–D model when the proportion of early diers tends to zero. This provides a useful benchmark for measuring the exposure of the interbank system to market discipline in our multibank model. Let μ denote the proportion of early diers and u be the Von Neumann Morgenstern utility function of depositors, with $u' > 0$ and $u'' < 0$. The optimal deposit contract (c_1, c_2) maximizes $\mu u(c_1) + (1 - \mu)u(c_2)$ under the constraint $\mu c_1 + (1 - \mu)c_2/R = 1$. Together with the budget constraint, this optimal contract is characterized by the first order condition:

$$u'(c_1) = Ru'(c_2). \tag{1}$$

When μ tends to zero, it is easy to see that c_2 tends to R and that c_1 tends to $D_0 = u'^{-1}(Ru'(R))$. Since $R > 1$ and u' is decreasing, we see immediately that $D_0 < R$. Therefore, if the bank is known to be solvent, no depositor has interest to withdraw unilaterally before he or she actually needs the money.

1.2. General Formulation of Consumption Across Space

Travel patterns, that is, which depositor travels and to which location, are exogenously determined by nature at $t = 1$ and privately revealed to each depositor. They result from depositors' payment needs arising from other aspects of their economic activities. For each depositor, initially at location i, nature determines whether he or she travels and in which location j he or she will consume at $t = 2$.[9] In order to consume at $t = 2$ at location j $(i \neq j)$ the travelers at location i can withdraw at $t = 1$ and carry the cash by themselves from location i to location j. The implicit cost of transferring the cash across space is the foregone investment return.[10] This motivates the introduction of credit lines between banks to minimize the amount of good not invested. The credit line granted by bank j to bank i gives the depositors of bank i going to bank j the right to have their deposits transferred to location j and obtain their consumption at $t = 2$ as a share of the assets at bank j at date $t = 2$.

A way to visualize the credit line granted by bank j to bank i is to think that consumers located at i arrive in location j at $t = 2$ with a check written on bank i and credited in an account at bank j. Bank i, in turn, gives credit lines to one or

8 This amount results from ex ante optimal contracting decisions that could be solved explicitly. For conciseness, we take D_0 as given. Notice that if R_i was verifiable, D_0 could be contingent on it and the risk of contagion could be fully eliminated.

9 More generally, depositors receive shocks to their preferences that determine their demand for the good indexed by a particular location.

10 We could also add an explicit cost of 'traveling with the cash' (that is, bypassing the payments system). It would not affect our results.

more banks as specified below.[11] At $t = 2$ the banks compensate their claims and transfer the corresponding amount of the good across space. The technology to transfer the good at $t = 2$ is available for trades between banks only.

To make explicit the values of the assets and the liabilities resulting from interbank relations we adopt the simplest sharing rule, namely:

Assumption 1. All the liabilities of a bank have the same priority at $t = 2$.

This rule defines how to divide bank's assets at $t = 2$ among the claim holders. It implies that credit lines are honored in proportion to the amount of the assets of the bank at date $t = 2$. In particular if D_i is the ex post value of a (unit of) deposit in bank i, then

$$D_i = \frac{\text{Bank}_i \text{ Total Assets}}{\text{Bank}_i \text{ Total Liabilities}}.$$

This assumption implies also that the banks cannot determine the location of origin of the depositors; thus depositors become anonymous and the banks cannot discriminate among them. Notice that more complex priority rules could be more efficient in the resolution of liquidity crises. However, we assume that they are not feasible in our context: this is a reduced-form assumption aiming at capturing the limitations of the information that is available in interbank networks. An additional assumption is needed to describe what happens in case a bank is closed at $t = 1$.

Assumption 2. If a bank is closed at time 1, its assets are shared between its own depositors only.

Assumption 2 simply means that when the bank is closed at time $t = 1$, only its depositors have a claim on its assets. Bank closure at time 1 may come from a decision of the regulator, or from the withdrawals of all depositors. Assumption 2 implies that when a bank is closed at time 1, it is deleted from the interbank network.

Let π_{ij} be the measure of depositors from location i consuming at location j, where i can take any value including j, and let t_{ij} be the proportion of travelers going from location i to j, $j \neq i$ (by definition, $t_{ii} = 0$). The matrix Π that defines where consumers go and in which proportions is related to the matrix T of travel patterns by

$$\Pi \equiv (1 - \lambda)I + \lambda T \tag{2}$$

where $\Pi = (\pi_{ij})_{ij}$, I is the identity matrix, and $T = (t_{ij})_{ij}$. This specification allows us to parameterize independently two features of the payment system: λ captures the

[11] For a similar characterization of credit chains in the context of trading arrangements, see Kiyotaki and Moore (1997).

intensity of interbank flows and the matrix T captures the structure of these flows. By definition, we have for all i, $\Sigma_j \pi_{ij} = 1$. For the sake of simplicity, unless otherwise specified (see Section 5), we will impose the following additional restrictions:

Assumption 3. For all j, $\Sigma_i \pi_{ij} = 1$.

In this way we discard the supply and demand imbalances at a specific location as the cause of a disruption in the payments system or in the interbank market. Because of the complexity of the transfers involved in an arbitrary matrix Π, we will illustrate our findings in two symptomatic cases:

- In the first one $t_{ij} = 1$ if $j = i + 1$ and $t_{ij} = 0$ otherwise, with the notational convention that $N+1 \equiv 1$. To visualize this case it is convenient to think that the consumers are located around a circle as in Salop's (1979) model. All travelers from i go to location $i + 1$, the clockwise adjacent location, where they must consume at $t = 2$. The payments structure implied by this travel pattern generates what we define as *credit chain interbank funding*, when the bank at location $i + 1$ provides credit to the incoming depositors from location i.
- In the second travel pattern $t_{ij} = 1/(N - 1)$ with $i \neq j$. Each two banks swap $\lambda/(N - 1)$ customers so that at time $t = 2$ at location j there are $\lambda/(N - 1)$ travelers from each of the other $(N - 1)$ locations. We will refer to this perfectly isotropic case as the *diversified lending case.*[12]

With *credit chain interbank funding*, credit flows in the direction opposite to travel. With *diversified lending* every bank gives credit lines uniformly to all other $N - 1$ banks. In terms of payments mechanisms, the interbank credit described above can be interpreted as a compensation scheme (net system) or a real-time gross system (RTGS) with multilateral credit lines.

Let us now introduce the players of the game, namely, the N banks and their depositors. At $t = 0$ banks decide whether to extend each others credit lines. In the absence of credit lines, all travelers have to withdraw at $t = 1$, which reduces the quantity that each bank can invest: this is what we call the *autarkic situation.* On the other hand, in the general case with credit lines, the value of final consumption at $t = 2$ is determined by a noncooperative game played by the banks' depositors. At $t = 1$ each depositor located at i and consuming at location j simultaneously and without coordination determines the fraction x_{ij} of his or her deposit to maintain in the bank. Accordingly, the percentage of investment remaining at location j where he or she must consume is

$$X_j \equiv \max\left[1 - \sum_k \pi_{jk}\,(1 - x_{jk})\frac{D_0}{\alpha}, 0\right]. \qquad (3)$$

[12] The structure of the payment flows in the credit chain interbank funding and in the diversified lending is very similar to that studied by Allen and Gale (1998).

Because of Assumption 1, the final consumption of depositors (i, j) results from a combination of a withdrawal at time $t = 1$ in bank i (that is, $(1 - x_{ij})D_0$) plus a proportion x_{ij} of the value at $t = 2$ of a deposit D_j in bank j. To determine the possible equilibria of the depositors' game, we have to compare D_0 with the (endogenous) values of the deposits $D_1, \ldots, D_N$ in all the banks at $t = 2$. Now, to determine D_i, consider the balance sheet equation for bank i at time $t = 2$

$$X_iR_i + \sum_j \pi_{ji}x_{ji}D_j = (\sum_j \pi_{ji}x_{ji} + \sum_j \pi_{ij}x_{ij})D_i, \tag{4}$$

where the left-hand side (right-hand side) represents the assets (liabilities) of bank i, X_iR_i is the return on its investment, $\Sigma_j \pi_{ji}x_{ji}D_j$ are the credits of bank i due from other banks, $(\Sigma_j \pi_{ji}x_{ji})\ D_i$ are its debts with other banks, and $\Sigma_j \pi_{ij}x_{ij}D_i$ are its deposits. Notice that Assumption 2 implies that the above equation does not apply when bank i is closed at $t = 1$. In this case $X_i = D_i = 0$.

The optimal behavior of each depositor (i, j) is $x_{ij} = 1 \Leftrightarrow D_j \geq D_0$, $\forall i, j$. Since it depends only on j, we denote by x^j, the common value of the x_{ij} where $x^j = 1$ if $D_j > D_0$ and $x^j = 0$ otherwise. This allows a simplification of (4)

$$X_iR_i + \left(\sum_j \pi_{ji}D_j\right) x^i = \left[\left(\sum_j \pi_{ji}\right)x^i + \sum_j \pi_{ij}x^j\right]D_i. \tag{5}$$

We establish the following notation: $\mathrm{D} = (D_1, \ldots, D_N)'$, $\mathrm{R} = (R_1, \ldots, R_N)'$, and Π' is the transpose of $\Pi = (\pi_{ij})_{i,j}$. For a given strategy vector $(x_{ij})_{i,j}$ one can compute the assets in place at bank $i(X_i)$ and the return on a deposit at bank $i(D_i)$. Then we check whether the strategies are optimal:

$$x^*_{ij} = \begin{cases} 1 & \text{if } D_j > D_0 \\ 0 & \text{if } D_j < D_0. \end{cases} \tag{6}$$

Any fixed point of this algorithm (that is, $x^*_{ij} \equiv x_{ij}$) is an equilibrium of our game.

When the mechanism of interbank credit functions smoothly, $x_{ij} \equiv 1$ for all (i, j) and depositors' welfare is greater than in the autarkic situation. This is because interbank credit lines allow each bank to keep a lower amount of liquid reserves and to invest more. However, the system is also more fragile. As we show in the next sections, the noncooperative game played by depositors has other equilibria than $x_{ij} \equiv 1$.

2. PURE COORDINATION PROBLEMS

We first analyze the equilibria of the game when all deposits are invested at $t = 1$, investment returns are certain, and all banks are solvent so that the only issue is the coordination among depositors. Disregarding the mixed strategy equilibria where depositors are indifferent between withdrawing their deposits and transferring them to the recipient banks, we obtain our first result:

Proposition 1. *We assume $R_i > D_0$ for all i (which implies that all banks are solvent). There are at least two pure strategy equilibria: (i) the inefficient bank run* *allocation where* $x^* = 0$ *(speculative gridlock equilibrium) and (ii) the efficient allocation where* $x^* = 1$ *(credit line equilibrium).*

Proof. See the Appendix.

Several comments are in order. In the credit line equilibrium there is no liquidation while in the speculative gridlock equilibrium all the banks' assets are liquidated. Since liquidation is costly and all banks are solvent, the credit line equilibrium dominates the speculative gridlock equilibrium as well as any other equilibrium where some liquidation takes place. The speculative gridlock equilibrium arises as a result of a coordination failure like in D–D. If depositors rationally anticipated at $t = 0$ a speculative gridlock equilibrium, they would prefer the autarkic situation.

In the credit line equilibrium with diversified lending, bank i extends credit lines to all the other banks and receives credit lines from them. In equilibrium the debt arising from bank i's depositors at $t = 2$ using bank i's credit lines with the other banks is repaid at $t = 2$ by bank i serving the depositors from the other banks. It is precisely because the behavior of one bank's depositors is affected by the expectation of what the depositors going to the same location will do, that this equilibrium is vulnerable to a coordination failure. If the depositors in a sufficiently large number of banks believe that they will be denied consumption at the location where they have to consume, it is optimal for them to liquidate their investment, which makes it optimal for the depositors in all other banks to do the same. The speculative gridlock equilibrium is related to the notion of domino effect that may arise in payments systems as a result of the settlement failure of some participant. Still, it may occur here even if all banks are solvent. Notice that banks do not play any strategic role: only depositors play strategically.

From the efficiency viewpoint, when all the banks are solvent the credit line equilibrium dominates autarky which in turn dominates the speculative gridlock equilibrium.[13] Hence there is a trade-off between a risky interbank market based on interbank credit and a safe payment mechanism that foregoes investment opportunities.[14]

Both the gridlock and the credit line equilibria involve the use of credit lines. In both equilibria banks extend and honor credit lines up to the amount of their $t = 2$ resources. In the speculative gridlock equilibrium it is not the banks that do not honor the credit lines, rather the depositors, by forcing the liquidation of the investment, reduce the amount of resources available at $t = 2$.

[13] When $\alpha = 1$ the last two are equivalent. The cost of the gridlock equilibrium is proportional to $1 - \alpha$. Notice that autarky is equivalent to a payment system with fully collateralized credit lines like TARGET (Trans-European automated real-time gross settlement express transfer), the payment system designed to handle transactions in the Euro area.

[14] For an analysis of this trade-off in a related setting see Freixas and Parigi (1998). However, even a real-time gross system like TARGET is not immune to a systemic crisis. As Garber (1998) points out, if there is a risk that a currency will leave the Euro currency area, the very infrastructure of TARGET, where national central banks of the participating countries extend to each other unlimited daily credit, provides the perfect mechanism to mount speculative attacks on the system.

There is a clear parallel between these two equilibria in our economy with N locations and the equilibria in a one-location D–D model. These results are also related to the papers by Bhattacharya and Gale (1987) and Bhattacharya and Fulghieri (1994) that consider N-location D–D economies without geographic risks.

The credit line equilibrium can be implemented in several ways: through a compensation system where credits are netted, by a RTGS (real-time gross settlement) system with multilateral or bilateral credit lines, through lending by the central bank, and through deposit insurance.

In this basic version of the model, in the event of a gridlock, every bank is *solvent* although *illiquid*. Thus, no difficulty in distinguishing between insolvent and illiquid banks arises for the central bank.[15] The central bank has a simple coordinating role as a LOLR in guaranteeing private-sector credit lines or in providing fiat money, both backed by the authority of the Treasury to tax the return on the investment.[16]

Similarly, by guaranteeing the value of deposits at the consumption locations, deposit insurance eliminates any incentive for the depositors to protect themselves by liquidating the investment, thus making it optimal for banks to extend credit to each other.

Like deposit insurance that is never used in equilibrium in the D–D model, the coordination role of the central bank costs no resources (excluding moral hazard issues), since in equilibrium it will not be necessary for the central bank to intervene. However, in a richer model credit line guarantees and deposit insurance would not have the same effect. In fact, unlike credit lines guarantees, deposit insurance penalizes the managers of distressed banks, and might offer better incentives to managers to monitor each other.

3. RESILIENCY AND MARKET DISCIPLINE IN THE INTERBANK SYSTEM

In the next two sections we tackle the issue of the impact of the insolvency of one bank on the rest of the system. In this section we investigate under which conditions the losses of one bank can be absorbed by the other banks without provoking withdrawals by depositors (this is what we call resiliency) and what are the implications in terms of market discipline. In the next section we consider the issue of contagion. That is, we investigate whether the closure of an insolvent bank generates a chain reaction causing the liquidation of solvent banks.

In order to model the possibility of insolvency in a simple way, we make the extreme assumption that the return R_i on the investment at location i can be either

[15] For an analysis of this issue see the companion paper by Freixas, Parigi, and Rochet (1998).

[16] For example, in the Canadian electronic system for the clearing and settlement of large value payments the central bank guarantees intraday credit lines (Freedman and Goodlet 1998).

$R \geq D_0$, or 0. If $R = 0$, bank i is insolvent, in which case it is efficient to liquidate it, absent contagion issues. For the remainder of this paper we assume that the probability of $R = 0$ is sufficiently low that it is optimal for the banks to invest all deposits at $t = 0$.[17] Returns are publicly observable at $t = 1$ but verifiable only at $t = 2$ so that no contract can be made contingent on these returns. Notice that by Assumption 1 the public information that bank 1 is insolvent cannot be used by the other banks to distinguish and discriminate the depositors of the insolvent bank. The efficient allocation of resources requires that banks be liquidated if and only if they are insolvent:

$$X_i = \begin{cases} 0 & \text{if } R_i = 0 \\ 1 & \text{if } R_i = R \end{cases} \tag{7}$$

Whether this efficient closure rule is a Nash Equilibrium of the noncooperative game between depositors will depend on the structure of the interbank payment system. To illustrate this, we focus on the case in which one bank (say, bank 1) is insolvent, and we investigate under which conditions $x = (1, \ldots, 1)$ is still an equilibrium, that is, under which conditions $D_i \geq D_0$ for all i. When $x = (1, \ldots, 1)$ and $R_1 = 0$ the balance sheet equations give

$$\mathrm{D} = (2I - \Pi')^{-1} \begin{pmatrix} 0 \\ R \\ \vdots \\ R \end{pmatrix} = R(2I - \Pi')^{-1} \begin{pmatrix} 0 \\ 1 \\ \vdots \\ 1 \end{pmatrix} \tag{8}$$

From (8) we define by γ the minimum of the components of the vector

$$(2I - \Pi')^{-1} \begin{pmatrix} 0 \\ 1 \\ \vdots \\ 1 \end{pmatrix} \tag{9}$$

We establish the following proposition:

Proposition 2. *(Resiliency and Market Discipline) When $R_1 = 0$, necessary condition for $x = (1, \ldots, 1)$ to be an equilibrium is that the smallest value of time $t = 2$ deposits $(R\gamma)$, which depends on the structure of interbank payment flows, exceeds D_0.*

Proof. From (8) and the definition of γ we see that $D_i \geq D_0$ for all i if and only if $\gamma \geq \frac{D_0}{R}$.

Several comments are in order. Proposition 2 highlights an important aspect of the tension between efficiency and stability of the interbank system. On one hand it establishes the conditions under which the system can absorb the losses of one

[17] For a large probability of failure, it is optimal to use the storage technology only.

bank without any deposit withdrawal. Resiliency, however, entails the cost of forbearance of the insolvent bank. On the other hand, it establishes the conditions under which $x = (1, \ldots, 1)$ is no longer an equilibrium. If a bank is known at $t = 1$ to be insolvent, depositors may withdraw and withdrawals may not be confined to the insolvent bank; hence market discipline entails the cost of possibly excessive liquidation. We interpret γ as a measure of the exposure of the interbank system as a whole to market discipline when one bank is insolvent.[18]

We now study how γ varies with λ (the proportion of travelers) and N (the number of locations) in the two cases of credit chain and diversified lending.

Proposition 3. *Both in the credit chain case and in the diversified lending case, γ increases with λ and N; that is, when the proportion of travelers increases or the number of banks increases, the system becomes less exposed to market discipline.*

Proof. See the Appendix.

When the number of banks increases, the insolvency of one bank has a lower impact on the value of the deposits in the other banks. Similarly an increase in the fraction of travelers spreads on the other banks a larger fraction of the loss due to the insolvency of one bank. This seems quite intuitive for the diversified lending case, since the banks hold more diversified portfolios of loans. The novelty is that this result holds true also for the credit chain case where banks have the possibility to pass part of their losses to other banks through the interbank market.

We now compare the two systems for given values of λ and N. We then compare the exposure to market discipline of the credit chain and the diversified lending structures.

Proposition 4. *In case of the insolvency of one bank, the system is more exposed to market discipline under diversified lending than under credit chains; that is, $\gamma^{CRE} > \gamma^{DIV}$.*

Proof. See the Appendix.

Proposition 4 may appear counterintuitive since diversification is usually associated with the ability to spread losses. The result depends on the proportion of the losses on its own portfolio that the insolvent bank is able to transfer to other banks through the payments system. In a diversified lending system there is more diversification so that solvent banks exchange a larger fraction of their claims. As a consequence in a diversified lending system the insolvent bank is able to pass over to the solvent banks a smaller fraction of its losses.

[18] As a benchmark consider again the limit of the D–D optimal contract when the proportion of early diers tends to zero. If we compute D_0 when $u(c) = c^{1-a}/(1-a)$ (CRRA utility function), from (1) we have $D_0/R = R^{-a}$, which is decreasing in R. Therefore, more profitable assets decrease the exposure of the bank to market discipline.

The case with three banks ($N = 3$) and everybody traveling ($\lambda = 1$) provides a good illustration. In a diversified lending system the balance sheet equations (5) become

$$D_i = \frac{1}{2}\left[R_i + \frac{1}{2}(D_{i-1} + D_{i+1})\right] \quad i = 1, 2, 3. \tag{10}$$

This means that if bank 1 is insolvent (that is, $R_1 = 0$), depositors at banks 2 and 3 obtain an equal share of total surplus, while bank 1 depositors receive 50 percent less. After easy computations, we find that bank 1 depositors receive $\frac{2}{5}R$, or equivalently bank 1 is able to pass $\frac{3}{5}R$ of its losses to the solvent banks whose depositors end up receiving $\frac{4}{5}R$.

Consider now the case of credit chains. Still assuming $\lambda = 1$, the balance sheet equations give

$$D_i = \frac{1}{2}[R_i + D_{i+1}] \quad i = 1, 2, 3. \tag{11}$$

We can compute the losses experienced by each bank (with respect to the promised returns R) and it is a simple exercise to check that the only solution is

$$D_1 = \frac{3}{7}R; \quad D_3 = \frac{5}{7}R; \quad D_2 = \frac{6}{7}R. \tag{12}$$

Therefore, bank 1 is able to pass on a higher share of its losses than in the diversified lending case, which explains the lower exposure of the interbank system to market discipline in the credit chain system.

The results of this section highlight another side of interbank markets in addition to their role in redistributing liquidity efficiently studied by Bhattacharya and Gale (1987). Interbank connections enhance the 'resiliency' of the system to withstand the insolvency of a particular bank. However, this network of cross liabilities may loosen market discipline and allow an insolvent bank to continue operating through the implicit subsidy generated by the interbank credit lines. This loosening of market discipline is the rationale for a more active role for monitoring and supervision with the regulatory agency having the right to close down a bank in spite of the absence of any liquidity crisis at that bank.

The effect of a central bank's guarantee on interbank credit lines would be that $x = (1, \ldots, 1)$ is always an equilibrium, even if one bank is insolvent. The stability of the banking system would be preserved at the cost of forbearance of inefficient banks.

4. CLOSURE-TRIGGERED CONTAGION RISK

4.1. Efficiency versus Contagion Risk

We now turn to the other side of the relationship between efficiency and stability of the banking system, and investigate under which conditions the closure at time $t = 1$ of an insolvent bank does not trigger the liquidation of solvent banks in a contagion fashion. Suppose that bank k is closed at $t=1$. Assumption 2 implies that $X_k=0$ and $D_k=0$. Closing bank k at $t=1$ has two consequences. First, we have an *unwinding* of the positions of bank k since $\pi_{ki}D_k$ assets and $\pi_{ki}D_i$ liabilities disappear from the balance sheet of bank k. In a richer setting this is equivalent to a situation in which the other banks have reneged on their credit lines toward bank k, possibly as a result of the arrival of negative signals on its return. Second, a proportion π_{ik} of travelers going to location k will be *forced to withdraw early* the amount $\pi_{ik}D_0$ and bank i will have to liquidate the amount $\pi_{ik}(D_0/\alpha)$. If $\pi_{ik}(D_0/\alpha)$ is sufficiently large, bank i is closed at $t=1$; otherwise the cost at $t=2$ of the early liquidation is $\pi_{ik}\,((D_0/\alpha)R-D_i)$.

Notice that if $\pi_{ik}(D_0/\alpha)\geq 1$, then $X_i=0$, that is, bank i is liquidated simply because there are too many depositors going from location i to location k, the bank is closed at $t=1$. The type of contagion that takes place here is of a purely mechanical nature stemming simply from the direct effect of inefficient liquidation. Since this case is straightforward let us instead concentrate on the other case, namely, $\pi_{ik}(D_0/\alpha)<1$. Because of unwinding and forced early withdrawal, the full general case is more complex. Since $x^k=0$, we have to suppress all that concerns bank k from the equations (5). We obtain

$$X_{i(k)}\,R_i+\sum_{j\neq k}\pi_{ji}D_jx^i=\left(\sum_{j\neq k}\pi_{ij}x_j+\sum_{j\neq k}\pi_{ji}\,x^i\right)D_i\,, \tag{13}$$

where

$$X_{i(k)}=\max\left[1-\pi_{ik}\frac{D_0}{\alpha}-\sum_{j\neq k}\pi_{ji}(1-x^j)\frac{D_0}{\alpha},0\right]. \tag{14}$$

We now have to check whether $x_{ij}\equiv 1$ for all i, $j\neq k$, can correspond to an equilibrium. In this case, $X_{i(k)}=\max[1-\pi_{ik}(D_0/\alpha),0]$ and system (13) becomes

$$R_i=\left(\sum_{j\neq k}\frac{\pi_{ij}+\pi_{ji}}{X_{i(k)}}\right)D_i-\sum_{j\neq k}\frac{\pi_{ji}}{X_{i(k)}}D_j\,. \tag{15}$$

Since by assumption $R_i\equiv R$ for all $i\neq k$, (15) becomes

$$\left(1-\pi_{ik}\frac{D_0}{\alpha}\right)R+\sum_{j\neq k}\pi_{ji}D_j=(2-\pi_{ik}-\pi_{ki})D_i\,. \tag{16}$$

This allows us to establish a result analogous to Proposition 2.

Proposition 5. *(Contagion Risk): There is a critical value of the smallest time $t=2$ deposits below which the closure of a bank causes the liquidation of at least another bank. This critical value is lower in the credit chain case than in the diversified lending case. The diversified lending structure is always stable when the number N of banks is large enough whereas N has no impact on the stability of the credit chain structure.*

Proof. It follows the same structure of the proof of Proposition 2. Denoting by M_k the inverse of the matrix defined by system (16), stability is equivalent to

$$\begin{pmatrix} D_1 \\ \vdots \\ D_N \end{pmatrix} = RM_k \begin{pmatrix} 1 \\ \vdots \\ 1 \end{pmatrix} > D_0 \begin{pmatrix} 1 \\ \vdots \\ 1 \end{pmatrix}. \tag{17}$$

One can see that all the elements of M_k are non-negative,[19] thus stability obtains iff $(D_0/R) \leq \psi_k$, where ψ_k denotes the minimum of the components $M_k \begin{pmatrix} 1 \\ \vdots \\ 1 \end{pmatrix}$. The computation of ψ_k is cumbersome in the general case but easy in our benchmark examples (where, because of symmetry, k does not play any role). One finds:

$$\psi_{\text{cre}} = 1 - \lambda\left(\frac{D_0}{\alpha} - 1\right); \quad \psi_{cre} = 1 - \lambda\left(\frac{\frac{D_0}{a} - 1}{N - 1 - \lambda}\right); \tag{18}$$

in the credit chain example, and in the diversified lending case, respectively. It is immediate from these formulas that $\psi_{\text{cre}} < \psi_{\text{div}}$ (for $N \geq 2$) and that ψ_{div} tends to 1 when N tends to infinity while ψ_{cre} is independent of N.

4.2. Comparison with Allen and Gale (1998)

It is useful to compare our results with those of Allen and Gale (1998). Proposition 2 establishes that systemic crises may arise for fundamental reasons, like in Allen and Gale. However, the focus of the two papers is different. Allen and Gale are concerned with the stability of the system with respect to liquidity shocks arising from the random number of consumers that need liquidity early in the absence of aggregate uncertainty. They show that the system is less stable when the interbank market is incomplete (in the sense that banks are allowed to cross-hold deposits only in a credit chain fashion) than when the interbank market is complete (in the sense that banks are allowed to cross-hold deposits in a diversified lending fashion).

In our paper interbank links arise, instead, from consumers geographic uncertainty and the focus is on the implications of the insolvency of one bank in terms of market discipline and stability of the system. In particular in Proposition 4 we show how the structure of interbank links allows to spread over other banks the losses of one bank. We show that a diversified lending system is more exposed to market discipline (that is, less resilient) than a credit chain system because in the latter the insolvent bank is able to transfer a larger fraction of its losses to other banks, thus reducing the incentives for its own depositors to withdraw. In Proposition 5 we are concerned with the stability of the system with

[19] The fact that the matrix M_k has non-negative elements follows from a property of diagonal dominant matrices (see, for example, Takayama 1985, p. 385).

respect to contagion risk triggered by the efficient liquidation at time $t = 1$ of the insolvent bank.

5. TOO-BIG-TO-FAIL AND MONEY CENTER BANKS

Regulators have often adopted a too-big-to-fail approach (TBTF) in dealing with financially distressed money center banks and large financial institutions.[20] One of the reasons is the fear of the repercussions that the liquidation of a money center bank might have on the corresponding banks that channel payments through it. Our general formulation of the payments needs, where the flow of depositors going to the various locations is asymmetric, offers a simple way to model this case and to capture some of the features of the TBTF policy. We interpret the TBTF policy as designed to rescue banks that occupy key positions in the interbank network, rather than banks simply with large size.[21]

Consider, for example, the case where there are three locations ($N = 3$). Locations 2 and 3 are peripheral locations and location 1 is a money center location. All the travelers of locations 2 and 3 must consume at location 1, and one-half of the travelers of location 1 consume at location 2 and the other half at location 3. That is, $t_{12} = t_{13} = \frac{1}{2}$ and $t_{21} = t_{31} = 1$, $t_{23} = t_{32} = 0$.[22] This implies that

$$X_1 = \max\left\{1 - \frac{D_0}{\alpha}\left[1 - (1-\lambda)x^1 - \lambda\left(\frac{x^2 + x^3}{2}\right); 0\right]\right\}, \tag{19}$$

and

$$X_2 = \max\left\{1 - \frac{D_0}{\alpha}\left[1 - (1-\lambda)x^2 - \lambda x^1\right]; 0\right\}$$

$$X_3 = \max\left\{1 - \frac{D_0}{\alpha}\left[1 - (1-\lambda)x^3 - \lambda x^1\right]; 0\right\} \tag{20}$$

Suppose now that one of these banks (and only one) is insolvent (this is known at $t = 1$). The next proposition illustrates how the closure of a bank with a key position in the interbank market may trigger a systemic crisis.

Proposition 6. *(i) If $\lambda > \alpha[(1/D_0) - (1/R)]$, the liquidation of bank 1 triggers the liquidation of all other banks (too-big-to-fail); (ii) If $\lambda < (2\alpha/D_0)$, liquidation of banks 2 or 3 does not trigger the liquidation of any of the other two banks.*

[20] See, for example, the intervention of the monetary authorities in the Continental Illinois debacle in 1984 and, to some extent, in arranging the private-sector rescue of Long Term Capital Management.

[21] The Barings' failure of 1996 is an example of the crisis of a large financial institution that did not create systemic risk.

[22] Notice that we now abandon Assumption 3 (the symmetry assumption).

Proof. To prove (i) notice that if bank 1 is closed, then $X_1 = 0$ and $x^1 = 0$. Then $D_2 = X_2R = (1 - (D_0/\alpha)\lambda)R$. Thus $x^2 = 0$ if

$$\left(1 - \frac{D_0}{\alpha}\lambda\right)R < D_0 \Leftrightarrow \lambda > \alpha\left(\frac{1}{D_0} - \frac{1}{R}\right).$$

To prove (ii) notice that if bank 2 is closed, then $x^2 = 0$. If (1, 0, 1) is an equilibrium, the balance sheet equations become, when $(D_0\lambda/\alpha) < 2$:

$$D_1\left(1 - \frac{\lambda}{2}\frac{D_0}{\alpha} + \lambda\right) = \left(1 - \frac{D_0}{\alpha}\frac{\lambda}{2}\right)R_1 + \lambda D_3$$

$$D_3\left(1 + \frac{\lambda}{2}\right) = R_3 + \frac{\lambda}{2}D_1. \tag{21}$$

If $R_3 = R_1 = R$, this yields $D_3 = D_1 = R$. This implies that $x = (1, 0, 1)$ is an equilibrium whenever $(D_0\lambda/\alpha) < 2$.

Our last result concerns the optimal attitude of the central bank when the money center bank becomes insolvent ($R_1 = 0$). When D_0/R is low, no intervention is needed. When D_0/R is large, the central bank has to inject liquidity. More precisely we have

Proposition 7. *When $R_1 = 0$, $x = (1, 1, 1)$ is an equilibrium if D_0/R is sufficiently low (no central bank intervention is needed). In the other case, the cost of bailout increases with D_0/R.*

Proof. When $R_1 = 0$, $x = (1, 1, 1)$ can be an equilibrium if $\mathrm{D} > D\begin{pmatrix}1\\ \vdots\\ 1\end{pmatrix}$. When $x = (1, 1, 1)$, the balance sheet equations (5) become

$$R_1 + (D_2 + D_3) = 3D_1 \tag{22}$$

$$R_2 + \tfrac{1}{2}D_1 = \tfrac{3}{2}D_2, \qquad R_3 + \tfrac{1}{2} = \tfrac{3}{2}D_3\ . \tag{23}$$

Solving (22) and (20) when $R_1 = 0$, $R_2 = R_3 = R$ yields $\mathrm{D}_1 = \frac{4}{7}\mathrm{R}$, $D_2 = D_3 = \frac{6}{7}R$, which is an equilibrium iff $(D_0/R) < \frac{4}{7}$. The cost of bailout is 0 iff $(D_0/R) < \frac{4}{7}$, it is $D_0 - \frac{4}{7}R$ iff $\frac{4}{7} < (D_0/R) < \frac{6}{7}$. When $(D_0/R) < \frac{6}{7}$, the central bank also has to inject liquidity in the solvent banks. The total cost to the central bank becomes $3D_0 - \frac{16}{7}R$.

6. DISCUSSIONS AND CONCLUSIONS

We have constructed a model of the banking system where liquidity needs arise from consumers' uncertainty about where they need to consume. Our basic insight is that the interbank market allows banks to minimize the amount of resources held in low-return liquid assets. However, interbank links expose the system to the possibility that a number of inefficient outcomes arise: the excessive liquidation of productive investment as a result of coordination failures among depositors; the reduced incentive to liquidate insolvent banks because of the implicit subsidies offered by the payments networks; the inefficient liquidation of solvent banks because of the contagion effect stemming from one insolvent bank.

6.1. Policy Implications

We use this rich setup to derive a number of policy implications (summarized in Table 1) with respect to the interventions of the central bank.

First, the interbank market may not yield the efficient allocation of resources because of possible coordination failures that may generate a 'gridlock' equilibrium. The central bank has thus a natural coordination role to play which consists of implicitly guaranteeing the access to liquidity of individual banks. If the banking system as a whole is solvent the costs of this intervention are negligible and its distortionary effects may stem only from moral hazard issues (Proposition 1).

Second, if one bank is insolvent, the central bank faces a much more complex trade-off between efficiency and stability. Market forces will not necessarily force the closure of insolvent banks. Indeed, the resiliency of the interbank market allows them to cope with liquidity shocks by providing implicit insurance, which weakens market discipline (Proposition 2). Therefore, the central bank has the responsibility to provide ex ante monitoring of individual banks. However, the closure of insolvent banks may cause systemic repercussions (Proposition 5) for

Table 1. *Summary of Central Bank interventions*

Problem	Type of Central Bank Intervention	Costs	Result
Speculative gridlock	Coordinating role of central bank • Guarantee credit lines • Deposit insurance	Never used in equilibrium; no cost, apart from moral hazard	Proposition 1
Insolvency in a resilient interbank market	Ex ante monitoring and supervision	Imperfect monitoring leads to forbearance and moral hazard	Proposition 2
Insolvency leading to contagion	Orderly closure of insolvent bank and arrangement of credit lines to bypass it	No cost, apart from moral hazard and money center banks; in case of money center banks it may be too costly or even impossible to organize orderly closure	Proposition 5; Proposition 6
	Bailout	Transfer of taxpayer money	Proposition 7

which the central bank has the responsibility to handle. In this case two courses of actions are available: orderly closure or bailout of insolvent banks. Given the interbank links, the closure of an insolvent bank must be accompanied by the provision of central bank liquidity to the counterparts of the closed bank.[23] This is what we called orderly closure. Assuming that this is possible, theoretically it entails no costs apart from moral hazard. However, the orderly closure might simply not be feasible for money center banks (Proposition 6) in which case the central bank has no choice but to bailout the insolvent institution, with the obvious moral hazard implications of the TBTF policy.

Our model can be extended in various directions some of which are discussed below.

6.2. Imperfect Information on Banks' Returns

In reality, both the central bank and the depositors have only imperfect signals on the solvency of commercial banks (although the central bank's signals are hopefully more precise). Therefore, the central bank will have to act knowing that with some probability it will be lending to (guaranteeing the credit lines of) insolvent institutions and with some probability it will be denying credit to solvent institutions. Also, depositors may run on all the banks that have generated a bad signal.

The consequences are different depending on the structure of the interbank market. In the credit chain case, the central bank will have to intervene to provide credit with a higher probability than in the diversified lending case. Therefore, in the credit chain case the central bank has a higher probability of ending up financing insolvent banks. Ex ante, therefore, the central bank intervention is much more expensive in the credit chain case, so that in this case a fully collateralized payments system may be preferred.

6.3. Payments among Different Countries

Systemic risk is often related to the spreading of financial crisis from one country to another. Our basic model can be extended to consider various countries instead of locations within the same country. When depositors belong to different countries, travel patterns that generate a consumption need in another location have the natural interpretation of demand of goods of other countries, that is, import demand. Goods of the other country can be purchased through currency (like in autarchy in the basic model) or through a credit line system whereby the imports of a country are financed by its exports. Our results extend to the model with different countries but the role of the monetary authority is somewhat different. While in our setup the lending ability of the domestic monetary authority was

[23] For instance, in the credit chain case, if bank k is closed, the central bank can borrow from bank $k-1$ and lend to bank $k+1$, thus allowing the interbank arrangements to function smoothly.

backed by its taxation power, the lending ability of an international financial organization is ultimately backed by its capital. Hence, the resources at its disposal are limited and in case of aggregate uncertainty its ability to guarantee banks' credit lines is limited.[24]

APPENDIX

NOTATION

Define

$$M(\lambda) \equiv [2I - \Pi']^{-1} = [(1+\lambda)\, I - \lambda T']^{-1} = \frac{1}{1+\lambda}\left[I - \frac{\lambda}{1+\lambda} T'\right]^{-1} \tag{A1}$$

where I is the identity matrix. We first need a technical lemma:

Lemma 1. *All the elements of $M(\lambda)$ are non-negative: $m_{ij}(\lambda) \geq 0$ for all i,j. Moreover for all i, $\Sigma_j m_{ij}(\lambda) = 1$. As a consequence, if $R_i < D_0$ for all i, then*

$$M(\lambda)\mathrm{R} > D_0 \begin{pmatrix} 1 \\ \vdots \\ 1 \end{pmatrix}. \tag{A2}$$

Proof. $M(\lambda) = (2I - \Pi')^{-1}$. Since Π' is a Markov matrix (because of assumption 3), all its eigen values are in the unit disk and $M(\lambda)$ can be developed into a power series:

$$M(\lambda) = \frac{1}{2}\left(I - \frac{\Pi'}{2}\right)^{-1} = \sum_{k=0}^{+\infty} \frac{\Pi'^k}{2^{k+1}}. \tag{A3}$$

This implies that $M(\lambda)$ has positive elements. Moreover $\begin{pmatrix} 1 \\ \vdots \\ 1 \end{pmatrix}$ being an eigen vector of Π' (for the eigen value 1), it is also an eigen vector for $M(\lambda)$. □

Proof of Proposition 1.

(i) Because of Assumption 2, $D_i = 0$ when $x_{ij} = 0$ for all j. Therefore $x^*_{ij} \equiv 0$ is always an equilibrium.

[24] See the role of the IMF in the 1997 Asian crises and the 1998 Russian crisis.

(ii) $x^j = 1 \Rightarrow X_j = 1$. Using the assumption that $\Sigma_j \pi_{ji} = 1$ equation (2.5) becomes

$$2D = R + \Pi' D. \quad \text{(A4)}$$

For $x^j = 1$ to be an equilibrium for all j, it must be

$$D = [2I - \Pi'] - 1\,R = M(\lambda)R \geq D_0 \begin{pmatrix} 1 \\ \vdots \\ 1 \end{pmatrix} \quad \text{(A5)}$$

This is an immediate consequence of the above lemma, which implies that $x = (1, \ldots, 1)$ is always an equilibrium when all banks are solvent. There are no other equilibria when $\alpha = D_0$. Indeed, if $x^i = 0$ then equation (5) implies that $X_i = 0$ or $D_i = R_i$. But X_i cannot be zero (unless all x^j are also zero) and $D_i = R_i > D_0$ contradicts the equilibrium condition. Notice, however, that $\alpha < D_0$, X_i can be zero even if some of the x^j are positive, which implies that other equilibria may exist. □

Before establishing Proposition 3 we have to compute the expression of matrix $M(\lambda)$ in the two cases of credit chain and diversified lending.

Consider the credit chain case first, where the matrix T is given by:

$$T = \begin{pmatrix} 0 & 1 & 0 & \ldots & 0 \\ & & \ldots & & \\ & & & \ldots & \\ 0 & \ldots & & 0 & 1 \\ 1 & 0 & \ldots & 0 & 0 \end{pmatrix} \quad \text{(A6)}$$

Therefore $T'^N = I$, so that $T'^k = T'^{k+N} = T'^{k+2N} \ldots$. Now

$$M(\lambda) = \left(\frac{1}{1+\lambda}\right) \sum_{k=0}^{\infty} (\theta T')^k, \quad \text{(A7)}$$

where $\lambda/(1+\lambda) = \theta$. Let $\Theta = \{1 + \theta + \theta^N + \theta^{2N} \cdots\}$. Thus

$$M(\lambda) \equiv \frac{\Theta}{1+\lambda}[I + \theta T' + (\theta T')^2 + \cdots + (\theta T')^{N-1}] = \frac{1-\theta}{1-\theta^N} A \quad \text{(A8)}$$

where

$$A \equiv [I + \theta T' + \cdots + (\theta T')^{N-1}]$$

$$= \begin{pmatrix} 1 & \theta^{N-1} & \ldots & \ldots & \theta^2 & \theta \\ \theta & 1 & \theta^{N-1} & \ldots & \ldots & \theta^2 \\ \ldots & \ldots & \ldots & \ldots & \ldots & \ldots \\ \ldots & \ldots & \ldots & \ldots & \ldots & \ldots \\ \ldots & \ldots & \ldots & \ldots & 1 & \theta^{N-1} \\ \theta^{N-1} & \ldots & \ldots & \theta^2 & \theta & 1 \end{pmatrix} \quad \text{(A9)}$$

Consider now the diversified lending case, where the matrix T is given by

$$T = \frac{1}{N-1}\begin{pmatrix} 0 & 1 & \dots & \dots & 1 \\ 1 & 0 & 1 & \dots & 1 \\ \dots & \dots & \dots & \dots & \dots \\ 1 & \dots & 1 & 0 & 1 \\ 1 & \dots & \dots & 1 & 0 \end{pmatrix}. \tag{A10}$$

It follows that $T = T'$. Now

$$M(\lambda) = \frac{1}{1+\lambda}\left[I - \frac{1}{1+\lambda}T'\right]^{-1} = (1-\theta)\sum_{k=0}^{\infty}(\theta T')^k. \tag{A11}$$

Notice that

$$T'^2 = \frac{1}{N-1}I + \frac{N-2}{N-1}T',$$

$$T'^3 = \frac{1}{N-1}T' + \frac{N-2}{N-1}T'^2 = \frac{1}{N-1}T' + \frac{N-2}{N-1}\left[\frac{1}{N-1}I + \frac{N-2}{N-1}T'\right].$$

Finally,

$$T'^3 = \frac{N-2}{(N-1)^2}I + \left[1 - \frac{N-2}{(N-1)^2}\right]T'. \tag{A12}$$

Recursively we obtain

$$T'^k = \beta_k I + (1-\beta_k)T', \tag{A13}$$

where

$$\beta_k = \frac{1}{N}\left[1 - \left(\frac{-1}{N-1}\right)^{k-1}\right]. \tag{A14}$$

Therefore,

$$M(\lambda) = (1-\theta)\sum_{k=0}^{\infty}(\theta T')^k = (1-\theta)\sum_{k=0}^{\infty}[\theta^k\beta_k I + \theta^k(1-\beta_k)T']. \tag{A15}$$

Proof of Proposition 3.

If $\mathbf{R} = \begin{pmatrix} 0 \\ R \\ \vdots \\ R \end{pmatrix}$ the necessary condition for $x = (1, \dots, 1)$ to be an equilibrium becomes

$$\mathbf{D} = M(\lambda)\mathbf{R} = M(\lambda)\begin{pmatrix} 0 \\ R \\ \vdots \\ R \end{pmatrix} \geq D_0. \tag{A16}$$

In the credit chain case equation (A9) implies that the first row of condition (A16) becomes

$$\frac{1-\theta}{1-\theta^N}(\theta^{N-1}+\cdots+\theta)R \geq D_0 \tag{A17}$$

or

$$\frac{D_0}{R} \leq 1 - \frac{1}{1+\theta+\cdots+\theta^{N-1}} \equiv \gamma_N^{\mathrm{CRE}}. \tag{A18}$$

It is easy to see that γ_N^{CRE} increases in N and in θ (and therefore in γ). Notice that $\gamma_\infty^{\mathrm{CRE}} = \theta$.

Under diversified lending, $M(\lambda)$is given by (A15). Checking the first row of (A16) and dividing by R yields

$$\frac{D_1}{R} = (1-\theta)\sum_{k=1}^{\infty}\left[\theta^k(1-\beta_k)\frac{N-1}{N-1}\right] \equiv \gamma_N^{\mathrm{DIV}} \geq \frac{D_0}{R}. \tag{A19}$$

Using

$$\beta_k = \frac{1}{N}\left[1-\left(\frac{-1}{N-1}\right)^{k-1}\right], \tag{A20}$$

equation (A19) becomes

$$\gamma_N^{\mathrm{DIV}} = (1-\theta)\sum_{k=1}^{\infty}\theta^k\left(1-\frac{1}{N}\left[1-\left(\frac{-1}{N-1}\right)^{k-1}\right]\right), \tag{A21}$$

or

$$N\gamma_N^{\mathrm{DIV}} = (1-\theta)\left[(N-1)\sum_{k=1}^{\infty}\theta^k + \sum_{k=1}^{\infty}\theta^k\left(\frac{-1}{N-1}\right)^{k-1}\right]. \tag{A22}$$

Since

$$(1-\theta)\sum_{k=1}^{\infty}\theta^k = \frac{(1-\theta)\theta}{(1-\theta)} = \theta, \tag{A23}$$

and

$$\begin{aligned}(1-\theta)\sum_{k=1}^{\infty}\theta^k\left(\frac{-1}{N-1}\right)^{k-1} &= \theta\,(1-\theta)\sum_{k=0}^{\infty}\theta^k\left(\frac{-1}{N-1}\right)^{k}\\ &= \frac{\theta(1-\theta)}{1+(\theta/N-1)} = \frac{(N-1)\theta(1-\theta)}{N-1+\theta},\end{aligned} \tag{A24}$$

equation (A22) becomes

$$N\gamma_N^{\mathrm{DIV}} = (N-1)\theta + \frac{(N-1)\theta(1-\theta)}{N-1+\theta} = \frac{(N-1)\theta[N-1+\theta+1-\theta]}{N-1+\theta} \tag{A25}$$

from which

$$\gamma_N^{\text{DIV}} = \frac{(N-1)\theta}{N-1+\theta} = \frac{1}{(1/\theta)+(1/N-1)}. \tag{A26}$$

Recalling that $\theta = \lambda/(1+\lambda)$, we see that γ_N^{DIV} increases with λ and N, and that $\gamma_\infty^{\text{DIV}} = \theta$.

Proof of Proposition 4.

Comparing γ_N^{DIV} and γ_N^{CRV} we obtain

$$\frac{\gamma_N^{\text{DIV}}}{\theta} = \frac{(N-1)}{N-1+\theta} = \frac{1}{1+(\theta/N-1)}, \tag{A27}$$

and

$$\frac{\gamma_N^{\text{CRE}}}{\theta} = \frac{1-\theta^{N-1}}{1-\theta^N} = \frac{1+\theta+\theta^2+\theta^3+\cdots+\theta^{N-2}}{1+\theta+\theta^2+\theta^3+\cdots+\theta^{N-1}}$$

$$= \frac{1}{1+\theta^{N-1}/(1+\theta+\theta^2+\theta^3+\cdots+\theta^{N-2})}. \tag{A28}$$

Since $\theta^{N-2} < \theta^{N-3} < \theta^{N-4} \ldots$, then

$$\frac{\theta^{N-2}}{1+\theta+\theta^2+\theta^3+\cdots+\theta^{N-2}} < \frac{1}{N-1}. \tag{A29}$$

Thus

$$\frac{\theta^{N-1}}{1+\theta+\theta^2+\theta^3+\cdots+\theta^{N-2}} < \frac{\theta}{N-1} \Rightarrow \frac{\gamma_N^{\text{CRE}}}{\theta} > \frac{\gamma_N^{\text{DIV}}}{\theta}. \tag{A30}$$

REFERENCES

Allen, Franklin, and Douglas Gale. 'Financial Contagion.' Mimeo, The Wharton School, University of Pennsylvania, 1998.

Berger, Allen N., Diana Hancock, and Jeffrey C. Marquardt. 'A Framework for Analyzing Efficiency, Risks, Costs, and Innovations in the Payments System.' *Journal of Money, Credit, and Banking* 28 (November 1996, Part 2), 696–732.

Bhattacharya, Sudipto, and Paolo Fulghieri. 'Uncertain Liquidity and Interbank Contracting.' *Economics Letters* 44 (1994), 287–94.

Bhattacharya, Sudipto, and Douglas Gale. 'Preference Shocks, Liquidity and Central Policy.' In *New Approaches to Monetary Economics*, edited by W. Barnett and K. Singleton. Cambridge: Cambridge University Press, 1987.

Brimmer, Andrew F. 'Distinguished Lecture on Economics in Government: Central Banking and Systemic Risks in Capital Markets.' *Journal of Economic Perspectives* 3 (1989), 3–16.

Calomiris, Charles W., and Charles M. Kahn. 'The Role of Demandable Debt in Structuring Optimal Banking Arrangements.' *American Economic Review* 81 (1991), 497–513.

Calomiris, Charles W., and Joseph R. Mason. 'Contagion and Bank Failures during the Great Depression: The June 1932 Chicago Banking Panic." *American Economic Review* 87 (1997), 863–83.

De Bandt, Olivier, and Philipp Hartmann. 'Systemic Risk: A Survey.' Mimeo, European Central Bank, Frankfurt, 1998.

Diamond, Douglas W., and Philip H. Dybvig. 'Bank Runs, Deposit Insurance, and Liquidity.' *Journal of Political Economy* 91 (1983), 401–19.

Flannery, Mark J. 'Financial Crises, Payment System Problems, and Discount Window Lending.' *Journal of Money, Credit, and Banking* 28 (November 1996, Part 2), 805–24.

Freedman, Charles, and Clyde Goodlet. 'The Canadian Payments Systems: Recent Developments in Structure and Regulation.' In *Payments Systems in the Global Economy: Risks and Opportunities*, Proceedings of the 34th Annual Conference of Bank Structure and Competition, Federal Reserve Bank of Chicago, 1998.

Freeman, Scott. 'Clearinghouse Banks and Banknote Over-Issue.' *Journal of Monetary Economics* 38 (1996a), 101–15.

—. 'The Payment System, Liquidity, and Rediscounting.' *American Economic Review* 86 (1996b), 1126–38.

Freixas, Xavier, and Bruno M. Parigi. 'Contagion and Efficiency in Gross and Net Payment Systems.' *Journal of Financial Intermediation* 7 (1998), 3–31.

Freixas, Xavier, Bruno M. Parigi, and Jean-Charles Rochet. 'The Lender of Last Resort: A Theoretical Foundation.' Mimeo, IDEI, 1998.

Garber, Peter M. 'Notes on the Role of TARGET in a Stage III Crisis.' National Bureau of Economic Research, Working paper no. 6619, 1998.

Gorton, Gary. 'Banking Panics and Business Cycles.' *Oxford Economic Papers* 40 (1988), 751–81.

Greenspan, Alan. 'Testimony before the Committe on Banking and Financial Services, U.S. House of Representatives.' Washington, D.C., October 1, 1998.

Kaufman, George G. 'Bank Contagion: A Review of the Theory and Evidence.' *Journal of Financial Services Research* 8 (1994), 123–50.

Kiyotaki, Nobuhiro, and John Moore. 'Credit Chains.' Mimeo, London School of Economics, 1997.

Reid, M. 'Flight to Quality.' *Banking World*, September 1991.

Rochet, Jean-Charles, and Jean Tirole. 'Interbank Lending and Systemic Risk.' *Journal of Money, Credit, and Banking* 28 (November 1996, Part 2), 733–62.

Salop, Steven C. 'Monopolistic Competition with Outside Goods.' *Bell Journal of Economics* 10 (1979), 141–56.

Saunders, Anthony, and Berry Wilson. 'Contagious Bank Runs: Evidence from the 1929–1933 Period.' *Journal of Financial Intermediation* 5 (1996), 409–23.

Schoenmaker, Dirk. 'Contagion Risk in Banking.' LSE Financial Markets Group, Discussion paper no. 239, 1996.

Summers, Bruce J., ed. 'The Payment System, Design, Management, and Supervision.' International Monetary Fund, Washington, D.C., 1994.

Takayama, Akira. *Mathematical Economics*, 2d ed. Cambridge: Cambridge University Press, 1985.

Townsend, Robert M. 'Economic Organization with Limited Communication.' *American Economic Review* 77 (1987), 954–71.

Wallace, Neil. 'Another Attempt to Explain an Illiquid Banking System: The Diamond-Dybvig Model with Sequential Service Taken Seriously.' *Quarterly Review*, Federal Reserve Bank of Minneapolis 12 (1988), 3–16.

Wall Street Journal, The. 'A Hedge Fund Falters, So the Fed Persuades Big Banks to Ante Up.' Interactive edition, September 24, 1998.

PART IV

AN INTERNATIONAL LENDER OF LAST RESORT?

20

Can there be an International Lender-of-Last-Resort?

FORREST CAPIE

I. INTRODUCTION

Around the world, from Asia to Russia and beyond, there is considerable financial turmoil. There is widespread talk of financial crises, and there are many suggestions being advanced for their resolution. One frequently suggested remedy is that there should be an international lender-of-last-resort. Kindleberger (1989) devoted a chapter to the 'International lender of last resort', in his *Manias, Panics, and Crashes.* A recent suggestion has been made that the Bank for International Settlements could be made an international lender-of-last-resort. And in *The Economist* of 10 October 1998 consideration was given again to the possibility of the International Monetary Fund (IMF) being the international lender-of-last-resort.

This paper is not in any way a proposal for reforming the IMF or making suggestions as to how it can perform the function of a lender-of-last-resort. The argument is rather that a proper understanding of that term shows that there cannot be an international lender-of-last-resort. The IMF or some other body like it may still have a function in the international financial system. However, it is perhaps worth noting that the IMF's rescue of countries in recent times is seen by some as creating the moral hazard which produces further problems of the same kind. This issue of bailout is key in an understanding of the role of the lender-of-last-resort.

The paper outlines first the nature of a financial crisis, before defining the lender-of-last-resort and considering who can carry out the function. This is followed by a brief discussion of the evolution of the lender in the history of thought, some domestic British experience and noting differences in Europe. Some consideration is then given to what might be an important element in the story–the place anonymity plays in the execution of the role. Finally, if all this is accepted, the conclusion that seems inevitably to follow is that there can be no international lender-of-last-resort.

The starting question is: is the banking system fragile or robust? Banks in fractional reserve systems take deposits and make loans, and by doing so multiply the stock of money. Similarly, when they fail, or take steps to reduce their assets, they reduce the stock of money, and in the face of wage and price stickiness that

This article first appeared in *International Finance* 1 (2), 1998. © Blackwell Publishers Ltd, 1998.

has a deleterious impact on real output. The danger of one bank failure leading to others failing increases the danger of a major collapse in the stock of money, and hence a severe recession in the real economy. Avoiding financial instability and the dangers it carries is therefore a concern.

But first, how should we recognize a financial crisis? The most operationally useful definition would seem to be that of Schwartz (1986). A crisis is where there is a threat to a country's money supply. This should be distinguished from a situation in which a major bank or financial institution or other institution fails.

The threat to the money stock can be illustrated by means of the simple money/multiplier model—a model whose application has proved powerful over the long historical period for different countries. The broad money supply is equal to the money multiplier times the money base:

$$M = \left[\frac{1 + \frac{C}{D}}{\frac{C}{D} + \frac{R}{D}} \right] B$$

where M is broad money, B is the monetary base, C/D is the public's currency/deposit ratio, and R/D is the banks' cash reserve/deposit ratio. This is simply an accounting framework and does not imply causality. Neither does it matter that central banks did not see themselves as behaving as if they were conscious of this framework. It is simply a useful way of setting out the issue. So, for example, it shows how the public have a role to play in determining the money stock in the way in which they hold cash and deposits. And it shows how the banks have a role to play in the way they hold their cash reserves in relation to deposits. Together these give the money multiplier. The monetary authorities control the monetary base, or it is determined via the balance of payments. In a financial crisis the public withdraw deposits and hold cash. And the banks, as they see the demand for cash rising, try to cope with this by raising their cash reserves. Both of these actions have the effect of reducing the money multiplier, and unless the monetary authorities take counteraction there will be a collapse in the money stock. In these circumstances the monetary authorities need to raise the supply of monetary base—sometimes dramatically so.

This is the purpose of the lender-of-last-resort. Yet, it is an issue that has been the cause of a certain amount of confusion in monetary economics, and monetary and financial history. There is disagreement as to how the role should be defined, and some debate as to how it should operate. There are two principal views on the issue. The first is that it means the rescue of an individual institution; the second that it should mean the rescue of the market as a whole—the provision of liquidity to allay widespread panic. It is in the first that the misconception lies, and it is important to dispose of that first.

Any commercial bank may, from time to time, extend additional loans to clients who are temporarily illiquid, or even by some accounting standards insolvent. They may do so even when the present expected return from the new loan itself is zero or negative, if the wider effects, for example on their own reputation for commitment to clients, or the knock-on effects of the failure of the first client on other customers, should warrant it. By the same token, a nascent central bank—an institution still some way short of maturity as a central bank—may 'rescue' some client correspondent bank, just as the commercial bank may support its business customer. But we would not want to describe such occasional, and ad hoc, exercises as involving a conscious assumption of a systematic lender-of-last-resort function. Nor would we want to see a mature central bank rescuing individual banks since there is too much moral hazard involved.

No central bank would want to pre-commit itself to giving special support to *any* individual bank which was running into liquidity problems. Especially with the development of efficient, broad interbank and other short-term money markets, a bank liquidity problem that is not caused by some technical problem is likely itself to be a reflection of some deeper suspicions about solvency. Consequently, an unqualified pre-commitment to provide assistance would involve too much moral hazard. Indeed any individual act of rescue involves a degree of moral hazard.

The proper view of the lender-of-last-resort involves the bank declaring its position to the market; what is known today as pre-commitment. This role is quite well defined in the literature on English monetary economics in the nineteenth century; and further, the particular institutional arrangements that evolved in England in the nineteenth century were perhaps close to ideal for its execution. The Bank of England was a fully fledged lender-of-last-resort by the 1870s, coming to the rescue of the market in an appropriate fashion through the buffer of the discount houses (as discussed later). It could be argued by extension that the continental European counterparts did not and could not act in this way until at least the end of the nineteenth century, and in most cases probably not until the beginning of the twentieth century. This had implications for the stability of the respective systems.

The role of lender-of-last-resort can be said to appear when the institution accepts a responsibility for the stability of the banking system as a whole, which should override any (residual) concern with its own private profitability. Thus, we would argue that it is the intellectual basis and reasoning of institutions for providing such support, rather than the individual act of rescue of the market itself, that determines whether the institution had become a lender-of-last-resort in fact. But while rescues can be clearly dated, shifts in mental perceptions are harder to date. As Fetter (1978) shows, the Bank of England's Court remained divided and uncertain over this issue at least until after the publication of *Lombard Street*; and we have less insight into the appropriate date in other countries with early founded government banks. However, by about 1900, this function was widely accepted as a core function of any newly established central bank.

The main points to be made are that the lender should not rescue individuals in distress, but supply liquidity to the market as a whole. It is important to stress that it is the peculiar position of the monopoly note issuer and holder and provider of the ultimate means of payment that allows—almost obliges—it to behave as the lender-of-last-resort. That is the only institution that can supply *without limit* (but at an increasing price) the ultimate means of payment. It is the knowledge in the markets that supply cannot run out that serves to assure the market and allay the panic.

Who carries out the function? It is mainly central banks, though of course it need not be. Central banks have two main functions. One is macro, the preservation of price stability; the other is micro, the preservation of financial stability. And the two are of course related. It is the latter, though, that really defines central banking. And it soon becomes clear that central banks and lenders-of-last-resort are close to being synonymous. It is in pursuit of its goal of price stability that the central bank seeks to keep a broad monetary target stable and it is that which on occasions obliges it to supply a greater quantity of base money. The institutions that we know as central banks have evolved over a long period and acquired, or developed and extended, their functions according to circumstances and the economic and political environment in which they found themselves. It is worth recalling the essential features of their origin and development. Some like to see the origins lying in the acquisition of the right to monopoly of note issue, and there is a case to be made for this, or at least that it is an important element in the make-up of a central bank. Others have emphasized what is often seen as the key function, the lenders-of-last-resort. Goodhart (1988) has drawn attention to the potential conflict of interest that exists if the 'central bank', the institution set up by government, given the monopoly of its business and a generally privileged position in the monetary system, continues to do a substantial amount of commercial business. The conflict of interest arises in the following way. If the commercial banks get into difficulties there is an incentive for the central bank to allow them to fail, or at least to suffer, and to capture more business for itself. This is the antithesis of the last resort role.

Prior to the latter part of the nineteenth century, central banks were generally expected to carry out a commercial banking function; in some cases, in the European countries when they were first established, they offered the only sources of commercial banking services (for example, Scandinavia), and they were often the most important and largest commercial bank in their country. Consequently, the early relationships between central banks and commercial banks were often ones of business rivalry and competition. This adversarial relationship was resolved around the early twentieth century in most cases, with a few exceptions (for example, Australia), by a largely uncodified concordat, whereby, in return for the central bank's withdrawal from commercial banking, the commercial banks voluntarily accepted the central bank's leadership.

But difficulty remains in defining central banking. The Bank of England was established in 1694, but at that time there was no concept of central banking.

Something close to a modern conception had emerged by the end of the eighteenth century, and Henry Thornton probably regarded the Bank of England as a central bank in a modern sense of the term, albeit recognizing some deficiencies in its behaviour. But there are others who would prefer to date it from 1844 or at least to see the Bank Charter Act 1844 as an important landmark, since that bolstered the Bank's monopoly privileges. For others still it would have to wait until the 1870s when the Bank accepted its function as a lender-of-last-resort and effectively withdrew from any rivalry with the commercial banks. We incline to the last mentioned.

We turn here to the issue as it is captured in the writings of the two most distinguished contributors to the subject in the nineteenth century, Henry Thornton and Walter Bagehot. The justification for this is that England industrialized first and became the earliest example of an industrial economy with a modern banking system, and hence the birthplace of monetary economics.

II. THE CLASSIC POSITION

Henry Thornton has been described as the father of the modern central bank. Thornton's classic monograph *Paper Credit* (1802) is the source of his principal ideas. Joseph Schumpeter called it the Magna Carta of central banking.

The essence of central banking for Thornton is contained in the following quotation:

> To limit the amount of paper issued, and to resort for this purpose, whenever the temptation to borrow is strong, to some effectual principle of restriction; in no case, however, materially to diminish the sum in circulation, but to let it vibrate only within certain limits; to afford a slow and cautious extension of it, as the general trade of the kingdom enlarges itself; to allow of some special, though temporary, increase in the event of any extraordinary alarm or difficulty, as the best means of preventing a great demand at home for guineas; and to lean to the side of diminution, in the case of gold going abroad, and of the general exchanges continuing long unfavourable; this seems to be the true policy of the directors of an institution circumstanced like that of the Bank of England. To suffer either the solicitations of merchants, or the wishes of government, to determine the measure of the bank issues, is unquestionably to adopt a very false principle of conduct. (Thornton 1802, p. 259)

This is a remarkably clear statement given its date and the state of development in the money market. It describes the ideal daily operation of a central bank. But how should the lender-of-last-resort behave in a crisis? Thornton acknowledged the danger of the failure of one bank leading to the spread of fear and possibly panic and the failure of many banks—a common occurrence in the England he was describing, that of the late eighteenth century when there were hundreds of small banks:

> If any one bank fails, a general run upon the neighbouring ones is apt to take place, which if not checked in the beginning by a pouring into the circulation a large quantity of gold, leads to very extensive mischief. (Thornton 1802, p. 180)

The remedy for such an occasion was for the Bank to provide liquidity:

> . . . if the Bank of England, in future seasons of alarm, should be disposed to extend its discounts in a greater degree than heretofore, then the threatened calamity may be averted through the generosity of that institution. (Thornton 1802, p. 188)

Thornton even allowed that several institutions could fail but that the central bank may nevertheless not feel the need to save them:

> It is by no means intended to imply, that it would become the Bank of England to relieve every distress which the rashness of country banks may bring upon them: the bank, by doing this, might encourage their improvidence. There seems to be a medium at which a public bank should aim in granting aid to inferior establishments, and which it often must find it very difficult to be observed. The relief should neither be so prompt and liberal as to exempt those who misconduct their business from all the natural consequences of their fault, nor so scanty and slow as deeply to involve the general interests. These interests, nevertheless, are sure to be pleaded by every distressed person whose affairs are large, however indifferent or even ruinous may be their state. (Thornton 1802, p. 188)

Thornton's view of the lender-of-last-resort was one that placed the emphasis on responsibility to the market, and not to an individual institution. The central objective is to prevent the collapse of the money stock. This is what we take to be the classic position.

Bagehot was the great developer and expounder of these views in the nineteenth century. He first wrote on this subject in 1848 in the first article that he published (Bagehot 1848). He was writing first of all about the previous year's financial crisis and commenting at the same time on the Act of 1844. His article is remarkable for one so young (he was only 21 at the time) and is worth quoting at length:

> The currency argument is this: It is a great defect of a purely metallic circulation that the quantity of it cannot be readily suited to any sudden demand; it takes time to get new supplies of gold and silver, and, in the meantime, a temporary rise in the value of bullion takes place. Now as paper money can be supplied in unlimited quantities, however sudden the demand may be, it does not appear to us that there is any objection on principle of sudden issues of paper money to meet sudden and large extensions of demand. It gives to a purely metallic circulation that greater constancy of purchasing power possessed by articles whose quantity can be quickly suited to demand. It will be evident from what we have said before that this power of issuing notes is one excessively liable to abuse because, as before shown, it may depreciate the currency; and on that account such a power ought only to be lodged in the hands of government . . . . It should only be used in rare and exceptional circumstances. But when the fact of a *sudden* demand is proved, we see no objection, but decided advantage, in introducing this new element into a metallic circulation. (Bagehot 1848, p. 267)

That is one of the clearest statements on the need for liquidity and the form its provision should take. The English banking system was continuing to evolve, sometimes in ways that Bagehot did not entirely approve of. He would rather there had been no central bank and that competition prevailed, but accepted that the system that had emerged had to be lived with.

Before 1870 there had been no consistency in the behaviour of the Bank of England. Sometimes it came to the rescue of the market and sometimes did not. Sometimes it bailed out insolvent institutions and at other times did not. In the context of these developments Bagehot set out his views first in the pages of *The Economist*, of which he was editor in the middle decades of the century, and then in *Lombard Street* (1873). It was in the latter that Bagehot set out what is taken to be his definitive position.

Where in Thornton's time of writing there were no joint stock banks, by 1870, when Bagehot embarked on *Lombard Street*, there were many such banks, and they were beginning to dominate the system. The risk of panic was clearly increased if a large joint-stock bank collapsed:

> . . . no cause is more capable of producing a panic, perhaps none is so capable, as the failure of a first-rate joint stock bank in London. (Bagehot 1873, p. 251)

Following Thornton, though, the solution was the same:

> A panic, in a word, is a species of neuralgia, and according to the rules of science you must not starve it. The holders of the cash reserve must be ready not only to keep it for their own liabilities, but to advance it most freely for the liabilities of others. (Bagehot 1873, pp. 51–52)

He goes on:

> That in a panic the bank, or banks, holding the ultimate reserve should refuse bad bills or bad securities will not make the panic really worse; the 'unsound' people are a feeble minority, and they are afraid even to look frightened for fear their unsoundness may be detected. The great majority, the majority to be protected, are the 'sound' people, the people who have good security to offer. (Bagehot 1873, p. 188)

This brings the emphasis back to the security on offer and thus to the market as a whole. But in addition Bagehot argued that these large joint-stock banks should provide more information about their activities, so that the sound might be separated from the unsound.

These two writers, Thornton and Bagehot, provide the classic view of the essence of central banking. The ideal form of the lender-of-last-resort was one in which there should be no individual bailout, but rather an acceptance to discount good quality paper irrespective of where it came from.

Some of these quotations cited above are of course open to different interpretation, and especially so since the monetary and banking systems were undergoing continual change. Not surprisingly, there continues to be some disagreement over the precise meaning of the lender-of-last-resort. It is clearly not easy to date the function, as it was something that was groped towards. A central bank in the making could come to the rescue of one of its customers (a bank) who was temporarily illiquid or even insolvent. Our argument is that such a rescue is analogous to the commercial bank rescuing one of its customers—simply good business practice. If we were to take this as a measure of the last resort function then the Bank of England became such a lender in the eighteenth century. But as we stressed, no central bank could pre-commit itself to coming to the rescue of any individual bank that was confronted with liquidity problems. That would result in serious moral hazard.

A central bank assumes the function of lender-of-last-resort when it accepts responsibility for the banking system as a whole, and that should override any residual concern with its own profitability. It is the appreciation of how they should behave in a crisis, rather than any individual act of rescue, that should date the acceptance of the role.

III. THE CASE OF ENGLAND

The history of the Bank of England (the Bank) is quite well known, and may easily be summarized and placed in the context of the framework outlined above. Founded in 1694, it was the government's bank from that date on. Joint-stock banking was prohibited, but a vigorous banking system developed in the next 100 years. The phrase 'lender-of-last-resort' entered the language at the end of the eighteenth century but, as we have argued, the Bank was not such a lender at that time. It did begin to acquire the monopoly of note issue with the 1844 Act, though in effect the monopoly had to wait until the 1870s.

It was also in the 1870s that the Bank accepted that its public responsibility greatly outweighed its pursuit of profit, and it became the lender-of-last-resort. There is no explicit statement to this effect, but following the exhortation of Bagehot first in *The Economist* in the 1860s, and then more persuasively in *Lombard Street* (1873), it seems the Bank accepted that public responsibility. Its commercial business continued, but was not significant.

In the 100 years after 1870 there seems to be ample demonstration that the British financial, and particularly banking, system was enormously stable, and that that stability was due in some good part to the operations of the Bank of England. The value of the currency was maintained, apart from wartime experience, for most of that period. More significantly, there were no financial crises in the period. Where crises had been periodic before 1870, there were none after that date. Admittedly that requires a little more elaboration. But following Schwartz's (1986) definition of a financial crisis—something that threatens or actually produces a collapse in the money stock—seems sensible. There will be occasions when banks, like other firms, fail, but that does not constitute a financial crisis. Exceptions may be taken to this definition, but it does seem to provide the most useful approach, in that it allows some harder assessment of a crisis, in terms of cash and reserve ratios.

There were occasions in this period after 1870 when there was the appearance of crises and some of these have been so described. For example, in 1878 the City of Glasgow Bank failed, and that had some repercussions in the banking sector, even if these were not serious. An examination of the public's currency/deposit ratio shows no rush to cash. Neither did the banks build up or lose their reserve/deposit ratio. The Bank of England did nothing to help, and rightly so, since the Glasgow

Bank was corruptly run. The approach is useful again in describing the events of 1890—sometimes called 'The Baring Crisis'—and correctly so since there was a crisis for one bank but not for the system. Baring's did indeed fail and was reconstituted. The Bank of England participated in that it organized a 'lifeboat', but it did not bail out an over-stretched bank.

In other years when there were crises around the world, and generally transmitted by means of the fixed exchange-rate system, they nevertheless did not appear in Britain. 1907 is an example. By then, of course, it was accepted in Britain that the Bank knew how to behave, and signs of panic abroad did not spark panic in England. The same is true of the interwar years, when again British banking was enormously stable. There was a crisis in 1931, but it was an exchange rate crisis. No banks failed, even if there was a little fudging of that issue. And, generally speaking, bank profits were not badly dented. This contrasted starkly with most of the rest of the world, with one or two exceptions such as Canada and The Netherlands.

Furthermore, it has been shown that for the years after 1870 the Bank of England acted to avoid panics and did so very successfully (Ogden 1991). Of course there were other factors in the British experience that contributed to stability. The most important was the structure of the banking system. It was increasingly a thoroughly branched system that allowed banks considerable diversification. At least in the years before 1914, this stability did not depend on the cartel, which had barely come into being at that date. Separating the respective contributions of these factors is a task yet to be tackled. Structure may well turn out to have been the more important, but the stabilizing presence of a trusted central bank must have made its own important contribution.

Continental European experience was mixed. In almost all European countries there were, from an early date (early according to their industrial development), relatively large joint-stock banks, and they competed with the government's bank. The latter's function was essentially the preservation of the value of the currency–metal convertibility. This could conflict with its pursuit of commercial business, and its role as banker to the other banks. As we noted, there were occasions when European banks moved their discount rate in a direction that appeared to be at odds with the preservation of the value of the currency. More research is required on these episodes with a view to ascertaining what pressures were found in the foreign-exchange markets and how these were dealt with. But the main point to make is that there were a number of impediments to the proper functioning of a central bank; impediments that did not disappear in the main, until the twentieth century.

IV. ANONYMITY

It is possible that a crucial element in this story is that anonymity is of fundamental importance in the execution of the lender-of-last-resort function. The lender-of-last-resort supplies funds to the market in times of need. It does not supply individual institutions. In its proper form it should not engage in bailing out firms of any kind, be they banks or non-banks. Therefore, if the operation could be carried out where the identity of those seeking funds was not known to the Bank that would be ideal.

The mechanism can be thought of as the central bank with a discount window which is of frosted glass, and is raised just a few inches. Representatives of institutions could therefore appear at the window and push through the paper that they wanted discounted. The central banker would return the appropriate amount of cash, reflecting the going rate of interest. The central banker does not know, nor does he care, who is on the other side of the window. He simply discounts good quality paper—or lends on the basis of good collateral. In this way institutions holding good quality assets will have no difficulty in getting hold of the funds they need. Institutions with poor quality assets are likely to suffer. In times of panic the interest rate would rise.

By something of a happy accident, this was in effect the system that developed in England. At the beginning of the nineteenth century the Bank of England monopoly aroused the ire of the banking community. Such was the antipathy between the Bank of England and the new joint-stock banks that they preferred to keep a distance between each other. Discount brokers emerged who conveniently transacted business between them. These discount brokers gradually acquired the capital base to finance their own portfolios, and by the third quarter of the nineteenth century had developed their modern form of the discount house.

When the commercial banks were under pressure in a liquidity squeeze, their first line of defence was to call in their loans to the discount houses, and this in turn sent the discount houses off to the Bank of England where they had special access. If the commercial banks had to cash in bills, they would do this at the discount houses, and the latter would in turn take them to the Bank. In this way the central bank never needed to know where the great bulk of the demand was coming from. It is our point that where it comes from is largely an irrelevance. Good bills get discounted.

In practice, of course, we know that individual institutions did take bills directly to the Bank, and borrowed on good security from the Bank when pressure developed. These were in the main its own customers (Ogden 1991).

It is interesting to speculate that some confusion in the discussion over the nature of the lender-of-last-resort function may have arisen from too cavalier a treatment of this model. Central banking was more advanced in Britain than in other countries, and the British model of central banking was often adopted elsewhere. But the actual mechanism did not exist elsewhere. Thus, a key feature of the British system, its inbuilt protective device for anonymity, was ignored. This meant that in most other countries the institutions themselves went to the 'central bank' and anonymity was lost. Difficulties were exacerbated when the government's bank and the commercial banks were in competition for commercial business. This seems to have been ignored in the literature, and it may be that it is this that has allowed the confusion over bailing out to develop as it has.

V. INTERNATIONAL LENDER-OF-LAST-RESORT

What does all this mean for an international lender-of-last-resort? If the argument is persuasive, it leads inevitably to the conclusion that there can be no such international equivalent of the lender-of-last-resort. First, it is the fact that it is the ultimate issuer of the currency that allows a central bank to be the lender-of-last-resort. The fact that there is no currency beyond the national boundary of that currency means the lender's jurisdiction is limited to these national boundaries. Thus, there was no international lender-of-last-resort under the gold standard. The suggestion has on occasion been made that the Bank of England, at the centre of the system and described as the 'conductor of the orchestra', was such a lender. But that is not the case. For example, if a financial crisis flared in France, that may have found the Bank of France appealing to the Bank of England for assistance, or indeed to anyone else who might lend to it. But only the Bank of France can act in France as the lender-of-last-resort by issuing francs in sufficient quantities to quell the panic.

In the world before 1914 there were episodes that bore some resemblance to this; not necessarily with central bank cooperation, but sometimes help was organized by means of a loan brokered by a banker such as Rothschild. These arrangements were to help some country through difficulties that threatened their ability to remain on the pegged exchange-rate system. Similarly, in the interwar period, stabilization loans were made initially to help countries back to the restored gold standard. However, the system that was restored was a flawed one, and further stabilization loans were required, and organized, through the League of Nations. The problem at base was the inappropriate policies being pursued by the USA and France, but in any case the problem was not of financial crises and no lender-of-last-resort was involved.

The IMF, designed at Bretton Woods in 1944, was an attempt to overcome these interwar problems. The IMF's primary function was to provide temporary assistance to countries with current account imbalances in a world of limited capital mobility. That it proceeded to do, and the system worked as planned, at least after the restoration of convertibility of currencies in 1958 and up to 1971. Even after that, the loans that continued to be made right up to the 1980s were attempts to allow countries to stay on pegged exchange-rate systems. Taxpayers were not being called upon. But in the 1990s, loans on a scale previously barely conceived of, have been made to countries not to help them stay on pegged rates but after their exchange-rate regime has broken down. Worse than that, the scale of the loans has meant there have been substantial transfers from ordinary taxpayers to a wealthier class.

Even if we were to turn a blind eye to this violation of the basic principle of the lender-of-last-resort—that is that bailouts have been carried out—we have seen that the IMF is actually incapable of coming to the rescue of some of those in difficulty. It does not have the resources. It was in fact unable in 1995 to extend to Mexico the necessary funds. The only way it could have such funds would be if individual central banks ceded to it the right to issue their currencies—dollars, pounds, euros and so on. That, however, takes us into wild political fantasy, and in any case does nothing to confront the problem of serious moral hazard involved in rescuing individual countries.

So, currently, neither the IMF, nor any institution like it, can be an international lender-of-last-resort. There is no world currency and neither is there likely to be one, so there can be no international lender-of-last-resort. It is as well to face that, so that energies can be directed to improved analysis and policies.

REFERENCES

Bagehot, W. (1848), 'The Currency Problem', *Prospective Review*, 297–337, in N. S. J. Stevas (ed.) (1986), *Collected Works*, 9. London: The Economist.

Bagehot, W. (1873), *Lombard Street*, (14th edn). London: Kegan Paul.

Bordo, Michael D. (1990), 'The Lender of Last Resort Alternative Views and Historical Experience', *Federal Reserve Bank of Richmond*, 76(1).

Capie, Forrest, Charles Goodhart, and Norbert Schnadt (1994), *The Development of Central Banking*. Cambridge: Cambridge University Press.

Fetter, F. W. (1978), *Development of British Monetary Orthodoxy*. New York: Augustus Kelley.

Goodhart, C. A. E. (1988), *The Evolution of Central Banks*, Cambridge, MA: MIT Press.

Kindleberger, C. P. (1989), *Manias, Panics and Crashes*. London: Macmillan.

Lovell, Michael (1957), 'The Role of the Bank of England as Lender of Last Resort in the Crises of the Eighteenth Century', *Explorations in Entrepreneurial History*, 10(1).

Ogden, E. (1991), 'An Analysis of Bank of England Discount and Behaviour', in Foreman-Peck (ed.), *New Perspectives on the late Victorian Economy*. Cambridge: Cambridge University Press.

Schwartz, Anna J. (1986), 'Real and Pseudo Financial Crises', in Forrest Capie and G. E. Wood (eds), *Financial Crises and the World Banking System*. London: Macmillan.

The Economist (1998), 'Lender without Limit', 10 October, 124.

Thornton, H. (1802), *An Enquiry into the nature and effects of Paper Credit of Great Britain*. Reprinted. New York: Augustus Kelley.

21

Earmarks of a Lender of Last Resort

ANNA J. SCHWARTZ

Some observers of the financial distress of countries in Asia and Latin America in recent years have suggested that what the world needs is an international lender of last resort. The institution that could serve this purpose, it is claimed, is the International Monetary Fund (IMF), either as presently constituted, or perhaps with some minor adjustments of its mandate.

In the first part of this lecture, I define the role of a lender of last resort in a domestic setting, give the historical context of the origin of the institution and cite examples of a lender of last resort that performed well and examples of a lender of last resort that performed poorly. I then describe modifications in this century of the time-honoured rules for a lender of last resort, and sum up the discussion by listing the attributes of a lender of last resort in a domestic context. In the second part of the paper, I examine the changing role of the International Monetary Fund since its creation in 1944. I then ask whether it is possible for an international institution like the IMF to possess the attributes of a lender of last resort. The answer, I believe, is negative. In the third part of the paper I conclude that world capital markets are prepared to hasten the recovery of countries in financial distress by lending to them on appropriate terms, putting in question the need for IMF lending.

1. THE DOMESTIC CONTEXT

Definition of a Lender of Last Resort

A responsibility of a central bank, the institution that occupies a central position within a country's financial system, is to serve as a lender of last resort in order to maintain an unimpaired payments system. Let me first note what the term 'payments system' refers to, and then how a payments system becomes impaired and what a lender of last resort does to prevent it from happening. A payments system refers to the procedures used to arrange transfers and advances of money between individuals and firms in an economy.

To answer the question about how a payments system becomes impaired, it is necessary to describe a modern banking system. It is a fractional reserve requirements banking system. In such a system, ordinary banks meet their reserve requirements—a fraction of the deposits on their books—by holding as vault cash the notes of the central bank and maintaining reserve balances with the central bank. Central banks control both the issue of bank notes and bank reserves—the sum of which is known as high-powered money.

One way a payments system may become impaired is when depositors fear for the safety of their deposits and run on banks. By withdrawing their deposits in cash, they squeeze the reserves of the banking system, threatening continued convertibility of deposits into cash. The fear that demands of depositors for cash cannot be met leads to a scramble for high-powered money. In a futile attempt to restore reserves, banks may call loans, refuse to roll over existing loans, or resort to selling assets. This is the sequence of events that impairs the payments system. It can also happen when fears prevail that funds are unavailable at any price to enable sound debtors to make payments that are due. The entire financial system is then at risk, as financial services are disrupted, and economic activity is reduced.

Central Banks as Lenders of Last Resort

During the nineteenth century, central banks had to learn the role of lender of last resort. They learned initially to provide the banks with additional reserves to cut short a panic once it had begun, but eventually learned to act in advance to avert its occurrence. The traditional way to discharge the responsibility was to extend loans of high-powered money to all solvent banks and all solvent borrowers that were temporarily illiquid. The only institution that had the resources to provide such loans in a crisis was the central bank, which could create high-powered money without limit, and hence was the lender of last resort.

The prescription for the exercise of lender of last resort responsibility was developed by Henry Thornton in 1802 and by Walter Bagehot in 1873. They advised that eligibility for loans be limited to solvent banks, that the banks pay a penalty rate for the loan, that is, a rate higher than the prevailing market interest rate, and that the banks offer good collateral. The offer of good collateral was one indication that the bank requesting the loan was indeed solvent. It was also important for the central bank to give timely and predictable signals to market participants of institutional readiness to make available an augmented supply of funds. The signal in and of itself was often sufficient to allay alarm, so that the funds were never drawn on.

The British Model of a Lender of Last Resort

The Bank of England was a slow learner of the need for lender of last resort assistance. A series of financial panics in 1825, 1847, 1857, and 1866 occurred before it developed the appropriate response to restore public confidence in the financial system. It was ineffective in quelling each of these four panics. It provided some assistance but not enough, and it did so hesitantly, so financial markets were not reassured. The panic of 1866, however, was the last one that the British experienced. After that date, the Bank of England was alert to the threat of panic and took actions that prevented the effects of individual bank failures from spreading to the entire financial system.

Evolution of the Concept of the Lender of Last Resort in the US

In this country the First Bank (1791–1811) and the Second Bank (1818–36) of the United States were precursors of a central bank, but it was not until 1913 with the founding of the Federal Reserve System that the idea of a lender of last resort was given substance. The immediate cause for the implementation of the concept was the panic of 1907, the last of a series after the Civil War (1873, 1884, 1890, 1893) that had destabilized US financial markets, though, as I have noted, there were no comparable British panics after 1866. This difference in the experience of panics in the two countries was explained in part by the unit banking system and undiversified asset portfolios of US banks and the highly concentrated British banking system with well-diversified asset portfolios. Hence US banks were more prone to fail than were British banks. The other part of the explanation was the absence in this country of a lender of last resort comparable to the Bank of England.

The institution that had been corralled into service during panics before 1914 in the absence of a US lender of last resort was the regional clearinghouse association of banks in selected cities (New York, St. Louis, New Orleans, Baltimore, and Atlanta). During panics, the clearinghouses issued loan certificates that banks used as if they were legal reserves. Loan certificates have been described as 'quasi-high-powered money.'

The most usual feature of a panic, when depositors sought to convert deposits into cash, was the decision by banks to restrict cash payments, that is, the banks restricted the amount a depositor could withdraw as cash, say, to $10 a week, when the deposit account was a large multiple of that amount. The issue of loan certificates by the clearinghouses for which the banks were charged interest halted the impairment of the payments system. Clearinghouses during panic times enabled banks to continue lending without having to pay out their reserves, and firms and households had the means to pay their debts.

It was dissatisfaction with this ad hoc arrangement to cope with panics that led to the creation of the Federal Reserve System. During the 1920s many banks failed but no panic developed. The first test of the Federal Reserve as a lender of last resort came in November 1930, when a run started on a large investment banking firm in the South, and in December 1930, when a run on a large New York City bank led to panic conditions. The Federal Reserve failed that test as well as subsequent ones during panics in 1931, 1932, and 1933. The toll of bank failures and the one-third reduction in the quantity of money that it entailed over this period resulted in the adoption of deposit insurance, when an effective lender of last resort would have obviated the need for such an agency.

Lenders of Last Resort Since the Great Depression

Neither the Bank of England nor the Federal Reserve has conducted lender of last resort operations in recent years according to the principles established by Thornton and Bagehot. The injunction to lend freely has been modified by involving other commercial institutions in addition to the central bank in rescuing troubled institutions. In the case of the Bank of England, this modification started as early as 1890, when the Bank arranged for other banks to join in the rescue of Baring Bros. This practice also occurs in France and Germany. In the US, the recent rescue of Long Term Capital Management was organized by the Federal Reserve Bank of New York in 1998, but only with private contributions.[1] In addition, banking problems are often resolved by the deposit insurance agency, not the central bank.

A second modification has characterized the injunction to lend only to temporarily illiquid but solvent banks. The justification for this change is the allegation, first, that during a crisis, the lender of last resort cannot distinguish between an illiquid and an insolvent bank and, second, that it may be desirable to rescue an insolvent bank because of contagion effects on sound banks. Neither of these allegations is convincing to me.[2] The practice of central banks, however, has been to prop up banks 'too big to fail,' and, if insolvent banks are shut, to do so only in the case of small banks. The Federal Reserve in 1989–90 gave discount window assistance to insolvent banks until the deposit insurance agency was in a position to resolve their future.[3]

Finally, the injunction to lend at penalty rates on good collateral has not been observed. Central banks have given assistance at market rates or below market rates. In addition, far from signaling in advance their intention to provide the financial markets with assistance, central banks have preferred to be ambiguous, so banks would not presume that they would be bailed out in case of difficulties. 'Constructive ambiguity' supposedly constrains excessive risk taking by banks.

These modifications of the time-honoured rules, it seems to me, replace them with discretion and, contrary to the briefs by central banks in their defense, invite forbearance on their part.

Lender of Last Resort Problem in an Emerging Market Country

Central banks in emerging market countries can serve as lenders of last resort for domestic borrowers with domestic-currency-denominated liabilities. They can always print any amount of domestic currency to accommodate a sudden surge in

[1] See Edwards (1999), who believes that 'traditional lender-of-last-resort approach' would probably not have failed in the case of LTCM's collapse, it was 'almost certainly not' 'the most efficient way for the Federal Reserve to provide assistance.'

[2] See Chari and Kehoe (1999), who explain: 'The prospect of receiving funds from the lender of last resort, even if the bank is insolvent, reduces the extent to which interest rates on deposits vary with the riskiness of the bank's portfolio. Thus, the lender of last resort implicitly subsidizes the risk taking by banks. The subsidy leads banks to take on excessive risk and paradoxically can make financial panics more frequent and more severe when they occur. One way the lender of last resort could avoid moral hazard is to lend only to illiquid but solvent banks' (p.14).

[3] See Anna J. Schwartz, 'The Misuse of the Fed's Discount Window,' *Federal Reserve Bank of St. Louis Review* 74(5), September/October 1992, pp. 58–69. The FDIC Improvement Act of 1991 limits the use of the discount window for long-term loans to troubled banks. It also curtails the regulator's discretion regarding when to intervene in the case of an undercapitalized bank.

demand. In emerging market countries, however, ordinary banks may borrow foreign currency and make domestic loans not only in domestic currency but also in foreign currency. If there is a surge in demand for foreign currencies, central banks can provide only the available foreign exchange reserves they hold; they cannot create more. I mention a possible solution to this problem at a later point.

A Summary of the Domestic Context

A domestic lender of last resort can create high-powered money denominated in its own national currency. It can exercise its own discretion in allocating the resources it commands. Time-honoured rules for the decisions it makes about how much to lend to which institutions on what conditions have been bent over the years since the rules were formulated. Nineteenth and twentieth century-type panics are no longer observed. Instead, lenders of last resort intervene whenever they believe there is a risk of contagion. I defer consideration of the validity of the idea of contagion until I deal with the claims of the International Monetary Fund that it can serve as an international lender of last resort.

2. THE INTERNATIONAL CONTEXT

The Changing Mission of the International Monetary Fund

I shall first describe the evolution of the IMF's mission from what it was originally conceived to be. It was created in 1944 by the framers of the Bretton Woods Articles of Agreement. They believed that international capital flows had destabilized the 1930s, and that floating exchange rates had encouraged competitive devaluation of national currencies. Therefore, the Bretton Woods design for the postwar world permitted government controls to limit international capital flows and provided for exchange rates pegged in terms of the US dollar or gold to achieve exchange rate stability.

In this set-up, the IMF's role was to enforce the rules in the pegged exchange rate system about when fundamental disequilibrium justified changing the peg, and to provide temporary loans to countries with a balance-of-payments deficit. The source of IMF resources was initially \$8.8 billion in quotas that members contributed (25 per cent in gold, 75 per cent in currencies)—quotas that could be raised every five years—plus in 1961, up to \$6 billion in their currencies that 10 industrial countries agreed to lend the Fund. A further addition to IMF resources was the creation of Special Drawing Rights (SDRs) by a 1967 amendment to the Articles of Agreement—so-called paper gold—and their first allocation in 1970. SDRs allowed the IMF to provide credit to member countries in excess of their quota subscriptions. Central banks, when allocated SDRs, can monetize them by issuing their equivalent value in national currencies.

The Bretton Woods system broke down in 1971, for reasons that do not need to be reviewed here. What is pertinent to this discussion is that the collapse destroyed the IMF's purpose. Floating exchange rates, the successor to the Bretton Woods pegged exchange rates, eliminated the IMF's exchange rate regulatory role, and changed the character of balance-of-payments problems. Since 1971, the IMF has been seeking a redefinition of its role.

In the international context, one important change in the environment in which the IMF operated under the Bretton Woods system is that since its demise, a highly liquid international financial system has arisen, and the world capital market has become increasingly mobile. The significance of this change is the basis for the view that I present in the third part of this lecture.

During the 1970s and 1980s, the direction the IMF pursued for itself was the provision of advice and information to its members numbering over 180 countries. The Mexican bailout in 1995 that the Clinton administration engineered, however, pointed the IMF in a new direction. After some false starts, the administration orchestrated a $50 billion rescue package—Mexico did not in fact obtain the full amount—to be provided by the Federal Reserve, the Treasury's Exchange Stabilization Fund, the IMF, and the Bank for International Settlements. This experience planted the idea that the IMF could function as an international lender of last resort.

Why the IMF Cannot Be a Lender of Last Resort

In a luncheon speech at the American Economic Association meeting on January 3, 1999, Stanley Fischer, the first deputy managing director of the IMF, argued the case, in a reformed international financial system, for 'an agency that will act as lender of last resort for countries facing a crisis.' He asserted that there was a need for such an agency and 'that the IMF is increasingly playing that role, and that changes in the international system now under consideration will make it possible for it to exercise that function more effectively.'[4] The speech raises the question whether it is true that the IMF possesses the attributes of a lender of last resort.

I have shown that central banks have the capacity to serve as their banks' and, more generally, their financial system's lender of last resort. They can create high-powered base money in their own national currency, they can act quickly, and they need the consent of no other agency to act. The IMF lacks each of these attributes. It cannot create high-powered money in any national currency, so it cannot create international reserves. Fischer's answer is that the IMF 'has access to a pool of resources, which it can onlend to member countries.' He notes that, if the IMF's resources bore the same size relative to output, to the quota formula, to the volume of world trade, as in 1945, its resources would be three, five, or more than nine

[4] See Stanley Fischer, 'On the Need for an International Lender of Last Resort,' revised version of a paper delivered at the American Economic Association and the American Finance Association, New York, January 3, 1999. Available at: http://www.imf.org/external/np/speeches/1999/010399.HTM. Fischer is not the only one to propose a lender of last resort role for the IMF. See also Steven Radelet and Jeffrey Sachs (1997) and George Soros (1998).

times larger than they will be in 1999. Is there an implication that quota increases that have been sought every five years since the IMF's founding will in future be sought more often?

Fischer also counts on the IMF's use of authorization to create SDRs as a supplement to its resources as well as its ability to borrow. One major difference between a central bank lender of last resort and the IMF, to which Fischer does not allude, is that the IMF needs a vote of its Executive Board to take any action. It has no independent authority, such as a central bank has, even one subject to the consent of the minister of finance. The IMF cannot issue SDRs and cannot borrow except if authorized by vote of the member countries.

The IMF cannot act quickly. Before the IMF provides money to a borrowing country, it first engages in lengthy negotiations to introduce a reform program. If it abides by time-honoured principles, a national lender of last resort rescues solvent banks temporarily short of liquidity. It does not rescue insolvent institutions. The IMF has no such inhibitions.

Fischer refers to a complaint that the Fund is too slow in emergencies, but counters that the Emergency Financing Mechanism, introduced after the Mexican crisis, enables it to move very rapidly. Very rapidly means after weeks or months, while an agreement with the distressed country is produced. Lending with conditionality and providing money only in tranches do not meet the requirements for overcoming a shortage of liquidity. A national central bank can promptly provide liquidity to the money market without administrative complications.

The IMF, it is clear, is only a simulacrum of a lender of last resort. It is not the real thing. What will its function be? There will be changes in the international financial system that Fischer describes—a shift to floating exchange rates by emerging market countries, their holdings of international reserves will be larger, private sector institutions will be involved in rescues of countries in distress, and those countries will adopt international standards—but he does not enumerate any changes in the way the IMF operates. It will still provide loans to pay off a country's foreign debts, although since 1998 no longer at subsidized interest rates, and will impose fiscal and monetary conditions and micromanage institutional behaviour.

Fischer proposes that in the future the IMF will lend on Bagehot's rules through the Supplementary Reserve Facility. Given global capital markets that will be ready to lend to countries that are willing to pay a penalty rate of interest and to offer good collateral, is there a need for an IMF? Fischer parses lending freely as meaning 'ready to lend early and in sufficient amounts to other countries that might be affected by contagion from the crisis.' He nowhere defines contagion or justifies the assumption that it occurs.

The Myth of Contagion

Will an individual country that has mismanaged its affairs precipitate an international financial crisis? One myth is that the loss of creditworthiness by the country in question has a tequila effect. The supposed tequila effect is that other countries without the problems of the troubled country are unfairly tarnished as also subject to those problems. In this way, it is said, contagion spreads the crisis from its initial source to other innocent victims. The second myth is that a bailout of the troubled country is essential. The rationale is again the idea of contagion. Failure to organize a bailout will create an international financial crisis by a domino effect. Rescuing the troubled country saves the rest of the world from unwarranted financial collapse.

Contagion, if the term is used accurately, occurs only in circumstances in which other countries are free of the problems of the country that first experienced trouble and yet suffered capital flight. It has become a dogma since the 1995 Mexican bailout that there was a tequila effect as a result of its distress. The evidence that has been offered since then is that the currencies and stock markets of countries (other than the original one to surface with problems) have declined. What is overlooked or deliberately omitted is that the countries said to be victims of contagion had the same problems as were present in the country that was supposedly the source of contagion.

Glib references to spillovers from disturbances that originate elsewhere are common in the current literature on international financial crises. The truth is that it is not necessary to invoke spillovers to account for multi-country financial disturbances. Capital flight from countries with similar unsustainable policies is not evidence of contagion. Proponents of the contagion dogma do not explain the absence of contagion from the New York stock market crash of 1987 nor from the 1990 Tokyo stock market and property bubble crashes.

It is ironic that the Mexican bailout of 1995 has inspired the model of what needs to be done. The emphasis by the IMF is on a standing procedure and faster access to funds. It thinks of itself as a financial panic lender. Lending by the IMF and the other rescuers, however, was not directed to the Mexican money market. The question that should be asked is, for whose benefit was the Mexican rescue arranged? Is there any doubt that the loan package was designed to pay dollars to Mexicans and nationals of other countries who invested in government tesobonos and cetes as well as dollar-denominated loans to Mexican nonfinancial firms? Is that the reason emergency loans are needed? To eliminate risk from investment in high-yielding foreign assets?

People in countries that pursue unsound economic policies pay a heavy price for those mistakes—slower if not negative growth, government austerity, and unemployment. But US-backed bailouts protect investors who lent money to governments or private sector institutions, not the people who suffer the consequences of unsound policies. In the absence of the IMF loans, investors would have taken a hit, but economic conditions in Mexico would have been no worse than they were with the loan, and Mexico would not have had the burden of repaying the loan. The East Asian countries and Brazil that were recipients of IMF loans are further examples of bailouts that limit wealth losses by investors in advanced countries, without benefit to the local populations.

Moreover, the Mexican bailout may well have fostered the belief among foreign investors in the East Asian countries that they were extending riskless loans because the IMF would provide the funds to pay them off. That in itself is enough reason to question the ground for the IMF's intervention. And there are surely other reasons related to the IMF's policy recommendations as conditions for its loans that could be challenged.

In my view, an emerging country that gets into trouble does not need the ministrations of the IMF to overcome its difficulties. Instead of bailouts that create conditions that promote the spread of financial crisis, the country can travel a different road to recovery.

3. RECOVERY WITHOUT THE IMF

It is important to distinguish between a financial panic and a financial crisis. A financial panic occurs in the money market and is a threat to the economy's payments system. A panic can be quickly ended by a lender of last resort. The recent difficulties of emerging market countries have involved financial crises rather than financial panics. A financial crisis occurs when asset prices plunge, whether prices of equities, real estate, or commodities, when the exchange value of a national currency experiences substantial depreciation, when a large nonfinancial firm or a financial industry faces bankruptcy, or a sovereign debtor defaults. A financial crisis is a prolonged disturbance that is resolved by government agencies other than the lender of last resort, although at some stage it may provide liquidity to the market through the discount window or open market purchases.

In this country, the collapse of the savings and loan industry was an example of a financial crisis that initially involved the deposit insurance agency and subsequently a new agency—the Resolution Trust Corporation—to deal with the problem. Resolving the savings and loan crisis was not a lender of last resort responsibility.

The IMF thinks of itself not only as a financial panic lender but also as a crisis manager. It can fill neither role. Only the emerging market country can do so. If the banking system is short of liquidity, the domestic central bank, not the IMF, must create high-powered domestic money to calm depositor fears. If the problem is a shortage of foreign money, the answer again is not the IMF. Some emerging market countries have devised schemes to deal with a sudden demand for foreign currency. The Argentine central bank has an option that cost it 33 basis points, under a repurchase agreement with 14 international banks to swap Argentine government securities for up to $7 billion US dollars, for which it will pay LIBOR plus 205 basis points. The length of the loan varies from two to five years, depending on the counterparty bank. Mexico has an arrangement with 31 commercial banks for a $2.5 billion foreign currency credit line. These are emerging market country, not IMF initiatives.

Correction of the conditions that produced a financial crisis must fall on the troubled country, not the IMF. If the country cannot service or amortize its foreign borrowings, the country, not the IMF has to negotiate a workout with the foreign lenders. The same applies to firms or banks that cannot repay on due dates what they have borrowed. If individual banks, other financial institutions, corporate and nonfinancial businesses are insolvent, domestic agencies either exist or must be established to recapitalize them or shut them down.

Currency crises and severe banking problems have accompanied recent financial crises. Emerging market countries that peg the exchange rate of their currencies to the currency of a developed country are prone to currency crises. When foreign investors believe that the nominal parity of the currencies is inconsistent with economic fundamentals, they sell off the currencies. Efforts by the emerging market countries to support the pegged value by deploying foreign exchange reserves ultimately collapse, and they have no alternative but to allow the exchange value to float. Domestic entities with debts denominated in foreign currencies suffer. A depreciated exchange value of a national currency will recover when reformed internal policies signal to the market that the economy's health is improving.

Flaws in the operation of the banking systems of emerging market countries have been uncovered in the course of financial crises. Bad loans are a pervasive problem of their portfolios. The best hope to remedy a shortage of bank capital is for foreign banks to acquire an interest in the banks of emerging market countries.

Financial crises, unlike panics, are not quickly ended. They may require fiscal support, and the resolution may not be attained for months or years. Compensating for the loss of wealth that a financial crisis imposes may exact a reduction in personal consumption and increased national saving over an extended period. This is what troubled countries have to endure. The IMF does not spare them these bleak consequences. Every country that has been a recipient of IMF loans has suffered a severe decline in output, punishing high interest rates, and accelerating inflation, despite IMF loans.[5]

The IMF was established in 1944 to serve as a lender to countries when private international capital markets were limited and repressed. IMF lending had a proper role in that regime but it no longer exists. Nowadays, private international capital markets are deregulated and flush with funds. IMF lending in the regime that now exists is a carryover for which there is no proper role. Every day brings news of the success of emerging market countries in raising funds from pension, mutual, and hedge funds, even countries barely over a financial crisis. South Korea, five months after its crisis in November 1997, sold a bond offering of $4 billion to international investors. Colombia sold $500 million in bonds in March 1999 six months after its crisis. Thailand, Mexico, and Argentina in the past year also had similar success in raising funds. Peru sought a loan but rejected the offer because it was unwilling to pay the credit risk interest premium.

What is the secret of access to capital markets? Countries that need to borrow abroad can count on finding private sector lenders if they will pay a penalty rate and offer good collateral. These are the terms, according to Fischer, on which the

[5] Thus far, Brazil has not experienced high inflation in the aftermath of its financial crisis. The delinking of wages and the exchange rate before the onset of crisis conditions appears to be the explanation for this result.

IMF in the future will lend. Does the IMF see itself as a lender in competition with capital markets?

Some countries that cannot meet the conditions for borrowing that the private market sets may require financial aid. Outright gifts to them from an international agency may be the right solution. A case can be made for such gifts to countries that have endured earthquakes, hurricanes, monsoons, plagues.

For economic development, however, emerging market countries that are reforming their banking structures, creating the proper mix of regulation, oversight, and market discipline to enforce acceptable rules of conduct in lending and investing, pursuing sound monetary and fiscal policies, and encouraging open capital markets will be well on the way to recovery from recent financial crises.

Concluding Comments

To create a more stable international financial system, each country should have in place a lender of last resort. A lender of last resort can forestall threats to the payments system associated with bank runs and stock market crashes. Despite references to the IMF as an international lender of last resort, it lacks the attributes of such an authority either in a domestic or global setting.

Financial crises differ from financial panics. Crises require the involvement of domestic agencies other than the lender of last resort. The IMF is no substitute for these crisis resolvers.

Crises and panics differ from currency crises, depreciation of the exchange value of a national currency as the result of a loss of confidence by investors in the currency of a country pursuing unsustainable policies, encompassing large current account deficits, excessive credit growth and misallocation of investment funds, excessive monetary expansion, and fiscal laxness. Currency crises occur when the nominal exchange rates at which countries peg their currencies are inconsistent with the economic fundamentals.

The widening and deepening of world capital markets in recent decades have established them as providers of loans to creditworthy countries, putting in question the need for IMF lending.

REFERENCES

Bagehot, Walter (1873). *Lombard Street: A description of the money market*, London: Henry S. King and Company.

Chari, V. V. and Patrick J. Kehoe (1999). Asking the Right Questions About the IMF. *The Region* 13 (May); 2–26. Federal Reserve Bank of Minneapolis.

Edwards, Franklin R. (1999). Hedge Funds and the Collapse of Long-Term Capital Management. *Journal of Economic Perspectives*, 13(2) Spring: 189–210.

Fischer, Stanley (1999). On the Need for an International Lender of Last Resort. Available at http:/www.imf.org/external/np/speeches/1999/010399.HTM.

Radelet, Steven and Jeffrey Sachs (1997). What have we learned, so far, from the Asian financial crisis? mimeo, Harvard Institute for International Development. Available at: www.hiid.harvard.edu.

Schwartz, Anna J. (1992). The Misuse of the Fed's Discount Window. *Federal Reserve Bank of St. Louis Review*, 74(5): September/October, pp. 58–69.

Soros, George (1998). The Crisis of Global Capitalism. *Wall Street Journal*, September 15, 1998.

Thornton, Henry (1802[1965]), *An inquiry into the nature and effects of the paper credit of Great Britain*. Edited with an Introduction by F. A v. Hayek. New York: Augustus M. Kelley.

22

Meltzer Report of the International Financial Institution Advisory Committee (*excerpts from Chapter 2*)

RECOMMENDATIONS

Six core principles guide our recommendations. These are

- sovereignty—the desire to ensure that democratic processes and sovereign authority are respected in both borrowing and lending countries;
- separation—the desire to define a set of tasks for the IMF that are distinct from the tasks of other multilateral agencies, to avoid counterproductive overlap;
- focus—establishing clear priorities and placing credible bounds on authority to ensure that the IMF does not continue to experience mission creep;
- effectiveness—designing mechanisms that are likely to achieve desired objectives at reasonable cost while avoiding corruption and other undesirable side effects;
- burden-sharing—ensuring that the burden of financing IMF operations is shared equitably among nations;
- accountability and transparency—ensuring that the governance and accounting structure of the IMF provide accurate information about IMF actions, that IMF officials are accountable for their actions, and that reports are available and understandable.

The Mission of the New IMF

The Commission recommends that the IMF be restructured as a smaller institution with *three unique responsibilities* which, if properly performed, would increase global stability, improve the functioning of markets, and help countries improve domestic monetary and fiscal policies.

(1) *To act as a quasi-lender of last resort to solvent emerging economies* by providing short-term liquidity assistance to countries in need under a mechanism designed to avoid the abuse of liquidity assistance to sponsor bail outs and under a system that would not retard the development of those institutions within the recipient country that would attract capital from commercial sources;

(2) *To collect and publish financial and economic data from member countries, and disseminate those data in a timely and uniform manner* that permits market participants to draw useful information about member countries' economic performance across time and across countries; and
(3) *To provide advice (but not impose conditions) relating to economic policy* as part of regular 'Article IV' consultations with member countries. Except in unusual circumstances, where the crises poses a threat to the global economy, loans would be given only to countries in crises that have pre-conditions that establish financial soundness.

The IMF should be precluded from making other types of loans to member countries. The current practice of extending long-term loans in exchange for member countries' agreeing to abide by conditions set by the IMF should end. Doing so would avoid duplication with other agencies and ensure that the IMF focuses on a clearly defined set of economic objectives.

The Commission recommends that long-term institutional assistance to foster development and encourage sound economic policies should be the responsibility of the reconstructed World Bank or regional development banks under a new mechanism—one designed to increase the probability of achieving bona fide objectives, without exerting excessive control over member countries' policies. The IMF's Poverty and Growth Facility should be closed.

Participation in IMF Programs

All IMF members should be expected to provide accurate economic and financial information in a timely manner. Increased reliance on private capital flows makes it imperative to improve the quantity, quality, and timeliness of information. Accurate information increases the number of market participants and improves market stability and efficiency.

Developed countries report on their economies and policies to the OECD. Central bankers discuss these topics at the BIS. Finance ministers of the G-7 countries exchange information and report on their problems and prospects at G-7 meetings. OECD members should be allowed to opt out of IMF Article IV consultations. All other countries should be required to participate.

IMF consultations are valuable. They force countries to review systematically and explain their policies and contribute to the development of data sources. To enhance the value of Article IV consultations, all reports should be published promptly. The IMF has shown leadership in recent years by encouraging publication and dissemination of its reports. We recommend that publication become mandatory.

The Commission recommends two types of restriction on the IMF's role as quasi-lender of last resort. First, the central banks of large, industrial countries should continue to function as lenders of last resort for their own currencies and financial systems. The IMF does not have, and cannot be expected to have, the resources to protect the payments systems of advanced industrial countries against an internal drain. And these countries have fluctuating exchange rates, so they do not have to respond to an external drain.

Second, to be eligible to borrow in a liquidity crisis, a member should meet minimum prudential standards. Countries that meet the standards would receive immediate assistance without further deliberation or negotiation. The IMF would not be authorized to negotiate policy reforms. The policies necessary to improve economic performance and end a crisis are well-known. The IMF's role would be to provide liquidity, promptly, in a financial crisis under strict rules. These rules reflect experience in many financial crises where fragile financial systems could not bear the strain caused by repatriation of foreign capital or reductions in foreign lending. Further, IMF assistance should be limited to illiquid not insolvent borrowers. IMF (or Development Bank) lending should not be used to salvage insolvent financial institutions, directly or indirectly, or to protect foreign lenders from losses.

Rules for IMF Lending

First, to limit corruption and reduce risk by increasing portfolio diversification, eligible member countries must permit freedom of entry and operation for foreign financial institutions in a phased manner over a period of years. Foreign institutions hold a highly diverse portfolio of loans to borrowers in many countries and different industries. They would be expected to act in much the same way as global industrial companies with assets in many countries; they would stabilize and develop the local financial system. They would benefit by diversifying their risks on the international financial marketplace. Countries would gain from increased stability, a safer financial structure, and from the management and market skills that global banks would impart. A competitive banking system would limit use of local banks to finance 'pet projects,' or lend to favoured groups on favourable terms.

Second, consistent with the Basel Commmittee's recent reform proposal, the Commission believes that bank regulation should incorporate market discipline as a means of measuring and enforcing prudential capital standards. To establish market discipline in the domestic financial sector and protect the soundness of financial institutions, commercial banks must be adequately capitalized. This can be achieved in different ways including a significant equity base and the issuance of uninsured subordinated debt to non-governmental and unaffiliated entities. The function of the subordinated debt is to encourage prudent behaviour by banks and monitoring by the subordinated investors.

Third, to encourage prudent behaviour, safety and soundness every country that borrows from the IMF must publish regularly the maturity structure of its outstanding sovereign and guaranteed debt and off-balance-sheet liabilities in a timely manner. Lenders need accurate information on the size of short-term liabilities to assess properly the risks that they undertake.

Fourth, the IMF should establish a proper fiscal requirement to assure that IMF resources would not be used to sustain irresponsible budget policies.

Under any system of minimum standards for access to assistance, including the standards used by the central banks of the industrialized countries, the entire financial structure may be put at risk by the inability of one large participant to meet the minimum standards for assistance. This 'too big to fail' argument has been used to rescue many insolvent institutions. The responsibility of the lender of last resort should be to the market, not to the individual participant. In recent decades, the collapse of the Penn Central, Drexel Burnham, and Russia have been met by loans to the market and solvent borrowers. Direct assistance was not given to the insolvent entity.

Terms for Lending

The Commission envisions a liquidity assistance mechanism that would be used to alleviate crises when private sector financing is temporarily unavailable. Historical experience suggests that liquidity crises typically last for a matter of weeks or, in extreme cases, for several months. To ensure that liquidity assistance is only used as a last resort, IMF loans (1) should have a short maturity (e.g., a maximum of 120 days, with only one allowable rollover), (2) should pay a penalty rate (that is, a premium over the sovereign yield paid by the member country one week prior to applying for an IMF loan), and (3) should specify that the IMF be given priority in payment over all other creditors, secured and unsecured.

The penalty rate premium could increase with the length of time the loan remains outstanding. This would provide an incentive for early repayment.

Phase in

The new rules should be phased in over a period of three to five years. If a crisis occurs before the new rules are in place in most countries, countries should be permitted to borrow at an interest rate above the penalty rate. The 'super penalty rate' would give countries an additional incentive to adopt the new rules.

Some countries may choose not to adopt the proposed rules. The names of the countries should be disclosed along with their ineligibility for IMF lender-of-last-resort services. Defaults should not always be prevented in these countries or elsewhere.

Ensuring Priority of IMF Claims on Sovereigns

One way to ensure priority of IMF claims is to require security or collateral. There are some practical difficulties in this approach for many countries. For example, commodity exports can serve as collateral, but this is a cumbersome process. Also, it may unintentionally encourage countries not to privatize important export-producing sectors (so that the government can retain control over exports to serve as collateral).

Second, 'negative pledge clauses' may prevent some governments from effectively subordinating existing creditors by pledging collateral on new loans. Many existing sovereign debt contracts specifically exempt from negative pledge clauses short-term debt, debt to foreign monetary authorities and multilateral institutions, and debt which is not publicly offered. There are various possible approaches to resolving the legal and practical problems of ensuring IMF priority when negative pledge clauses apply. For example, IMF advances can be treated as 'exchanges of assets,' rather than as loans, to avoid the application of negative pledge clauses. Another approach, in a crisis, would take advantage of the grace period allowed before the enforcement of negative pledge clause violations (typically 90–120 days). This would permit collateralized (secured) IMF loans of sufficiently short maturity.

Perhaps the most promising and simple approach to ensuring IMF seniority, while waiting for markets and governments to resolve the practical and legal problems of providing collateral, would be to require IMF members to agree to three debt management rules as part of the prequalification requirement for access to IMF liquidity assistance: (1) Member countries must specifically exempt the IMF from the application of negative pledge clauses in all new sovereign debts issued by the member country. Most sovereign debt outstanding by developing economies is of relatively short maturity. Within a period not much longer than the phase in, contracts could be amended to give priority to the IMF. Issuers interested in hastening the conversion process could also repurchase outstanding debt, or ask creditors to accept an exchange of new debt (containing the exemption) for old debt. (2) Borrowers would give the IMF explicit legal priority with respect to all other creditors, secured and unsecured. (3) Member countries that default on their IMF debts would not be eligible for loans or grants from other multilateral agencies or other member countries.

Credit Limits

Credit limits are necessary to restrict the amount of assistance that a country can receive from the IMF. The limit should reflect the capacity of the sovereign to repay its debt to the IMF. A borrowing limit equal to one year's tax revenues might be a reasonable credit limit.

Other Recommendations

Extraordinary Events. The Commission recognizes that countries may need to borrow for reasons other than a liquidity crisis. In such cases, vehicles other than the IMF are available. For example, countries should apply to a multilateral development bank or a United Nations' agency, if emergency assistance to alleviate starvation or disease is called for. Or, if a country undertakes institutional reform or poverty alleviation programs, it should apply for assistance to the development banks.

If extraordinary political events lead some group of countries to determine that they wish to act jointly to provide foreign aid or loans to another nation (as, for example, appears to have been the determination of the G-7 finance ministers in the case of Russia in the late 1990s), the lending countries—acting through appropriate constitutional and parliamentary procedures—should provide the aid directly.

Following a financial crisis, a country will often find that it wishes to undertake institutional reforms. It may want to spread the burden of adjustment to the crisis differently than the market solution. For example, it may wish to shield the weakest or poorest parts of the society from bearing the full burden determined by market processes. Expenditures for these purposes can be financed either domestically, or by borrowing abroad if the country has established credit, or from multilateral development institutions, if the access to capital markets is restricted.

The IMF should not be used as a 'slush fund' to satisfy decisions of the G-7 finance ministers or other groups of powerful members. Such practices undermine the IMF's role as a supplier of liquidity, distort the incentives of lenders and borrowers in international capital markets, bypass the budget process in the lending countries and, by imposing conditions, undermine the development of responsible, democratic decision-making in the borrowing countries.

Exchange Rates. A pegged exchange rate is neither permanently fixed nor flexible. A country commits to maintain its exchange rate only as long as it chooses to do so. Pegged exchange-rate systems have proved to be costly and usually unsustainable in a crisis.

Countries have spent billions of dollars and raised domestic interest rates to unsustainable levels in fruitless attempts to prevent devaluation. Stanley Fischer, First Deputy Managing Director of the IMF, summarizes the experience in the 1997–98 Asian crises.

> It is a fact that all countries that had major international crises . . . relied on a pegged or fixed exchange-rate system before the crisis; and it is also true that some countries that appeared vulnerable but that had flexible exchange rates avoided such crises. Countries with very hard [firm, non-adjustable] pegs have been able to sustain them. Accordingly, we are likely to see emerging market countries moving toward the two extremes of either a flexible rate or a very hard peg—and in the long-run, the trend is almost certainly to be towards fewer currencies.[1]

A majority of the Commission agrees with this conclusion. Countries should choose either firmly-fixed rates or fluctuating rates. Neither system is ideal for all countries, at all times, and under all conditions. Mixed systems typically work poorly, as they did in Asia.

Rigidly-fixed systems require large reserves or lines of credit. They acquire needed credibility gradually, often only after the country surmounts a crisis. To increase credibility, some countries, adopting a fixed exchange rate, have chosen

[1] Stanley Fischer, 'Presentation to the International Financial Institution Advisory Commission.' Washington: International Monetary Fund, February 2, 2000, p. 12.

to establish a currency board or, in a few cases, have taken a strong foreign currency—such as the dollar or the Euro—as their domestic money. The eleven countries that joined the European Central Bank have taken a different route, a common currency internally and a fluctuating exchange rate against the rest of the world.

A critical point is often overlooked. The long-run position of an economy does not depend on the choice of the exchange-rate system. Exchange-rate systems determine how a country adjusts to external events or domestic policies. A fluctuating exchange-rate system adjusts by currency appreciation or depreciation. A fixed exchange-rate system adjusts by raising or lowering the domestic price level relative to foreign prices. The adjustment cannot be prevented in either system, and it occurs quickly with capital mobility.

Two important lessons of experience under many different exchange-rate regimes are: First, countries that follow stabilizing monetary, fiscal (and other) policies can successfully maintain either a fixed or a fluctuating exchange rate. Second, countries that adopt policies that are excessively expansive or contractive have difficulty maintaining a fixed exchange rate or avoiding appreciation or depreciation of a fluctuating rate.

Stabilizing policies are more important than the choice of exchange-rate regime. If domestic policies, or external events, destabilize a country, the country will have to adjust. It is not an accident, but instead a necessary consequence of the adjustment process, that countries with fixed exchange rates—China, Hong Kong, and Argentina—experienced deflation in the late 1990s, while Australia, Canada, the United States, and the Euro adjusted by allowing their exchange rates to appreciate or depreciate.

The Commission recommends that countries avoid pegged or adjustable rates. The IMF should use its Article IV consultations to make countries aware of the costs and risks of pegged or adjustable rates.

Debt Renegotiation. The Commission does not approve of the IMF's policies in Latin America in the 1980s and in Mexico in 1995, or in many other cases. IMF loans to these countries protected US and other foreign banks, financial institutions, and some investors at great cost to the citizens of the indebted countries. The loans delayed resolution of the 1980s crises by permitting lenders and borrowers to report the debt as fully serviced.

Many suggestions have been made to change contractual terms or to impose costs on private lenders in a crisis. Most of these proposals seek to share the costs of resolving crises between the public and private sector. The Commission believes that lenders who make risky loans or purchase risky securities should accept the true losses when risks become unpleasant realities.

Proposals for bankruptcy courts, collective action clauses and other contractual changes, or other attempts to share losses between private and public lenders and institutions, raise many unresolved problems. None is problem free. Unlike bank debt, there are often many holders of emerging market bonds, each interested in protecting their own, frequently divergent, interests.

Lee C. Buchheit, an expert on these issues, points out that debt renegotiation practices are evolving rapidly, without official intervention.[2] The Commission believes that the development of new ways of resolving sovereign borrower and lender conflicts in default situations should be encouraged but left to the participants until there is a better understanding by debtors, creditors, and outside observers of how, if at all, public-sector intervention can improve negotiations.

Finance and Accounting Reforms. The IMF's accounting system should be simplified and rationalized to improve transparency. The recent use of gold sales and repurchases as an accounting device for forgiving HIPC debt is an example of budgetary obfuscation which is substantively unrelated to the act of forgiving debt. Contrivances of this kind have no place in a multilateral lending agency dedicated to increasing transparency of member governments' policies and operations.

IMF accounts should be reformed to mimic standard accounting procedures for representing assets and liabilities and income and expenses. Loans should be specifically identified in IMF accounts (as opposed to the current practice of including loans under currency and securities holdings), and loans should be divided according to their maturity and delinquency status unlike current practice. Currency holdings should be divided into categories that make their usefulness as a funding resource clear. Currencies should be divided into G-5 currencies, other currencies considered useful for intervention purposes, and nonusable currencies. Liabilities should be separated from equity. Undrawn commitments under operative credit arrangements should be disclosed. Quotas, reserves, and deferred income should be set forward under a separate heading as equity. Quotas should be divided according to whether they represent contributions from G-5 countries, other possibly useful subscriptions, or subscriptions from countries with non-usable currencies. Undrawn borrowing capacity should be similarly divided into three groups separating G-5 currencies, other usable currencies, and non-usable currencies. Income accounts should recognize all implicit subsidies to borrowers (which would no longer occur under the proposed lending rules).

The 'SDR Department' accounts should be incorporated into the IMF's overall accounts, recognizing countries with SDR holdings above cumulative allocations as net suppliers of credit and countries with holdings below cumulative allocations as net recipients of credit. These net positions should be combined with the countries' reserve positions in the 'General Department' to obtain an accurate view of net providers and users of subsidized funding. The Appendix shows a recommended pro forma balance sheet for the IMF.

The Commission's proposal would make the IMF a stand-by lender. Lending would decline, so fewer resources would be required. In keeping with the greatly reduced lending role of the IMF, the Commission recommends against further quota increases for the foreseeable future. The IMF's current resources should be

[2] Lee C. Buchheit. 'Sovereign Debtors and their Bondholders'. Prepared for the Commission and presented on February 1, 2000.

sufficient for it to manage its quasi-lender of last resort responsibilities, especially as current outstanding credits are repaid to the IMF.

In a crisis the Fund should borrow convertible currencies as needed to finance short-term liquidity loans. IMF members would be jointly liable for its borrowings, on a pro rata basis depending on quota shares. Borrowing could either be made from the private sector or from credit lines of member countries.

Transparency. The IMF should conduct its operations in a fully transparent manner. The IMF should maintain and publish full details of its assistance to each country in a timely manner and should publish its Article IV consultations.

The IMF should take and record votes at Executive Board meetings and publish summaries of its meetings after a reasonable lag.

Debt Relief. Debt of HIPC countries cannot be repaid under any foreseeable future developments. IMF or other lending to make debt service appear current repeats the mistake made in Latin America in the 1980s.

Private ownership, open markets, and the rule of law encourage growth and development. HIPC debt should be forgiven in its entirety conditional on the debtor countries implementing institutional reforms and an effective development strategy.

23

The Asian Crisis: Lessons for Crisis Management and Prevention

RICHARD BREALEY

I. INTRODUCTION

Woody Allen, in a graduation day speech, remarked: 'More than any other time in history, mankind faces a crossroads. One path leads to despair and utter hopelessness. The other to total extinction. Let us pray we have the wisdom to choose correctly.' The international financial institutions must have felt that they confronted a similar predicament when faced by the successive financial crises in Asia, Russia and Brazil. These events have prompted renewed debate about crisis prevention and resolution. In particular, it has been argued that the IMF should serve as an international equivalent of the domestic lender of last resort, which can assist countries hit by a creditor panic or currency flight. The difficulties for the IMF in fulfilling this role are its relative lack of resources and the problem of distinguishing between the illiquid and insolvent borrower. Moreover, as we show later, the behaviour of asset prices on the announcement of IMF assistance provides little encouragement for the view that the IMF's intervention helps countries to resolve a problem of financial panics. An alternative role for the IMF is to use its leverage to enforce policy changes on affected countries. This role does not assume that a country's creditors are subject to contagious panics, and the form and quantity of assistance that are needed to impose conditions are not the same as are required to stem a creditor panic.

The fact that IMF support has been a response to the withdrawal of funds by international banks (and capital flight by domestic investors) has led to concern that the IMF is simply bailing out the banks and thus to calls for a redistribution of the burden. This view seems to be coloured by the assumption that international banking is not a competitive activity, so that the banks are able to collect economic rents from the IMF's assistance. Proposals for burden-sharing further assume that the form of private sector lending would be unaffected by attempts to 'bail in' the private sector. A related concern is that the prospect of IMF assistance to troubled countries leads to a moral hazard problem on the part of both lenders and borrowers. This moral hazard argument does not sit well with the huge losses that have been made by foreign investors in the affected countries, nor with the extreme reluctance on the part of borrowers to seek IMF assistance.

This article first appeared in *International Finance* 2 (2), 1999.

The strong limitations on the international community to resolve a major international financial crisis suggest that the focus of public policy should be on crisis prevention rather than resolution. It is foolish to look for a single panacea. Debate has focused *inter alia* on alternative exchange rate systems, the structure of banking and bank supervision in emerging markets, and the systems of corporate governance and control ('crony capitalism'). Rather less attention has been given to the issues of capital structure. It is clear, however, that the capital structures of governments, financial institutions and corporations contributed to the severity of the crises in the affected countries. In particular, the high levels of bank borrowing and the maturity and currency mismatches incurred by the banks endangered the solvency of the banks and limited the policy responses of governments.

The next section of this paper provides some brief background material on the Asian crisis and the events that led up to it. Section III discusses the role of the IMF and the related issues of burden-sharing and moral hazard. Section IV turns to the topic of crisis prevention and discusses the role of capital structure in reallocating the real risks in emerging market economies. Section V reviews briefly some of the policy implications and Section VI concludes.

II. THE ASIAN FINANCIAL CRISIS

A. The Onset of the Asian Financial Crisis

The float of the Thai baht in July 1997 was the first step in a series of financial crises that first swept through Thailand, the Philippines, Malaysia, Indonesia and Korea, and subsequently spread to Russia and on to Brazil. In each of the affected Asian countries there was a substantial flight of capital by both domestic and international investors. Foreign exchange reserves, which had been growing rapidly, were depleted even more rapidly, with Korea losing US$25 billion in usable reserves in just over a month. Throughout the region governments attempted with little success to stem this pressure on reserves by increasing short-term interest rates, which in the case of Indonesia rose to over 80%. The capital flight resulted in a remarkable period of turbulence in the foreign exchange markets. Volatility in the rupiah, which had been a fraction of 1% per day under the crawling peg, reached 12% per day (International Monetary Fund, September 1998), roughly the annual volatility of most Western equity markets. By its low point in 1998 the rupiah had lost 80% of its value in nominal terms and about 70% in real terms. Each of the other affected Asian currencies depreciated by more than 38%.

Many of the crisis countries found themselves in a debt trap, where the cost of rolling over loans forced them into spiralling debt levels and public sector deficits. In such cases the reduction in the wealth levels of the citizens, needed to escape from such a trap, was politically infeasible. Raising interest rates to protect the currency increased the burden of servicing domestic government debt and drove the government into yet larger deficits, while allowing the currency to depreciate increased the cost of foreign currency debt and threatened the solvency of the banking system through which much of the foreign currency debt was channelled.

Concerns over possible defaults caused the spread over US Treasuries to widen to between 8 and 18% for the affected Asian countries. Each country also experienced a run on the banks. Since the second half of 1997 several hundred financial institutions have been closed down, suspended or nationalized, and recapitalization needs are estimated to range between 18 and 34% of GDP for the crisis countries.

The consequences for all the affected countries have been severe. In Indonesia GDP fell by 14% in 1998 and by an average of over 7% in the five affected Asian countries, though that still leaves income per head substantially higher than it was at the start of the decade. In the region of US$120 billion of capital has left these countries. Would-be borrowers in many developing countries have been effectively cut off from access to the capital markets, while liquidity has been severely affected, and spreads have increased. The losses to foreign creditors and equity investors in East Asia and Russia amount to an estimated $350 billion.[1]

The East Asian story has since been more or less repeated in the other crisis countries. In each case capital flight has put pressure on reserves, which the government has attempted to fight by very high domestic interest rates and fiscal restraint. In Russia the depth of the problem and the reluctance of the government to pass needed reforms has resulted in a debt moratorium and *de facto* default.

B. The Seeds of the Crisis

What at the time seemed so surprising about these events was that many of the countries had seemed models of economic success. In the words of one commentator, 'From 1945 to 1997 the Asian economic miracle fueled the greatest expansion of wealth, for the largest number of persons, in the history of mankind' (Jackson 1999). In the affected Asian countries growth in real GDP had averaged 7% a year since 1990, with relatively little pressure on consumer prices. Brazilian real GDP grew at an annual rate of 4.5% between 1993 and 1996, while in five years inflation fell from 2,500% to under 3%. Even Russia appeared to be making progress with its problems. Inflation in 1997 was below 15% compared with nearly 900% five years earlier. The rouble had stabilized and GDP in 1997 grew slightly after declining in each of the previous five years.

However, it is easy with hindsight to see that the seeds of the emerging market crisis of 1997/8 were sown earlier in the 1990s, when improvements in the access to financial markets and apparent high returns on investments caused a surge of capital inflows into many emerging markets. By 1996 the total net private capital inflow to the affected Asian countries had reached US$73 billion, up from just $25 billion six years earlier.

The risks involved in this huge capital inflow to Asian emerging markets were exacerbated by the fact that most of it was in the form of bank debt. In 1996, the

[1] Quoted in Institute of International Finance (1999b).

year preceding the Asian crisis, 61% of the capital flows to the affected countries consisted of bank lending (Institute of International Finance 1999a). Most of the external debt was contracted by the private sector and, except in Indonesia, the money was largely channelled through local banks that relent the money to local businesses. Net interbank borrowing by banks in the five most troubled Asian countries amounted to about US$43 billion annually during 1995 and 1996. Most of this lending was denominated in dollars. Foreign bank debt amounted to 45% of GDP in Thailand, 35% in Indonesia and 25% in Korea. This debt generally had a maturity of less than one year.[2] In contrast, the average maturity of the loans made to local companies by the banks was longer than a year and the loans were commonly denominated in the local currency. Thus banks assumed both a maturity mismatch and a currency mismatch. In Thailand, where there are restrictions on the open foreign exchange positions of banks, the banks limited their currency risk by relending in dollars. However, since their clients did not have the foreign currency earnings to repay these debts, the banks simply traded a currency risk for a credit risk.

During the 1990s bank credit in most Asian countries grew rapidly by between 12 and 18% per annum in real terms. In many countries this resulted in large exposures to particular sectors, notably property,[3] and to overconcentration to single borrowers. In Korea the average book debt-to-equity ratio of the corporate sector reached nearly 200% and the top 30 chaebols had a debt–equity ratio of more than 400%. This is despite the fact that even before the onset of the crisis these chaebols were barely profitable.[4] The weakness in the banking system was (as so often) hidden by the gap between the book and market value of the loans. In Indonesia, Moody's has estimated that the proportion of loans that are non-performing could be as high as 75%. In Korea, non-performing loans may amount to 150 trillion won.

Most currencies were pegged principally against the dollar, despite the fact that a high and increasing proportion of external trade was with countries in the Asian region. These currency pegs had the effect of disguising the risks involved in the foreign currency loans and offered apparent low-risk profits on investment in local fixed interest markets. Thus the capital inflow reflected in part 'arbitrage' activity by banks and investors, who were able to borrow dollars and relend in the local currency at a profit as long as the peg to the dollar was maintained. The currency peg also meant that the risk was largely a jump risk, where the high probability of a small profit disguised the smaller chance of a substantial loss. Thus, when the currencies began to depreciate, there was little opportunity for banks to take corrective action by lifting their positions.

What made the currency pegs unsustainable was the sharp fall in the growth in exports from the region. This stemmed from a combination of an appreciation in

[2] In a probit analysis of financial crises in emerging markets, Radelet and Sachs (1998) find that the ratio of short-term debt to reserves is strongly associated with the onset of a crisis.

[3] In 1996 property lending as a percentage of total lending was 25% in Malaysia, 20% in Indonesia, and 18% in Thailand (International Monetary Fund 1998b).

[4] For example, in early 1997 six chaebols filed for bankruptcy (International Monetary Fund 1998b).

the real exchange rates, particularly relative to the yen, the weak Japanese economy, increasing competition in export markets from China and Mexico and excess capacity in many exporting industries, such as the semiconductor, petrochemical and automobile industries. By 1996, the current account deficit in the five Asian countries had reached $55 billion.

III. THE INTERNATIONAL RESPONSE TO FINANCIAL CRISES

The events of 1997–98 have prompted increased debate about the international response to such financial crises. This section considers the role of international institutions in crisis prevention and management. Specifically, it seeks to answer the following questions:

1. What is the role of the IMF?
2. Who benefits from IMF assistance?
3. How should the burden be shared?
4. How serious is the problem of moral hazard?
5. How can the IMF help with crisis prevention?

A. What Is the Role of the IMF?

The IMF was established in 1947 to buttress the Bretton Woods system of fixed exchange rates, and was intended to provide temporary assistance in the event of destabilizing speculation and consequent balance of payments difficulties. But its role has changed to one of engineering major structural reforms and providing assistance in the face of possible default on international loans.

Much of the debate on the effectiveness of the IMF in the recent international crises has centred on the appropriateness of its programmes. But there have also been more fundamental questions about its role in crisis management and prevention. Why would the private sector not be prepared to lend to affected countries at 'fair market rates'? Is there an imperfection in the private capital markets that justifies the existence of an international lender of last resort? Are there multiple equilibria in financial markets, so that a simple nudge from an international financial institution could transport us safely from a bad equilibrium to a good one? Unless these questions can be answered, we do not know whether an IMF is needed at all or in what circumstances and in what form it should provide assistance.

The following quotations may illustrate the sharp divergence of opinion over these issues:

> The crises have brought home the absolute indispensability of the IMF as the core provider of emergency, conditioned international support to countries in financial difficulty. . . . Without the IMF, even those countries that are committed to reform might face default. . . which could have devastating effects on their own economies and significantly raise the risks of contagion in other markets. (Summers 1998)

[T]he question is whether there is a need for an agency that will act as lender of last resort for countries facing a crisis. There is such a need: it arises both because international capital flows are not only extremely volatile but also contagious, exhibiting the classic signs of financial panics, and because an international lender of last resort can help mitigate the effects of this instability, and perhaps the instability itself. . . . I will argue not only that the international system needs a lender of last resort, but also that the IMF is increasingly playing that role and that changes in the international system now under consideration will make it possible for it to exercise that function more effectively. (Fischer 1999)

IMF resources have been used to 'bail out insolvent emerging market banks and international bank lenders' The costs have been: (1) undesirable redistributions of wealth from taxpayers to politically influential oligarchs in developing economies; (2) the promotion of excessive risk taking and inefficient investment; (3) the undermining of the natural process of deregulation and economic and political reform which global competition would otherwise promote. (Calomiris 1998)

The role of a lender of last resort is not to bail out failed banks. Its job is to assure that solvent financial institutions do not fail because of lack of liquidity. . . . Since 1971, the IMF has been looking for new things to do. It has now solved its problem by creating moral hazard, allowing international banks to avoid the risks they undertake by imprudent lending. The IMF encourages the behavior that creates the problems. (Meltzer 1998)

In common with most advocates of active IMF involvement, both Summers and Fischer emphasize the danger of 'panics' in financial markets and of consequent 'contagion'. By contrast, Calomiris and Meltzer place more weight on the dangers of moral hazard that result from the prospect of an IMF 'bail-out'.

One of the roles envisaged for the IMF, and suggested in Stanley Fischer's 1999 paper, is as an international equivalent of the domestic lender of last resort.[5] The function of the domestic lender of last resort is to prevent destabilizing runs on the banking system. One way that this could arise is from a liquidity mismatch. For example, a bank may be solvent as long as all depositors agree to maintain their investment, but subject to a run if each depositor is concerned that others are about to withdraw their cash. This possibility stems from the fact that depositors cannot coordinate their actions. One solution is to establish a benevolent lender of last resort that can prevent such runs simply by standing ready to provide whatever liquidity is needed.[6]

In practice, pure liquidity panics are rare and bank runs are more often motivated by insolvency worries. Here too problems may arise because depositors are unable to coordinate their actions or pool their information. For example, each depositor may rationally draw inferences about the bank's solvency from the actions of the other depositors. So a small initial loss of deposits can lead to a cascade of withdrawals.[7] If a lender of last resort has superior information or can pool

[5] See also Sachs (1995).

[6] The role of a lender of last resort in preventing liquidity runs was first suggested by Thornton (1802) and developed by Bagehot (1873). A formal model of bank runs is provided by Diamond and Dybvig (1983).

[7] For early models of rational cascades see Banerjee (1992) and Welch (1992).

the information available to individual depositors, it may be able to distinguish a bad cascade from a good cascade and nudge the market towards the appropriate outcome.[8]

The liberalization of the world's capital markets in the past 20 years has led to large capital flows into and out of emerging markets. While this is not necessarily a cause for concern, it may leave countries exposed to the type of liquidity or information-motivated panics that are used to justify a domestic lender of last resort. An international lender of last resort is clearly not necessary to protect a country's banking system against runs on its domestic book, but may, for example, be needed where banks have large foreign currency books.

This view that there is an important role for an international lender of last resort relies heavily on the view that financial markets are prone to bubbles, panics and contagion. However, while models of rational multiple equilibria that produce bubbles and panics are fun to construct, it is not clear that they work better than simpler models. For example, analyses of bank runs suggest that these runs generally reflect shared and justified worries about the bank's solvency and that well capitalized banks are not subject to runs (see, for example, Kaufman 1994). If financial markets do function well most of the time and aggregate information efficiently, then the capital withdrawals that have been experienced in a number of emerging markets are more likely to indicate basic structural weaknesses in the country's banking and exchange rate system than a failure of coordination between lenders. Thus, the case for an international lender of last resort depends heavily on the lender's access to superior information on the solvency of the country's banking system.

Unlike a domestic lender of last resort, the IMF's ability to respond to a liquidity run is limited by its lack of resources. For example, between 1992 and 1996 the net amount disbursed by the IMF under the Standby Arrangements and Extended Fund Facilities was about US$18 billion. During the same period the total net private capital flows to emerging markets were over $1 trillion. The events of 1997–98 led to an increase of two-thirds in the IMF's net lending. Nevertheless, at the end of January 1999 the total amount owing to the IMF under Standby Arrangements and Extended Fund Facilities was still only $41 billion, far smaller than the amount of private capital that has been withdrawn from emerging markets.

This lack of resources may be less crucial in the case of a solvency run. If the IMF does have superior information that allows it to distinguish between solvent and insolvent countries, then its willingness to put its money where its mouth is could serve as an important signal to the private sector. Such a signal could bring large welfare gains to the country in the form of reduced costs of further private sector credit (and an unrecoverable windfall gain to the value of existing loans by private sector banks).

Unfortunately, the signals provided by the IMF's involvement are likely to be mixed. Recourse to the IMF generally occurs only when the patient is in need of

[8] It is also sometimes argued that an international lender of last resort is needed to counter attempts at market manipulation or irrational speculation that leads to excess volatility in asset prices.

intensive care. As Radelet and Sachs (1998) suggest, the 'arrival of the IMF gives all the confidence of seeing an ambulance outside one's door'. Thus, news that the IMF is willing to provide assistance may be overshadowed by the news that the country needs it. Moreover, even if the IMF is particularly well qualified to assess country prospects, it is often under strong political pressure to extend assistance to borrowers, such as Russia, where there are clear doubts about the country's ability to service its debts. This muddies the signal provided by IMF assistance.

An alternative rationale for the IMF is that while private sector lenders may wish to impose conditions on the local government, they find it difficult to do so. Thus, the IMF may be able to attach conditions that would be impossible for the private sector.[9] If this is the case, there could be an overall welfare gain. Of course, this raises the question as to why the government could not voluntarily bind itself to the same courses of action at the time that the loan is needed. The answer may lie partly in the difficulty of specifying these actions ex ante (hence the use of staged IMF lending) or in the fact that a populist government may find it easier to justify to its citizens conditions that have been imposed by an external body. The fact that the required reforms are packaged with IMF lending both allows the IMF to exert leverage and provides an incentive for it to monitor the implementation of the reforms. However, the gains in this case may be linked only weakly to the extent of the support.

These two models of the IMF's role do not sit happily together and have different implications for the form of its assistance. For example, there is little place for staged lending or conditionality for a lender of last resort, whose function is to stem a panic resulting from liquidity or solvency concerns. On the other hand, staged lending is an essential tool for enforcing policy changes.

B. Who Benefits from IMF Assistance?

It is not easy to measure the effect of IMF programmes and more often than not the debate is liable to get mired in counterfactual speculation about what might have happened in the absence of support. An alternative approach is to focus on changes in asset values at the time of the announcement of IMF assistance. In some ongoing research with Evi Kaplanis of the London Business School, I have been looking at the relative performance of equities, bonds and currencies in the weeks surrounding the announcement of IMF support.[10] The results are preliminary, but they suggest three things:

1. During the two years preceding the announcement of support there is a sharp relative fall in equity prices in the affected countries. Bond prices and exchange rates also decline sharply, though this fall is over a shorter period.

[9] The IMF's experience in dealing with crisis situations may also give it an important consultancy role in determining the appropriate policy response.

[10] Returns are measured relative to returns on similar assets in a sample of emerging markets. The results of the exercise are similar regardless of whether the announcement date is defined by a news or press release by the IMF or by press comment that may precede such a release.

2. In the days immediately following the announcement of IMF support there is no statistically significant change in the value of each asset class.
3. In the months following the announcement of IMF support, asset prices show little abnormal movement. This is exactly what any believer in efficient markets would predict, but it does not support those who believe that markets are sized by irrational panics that cause them to overshoot.

If these results stand up to further analysis, then it is difficult to argue that the IMF decision to provide assistance is an important signal as to the health of the beneficiary or that it provides information to the markets about the recipient's willingness to accept desirable reforms. However, the tests are insufficiently powerful to determine whether there is a gain in asset values that exceeds the very limited degree of subsidy in the IMF assistance.

C. How Should the Burden Be Shared?

IMF assistance is typically a response to a flight of private capital from the affected country. Often the cash helps the country to repay maturing debts. This has prompted concern that the IMF is simply bailing out the international lending banks and that there should be some form of burden-sharing.

It seems unlikely that IMF aid simply goes into the pockets of the international lending banks. International banking is a highly competitive activity and therefore the prospect that IMF support may be available in the event of difficulties is likely to be reflected in the interest rates that banks charge. Of course, in this case IMF assistance would be simply a form of Third World aid, the benefits of which are shared between the fortunate countries that do not subsequently require assistance and the unfortunate ones that do.

If IMF assistance enables countries to repay maturing bank debts, any unanticipated announcement of assistance would result in an increase in the value of the equity of lending banks. In practice, there do not appear to be any abnormal returns in equity prices of international banks, which may suggest either that the IMF assistance is regarded as an automatic response to a balance of payments crisis and is therefore fully anticipated, or (more likely) that the news of IMF assistance percolates slowly and the amount of the subsidy is too small to observe.

If IMF support does result in increases in the value of private sector debt, the IMF could try to recapture some of these value enhancements by arranging, for example, a moratorium on private sector debt. Certainly, the IMF may have a coordinating role between private lenders, in cases where they have a common interest in renewing their lines. This is the crisis manager role that has been described by Stanley Fischer (1999). However, the suggestion of compulsion would not sit well with the arguments that have been made for an international lender of last resort. If private sector lenders are reluctant to continue to lend even when the IMF has offered assistance, there is a message that one would do well to heed.

If some form of enforced 'burden-sharing' was anticipated, it would be reflected in higher interest rates on developing country debt. It is also dangerous to assume that the structure of private-sector lending would be independent of attempts to recapture any value enhancement. In particular, lenders would have an incentive to structure the debt to make it easier to exit before the imposition of a moratorium. This is exactly the opposite of the financial structures that one would like to see in developing countries.

D. How Severe Is the Problem of Moral Hazard?

Critics of the IMF's role commonly contend that the prospect of IMF assistance leads to a moral hazard problem. International banks, it is suggested, are tempted to lend recklessly to emerging markets, and the governments and banks in these countries are tempted to borrow excessively. The first point to make is that this does not necessarily reduce social welfare, for it is arguable that, given the under-developed equity markets in developing economies, these countries have suffered from a shortage of risk capital rather than an excess. While this suggests the need to encourage the supply of equity capital, the existence of an international financial institution that partially underwrites the risk of the lending banks may serve as a second-best solution to the shortage of risk capital.

There is little doubt that the prospect of IMF assistance creates a potential moral hazard, but, while it is difficult to provide convincing evidence, it seems likely that the danger is often overstated. The subsidy in IMF loans is negligible compared with the losses that have been suffered by investors in East Asia, Russia and Brazil. Neither the promised yields nor the volatility of emerging market debt are consistent with the notion that investors regarded these loans as low risk. Nor does the rapid capital outflow at the onset of a crisis suggest that investors were confident of being bailed out if they maintained their positions. Given the heavy losses that investors have taken on their emerging market books, their caution was right.[11]

Nor is it clear that the debtors take much comfort in the prospect of IMF assistance. Not only are governments generally reluctant to call on IMF help, but the financial crises in these markets typically impose considerable costs on all the country's citizens. In almost all cases the appeal for IMF assistance has led to considerable domestic unrest, a fall in the government and a change in the governor of the central bank. It is difficult, therefore, to believe that politicians and business people are tempted to pursue reckless policies in the belief that they will not suffer the consequences.

E. The Role of the IMF in Crisis Prevention

Financial crises have resulted in large wealth losses, but there is relatively little that the IMF can do to replace this lost wealth. Despite the popular image of huge bailouts, the subsidy provided by the IMF (or 'burden' in the eyes of its critics) is

[11] Share prices of banks with large exposures to emerging markets have also reflected investor concern about potential losses.

negligible compared with the wealth losses that the borrowing countries have experienced. This suggests that prevention of international crises should take precedence over cure.

An interesting issue is how far the IMF can play a role here beyond that of an experienced consultant. One problem for the IMF has been that countries are reluctant to seek assistance and do so only as a last resort. This shows up in the preceding asset returns. For example, over the two years before a country seeks IMF support, equity prices on average experience a relative decline of 35%. In the case of bank stocks the relative decline is about 40%. It is possible, therefore, that the need for IMF assistance would be reduced if countries could be encouraged to make earlier policy changes. This seems to be the motive behind President Clinton's proposal for contingent credit lines.

Unfortunately, it has proved difficult to devise a scheme that maximizes the Fund's ability to influence economic policies without at the same time risking excessive strain on the Fund's resources. Suppose, for example, that the IMF offered a committed line of credit that would be rolled over as long as the country continues to follow IMF-approved policies. A country that entered into such an arrangement would be induced to follow the agreed policies because it wished both to maintain the insurance of the line of credit and to avoid the negative signal associated with a refusal to renew the line. However, such a scheme would also leave the IMF with a potentially large open liability. It is probably for this reason that the agreed facility does not involve a firm commitment on the part of the Fund. Instead, loans under the facility will depend on the health of the IMF's resources,[12] evidence that the country is the victim of 'contagion' that is largely outside its control and the country's willingness to pursue a further agreed set of policies. By seeking to retain leverage at the time that the funds are released, the IMF is giving up most of the leverage at the time that the facility is entered into and is reducing the incentives for any country to apply for the facility. Thus, in the trade-off between exerting leverage and retaining flexibility, the Fund has placed almost exclusive emphasis on flexibility.

IV. CRISIS PREVENTION AND THE LESSONS FROM THE ASIAN CRISIS

We argued above that there are strong limitations to the ability of any international financial institution to resolve a major financial crisis and that the focus of public policy should be on prevention rather than cure.

Debate about possible policy responses has focused on a number of issues. First, part of the blame for recent financial crises has been laid at the door of pegged exchange rates, and this has led to the view that countries need to choose between freely floating currencies on the one hand and currency boards or enlarged

[12] The agreed contingent credit line scheme envisages that a country will normally have access to between 300 and 500% of its Fund quota.

currency areas on the other.[13] Second, the substantial capital flows to and from the affected countries have prompted concern about excessive speculation and raised the question of whether governments should throw sand into the speculative works in the form of a Tobin tax or capital controls.[14] A third set of issues centres on corporate ownership and governance in the affected countries, for it has been argued that discipline has been weakened by the degree of conglomeration in corporate structures and the close relationships between non-financial corporations and banks.[15]

This paper by-passes these issues and focuses instead on the role of capital structure in the recent financial crises. One of the principal lessons from recent events centres on the distribution of risk. The Asian crisis occurred first in the real economy, where huge overcapacity and increasing costs led to a sharp fall in profitability. The crisis in the real economy showed up in the financial sector in the form of large capital outflows, falling asset prices and insolvencies in financial institutions. There are always likely to be shocks in the real economy, but countries and their institutions can adopt financial structures which ensure that the consequences of these shocks are distributed efficiently. Two features of the financial structure in the affected Asian countries were a particular source of difficulty.

- Many of the banks borrowed dollars and reinvested in domestic currency loans. Their willingness to do so was enhanced by their belief that the governments were committed to maintaining the currency pegs. Some banks believed that they had hedged the currency risk by also making dollar loans to local companies. But, since the borrowers had no dollar income with which to repay these loans, the banks found that they had merely substituted credit risk for currency risk.
- The currency mismatch was also accompanied by a maturity mismatch, with banks funding in the short-term interbank market and then relending at longer maturities. Thus banks faced a problem of rolling over existing loans as they matured and could do so only on very unfavourable terms. Governments also funded themselves with very short-term debt, so that they too were faced with the problem of rolling over maturing loans at very high rates. This created a conflict between the need to reduce the government deficit and the need to raise interest rates to protect the currency and thus the cost of foreign currency debt, much of which was incurred by the banking system.

The choice of financial structure is largely a problem in risk distribution. Capital can be provided in the form of either equity or debt. The heavy reliance on debt finance by many East Asian companies meant that only a small reduction in profitability was needed to produce financial distress and default, the costs of which

[13] If financial crises are a consequence of fixed exchange rates, then it is arguable that the IMF should abandon its traditional role of providing funds to countries to defend a currency peg. This view was expressed forcefully by Robert Rubin (1999).

[14] For a discussion of the role of capital controls see, for example, Dooley (1996) and Eichengreen *et al.* (1998).

[15] For relevant discussions on these issues, see Myers (1998) and Rajan and Zingales (1998).

were borne largely by local banks. This points first to the need to improve the supply of equity in these countries. This is particularly important in the case of capital inflows. Since developing economies are often relatively undiversified, foreign equity ownership has the advantage of spreading that risk widely.

Foreign equity investment can be in the form of either portfolio investment or direct investment. Portfolio investment is more easily reversed than direct investment. Thus, heavy net purchases of East Asian equities by foreign investors were replaced by modest net sales in 1997 (Institute of International Finance 1999a). Although these sales were necessarily taken up by domestic investors, many of the foreigners who sold their stock converted the proceeds to dollars, and this contributed to the pressure on exchange rates. In contrast to portfolio investment in equities, foreign direct investment in the affected Asian countries declined only modestly, while for Asia as a whole it actually increased.[16]

Unlike equity, debt brings with it the risk of default, but debt instruments may differ on a number of dimensions that affect the allocation of risk.

- *Currency.* The recent financial crises have highlighted the risks for governments, banks and industrial companies of unmatched foreign currency borrowing. Clearly, loans between different currency zones must always involve a currency risk for some party, but it is undesirable that these risks should be concentrated in the developing country and particularly in its banking system.
- *Maturity.* Borrowers that finance with a succession of short-term loans must roll over their loans at rates that reflect their changing credit risk. As the debt maturity is lengthened, more of that default risk is passed to the lender. Thus, long-term debt effectively provides the borrower with insurance against a rise in the default premium. Of course, such insurance does not come free, for the lenders will charge a higher rate of interest on long-term risky loans (Merton 1974).[17]
- *Guaranteed lines of credit.* A related mechanism for risk-shifting involves guaranteed lines of credit. For example, a group of foreign banks have entered into a firm commitment (that is, without a 'material adverse change' clause) to lend Argentina up to US$7 billion against collateral at 200 b.p. above LIBOR. Similarly, Mexico has arranged a simple overdraft facility for about $3 billion. In both cases the governments paid a commitment fee and in exchange the banks took on the risk of movements in the default premium.

[16] While foreign direct investment accounted for about half of private capital inflows into all emerging Asian markets before the crisis, it accounted for only about one-sixth of the private flows to the affected countries. This difference between the liquidity of direct and portfolio investment may go some way towards explaining why some countries were relatively insulated from the shocks that affected other parts of the region. For example, while China shared the problems of a chronically weak banking system, an overlevered corporate sector, excess capacity in many industries and a sharp expansion of domestic credit, the ratio of foreign direct investment to financial investment in China was substantially higher than in the most affected countries (Lardy 1999). As a result, China did not experience the capital outflows of its neighbours.

[17] Note that this does not imply that longer-term debt raises the cost of capital for emerging markets. Capital structure irrelevance propositions are not violated simply by changes in debt maturity.

- *Interest rate.* Long-term *variable-rate* debt shifts the risk of changes in the default premium from the borrower to the lender. With long-term *fixed-rate* debt, both the default premium and the risk-free interest rate are fixed. In the case of corporate debt, the impact on risk depends on the effect of interest rate changes on the value of the firm's assets. However, since major financial crises typically involve both a sharp rise in real interest rates and a fall in the nominal value of corporate assets, the issue of fixed rate debt avoids the prospect of an increase in debt-servicing costs at the time of declining profits. Since increases in the domestic short-term interest rate are a common response to a financial crisis, long-term fixed-rate government debt frees the government from the conflict between raising interest rates to protect the currency and holding down its borrowing costs. Governments have a further reason to prefer the issue of fixed-rate, long-term debt, since it plays a role for governments which is similar to that of equity. Governments have uncertain income. If there is an unanticipated fall in the real value of this income stream, then the government can seek to recover the deficit from its citizens in the form of higher taxes or poorer services. However, particularly in developing countries, it may be infeasible to require the citizens to bear all the risk of the government's activities, so that the bondholders may need to take on part of the risk. The adjustment to interest rates that is needed to enforce real wealth losses on the bondholders is much smaller if the government is financed largely by long-term nominal debt denominated in its domestic currency.
- *Call provisions.* Call provisions on bonds may have both a signalling and an incentive effect, since a borrower that is prepared to pay a premium for the right to repay early has an incentive to maintain the value of its debt and credibly signals its confidence that it can do so.
- *Structured debt.* Structured debt makes it possible to tailor debt service more closely to the borrower's ability to pay. This may be particularly important for sovereign governments that cannot issue equity directly. One possible response, suggested by the insurance industry, is to issue catastrophe or 'forgiveness' bonds, the payments on which are reduced in the event of a defined catastrophe. An alternative is to index the debt service to some measure of economic output. Thus, Mexico has issued oil-linked bonds, while Bulgaria has issued GDP-indexed bonds. A somewhat simpler solution is to combine an issue of straight debt with simultaneous commodity or equity swaps. For example, a government could gain considerable protection against the effects of an economic crisis by entering into an equity swap whose payments are linked to the level of its domestic equity index.[18]
- *Debt conversion.* Debt brings with it the risk of default and, in countries where the bankruptcy code is undeveloped or its application unpredictable, this may raise the cost of debt. A somewhat unconventional solution might be to develop

[18] An alternative which would largely eliminate the possibility of moral hazard would be to link payments to a regional equity index.

debt that converts automatically to equity as the value of the borrower's assets declines. Since the role of bankruptcy codes is to ensure the orderly transfer of ownership to the debtholders in the event of default, such a security would build the bankruptcy mechanism directly into the debt contract and would therefore substitute for local bankruptcy law.

- *Securitization.* The Asian crisis highlighted the problems caused by domestic banks which acted as intermediaries between international lending banks and local corporate borrowers. The cost of financial distress in the corporate sector therefore fell first on the local banking system. This could be avoided if the debt was securitized or was raised directly from the overseas banks.

We have argued that the financial crisis in Asia was exacerbated by the financial structure of the countries, notably the high degree of corporate leverage, the dominance of local bank financing and the currency and maturity mismatch of this bank lending. The result was that risk was poorly diversified and unduly concentrated on the country's banking system. There is no single optimal capital structure for either corporations or governments. We cannot say, for example, that local currency debt is always less risky than foreign currency debt or that fixed rate debt is preferable to variable rate debt. Our discussion, however, illustrates the importance of both the level and design of debt in allocating risk.

Notice that changes in capital structure redistribute risk and can therefore mitigate the consequences of future wealth losses. But the time to redistribute risk is before you lose all your wealth. The bankrupt gains little by resolving never to go to the casino again. Once the losses have occurred, they cannot be recovered by voluntary debt restructuring. Voluntary restructuring can shift the time pattern of cash flows and their risk; it cannot affect value. It is part of crisis prevention; it has little role to play in crisis resolution.

V. POLICY IMPLICATIONS

In this section we sketch some of the policy implications for developing countries, most of which flow fairly directly from our analysis of the issues. We begin with the role of foreign capital.

Since a high proportion of foreign investment in developing countries has been in the form of short-term debt, it has provided little risk pooling and has led to substantial capital outflows with an associated pressure on reserves. Policy, therefore, needs to be aimed at increasing the proportion of foreign capital that is in the form of foreign direct investment or equity portfolio investment. In particular, liberalization of foreign direct investment or inward equity portfolio investment needs to be undertaken in parallel with that of short-term banking flows.

There are some encouraging indications that an increasing proportion of foreign capital in emerging markets is of a long-term nature. For example, foreign direct investment in emerging markets has increased by 30% a year since 1990 and by 1997 had reached nearly 50% of private capital inflows to emerging markets (though it remained relatively unimportant in South East Asia).[19] Foreign direct investment depends in part on the absence of government constraints that are often designed to protect particular local industries, but it is also heavily dependent on a benign political, legal and institutional infrastructure.

Since 1980, an increasing fraction of the indirect investment in emerging markets has been securitized, with the result that both equity and bond investment have grown at the expense of bank lending. This has had two advantages. While these portfolio flows have been more volatile than direct investment, they are at least more stable than short-term banking flows. Further, proportionately more of the risk has been borne by foreigners and thereby pooled. In some countries the growth in foreign equity investment has been hampered by direct restrictions on ownership. For example, before May 1997 foreign equity investment in Korea was inhibited by the fact that investors as a group were not permitted to hold more than 20% of the shares of any Korean firm.[20] But, even where there have been no such formal constraints on foreign equity holdings, investment has been restricted by the costs of accessing overseas markets. There are various actions that may help to cut these access costs. For example, trading costs could be reduced by making it easier for firms to list on overseas exchanges and by deregulating the domestic exchanges. Other (and potentially much larger) costs arise from the difficulties of acquiring information about an overseas market and therefore depend among other things on the quality of accounting data and the regulation of trading activity. The growth of specialist country funds suggests that investing through such funds may have helped to economize on the costs of collecting information.[21]

We have stressed the role of short-term bank loans in the Asian crisis. Such short-term loans shift risk from the lender to the borrower, who must take on the uncertainty about the default premium when the loans are rolled over. Therefore, contrary to some recent suggestions, the regulatory authorities who are responsible for the solvency of the *lending* banks have no reason to encourage them to increase the maturity of their interbank loans. However, the regulators for the *borrowing* banks do need to be concerned about both the maturity and currency mismatch of the bank portfolios. Moreover, the heavy sectoral concentration of these loan portfolios and the very high leverage of many corporate borrowers emphasize the need for much stronger supervision of the lending practices of the local banks and of the valuation of their loans.

While there are dangers in abrupt increases in competition, there is a strong case in many developing economies for reducing barriers to entry by foreign banks, which would facilitate direct loans from these banks to corporates, rather than

[19] As a result of the capital outflow in 1998 from crisis countries, direct investment rose in that year to 84% of net private flows to emerging markets (Institute of International Finance 1999a).

[20] This proportion was increased progressively to 50% in December 1997. Restrictions on foreign investment in long-term Korean corporate bonds have been even more severe.

[21] Between 1990 and 1995 the number of US country funds increased about fivefold and the assets under management increased from $13 billion to $109 billion (Serra 1999). For evidence that country funds economize on information costs, see Frankel and Schmukler (1997).

loans by way of the interbank market. Such competition is also likely to be the best antidote to uncommercial lending practices by domestic banks.

Corporations in the crisis countries had not only expanded productive capacity with little regard for prospective returns, but financed this expansion largely by borrowing. Thus, a relatively small decline in economic activity led to widespread defaults, the cost of which was borne by the banking system. This suggests three further policy aims. The first is to promote greater use of equity finance. Deregulation of the underwriting market can help to reduce the costs of issuing equity, while the supply of equity finance can be enhanced by encouraging foreign equity ownership and by increasing domestic institutional ownership.[22] The second policy aim should be to reduce the cost of default by improved bankruptcy procedures. The third is to reduce the probability of default by encouraging more efficient hedging. In some cases there already exist efficient hedging instruments. For example, the development of the swap market has provided borrowers with a low-cost way to separate the currency of the loan from their exposure to that currency. The problem, therefore, was not that the means for hedging were absent, but that Asian corporations and banks were confident that the currency pegs would be maintained and were content to take on the risks of foreign currency borrowing. But currency fluctuations are not the only macro risks that threaten corporations and governments in developing countries. Particularly for governments, which are unable to issue equity explicitly, there is a clear need for them to design debt structures that hedge against the principal risks. There is much talk about involving the private sector in crisis prevention.[23] The greatest potential contribution of commercial and investment banks to crisis prevention would be to devise and market efficient hedging instruments to corporations and governments.

VI. CONCLUSION

Underlying public policy towards international crises is the view that markets are subject to a succession of contagious bubbles and panics, which the authorities can, and should, intervene to ameliorate. However, significant progress in developing policy will be made only when it is recognized that financial markets generally function well and that international financial institutions have neither the resources nor the superior information to stem the wealth losses that these crises cause. Thus, the principal function of the IMF is not to counteract supposed failures of financial markets by acting as a lender of last resort, but instead should be to use its ability to impose conditions that would be difficult for private institutions to require.

There has been considerable concern that the primary beneficiaries of IMF assistance are the major international banks, which have been able to avoid the

[22] This is frequently associated with the development of private pension schemes.

[23] See, for example, International Monetary Fund (1999) and Institutue of International Finance (1999b).

consequences of their imprudent lending and therefore have little reason to be any more prudent in the future. These concerns are almost certainly misplaced. International banking is a competitive activity and there is no reason to suppose that the banks have been able to appropriate to themselves the (very small) subsidy in IMF loans. Nor does the yield and volatility of developing country debt suggest that lenders regard that debt as underwritten by the IMF. Moves to 'bail in' private lenders by (say) a moratorium on debt service are likely to be counterproductive, since they are likely to increase the cost of private sector debt and induce banks to exit even more rapidly.

The emphasis of public policy should be on crisis prevention rather than resolution. The Asian crisis was prompted by huge industrial overcapacity and increasing costs, which led to a sharp fall in profitability. This crisis in the real economy showed up in the financial sector in the form of large capital outflows and considerable strains on the domestic banking system. This suggests the need to develop financial structures that can distribute more efficiently risks in the real economy.

A large proportion of foreign capital was in the form of short-term, foreign currency interbank loans. Not only was this capital inflow easily reversed, but the risks were concentrated in the developing countries' banking systems. Where capital consisted of foreign direct investment or equity portfolio investment, capital flows were much more stable and the risk was efficiently pooled with foreign investors.

Unlike equity, debt brings with it the risk of default. This risk, however, is influenced by the structure of the debt. For example, we noted how the risk of changes in the default premium can be reduced by an extension in debt maturities and we showed how structured debt can be used to reduce the risk of default. It is also undesirable that default risk should be borne solely by domestic banks. The pool of lenders can be widened both by encouraging the entry of foreign banks and by securitization of corporate debt.

There are some encouraging signs that some of these changes in financial structure have already been taking place. For example, an increasing proportion of capital inflows into emerging markets has been in the form of foreign direct investment and more of the indirect investment has consisted of bond and equity investment rather than bank loans. Nevertheless, there are a number of possible institutional reforms that could help to accelerate these processes.

REFERENCES

Bagehot, W. (1873), *Lombard Street.* London: Kegan Paul.

Bancrjee, A. V. (1992), 'A Simple Model of Herding Behavior', *Quarterly Journal of Economics*, 107, 797–818.

Calomiris, C. W. (1998), 'The IMF's Imprudent Role as Lender of Last Resort', *The Cato Journal*, 17, 275–94.

Diamond, D. and P. Dybvig (1983), 'Bank Runs, Liquidity, and Deposit Insurance', *Journal of Political Economy*, 91, 401–19.

Dooley, M. P. (1996), 'A Survey of Literature on Controls over International Capital Transactions', *IMF Staff Papers*, 43, 639–87.

Eichengreen, B., M. Mussa *et al.* (1998), 'Capital Account Liberalization: Theroretical and Practical Aspects', *IMF Occasional Paper No.172*.

Fischer, S. (January 1999), *On the Need for an International Lender of Last Resort*. Washington, DC: International Monetary Fund.

Frankel, J. A. and S. L. Schmukler (1997), 'Country Funds and Asymmetric Information', working paper, Center for International and Development Economics, University of California, Berkeley, May.

Institute of International Finance (1999a), *Capital Flows to Emerging Market Economies*. Washington, DC: Institute of International Finance.

Institute of International Finance (1999b), *Involving the Private Sector in the Resolution of Financial Crises in Emerging Markets*. Washington, DC: Institute of International Finance.

International Monetary Fund (1998a), *International Capital Markets: Developments, Prospects and Key Policy Issues*. Washington, DC: IMF.

International Monetary Fund (1998b), *The World Economic Outlook: Financial Turbulence and the World Economy*. Washington, DC: IMF.

International Monetary Fund (1999), *Involving the Private Sector in Forestalling and Resolving Financial Crises*. Washington, DC: IMF.

Jackson, K. D. (1999), 'Introduction: the Roots of the Crisis,' in K. D. Jackson, ed., *Asian Contagion: the Causes and Consequences of a Financial Crisis*. Boulder, CO: Westview Press.

Kaufman, G. (1994), 'Bank Contagion: a Review of the Theory and Evidence', *Journal of Financial Services Research*, 8, 123–50.

Lardy, N. (1999), 'China and the Asian Financial Contagion', in K. D. Jackson, ed., *Asian Contagion: the Causes and Consequences of a Financial Crisis*. Boulder, CO: Westview Press.

Meltzer, A. H. (1998), 'Asian Problems and the IMF', *The Cato Journal*, 17, 267–74.

Merton, R. (1974), 'On the Pricing of Corporate Debt: Risk Structure of Interest Rates', *Journal of Finance*, 29, 449–70.

Myers, S. C. (1998), 'Financial Architecture', *European Financial Management*, 5, 133–41.

Radelet, S. and J. Sachs (1998), 'The East Asian Financial Crisis: Diagnosis, Remedies, Prospects', unpublished paper, Harvard Institute for International Development, 20 April.

Rajan, R. G. and L. Zingales (1998), 'Which Capitalism? Lessons from the East Asian Crisis', unpublished paper, University of Chicago, September.

Rubin, R. E. (1999), 'Remarks on Reform of the International Financial Architecture to the School of Advanced International Studies', 21 April.

Sachs, J. (1995), 'Do We Need an International Lender of Last Resort?', Frank Graham Memorial Lecture, Princeton University.

Serra, A. P. (1999), 'Tests of International Capital Market Integration: Evidence from Emerging Markets', PhD dissertation, London Business School.

Summers, L. (1998) 'Opportunities Out of Crises: Lessons from Asia', remarks to the Overseas Development Council, 19 March.

Thornton, H. (1802), *An Enquiry into the Nature and Effects of Paper Credit of Great Britain*. New York: August Kelley.

Welch, I. (1992), 'Sequential Sales, Learning and Cascades', *Journal of Finance*, 47, 695–732.

24

On the Need for an International Lender of Last Resort

STANLEY FISCHER

The frequency, virulence, and global spread of financial crises in emerging market countries in the last five years—Mexico in 1994, with the subsequent tequila contagion in Latin America and for a day or two in east Asia; east Asia in 1997 and 1998, with contagion spreading crisis within the region; Russia in 1998, itself affected by Asian contagion, with the Russian contagion spreading to Latin America in addition to eastern Europe and the rest of the former Soviet Union—has led to the most serious rethinking of the structure of the international financial system since the breakdown of the Bretton Woods system in 1971. In the coming months and years, governments and international institutions will be putting in place a series of changes designed to strengthen the international financial system.

The vision that underlies most proposals for reform of the international financial system is that the international capital markets should operate as well as the better domestic capital markets. To express the goal in this way is to drive home the point that volatility and contagion cannot be banished, for asset prices inevitably move sharply, and in ways that are significantly intercorrelated. But while volatility and contagion will always be with us, we can surely do better in reducing the frequency and intensity of emerging market financial crises, and the extent of contagion, than we have in the last five years.

As we consider how to make the global capital markets operate better and how to reduce the frequency and virulence of financial crises, I would like to revisit a literature that emerged out of the financial crises of the nineteenth century, that on the lender of last resort. The best-known classic writing on the lender of last resort is Walter Bagehot's (1873) *Lombard Street.*[1] The most famous lesson from Bagehot is that *in a crisis, the lender of last resort should lend freely, at a penalty rate, on the basis of collateral that is marketable in the ordinary course of business when there is no panic.*

I will start by reviewing the case for a lender of last resort in the domestic economy, and the set of rules that the lender of last resort is supposed to follow.

[1] Henry Thornton's (1802) analysis of the role of lender of last resort is also remarkably sophisticated. For an historical discussion of the lender of last resort, see Humphrey and Keleher (1984).

This article first appeared in the *Journal of Economic Perspectives* 13(4), 1999. © American Economic Association.

I will then discuss the moral hazard problem that is created by the existence of a lender of last resort—that is, the problem that the existence of a lender of last resort may create incentives for risky behavior which raise the chances of financial crises—and measures to mitigate it. I then turn to the international system and will argue that it too needs a lender of last resort. I will argue that the International Monetary Fund, although it is not an international central bank, has undertaken certain important lender of last resort functions in the current system, generally acting in concert with other official agencies—and that its role can be made more effective in a reformed international financial system.[2]

THE DOMESTIC LENDER OF LAST RESORT

The role of lender of last resort for the central bank is associated with the prevention and mitigation of financial crises. Financial crises and panics have been taking place for centuries (Kindleberger, 1996; MacKay, 1841). They are typically associated with a sudden loss of confidence in the standing of some financial institutions or assets. Because the chain of credit is based on tightly interlinked expectations of the ability of many different debtors to meet payments, a sense of panic can spread rapidly, contagiously, through the financial system, and if unchecked, have significant effects on the behavior of the real economy. The role of the lender of last resort is to offer an assurance of credit, given under certain limited conditions, which will stop a financial panic from spreading—or better still, stop it from even getting started.[3]

While there is considerable agreement on the need for a domestic lender of last resort, some disagreements persist about what the lender of last resort should do. I will start with the traditional Bagehot (1873) conception, as summarized and developed by Meltzer (1986, p. 83):

> The central bank is called the lender of last resort because it is capable of lending—and to prevent failures of solvent banks must lend—in periods when no other lender is either capable of lending or willing to lend in sufficient volume to prevent or end a financial panic.

[2] Among those who have sought to build on and develop the analysis of the role of lender of last resort in recent years, see Benston *et al.* (1986), Freixas (1999), Garcia and Plautz (1988), Goodhart (1995), Goodhart and Huang (1998), Goodfriend and Lacker (1999), Holmstrom and Tirole (1998), Kindleberger (1996, first edition 1978), Meltzer (1986), Mundell (1983), Schwartz (1988), Solow (1982), and Wijnholds and Kapteyn (1999). Claassen (1985) provides an interesting discussion of the role of an international and domestic lenders of last resort in an international context. Recent discussions of the potential role of the IMF as an international lender of last resort include Calomiris (1998), Calomiris and Meltzer (1998), Capie (1998), Chari and Kehoe (1999), Giannini (1998), Jeanne (1998), and Meltzer (1998). Mishkin (1999) and Radelet and Sachs (1998) take up lender of last resort issues in the context of the Asian crisis.

[3] In economic theory panics can be modeled as cases of multiple equilibria, possibly dependent on herd behavior. The classic reference is Diamond and Dybvig (1983). For a related model in the international context, see Chang and Velasco (1998).

Meltzer lists (pp. 83–4) five main points concerning a lender of last resort, the first four derived from Bagehot:

> The central bank is the only lender of last resort in a monetary system such as [that of the United States].
>
> To prevent illiquid banks from closing, the central bank should lend on any collateral that is marketable *in the ordinary course of business when there is no panic* [emphasis added]. It should not restrict lending to paper eligible for discount at the central bank in normal periods.
>
> Central bank loans, or advances, should be made in large amounts, on demand, at a rate of interest above the market rate. This discourages borrowing by those who can obtain accommodation in the market.
>
> The above three principles should be stated in advance and followed in a crisis.
>
> Insolvent financial institutions should be sold at the market price or liquidated if there are no bids for the firm as an integral unit. The losses should be borne by owners of equity, subordinated debentures, and debt, uninsured depositors, and the deposit insurance corporations, as in any bankruptcy proceeding.

Meltzer's (1986) statement for the most part agrees with other formulations, but does not emphasize the view, summarized for instance by Humphrey (1975) and attributed to Thornton (1802), that the overriding objective of the lender of last resort should be to prevent panic-induced declines in the aggregate money stock, and thus that the lender of last resort role can be viewed as part of a central bank's overall task of monetary control. In some more recent formulations, this view has been extended to what could be considered a sixth precept, which could be added to the above list: 'In the event of a panic, the central bank should assure liquidity to the market, but not necessarily to individual institutions.'[4]

With this notion of the lender of last resort in mind, I will take up six questions about the role of the domestic lender of last resort.

Is the Central Bank the Only Lender of Last Resort?

Lenders of last resort have generally undertaken two roles: *crisis lender* and *crisis manager*. The crisis lender provides financing to deal with a crisis. The crisis manager takes responsibility for dealing with a crisis or potential crisis, whether or not the institution itself lends for that purpose. In the midst of a financial crisis, there is often a potential managerial (or facilitating or coordinating) role in which other agents or institutions may be encouraged to act in the right way, for instance by extending a loan to an institution whose failure could have systemic consequences.

While historically the central bank has generally been both the crisis manager and the crisis lender, neither role has to be carried out by the central bank. If a certain authority, and access to resources, are necessary for taking this coordinating role, then a Treasury may be able to do it as well as a central bank. At various times in U.S. history, institutions other than the central bank have played one or both of these

[4] In private conversation, Meltzer has indicated that he sees no advantage to the rule that the central bank should lend only to the market rather than on occasion if necessary also to individual institutions.

roles, including: the U.S. Treasury; private institutions, such as clearing-houses; and in 1907, J.P. Morgan (Kindleberger, 1996, pp. 133–5).[5] Indeed, the separation of the roles of crisis lender and crisis manager could become more frequent as the task of supervision of the financial sector is separated from the central bank, as it has been in the United Kingdom and elsewhere.

Does the Lender of Last Resort Need the Ability to Create Money?

There is no question that a lender of last resort will often find it useful to have the power to create money. The clearest example is when a panic takes the form of a run from bank deposits into currency. Then the central bank is well-positioned to create quickly the currency needed to deal with the panic, and at no first-round cost to the taxpayer.[6]

However, panics caused by a demand for currency are rare (Kaufman, 1988; Schwartz, 1988). More generally, a panic may take the form of a run, possibly enhanced by contagion, in which deposits shift from those banks and financial institutions deemed unsound to those thought to be healthy. In these cases, creating additional money may be unnecessary. At least in principle, the liquidity can simply recirculate from the institutions gaining money back to those losing it. Again in principle, the market can accomplish this shift, if it is able to distinguish the merely illiquid from the insolvent companies.

But—and this is the critical point—*the line between solvency and liquidity is not determinate during a crisis.* If a crisis is well-managed, the number of bankruptcies may remain small; if it is badly managed, it may end in general illiquidity and insolvency. A skilled lender of last resort, able to assure the markets that credit can and will be made available to institutions that would be solvent in normal times, can help stem a panic and reduce the extent of the crisis.

All this is straightforward, provided the central bank is free to create money. However, at the time that Bagehot (1873) wrote *Lombard Street*, the Bank of England was bound by gold standard rules; that is, money could only be created in accordance with the amount of gold held by the Bank, and the Bank did not have the ability to create gold. Nonetheless, Bagehot enjoined the Bank to act as lender of last resort. In the three financial crises preceding the writing of *Lombard Street*, the Bank of England was given permission to break the gold standard rule, and since Bank of England credit was accepted as being as good as gold, it managed to stay the panics. The key was not the legal right to create money, but the effective ability to provide liquidity to the market.

[5] Although some have pointed with approval to the role of clearing-houses in financial panics, note Kindleberger's quotation (1996, p. 134) from Jacob Schiff in 1907: 'The one lesson we should learn from recent experience is that the issuing of clearing-house certificates in the different bank centers has also worked considerable harm. It has broken down domestic exchange and paralyzed to a large extent the business of the country.'

[6] Accordingly, Schwartz (1988) argues that the central bank should act as lender of last resort only in the event of a run from banks into currency.

A similar question, of whether there can be a lender of last resort when the central bank is constrained in the creation of money, arises today in countries with currency boards, where foreign exchange holdings constrain the domestic money supply. If the question is how to deal with domestic financial institutions that may suffer liquidity problems, one solution adopted in Bulgaria, where the banking department of the central bank is assigned the task of (limited) lender of last resort, is to set up an agency that is endowed with sufficient resources to lend in the event of a panic or banking sector problems. If the problem is how to deal with a potential external shock that puts pressure on the domestic banking system, then the country may either hold excess foreign exchange reserves, or as in the case of Argentina, borrow from the markets and the official sector and put in place international lines of credit. In these cases, the private and public sector lenders to the central bank are acting as the crisis lender, while the central bank is acting as crisis manager.[7]

These examples make the point that lender of last resort need not have the power to create money, as long as it can provide credit to the market or to institutions in trouble. It is possible to set up an agency to deal with potential banking sector problems and endow it with sufficient funds—perhaps from the Treasury—to cover the anticipated costs of normal crises. In dealing with banking crises, the lender of last resort has more often acted as crisis manager, as coordinator, without putting up its own funds, than as outright lender. In the 20-year period ending in 1993, taxpayer or deposit insurance money was used in over half the 120 banking rescue packages studied by Goodhart and Schoenmaker (1995), in part because the central bank simply did not have the real resources that were required to deal with the banking problem. In any case, the costs of major financial system difficulties will one way or another be borne by the fiscal authority, either explicitly or implicitly, in the form of lower central bank profits over an extended period of time.[8]

This point—that while it is advantageous for the lender of last resort to be able to create money, it is not an essential attribute of the lender of last resort—is both central to the argument of this paper, and controversial. I make the argument on logical and historical grounds, namely, that it is possible to conceive of an institution that does not have the ability to create money acting usefully as both crisis manager and crisis lender and that as a historical matter, such institutions have usefully undertaken such roles. Others would argue that without the ability to create unlimited amounts of money, the would-be lender of last resort lacks credibility and thus cannot stabilize a panic. Those who take the latter view should interpret the argument of this paper as being that there is a useful role to be played

[7] Of course, the question arises why any external financing is needed in response to a currency shock if the rules of the currency board are strictly applied. The answer is that the monetary authority may want to mitigate the adverse effects of an external shock on the banking system and the economy.

[8] Not all financial crises need ultimately to be costly to the public sector; indeed, if the lender of last resort intervenes in a pure panic and manages to stabilize the situation, it should expect to come out ahead when its lending is repaid. Apparently both the Swedish and Norwegian bank restructuring agencies that were set up in the crises of the early 1990s have come close to meeting this criterion. (I am indebted to my colleague Stefan Ingves for this information.)

by an institution that can be both crisis manager and crisis lender, even if—according to their own definition—it cannot be a lender of last resort.

Why Should a Lender of Last Resort Lend Only Against Collateral, Especially Collateral Evaluated at its Value in Noncrisis Times?

By basing the decision to lend on the availability of acceptable collateral, the lender of last resort applies a rough but robust test of whether the institution is in trouble because of the immediate panic, or because of an insolvency that will persist even after the panic. Moreover, when financial institutions know that the lender of last resort will demand collateral, they have an incentive to reduce risks in their portfolios by holding assets that would be accepted as collateral.

The requirement that the collateral be good in normal times is the critical insight. The implicit view behind the requirement that the lender of last resort require collateral, and that the collateral be valued at noncrisis levels, is that there is a good equilibrium towards which the lender of last resort is trying to steer the system. By lending on the basis of the value of collateral in normal times, the lender of last resort helps prevent the panic in the market from becoming self-fulfilling.

More broadly, this rule also suggests that the lender of last resort should apply the rules of collateral generously. In a famous passage bearing of this point, Bagehot (1873[1924 edition, p. 52]) quotes the Bank of England in 1825: 'We lent it by every possible means and in modes we had never adopted before; we took in stock on security, we purchased Exchequer bills, we made advances on Exchequer bills, we not only discounted outright but we made advances on the deposit of bills of exchange to an immense amount, in short by every possible means consistent with the safety of the bank, and we were not on some occasions over-nice.' In a similar spirit, the Governor of the Bank of England described the Bank's reaction to the Overend financial crisis in May 1866 (as quoted in Clapham, 1944, Volume II, pp. 283–4): 'We did not flinch from our post... we made advances which would hardly have been credited... before the Chancellor of the Exchequer was perhaps out of his bed we had advanced one-half of our reserves... I am not aware that any legitimate application for assistance made to this house was refused.'

Why Should the Lender of Last Resort Charge a Penalty Interest Rate?

The penalty interest rate serves several functions. It limits the demand for credit by institutions that are not in trouble. It reduces the risk that financial institutions will take excessive risks in normal times, secure in the knowledge that they will be able to borrow cheaply in tough times. It encourages institutions to repay the lender of last resort as soon as possible after the crisis, in preference to other outstanding loans.[9]

[9] Mints (1945, pp. 191) attributes Bagehot's advocacy of a high lending rate to his view that internal and external drains typically accompany each other; that is, an internal financial panic under a gold standard was often accompanied by gold leaving the country. The high interest rate was designed to

But just as the requirement for collateral is not intended to stifle the lender of last resort, neither is the application of penalty interest rates. The penalty rate need not be defined relative to the rate at which institutions would lend to each other in the market during a panic. Instead, the penalty must be relative to the interest rate during normal times. In practice, the lender of last resort has frequently lent at a nonpenalty rate (Giannini, 1998).

Should the Lender of Last Resort Lend Only to the Market, and Not to Individual Institutions?

This view holds that, given the provision of sufficient liquidity to the markets, the private sector will be able to decide which institutions should be saved. Moreover, by providing liquidity to the market, the lender of last resort avoids the political hazards of lending to individual institutions.

This idea is a worthy one that should be followed when possible. But given the uncertainties in the midst of a panic over what market conditions will exist in the future, and thus over which institutions should survive, the precept cannot be accepted as a general rule of conduct for the lender of last resort. Almost by definition of a financial panic, a market in the throes of a panic will not do a sound job of allocating credit across institutions. Indeed, Goodhart and Huang (1998) argue that adopting the view that the lender of last resort should lend only to the market is to reject the notion of the lender of last resort.

Should the Principles on Which the Lender of Last Resort Would Lend be Clearly Stated in Advance?

During a crisis, the knowledge that there is an effective lender of last resort should tend to reduce the incentive for runs on otherwise healthy institutions. However some, who fear that market participants will have an incentive to take excessive risks if they believe a lender of last resort will always be available to stem panics, argue for *constructive ambiguity* about the circumstances in which a lender of last resort will step in to seek to stabilize a crisis. The uncertainty generated by such ambiguity should encourage market participants to take fewer risks.[10]

Some ambiguity is simply unavoidable: no central bank or lender of last resort will ever be able to spell out precisely in advance the circumstances under which it would act as either a crisis lender or crisis manager and the conditions it will lay down at that time. But unnecessary ambiguity is not constructive, for it implies that occasions will occur when the putative lender of last resort is expected to deliver, but does not—for example in the Russian crisis of August 1998, when

stop the external drain of gold, and lending freely would stop the internal drain—a reading that is consistent with Bagehot.

[10] Freixas (1999) develops a theoretical case for constructive ambiguity by the lender of last resort.

many market participants expected the official sector to prevent a Russian devaluation. In such a setting, ambiguity makes the economic costs of a given financial crisis worse; indeed, Guttentag and Herring (1983, p. 24) describe as the worst possible system one in which a lender of last resort is expected to take action, but the relevant institution cannot or does not provide the function.

There are three reasons for a lender of last resort to spell out its rules to the extent possible. First, by specifying a good set of rules, the central bank reduces the likelihood of unnecessary self-justifying crises. This was Bagehot's (1873) justification. Second, by announcing and implementing a particular set of rules, the lender of last resort provides incentives for other stabilizing private sector behavior; for instance, in the holding of assets good for collateral. Third, by spelling out the rules in advance, the lender of last resort somewhat limits its own freedom of action after the event, which reduces risks of politically motivated or spur-of-the-moment actions. Of course, *in extremis* the rules could be broken as they were by the Bank of England when it violated the gold standard rules to provide additional credit during crises in the nineteenth century. Spelling out the rules would nonetheless serve a useful purpose, since the lender of last resort would hesitate before incurring the cost of breaking them.

Much of the discussion of these six questions revolves around a common topic, the issue of moral hazard, to which I will now turn.

MORAL HAZARD

'Moral hazard,' notes Guesnerie (1987, p. 646), 'refers to the adverse effects, from the insurance company's point of view, that insurance may have on the insuree's behaviour.' The standard but extreme example is that of an individual with fire insurance who burns down the property; the less extreme example is of a fire insurance holder who, after becoming insured, takes less care to prevent a fire. More generally, the idea of moral hazard applies to any situation where a perceived reduction in the risk it faces leads a party to take riskier actions, or to neglect precautionary measures.

In the case of the domestic lender of last resort, moral hazard problems could arise with respect to both the actions of managers of financial institutions who believe they are better protected against risk because they would receive loans from the lender of last resort during a crisis, and the actions of investors in those financial institutions (Hirsch, 1977). If the lender of last resort was able to intervene only to stop unwarranted panics, leaving institutions that would be insolvent in normal times to fail, the managers of these institutions and their investors would face the right incentives and there would be no moral hazard created by the existence of the lender of last resort. But the lender of last resort is unlikely to be able to distinguish perfectly between warranted and unwarranted crises. Moreover, financial institutions already know that because of the existence of deposit insurance and the too-big-to-fail doctrine that the government has an incentive to prevent them from failing and thus already have a moral hazard motivation to believe that a government rescue of some sort will be forthcoming. For all these reasons, measures to offset the moral hazard of both managers of financial institutions and investors would be helpful.

In considering how to reduce moral hazard, it is important to recognize that the problem has no perfect solution. Instead, appropriate policies will generally combine the provision of insurance with measures to limit moral hazard. In the case of moral hazard resulting from the existence of a lender of last resort (as well as resulting from deposit insurance and too-big-to-fail provisions), there are three categories of measures to limit moral hazard: official regulation; encouragement for private sector monitoring and self-regulation; and the imposition of costs on those who make mistakes, including enforcement of bankruptcy procedures when appropriate (Stern, 1999). I consider these in turn.

First, to be eligible for loans from a lender of last resort, banks' portfolio activities are regulated. The regulations are intended to limit the likelihood of panics and the need for a lender of last resort, while not preventing well-informed risk-taking by investors.

Second, the system seeks to encourage private sector monitoring of financial institutions, particularly by sophisticated investors. Requirements for the provision of information to investors are helpful in this regard. The limit on the size of bank accounts covered by deposit insurance is intended to provide an incentive for large depositors to monitor banks (along with limiting government liability in the case of a bank failure); however, because of concerns that large institutions are too big to fail without threatening financial contagion, these limits rarely operate when large institutions get into trouble. In addition, when the lender of last resort, acting as crisis manager, arranges a bank rescue package financed by the private sector, it encourages more careful monitoring by such institutions in the future.

Third, the lender of last resort should seek to limit moral hazard by imposing costs on those who have made mistakes. Lending at a penalty rate is one way to impose such costs. Changes in management of an institution that is being helped should typically occur, and, as specified in Meltzer's fifth law stated above, equity-holders and holders of subordinated claims on the firm should suffer losses. In the case of insolvency, institutions should be sold or liquidated under the provisions of well-defined bankruptcy laws, which help ensure that workouts for insolvent firms are carried out in an orderly way.

How well do these devices work to limit moral hazard? A first judgment, based on the frequency of financial crises around the world during the last two decades, is this: Not very well. But this answer is too sweeping. Moral hazard is something to be lived with and controlled, rather than fully eliminated; some crises are bound to happen in any system that provides appropriate scope for private sector risk taking; and many financial crises have been caused by waves of euphoria and depression, not by the existence of a lender of last resort—for after all, the long history of financial crises predates lenders of last resort and deposit insurance. The right comparison is not between the real world and a hypothetical world with no financial crises, but rather between the operation of a system with a lender of last resort (and deposit insurance) and one without them. I am not aware of careful studies that have attempted to make this more sophisticated judgment. However, I suspect that such a study, while likely to absolve the presence of various official forms of financial insurance, including the assumption that there is a lender of last resort, from blame for much financial instability, would conclude that it is important to do a better job of controlling moral hazard in the domestic financial system.

AN INTERNATIONAL LENDER OF LAST RESORT?

The case for a domestic lender of last resort is broadly accepted. In the aftermath of the global financial turmoil of the last five years, the question arises of whether the international financial system needs a lender of last resort.

The issue is whether there is a useful role for an institution that takes responsibility for dealing with potential and actual crises, either as a crisis lender, or as a crisis manager, or both. This differs from the question that is sometimes asked as to whether leading central banks should accept some responsibility for the performance of the global economy, along with their national economy. For instance, when Kindleberger (1986) blames the Great Depression on the absence of an international lender of last resort, he means that no agency—and the natural candidates were the Bank of England, the Banque de France, and the U.S. Federal Reserve—pursued a monetary policy that took account of the international dimensions of the crisis in which it found itself. Kindleberger would probably say, approvingly, that in the late 1990s, the Fed *has* acted as international lender of last resort in that sense, even though it was taking actions in the interests of the United States.

I will focus specifically on the case for an international agency to act as lender of last resort for countries facing an external financing crisis. In such a crisis, a country—and by this I mean both the official and private sectors within the country—faces a typically massive demand for foreign exchange. The domestic central bank cannot produce this currency. Thus, the fact that the country may have its own central bank capable of creating the domestic currency is typically irrelevant to the solution of an external financing problem.

There is a potential need for such assistance to a country both because international capital flows are not only extremely volatile but also contagious, exhibiting the classic signs of financial panics,[11] and because an international lender of last resort can help mitigate the effects of this instability and perhaps the instability itself. At the macroeconomic level, a country faced with a sudden demand for foreign exchange can permit its exchange rate to adjust and/or can restrict domestic demand to generate a current account surplus. At the microeconomic level, foreign creditors can attempt to collect on obligations and financial institutions and corporations can—if necessary, and if the domestic legal system is adequate—be put

[11] For models with multiple equilibria in an international context, see Chang and Velasco (1998) and Zettelmeyer (1998).

into bankruptcy. However, all such measures are likely in a panic to result in a considerable overshooting of the needed adjustment, and there is accordingly a case for the public sector both to provide emergency foreign exchange loans and to assist the domestic authorities in attempting to manage the crisis.

The argument rests also on the view that international capital mobility is potentially beneficial for the world economy, including for the emerging market and developing countries. Critics of this view argue that neither the theoretical nor empirical evidence supports a positive link between openness to international capital markets and growth. Indeed, both China and India have grown rapidly during the 1990s with only limited openness to international capital markets and appeared relatively immune from the east Asian financial crisis. It is true that there is as yet little convincing econometric evidence bearing on the benefits or costs of open capital markets. However, all the economically most advanced countries are open to international flows of capital, which suggests that this should be the eventual goal for other countries. In addition, countries that close themselves off to international flows of capital also thereby protect the financial sector from foreign competition, which reduces the efficiency of this important industry. Finally, I suspect, but cannot of course establish, that with regard to empirical work on the benefits of capital account liberalization, the economics profession is a little behind where we were a decade ago on trade liberalization, when empirical work showing its benefits was widely regarded as highly suspect, too.

But the critics of international capital mobility are correct to this extent: its potential for economic benefit can only be realized if the frequency and scale of financial crises can be reduced. The founders of the Bretton Woods system provided for the use of controls on international capital flows to reduce the likelihood of such crises. Some controls—particularly controls that seek to limit short-term capital *inflows*—can be envisaged as a useful part of a transitional regime while the macroeconomic framework and financial structure of an economy are strengthened. The use of controls to limit capital *outflows* has been advocated in the recent crises by several academics and adopted by Malaysia. But it is surprising and impressive how few countries have enacted capital controls in recent years. Indeed, policymakers in Latin American countries that often had such controls in the 1980s have rejected them this time around, emphasizing that the controls were inefficient, widely avoided, and had cost them dearly in terms of capital market access. It remains an open question whether more countries will turn to capital controls in the next few years, either in normal times or in the midst of crises. The answer will depend to an important extent on the success of other financial reforms that are implemented in the next few years.

I will argue not only that the international system needs a lender of last resort, so that the global economy can reap greater net benefits from international capital mobility, but also that the IMF has increasingly been playing the role of crisis manager for the last two decades (Boughton, 1998). Changes in the international system now under consideration—particularly those relating to efforts to bail in the private sector—should make it possible for the IMF to exercise the lender of last resort function more effectively.

In focusing on the Fund's potential role as lender of last resort, I leave aside its other important functions. For example, Article I(i) of the Articles of Agreement, as enacted in 1944, describes the first of its fundamental purposes as being: '[t]o promote international monetary cooperation through a permanent institution which provides the machinery for consultation and collaboration on international monetary problems.' Other functions of the Fund include lending for current account purposes to countries that lack market access; surveillance and the associated provision of information; and technical assistance, including policy advice and monitoring.

Let me immediately turn to the argument that the IMF cannot act as a lender of last resort because it is not an international central bank and cannot freely create international money. As discussed earlier, even the domestic lender of last resort—whether as crisis lender or as crisis manager—is not necessarily the central bank. The IMF has resources to act as a crisis lender, because its financial structure, close to that of a credit union,[12] gives it access to a pool of resources which it can lend to member countries. The IMF also has been assigned the lead as crisis manager in negotiating with member countries in a crisis and helping to arrange financing packages. Finally, as will be discussed below, it also has the ability—not so far used—to create international reserves in a crisis.

The question arises whether the IMF, as crisis lender, has sufficient resources to do the job. The Fund has reached its present size as a result of a series of increases in countries' quotas—that is, the amount which members of the IMF agree to deposit in the Fund in their own currencies. Relative to the size of the world economy, the IMF has shrunk significantly since 1945. If the Fund were today the same size relative to the output of its member states as it was in 1945, it would be more than three times larger.[13] If the quota formula applied in 1945 were used to calculate actual quotas today, the Fund would be five times its present size. If the size of the Fund had been maintained relative to the volume of world trade, it would be more than nine times larger; that is, the size of the Fund would be over $2.5 trillion. Since the Fund was set up at a time when private capital flows were very small, its scale relative to private capital flows has declined even more than its size relative to trade flows.

Despite this significant shrinkage relative to the original conception, the Fund as lender of last resort is still able to assemble a sizeable financial package in response to a crisis. In case of systemic problems, the Fund can augment the use of its own resources by borrowing. Further, as demonstrated in the recent Brazilian and east Asian financial rescue packages, member governments and other international financial institutions may add significantly to these packages in cases they deem to be of particular importance. Whether the Fund will in future be large enough relative to the scale of problems will depend on the future scale and volatility of

[12] The analogy is due to Kenen (1986).

[13] Total quotas are approximately $300 billion. The effective availability of resources to lend is smaller, since the weaker currencies held by the Fund are not in practice usable for lending.

international capital flows, which will in turn depend on the effectiveness of reforms, including measures to deal with problems of moral hazard.

The earlier discussion noted in the domestic case that while it is not essential that the lender of last resort be the central bank, it is helpful. Would it be useful for the IMF to be able to create reserves? Under Article XVIII of the Articles of Agreement, the Executive Board of the Fund can by an 85 percent majority allocate Special Drawing Rights (SDRs) 'to meet the long-term global need, as and when it arises, to supplement existing reserve assets.' These SDRs would augment the reserves of member countries. It is easy to envisage circumstances under which a targeted increase in reserves would be useful to prevent a seizing up of flows of credit in the world economy; indeed, for a short period that seemed to be the case in the fall of 1998. However, a general allocation of SDRs has to be made in proportion to quota holdings and so this mechanism would not in its current form be well-suited to dealing with a problem that affects a specific group of countries.

The IMF thus has the capacity to act as crisis lender to individual countries, and in specified circumstances, through an issue of Special Drawing Rights, could lend more broadly. It also acts as crisis manager. Kindleberger (1996, p. 188) complains that the Fund is too slow in emergencies, but in Korea in late 1997 the IMF has demonstrated an ability to move very rapidly, using the Emergency Financing Mechanism introduced after the Mexican crisis in 1994. The main constraint on the IMF's ability to react speedily in a crisis is that governments suffering a financial crisis delay too long in approaching it, in part because excessive delay is a common characteristic of governments that experience financial crises, but also because they hope to avoid taking the actions that would be needed in a Fund program.

THE EVOLVING CONTEXT OF THE INTERNATIONAL FINANCIAL SYSTEM

The IMF already acts in important respects as international lender of last resort, but the job can surely be done better. However, before addressing that issue directly, I will discuss four central elements in the ongoing evolution of the international financial system: exchange rate systems; reserve holdings; measures to bail in the private sector; and international standards.

In regard to the first subject, over a century of controversy has produced no clear answer to the question of which exchange rate system or monetary regime is best. The best exchange rate for a country seems to depend on the country's economic history, particularly its history of inflation. Nonetheless, it is striking that the major external financial crises of the last three years—in Thailand, Korea, Indonesia, Russia and Brazil—have affected countries with more or less pegged exchange rates. Further, the assumption within these countries that the exchange rate was stable profoundly affected economic behavior and certain kinds of risk taking, especially in the banking system, and contributed to the severity of the post-devaluation crises.

The link between pegged exchange rates and susceptibility to crisis is far from ironclad, however. Several countries with very hard pegs, particularly Argentina and Hong Kong, have succeeded with fixed exchange rates. Some countries with flexible rates, among them Mexico, South Africa and Turkey, have been severely affected by the global economic crisis. Nor should we forget that many countries benefitted from using a pegged or fixed exchange rate as a nominal anchor in disinflation efforts and that the fear of devaluation is often a vital discipline for weak governments. Nonetheless, the virulence of the recent crises is likely to shift the balance towards the choice of more flexible exchange rate systems, including crawling exchange rate pegs with wide bands.

But while the number of nominal exchange rate pegs may decline in the coming years, the world is unlikely to move to a system in which exchange rates for all countries float freely. If countries desire to fix their exchange rates, they may well want to do so definitively, through a currency board. In the longer run, if Europe's move to a single currency succeeds, the result may be additional currency unions and fewer currencies. Because sharp shifts in international investor sentiment regarding even a country with a floating rate can set off a panic and contagion, and because some countries will continue to peg their rates, the need will still exist for an international lender of last resort.

Second, regarding the issue of reserves, there has been surprisingly little emphasis on the fact countries with very large foreign exchange reserves have generally fared better in the recent economic crises than those with small reserves. However, a number of countries, particularly Korea, have recognized that ratio of reserves to short-term external liabilities is an important factor determining the likelihood of a financial crisis (Calvo, 1995), and are accumulating reserves accordingly.[14]

Foreign exchange reserves can be built up in several ways. The most obvious approach is to run a current account surplus; indeed, it is likely that a general desire by emerging market countries to build up reserves by running current account surpluses will impart a deflationary impact to the world economy in the next few years. Reserves can be borrowed, although the interest costs are typically well above the return on reserves. Argentina and a few other countries have put into place a variation on the idea of borrowing reserves, which is to arrange for precautionary or contingent lines of credit, which can be drawn on at short notice if needed. International reserves might also be increased by international agreement on, for example, an issue of Special Drawing Rights. It is not possible without a more detailed analysis to decide which approach is preferable: the approaches differ in terms of effects on aggregate demand, the distribution of seigniorage and other variables. However, I expect that one way or another, the recent experience of crises will lead to larger holdings of reserves.

[14] The focus in the text is on the numerator of the ratio of reserves to short-term debt; however, countries need also to ensure that the denominator stays under control. This element plays an important role in the evolving international architecture, but I shall not pursue it here.

Third, no topic in the new international financial architecture has received as much public attention as the need to involve the private sector in the resolution of financial crises. The arguments are simple and compelling. At the economic level, as the role of private capital flows in the international economy increases, the public sector should not take upon itself the full responsibility for financing countries from which the private sector is withdrawing, for to do so is to court moral hazard on a major scale, to set the wrong incentives for private sector investors and to accept an impossible task—since the public sector will not in the end have enough resources to carry out such a commitment. At the political level, elected officials are unwilling to make public money available for unlimited bailouts of previously incautious private investors.

One approach, just mentioned, is to put in place precautionary lines of credit from private sector lenders. Such lines of credit can serve as a useful supplement to the holding of reserves, and might well be cheaper than actually increasing reserves. A second approach, suggested in a report by the G-10 deputies after the Mexican crisis, is the proposal that bond contracts should be modified to facilitate the rescheduling of payments in the event of a crisis, including permitting creditors to make decisions by majority rather than unanimity.[15] Yet another suggestion, associated with Jeffrey Sachs, is the possibility of a mechanism which would formally impose or allow a stay on payments by a country in financial crisis, a proposal which is sometimes referred to as international bankruptcy. Some developing countries object that such measures would make it more expensive for them to borrow, but most likely that would reflect a more appropriate pricing of risks.

Private sector involvement in external financing crises needs to be approached carefully, lest proposed solutions increase the frequency of crises. For instance, it is sometimes proposed that banks (or other creditors) should always be forced to share in the financing of IMF programs. But if such a condition were insisted on, the creditors would have a greater incentive to rush for the exits at the mere hint of a crisis. This problem suggests that even with private sector involvement, a lender of last resort will continue to be necessary. It also suggests that the involvement of the private sector should differ according to the circumstances of each country: sometimes a formal approach may be necessary, as in Korea at the end of 1997; at other times less formal discussions could serve better; and on occasion, if a country enters an IMF program sufficiently early, perhaps private creditors need not be approached at all.

Fourth, because weaknesses in financial sectors and in the provision of information were such an important factor in the recent crises, a major effort is now underway to encourage emerging market countries to meet agreed international standards of financial and corporate sector behavior, as well as the provision of information. The best-known standards are those for banking, defined by the Basel

[15] This possibility is developed in the report of the [G-22] Working Group on *International Financial Crises*. See also the speech by Gordon Brown (1998).

committee on Banking Supervision. The IMF's Special Data Dissemination Standard has just gone into full operation. Codes of fiscal practice and monetary and financial transparency are also being prepared by the IMF in cooperation with other institutions. A major international effort will be undertaken to improve banking standards, in part through international monitoring and IMF surveillance in cooperation with the World Bank. Among other important international standards already developed or in the process of development are international accounting standards, International Organization of Securities Commissions (IOSCO) standards for the operation of securities markets, and an international standard for bankruptcy regulations.

The main incentives for a country to adopt any of these standards are the expectation that the economy would operate more efficiently and the hope that international investors would treat the economy more favorably. In fact, most leading emerging market countries have subscribed to the IMF's Special Data Dissemination Standard, which suggests that these incentives may suffice to encourage participation in international standards. Nonetheless, further incentives may prove useful; for instance, the risk weights assigned by regulators in creditor countries could reflect the recipient country's observance of the standards. Further incentives can be provided by the appropriate design of official lending facilities.

IMPROVING THE FUNCTIONING OF THE INTERNATIONAL LENDER OF LAST RESORT

At the end of 1997, the IMF introduced the Supplemental Reserve Facility (SRF), which can make short-term loans in large amounts at penalty rates to countries in crisis. SRF loans have been made to Korea, Russia, and Brazil, subject to conditions that certain economic policies be followed. In addition, in April 1999, the Executive Board of the IMF established the Contingent Credit Line (CCL) facility, designed to provide countries with a line of credit that can be drawn on in the event they are struck by contagion from an external crisis. To qualify for a CCL, a country must be pursuing good macroeconomic policies, have a strong financial sector and either meet or be moving towards meeting international standards in a variety of areas. The CCL is thus intended to provide an element of insurance and reassurance for countries with good policies, and incentives for others to pursue good policies, rather than to come to the assistance of countries that are already in trouble. The lending terms for the CCL are similar to those for the SRF. No CCLs have yet been arranged.

Calomiris (1998) and Calomiris and Meltzer (1998) recommend that the IMF act only as lender of last resort, under Bagehot rules, and only to countries that meet a stiff set of requirements, most importantly on the banking system. Among these conditions is the requirement that foreign banks be allowed to operate in the country, a reform that countries should adopt in any case. Loans would be made to qualifying countries on the basis of collateral, and without policy conditionality.

Without going into the overall merits of their analysis,[16] I would like to note that the CCL goes some way towards meeting their proposals. It would further be desirable if the rate charged for access to the CCL and the SRF depended on the extent to which countries meet the relevant international standards. For example, a non-qualifying country might pay a higher penalty interest rate, or be subject to tougher policy conditionality, or in extreme cases, be denied access to the lender of last resort funds.

IMF lending under the Supplemental Reserve Facility incorporates the classic Bagehot (1873) prescription that crisis lending should be at a penalty rate. Policy conditionality can be interpreted as a further element of the penalty, as seen from the viewpoint of the borrower country's policymakers. But what about the Bagehot prescriptions that lending should take place on good collateral, and that institutions that would be bankrupt in normal times should not be saved?

The Articles of Agreement permit the Fund to ask for collateral, but it has rarely done so. The Fund and the World Bank are regarded as preferred creditors, who have a first claim on payments made by countries in debt to them, and their collateral is thus the threat of denying access to global capital markets to countries that default. That is the main, and a powerful and effective, incentive for countries to repay—which is almost always done, in full and on time. While collateralized lending should remain a possibility for the Fund, it does not seem to be essential given the Fund's preferred creditor status.

The more general Bagehot prescription that institutions which are truly bankrupt should not be saved by a lender of last resort is difficult to apply in the international context. To the extent that foreign creditors have claims on private sector corporations in a debtor country, the bankruptcy rules for the debtor country should apply and the Bagehot prescription would be relevant. But it has to be recognized that bankruptcy regulations in many emerging market countries have been ineffective, which is why an effort is now underway to develop an international standard for a domestic bankruptcy code. For a sovereign debtor, the ability to generate repayments is more a matter of political than of economic feasibility. There is no bankruptcy status for a sovereign, but workout procedures, including those of the Paris and London Clubs, and possibly those to be developed as private sector bail-ins are considered further, play a similar role.

The one Bagehot prescription that does not apply in an international crisis is that of lending freely, if by freely is meant without limit. As already discussed, such a policy would create too much moral hazard.[17] How can an international crisis lender and manager deal with moral hazard problems? Charging a penalty rate of interest should help discourage borrower moral hazard, but moral hazard for borrowers is of much less concern than for investors. Borrower moral hazard is

[16] I note for the record that the suggestion that the IMF should operate only as lender of last resort either overlooks or grossly undervalues the other functions carried out by the IMF, which were noted earlier in this discussion.

[17] To say this does not, however, determine the optimal size of crisis loans.

already deterred by the requirements of policy conditionality. Governments try to avoid going to the IMF—indeed they frequently delay too long—and policymakers who preside over a crisis and then have to turn to the IMF generally lose office, as witness the Asian crisis countries and Russia.

Investor moral hazard—that a lender of last resort would encourage investors to loan unwisely—is a more serious concern. In considering this issue, it is important to distinguish the hazards associated with different types of international capital flows.[18] In the case of equity investment, for example, the investor needs to be held responsible—and they have been, for equity investors have taken large losses in the recent crises. In the case of interbank lines of credit, however, the responsibility for addressing the risk of unwise lending because of moral hazard lies as much with the government of the lender as with the borrower government, for it is the former which supervises and tends to protect its banks. Lender supervisory authorities will have to recognize the responsibilities of their institutions to participate in workout procedures and private sector bail-ins when necessary.

The single most important change in the international system that will tend to limit moral hazard by encouraging better monitoring and self-regulation by capital market participants is the adoption of better methods of involving the private sector in financing the resolution of crises. As discussed above, the issues here are immensely difficult; they are also immensely important. Unless better ways of involving the private sector are found, the IMF will not be able to perform its proper function as international lender of last resort, both as crisis lender and crisis manager. At present, the official sector is seeking to involve private sector lenders in several countries in crisis; as this experience is analyzed within the coming months, some general principles for how to involve the private sector should be distilled and begun to be implemented in cases of crisis lending by the IMF and other official institutions.

The crises of the last five years have revealed major weakness in the structure of the international economy. It is urgent to start developing and implementing the constructive solutions that have been proposed, among them improvements in transparency, the adoption of appropriate exchange rate systems, the development and monitoring of international standards, including a bankruptcy standard, the development of precautionary lines of credit, and methods to involve the private sector in financing the resolution of emerging market crises. Important progress has been made during the last twelve months. As these changes continue to be implemented, the role of the international lender of last resort will become both better defined and more effective.

REFERENCES

Bagehot, Walter. 1873. *Lombard Street: A Description of the Money Market.* London: William Clowes and Sons.

[18] I am grateful to Mervyn King for emphasizing this point.

Benston, George, Robert Eisenbeis, Paul Horvitz, Edward Kane and George Kaufman. 1986. *Perspectives on Safe and Sound Banking: Past, Present, and Future.* Cambridge, Massachusetts: MIT Press.

Boughton, James. 1998. 'From Suez to Tequila: The IMF as Crisis Manager.' Unpublished; Washington: International Monetary Fund.

Brown, Gordon. 1998. 'Rediscovering Public Purpose in the Global Economy.' Speech delivered at the Kennedy School, December 15.

Calomiris, Charles. 1998. 'Blueprints for a New Global Financial Architecture.' Unpublished; New York: Columbia Business School.

— and Allan H. Meltzer. 1998. 'Reforming the IMF.' Unpublished; New York: Columbia Business School.

Calvo, Guillermo. 1995. 'Varieties of Capital Market Crises.' University of Maryland Center for International Economics, Working Paper 15.

Capie, Forrest. 1998. 'Can there be an International Lender of Last Resort?' Unpublished; London: City University Business School.

Chari, V. V. and Patrick J. Kehoe. 1999. 'Asking the Right Questions about the IMF,' in *The Region*, 1998 Annual Report of the Federal Reserve Bank of Minneapolis, pp. 3–26.

Claassen, Emil-Maria. 1985. 'The Lender-of-Last-Resort Function in the Context of National and International Financial Crises.' *Weltwirtschaftliches Archiv.* 121:2, pp. 217–37.

Clapham, Sir John. 1944. *The Bank of England.* Cambridge: Cambridge University Press.

Chang, Roberto and Andres Velasco. 1998. 'The Asian Liquidity Crisis.' NBER Working Paper 6796, November.

Diamond, Douglas and Philip Dybvig. 1983. 'Bank Runs, Deposit Insurance, and Liquidity.' *Journal of Political Economy.* June, 91:3, pp. 401–19.

Freixas, Xavier. 1999. 'Optimal Bail Out Policy, Conditionality and Creative Ambiguity.' Unpublished; Bank of England.

Garcia, Gillian and Elizabeth Plautz. 1988. *The Federal Reserve: Lender of Last Resort.* Cambridge, Massachusetts: Ballinger.

Giannini, Curzio. 1998. 'Enemy of None but a Common Friend to All? An International Perspective on the Lender-of-Last-Resort Function.' Unpublished; Washington: International Monetary Fund.

Goodfriend, Marvin and Jeffrey M. Lacker. 1999. 'Limited Commitment and Central Bank Lending.' Federal Reserve Bank of Richmond, Working Paper January, 99:2.

Goodhart, Charles A. E. 1995. *The Central Bank and the Financial System.* Cambridge, Massachusetts: MIT Press.

— and Haizhou Huang. 1998. 'A Model of the Lender of Last Resort.' Unpublished; Washington: International Monetary Fund.

— and Dirk Schoenmaker. 1995. 'Should the Functions of Monetary Policy and Bank Supervision Be Separated?' *Oxford Economic Papers.* 47, pp. 539–60.

Guesnerie, Roger. 1987. 'Hidden Actions, Moral Hazard and Contract Theory,' in *The New Palgrave: A Dictionary of Economics.* Eatwell, John, Murray Milgate and Peter Newman, eds. Volume II, pp. 646–51. London: The Macmillan Press.

Guttentag, Jack and Richard Herring. 1983. 'The Lender-of-Last-Resort Function in an International Context.' *Princeton University Essay in International Finance.* No. 151, May.

Hirsch, Fred. 1977. 'The Bagehot Problem.' *The Manchester School.* September, 45:3, pp. 241–57.

Holmstrom, Bengt and Jean Tirole. 1998. 'Private and Public Supply of Liquidity.' *Journal of Political Economy.* February, 106:1, pp. 1–40.

Humphrey, Thomas. 1975. 'The Classical Concept of the Lender of Last Resort.' *Federal Reserve Bank of Richmond Economic Review*. February, 61, pp. 2–9.

— and Robert Keleher. 1984. 'Lender of Last Resort: An Historical Perspective.' *Cato Journal*. 4:1, pp. 275–321.

Jeanne, Olivier. 1998. 'The International Liquidity Mismatch and the New Architecture.' Unpublished; Washington: International Monetary Fund.

Kaufman, George. 1988. 'The Truth about Bank Runs,' in *The Financial Services Revolution: Policy Directions for the Future*. England, C. and T. Huertas, eds. Boston: Kluwer Academic Publishers.

Kenen, Peter. 1986. *Financing, Adjustment, and the International Monetary Fund*. Washington: Brookings Institution.

Kindleberger, Charles. 1986. *The World in Depression, 1929–1939*. Revised and enlarged edition. Berkeley: University of California Press.

— 1996. *Manias, Panics, and Crashes: A History of Financial Crisis (Wiley Investment Classics Series)*. New York: John Wiley and Sons, 3rd edition. (First edition, 1978).

MacKay, Charles. 1841. *Extraordinary Popular Delusions and the Madness of Crowds*. New York: Farrar, Straus and Giroux (reprint, 1932).

Meltzer, Allan. 1986. 'Financial Failures and Financial Policies,' in *Deregulating Financial Services: Public Policy in Flux*. Kaufman, G. G. and R. C. Kormendi, eds. Cambridge, Massachusetts: Ballinger.

Meltzer, Allan. 1998. 'What's Wrong with the IMF? What Would be Better?' Paper prepared for Federal Reserve Bank of Chicago Conference: *Asia: An Analysis of Financial Crisis*, October 8–10.

Mints, Lloyd W. 1945. *A History of Banking Theory*. Chicago: University of Chicago Press.

Mishkin, Frederic S. 1999. 'Lessons from the Asian Crisis.' National Bureau of Economic Research Working Paper 7102, April.

Mundell, Robert. 1983. 'International Monetary Options.' *Cato Journal*. 3:1, pp. 189–210.

Radelet, Steven and Jeffrey D. Sachs. 1998. 'The East Asian Financial Crisis: Diagnosis, Remedies, Prospects.' *Brookings Papers on Economic Activity*. 1, pp. 1–74.

Schwartz, Anna. 1988. 'Financial Stability and the Federal Safety Net,' in *Restructuring Banking and Financial Services in America*. Haraf, W. S. and G. E. Kushmeider, eds. Washington: American Enterprise Institute.

Solow, Robert. 1982. 'On the Lender of Last Resort,' in Kindleberger, C. P. and J. P. Laffargue, eds. Cambridge: Cambridge University Press.

Stern, Gary. 1999. 'Managing Moral Hazard.' *The Region*. Federal Reserve Bank of Minneapolis, June, 13:2.

Thornton, Henry. 1802. *An Enquiry into the Nature and Effects of the Paper Credit of Great Britain*, Hayek, F. A., ed. Fairfield: Augustus M. Kelley Publishers (reprint, 1978).

Wijnholds, Onno and Arend Kapteyn. 1999. 'The IMF: Lender of Last Resort or Indispensable Lender.' Unpublished; International Monetary Fund, June.

Zettelmeyer, Jeromin. 1998. 'International Financial Crises and Last Resort Lending: Some Issues.' Unpublished. Washington: International Monetary Fund.

25

Pitfalls in International Crisis Lending

CURZIO GIANNINI

1. INTRODUCTION

The unprecedented wave of foreign-exchange and financial crises which marked the last years of the millennium has spurred a wide-ranging debate on international institutional reform. The Bretton Woods architecture laid out in 1944 was explicitly aimed at keeping financial instability a national concern. This was achieved by making capital controls the rule rather than the exception in international relations and by forbidding the International Monetary Fund (IMF) to make its resources available to finance a sustained outflow of capital. Accordingly, no provision was made in the otherwise comprehensive Bretton Woods agreement for coordinating bank supervision across countries or for establishing last-resort lending facilities for either international banks or countries.

There is now nearly unanimous consensus on the need to move beyond this structure. Already in the 1980s, the authorities of G10 countries became increasingly aware that as the degree of integration of financial markets worldwide increased, supervisory activities needed to be more strictly coordinated. What the more recent wave of crises has now brought home is the need to establish some form of emergency lending at the supranational level. Starting from Sachs (1995), a number of proposals have been put forward to this effect.[1]

Most proposals, including the most influential of them all, the one put forward by the Meltzer Commission (2000), revolve around Walter Bagehot's classic maxim that a lender of last resort should 'lend freely to illiquid but fundamentally solvent institutions, at penalty rates and on good collateral'. But this raises a problem. As is becoming increasingly clear, the belief that national practices closely conform to Bagehot's maxim is largely a myth (Goodhart 1999; Giannini 1999). At the national level, lending of last resort in our days hinges on *constructive ambiguity*, because the distinction between illiquidity and insolvency, the penalty rate, and the 'good' collateral prescription have all proved poor guide for action in crisis times (Freixas *et al.*, 2000). Thus, what lenders of last resort throughout the world

This essay revisits and updates the theses of a piece published in June 1999 in the Princeton Essays series. I am grateful to Stan Fischer, Charles Goodhart, and Gerhard Illing for a number of insightful observations and comments on previous drafts. Neither they nor the organization for which I work, the Banca d'Italia, bear any responsibility for the views expressed herein.

[1] See Rogoff (1999) for a survey of the main proposals.

have learned to value most is *flexibility* to decide each crisis in its own merit. But flexibility may easily be abused. To avert this risk, most countries have undergone far-reaching institutional changes in the course of the twentieth century, meant on the one hand to sustain the legitimacy of the lender of last resort, namely the central bank; on the other, to contain moral hazard—the danger that flexibility be used in such a way as to increase the likelihood of crises, and ultimately the social costs associated with financial instability.

It seems unreasonable to expect that Bagehot's maxim, outdated at the national level, should now prove a *panacea* in the much more complex international environment. But replicating constructive ambiguity at the international level is no small task, for three reasons, two of which pertain to the peculiarities of the institutional environment and another to the nature of the problem itself.

First of all, financial emergencies typically entail much uncertainty as to underlying causes and possible outcomes. Since political accountability at the international level is limited, it may be rational for individual governments to retain a fairly large degree of control on the actions of the institution serving as lender of last resort. Timely and effective action may hence be hard to obtain because of cooperation failures. Second, while a national lender of last resort, typically deals with financial firms, namely entities with a well-defined governance structure and subject to the nation's legal system, at the international level the beneficiaries of lending of last resort are countries. When dealing with countries, a whole host of new issues arise, from how to define collateral to finding a meaningful way to distinguish between illiquidity and insolvency. Perhaps more importantly, countries are subject to domestic political shocks that may translate into policy reversals and, in extreme circumstances, lead to the reneging of past commitments. It may therefore be rational for an international lender of last resort, to make up for the lack of enforcement powers, to ration its credit and to resort to forms of time-consuming and politically controversial policy conditionality. Finally, national sovereignty also implies that the creditors of the countries hit by financial crisis are subject to different jurisdictions. Problems and conflicts of interest may thus arise among authorities in ensuring effective control over the institutions falling within their jurisdiction. In other words, *international creditors* are largely beyond the reach of *international organizations*. Containing moral hazard on the creditor side is therefore far from trivial.

The paper's main message is that, in light of these complexities, 'optimal' international arrangements and procedures for crisis lending are likely to look different from national practices. In particular, given the political and economic drawbacks of a purely discretionary regime and the impracticality of direct control of private creditors, one should aim at establishing a framework which places less emphasis on crisis lending and more on ex ante incentives and ex post creditor coordination procedures. Within the suggested framework, the institution at the centre of the system, the IMF, would retain discretion to address individual crises on a case-by-case basis, providing emergency finance when necessary. But crisis lending would be subjected to strict limits; moreover to make these limits credible, tools should be developed to ensure creditors' coordination, including collective action clauses and temporary standstills.

The main stumbling block to be overcome on this reform path is the gross inadequacy of the IMF's statute—the Articles of Agreement—in the present financial environment. Chastened by the previous four rounds of amendments, political authorities have so far shied away from the complex task of updating the Articles. But the various experiments on creditor coordination conducted in a number of countries after the Asian crises have only confirmed that, if there ever was a time when an amendment was needed, this is the present one. A revision of the Articles should aim at giving the IMF an explicit mandate to promote orderly and well-sequenced capital account liberalization. As part of this mandate, the IMF would also be legitimized to endorse a suspension of creditor rights when all other options have been exhausted and the debtor is making a goodwill effort at economic adjustment.

The paper is organized as follows. Section II is devoted to analysing the peculiarities of the international domain. I describe the trade-off between discretion and resources that has marred international organizations in many fields, hampering their effectiveness in emergency situations, and then discuss the reasons that may explain this regularity. I then analyse the consequences the notion of national sovereignty has for the authority of international institutions and, by implication, for their speed of response. Finally, I address the specific problems posed by the fact that international creditors fall largely beyond the reach of the international crisis manager, owing to the still unchanged national bases of financial supervision and regulation. Section III moves on to the issue of what can realistically be done to adapt the existing institutional set-up in the light of the previous analysis and of the experience accumulated in recent years. I first discuss the record and prospects of regional financial arrangements. Subsequently, I deal with the role of the IMF in the new international financial environment, discussing also the recommendations of the Meltzer Report. Finally, I discuss principles and practices of private sector involvement, as well as the benefits that may derive from an amendment of the IMF's Articles of Agreement. Section IV gathers up the various threads.

II. WHY THE INTERNATIONAL DOMAIN IS DIFFERENT

II.1. Rules and Discretion at Multilateral Organizations

The most interesting issue raised by the existence of institutions is how they ever manage to legitimize their actions. All institutions must have at their roots some means by which the rules and procedures of decisionmaking they embody can credibly constrain individual and collective behaviour. National institutions have the advantage of being cumulative in this respect, in that they can rely on previous, successful, acts of institution-making, such as the establishment of a credible legal system, or of rules of political representation. An international institution in a world of independent, politically sovereign, entities, must, by contrast, be self-enforcing. For such an institution to be credible, member countries must clearly perceive that they have a long-run, broad-ranging interest to stick to, rather than to defect to pursue short-run gains. This is but another way to say that any obligation arising from international conventions, customary laws, or treaties depends for its execution on the continuing consent of the obligor (De Bonis, Giustiniani and Gomel 1999).

Recent theoretical reflection on the political economy of cooperation has shown that, short of recourse to force or to the enforcement services of a hegemonic power, international collective action requires a notion of reciprocity, whereby each member can be sure that there will be a balanced distribution of whatever gain (or loss) derives from the cooperative effort.[2] The notion of 'balanced distribution of gains and losses' is clearly ambiguous. A fairly unassuming interpretation, however, would take it as implying that there should be no systematic pattern of gains and losses among a given institution's membership. In highly structured contexts, the principle of reciprocity can work marvels, testifying to the general invalidity of the 'extreme realist' argument that credible international institutions are not feasible. Crisis management, however, is different, for at least two reasons. First, by the very definition of 'crisis' the payoff structure tends to vary from one crisis to another, making it difficult ex ante to estimate gains and losses with any accuracy. Second, dealing with a crisis entails shifting resources from one section of the membership to another, if only on a temporary basis. If certain members are more crisis prone than others, legitimizing the crisis manager may prove difficult, unless it is clearly understood—notwithstanding payoff uncertainty—that ending the crisis is in everyone's interest.

This does not mean that effective crisis management is impossible. It only means that the issue of control is, if anything, magnified when shifting from the national to the international level. To contain the risk of abuse, countries will want to make sure they have all the relevant information before committing their own resources in each particular case. Alternatively, if they ever agree on a more structured response—for instance, by establishing a specialized crisis-management organization—they are likely to devise a control structure that circumscribes possible losses. This could be done, for instance, by reducing the amount of committed resources, or the technical discretion of the crisis manager, or both. A response of this kind, it needs to be understood, would be rational, given the circumstances under which the 'game' is supposed to take place.[3] Its practical consequence, however, would be to reduce the effectiveness of international crisis management.

Postwar international monetary relations, with the structure of the institution placed at the centre, namely the IMF, bear witness to the practical importance of these considerations.[4] The IMF was built on two foundation stones: one, financial; the other, operational. On the financial side, it was agreed at Bretton Woods that the new institution would operate, not as a financial intermediary (let alone as a

[2] See Milner (1992). As an alternative to reciprocity, international cooperation could be structured so as to produce side-payments of different kinds to the various parts involved. This option, however, which implies continuous renegotiations, seems to be more relevant to ad hoc or relatively unstructured forms of cooperation than to the more institutionalized ones considered in this essay.

[3] For a formalization of this assertion, see Calvert (1995).

[4] The evolution of international cooperation in the field of public health and the history of the United Nations are two other cases in point. See Cooper (1989) on the former and Nicholson (1998) on the latter.

central bank), but as a *credit union*, 'with relations among its members based on the principle of mutuality' (Kenen 1986, p. 3). Accordingly, each member's access to balance-of-payments finance was to be based on the quota it contributed to the common pool and on a reciprocal commitment to grant credit to other members. On the operational side, it was mandated that the institution would base its actions on the principle of universality, according to which no discrimination should ever be made among member countries or groups thereof.

The concepts of reciprocity and lender of last resort are, nonetheless, basically at odds with one another. The lender of last resort must either be in a position to create its own resources—which would be incompatible with the credit-union concept—or to channel resources systematically from those who have them to those who do not. Moreover, the lender of last resort has to act swiftly, decisively, but also selectively, inflicting losses (varying according to circumstances) on at least some of the affected parties. The framers of the international monetary architecture seem to have been aware of this tension, because they took a number of steps to make sure that the IMF would *not* develop a lender-of-last-resort role, either by statute or by spontaneous endogenesis. The first step involved renouncing capital mobility, contrary to the original intentions of the White plan. The objective of exchange-rate stability, which was the ultimate goal of the endeavour, was pursued through a double-pronged strategy based on capital controls and individual countries' access to short-term current-account financing. Furthermore, to make clear that this adjustment-smoothing function should not be interpreted as envisaging a lender-of-last-resort role for the new institution, a passage in the IMF's Article VI explicitly forbade the provision of IMF resources to countries experiencing 'a large or sustained outflow of capital.' A further step was the avoidance, throughout the Articles, of the language of credit, the main effect of which was to make the IMF charter almost unreadable. Finally, the procedures, terms, and purposes to which the institution should adhere in the daily conduct of its business were all carefully spelled out in the Articles—in stark contrast to the vagueness, even recklessness, with which the mission and operational content of central banking were at the time laid out in comparable national documents.

This strategy could be expected to work only so long as capital controls operated effectively. Thus, the tension between reciprocity and effective lender-of-last-resort action was bound to resurface when, in the early 1960s, the effectiveness of capital controls began to diminish as a result of the restoration of current-account convertibility. The US and UK authorities, in particular, soon began to look for an emergency mechanism that could rapidly be relied upon in times of crisis—but emphatically not in ordinary circumstances—to sustain the exchange value of reserve currencies in the presence of sudden capital reversals. They intended that 'rapidly' should mean that resources would have to be provided on a quasi-automatic basis, without the borrowing country needing to subject itself to the close scrutiny of the multilateral organizations or to undertake extensive negotiations with ultimate lenders (James 1996). The mechanism eventually took the form of the General Arrangements to Borrow (GAB). The main novelty of the GAB, which was also what made it acceptable to its various country contributors, was that the funds under GAB control were distinct from the pool of resources available to the general membership. Quotas would not be affected by it, and as a result, the IMF could not draw on the GAB to finance the balance-of-payments difficulties of members not participating in the arrangement. As Kenen (1986) has remarked, the GAB was a kind of credit union writ small, made possible by derogation from the principle of universality. Departure from universality, however, was not enough to make the arrangement as rapid and flexible as its proponents had hoped. In fact, the notion of quasi automaticity was eventually dropped, because a number of contributors demanded that activation require the consent of each participant in the scheme. Consequently, the GAB carried a 'double lock' in that any drawing would have to be approved both by individual GAB members and by the IMF Executive Board. James (1996, p. 164) describes this innovation as 'a major dent in the Fund's claim to universality and to a capacity to judge by itself the conditions of assistance in dealing with balance of payments problems.'[5]

It would be perfectly possible to argue that the GAB's story is but one episode in the learning process that has been occurring worldwide ever since financial liberalization began. According to this argument, it would only be a matter of time before the dismal experience of recent crisis management led authorities to start devising a more effective way of discharging the lender-of-last-resort function at the international level. There seems to be ample ground for skepticism, however, in view of the responses the recent crises have so far elicited with respect to funding and operations of the IMF.

On the funding side, the response can be described as 'more of the old medicine' rather than a new prescription. At Halifax, in June 1995, the G-7 leaders called for the opening of negotiations 'with the objective of doubling as soon as possible the amount currently available under the GAB to respond to financial emergencies.' The arrangement that has emerged from such negotiations, the New Agreements to Borrow (NAB), reproduces the GAB structure in all important respects, including the double-lock principle.[6] On the operational front, Article VI's prohibition of

[5] Indeed, the subsequent record of the GAB was far from satisfactory. The high point of the arrangement came between 1977 and 1978, when the IMF resolved to borrow almost SDR 4 billion to finance drawings by Italy, the United Kingdom, and the United States. By contrast, the way the GAB had been conceived meant that it could play no role in the debt crisis of the early 1980s. In light of that experience, the system was modified in 1983 to give the IMF permission to use the GAB to finance transactions with nonparticipants. This departure from the credit-union principle, however, proved purely formal, because the double-lock principle prevented recourse to the arrangement in all the following crisis episodes, including the recent Mexican and Asian ones. The only subsequent activation of the GAB occurred in the context of the failed Russian rescue package, when it was made practically inevitable, as well as ineffective, by the exhaustion of all other possible sources of funds.

[6] Thus, the NAB can be activated to cope with financial crises of systemic importance even when these originate in a country that is not a member of the IMF. The main advantage of the NAB over the GAB, which will be kept in place, consists in the number of contributors, which has been significantly expanded. The coexistence of the two mechanisms, however, has made the activation procedure even more cumbersome, because rules have had to be devised to ensure that the same country will not be

capital-account financing still stands. Indeed, even though the IMF staff has called for its repeal on several occasions (see, e.g., Quirk *et al.*, 1995), the amendment envisaged to give the IMF authority over capital-account liberalization does not contemplate such a bold step. To be sure, the present language of Article VI did not prevent either the Mexican or the Asian packages, because in both cases, there happened to be a current-account imbalance. The fact that the nature of those crises had little to do with the current account was and is clear to everybody, however, so much so that the IMF has felt the need to set up a special window, the Supplemental Reserve Facility (SRF), to deal explicitly with capital-account problems. Created in December 1997, the SRF has since been utilized for the Brazilian, Korean, Russian, and, more recently, Turkish and Argentine packages. Inevitably, however, this has meant a direct confrontation with Article VI. This time, the justification for the facility could not be found in the adjective 'large' as had been the case in the early 1960s, because the recent packages were large by any standard. The activation of both the GAB and the NAB, moreover, which are obvious sources of funding for such a facility, depends on there being a systemic threat to the international monetary system, which would be unlikely if the capital outflows were 'small'. The only way out of the impasse was to work on the adjective 'sustained' interpreting it as referring to the future, rather than the past. Accordingly, the SRF has been described as aiming not so much at financing a given outflow, no matter how big or sustained up to that moment, but rather at halting the outflow by rebuilding the country's reserves.

It would be difficult not to view this as a form of rule-bending based on 'fancy legal footwork' (Polak 1998, p. 49). Rule-bending has at least one significant drawback, however. If it is protracted or applied to core, rather than to marginal, functions, it risks putting the legitimacy of the rule-bending institution at great peril. If its legitimacy is called into question, the institution will have little choice but to seek the support of its most powerful members, by putting their interest first. One way or the other, any pretense of universality and reciprocity would become illusory.

One may be tempted to consider all this as irrelevant. After all, not only have a number of jumbo rescue packages been mounted and put into place in recent years, but none of the members of the IMF has suggested so far abolishing the SRF. Quite the contrary. A new crisis facility, the Contingent Credit Line (CCL), has been added to the panoply, with the aim of stemming international contagion.[7]

The temptation should be resisted. On the one hand, large as they have been in relation to individual countries' quotas, recent packages have remained small both relative to GDP and, what matters more, relative to the outstanding stock of external

called upon to contribute twice for the same operation, as a member of both the GAB and the NAB. Such rules also make it difficult to estimate the exact amount of resources that can be drawn in any particular instance. Thus, even though the NAB, like the GAB in its post-1983 version, goes beyond the principle of reciprocity, it does so in a way that raises doubts about its effectiveness as a pool of resources for lender-of-last-resort functions. This concern is strengthened by the fact that at no time during the negotiations that led to the NAB was the next most obvious alternative, the IMF borrowing directly from the market, seriously contemplated.

[7] More on the CCL in Section III.2.

debt. That is, recent bail-outs fall in the category of *partial* bail-outs. In the case of Indonesia and Korea, in 1998, to circumvent the resistance of the IMF Board, the notion of a 'second line of defense', according to which a number of creditor countries would be ready to provide additional financial support on a bilateral basis, was broached. But the promise failed to persuade the markets, and these funds were never disbursed. As it happens, partial bail-outs have a number of drawbacks for crisis management purposes, which may make them, under certain conditions, inferior to the no-bail-out option (Zettelmeyer 2000). On the other hand, the perception that crisis facilities might be abused has led a number of prominent IMF members, in the context of the review of IMF facilities now underway, to invoke the introduction of special majority voting procedures for granting countries access above quota to the SRF and the CCL. Such procedures would have the effect of severely curtailing the discretion of the IMF in crisis management. Whether such a change will ever win sufficient consensus to come into effect is a different question. But what matters for our purposes is to realize that the rules versus discretion issue in international emergency lending is far from settled. Past experience and theoretical insight both advise us to remain skeptical that it ever will.

II.2. The Rationale and Limits of Policy Conditionality

International financial crises need not be sovereign crises. However, the lessons of the last twenty years suggest that major private-sector crises tend rapidly to become sovereign crises as domestic public opinion forces the government to bail out the banking system or an important segment of the corporate sector. Indeed, as recent experience has shown, international rescue packages may make this transmutation inevitable. Thus, a distinction between private-sector and sovereign crises may be very difficult to draw.

Sovereignty is a political, not an economic, concept and is thus not easily squared with the economist's standard toolbox. A way around the problem consists of treating sovereign entities as if they were utility-maximizing individuals with well-defined preferences and endowments. There is an important distinction between the sovereignty of an individual and the sovereignty of a state, however. The sovereignty of an individual ceases the moment a choice has been made, because once a contract is entered into, the parties can rely on external institutional arrangements to see that it is enforced. A state, by contrast, is legally sovereign in that it recognizes no authority as superior to itself.

An important implication of the notion of sovereignty is that countries lack a foolproof way to commit themselves to a given course of action.[8] Failure to come

[8] This does not mean that the authorities will be unable to commit themselves credibly under all possible circumstances. Rather, it means that, because there is no independent—that is, third-party-enforced—commitment technology, the credibility of policy announcements is not to be taken for granted, for it will depend on the characteristics of the overall institutional environment, as well as on the specific payoffs from reneging on the commitment.

to grips with this problem goes a long way toward explaining why the Bretton Woods arrangements did not operate as their architects had expected. The excessive rigidity of exchange rates, which is often singled out as the most important factor behind the system's eventual collapse, was largely the outcome of the national authorities' attempt to limit their own freedom of action so as to ensure the 'credibility' of their policies (Eichengreen 1996). That is, exchange-rate rigidity was largely brought about by the search for a dependable commitment technology, contrary to the belief—widespread in the postwar period—that constraints on 'enlightened' domestic-policy management should be avoided to the greatest possible extent (Dam 1982). With the demise of the system of fixed exchange rates, the role of enforcer of policy announcements has come to be performed predominantly by the capital markets. Authorities have gradually come to realize that by liberalizing capital markets, both domestically and internationally, they would not only foster a better allocation of resources in the long run, but would also acquire credibility. At bottom, the various monetary-reform strategies that have been tried over the last fifteen years or so in the industrial world—from central-bank independence, to inflation targeting, to investing in anti-inflationary reputations—are all predicated on the assumption that there is a market watching what the authorities are doing (Cottarelli and Giannini 1997). In this sense, one can say that today's international monetary system is market-led (Padoa-Schioppa and Saccomanni 1994). The proposal to add the goal of capital-account convertibility to the IMF charter, much discussed around the mid-1990s and subsequently side-stepped by more pressing necessities, is no more than a way to formalize what is already a fact for an increasing number of countries.

The lack of an 'objective' commitment technology for sovereign countries is often taken to mean that a strong market penalty, in the form of denial of access to foreign finance for an indefinite time after default, is the only deterrent against policy misdeeds.[9] But this risks being a gross oversimplification, hard to reconcile with historical evidence, at least insofar as our century is concerned. In the aftermath of the debt defaults of the 1930s, for instance, the loss of capital-market access was hardly discernible (Eichengreen 1991). Countries that continued to service their debts throughout the 1930s did not subsequently enjoy superior access to credit markets.[10]

This absence of penalty probably has much to do with a second, difficult to capture, implication of the notion of sovereignty: unlike individuals, countries can undergo pervasive regime changes. Institutional reform or a change in the ruling

[9] This is the typical result one gets by factoring the notion of sovereignty into an otherwise standard model of debt optimization; see Eaton and Fernandez (1995).

[10] Argentina, for example, did not enjoy better capital-market access as a faithful repayer than did the less faithful Brazil (Cardoso and Dornbusch 1989), and Eichengreen (1989) finds no evidence for the period from 1945 to 1955 that the volume of external capital a sovereign borrower could obtain was negatively affected by its prior default. Indeed, going back to the 1930s, gross national product and industrial production appear to have recovered more quickly in countries that defaulted than in countries that continued to honor their debts (see Eichengreen and Portes 1989).

coalition can, by signaling a systematic change in policy, offset the reputational effects of prior actions, including default (Fishlow 1989). In the nineteenth century, for example, resumption of gold convertibility was perhaps the clearest way to signal the return to the regime of sound money after a lapse into policy laxity. Today, one can argue that this function has been taken over by the act of establishing independent technical authorities and by IMF conditionality. So, although market monitoring is needed ex ante to discipline the government's behaviour, a long punishment by markets in the face of default may not be the socially optimal response. The correct answer is, rather, that it depends.

Regime changes are more likely to occur in the aftermath of a major crisis, because such an event tends to heighten awareness of the costs implicit in the existing policy and institutional framework (see Olson 1982). Indeed, foreign-exchange crises, whether or not they end in outright default, tend to be very costly. Eichengreen and Portes (1989) show, for the 1930s, that the supply of money, imports, and GDP growth all contracted more sharply in the countries that defaulted than in those that did not.[11] Credible regime changes cannot happen overnight, however, because the probability of a set of reforms being carried through ultimately depends on the continuing support of the country's population. The extent and persistence of such support will itself depend on the population's judgment that the program will succeed and that the outcome will be in the individual self-interest of the average citizen (Johnson 1997). Achieving and maintaining the necessary consensus is therefore likely to entail a continuous exchange of signals between the government and its constituency. A credible regime change is, thus, better portrayed as a process, an intrinsically fragile process, than as a single action.

The need for a regime change to take place in real time is the source of a number of complications for an international lender of last resort. Suppose the lender of last resort wants to gauge the probability that the regime change will be credible. Where will it look? Considering the country's fundamentals, although useful, will not be enough, because the existence of a political constraint might imply that the country stops being willing to pay far sooner than it reaches its technical ability to pay. It can then look at the country's past record in terms of policies, political stability, or compliance with surveillance exercises. But here again, the very definition of a regime change is that what has occurred until the very moment such a change takes place matters only up to a point. The only possibility remaining is to look at the extent of the reforms the authorities are willing to commit themselves to and at the determination with which they are introduced and

[11] In more recent times, the $50 billion rescue package that allowed the Mexican authorities to continue to service their debt did not avert a 6 per cent decline in real output in 1995—Mexico's deepest recession in fifty years. In the cases of Indonesia, Korea, and Thailand, the IMF World Economic Outlook forecast as late as May 1997 that real output would grow in 1998 by 7.5, 6.3, and 7.0 percent, respectively. Actual figures show a contraction, instead, of about 13, 7 and 10 per cent, respectively (IMF, 2000a). The psychological and economic impact of a foreign-exchange crisis, moreover, ensures that, despite the lack of international bankruptcy procedures, the 'management' of a country hardly ever remains in office to see the crisis through.

defended. The very determination with which the new government pursues its policies, however, may undermine the consensus around the new policy course. If this is the case, it may be advisable to relax the new policy somewhat at the margins, rather than to insist on adhering to its original stance. The international lender of last resort is not in a position, however, to evaluate with the necessary precision whether such a modification of the agreed upon course of action is warranted. There is a fundamental asymmetry between international organizations and domestic authorities, in that domestic authorities are to a large extent the producers and guarantors of the information on which the assessment of the regime change is to be based. A further complication of the existence of a political constraint is that foreign creditors of sovereign debtors will, in deciding their strategies, typically lack a well-specified outside option (namely, the liquidation value) to determine their own bargaining power (Eichengreen and Portes 1995). Another important lesson borne out by recent crises is that the effectiveness of multilateral surveillance in a world where most information is produced locally depends crucially on the collaboration and provision of timely and transparent information by the authorities concerned. The result of all this is that although a domestic lender of last resort can count on prior information (the supervisory track record) and can expect its decisions to be carried through whatever their content, an international lender of last resort is bound to act under a far more extensive veil of ignorance. It must remain exposed to the risk of a policy reversal until the implementation process has been pushed to the point at which the cost of going back precludes a reversal.

The combination of all these features, which are nonexistent or of only limited importance at the national level, appears to put international crisis management in a class of its own. The possibility of a regime change makes sovereign crises more manageable in principle, if a way can be found to sustain the credibility of such a change. At the same time, the inevitable complexities of political decisionmaking create the possibility of a self-fulfilling debt run, while the fundamental information asymmetry between national authorities, on the one hand, and multilateral organizations and private creditors, on the other, works against the creation of a climate of trust once a crisis emerges, and might even stand in the way of mobilizing public support for the government's program. A nonconflictual relationship between a sovereign debtor and its creditors (and, of course, international organizations) may be further hindered by the lack of an objective benchmark (the liquidation value) against which to establish the bargaining power of the two sides. Thus, although *timely action* is crucial to effectively carrying out the lender-of-last-resort function in a national context, *gaining time* before any irreversible action is taken, so as to permit a more thorough and less emotional assessment of the respective parties' options and payoffs, is likely to be a more important aim at the international level.

II.3. Controlling Creditors' Behaviour

Any form of insurance, and lending of last resort is no exception in this respect, creates moral hazard, if the behaviour of the insured party can influence the probability of the event insured against. At the national level, the moral hazard implicit in the protection granted to banks and their main creditors (i.e. depositors) through lending of last resort and the related notion of deposit insurance has been controlled—more or less successfully depending on circumstances—through a blend of regulation, supervision, and outright threats to close the affected bank or change its management. The important point to be made here is that all this required—mainly in the inter-war years of the twentieth century—a massive effort in legal and institutional adaptation throughout the industrial world. As a result, in our days national lending of last resort is surrounded by a host of supportive legal institutions and concepts, from which central banks draw at once capacity and legitimacy to act swiftly to counter both liquidity and solvency crises.

The international environment lies in stark contrast with this picture. On the one hand, the IMF, the most obvious candidate for the job of international lender of last resort, lacks both supervisory and regulatory powers. All it can do is to impose conditionality on debtor countries, and this only as part of its actual lending (whereas at the national level supervision can be exerted even if banks do not borrow from the central bank). But there is nothing whatsoever it can directly do to control creditors' behaviour. On the other hand, the international legal framework is highly defective, in that not only does it lack a coherent bankruptcy component; it also comprises several competing national legal systems whose principles, design, and operations are often incompatible. With international investors falling largely outside the sphere of influence of international organizations as well as of individual national authority, it may be difficult to make investors internalize the costs associated with the availability of this implicit form of insurance. Moral hazard consequently tends to be a more serious problem at the international level.

Measuring the actual extent of moral hazard, however, is no easy task, for lack of a clear counterfactual, that is, the costs that would have materialized had a rescue not been mounted. Thus, it might well be that, even if some moral hazard were created, the overall effect of having a lender of last resort ready to intervene could still turn out to be positive, because the total costs of a crisis cannot be taken as given. After all, if lending of last resort were a zero-sum game, it would have no social value.

Those who have tried to measure moral hazard by looking at the behaviour of spreads and capital flows in the aftermath of the announcement of an IMF rescue package have generally come to the conclusion that its incidence is negligible (Haldane 1999; Lane and Phillips 2000; Zhang 1999; Spadafora 2001). If anything, one is struck by the failure of the announcement to rapidly bring risk premia back to pre-crisis times, as over-pricing of country risk remained a feature of international capital markets long after the international authorities had decided to intervene. This is probably related to the fact, already noticed in Section II.1, that although large in absolute terms, rescue packages of the recent past have often been small relative to the external exposure of the countries concerned.

The indirect evidence that rescue packages did not come free—and therefore by themselves could not fuel mortal hazard—is even more compelling if one looks at the size of current account reversals or exchange rate adjustments in the months immediately after the crisis. In Asia, for example, comparing 1998 with 1996, the current account adjustment amounted to 63$ billion in Korea (or 16.8 per cent of GDP) $29 billion in Thailand (20 per cent), $12.2 billion in Indonesia (8 per cent). Likewise, in Indonesia the exchange rate fell by 60 per cent in 1997 and output contracted by 14 per cent the following year. The comparable figures are 47 per cent and 5.5 per cent for Korea, 45 per cent and 8 per cent for Thailand (Haldane 1999).

Any complacency based on the above evidence would be misplaced, though. Arguing that IMF rescue packages did not create moral hazard does not imply that moral hazard could not be already there before the crises erupted. The behaviour of capital flows to emerging markets and of risk spreads in the course of the 1990s is indeed very hard to explain on the basis of fundamentals only (Cline and Barnes 1997). Moreover, the bulk of the upsurge of capital flows to Mexico in 1994 and to Asia in the years immediately before the crises of 1997–98 was accounted for by international interbank lending. As it happens, the international interbank market is widely perceived by market participants as too important for authorities in the major countries to tolerate its disruption or even milder forms of instability (Bernard and Bisignano 2000). Authorities, perhaps unwittingly, did encourage this belief on a number of occasions through their deeds and pronouncements.[12]

Several accounts of recent crises in emerging markets have put the blame squarely on the 'excessive' guarantees provided to international investors by *national* authorities, although there are differences as to which national authorities are to blame more.[13] Indeed, that moral hazard might have been an important factor in the 1990s is by now accepted by the authorities themselves. The report on 'Supervisory Lessons to be drawn from the Asian Crisis' issued by the Basel Committee in 1999 states

> some foreign investors, including G10 banks, may have assumed that implicit government guarantees existed on these claims, in particular on banking sector claims. Accordingly, as in past crises, a significant element of moral hazard may have existed, but with a greater emphasis on an implied extension of government protection to private sector counterparties. [. . .] Thus, participants in the local economy and foreign counterparties alike had little incentive to manage potential risks and in many cases assumed implicit government backing of private claims (p. 14).

The way the Korean crisis unfolded is further confirmation of this. Spreads hardly reacted to the announcement of the IMF package. But they dropped abruptly in March 1998, after the announcement of the conversion of $24 billion of short-term bank debt into debt with one to three-year maturities, all but $4 billion guaranteed by the Korean government. This move had the effect of reassuring

[12] This is brought out, among other things, by the risk weighting in the Basel Accord on capital requirements and by the way interbank credit lines were singled out as 'special' in the G10 *Report on the Resolution of Sovereign Liquidity Crises*, issued in 1996 in the aftermath of the Mexican crisis. See Giannini (1999) for more detail.

[13] Krugman (1998), for example, emphasizes the responsibilities of local authorities in recipient countries. Levy Yeyati (1999), by contrast, blames the attitude of authorities in creditor countries.

international banks that their prior belief about the degree of protection granted to interbank lending would not be disproved. On the whole, estimates of losses from the various crises tend to agree that, although those stemming from underwriting and portfolio flows were quite sizable, those that can be attributed to loan defaults are all but negligible (Baily, Farrell and Lund 2000; Institute of International Finance 1999).

That the implicit guarantee given to the international interbank market should all of a sudden be removed is unthinkable in light of the importance this market has for the global distribution of liquidity and the adverse selection problems that mar this particular market. At a minimum, if the subsidy was removed, the market would likely be closed to most banks in emerging market economies. The subsidy, as Bernard and Bisignano (2000) conclude, has to be managed, rather than removed. This state of affairs places an international lender of last resort such as the IMF in an awkward position, however, because the impact of its actions will depend on the degree of control that a host of other authorities are willing and able to exert, both individually and collectively, over international investors, most notably banks. With the establishment in 1999 of the Financial Stability Forum and the revision of the Capital Accord underway at the Basel Committee, national authorities are trying to respond to the challenge. But there is a long way to go, and the coordination of national supervisory authorities among themselves, let alone with the IMF, which has no institutional relationship with the FSF apart from being one of its members, can hardly be taken for granted.

Then there is a further problem. Can one assume that the way the burden of crisis resolution is allocated among creditors and debtors is socially irrelevant? Lane and Phillips (2000), among others, answer affirmatively, arguing that such costs would be factored into prices anyway. But this answer is unconvincing, in light of the different nature of the parties involved in international contracts and the imperfections that mar international markets for sovereign debt. Indeed, the very fact that the phenomenon of over-pricing tends to persist after the announcement of a rescue package, as shown by Haldane (1999), points to the possibility that this way of coping with what is basically a coordination problem among creditors may be socially inefficient. It is misleading to portray this problem, as is often done, as one of achieving a 'more equitable burden-sharing' between debtors and creditors. When resources have been misallocated, the question of who was responsible in the first place is of little economic relevance. What matters is that the misallocation be dealt with in the least costly way and with the least recourse to the money of third parties, ultimately the taxpayers. Using the terminology of lawyers, costs should be assigned to the 'cheapest cost avoider' of whatever causes the losses, so as to minimize the chance of the loss occurring.[14] At the international level, there exists a long-standing tendency for the burden to be borne mainly by

[14] For the notion of 'cheapest cost avoider', see Calabresi (1970).

debtors, irrespective of the international financial regime (Eichengreen 1991). But it is debatable whether debtor countries are actually the cheapest cost avoider, for the very reasons mentioned in Section II.2. Responding to crises will take time, because of the mechanics of the political process. Moreover, even if a policy package is put together, its chances of being implemented may depend on the graduality with which authorities go about it. That is, in some circumstances the debtor country may fail to meet one of the essential preconditions Calabresi (1970) identifies as being the cheapest cost avoider—that of being in a position to take immediate and effective action to minimize losses. If so, then turning to creditors is the only alternative. No one likes to be considered the cheapest cost avoider, of course. But the wide-ranging debate on private sector involvement takes a whole new light when seen in these terms. This is why, whatever we think of the merits of the rescue packages mounted in Latin America and in Asia in the second half of the 1990s, containing moral hazard and the losses associated with crisis resolution at the international level is likely to remain the key challenge for the years ahead.

III. INTERNATIONAL CRISIS MANAGEMENT: LESS LENDING, MORE COORDINATION

The main message of the previous section is that the extension of lender-of-last-resort practices to the international domain encounters severe problems. Limited resource availability does not seem to be a significant hindrance overall. The frequently heard claim that the lender of last resort needs to be able to create liquidity for its actions to be effective has been disproved by national experience. Moreover, the latest IMF quota increase, the availability of both the GAB and the NAB, and the possibility of activating bilateral contributions have, taken together, significantly increased the resources the IMF can mobilize in case of need. The real problems seem to lie at a deeper level. First of all, given the imperfect control structure of international organizations—itself the consequence of the lack of third-party enforcement powers—a crisis manager endowed with ample resources is likely to see its technical discretion to act selectively seriously curtailed, in practice if not in principle. The organization's main political principals will find it difficult ex ante to assess with sufficient accuracy the probability of success—and the associated pay-off for themselves—of a rescue package requiring wide-ranging policy changes, a lot of political determination, and, inevitably, a rather long gestation to come to fruition. The ultimate effect of this state of affairs would be either a politicization of the decisions of the lender of last resort or a significant loss of flexibility, and ultimately effectiveness, in the conduct of the organization's business. The issue of containing moral hazard, moreover, is far from settled. It is true that the development of surveillance and conditionality has decreased moral hazard with respect to debtors over the past few decades, but individual countries must perceive that they have an interest in cooperating with the international enforcer if those tools are to be effective. There is an important difference between the international domain and the domestic context, where the lender of last resort can rely on a complex regulatory structure that gives force to the threat of 'punishment'. Moreover, the problem of moral hazard with respect to the creditor lies largely beyond the reach of the lender of last resort, because it is related to the degree of protection creditors receive in their home country as well as in recipient countries. To protect its resources, the international lender of last resort thus has to rely on the actions of other actors, over which it has very little leverage. This is a very uncomfortable situation, which domestic lenders of last resort have consistently tried to avoid.

These considerations help make sense of the less-than-satisfactory performance of international rescue packages in the last few years. They also help to explain why a number of countries, such as Chile and Malaysia, have preferred to protect themselves from financial instability through unilateral recourse to capital controls. In the long run, however, such a response appears self-defeating. The move away from capital controls did not occur by chance, or just through sheer technological progress. It was primarily a response to two deeply felt needs that the Bretton Woods framework met imperfectly, if at all: the need for a better allocation of resources worldwide and the need for a mechanism to strengthen the credibility of domestic policymaking. Even if the clock could be set back, reinstating reliance on controls as the rule rather than the exception, it remains unclear how this reliance could be reconciled with reasonably fast growth and sound domestic policymaking. Thus, there appears to be ample scope for exploring middle-course solutions–working on the assumption that the leave-it-to-the-market option simply does not exist. This is the task to which I now turn.

III.1. A Regional Lender of Last Resort?

All the three pitfalls identified in Section II are more or less directly connected to the notion of sovereignty. An international lender of last resort is likely to have a hard life because the ultimate source of power and legitimacy in the present institutional environment is still the nation-state. But if surrendering part of sovereign powers to a truly universal institution is still an unpalatable option, there are already a number of examples of regional institutions–with the European System of Central Banks being the most remarkable epitome–which do enjoy close-to-sovereign powers. Should not regional emergency arrangements therefore be a somewhat natural alternative to a truly international lender of last resort? That is, one can envisage a world in which this function would be discharged either by a recognized hegemon within a given area or by an area-wide, cooperative institution explicity endowed with lender-of-last-resort faculties. An obvious structure would be one in which each of the three main trading blocs–Asia, the Western Hemisphere, and Europe–would separately oversee financial stability in its own region, each in its own way, tailoring its oversight to local traditions and existing practices and institutions.

A regional lender of last resort would, in principle, have three advantages over a universal one. First, mustering sufficient resources is likely to prove less troublesome, because geographical proximity, insofar as it can be taken as an indicator of economic integration, tends to strengthen perceptions of the social cost of inaction in the face of a crisis. Second, winning consensus about the need for concerted action and the form it should take might be easier, because the number of countries involved in each region would be relatively small. Devising country-specific forms of compensation for joining in the collective lender-of-last-resort effort might also prove simpler, given that relations among the states in a region will normally go beyond purely financial matters. Finally, relatively deep-rooted cultural ties—again, a natural outcome of proximity—may provide a favourable terrain for the establishment of an 'epistemic community', namely, a 'professional group that believes in the same cause-and-effect relationships, truth tests to accept them, and shares common values, so that its members show a common understanding of a problem and its solution' (Haas 1990, p. 55).

Geographical proximity is by far the greatest advantage. For all the talk of globalization, much of today's trade remains regional, rather than truly global. In fact, the growth of intraregional trade flows is probably the distinguishing feature of the remarkable increase in overall world trade in the last two decades. The flourishing of areawide trade initiatives, such as the Single Market, Asia-Pacific Economic Co-operation, and the North American Free Trade Agreement (NAFTA), can itself be viewed as reflecting this underlying trend. Indeed, the pressure of economic integration can be so strong as to push beyond a regional lender of last resort, toward full-fledged monetary union. Eichengreen (1996), for one, has forcefully argued that monetary union in Europe can be viewed as a response to the 'ineluctable rise in international capital mobility' which risked undermining, by the attendant increase in exchange-rate volatility, intra-European trade flows and the very possibility of pursuing domestic objectives. The economic rationale of monetary union, in short, is that 'relatively large, relatively closed economies are able to pursue domestic objectives without suffering intolerable pain from currency swings'.

Regional lending of last resort should thus be seen as an option both for countries in the process of transition to monetary union and for others that, while recognizing their common interest in exchange-rate stability, even to the point of being ready to peg the external value of their currency unilaterally, are not yet in a position to contemplate a total surrender of monetary sovereignty.

Defined in this way, however, regional lending of last resort has two shortcomings. No matter how strong the trade links are, and how well-developed cooperative initiatives in the trade field are, designing a credible structure for lender-of-last-resort purposes is likely to be complex. If countries are unwilling to contemplate surrendering monetary sovereignty altogether, either as an immediate option or over a more distant horizon, it must be because they want to retain some autonomy for their domestic economic policies. Assembling a rescue package is likely to entail, at least in the short-run, some deviation from the pattern of domestic policies otherwise deemed desirable in some of the countries in the area. The outcome of such an effort is therefore bound to remain highly uncertain. A credible commitment from the borrowing country to adjust can be made only as part of a broader web of interlocking agreements.[15] This can be seen as no more than a variation on the control issue evoked in the previous section. The importance of the concern is underscored by two recent pieces of evidence. The first, and probably foremost, is the ERM crisis of 1992–93. Lack of economic convergence certainly played a leading role in straining the European multilateral peg, just as it had strained the Bretton Woods exchange-rate system back in the early 1970s, but there is now a broad consensus that the scale and persistence of the ERM crisis can be explained only by invoking an element of self-fulfilling behaviour on the part of market investors. This behaviour could have been addressed had core countries been willing to provide more extensive lender-of-last-resort services for the area as a whole. What makes the European experience all the more remarkable is that the failure to organize an effective areawide defense against speculative flows took place in the context of an otherwise highly advanced process of institutional, and even political, integration.

A further example is provided by the failed US attempt, in early 1995, to assemble an all-American rescue package to deal with Mexico's difficulties. The problem with the initiative was that it could not be funded sufficiently through the Exchange Stabilization Fund (ESF), which was at the immediate disposal of the US Treasury. It therefore required congressional approval, which intense behind-the-scenes consultations in Washington made clear could not be taken for granted. Announcing a rescue package without the certainty that Congress would make the necessary appropriation involved political risks that the US authorities were understandably unwilling to take. Thus, the all-American plan was dropped in favour of an orchestrated IMF package, in which the United States had a stake roughly equivalent to the sums available in the ESF (Fraga 1996). Again, it is noteworthy that the episode did not take place in an institutional vacuum, but in the context of a deep political commitment to NAFTA, both in Mexico and in the United States.

There is a second shortcoming to regional lending of last resort. Geographical proximity may increase awareness of the social cost of inaction to the point of making regional authorities overemphasize financing to the detriment of adjustment. In the absence of conditionality, moral hazard might loom large for such debtor countries. Even though the region might form a relatively closed economic bloc, the risk of worldwide contagion through purely financial channels can hardly be exaggerated in the present reality of global capital. As recent experience shows, especially after Russia's unilateral suspension of debt service, there is nothing to guard against global spillovers of regional regulatory and policy failures. This risk may be subdued only if the regional arrangement is built around a clear

[15] After surveying a number of indicators of economic integration, for instance, Bayoumi, Eichengreen and Mauro (2000) conclude that the differences between the countries participating in ASEAN and the European Union as to the degree of economic convergence do not appear very large. What makes monetary integration in Asia unlikely, in their view, is the institutional and political gap.

and uncontested hegemon, with the authority to impose policy conditions as part of an emergency package. This was perhaps the main objection to the attempt made in the early months of the Asian crisis by some countries in the area to organize a $100 billion regional emergency fund, to be known as the Asian Monetary Fund. The initiative was announced by the Japanese finance minister during the joint IMF-World Bank meetings in Hong Kong. Nothing was said at the time about how the Asian Monetary Fund would operate or about the conditions that would be attached to individual rescue packages. After the other G-7 countries had made it clear that they would go along with the initiative only if the IMF were involved, the plan was dropped—which suggests that it had more to do with avoiding conditionality than with fundraising.[16]

The moral of all this is that, for the foreseeable future, an integrated system of regional lending of last resort is unlikely to emerge, unless as a reaction to a dramatic setback in international financial cooperation, as signaled for instance by the abolition of the IMF (Goodhart 1999). Such an extreme scenario, however, seems at the moment highly unlikely. At most, elaborating on the Japanese idea for an Asian Monetary Fund, one might envisage at this stage the creation of a number of regional pools of resources that could be activated exclusively for countries belonging to the region. To be viable, however, such a structure would need to be coherently designed and managed, according to a unique code of conduct. In the trade field, there are those who argue that the trend toward regionalism is made more acceptable by its occurring in the context of an ever stronger global institutional arrangement, represented by the World Trade Organization and the conflict-solving procedures over which it presides. In such a context, regionalism can be interpreted as but one layer within a multilayered, but internally coherent, institutional framework (Lawrence, Bressand and Ito 1996). Coordination in trade is desirable, but not strictly necessary, because each region can benefit from liberalization even if all the other regions maintain their trade restrictions. Coordination in finance, however, appears to be vital, for the potential for contagion across regions is significant. Leaving each region to decide the rules according to which lender-of-last-resort services should be provided may well result in a system of destructive, rather than constructive, ambiguity.

III.2. The Evolving Role of the IMF and the Meltzer Report

Ever since its establishment, in 1945, the IMF has witnessed a gradual, but nonetheless deep, evolution of its mission and range of activities. As mentioned in Section II.1, the institution was entrusted at Bretton Woods with a conceptually simple task: to protect the fixed-exchange-rate system through the provision of

[16] Even though no concrete step towards an Asian Monetary Fund has been made yet, a number of Asian countries (ASEAN plus China, Korea, and Japan) are working at establishing a region-wide system of currency swaps, along the lines of the G10 system. For the latest developments in this area, see Bergsten (2000b).

adjustment-smoothing finance. Article I(v) states that one of the fundamental purposes of the organization is 'to give confidence to members by making the general resources . . . temporarily available . . . under adequate safeguards.' Two points are worth emphasizing in this passage. 'Confidence' is to be given to countries, not to their lenders, because capital mobility is expected to be restricted. And access to adjustment-smoothing finance will not come cheap, because it will be made conditional on the existence of 'adequate safeguards'—the origin of the notion of conditionality that was derived later.

This is basically the framework within which the IMF operated until the breakdown of the Bretton Woods System in the early 1970s. With the switch to flexible exchange rates, the IMF's mission was somehow left hanging in the air. This inevitably entailed a certain loss of legitimacy, and 'an accompanying perception of increased IMF obtrusiveness' (Guitián 1992, p. 25). A legal fix was eventually found with the Jamaica amendment of the Articles of Agreement, which gave the IMF a new mission—that of administering the 'code of conduct' laid out in the newly drafted Article IV, which states the aim of 'assuring orderly exchange arrangements and promoting a stable system of exchange rates'.

At first, this legal change meant little in terms of the way in which the IMF was perceived, especially in developing countries. In fact, the outbreak of the debt crisis in the early 1980s probably marked the lowest point of IMF popularity (James 1996). Starting in the late 1980s, however, something changed. An increasing number of countries began to realize that in a world of increasing capital mobility, the IMF could play a useful role as provider of credibility, beside and even above the more traditional role of lender of resources. This change of attitude in the countries tapping the IMF is supported by three pieces of evidence. First, the share of net IMF credit relative to total net external financing to developing countries dropped from 4.5 per cent during the 1980s to less than 1 per cent in the period from 1990 to 1996. Second, there has been a rapid increase in recent years in the number of so-called precautionary programmes, that is of programmes undertaken without the immediate intention of borrowing funds. About one-third of IMF programmes under Standby and Extended Fund Facility arrangements fall into this category. Finally, although the ratio between actual and potential borrowing in all outstanding IMF arrangements—excluding off-track arrangements—has declined since the early 1980s and reached a historical low, the number of countries with an IMF programme has risen to all-time peaks. The message of all this is fairly simple: the IMF stamp of approval is being used by an increasing number of countries to enhance the credibility of country authorities in association with adjustment programmes predicated on the availability of private international finance. The IMF has gradually shifted, for a large part of its membership, from providing confidence to governments to providing confidence to the markets that are supplying the finance needed by the governments to make their policies succeed (Cottarelli and Giannini 1999).

As a result, the IMF has already developed the means, and to a large extent the skills, to sustain the credibility of member countries in adverse circumstances. This does not mean that it has played the role of credibility provider, or of confidence-enhancing mechanism, in the best possible way in all possible circumstances, and recent crises have certainly taught a number of lessons in this respect. Nonetheless, that there is a growing demand for the credibility services of the IMF among its membership appears undeniable. The issue is whether and to what extent this demand can be met to make the management of foreign-exchange crises a smoother process than it is at present.

A somewhat 'natural' evolution would seem to consist in shifting the emphasis of conditionality from what a country does *after* borrowing from the Fund to what it does *before*—what might be called ex ante conditionality. After all, this is very similar to what central banks do within their national domain: they supervise banks ex ante, and when a crisis strikes, they discriminate between good and bad banks on the basis of both the availability of collateral, and of what they know about the ailing bank from the supervisory record (Freixas *et al.*, 2000).

That the IMF should behave like a national central bank is the thrust of the Meltzer Report, drafted by a Commission established in 1998 by the US Congress as part of the legislation authorizing $18 billion of additional funding for the IMF (Meltzer Commission 2000). The report's recommendations echo and elaborate upon similar proposals made by Charles Calomiris (1998) and Stanley Fischer (1999). Access to IMF resources, according to the suggested scheme, would be made conditional on the compliance by borrowing countries with four requirements: adequate capitalization of domestic banks; freedom of entry for foreign banks; adoption by debtor countries of internationally agreed fiscal standards; disclosure by debtor countries' governments of comprehensive, timely and accurate financial information. Requests for funds from qualifying countries would be met automatically, at penalty rates but free from any form of ex post conditionality. The funds provided would be short-term (a maximum of 120 days, with only one allowable rollover) and would be given seniority status over private lending.[17] The proposal to grant IMF loans effective seniority over other forms of lending, which does not depart from current practice, is offered as a second-best option to posting collateral—Fischer's (1999) preferred option—since in the present international environment the latter runs against a number of legal and practical difficulties.

According to the report all other forms of lending should be ceased, since they are seen as unnecessary and possibly detrimental in a world in which capital markets have replaced official financing as the main source of external funding for sovereign countries.

The approach of the Meltzer Report is clearly reminiscent of Bagehot's doctrine that a lender of last resort should lend freely to illiquid debtors only, at penalty rates, and on good collateral.[18] But Bagehot's doctrine, perhaps appropriate in the

[17] The report is less clearcut on access limits, suggesting that 'the limit should reflect the capacity of the sovereign to repay its debt to the IMF' and that in this respect 'one year's tax revenues' might be a 'reasonable limit'.

[18] I do not deal here with other aspects of the Meltzer Report, such as whether the IMF should withdraw from long-run lending and poverty reduction or the recommendations concerning a number of other multilateral institutions. See Bergsten (2000a) on these aspects.

context of the London capital market in the second half of the nineteenth century, is no longer relevant to describe national practices in this area—essentially because the distinction between illiquidity and insolvency has proven a poor guide for action for central banks.[19] Moreover, the experience of industrial countries over the last two decades shows that compliance with rather general requirements (as the envisaged requirements must of necessity be) is no guarantee against the risk of either regulatory or macroeconomic failures. Finally, past compliance will be no guarantee of future compliance, that is, after liquidity assistance has been provided, once the possibility of policy regime switches is conceded. Conversely, when the crisis erupts, it could prove socially desirable to provide liquidity assistance even to countries that have failed to meet the prescribed requirements ex ante.

Some of the Meltzer Report's recommendations are already embodied in the Contingent Credit Line (CCL), the facility established by the IMF Board in April 1999 to provide countries with a line of credit to be drawn in the event they are struck by contagion from an external crisis. To qualify for the CCL, a country must be pursuing good macroeconomic policies, have a strong financial sector and either meet or be moving towards meeting international standards in a variety of areas. The lending terms of the CCL are the same as those of the Supplemental Reserve Facility, that is the facility used to deal with Asian crisis, and are therefore penalizing with respect to ordinary IMF charges.

As of the time of writing (September 2001), no country has applied for the CCL, in spite of the fact that the preconditions for drawing are somewhat laxer than those recommended in the Meltzer Report. The main reason is that debtor countries fear that by applying for the CCL, and therefore by accepting to be dealt with at penalty rates, they would signal to the markets a state of financial uneasiness that could risk precipitating the crisis they are struggling to avoid. This concern is made more compelling by the very availability of the SRF, which can be activated ex post on practically the same terms, except for possibly stronger policy conditionality. Thus, if one were to follow the logic of the Meltzer Report to the extreme, the SRF should be suppressed and the rate of charge on the CCL should be brought down to below-market rates, to signal that the IMF considers a given country more creditworthy than the market perceives in the midst of a crisis.[20]

But would such a framework be a credible antidote to moral hazard? There is reason to doubt it. The logic of the reinforced CCL would require that a country be expelled from the list of eligible borrower as soon as it ceases to meet even one of the preconditions. But on the one hand no domestic lender of last resort has ever announced publicly that it would not support a given institution because it failed to comply with supervisory standards—for fear of precipitating a crisis. It is

[19] I have described in detail the discrepancy between the theory and the practice of national lending of last resort elsewhere; see Giannini (1999). For a survey of the literature, see also Freixas *et al.* (2000).

[20] To make the CCL more attractive to potential applicants, in fact in September 2000 the IMF Board has agreed to lower the interest charge below that of the SRF, keeping it, however, penalizing with respect to ordinary charges.

unreasonable to expect that of an international organization enjoying less technical discretion and political legitimacy than ordinary central banks. On the other hand, the preconditions are sufficiently vague and their relationship to the actual capacity of the debtor country to honour its debt sufficiently debatable as to allow much room for interpretation. The threat of expulsion would thus not be credible.

Those who conceived the CCL were aware of this problem, and suggested that it could be solved on a case by case basis by adjusting the terms and conditions attached to the borrowed funds. For example, Fischer (1999, p. 101) states that 'a non-qualifying country might pay a higher penalty interest rate, or be subject to tougher policy conditionality, or in extreme cases, be denied access to the lender of last resort funds.' Indeed, something like this is already embedded in the structure of the CCL, since the fourth precondition for its activation is that the borrowing country should have in place 'a satisfactory economic and financial program, which the member stands ready to adjust as needed'. But all this amounts to admitting that no international lender of last resort will ever be able to act in an automatic fashion on the basis of a limited set of binary parameters.

III.3. Private Sector Involvement

In the light of the IMF's difficulties in developing into a lender of last resort proper and the impracticality of regional arrangements, it is not surprising that already at an early stage in the post-Asia reflection, in October 1998, the G7 should have called for '. . . greater participation by the private sector in crisis prevention and resolution'. Ever since, this has become a hot topic in the debate on reforming the international architecture, even though terminological confusion, double thought, and sheer rhetoric have not been lacking.[21]

Although the notion of private sector involvement (henceforth, PSI) as such is quite new, the practice is time-honoured. As a matter of fact, many lender-of-last-resort operations from the nineteenth century down to recent times have taken the form of concerted rescues, in which private banks played an important role (see Goodhart and Schoenmaker 1995; Giannini 1999). As mentioned in Section II.3, there are two distinct reasons why PSI might be desirable. One is moral hazard reduction; the other is greater efficiency in crisis resolution in a world in which a crisis is mainly a manifestation of a coordination problem among private creditors. It is useful to distinguish three forms of PSI: contractual, voluntary and coercive. Let us examine each of them in turn.

Contractual PSI. Lending of last resort is a form of implicit insurance against the risk of illiquidity. If implicit insurance can be expected to work only imperfectly in an international context, why not try explicit insurance? The latter could take the form, for example, of an option-like contract giving the borrowing country the right to access extraordinary sources of financing should pressure develop

[21] See Haldane (1999) for a discussion of the analytics of private sector involvement. IMF (2000) contains a very informative survey of the experience so far accumulated in this field.

in its own foreign-exchange market. Because such an agreement would be voluntary, the premium could compensate the insurers for the risk they run.

Argentina and Mexico, plus a number of minor countries, are experimenting with contingency financing arrangements of this sort (Institute of International Finance 1999). The structure of such contractual arrangements raises a number of questions. Can the market be expected to provide enough insurance, given the nature of the event that is being insured against? Moreover, suppose the market is reacting correctly to an imbalance in the country's fundamentals: will the facility still be beneficial to the country itself and to the international community at large?

Neither the Argentine nor the Mexican arrangement is 'large' in comparison with the latest rescue packages, so it seems unrealistic to expect that such arrangements might act as a perfect substitute for public money. But the main problems seem to lie elsewhere. First, the existence of margin calls implies that, in case of large price swings, which clearly cannot be ruled out given the type of event these countries are trying to insure against, the arrangement could very well unwind. Perhaps more important, the banks participating in the arrangement might wish to hedge their exposure. They might start selling government securities short, for example, when called to provide 'additional' finance under the arrangement. If they choose to do so, the overall amount of foreign finance available to the borrowing country will remain unchanged. Furthermore, the very automaticity of the arrangement, that is, its unconditional nature, might prove to be an undesirable feature. Once the existence of the facility becomes publicly known, authorities might come under pressure to draw on it rather than take potentially unpopular measures to stem an incipient crisis. A careful drafting of the conditions for a drawdown might reduce this risk, but the overall record of the market with regard to surveillance suggests that the facility might be used to delay needed policy adjustments.

Mexico's decision, in September 1998, to draw $2.66 billion from its contingent facility—the first such drawing ever—aroused much controversy among the thirty-three banks participating in the arrangement. The banks complained that the interest rate at which the drawing occurred (1 per cent above LIBOR) had been negotiated eighteen months earlier and had, in the meantime, fallen considerably below market. This could hardly be blamed on Mexico, though, and in fact it did not prevent a drawing under the original agreement. The creditors' discontent, however, shows that the risk inherent in such facilities might have been originally underestimated; as a consequence, one can expect that future drawings will be made either more costly for the borrower or less 'automatic' (see Institute of International Finance 1999, regarding this episode). In short, while contingency financing arrangements might be a means to increase awareness of debtor countries and their creditors of the risk of illiquidity, it is unlikely that they could ever become in themselves a 'key' tool for managing or even preventing crises.

Voluntary PSI. Voluntary agreements among creditors for the maintenance of exposure or even for providing fresh money in crisis times have played an important role in a number of recent crisis episodes. One may wonder to what extent a 'voluntary' agreement is really voluntary, but this is beside the point. It is one of the authorities' responsibility to exert moral suasion or any 'elbow nudging' activity to induce private creditors into actions that they would otherwise not undertake. What matters, in the end, is that private creditors act on the basis of what they perceive to be their own interest, based on the information they have and the incentives provided by the authorities. The problem with voluntary arrangements is that they can be expected to work only when creditors are relatively homogeneous and have an interest in maintaining a long-term business relationship with the borrower. In Korea, for example, the concerted rollover promoted through moral suasion by the world's main central banks worked only because on the one hand interbank lending accounted for the bulk of the country's external exposure, and, on the other, the intervention took place after most creditors had already drastically reduced, or cancelled altogether, their exposure, leaving in the market only a few big institutions which had an interest in maintaining their stake. In subsequent crisis episodes, most notably in Turkey and Argentina, voluntary PSI has failed to meet the official sector's expectations, forcing the IMF to increase its financing to fill the gap.[22]

Faced with a similar difficulty, back in the early 1980s, the IMF's response was to condition its disbursements on the markets first agreeing to provide new money. The underlying idea was that the knowledge that a sovereign default would be forthcoming if they failed to organize a rescue, would encourage private investors to find ways around their collective action problem. But this strategy can be applied only to captive investors, not to investors whose claims can be liquidated on secondary markets. When such claims are an important component of the country's external exposure, announcing that the IMF will withhold its financing until an agreement has been reached only 'arms the private creditor with an additional weapon to be used in their skirmish with the country' (Eichengreen and Ruehl 2000, p. 8). This is why the IMF subsequently developed the notion of 'lending into arrears' (LIA), which consists in providing limited finance to a country even when the latter is in arrears to private creditors, so long as it is making good-faith efforts at negotiating a consensual restructuring. But LIA is a two-edged sword. What if creditors refuse to provide new money or to renew their exposures, or if negotiations are extended indefinitely? LIA would then result only in a substitution of private finance with official finance. Aware of this further difficulty, the IMF's next step has been to condition its financing on the country's reaching a target for foreign exchange reserves which implies that some debts are not honoured as scheduled, namely that the country first secure the contribution of its creditors to the package. All the recent experiments in crisis management (Romania, Ukraine, Pakistan, Ecuador and Nigeria) revolve around this simple

[22] A further problem is that foreign creditors can be expected to learn from past experience and adjust their policies accordingly to reduce the risk of being 'voluntarily' involved. An instance of this behaviour can be found in the unfolding of the Brazilian crisis of 1998–99, where some international banks with local operations acted preemptively and cut their interbank lines to these local operations at the mere rumour that the international authorities were considering to intervene. See IMF (2000).

mechanism. This is not the place to review these experiments in detail. Suffice it to say that commentators agree that on the whole they have yielded unsatisfactory results (Eichengreen and Ruehl 2000; IMF 2000). The reason is that, lacking a credible threat of default on the part of the sovereign and there being no credible limit to IMF financing, the various statements issued by the IMF in the course of a crisis have mainly the effect of 'allowing a large, loose collection of creditors to hold official money hostage' (Eichengreen and Ruehl 2000, p.23). So the real issue here is why is the threat of default not credible? This brings us to consider coercive forms of PSI.

Coercive PSI. The coercive measure *par excellence* barring outright default, is a standstill on foreign payments.[23] With perfect information, a standstill would be hard to justify. But Gorton (1985) and Wallace (1988) have shown that partial suspension schemes may dominate a lender-of-last-resort scheme unless the government or some external agency has superior information about the nature and size of the run. Information asymmetries, as it happens, are a constituent feature of the financial environment, and one could argue that this problem is likely to be more serious when countries are concerned. The risk of a run, moreover, is magnified in this case by the lack of a clear 'liquidation' value for the individual country's assets. When these conditions prevail, it may be rational for investors to run, acting on the basis of some noisy, but nonetheless meaningful, indicator. The suspension of convertibility may hence be the rational course of action for the debtor, because the debtor, who by definition enjoys superior information, is thus afforded the time to signal to creditors that the continuation of the relationship may be mutually beneficial.[24] When dealing with sovereign debtors, however, one must be aware of two complicating factors. First, a country may declare a standstill not because it is unable to pay, but rather because it is unwilling to do so. The two cases obviously have different implications, and should be distinguished. Second, after suspending convertibility a bank can go about the rest of its business for a while without much external pressure, because as a financial intermediary, it does not need interim liquidity. This is clearly not the case with countries, which are typically brought to suspend external payments in situations where they still need foreign money to finance a budget or current-account deficit. Recourse to suspension therefore makes sense only if a source of interim finance can be found to keep the country afloat until full convertibility is restored.

The possibility of resorting to standstills as a policy tool was first envisaged after the Mexican crisis by the G-10 in its report on *The Resolution of Sovereign Liquidity Crises* (1996), also known as the Rey Report, where it is stated that 'a temporary suspension of debt payments by the debtor may be unavoidable as part of the process of crisis resolution and as a way of gaining time to put in place a credible adjustment program.' Since then, the view has been reiterated several times in official documents, the latest of which is the press communiqué issued in Prague in

[23] A milder coercive measure is the 'hair-cut' scheme proposed by Litan and Herring (1998).

[24] This argument has been formalized by Miller and Zhang (2000). See also Zettelmeyer (2000).

September 2000 after the Annual Meetings of the IMF. But to date official declarations have not been followed by concrete steps. One reason for this discrepancy between words and deeds is the strong resistance to the notion of standstills put up by the private sector. Immediately after the publication of the Rey Report, the Institute of International Finance issued a statement in which the G-10 recommendations on standstills and LIA were called 'misguided' on the ground that they would face enormous implementation problems and, if implemented, would fuel moral hazard with respect to debtors (Institute of International Finance 1996). A few years later the Institute of International Finance issued a full-fledged counter-report, which this time criticized moratoria on the two-fold ground that they would run against the principle that contracts should be honoured and would be contradictory with the official sector's objective of prompt restoration of market access for countries hit by a crisis (Institute of International Finance 1999). The private sector's view has proven highly influential on the negotiating position of the most important official actor, the US Treasury.[25]

The objections to standstills based on the sanctity of contracts and on debtor moral hazard, however, are easily disposed of. The principle that in some circumstances interrupting the validity of contracts may be in the interest not only of the debtor, but also of creditors themselves, has long been accepted in national legislation. It is difficult to see why it should not be so at the international level, if appropriate ways were found to reassure creditors that this option would not be abused. Furthermore, debtor moral hazard cannot be so serious a problem, since the need for interim finance will allow international organizations to keep a sovereign debtor under the hold of policy conditionality even while the standstill is in place.

Another, more worrisome, concern is that a standstill might accelerate the withdrawal of private capital from the country concerned, and possibly from other countries in the same risk class, thereby fuelling international financial instability through contagion (IMF 2000). This risk, while difficult to estimate with any accuracy, is real, but it need not paralyse international authorities. On the one hand, a credible threat of default may in some circumstances help facilitate a voluntary agreement among the parties, particularly when many creditors have claims maturing in the same time frame, so that a rush for the exit would not be the optimal strategy.[26] On the other, much can be done to make standstills more orderly by improving 'at the margin' the institutional environment in which they take place. No form of intervention to make markets 'work better' can be expected to be effective without a number of supporting institutions and legal practices. While, as I have argued in Section II, a larger dose of realism is needed when dealing with the

[25] As proof of this assertion, see Summers (2000), where standstills are mentioned only in a footnote as a theoretical possibility with no bearing to the real world.

[26] One may mention the 1982 agreement between Mexico and its creditors, or more recently the cases of Pakistan and Ukraine, as evidence of voluntary agreements reached against a risk of default perceived to be credible by creditors.

international environment than with the more reform-friendly national one, there seem to be at least three areas in which progress can be made.

The first area is that of debt contracts. The Rey Report was particularly adamant in stressing the desirability of inserting collective action clauses (CACs) into standard international bond contracts, to facilitate the collective representation of dispersed bondholders in case of sovereign default.[27] While still part of the official sector's strategy, this specific recommendation has come to nothing because neither the developed countries, nor, understandably, the less developed ones, wanted to make the first move, for fear of an adverse market reaction. Needless to say, this failure has deprived the international reform effort of an important leg, since, as forcefully argued by Eichengreen and Ruehl (2000), 'encouraging countries to suspend payments as a way of driving the bondholders to the bargaining table will be disastrous so long as there is no bargaining table to which they can be driven'.[28]

A second area concerns the provision of interim finance. The IMF has already developed an important tool, in the form of LIA. But LIA was never thought as a substitute for private finance; rather, its role was to encourage the private sector to do its part, knowing that the debtor's actions carried the implicit endorsement of the IMF. But the encouragement has not proven strong enough, and for understandable reasons: why should private creditors provide fresh money knowing that these claims will enjoy no special protection with respect to either past loans or the new finance provided by the IFIs themselves? Only treating new debt as senior to existing debt can really persuade creditors to act cooperatively. But this can be done only with the explicit or implicit backing of the IFIs themselves, since the seniority structure once established in the markets has in the meantime fallen victim to the case-by-case approach so far followed in sovereign debt restructurings. And after all the principle that an insolvent firm can raise new financing that is senior to outstanding debt, subject to the agreement of the court, forms an integral part of the bankruptcy code of most developed countries.

The third and final area where advance may be made is that of the legal bases of standstills. Unlike traditional lending of last resort, LIA tends to run against the creditors' immediate interest by giving the distressed country the means to afford, so to speak, a standstill. It is thus confrontational in a way that traditional lending of last resort has never been. It consequently raises the issue of its impact on creditors' recourse to courts, on the programme's chances of success and, ultimately,

27 See Dixon and Wall (2000) for a comprehensive review of CACs and their implications.

28 After the Rey Report was published, it became known that some international bonds, those issued under British law, already contained provisions for the collective representation of bondholders. These CACs played a role in the resolution of both Pakistan's and Ukraine's foreign debt problems, although only in the latter case were they actually invoked. However, the activation of CACs was not part of the official sector's strategy in either case; moreover, the experience of Romania—which in the midst of its own debt crisis was pressed by foreign investors to issue, contrary to previous practice, New York style bonds—shows that, lacking a more sanguine support from the official sector, the diffusion of CACs may in the long run decrease rather than increase. An even stronger response, suggested by Rogoff (1999), would consist in measures restricting countries' ability to waive sovereign immunity, as a way to discourage the mediation of debt contracts in industrialized country courts.

on the IMF's resources. The risk is that aggressive litigation on the part of creditors, involving extensive seizure of assets, could effectively prevent balance-of-payments adjustment and thus derail the whole programme. When LIA took its present form, in the late 1980s, litigation did not prove to be a major problem. Creditors generally did not resort to legal remedies, and a number of agreements were reached within a reasonably short time after the IMF's announcement that it would support a debtor, notwithstanding its arrears. The creditors at the time, however, were primarily commercial banks, and competition in the industry was not yet as fierce as it is today. As a result, national central banks could play an important role behind the scenes in encouraging financial institutions to accept a cooperative settlement. Such forbearance cannot be expected of all creditors—certainly not of bondholders in general, and possibly not even of many internationally active banks of our days. Indeed, investment-fund managers and other similar financial agents are likely to have a fiduciary obligation to customers to make the most of their holdings of distressed securities. A worst-case scenario would also need to contemplate the possibility that the IMF, having endorsed a standstill, or even having made it a condition for initiating a programme, might be dragged into the litigation.

It is difficult to say how much emphasis should be laid on this problem. In recent debt restructurings, legal disputes have played a minor role. Moreover, the problem could be mitigated if the official sector accepted a lower degree of seniority for sovereign and multilateral lending, since this would reduce the conflict of interest between the roles of creditor and enforcer (implicit or whatever) of standstills. But recent experience may not constitute a reliable precedent, as the logic of the coercive approach has never been pushed to the limit. As to the seniority structure of international claims, recent official declarations go, if anything, in the opposite direction.

Thus, a coercive approach to be used in extreme circumstances is unlikely to be credible unless the international community develops legitimate means for temporarily suspending the creditors' legal rights, while at the same time credibly constraining access to IMF resources. But how is this going to be achieved? The obvious place to look is in the IMF's Articles of Agreement. As mentioned above, Article VI.1 (a) empowers the IMF to require that a member impose controls on the outflow of capital as a condition for the use of its resources. In turn, Article VIII.2(b) states that 'exchange contracts which involve the currency of any member and which are contrary to the exchange control regulations of that member maintained or imposed consistently with this Agreement shall be unenforceable in the territories of any member'.

Invoking Article VIII in its present form to justify a standstill, however, would require some measure of creative textual interpretation. The IMF Board could state that the expression 'exchange contracts' is to be interpreted as encompassing credit agreements. Interpreted this way, Article VIII would make claims arising from sovereign default temporarily unenforceable following a decision by the board. It is debatable whether this would really settle the matter, however. Rule bending may be acceptable in dealing with sovereign entities that find the expanded interpretation in their own interest, but it can hardly be expected to be effective when it involves private creditors who might take their case to a perhaps unsympathetic national court. Thus, if standstills are to be credibly added to the panoply of tools available for dealing with foreign-exchange crises, changing the language in Article VIII appears highly advisable—perhaps in the context of a general revision of the IMF's mandate as regards the capital account. By giving the IMF responsibility for fostering orderly and well-sequenced capital account liberalization, a clear signal would be sent to the financial markets that they are seen to perform an important function both in allocating resources worldwide and in disciplining domestic economic policies.[29] At the same time, by explicitly contemplating standstills as a policy tool, to be used only as an ultima ratio expedient, and in the context of a strong adjustment effort, the authorities would make it clear that there is no reason to believe that international financial markets are immune from the imperfections that have prompted the development of an extensive regulatory framework at the national level.

IV. CONCLUSION: TOWARDS A REGIME OF 'CONSTRAINED DISCRETION'

Financial markets do not manage themselves. This is, in essence, the reason why central banks exist. It is not clear—as the recent wave of crises has taken the trouble to show—why this truth should be less compelling at the international than at the national level. The Bretton Woods architects tried to dispose of the problem by insulating national financial markets to the greatest possible extent. By doing so, they reasoned, financial instability would also be kept a national problem, and could accordingly be taken care of with the machinery of the then rampant nation-state.

Technological and financial innovation has now made this strategy irremediably outdated. Unfortunately, the issue of extending lender-of-last-resort practices beyond national borders is anything but straightforward—the more so since the received doctrine on lending of last resort seems increasingly at variance with actual practice even at the national level. This is why reform proposals of recent years differ wildly, ranging from the Meltzer Commission's (2000) suggestion that the IMF should be transformed into a semi-automatic lender of last resort organized along Bagehotian lines, to Schwartz's (1998) plea for abolishing the IMF and 'let the market work'.

In this paper, I have argued against extreme solutions, because they seem to me to contradict what is perhaps the most interesting contribution of recent reflection on the theory and history of institutions—namely, that successful institutional adaptation tends to take place *at the margin*, rather than by quantum jumps. A Bagehotian lender of last resort no longer exists, if it ever did, even at the national level. How could it be established without fueling moral hazard in the much more 'unfriendly' international environment? At the other end of the reform spectrum,

[29] For a survey of the theoretical underpinnings and the practical implications of capital account liberalization, see Eichengreen *et al.* (1998).

recent decades have witnessed an increase, rather than a decline, in the services member countries demand from the IMF. In particular, besides providing loans against current account imbalances to countries with little or no access to capital markets, the IMF is increasingly been regarded as a signaling, or confidence-enhancing, device by governments eager to commit themselves credibly to sound policies but unable to do so for lack of sufficiently strong domestic institutions. What benefit could be drawn by setting the clock back to the pre-Bretton Woods era?

Against these concerns, I think that a middle-of-the-road approach has much to commend itself. Under such an approach, the IMF would still deal with foreign exchange crises on a case-by-case basis, also advancing emergency finance when needed. Its actions, however, would be constrained, on one side, by precise statutory limits to the amount of resources it may lend to any individual member; on the other, by the existence of legal tools and practices making it feasible for debtor countries to temporarily suspend creditors' rights under international supervision.

A strategy of constrained discretion would not necessarily be unfriendly to the market. It would clearly not be unfriendly, for instance, if standstills were credibly circumscribed to being used as a way to facilitate creditors' coordination only when no other option appeared workable (including private contingent facilities backed in part by the public sector), and to the extent that the country concerned was making a strong effort to adjust its policies.

To make the constrained discretion regime credible, however, the international community should lay greater emphasis than has been the case so far on institutional adaptation, especially as regards legal practices in the area of contract law and international bankruptcy. Moreover, a revision of the fundamental charter governing international monetary relations—the IMF's Articles of Agreement—seems highly advisable for two reasons. First, endorsing standstills without simultaneously asserting that a reasonable degree of freedom in the allocation of capital worldwide represents one of the fundamental aims pursued by the international community would encourage member countries to reverse whatever progress they had made toward capital-account liberalization, and even to contemplate a return to the Bretton Woods regime of all-encompassing capital controls. Second, the handling of standstills, without amending the Articles to legitimize a suspension of creditor rights in the presence of goodwill efforts at adjustment, could very well trigger a disorderly process and even risk to drag the IMF into legal disputes. I have accordingly suggested that the possibility of temporary standstills be made explicit through a change of language in Article VIII, to be made in the context of a broader revision of the Articles aimed at giving the IMF responsibility for encouraging appropriately sequenced, but nonetheless extensive, capital-account liberalization.

Amending the Articles is a time-consuming and politically demanding task. This explains why, while acknowledging the desirability of an amendment in principle, the two main official reports drafted in the aftermath of the financial crises of the 1990s—the G10's Rey Report (1996) and the G22 Report (1998)—both rejected the idea on practical grounds. But if the relatively modest move of changing Article VIII should really prove infeasible, it is hard to see how the far more ambitious goal of establishing a moral-hazard-free lender of last resort at the world level could ever be achieved. It is likely that sooner or later the most influential members of the IMF will wish to take a second look at the whole issue.

It may be worth emphasizing in closing that redefining the role of the IMF along the lines suggested above need not imply ruling out international bailouts altogether. In certain circumstances, helping a country through a foreign-exchange crisis might be desirable, economic objections notwithstanding. It would appear advisable, however, in keeping with national practices, to leave responsibility for politically motivated rescues to governments, so as to protect both the legitimacy and the resources of the technical agency placed at the center of the international monetary system. This was the choice made by the Bretton Woods architects. In retrospect, it does not appear to have been unwise.

REFERENCES

Baily, Martin N., Diana Farrell, and Susan Lund, 'The Color of Money', *Foreign Affairs*, Vol. 79, No. 2, March/April 2000.

Bayoumi, Tamim, Barry Eichengreen, and Paolo Mauro, 'On Regional Monetary Arrangements for Asean', *CEPR Discussion Paper* No. 2411, April 2000.

Bernard, Henry, and Joseph Bisignano, 'Information, Liquidity and Risk in the International Interbank Market: Implicit Guarantees and Private Credit Market Failure', *BIS Working Paper*, No. 86, Basle, Bank for International Settlements, March 2000.

Bergsten, Fred, *Meltzer Commission Report – Dissenting Opinion*, Senate Committee on Banking, Housing, and Urban Affairs, Washington, March 2000a.

— 'East Asian regionalism—Towards a Tripartite World', *The Economist*, July 15th, 2000b.

Calabresi, Guido, *The Costs of Accidents: A Legal and Economic Analysis*, New Haven: Yale University Press, 1970.

Calomiris, Charles W., 'Blueprints for a New Global Financial Architecture' paper presented at the Federal Reserve Bank of Chicago Conference, Asia. 'An Analysis of Financial Crisis', Chicago, October 8–10, 1998.

Calvert, Randall L., 'The Rational Choice Theory of Social Institutions: Cooperation, Coordination, and Communication' in Jeffrey S. Banks and Eric A. Hanushek, eds., *Modern Political Economy: Old Topics, New Directions*, Cambridge and New York, Cambridge University Press, 1995.

Cardoso, Eliana, and Rudiger Dornbusch, 'Brazilian Debt Crises: Past and Present' in Barry Eichengreen and Peter Lindert, eds., *The International Debt Crisis in Historical Perspective*, Cambridge, Mass., and London, MIT Press, 1989.

Cline, William R. and Kevin J.S. Barnes, 'Spreads and Risks in Emerging Markets Lending', *Institute of International Finance Research Papers*, No. 97-1, 1997.

Cooper, Richard, 'International Cooperation in Public Health as a Prologue to Macroeconomic Cooperation' in Cooper et al., *Can Nations Agree: Issues in International Cooperation*, Washington, D.C., Brookings Institution, 1989.

Cottarelli, Carlo, and Curzio Giannini, 'Credibility Without Rules? Monetary Frameworks in the Post-Bretton Woods Era', *IMF Occasional Paper*, No. 154, 1997.

—, 'Inflation, Credibility, and the Role of the International Monetary Fund', *IMF International Economic Policy Review*, Vol. 1, 1999.

Dam, Kenneth, *The Rules of the Game*, Chicago, University of Chicago Press, 1982.

De Bonis, Riccardo, Alessandro Giustiniani, and Giorgio Gomel, 'Crises and Bail-Outs of Banks and Countries: Linkages, Analogies, and Differences', *World Economy*, 22, January 1999.

Dixon, Liz, and David Wall, 'Collective Action Problems and Collective Action Clauses', *Financial Stability Review*, June 2000.

Eaton, Jonathan, and Raquel Fernandez, 'Sovereign Debt', *National Bureau of Economic Research Working Paper* No. 5131, Cambridge, Mass., National Bureau of Economic Research, May 1995.

Eichengreen, Barry, 'The US Capital Market and Foreign Lending, 1920–1955' in Jeffrey Sachs, ed., *Developing Country Debt and Economic Performance*, Chicago and London, University of Chicago Press, 1989.

—, 'Historical Research on International Lending and Debt', *Journal of Economic Perspectives*, 5, Spring 1991.

—, *Globalizing Capital*, Princeton, Princeton University Press, 1996.

—, Michael Mussa, Giovanni Dell'Ariccia, and staff, Capital Account Liberalization: Theoretical and Practical Aspects, *IMF Occasional Paper*, No. 172, 1998.

— and Richard Portes, 'After the Deluge: Default, Negotiation, and Readjustment during the Interwar Years,' in Barry Eichengreen and Peter Lindert, eds., *The International Debt Crisis in Historical Perspective*, Cambridge, Mass., MIT Press, 1989.

—, —, *Crisis? What Crisis? Orderly Workouts for Sovereign Debtors*, London, Centre for Economic Policy Research, 1995.

—, and Christof Ruehl, 'The Bail-in Problem: Systematic Goals, Ad Hoc Means', *CEPR Discussion Paper*, No. 2427, April 2000.

Fischer, Stanley, 'On the Need for an International Lender of Last Resort', *Journal of Economic Perspectives*, Vol. 13, No. 4, Fall 1999.

Fishlow, Albert, 'Conditionality and Willingness to Pay: Some Parallels from the 1890s' in Barry Eichengreen and Peter Lindert, eds., *The International Debt Crisis in Historical Perspective*, Cambridge, Mass., and London, MIT Press, 1989.

Fraga, Arminio, 'Crisis Prevention and Management: Lessons from Mexico' in Peter B. Kenen, ed., 'From Halifax to Lyons: What Has Been Done About Crisis Management?', *Princeton Essays in International Finance*, No. 200, October 1996.

Freixas, Xavier, Curzio Giannini, Glenn Hoggarth, and Farouk Soussa, 'Lender of Last Resort: What Have We Learned Since Bagehot?', *Journal of Financial Services Research*, Vol. 18, No. 1, 2000.

Giannini, Curzio, 'Enemy of None But A Common Friend of All'? An International Perspective on the Lender-of-Last-Resort Function', *Princeton Essays in International Finance*, No. 214, June 1999.

Goldstein, Morris, *The Asian Financial Crisis: Causes, Cures, and Systemic Implications*, Washington, D.C., Institute for International Economics, 1998.

Goodhart, Charles, 'Myths About the Lender of Last Resort', *International Finance* 2–3, 1999.

—, and Dirk Schoenmaker, 'Should the Functions of Monetary Policy and Bank Supervision Be Separated?' *Oxford Economic Papers*, 47, October 1995.

Gorton, Gary, 'Bank Suspension of Convertibility' *Journal of Monetary Economics*, 15, March 1985.

Group of Ten (G-10), *The Resolution of Sovereign Liquidity Crises: A Report to the Ministers and Governors*, Basle, Bank for International Settlements, and Washington, D.C., International Monetary Fund, May 1996.

Group of Twenty-Two (G–22), *International Financial Crises*, Washington, D.C., Group of Twenty-Two, 1998.

Guitián, Manuel, 'The Unique Nature and Responsibilities of the International Monetary Fund', *Pamphlet Series*, No. 46, Washington, D.C., International Monetary Fund, 1992.

Haldane, Andy, 'Private Sector Involvement in Financial Crises: Analytics and Public Policy Approaches', *Financial Stability Review*, November 1999.

Haas, Peter, *Saving the Mediterranean*, New York, Columbia University Press, 1990.

Institute of International Finance, *Resolving Sovereign Financial Arrears*, Washington, D.C., Institute of International Finance, 1996.

—, *Report of the Working Group on Financial Crises in Emerging Markets*, Washington, D.C., Institute of International Finance, January 1999.

International Monetary Fund, *World Economic Outlook*, Washington, D.C., May 1999.

—, 'Private Sector Involvement in Crisis Prevention and Resolution: Market Views and Recent Experience', in *International Capital Markets–Developments, Prospects, and Key Policy Issues*, September 2000.

James, Harold, *International Monetary Cooperation Since Bretton Woods*, Washington, D.C., International Monetary Fund, 1996.

Johnson, Omotunde E.G., 'Policy Reform as Collective Action', *IMF Working Paper*, No. 163, 1997.

Kenen, Peter, *Financing, Adjustment, and the International Monetary Fund*, Washington, D.C., Brookings Institution, 1986.

Krugman, Paul, 'What Happened to Asia?', mimeo, January 1998.

Lane, Timothy, and Steven Phillips, 'Does IMF Financing Result in Moral Hazard?', *IMF Working Paper*, No. 168, 2000.

Lawrence, Robert Z., Albert Bressand, and Takatoshi Ito, *A Vision for the World Economy*, Washington, D.C., Brookings Institution, 1996.

Levy Yeyati, Eduardo, 'Global Moral Hazard and International Bank Lending: The "Overlending Syndrome"', *IMF Working Paper*, No. 100, July 1999.

Litan, Robert E., and Richard J. Herring, 'Statement of the Shadow Financial Regulatory Committee on International Monetary Fund Assistance and International Crises', Statement No. 145, May 4, 1998.

Meltzer Commission, *Report of the International Financial Institution Advisory Commission* (Chairman: Allan Meltzer), Senate Committee on Banking, Housing, and Urban Affairs, Washington, March 2000.

Miller, Marcus, and Lei Zhang, 'Sovereign Liquidity Crises: The Strategic Case for a Payments Standstill', *The Economic Journal*, Vol. 110, No. 460, January 2000.

Milner, Helen, 'Review Article: International Theories of Cooperation among Nations. Strengths and Weaknesses,' *World Politics*, No. 44, April 1992, pp. 466–496.

Nicholson, Michael, *International Relations*, New York, New York University Press, 1998.

Olson, Mancur, *The Rise and Decline of Nations. Economic Growth, Stagflation, and Social Rigidities*, New Haven, Yale University Press, 1982.

Padoa-Schioppa, Tommaso, and Fabrizio Saccomanni, 'Managing a Market-Led Global Financial System' in Peter B. Kenen, ed., *Managing the World Economy*, Washington, D.C., Institute for International Economics, 1994.

Polak, Jacques J., 'The Articles of Agreement of the IMF and the Liberalization of Capital Movements' in Stanley Fischer *et al.*, 'Should the IMF Pursue Capital-Account Convertibility?', *Princeton Essays in International Finance*, No. 207, May 1998.

Quirk, Peter J., Owen Evans, and staff, 'Capital Account Convertibility, Review of Experience and Implications for IMF Policies', *IMF Occasional Paper*, No. 131, 1995.

Rogoff, Kenneth, 'International Institutions for Reducing Global Financial Instability', *Journal of Economic Perspectives*, Vol. 13, No. 4, Fall 1999.

Sachs, Jeffrey, 'Do We Need an International Lender of Last Resort?' Princeton University, Frank Graham Memorial Lecture, April 20, 1995.

Schwartz, Anna, 'Time to Terminate the ESF and the IMF', Foreign Policy Briefing, No. 48, Washington, D.C., Cato Institute, August 26, 1998.

Spadafora, Francesco, 'Financial Crises, Moral Hazard and the "Speciality", of The International Interbank Market', Banca d'Italia, *mimeo*, September 2001.

Summers, Lawrence H., 'International Financial Crises: Causes, Prevention, and Cures', *American Economic Review*, Vol. 90, No. 2, May 2000.

Wallace, Neil, 'Another Attempt to Explain an Illiquid Banking System: The Diamond and Dybvig Model with Sequential Servicing Taken Seriously', *Federal Reserve Bank of Minneapolis Quarterly Review*, 12(4), Fall 1988.

Zettelmeyer, Jeromin, 'Can Official Crisis Lending be Counter Productive in the Short Run?', *Economic Notes*, Vol. 29, No. 1, 2000.

Zhang Xiaoming, Alan, 'Testing for "Moral Hazard" in Emerging Markets Lending', *Institute of International Finance Research Papers* No. 99-1, August 1999.

Index